CAMBRIDGE STUDIES IN
ANGLO-SAXON ENGLAND

3

RELIGION AND LITERATURE IN
WESTERN ENGLAND,
600–800

CAMBRIDGE STUDIES IN ANGLO-SAXON ENGLAND

EDITORS

SIMON KEYNES

MICHAEL LAPIDGE

Editors' preface

Cambridge Studies in Anglo-Saxon England is a series of scholarly texts and monographs intended to advance our knowledge of all aspects of the field of Anglo-Saxon studies. The scope of the series, like that of *Anglo-Saxon England*, its periodical counterpart, embraces original scholarship in various disciplines: literary, historical, archaeological, philological, art-historical, palaeographical, architectural, liturgical and numismatic. It is the intention of the editors to encourage the publication of original scholarship which advances our understanding of the field through interdisciplinary approaches.

Volumes published:

1 *Anglo-Saxon Crucifixion Iconography and the Art of the Monastic Revival* by BARBARA C. RAW

2 *The Cult of the Virgin Mary in Anglo-Saxon England* by MARY CLAYTON

3 *Religion and Literature in Western England, 600–800* by PATRICK SIMS-WILLIAMS

RELIGION AND LITERATURE IN WESTERN ENGLAND 600–800

PATRICK SIMS-WILLIAMS

Fellow of St John's College, Cambridge
University Lecturer in the Department of Anglo-Saxon, Norse and Celtic

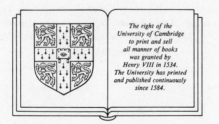

The right of the
University of Cambridge
to print and sell
all manner of books
was granted by
Henry VIII in 1534.
The University has printed
and published continuously
since 1584.

CAMBRIDGE UNIVERSITY PRESS

CAMBRIDGE

NEW YORK   PORT CHESTER

MELBOURNE   SYDNEY

mf

Published by the Press Syndicate of the University of Cambridge
The Pitt Building, Trumpington Street, Cambridge CB2 1RP
40 West 20th Street, New York, NY10011, USA
10 Stamford Road, Oakleigh, Melbourne 3166, Australia

© Cambridge University Press 1990

First published 1990

Printed in Great Britain at the University Press, Cambridge

British Library cataloguing in publication data
Sims-Williams, Patrick.
Religion and literature in western England, 600–800. –
(Cambridge Studies in Anglo-Saxon England; 3).
1. England. Anglo-Saxon religion. 2. English
literature – Critical studies.
I. Title.
293'. 0942

Library of Congress cataloguing in publication data
Sims-Williams, Patrick.
Religion and literature in western England,
600–800 / Patrick Sims-Williams.
p.   cm. – (Cambridge studies in Anglo-Saxon England; 3)
Includes bibliographical references.
ISBN 0–521–38325–0
1. West Midlands (England) – Civilization.
2. Anglo-Saxons – England – West Midlands – History
3. England – Church history – Anglo-Saxon period, 449–1066.
4. English literature – Old English, ca. 450–1100 – History and criticism.
I. Title.   II. Series: Cambridge studies in Anglo-Saxon England; v. 3
DA670.W49S56   1990
942.4'4015 – dc20   89–37968 CIP

ISBN 0 521 38325 0

CE

TO MARGED

Contents

Preface

Some topics relevant to this book have been dealt with more thoroughly in various preparatory papers listed in the bibliography. In them readers can find some discussion of the sixth-century background to this study and detailed evidence for various aspects which are simply summarized here so as to avoid duplication. I have tried to avoid methodological disquisitions and formal description and analyses of sources, but specialists should find my assessment of the sources to be implicit. The approach to the authenticity and interpretation of early charters is, I hope, broadly that of authorities such as Professor Brooks and Dr Scharer. Charters are cited by the number in Professor Sawyer's *Handlist*, in accordance with the policy of the series in which this book appears, but it should be understood that reference should also be made to the printed texts and secondary authorities cited in the *Handlist*; in particular, there is often relevant information in H. P. R. Finberg's *Early Charters of the West Midlands*. For archaeological evidence I have given references to available distribution maps, but I have refrained from providing new ones (with one exception in fig. 2), since new discoveries soon render them misleading. When the location of minor places is important, I have given National Grid References (in the form SP/1694, SO/8805, etc.); these can be found on all modern Ordnance Survey maps. To make the text as accessible as possible I have given quotations in translation, or have added translations in the footnotes.

I am grateful to everyone who has helped me. Professor Peter Sawyer was a stimulatingly critical examiner of very early versions of chs 1–5. Dr Catherine Hills, Mr Andrew Orchard and Dr Robin Glasscock kindly read subsequent drafts of chs. 3, 11 and 12 respectively, and my wife, Dr Marged Haycock, scrutinized many sections. The book is the better for their comments; its faults remain mine. In palaeography I had the invaluable advice of the late T. J. Brown. Professor Philip Grierson and Mr Mark Blackburn have advised me on numismatics, Dr H. M. Taylor on architecture, Mr Kenneth Harrison on chronology, and Dr Neil Wright, Mr Guy Lee and Professor J. A. Crook helped with Latin problems. Mr Steven Bassett has kindly sent me offprints and an advance proof of his chapter in *The Origins of Anglo-Saxon Kingdoms*. Mrs P. Hunter Blair generously gave me many useful items from the library of her late husband, who, with Professor Peter Clemoes, first encouraged me to stray into publishing outside Celtic studies. I should also record my gratitude to my parents, brothers and sister for their encouragement in those uncertain early years of research.

This work owes much to innumerable friends, teachers and colleagues in the universities of Cambridge and Birmingham. I must, however, note my debts at Birmingham to the much-missed inspiration of the late Geoffrey Shepherd, to the seminars of Professor R. H. Hilton, Dr Christopher Dyer, Professor R. H. C. Davis and Professor Wendy Davies, and to my fellow research student Dr David Rollason. Returning to Cambridge, I have had wise guidance from Dr Simon Keynes and Dr Michael Lapidge, first as colleagues and then as editors. Before the 'Cambridge Studies in Anglo-Saxon England' series was created, this book was intended for the 'Studies in Medieval Life and Thought' series and took shape with the encouragement of the late Walter Ullmann and two of his successors, Professors J. C. Holt and C. N. L. Brooke; I am especially indebted to Professor Brooke for many detailed comments. The book would have been even longer in the making had Mr Paul Bibire and Dr Martin Richards not helped me come to terms with computers, and had I not had the privilege of working in St John's College Library under the friendly eyes of Mr Malcolm Pratt, the late Norman Buck, M.A., and the other staff. St John's College paid for my trips to foreign libraries, and the British Academy's award of a research readership allowed me to see the volume through the press while pursuing other research. I hope all readers of this book will share some of the pleasure I have had in writing it.

Abbreviations

AAe	*Archaeologia Aeliana*
AB	*Analecta Bollandiana*
AC	*Annales Cambriae*, ed. Phillimore
AHDLMA	*Archives d'histoire doctrinale et littéraire du moyen âge*
AntJ	*Antiquaries Journal*
ArchJ	*Archaeological Journal*
ASC	*Anglo-Saxon Chronicle*, ed. Plummer, *Two Chronicles*; trans. *EHD*, no. 1
ASE	*Anglo-Saxon England*
ASSAH	*Anglo-Saxon Studies in Archaeology and History*
BAR	British Archaeological Reports
BBCS	*Bulletin of the Board of Celtic Studies*
BCS	*Cartularium Saxonicum*, ed. Birch
BGDSL	*Beiträge zur Geschichte der deutschen Sprache und Literatur*
BIHR	*Bulletin of the Institute of Historical Research*
BL	British Library (London)
BN	Bibliothèque Nationale (Paris)
BNJ	*British Numismatic Journal*
BOH	*Baedae Opera Historica*, ed. Plummer
CA	*Current Archaeology*
CBA	Council for British Archaeology
CCSL	Corpus Christianorum, Series Latina
CLA	Lowe, *Codices Latini Antiquiores* [cited by volume and no.]
CMCS	*Cambridge Medieval Celtic Studies*
CP	Stenton, *Preparatory to Anglo-Saxon England: Collected Papers*
CSEL	Corpus Scriptorum Ecclesiasticorum Latinorum
DEB	Gildas, *De excidio Britanniae*, ed. Winterbottom

DEPN	Ekwall, *Concise Oxford Dictionary of English Place-Names*
DP	*Description of Penbrokeshire*, ed. Owen
DR	*Downside Review*
Duemmler	*Epistolae Karolini Aevi* II, ed. Duemmler
ECWM	Finberg, *Early Charters of the West Midlands*
EEMF	Early English Manuscripts in Facsimile
EETS	Early English Text Society
	os original series
EHD	*English Historical Documents*, ed. Whitelock, 2nd ed.
EHR	*English Historical Review*
EL	*Ephemerides Liturgicae*
EPNS	English Place-Name Society
FS	*Frühmittelalterliche Studien*
Gl.	Gloucestershire
GP	William of Malmesbury, *Gesta pontificum*, ed. Hamilton
HB	*Historia Brittonum*, ed. Mommsen, *Chronica Minora* III, 111–219
*HBC*²	*Handbook of British Chronology*, 2nd ed., ed. Powicke and Fryde
*HBC*³	*Handbook of British Chronology*, 3rd ed., ed. Fryde *et al.*
HBS	Henry Bradshaw Society
He.	Herefordshire
HE	Bede, *Historia ecclesiastica*, ed. and trans. Colgrave and Mynors
HF	Gregory of Tours, *Historia Francorum*, ed. Arndt; trans. Thorpe
H&S	*Councils and Ecclesiastical Documents*, ed. Haddan and Stubbs
HThR	*Harvard Theological Review*
JBAA	*Journal of the British Archaeological Association*
JEGP	*Journal of English and Germanic Philology*
JEH	*Journal of Ecclesiastical History*
JEPNS	*Journal of the English Place-Name Society*
JTS	*Journal of Theological Studies*
KCD	*Codex Diplomaticus*, ed. Kemble [charter cited by number]
LH	*The Local Historian*
LL	*Text of the Book of Llan Dâv*, ed. Evans and Rhys [charter cited by page on which it begins, subdivided as a and b when two charters begin on the same page]

MA	*Medieval Archaeology*
MÆ	*Medium Ævum*
MGH	Monumenta Germaniae Historica
	Auct. antiq. Auctores antiquissimi
	SS. rer. Merov. Scriptores rerum Merovingicarum
MHB	*Monumenta Historica Britannica*, ed. Petrie and Sharpe
MLN	*Modern Language Notes*
MS	*Mediaeval Studies*
NA	*Neues Archiv der Gesellschaft für ältere deutsche Geschichtskunde*
NTBB	*Nordisk Tidskrift för Bok- och Biblioteksväsen*
O.S.	Ordnance Survey
Ox.	Oxfordshire
PBA	*Proceedings of the British Academy*
PBNHPS	*Proceedings of the Birmingham Natural History and Philosophical Society*
PG	Patrologia Graeca, ed. Migne
PIBA	*Proceedings of the Irish Biblical Association*
PL	Patrologia Latina, ed. Migne
PMLA	*Publications of the Modern Language Association of America*
PNE	Smith, *English Place-Name Elements*
PNGl	Smith, *Place-Names of Gloucestershire*
PNOx	Gelling, *Place-Names of Oxfordshire*
PNWa	Gover *et al.*, *Place-Names of Warwickshire*
PNWilts	Gover *et al.*, *Place-Names of Wiltshire*
PNWo	Mawer *et al.*, *Place-Names of Worcestershire*
PPRS	Publications of the Pipe Roll Society
PRIA	*Proceedings of the Royal Irish Academy*
QJGS	*Quarterly Journal of the Geological Society of London*
RB	*Revue bénédictine*
RC	*Revue celtique*
RCHM	Royal Commission on Historical Monuments (England)
RCHM Gl	RCHM, *County of Gloucester*
RES	*Review of English Studies*
RHE	*Revue d'histoire ecclésiastique*
RS	Rolls Series (Memorials and Chronicles of Great Britain and Ireland during the Middle Ages)
S	Sawyer, *Anglo-Saxon Charters: A Handlist* {charter cited by no.}

SC	Sources chrétiennes
SE	*Sacris Erudiri*
Settimane	*Settimane di studio del Centro italiano di studi sull'alto medioevo* (Spoleto)
Shr.	Shropshire
So.	Somerset
Tangl	*Die Briefe des heiligen Bonifatius und Lullus*, ed. Tangl
TBAS	*Transactions of the Birmingham Archaeological Society*
TBGAS	*Transactions of the Bristol and Gloucestershire Archaeological Society*
TBWAS	*Transactions of the Birmingham and Warwickshire Archaeological Society*
TCBS	*Transactions of the Cambridge Bibliographical Society*
TLSSAHS	*Transactions of the Lichfield and South Staffordshire Archaeological and Historical Society*
TPS	*Transactions of the Philological Society*
TRHS	*Transactions of the Royal Historical Society*
TSAS	*Transactions of the Shropshire Archaeological Society*
TWAS	*Transactions of the Worcestershire Archaeological Society*
TWNFC	*Transactions of the Woolhope Naturalists' Field Club*
VCH Gl	*Victoria County History of Gloucestershire*
VCH Wa	*Victoria County History of Warwickshire*
VCH Wo	*Victoria County History of Worcestershire*
VEHSRP	*Vale of Evesham Historical Society Research Papers*
VW	*Vita S. Wilfridi*, ed. and trans. Colgrave, *Life of Saint Wilfrid*
Wa.	Warwickshire
WMA	*West Midlands Archaeology* [CBA Group 8]
WMANS	*West Midlands Archaeological News Sheet* [CBA Group 8; continued as *WMA*]
Wo.	Worcestershire
ZKT	*Zeitschrift für katholische Theologie*

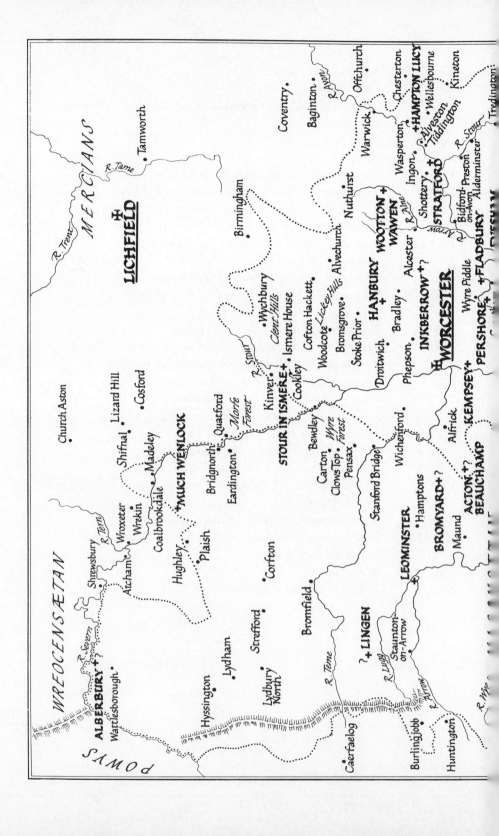

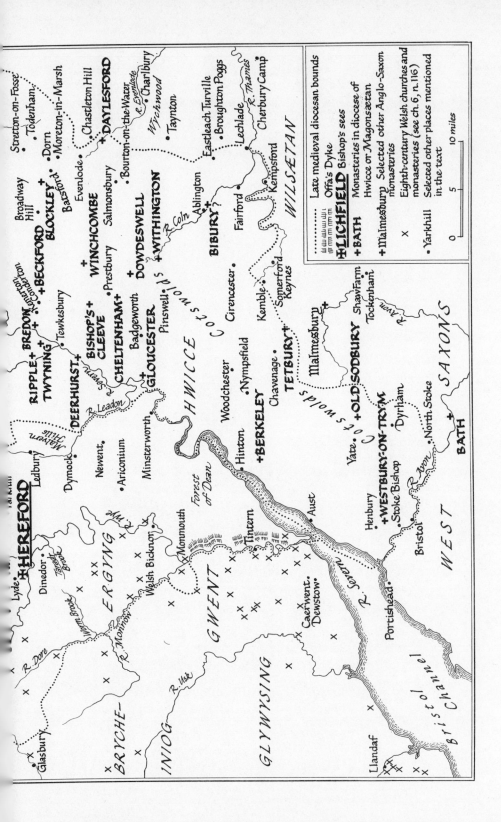

I

Introduction

King of the perennial holly-groves, the riven sandstone: overlord of the M5: architect of the historic rampart and ditch, the citadel at Tamworth, the summer hermitage in Holy Cross: guardian of the Welsh Bridge and the Iron Bridge: contractor to the desirable new estates: saltmaster: moneychanger: commissioner for oaths: martyrologist: the friend of Charlemagne.

'I liked that,' said Offa, 'sing it again.'

Geoffrey Hill, Mercian Hymns, no. 1

This book is an attempt to recover a coherent picture of two seventh- and eighth-century Anglo-Saxon kingdoms in western England, centred on the Avon and Severn valleys and bordering on Wales.[1] The Anglo-Saxons of this area are now almost forgotten, because, unlike their Northumbrian counterparts, they have left us no narrative history nor early saints' lives. Historians have had nothing like Bede's *Historia ecclesiastica* or Stephen's *Vita S. Wilfridi* to retell and reinterpret. Yet much can be pieced together from extant letters, poems, manuscripts and land charters; early charters in particular survived in large numbers, notably at Worcester, partly because the area lay outside the main sphere of Viking attacks in the ninth and tenth centuries. The range of fragmentary and disparate sources presents problems in assembling and interpreting the material, but I hope to show that the challenge of combining very varied types of evidence is worth taking up. For me, Wilhelm Levison's *England and the Continent in the Eighth Century* (The Ford Lectures for 1943) was a particularly inspiring demonstration that evidence often compartmentalized as 'literary' and 'historical' can be combined. I want to show that Levison's broad approach can in turn co-exist with the English tradition of interdisciplinary regional studies.

[1] I use 'west' (as opposed to 'south-west' and 'north-west') to refer to the area that used conveniently to be called the 'West Midlands' before that term was adopted as a new county name in the 1974 local government reorganization. Roughly speaking, my area covers the former counties of Gl., He. and Wo., and parts of Wa. and Shr.

This is essentially a work of description and interpretation. I have not approached my chosen period and area with a preconceived set of questions and hypotheses, preferring to allow these to emerge as the evidence was studied. While it would be naive to deny that the scope of this book reflects my own interests, preoccupations and assumptions, I believe that to a much greater degree it reflects the limitations of the surviving sources. These are simply inadequate to answer many standard historical questions. For example, the excellent studies by Hooke and Dyer reveal that the pre-800 evidence for even the best documented part of the area has little to offer the landscape- and socio-economic historian by comparison with the later Anglo-Saxon and post-Conquest evidence. Many tracts of land distant from churches and church estates went unrecorded; whole strata of society were too poor to be mentioned in the land charters that tacitly disposed of their labour, services and renders; and the charters' formal phraseology and terminology limit our insight into the social relationships of the secular aristocracy.[2] By contrast, the charters do enable us to build up a detailed picture of change, development and variety in the life of the church. Again, literary historians may be disappointed that the literature which can be localized in the area is predominantly ecclesiastical and exclusively Latin rather than vernacular. Theories that the Old English 'elegies' were composed near the Welsh border or that *The Ruin* describes the city of Bath cannot, alas, be proved, although we note with interest that seventh-century Worcester had close links with Whitby, where Cædmon composed Christian poetry in Old English.[3] On the other hand, if we cannot show that any extant Old English poem was composed in seventh-century Worcester, we can study a seventh-century abbess's biblical commentary,

[2] Hooke, *Hwicce* (cf. below, p. 363); Dyer, *Lords and Peasants*. For the basic problem that we cannot distinguish between sales and gifts cf. below, p. 96. The precise significance of the Latin terminology for aristocrats below the royal ranks of *regulus* and *subregulus* — *praefectus*, *comes*, *minister*, etc. — is all too frequently vague; see Loyn, 'The Term Ealdorman', 'Gesiths and Thegns', and *Governance*, pp. 48–9; Whitelock, 'Some Charters', pp. 89 and 97–8; Campbell, *Essays*, pp. 85–98; Thacker, 'Some Terms for Noblemen'; Wallace-Hadrill, *Commentary*, pp. 67 and 223. In this book I tend to prefer the familiar term 'thegn' where the sources may have meant *gesith* by *comes*. A fuller understanding of the aristocracy of the sub-kingdoms may come from an investigation of the witness-lists of the Mercian charters as a whole, a major desideratum.

[3] *HE* IV.23–4. Cf. *The Seafarer*, ed. I. L. Gordon (London, 1960), pp. 31–2; *Three Old English Elegies*, ed. R. F. Leslie (Manchester, 1961), pp. 33–4 and 36; R. I. Page, *Anglo-Saxon Aptitudes: An Inaugural Lecture* (Cambridge, 1985), pp. 20–4.

now in Germany, an eighth-century bishop's collection of Latin poetry, now in the United States; and even in the British Library we find a fascinating prayer book from Worcester, 'almost untouched ... when so much is poured forth in print, and by learned societies too, that signifies so little'.[4]

This book contains many personal and place-names, but, owing to the nature of the sources, no rounded personalities step off the page, and no palaces or monasteries rise up in splendour. A few individuals stand out – a sick brother in Wenlock monastery who reported a vision of the afterlife, a bishop of Worcester noted for his letter-writing and poetry-collecting – and glimpses of one or two places are caught from archaeological excavation. For the most part, however, we have to observe patterns in conglomerations of small pieces of evidence, such as the distribution of artefacts, place-names, monasteries and manuscripts, and then assess how far those patterns have been distorted, or even created, by the way in which the evidence has survived. For instance, most comparisons between the kingdoms of the Hwicce and Magonsætan are vitiated by the different degrees to which evidence has been preserved in the corresponding dioceses of Worcester and Hereford. Nearly all early records of the see of Hereford are believed to have been destroyed in 1055 when the Welsh sacked and burnt the cathedral 'with all its ornaments'.[5] By contrast, at Worcester we have the benefit not only of the massive so-called 'Hemming's Cartulary', which was compiled partly in the time of Bishop Wulfstan I (resigned 1016) and partly soon after the death of Wulfstan II in 1095, but also of the fact that many other cartularies, calendars of grants, and single-sheet charters survived at Worcester long enough after the Reformation to be preserved or copied by antiquaries.[6] Moreover, the fact that the monastic revivals of the tenth century and later were promoted less vigorously in Hereford diocese than they were by St Oswald, bishop of Worcester, and others in his diocese, meant that fewer independent monastic archives were

---

[4] BL, Royal 2. A. xx. Thus E. Bishop, *Liturgica*, pp. 179 and 391; but the former point, at least, still holds. Cf. N. Abercrombie, *The Life and Work of Edmund Bishop* (London, 1959), pp. 363–4.

[5] Cf. Sims-Williams, 'William', p. 13, n. 24.

[6] BL, Cotton Tiberius A. xiii, ed. Hearne, *Hemingi Chartularium* (cf. Ker, *Books, Collectors and Libraries*, pp. 31–59; Scharer, *Königsurkunde*, pp. 281–4). For other Worcester materials see.*ECWM*, pp. 11–18 (note further the calendars of grants to Worcester in *Hemingi Chartularium*, ed. Hearne II, 369; cf. BCS 1320) and in *Worcester Cartulary*, ed. Darlington, pp. 1–3); Sawyer, *Anglo-Saxon Charters*, pp. 44–67 (under relevant charters); and Sims-Williams, 'Cuthswith', pp. 6–8 and references.

conserved in Hereford diocese. As a result, although we may have a shrewd suspicion that many of the greater 'minster churches' of Herefordshire and Shropshire at the time of Domesday Book originated in seventh- or eighth-century monastic foundations comparable to monasteries in Worcester diocese such as Gloucester, Evesham and Pershore, this cannot be proved.[7]

While some of the limitations of the evidence are predictable, there is often no way of telling how representative the surviving evidence is. There were surely monasteries and writers and kings of whom we do not know even the names. The search for manuscripts will take us to Boulogne-sur-Mer, Würzburg, and Urbana, Illinois; but major codices may have disappeared without trace, and others, whose origin is unrecognized, may survive elsewhere in England or abroad. As Sisam remarked (speaking of *c.* 1000 AD), 'the movement of books from place to place must be reckoned common, not exceptional . . . Books tended to stay in one place when they were stillborn, or obsolete, or when the place was isolated. But the only way of disseminating texts, and one way of securing extra copies, was to send them from one place to another'.[8] Our jigsaw is so incomplete that we do not know how many pieces are missing, nor how big it is. I hope to show that it is still worth attempting.

The geographical limits of this study are those of the later medieval dioceses of Worcester and Hereford (see fig. 1), with some slight adjustments where these are known to be anachronistic.[9] Such anachronisms

---

[7] See, for example, the map by Blair, 'Secular Minster Churches', pp. 108–9. I have resisted the temptation to argue backwards from *unsupported* post-800 evidence. Cf. below, p. 133, n. 86.

[8] Sisam, *Studies*, p. 228.

[9] The later medieval diocesan boundaries, immediately before Henry VIII's reforms, are mapped on the O.S. map *Monastic Britain: South Sheet*, 2nd ed. (Southampton, 1954), on the basis of the maps of Gloucester, Hereford and Worcester dioceses in *Valor ecclesiasticus temp. Henr. VIII auctoritate regia institutus*, 6 vols., Record Commission (London, 1810–34) II and III; see also Rees, *South Wales and the Border*, and my map, fig. 1. The most complete earlier evidence for them is the thirteenth-century *Taxatio ecclesiastica Angliae et Walliae auctoritate P. Nicholai IV circa A.D. 1291*, Record Commission (London, 1802). The later Worcester boundary varies from the early Anglo-Saxon one in excluding Bath, which had been transferred from Mercia to Wessex in the tenth century (see Taylor, 'Bath', and J. A. Robinson, *The Saxon Bishops of Wells*, British Academy Supplemental Papers 4 (London, [1919]), p. 5), but it is also known to differ somewhat on the Hereford border (see below, p. 43). Cf. below, n. 12.

are few, for the diocesan boundaries seem to have remained remarkably stable down to the creation of the diocese of Gloucester in the sixteenth century. My study does not cover the area of the Midlands and northern Welsh marches that lay within the great Mercian diocese of Lichfield (later Chester and Coventry); this deserves separate treatment on a similar scale, by some other hand.

It is obviously appropriate to use diocesan boundaries in a book partly concerned with ecclesiastical affairs. A compelling reason for using them is the strong probability that they have fossilized the secular boundaries of the seventh and eighth centuries. At this period the area was dominated from the north by the Mercians (*Mierce*), who also controlled the Middle Anglian region to the east; they did not, however, control the West Saxon region to the south nor the Welsh kingdoms to the west. The area was divided into two kingdoms, the kingdom of the Hwicce and the kingdom of the Magonsætan (also spelt *Magansæte* etc.). Their kings or, later, sub-kings and ealdormen, were under the overlordship of the kings of Mercia. Documentary and place-name evidence shows that the kingdom of the Hwicce corresponded with remarkable precision to the medieval diocese of Worcester, whose bishops sometimes styled themselves *episcopi Hwicciorum*.[10] West of the river Severn we have much less evidence – there are fewer early charters and the English Place-Name Society has yet to cover Herefordshire and Shropshire – but what evidence there is, coupled with the analogy of the Worcester diocese and the known tendency of the church to follow existing political boundaries (and ignore them when they change), points to the conclusion that the Hereford diocese corresponded to the kingdom of the Magonsætan.[11] Hence as late as the sixteenth century the ecclesiastical boundaries perpetuated the early Anglo-Saxon secular boundaries much more accurately than did the later administrative districts across which they seemed to cut so anomalously: the shires of Warwick, Worcester, Gloucester, Hereford and Shrewsbury. These shires, together with the short-lived shire of Winchcombe, were West Saxon administrative units, imposed with complete disregard for local sentiment

[10] Smith, 'Hwicce' and *PNGl* IV, 31–3; Hooke, *Hwicce*, pp. 6 and 12–15. I need not rehearse the evidence.

[11] Here I agree with Finberg, *ECWM*, p. 228, and with Smith, 'Hwicce', p. 59, and *PNGl* IV, 32. A parallel case was the bishopric of the Middle Angles, which served the kingdom of the same name set up by the Mercians.

and tradition, after the decline of Mercian power under Viking and West Saxon pressure in the ninth century.[12]

The two kingdoms and dioceses had certain aspects in common. Both kingdoms became subservient to the Mercian kings. Both dioceses were created, probably in the 670s, by carving up the immense, unwieldy Mercian diocese of Lichfield. In both, an Anglian variety of Old English was spoken, as in Mercia.[13] On the other hand there are obvious physical differences. The kingdom of the Hwicce, centred on the Avon and lower Severn valleys, was relatively low-lying and was surrounded by other Anglo-Saxon kingdoms, whereas the Magonsætan occupied a frontier kingdom, both geographically, since it lay at the division between the Lowland and Highland zones of Britain,[14] and historically, since its western borders must have been established by force of arms against an indigenous Welsh aristocracy. Unfortunately the sources are simply inadequate to permit theses about the impact of the 'frontier' on the form and ethos of this western society;[15] a suggestion of a 'heroic age' may be gained, rightly or wrongly, from retrospective Welsh *englyn* poetry of the ninth or tenth centuries and, on the English side of the border, from the large number of place-names compounding *hlaw/hlæw* 'burial mound' with personal names of archaic or royal appearance.[16] The two kingdoms and

[12] See Stenton, *Anglo-Saxon England*, pp. 293 and 336–7; C. S. Taylor, 'The Origin of the Mercian Shires', in *Gloucestershire Studies*, ed. Finberg, pp. 17–51; Smith, 'Hwicce', p. 60 and n. 22; Finberg, *Agrarian History*, p. 479; Sawyer, *Roman Britain to Norman England*, p. 197. Taylor argues (pp. 19–20) that the Mercian shires must have originated after Alfred's reign since they disregard the line of division agreed with Guthrum (886–90). Stenton favours the last years of Edward the Elder (899–924 or 925). Taylor and Finberg favour 1007×1016 (regarding the *ASC* entry for 1006 as not quite contemporary); but Hemming's entry, quoted by Taylor (p. 25) and Finberg (*ECWM*, p. 234), may imply that the shires existed *before* the time of Eadric Streona. On Winchcombeshire see *ECWM*, pp. 228–35 and Bassett, 'Search', pp. 6–7. I have not seen J. Whybra, *A Lost English County: Winchcombeshire* (Woodbridge, 1989). I refer throughout to Wo., Gl., etc. simply for the sake of topographical convenience; cf. below, n. 21. A useful map of diocesan and shire boundaries (erroneous near Wenlock) is given by Barlow, *English Church 1000–1066*, p. 161.

[13] Except in the extreme south of Gloucestershire; cf. *PNGl* IV, 41 and 43.

[14] But on this distinction cf. Fowler, 'Lowland Landscapes'.

[15] Cf. *The Turner Thesis concerning the Role of the Frontier in American History*, ed. G. R. Taylor, 3rd ed. (Lexington, 1972); L. H. Nelson, *The Normans in South Wales, 1070–1171* (Austin, 1966), pp. 181–4; *Medieval Frontier Societies*, ed. R. Bartlett and A. MacKay (Oxford, 1989).

[16] Cf. below, p. 29, n. 61; Sims-Williams, 'Settlement', p. 4, n. 11.

dioceses studied in this book do not together constitute a meaningful region vis-à-vis the rest of Britain.

I would maintain, however, that each kingdom on its own can be regarded as a 'region' in a social and psychological sense. Admittedly, they cannot have been of any antiquity in the seventh century, for Anglo-Saxons are unlikely to have begun to settle the area in any numbers before the sixth century and there is no reason to ascribe a Celtic origin to the kingdoms. Indeed, it is possible that neither was created until the mid-seventh century, out of what was undoubtedly a diverse mixture of smaller population groups, some of which are known to us by name.[17] Yet, however ethnologically disparate each kingdom may have been originally, it would inevitably have been shaped into a region with an identity of its own by the reiterated activities of kings and their agents overseeing their estates, collecting their food-renders and exercising secular power in other ways, and by the work of bishops ministering to, ruling and visiting the diocese corresponding to the kingdom.[18] These multifarious administrative activities would have given some sense of social and perceptual unity to kingdoms which were not discrete linguistic or economic entities, though they had some geophysical basis.[19] They may even have encouraged linguistic and economic cohesion. As Dr Stafford remarks of the East Midlands, 'administrative boundaries played an important role in defining communities, turning groups on either side of an imaginary line in different directions, towards different groups and centres'.[20] We may compare the degree of loyalty which the originally artificial West Midland shires have now gained, as revealed by the storms of protest when central

---

[17] See below, p. 31.

[18] For bishops travelling round their dioceses see Bede's *Epistola ad Ecgbertum* (*BOH* I, 405–23; *EHD*, no. 170). No early itinerary is extant, but in later periods they give graphic evidence of diocesan cohesion. See, for example, that of the Bishop of Hereford in 1290, mapped by J. R. H. Moorman, *Church Life in England in the Thirteenth Century* (Cambridge, 1945), p. 189; cf. Dyer, *Lords and Peasants*, p. 55.

[19] See ch. 12 below for the kingdom of the Hwicce. Hilton's *A Medieval Society* is a successful socio-economic study of a thirteenth-century region (Worcester diocese, plus the rest of Gloucestershire and Warwickshire) which comprised areas which were 'strongly contrasted, topographically, economically and socially' (p. 12; cf. p. 8). A strict definition of 'region' by Hoskins is followed by Ford, 'Settlement Patterns', p. 280, but for a more fluid approach see Everitt, *Continuity and Colonization*, pp. 5–6 and 335–6.

[20] Stafford, *East Midlands*, pp. 138–9.

government imposed new counties such as 'Avon' and 'Hereford and Worcester' in 1974.[21]

Such regional loyalties in the seventh and eighth centuries are more easily inferred than demonstrated, because of the limitations of the evidence. For instance, in later periods the regional loyalties of laymen are sometimes revealed by their wills;[22] but no pre-ninth-century Anglo-Saxon wills survive. We may, however, note an account of a synod in (?)804, attended by the Mercian king and the bishops of Canterbury, Leicester, Worcester, Hereford and Lindsey, according to which a layman, Æthelric son of Æthelmund, bequeathed extensive lands in the kingdom of Hwicce to his mother, who may have been abbess of Berkeley, and to other religious houses, all within the kingdom: Deerhurst, Gloucester and the see of Worcester.[23] Again, oral poetry may have been fiercely regional, but the only relevant branch of early secular 'literature' which stood much chance of being written down and surviving was genealogy; and by the time that the extant Anglian collection of genealogies was redacted in the late eighth century, the expansion of Mercian power had made the royal lines of the Hwicce and Magonsætan politically expendable, and so their genealogies do not appear in it.[24] Yet the Mercian supremacy probably did not destroy local loyalties; indeed, reaction to Mercian hegemony may have reinforced them. Stenton held that the rulers of the Hwicce in their last charters 'assert, and even emphasize, the shadow of kingship that belonged to them'.[25] No literary tribute to this kingship has been preserved, but the unfavourable nature of the recording can hardly be overemphasized: had the Hwicce and Magonsætan proved to be dominant powers in later Anglo-Saxon England, their own traditions of early greatness might be as prominent in the record as those of the West Saxons are in the *Anglo-Saxon Chronicle*.[26]

A measure of a community's cohesion, it has been said, is its distrust of outsiders.[27] Such distrust is not explicitly revealed by our sources, but there are examples of inter-regional conflict which may be counted as a product and cause of distrust of neighbouring kingdoms and peoples. For

---

[21] Following the EPNS, I avoid using these units.   [22] See below, p. 94, n. 26.
[23] See below, pp. 38–9 and 174–6.   [24] See Dumville, 'Anglian Collection'.
[25] *Anglo-Saxon England*, p. 46. Cf. Scharer, 'Intitulationes', pp. 36–7.
[26] Cf. Sims-Williams, 'Settlement', pp. 26–41.
[27] G. C. Homans, *English Villagers of the Thirteenth Century* (Cambridge, Mass., 1942), p. 328.

instance, in 802 the ealdorman Æthelmund, probably the father of the Æthelric mentioned above, rode from the province of the Hwicce across the border at Kempsford on the Thames, 'and Ealdorman Weohstan with the Wilsætan [people of Wiltshire] met him, and a great battle took place, and both ealdormen were killed and the Wilsætan had the victory'.[28] Another dispute comes into the open the following year in the ecclesiastical sphere, at a council presided over by the archbishop of Canterbury: the bishops of Worcester and Hereford argue about their churches' ancient rights over the monasteries of Cheltenham and Beckford, and after witnesses have been heard and much said on both sides, the archbishop arranges a compromise.[29] Besides such conflicts among the Anglo-Saxon kingdoms or dioceses, there was also tension between them and their Welsh neighbours which would have encouraged self-definition on both sides. Offa's Dyke is the most enduring monument to this tension, but perhaps the most eloquent testimony is the early tenth-century ordinance on litigation among the Dunsæte ('hill-dwellers', or 'dwellers near *Dunre*, i.e. Dinedor'?), who were English and Welsh peoples dwelling on either side of a river usually identified as the Wye.[30] The secular distrust between English and Welsh spilled over into the ecclesiastical sphere, and neither group scrupled to sack the other's churches.[31] The 'ecclesiastical saga'[32]

[28] *ASC.* Cf. Loyn, *Governance*, p. 56; and below, p. 38.   [29] See below, pp. 138–9.

[30] *Die Gesetze der Angelsachsen*, ed. F. Liebermann (Halle, 1903–16) I, 374–9, II, 214–19, III, 355–6; facsimile of Cambridge, Corpus Christi College 383, and translation in Noble, *Offa's Dyke Reviewed*, pp. 103–9. Cf. *CP*, pp. 198 and 358–9; G. Garnett, '"Franci et Angli": The Legal Distinctions between Peoples after the Conquest', in *Anglo-Norman Studies VIII: Proceedings of the Battle Conference, 1985*, ed. R. A. Brown (Woodbridge, 1986), pp. 109–37, at 134. Derivation of *Dunsæte* from OE *dūn* 'hill' (see *PNE* II, 94) is preferable to the Welsh etymology (*dwfn*) given by Förster, *Themse*, p. 175, and to Noble's 'down river people' (p. 17). A connection with Dinedor Camp (SO/5236) was suggested by Jones, 'Early Historic Settlement', p. 130. This name contains Welsh *din* 'fort' < Celtic **dūno-*, but this element interchanged in bilingual areas with OE *dūn* (*PNE* I, 139, cf. Gelling, *Place-Names in the Landscape*, p. 141), hence the Domesday name for the vill and hundred of Dinedor (later part of Webtree hundred) was *Dunre* (with Welsh *-vre* < *bre* 'hill' or *-dre(f)* < *tref* 'hamlet' according to Charles, 'Archenfield and Oswestry', p. 86): O. S. Anderson, *The English Hundred Names* [Part I] (Lund, 1934), p. 168. The unnamed river usually identified with the Wye could be a smaller stream such as the Taradr (which runs by Dinedor) or the Worm, which together formed a significant cultural boundary; cf. below, p. 45 and n. 148.

[31] See below, pp. 29, n. 60, and 46, n. 149.

[32] N. K. Chadwick's apt phrase, *The Age of the Saints in the Early Celtic Church* (Oxford, 1961), p. 122 (cf. Wallace-Hadrill, *Commentary*, p. 126). See below, p. 78, n. 94.

relayed by Bede about St Augustine of Canterbury's frosty meeting with the British bishops at 'Augustine's Oak', on the borders of the Hwicce and West Saxons, may not tell us anything about historical events *c.* 600, but it does nevertheless bear witness to the deep mutual suspicion that existed between the English and Welsh churches by the early eighth century.

In short, then, we are quite justified in taking the kingdoms and dioceses of the Hwicce and Magonsætan as the limits of this study. But if these two units are not arbitrary, neither can they be regarded as self-contained. The same communication systems that tended to unify each also provided access to neighbouring regions and even further afield for persons of sufficient means.[33] The Roman road-system had indeed been expressly designed to subjugate British kingdoms, the boundaries of which, while different from those of the Anglo-Saxon kingdoms, also had some natural geographical basis. Some of the nodal points of the Roman system, such as Kenchester, Alcester and Droitwich, lay within the English kingdoms and would have helped to unify them; but others, such as Wroxeter, Gloucester and Bath, lay near their frontiers and would have had the opposite effect.[34] Place-name and other evidence suggests that the Roman roads continued to play their part in communications in the Anglo-Saxon period.[35] Some long-distance prehistoric tracks were presumably still in use, too, although it is difficult to find evidence for the relative importance, or even existence, of routes such as the 'Jurassic Way' along the Oolite ridge from Somerset to the Humber, or the Clun-Clee track from Cardigan Bay, which is supposed to ford the Severn at Bewdley and there bifurcate, with one branch leading up to the Clents and thence southwards along the 'Ridgeway' towards Alcester, and the other leading

---

[33] On roads in the area see D. Hooke, 'The Reconstruction of Ancient Routeways', *LH* 12 (1976–7), 212–20, *West Midlands*, pp. 300–14, and *Hwicce*, pp. 58–62, 120–2, 125 and 145–9; L. E. W. O. Fullbrook-Leggatt, 'Saxon Gloucestershire', *TBGAS* 57 (1935), 110–35 (pp. 116–19 and map); *RCHM Gl* i, xlv–xlviii.

[34] See Margary, *Roman Roads* ii, map, and the O.S. maps of *Roman, Dark Age*, and *Pre-Conquest Britain*.

[35] For references to Roman and other roads in charters, etc. see *PNWo*, pp. 2–9; *PNWa*, pp. 7–11; *PNGl* i, 15–21 and iv, 16–17, 21–4, 28 and maps. It has often been argued that Roman roads influenced the siting of Anglo-Saxon settlements, but the relevance of Roman roads to 'early' place-names, including those in *-hām* (see Gelling, *Signposts*, pp. 112 and 117), has been questioned; see D. Kenyon, 'The Antiquity of *hām* Place-Names in Lancashire and Cheshire', *Nomina* 10 (1986), 11–27; Copley, *Archaeology and Place-Names*, pp. 2–3, and *Anglian Regions*, p. 4.

to Worcester.[36] A further system of communications was provided by the spider's web of saltways which radiated far outside the Hwiccian kingdom from its vital brine springs at Droitwich. The reconstruction of these 'salterstreets' depends mainly on late Anglo-Saxon or later allusions, but seventh-century royal grants of rights over brine pits and salt pans at Droitwich imply that many of the saltways which carried the salt from Droitwich (Roman *Salinis*), and brought the fuel to its furnaces, were very old.[37] Besides these old routes, the political and economic needs of the kingdoms would be bound to give rise to new roads like the 'Portways' which led to Worcester in the late Anglo-Saxon period.[38]

Some indication of the area's links with the outside world is given by the distribution of seventh- and eighth-century coins, even though the number of surviving coins is too small for the evidence to stand interpretation in terms of chronological ebb and flow – for example, no coins of Offa (757–96) are known to have been found here apart from a penny at Woodcote near Chaddesley Corbett, Wo., and two pennies in the east, near Bidford-on-Avon, Wa.[39] If we leave aside, as presumably belonging

[36] O.S. *Map of Southern Britain in the Iron Age* (Southampton, 1962); W. F. Grimes, 'The Jurassic Way', in *Aspects of Archaeology in Britain and Beyond: Essays presented to O. G. S. Crawford*, ed. W. F. Grimes (London, 1951), pp. 144–71; Finberg, *Gloucestershire Landscape*, pp. 35–6 (for minor trackways in the Cotswolds, partly taken over by the Romans, see pp. 39–40, 42 and 71 and n.; cf. Margary, *Roman Roads* I, 132–4); L. F. Chitty, 'The Clun-Clee Ridgeway: A Prehistoric Trackway across South Shropshire', in *Culture and Environment*, ed. Foster and Alcock, pp. 171–92; Thorpe, 'Growth of Settlement', pp. 91–2 (for the Ridge Way see *PNWo*, p. 4). Healthy scepticism about 'routeways' is expressed by Christopher Taylor in his *Roads and Tracks of Britain* (London, 1979), pp. 38–9 (see pp. 32–3 and 184 on the 'Jurassic Way') and *Village and Farmstead*, p. 17.

[37] Besides the treatment in the EPNS volumes (above, n. 35), see Houghton, 'Salt-ways', with map; Hilton, *A Medieval Society*, pp. 11–12 (with map based on [W. T.] Whitley, 'Saltways of Droitwich District', *TBAS* 49 (1923), 1–15); Darby and Terrett, *Domesday Geography*, pp. 38–9 and 252–3; Hooke, *Hwicce*, p. 125, fig. 31. The element *wich* 'salt works, brine spring' is probably a ghost-word (*PNE* II, 260; cf. Gelling, *Signposts*, p. 67). For charter references to Droitwich see *ECWM*, p. 249; Hooke, 'Droitwich Salt Industry', and *Hwicce*, pp. 122–6. For a possible 'late Roman/early Saxon' timber structure at the 'Great Brine Pit' in Droitwich see J. Price, 'Droitwich, Upwich', *WMA* 27 (1984), 61–2.

[38] *PNWo*, pp. 3–4 (cf. *PNWa*, pp. 9–10; *PNGl* I, 18; *PNE* II, 70–1); Hooke, 'Hinter-land', and *Hwicce*, pp. 120–2.

[39] M. A. S. Blackburn and M. J. Bonser, 'Single Finds of Anglo-Saxon and Norman Coins – 2', *BNJ* 55 (1985), 55–78, at 59–60; Bidford coins from unpublished list by W. A.

in a late British context, finds of Roman coins 'from Augustus to Phocas AD 602' at Castle Mound, Worcester,[40] we see the distribution of the seventh-century gold coinage beginning to impinge on the south-eastern corner of the Hwiccian kingdom towards the middle of that century, with an Anglo-Saxon runic coin of *c.* 625 at Eastleach Turville, Gl., which may originate from the middle Thames valley, and a Merovingian (Meuse valley) coin of *c.* 650 at Bourton-on-the-Water, Gl.[41] The silver coinage of the last quarter of the century and the first half of the eighth does not reach the area until after *c.* 700, and never spreads to the Magonsætan. It comprises, first, four 'porcupine sceattas' at Worcester, at Alcester, Wa., and at Marl-cliff near Bidford-on-Avon, Wa. (two coins) – these probably originated in Frisia or the lower Rhineland;[42] and then ten native 'sceattas' at Alve-church, Badsey and Sedgeberrow, Wo., Chedworth and Temple Guiting, Gl., Bidford-on-Avon, Wa., and – a little to the south of the Hwicce – at Shakenoak near Witney, Ox. (three coins) and Portishead, Som.[43] Nine of

Seaby via Mr Blackburn. (There were also three pennies from Coenwulf's reign at Bidford, and Mr Blackburn tells me that another, of *c.* 800, was found near Tewkesbury in 1988.) For a map of Offa's coinage (made before these finds) see Hill, *Atlas*, p. 123.

[40] See below, p. 89, n. 10.

[41] See map by S. E. Rigold in *Sutton Hoo*, ed. Bruce-Mitford 1, 656 (his items 67a and 127), with review by D. M. Metcalf in *ASE* 6 (1977), 252–3; I. Stewart, 'Anglo-Saxon Gold Coins', in *Scripta Nummaria Romana: Essays presented to Humphrey Sutherland*, ed. R. A. G. Carson and C. M. Kraay (London, 1978), pp. 143–72, at 149 and n. 44; P. Grierson and M. Blackburn, *Medieval European Coinage* (Cambridge, 1986–) 1, 161 and 488, no. 490. The coin-like pendant from Compton Verney is not, in fact, a coin; see below, p. 69. The provenance of the Bourton coin depends on a ticket accompanying it, which Prof. Grierson would guess goes back near to the discovery in 1850; Mr Blackburn suggests the date *c.* 650 judging by the fineness.

[42] Metcalf, 'Monetary Affairs', p. 94; Rigold and Metcalf, 'Revised Check-List', p. 266; W. A. Seaby, 'Alcester', *WMA* 29 (1986), 47 (quoting Metcalf's identification of this coin as the VICO/VOIC type of Series E); R. Hingley *et al.*, 'Bidford-on-Avon', *WMA* 30 (1987), 41. For the Low Countries origin see Metcalf, 'Monetary Circulation', p. 32; Blackburn, 'Chronology', pp. 166 and 173; cf., differing in respect of VICO/VOIC, W. op den Velde *et al.*, 'A Survey of Sceatta Finds from the Low Countries', in *Sceattas*, ed. Hill and Metcalf, pp. 131 and 138–9.

[43] Metcalf, 'Monetary Circulation', pp. 64–5, and Rigold and Metcalf, 'Revised Check-List', s.nn. I know of the Bidford coin, discovered at Marlcliff in 1988, from an unpublished note by W. A. Seaby, via Mr Blackburn. A connection between the Temple Guiting coin and the hypothetical Anglo-Saxon secondary barrow burial is very uncertain; see O'Neil, 'Bevans Quarry', pp. 19 and 37. It is of a type – U (23e) – which may be as early as *c.* 720; cf. Blackburn, 'Chronology', pp. 166–7 and 168, n. 10.

these native coins (all except the one from Temple Guiting) belong to a distinct group which are modelled on London prototypes, and of which some examples elsewhere are of London provenance or bear more or less corrupt versions of the inscription *DE LVNDONIA*. Metcalf suggested that they may have been minted among the Hwicce, perhaps at Worcester, coming thence to London, where the bishops of Worcester engaged in trade.[44] On the other hand, the subsequent discoveries near Cambridge and near Royston, Hertfordshire, of two coins from the same die as the Badsey coin may point back to London or the south-east: they have suggested the hypotheses that the 'Hwiccian sceattas' may be 'a freak group possibly representing the survivors of one or more large payments from the Thames basin' or may be due to 'a relatively late extension of coin circulation into that [Hwiccian] region'.[45] Exchange for salt from Droitwich[46] or wool from the Cotswolds are possible contexts.

These finds are very few compared to south-eastern England, but in assessing this it must be borne in mind that the Midlands were on the edge of the area in which money circulated; judging by the negative numismatic evidence, so vast an administrative feat as Offa's Dyke was achieved without money changing hands.[47] Moreover, even the powerful Mercian kings of the central eighth century had most of their coinage minted in Kent, London and East Anglia,[48] and probably ran a balance-of-payments deficit with the southern kingdoms which controlled continental imports. Rather than dwelling on the negative aspect of the coin evidence, we should regard what survives as further proof of the area's links with the outside world.

The bulk of the population may have been mobile within even less than a

---

[44] Metcalf, 'Sceattas from the Territory of the Hwicce'; 'Monetary Affairs', pp. 99–100; 'Monetary Circulation', pp. 34, 36 and n. 21, 37, 47 and 64–5. Cf. below, p. 147.

[45] M. Blackburn and D. Sorenson, 'Sceattas from an Unidentified Site near Cambridge', in *Sceattas*, ed. Hill and Metcalf, p. 224; M. A. S. Blackburn and M. J. Bonser, 'Single Finds of Anglo-Saxon and Norman Coins – 3', *BNJ* 56 (1986), 64–101, at 73–4, where two further 'sceattas' from near Royston, similar to those from Chedworth and Portishead, are recorded.

[46] Cf. Hooke, *Hwicce*, p. 126.

[47] Cf. Hill, *Atlas*, pp. 75 and 123; Metcalf, 'Monetary Affairs', p. 91; Stewart, 'London Mint', p. 29. For the ninth-century cash economy see Dyer, *Lords and Peasants*, p. 31, citing BCS 309 (S 1431), for which see below, p. 138. Already in 704×709 we hear of six hundred *solidi* changing hands; see below, p. 191.

[48] Cf. Metcalf, 'Monetary Circulation', pp. 36 and n. 22, and 39; Stewart, 'London Mint'.

twenty- or thirty-mile radius of their place of birth (an estimate for the late thirteenth century),[49] and may thus have developed a more or less *unconscious* local identity. Persons of high status evidently travelled much more. Thus we find the thegns of the Mercian court attesting charters from centres much more widely scattered than those attested by the kings of the Hwicce or by the ealdormen of the Hwicce who replaced them; and while many abbots of minor monasteries attest no more surviving charters than the ones relating to the foundation of their own houses, the names of more important abbots occur frequently and widely. To judge by the records of church councils, the bishops of the Hwicce and Magonsætan travelled extensively within the southern province of Canterbury, though the bulk of their activities may have been centred on their own dioceses.[50] Worcester had the distinction, even before the monastic reform of the tenth century, of at least one bishop who had travelled to Rome (Oftfor in the late seventh century) and two who went to Germany (Milred in 753 and Cenwald in 929).[51] Wealthy laymen, like Æthelric son of Æthelmund, made the Roman pilgrimage, and even a brother of a monastery such as Wenlock may have been able to travel overseas.[52] These wider horizons may have made such persons *consciously* aware of the distinctiveness of their own regions.[53]

This said, however, it must be recognized that the Anglo-Saxons of the kingdoms of the Hwicce and Magonsætan display little regional consciousness in their surviving Latin writings. Land charters, despite their evocation of particular places, may be dismissed as functional documents,[54] and the same may be true of Bishop Cuthbert's verses on the tomb of his predecessors and of a *regulus* of the Magonsætan and his queen, which

---

[49] Hilton, *A Medieval Society*, p. 7. Cf. Dyer, *Lords and Peasants*, pp. 366–8.

[50] A map of Mercian royal councils is given by Hill, *Atlas*, p. 83. For church councils (some at unidentified places) see *HBC*[3], pp. 583–9 and Vollrath, *Synoden*. The texts are in H&S III.

[51] See below, pp. 193–4 and 229–37. On Cenwald, who was accompanied by Cynath, abbot of Evesham, see Keynes, 'Athelstan's Books', pp. 198–201. For later diplomatic missions in Germany by Ealdred, bishop of Worcester, see Barlow, *Edward the Confessor*, pp. 169, and n. 3, and 215; M. Lapidge, 'The Origin of CCCC 163', *TCBS* 8 (1981–5), 18–28, at 21–2.

[52] See below, pp. 174 and 243 (where, however, the suggested emendation would keep the monk at Wenlock).

[53] A later instance from the area is Walter Map.

[54] But cf. Barlow, *English Church 1000–1066*, p. 127, n. 2.

William of Malmesbury thought showed 'antiquitatem uiri, quantumque antecessores suos honorificauerit'.[55] The contents of the book of epigrams owned by Cuthbert's contemporary, Bishop Milred of Worcester, show some slight local bias – they may refer to abbots of Hanbury and Kempsey, for example – but this may be due as much to the selection of material to hand as to any particular regional predilection.[56] Similarly, a collection of prayers which may have been compiled at Worcester about his time gathers prayers composed in Lindsey (*Oratio Hygbaldi*) and Wales (*Oratio Moucani*), as well as material which may be of local origin (*Versus Cuð de sancta trinitate*).[57] Among ecclesiastics it was an age of internationalism, as is abundantly attested by those pages in Bede and Stephen about the spread of church music, architecture and learning; in everything the search was for unity and conformity, even if the searchers sometimes made off in opposite directions. Inevitably there were regional variations, for instance in script, but these were probably not deliberately promoted; indeed script could be remarkably standard over a wide area: witness modern scholars' difficulties in distinguishing Mercian and Kentish uncial.[58] Books and scribes were mobile: one manuscript reached the diocese of Worcester from Italy and travelled thence, expertly repaired, to Germany. The basic Christian Latin texts upon which the incipient, proudly imitative, Anglo-Latin literature was raised achieved a wide dissemination.[59] For all these reasons a regional approach would be artificial and parochial in a solely literary investigation. The justification for the inclusion of literary history in the present book is that it adds a dimension to the more conventionally 'historical' account of the kingdoms; it is *not* intended to demonstrate the existence of a peculiarly regional literature. This perspective also justifies consideration not only of texts composed in the area but also of manuscripts compiled or copied in it, or even merely imported at an early date. As André Wilmart remarked, manuscripts are the mirror as well as the vehicle of civilisation.[60]

[55] 'The man's uprightness [*or* sense of antiquity?] and how much honour he would give to his predecessors': *GP*, p. 299. On the verses see below, p. 342.

[56] See below, pp. 355–7. [57] See below, pp. 280, 320–3 and 357–9.

[58] Cf. Engelbert, 'Bemerkungen'. [59] See below, pp. 190–5, 211–42 and 328–59.

[60] 'Les manuscrits n'ont pas été seulement, en raison de leur contenu, le véhicule de la civilisation; ils en ont été aussi, quant à leur aspect, ils en sont toujours à nos yeux le miroir, miroir réduit, tant qu'on voudra, mais fidèle' ('Restes d'un très ancien manuscrit', p. 296).

2

The kingdoms of the Hwicce and the Magonsætan

THE ANGLO-SAXON SETTLEMENT

The early history of Mercia and its sub-kingdoms is obscure because no early traditions about the area have survived from Mercia itself, with a few exceptions such as the Mercian royal genealogies and probably the so-called *Tribal Hidage*.[1] We know about it from the traditions of Mercia's ancient enemies, who were interested in Mercian affairs only insofar as they impinged on their own histories. Neither Bede in Northumbria nor his Kentish and West Saxon informants seem to know much about the settlement of central England; neither do the Welsh sources nor the early part of the *Anglo-Saxon Chronicle*, which reflects the interests of the West Saxon royal house and, in any case, only begins to provide useful information in the seventh century. The Mercians do not appear in the *Historia ecclesiastica* until Bede has occasion to mention that two of Edwin of Northumbria's sons were born during Edwin's exile (that is, before 616) to Cwenburg, daughter of the Mercian king Ceorl.[2] Similarly the Hwicce first enter history because a Northumbrian, St Wilfrid, encountered a princess of their race in Sussex in about 680;[3] and the Magonsætan are not named at all by Bede. It is oddly symptomatic of the way the Mercians are known

---

[1] For the genealogies see Dumville, 'Kingship, Genealogy and Regnal Lists' and 'Anglian Collection'. For a guess that they were compiled at Winchcombe, see Thacker, 'Pre-Viking Mercia', pp. 11–12. On the *Tribal Hidage* see below, n. 5.

[2] *HE* II.14. On Bede's limited knowledge of Mercia see Kirby, 'Bede's Native Sources', pp. 368–70; Sawyer, *Roman Britain to Norman England*, pp. 7–8; Wallace-Hadrill, *Commentary*, p. 140. On the biasses and limitations of *ASC* see Hill, *Atlas*, pp. 20–1; Sims-Williams, 'Settlement', pp. 26–41.

[3] *HE* IV.13. See below, pp. 34 and 57. Cf. Harrison, *Framework*, p. 18.

from the point of view of their neighbours that their very name, *Mierce*, means 'frontier folk'.[4]

The *Tribal Hidage* is a presumably Mercian memorandum, of uncertain practical purpose, estimating the extent of various peoples.[5] It may be as old as the time of Bede, or still earlier, but the manuscripts are eleventh-century and later and the text has probably suffered a good deal of corruption and alteration. Although the compiler estimates the size of the peoples not in spatial units but in hides, a family unit, he clearly thinks of them in geographical terms, not as nebulous tribal groups. He lists them in roughly clockwise order round Mercia, and peoples with old folk-names, who may have had no fixed territory during the migration period, are listed on an equal footing with peoples whose very names, compounded with *-sætan/sæte*, like *W[r]ocensætan* 'dwellers near the Wrekin', show them to have been geographically fixed.[6] His sense of a correlation between particular peoples and particular territories is apparent in his geographical divisions of single peoples (such as the East and West *Wixan*), and is especially clear in the first item, where he distinguishes the land of the Mercians proper (which was centred on the Trent according to Bede) from the greater area they came to rule:

Myrcna landes is þrittig þusend hyda þær mon ærest Myrcna hæt.

Mircheneland est de triginta hidis ab eo loco ubi primum Mircheneland nominatur.[7]

The Hwicce (MSS *Hwinca*, etc.), like some important kingdoms such as Essex and Sussex, are assessed at 7,000 hides, a figure which may imply

---

[4] Which frontier is meant is uncertain; see Stenton, *Anglo-Saxon England*, p. 40; P. Hunter Blair, 'The Northumbrians and their Southern Frontier', *Archaeologia Aeliana*, 4th ser. 26 (1948), 98–126; Sawyer, *Roman Britain to Norman England*, p. 38; Wallace-Hadrill, *Commentary*, p. 227.

[5] BCS 297. Cf. Stenton, *Anglo-Saxon England*, pp. 295–7; Hart, 'Tribal Hidage'; Davies and Vierck, 'Contexts'; Sawyer, *Roman Britain to Norman England*, pp. 110–13; Hill, *Atlas*, pp. 76–7; Campbell, *The Anglo-Saxons*, pp. 59–61 and 99; Loyn, *Governance*, pp. 34–7; Stafford, *East Midlands*, pp. 94–6; Bassett, 'Search', p. 17.

[6] *DEPN*, p. xiii; Gelling, 'New Look', pp. 69–71; Freeman, 'Some Place-Names', pp. 63 and 72. Cf. below, p. 32, n. 75.

[7] 'Mercia, as originally named, is 30,000 hides.' On this passage of the *Tribal Hidage* cf. Scharer, 'Intitulationes', p. 50. For Bede's hidage see *HE* III.24. Cf. Stafford, *East Midlands*, p. 96. On the hide see below, p. 369.

important but dependent status.[8] The *Magonsætan* are absent, possibly because they were included in the large 30,000 figure for *Myrcna land* (quoted above), but more likely by an accident in transmission: the first few names after Mercia, where one might expect to find *Magonsætna*, are W[r]*ocensætna* ('Wrekin-dwellers', 7,000 hides), *Westerna* (7,000 hides) and *Pecsætna* ('Peak-dwellers', 1,200 hides), and another -*sætna* name may have fallen out by haplography. Alternatively, if the compiler began his clockwise circuit with the Wrekin-dwellers, he may have intended to end with the Magonsætan to their south but have forgotten to do so; or the entry may have been lost in this position, perhaps when the last entry, the 100,000 hides of Wessex, was added. Most recent commentators associate *Westerna*, which is simply the genitive plural of the adjective meaning 'western', with the Magonsætan, but in view of the roughly clockwise ordering at the start of the tract they may belong north of the Wrekin-dwellers, around Cheshire, where they were placed by Corbett and Stenton.[9]

Can we supplement the meagre historical record with linguistic and archaeological evidence for the Hwicce and Magonsætan? Unfortunately not, both because of chronological problems and because of the difficulty of co-ordinating the evidence provided by the three disciplines.[10]

The available linguistic evidence consists mainly of the distribution pattern of dialectal elements and phonological features in place-names. These names are difficult to handle because it is generally impossible to know how much older they are than the documents in which they are attested, which are never older than the late seventh century, and in many cases are transmitted in late copies which may have modified the orthography. Even in the case of names preserved in original charters, it is questionable whether their spelling reflects the 'grantor's dialect',[11] given our uncertainty about who drew up charters in the early Anglo-Saxon period. In any case, it is a mistake to try and correlate the distribution of

---

[8] Sawyer, *Roman Britain to Norman England*, pp. 110–11. Cf. W. J. Corbett in *The Cambridge Medieval History* II, ed. H. M. Gwatkin and J. P. Whitney (Cambridge, 1913), 551.

[9] *Ibid.*, p. 544; Stenton, *Anglo-Saxon England*, pp. 201 and 296. Cf. Hart, 'Tribal Hidage', pp. 139–41; Davies and Vierck, 'Contexts', p. 231; Loyn, *Governance*, p. 35. Is the name *Westernesse* in the Middle English romance *King Horn* perhaps relevant?

[10] See Wainwright, *Archaeology and Place-Names and History*.

[11] *PNGl* IV, 38. Only some of the problems are seen by T. E. Toon, *The Politics of Early Old English Sound Change* (New York, 1983).

dialects and languages with the distribution of named peoples, as defined by themselves or their contemporaries in written records.[12] Of course, there is often a broad correspondence – hence the use of terms like 'Anglian' and 'Saxon' for linguistic phenomena characteristic of the kingdoms which so styled themselves – but we cannot legitimately enlarge our knowledge of the prehistoric distribution of a people like the Hwicce by reference to such disparities as 'Saxon' forms like *throp* in southern Gloucestershire, within the historical kingdom of the Hwicce, or 'Anglian' forms in western Oxfordshire, outside it.[13] Dialect areas, ethnic groups and kingdoms are not necessarily contiguous.

Similar problems arise in trying to relate the early Anglo-Saxon kingdoms to the material-culture regions about which archaeology informs us; this should be obvious from the published distribution maps for pottery and spearheads.[14] In the area studied here the problems of correlation are especially severe because most of the archaeological evidence is provided by burials furnished with grave-goods, and such graves are concentrated in the east of what became the kingdom of the Hwicce and peter out in the seventh century when the kingdom is first attested historically.[15] While the sixth-century graves within what became the Hwiccian kingdom do share some recurrent features, both in grave-goods and in an unusual preference for orienting inhumations on a north–south axis,[16] they also reveal a material culture with close links with the neighbouring Anglo-Saxon areas: for example, graves in the Avon valley contained a series of five typologically related square-headed brooches which stretch from Beckford, Wo., north-east out of Hwiccian territory to Baginton, Wa. (there was a sixth at Cherbury Camp, Ox.), while a pair of saucer-brooches from the Broadway Hill cemetery, in the Avon valley, were from the same mould as

[12] See Wainwright, *Archaeology and Place-Names and History*.

[13] *PNGl* IV, 40; Smith, 'Hwicce', p. 61; *PNOx*, p. xix; Hooke, *Hwicce*, pp. 8–9.

[14] Cf. Sims-Williams, 'Settlement', p. 31.

[15] For the distribution of graves see Hooke, *Hwicce*, p. 25, fig. 3, but for the seventh century in particular see fig. 2 below, p. 63 (cf. below, n. 33). See now K. Pretty, 'Defining the Magonsæte', in *Origins*, ed. Bassett, pp. 171–83 and 277–9.

[16] M. E. Wilson, 'The Archaeological Evidence of the Hwiccian Area' (unpubl. PhD dissertation, Durham Univ., 1972); see also Pretty, 'Welsh Border'. For Hwiccian orientation see Faull, 'British Survival', p. 37 (this needs adjustment, since she treats all Warwickshire sites as Middle Anglian).

a pair from Broughton Poggs, Ox., on the other side of the Cotswolds.[17] This sort of correspondence in material culture could have arisen through intercourse of many sorts and it is impossible to say whether it testifies to interchange *across* or *within* ethnic and political boundaries. More confusion than historical insight has resulted from the way in which scholars like Leeds and Baldwin Brown used terms like 'West Saxon' in characterizing the material culture of the Avon valley cemeteries – often with more than half an eye on the dubious sixth-century annals in the *Anglo-Saxon Chronicle*.[18] The archaeological record is simply not suited to political interpretation.

The fact has to be faced that the whole area is prehistoric in the sixth century. The sole contemporary written source, the *De excidio Britanniae* of Gildas, cannot be dated or localized precisely enough to be very useful to us.[19] Perhaps the most that can be deduced from the distribution of the Anglo-Saxon cemeteries is that English settlement extended westwards along the Avon and its tributaries as far as Bredon Hill, along the Thames beyond Cirencester to Chavenage, and northwards from Chavenage along the Cotswolds.[20] The grave-goods show that these communities were in contact with (but not necessarily offshoots of) the contiguous Anglo-Saxon communities of the upper Avon and upper Thames valleys. Those river

---

[17] Leeds, *Square-Headed Brooches*, pp. 47–53; Hines, *Scandinavian Character*, pp. 129–32 and 362 (map); J. M. Cook, 'An Anglo-Saxon Cemetery at Broadway Hill, Broadway, Worcestershire', *AntJ* 38 (1958), 58–84, at 73; Pretty, 'Welsh Border', p. 72; Baldwin Brown, *Arts* III, 341, and IV, 661.

[18] Leeds, *Settlements*, pp. 63 and 73; Baldwin Brown, *Arts* IV, 613, 616–17 and 666; *PNWo*, p. xvi and n. 1 (envisaging an eastwards movement up the Avon). Thus the Hwicce have been assumed to be West Saxons (*PNWa*, pp. xv–xvi; Thorpe, 'Growth of Settlement', pp. 102 and 107) or an Anglian aristocracy imposed on a West Saxon population (*PNWo*, p. xviii). Smith, on the other hand, argues that the mixed Anglo-Saxon 'culture' of the Avon valley was imported from the mixed 'culture' of the Middle Anglian Nene valley ('Hwicce', p. 61 and nn.; *PNGl* IV, 42; cf. Baldwin Brown, *Arts* IV, 617 and 668–9). On the problem of the annals see Sims-Williams, 'Settlement', pp. 31–4.

[19] Sims-Williams, 'Gildas and the Anglo-Saxons'. Cf. *Gildas: New Approaches*, ed. Lapidge and Dumville.

[20] See fig. 2, below, p. 63. The possibility that the distribution of 'Anglo-Saxon' cemeteries reflects the diffusion of Anglo-Saxon burial rites among the British population outside the area of Anglo-Saxon settlement (Dickinson, 'Present State', p. 23) seems remote; the evidence points rather to Anglo-Saxon assimilation to Romano-British norms (see below, pp. 64–83). But cf. below, pp. 70 and 83, n. 117.

valleys had been densely settled from the earliest times and provided excellent agricultural land,[21] so there can be little doubt that the Anglo-Saxon settlers established themselves against the Britons by force or threat of arms; indeed their practice of inhuming their dead with shield, spear and other weapons may imply an assertion of warrior values.[22] Their relations with the indigenous Romano-British communities of the Avon valley and Cotswolds are obscure, not least because the sixth-century Britons left little archaeological trace. The survival of British place-names indicates some contact, but cannot be translated into demographic terms.[23] We cannot tell in what proportions Britons were slain, were enslaved, emigrated overseas, or moved to marginal territory – four possibilities offered by Gildas.[24] Some scholars, such as Finberg in his studies of Withington and Blockley in the Cotswolds, have deduced a continuity of population from the nearby siting of Anglo-Saxon and earlier Romano-British settlements,[25] but sceptics question the value of such topographical evidence, which, in Postan's words, may reflect only the 'predilection of conquerors for areas and places into which capital and labour had been sunk, and which were therefore capable of immediate exploitation', or even merely a 'similarity in the evaluation of land by the different waves of occupiers'.[26] Yet a clean sweep of the native population is unlikely in an early medieval agrarian context and certainly should not be deduced from Gildas's rhetorical and lurid account of the fifth-century devastations. At Stretton-on-Fosse radiocarbon evidence has been adduced

---

[21] For the Thames Valley see below, p. 384, n. 108. For the Avon Valley see below, pp. 371–5. For Anglo-Saxon burials in these areas see maps in J. R. Kirk, 'Anglo-Saxon Cremation and Inhumation in the Upper Thames Valley in Pagan Times', in *Dark-Age Britain*, ed. Harden, pp. 123–31, at 125; Dickinson, 'Present State', pp. 24–6; Ford, 'Settlement Patterns', p. 276; Hooke, *Hwicce*, p. 25; Hawkes, 'Early Saxon Period', p. 98.

[22] This rite is much more common than cremation in the Hwiccian area. On its antecedents and significance see Hills, 'Review', p. 302; James, 'Cemeteries', and 'Merovingian Cemetery Studies', pp. 37–9; Hines, *Scandinavian Character*, p. 274.

[23] See below, p. 24.

[24] *DEB*, c. 25. Cf. Sims-Williams, 'Gildas and the Anglo-Saxons', pp. 8–9. On the difficulty of interpreting Gildas's rhetoric see *ibid.*, pp. 9–12.

[25] Finberg, *Lucerna*, pp. 1–65, and *Gloucestershire Studies*, pp. 5–11. Cf. Reece, 'Cotswolds'. See also below, pp. 379 and 387. Cf. Finberg's remarks on Bourton-on-the-Water and Salmonsbury, *Gloucestershire Landscape*, pp. 47–8 (cf. Todd, 'Vici', p. 108).

[26] M. M. Postan, *The Medieval Economy and Society* (Harmondsworth, 1975), p. 11 (cf. p. 12).

for one of the adjacent Romano-British cemeteries overlapping in time with the large Anglo-Saxon inhumation cemetery. While the proximity of settlement which this presumably implies does not in itself indicate co-operation between the two communities – the unattractive soils of the Moreton Gap might tend to entice settlers onto the few patches of gravel like that at Stretton[27] – a degree of intermarriage is suggested by the discovery both of studded boots (burying these was a Romano-British rite) and of material woven by traditional Romano-British methods in the earlier female graves in the Anglo-Saxon cemetery.[28] Again, at another Avon valley site, Wasperton, variations in grave-goods and orientation among the two hundred inhumations in the late Romano-British/Anglo-Saxon cemetery have been plausibly interpreted in terms of a mixed 'British' and 'Saxon' population.[29] Such evidence, being unlikely to be merely the result of long-distance trade, is more suggestive than the appearance of Celtic penannular brooches in Anglo-Saxon grave assemblages, as in a rich sixth-century female grave at Bidford-on-Avon,[30] which was once held to 'give the lie to the extermination of British inhabitants in the areas of the settlements'.[31] Nevertheless, ethnological deductions from apparel, material culture and funerary practices are treacherous, and so far the

---

[27] Ford, 'Settlement Patterns, p. 274. Cf. Sawyer, *Roman Britain to Norman England*, p. 165; J. Malam, 'Stretton-on-Fosse (SP 222384)', *WMANS* 22 (1979), 13–14. For the topography see Gardner *et al.*, 'Stretton 1971–76', pp. 2–6, and below, pp. 386–7.

[28] Ford, 'Stretton-on-Fosse'; Clarke, *Lankhills*, pp. 329 and 406–8.

[29] SP/265585. G. Crawford, 'Excavations at Wasperton', *WMA* 25 (1982), 30–44; 26 (1983), 15–28; 28 (1985), 1–3. Cf. below, p. 82.

[30] W. J. Ford, 'Bidford-on-Avon, Warws. (SP 0998 5197)', *WMANS* 14 (1971), 21. At Bidford 'continuity of burial from the Roman to the Anglo-Saxon period' seems only an 'interesting possibility' (Hirst, 'Bidford', p. 55). Slater and Wilson suggested that the use of the Anglo-Saxon cemetery at Bridgetown just south of Stratford-upon-Avon overlapped with that of the nearby Romano-British cemetery serving the Romano-British settlement at Tiddington (*Stratford*, pp. 19 bis, 22 and 28–30), but this seems to be the result of a mistake, a 'Germanic' Type IB buckle from a female grave in the Anglo-Saxon cemetery (S. C. Hawkes and G. C. Dunning, 'Soldiers and Settlers in Britain, Fourth to Fifth Century', *MA* 5 (1961), 1–70, at 49, no. 14) being wrongly assigned to the Romano-British cemetery. In any case, any ethnic label for the buckle is uncertain; cf. Sims-Williams, 'Gildas and the Anglo-Saxons', p. 21, n. 94.

[31] E. T. Leeds, 'The Distribution of the Angles and Saxons Archaeologically Considered', *Archaeologia* 91 (1945), 1–106, at 46. For Bidford and other finds in the area see T. M. Dickinson, 'Fowler's Type G Penannular Brooches Reconsidered', *MA* 26 (1982), 41–68.

painstaking efforts of archaeologists have offered no more than interesting possibilities about Anglo–British contact. Indeed, it may never reveal the relative material status of the two populations; the Britons probably avoided elaborate grave-goods more because assertion of status in this fashion was alien to the Romano-British tradition than because they were relatively impoverished. We have advanced little since 1862 when Stubbs surmised that the Hwicce 'probably contained a fair sprinkling of native British Christians'.[32] There is still insufficient evidence to adjudicate between violent intrusion and peaceful assimilation.

No sixth-century Anglo-Saxon graves have been recognized in the Severn valley and beyond, in the southern Cotswolds and Vale of Gloucester and in the valley of the (Bristol) Avon.[33] This suggests that the Britons, though archaeologically invisible, still dominated this western area and that any Anglo-Saxon settlers here were assimilated, at least in their burial customs, to the British population. It is tempting to think of this east/west division in terms of the uneasy partition (*diuortium*) described by Gildas,[34] with the western area controlled by British tyrants of the sort castigated by Gildas, but there is no usable written or archaeological evidence. The ninth-century *Anglo-Saxon Chronicle* asserts that in 577 the West Saxon kings Cuthwine and Ceawlin

> fought against the Britons and killed three kings, Conmail, Condidan and Farinmail, at the place which is called Dyrham; and they captured three of their cities, Gloucester, Cirencester and Bath.

Unfortunately this entry raises some suspicions – for example, it is unlikely that Cirencester was in British hands as late as 577 – and it may be inspired by later West Saxon claims on southern Mercian territory.[35] Even taken at

---

[32] Stubbs, 'Cathedral, Diocese, and Monasteries', p. 238.

[33] Several graves on the Somerset side of the Avon, generally regarded as seventh-century Anglo-Saxon, may be British. See Rahtz and Fowler, 'Somerset', pp. 200–1, and below, p. 70. For an outlying seventh-century Anglo-Saxon cemetery at Bromfield, see below, p. 67. For outlying finds in non-funerary contexts see below, p. 66, n. 45.

[34] *DEB*, c. 10; cf. Sims-Williams, 'Gildas and the Anglo-Saxons', p. 27; D. N. Dumville, 'The Chronology of *De Excidio Britanniae*, Book I', in *Gildas: New Approaches*, ed. Lapidge and Dumville, pp. 61–84, at 74, 77, n. 65, and 82, n. 98.

[35] Sims-Williams, 'Settlement', p. 33 (on Cirencester, cf. Hooke, *Hwicce*, pp. 75–6). Dr Tania Dickinson tells me that in her unpublished DPhil. dissertation she gave further arguments suggesting that the early West Saxon annals were compiled in the context of rivalry with Mercia.

face value it is difficult to interpret; for instance, the verb *genamon* 'captured' does not necessarily signify permanent West Saxon occupation.[36]

Some Britons doubtless emigrated: the first element in the name of the early Welsh kingdom of Glywysing (later Morgannwg, Glamorgan) probably derives from *Gleuenses* (or *-is*) 'men (*or* man) of Gloucester'.[37] Other Britons must have stayed and come to favourable or unfavourable terms with the English settlers: they are probably commemorated in some of the place-names of the *Walcot* and *Comberton* type, though there is little point in mapping these, as in any particular instance the first element may be the personal names *Walh* or *Cumbra* rather than the words for 'Briton' from which these personal names derive (which is not to deny that the existence of such personal and place-names is significant in the context of Anglo–British relations in general).[38] Broadly speaking, the proportion of surviving Celtic place-names increases westwards, being low in Warwickshire, for instance, but increasing in Worcestershire and Gloucestershire.[39] There are surprising exceptions, however, which are not easily explained: thus the early Celtic element in the place-names of Gloucestershire west of the Severn and of central Shropshire has been found to be unexpectedly low.[40] Was the English settlement of these areas, though late, comparatively swift and thorough?

---

[36] Cf. the annal for 584.

[37] Welsh tradition derives the name *Glywysing* from an eponymous founder *Glywys* (< sg. **Gleuensis*?). See Sims-Williams, 'Some Functions of Origin-Stories in Early Medieval Wales', in *History and Heroic Tale*, ed. T. Nyberg *et al.* (Odense, 1985), p. 103 and n. 30; *Culhwch ac Olwen*, ed. R. Bromwich and D. S. Evans (Cardiff, 1988), p. xlviii, n. 91. Migration westwards is also suggested by the name *Ergyng*; see below, p. 45.

[38] *PNE* I, 119–20, and II, 242–4; *PNGl* IV, 26–7. For a more positive view of the value of such names see Dodgson, 'English Arrival in Cheshire', p. 31; M. L. Faull, 'The Semantic Development of OE *wealh*', *Leeds Studies in English* ns 8 (1975), 20–44, at 31–4, and 'British Survival', pp. 12–14; Gelling, *Signposts*, pp. 92–6; Thomas, *Christianity*, p. 258.

[39] *PNWa*, p. xx, quoted with approval by Gelling, 'Notes', p. 61; *PNGl* IV, 23; Gelling, *Signposts*, pp. 88–90.

[40] *PNGl* IV, 23 (for the evidence see pp. 28–30 and map at end); Gelling, 'Evidence', p. 204. See also Gelling, *Signposts*, pp. 62, 90 and 100. Cf. Charles, 'Archenfield and Oswestry'. Maps of British-derived names are given by Hooke, *Territorial Organization*, p. 19, and *Hwicce*, p. 33; Gelling, *Signposts*, p. 91, and 'New Look', p. 64.

PENDA AND THE RISE OF MERCIA

In the second quarter of the seventh century we get our first glimpses of Mercian history from the written sources. It is history of a typically Dark Age kind, focussed not on peoples and settlements, but on heroic dynasts, like the Mercian king Penda (d. 655). The earlier silence about Mercia in Bede, the *Anglo-Saxon Chronicle*, the *Annales Cambriae* and *Historia Britto-num* may indicate that it was not until Penda's time that the Mercians became important as allies or enemies of the Northumbrians, West Saxons and Britons. Penda's importance seems to be confirmed by the fact that the Mercian regnal list, compiled at the end of the eighth century, begins with him.[41] The only known earlier king of the Mercians, mentioned in passing by Bede, is the early seventh-century Ceorl, who appears in none of the regnal lists and genealogies.[42] Was his name a nickname for an upstart of less than aristocratic, 'churlish' stock?

Penda's origins and rise to power are obscure. He was 'of the royal stock of the Mercians' according to Bede, and his genealogy, which is first attested along with the Mercian regnal list in the late eighth-century context of the Anglian collection of genealogies, traces his ancestry back through Pybba, Crioda, Cynewald and Cnebba to Icel, and then beyond into the world of continental Germanic legend.[43] No early source states

---

[41] Dumville, 'Anglian Collection', pp. 29, n. 3, 33, 36 and 40, and 'Kingship, Genealogy and Regnal Lists', p. 100. It is not true that 'all extant Mercian regnal lists begin with Crida' (Davies, 'Annals and the Origin of Mercia', p. 22), and the extension back to him (*ibid.*, p. 27, n. 12) may be very late.

[42] *HE* II.14 (*Cearl*, a form of *Ceorl*: A. Campbell, *Old English Grammar* (Oxford, 1959), p. 118). Cf. *HBC*[3], p. 15. Henry of Huntingdon and later authorities indicate a royal succession: Crioda, Pybba, Ceorl, Penda. This may be taken from a regnal list (Davies, 'Annals and the Origin of Mercia'), but there is no evidence for it being ancient or authentic, and I am not convinced that it included regnal years. The names may be taken from Penda's pedigree and from Bede and their order may have been determined by equating Crioda with the person of the same name in *ASC* 593, with Pybba being placed so as to fill the gap between 593 and the *floruit* for Ceorl deducible from *HE* II.14. Davies suggests an explanation why some late authorites have Pybba succeed Crioda in 588 rather than 593 (p. 20). One cannot agree that the chronology of Crioda was not inspired by the 593 obit (p. 27, n. 11). Cf. Plummer, *Two Chronicles* II, 18; Stenton, *Anglo-Saxon England*, p. 30.

[43] Cf. Sims-Williams, 'Settlement', p. 23 and n. 98. The texts are edited by Dumville, 'Anglian Collection'. Mercian family trees are attempted by Searle, *Bishops, Kings and Nobles*, pp. 290–9, Hart, 'Kingdom of Mercia', and Stafford, *East Midlands*, p. 103.

that these immediate ancestors were kings. Descent from Icel, however, was regarded as a sign of royal blood in the eighth century; Felix, writing in the second quarter of that century, noted that:

In the days of Æthelred, the illustrious king of the Angles [king of Mercia, 674–704], there was a certain man of distinguished family of the Mercians, called Penwalh, whose dwelling was in the regions of the Middle Angles and was enriched by an abundance of diverse goods. The descent of this man came through the most noble names of illustrious kings in direct line back to Icel from whom it began in days of old.[44]

In view of the well-known Germanic customs of nomenclature,[45] it is quite likely that this Middle Anglian *Pen*walh was closely related to *Pen*da, who had set his son Peada to rule the Middle Angles.[46] A relationship is further suggested by the tradition that Mere*walh*, the first known ruler of the Magonsætan, was a son of Penda.[47] Some British alliance or intermarriage may be implied by the elements *walh* and *pen* in these names (cf. Welsh *pen* 'head, chief'), but this argument cannot be pressed.

When Penda became king is uncertain. He died in 655, and the *Chronicle*'s accession date of 626 may have been calculated backwards from this, employing its schematic-looking figures of fifty years of life before his accession and thirty after it; the first figure is unlikely on other grounds, and both suggest a background in legend and poetry rather than annal-keeping.[48] Bede, on the other hand, is supposed by Stenton and others to state that Penda began to rule in 633; but that is not quite what Bede says. Speaking of Penda's collaboration with the northern Welsh king Cadwallon against the Northumbrians in 633, he merely states:

---

[44] Cf. *EHD*, p. 771; *Life of Saint Guthlac*, ed. and trans. Colgrave, cc. 1–2; Chadwick, *Origin*, p. 14. On the date of this *Vita* see Whitelock, 'Pre-Viking Age Church', p. 15.

[45] *CP*, p. 89; *Medieval Nobility*, ed. Reuter, pp. 3 and 149–52.

[46] On Middle Anglia and Peada cf. Chadwick, *Origin*, p. 16; Campbell, *Essays*, pp. 85, 88, n. 21, and 91.

[47] See below, p. 47.

[48] Harrison, *Framework*, p. 132, n. 10; cf. Sims-Williams, 'Settlement', pp. 35–6. On the problem of the 50 years see Chadwick, *Origin*, p. 15; Stenton, *Anglo-Saxon England*, p. 81, n. 2; *EHD*, p. 161, n. 1. In view of these scholars' arguments, it is unlikely that Penda became king as early as *c.* 607 (Davies, 'Annals and the Origin of Mercia', p. 21). On this and other topics discussed in this section see now N. Brooks, 'The Formation of the Mercian Kingdom', in *Origins*, ed. Bassett, pp. 159–70 and 275–7.

auxilium praebente illi Penda uiro strenuissimo de regio genere Merciorum, qui et ipse ex eo tempore gentis eiusdem regno annis XX et duobus uaria sorte praefuit.[49]

In fact Bede may not have known how long before 633 Penda began to reign.

As a result of these uncertainties we cannot be sure, though it is the most natural and probable interpretation, that Penda was already king of the Mercians on his second appearance in the *Chronicle*, in 628:

In this year Cynegils and Cwichelm fought against Penda at Cirencester, and afterwards came to terms (*gepingodan*).

This is the first time in the *Chronicle* that the Mercians encounter the West Saxons (here led by Cynegils and his son Cwichelm). The implication seems to be that Penda got the upper hand. The terms may have included the marriage between Penda's sister and Cenwealh, Cynegils's son and Cwichelm's brother; this may have been an unwilling alliance, for Cenwealh later repudiated her and was therefore attacked by Penda and driven into a three-year exile in 645.[50] Perhaps the battle of Cirencester gave the Mercians control over the Hwiccian kingdom;[51] however, it may be that Mercian overlordship of the Hwicce and Magonsætan had to wait until the reign of Penda's son Wulfhere.

Penda's career needs to be seen in a wide context. According to Bede's famous heptad,[52] the kingdoms south of the Humber were at first dominated by four kings of Sussex, Wessex, Kent and East Anglia, but then by the Northumbrians Edwin (d. 633), Oswald (d. 641) and Oswiu

---

[49] 'Cadwallon was aided by Penda, a very able fighting-man [cf. Wallace-Hadrill, *Commentary*, p. 84] of the Mercian royal stock, who ruled the kingdom of that people through various fortunes for twenty-two years from that time': *HE* II.20. (This has been dated 632, but 633 is certainly what Bede intends; see Harrison, *Framework*, p. 86.) See Stenton, *Anglo-Saxon England*, p. 81; *EHD*, p. 161, n. 1; *HBC*[3], p. 15. But cf. *BOH* II, 115. Davies, 'Annals and the Origin of Mercia', p. 21, suggests that Penda sometimes ruled jointly with his brother Eowa, who is called *rex Merciorum* in *AC*, s.a. 644 and in *HB*, c. 65.

[50] *HE* III.7. Cf. *ASC* 645 and 658. The 645 date is taken from *ASC* and 'The Ramsey Computus', ed. C. Hart, *EHR* 85 (1970), 29–44.

[51] Thus Stenton, *Anglo-Saxon England*, pp. 45 and 67; Sawyer, *Roman Britain to Norman England*, pp. 38 and 43. The association of this annal with Wansdyke argued by C. and A. Fox was rejected by H. S. Green, on the basis of the non-relation of Wansdyke to parish boundaries; cf. Sims-Williams, 'Settlement', p. 28, n. 121.

[52] *HE* II.5; cf. Sims-Williams, 'Settlement', pp. 25–6.

(d. 670). Penda's achievement – unrecognized in the Northumbrian heptad – was to win the chance of a similar *imperium*, if not for himself, at least for his son Wulfhere. An important stage must have been to free Mercia from Northumbrian control; the *Historia Brittonum*, perhaps correctly, puts this in stark terms, saying of Penda that 'he first redeemed the kingdom of the Mercians from that of the Northerners' ('ipse primus reparauit regnum Merciorum a regno Nordorum').[53] His alliance with Cadwallon against Edwin in 633 was a major step. Possibly the Northumbrians first recognized full Mercian independence then; at least, that is a possible interpretation of Bede's words, quoted above. Seven years before this war, the West Saxon king Cwichelm had instigated an attempt at assassinating Edwin, in 626, hoping to deprive him of his kingdom – and, no doubt, of his *imperium* south of the Humber – and Edwin, once he had recovered from his poisoned wound, had led a successful campaign of revenge against the West Saxons.[54] As Chadwick saw, the battle at Cirencester in 628 may have formed part of this campaign, with Penda acting in Edwin's service;[55] at any rate Penda would have been able to rely on Edwin's support at his rear. By 633, however, having secured the settlement with the West Saxons, Penda switched his allegiances and began the series of attacks on Northumbria that lasted for the rest of his reign.

Alliances with Welsh kings were evidently important in bolstering Mercian independence. Cadwallon of Gwynedd (d. 634) was the ally in 633, and Penda's final defeat at the *Winwæd* (near Leeds) in 655 was partly due to the defection, on the night before the battle, of Cadafael of Gwynedd, one of the British kings who had accompanied him.[56] A seemingly contemporary Welsh elegy on Cynddylan, a prince of Powys, includes the line 'when the son of Pyd wished, how ready was he' (*pan fynwys mab pyd mor fu parawd*), apparently referring to an alliance between Cynddylan and Penda son of Pybba, whose nickname in Welsh sources is *Panna ap Pyd* ('Penda son of Danger').[57] The occasion may have been

53 *HB*, c. 65 (*EHD*, p. 263); Dumville, 'Kingship, Genealogies and Regnal Lists', p. 100 and n. 159.

54 *HE* II.9.   55 Chadwick, *Origin*, p. 6.

56 *HE* II.20 and III.24; *HB*, c. 65 (*EHD*, p. 263); Hughes, *Celtic Britain*, pp. 92–4.

57 '"Marwnad Cynddylan"', ed. Gruffydd, pp. 14 and 20 line 28; translated by T. Jones in J. Gould, '*Letocetum*: The Name of the Roman Settlement at Wall, Staffs.', *TLSSAHS* 5 (1963–4), 51–4. For Panna fab Pyd see E. Phillimore, 'Notes on Place-Names in English Maelor', *Bye-Gones Relating to Wales and the Border Counties* ns 1 (1889–90),

Penda's defeat of Oswald in 641 at Oswestry (Old English *Maserfelth*, Welsh *Cogwy*), for a later Welsh *englyn* on this battle states that 'Cynddylan was a helper' (*Cynddylan oedd kynnorthwy*).[58] These Welsh alliances need not have prevented Mercian expansion in the direction of Wales, and may even have aided it, for the Welsh kingdoms were no more united among themselves than the Anglo-Saxon.[59] In any case, alliances were soon broken when it appeared advantageous; subsequent lines in the elegy on Cynddylan refer to an attack on Lichfield, apparently after Penda's death.[60] Later Welsh *englynion*, of about the ninth or tenth centuries, which describe the English devastation of Cynddylan's lands in the Severn and Tern valleys around Wroxeter,[61] may owe more to imagination than to history. Nevertheless, by the time of Wulfhere's death in 674 or 675, when the foundation of monasteries in places like Bath and Much Wenlock is recorded by charters naming Mercian kings, more or less the whole of the kingdoms of the Hwicce and Magonsætan was clearly under Mercian control.[62] The subsequent political development of the two kingdoms, headed at first by *reges*, then by *reguli* and finally by *ealdormen* dependent by definition on higher royal authority, was to reflect the growth of Mercian central control.[63]

THE KINGDOM OF THE HWICCE

The strange name *Hwicce* has been thought to be a very old folk-name, perhaps going back to the pre-migration age, and possibly a term of

478–85, at 480. In my forthcoming edition of the *englynion y beddau* discussed by Phillimore I argue that the correct reading is 'the grave of Panna son of Pyd in the onrush of a river', comparing Bede's account of the flooding of the *Winwæd*, *HE* III.24.

[58] *Canu Llywarch Hen*, ed. Williams, pp. xxxiii and 48. The twelfth-century poet Cynddelw represents Cogwy as a battle between Powys and Oswald; see I. Williams, 'A Reference to the Nennian Bellum Cocboy', *BBCS* 3 (1926–7), 59–62.

[59] See the seemingly contemporary poems on Cynan Garwyn, Cadwallon and Cynddylan; for references and discussion see Sims-Williams, 'Gildas and Vernacular Poetry', p. 171.

[60] '"Marwnad Cynddylan"', ed. Gruffydd, p. 20, lines 52–62 (cf. pp. 15–16). The reference to a bishop suggests the Northumbrian interregnum (*HE* III. 21) or the reign of Wulfhere (*HE* III. 24). That a British bishopric is meant seems unlikely.

[61] *Canu Llywarch Hen*, ed. Williams, pp. 33–48. I have not yet seen J. Rowland, *Early Welsh Saga Poetry: A Study and Edition of the Englynion* (Woodbridge, 1989).

[62] For the date of Wulfhere's death see Harrison, *Framework*, p. 80; Wood, 'Bede's Northumbrian Dates', pp. 287–8 and 292. On the 'charter horizon' and early foundations see below, pp. 85–6.

[63] C. S. Taylor, 'Origin of the Mercian Shires', in *Gloucestershire Studies*, ed. Finberg, p. 19. Cf. Loyn, 'The Term *Ealdorman*'.

contempt (cf. Old Icelandic *hvikari* 'coward') later adopted by the people themselves. An alternative explanation derives it from *hwicce* 'ark, chest', which could refer to the appearance of their flat-bottomed valley, bounded by the Cotswold and Malvern hills.[64] Be this as it may, the unusual nature of the name means that it is easy to recognize it, and the derived personal names *Hwicc* and *Hwicca*, in place-names. Such place-names outside the kingdom of the Hwicce are Whiston in Northamptonshire, Witchley in Rutland (this is disputed) and Wychnor in Staffordshire (the site of an Anglo-Saxon cemetery near the junction of the Trent and the Tame and Mease).[65] A. H. Smith wrongly concluded from these place-names that the Hwicce may have been an Anglian folk who had migrated south-westwards along the Nene valley across the Northamptonshire watershed into the valley of the Warwickshire Avon;[66] he overlooked the alternative, that the places may be named from later migrants in the opposite direct-ion from the historical territory of the Hwicce. Smith's further argument that the distribution of grants by the Hwiccian kings shows the 'original territory' of the Hwicce to have been centred in the Avon valley falls down because land charters cannot be assumed to grant kings' personal estates.[67] It is indeed impossible to define the Hwiccian area until the

---

[64] See respectively Smith, 'Hwicce', p. 62, n. 1 – cf. the way in which Welsh *Gwyddyl* 'Irish', from *gwydd* 'wild', was adopted by the Goidels themselves (P. Mac Cana, 'Y Trefedigaethau Gwyddelig ym Mhrydain', in *Y Gwareiddiad Celtaidd*, ed. G. Bowen (Llandysul, 1987), p. 169, and compare modern names such as 'The Old Contempti-bles' or 'The Vermin Club' – and Gelling, 'New Look', p. 69.

[65] Smith, 'Hwicce', p. 64, n. 1; *PNGl* IV, 42; Phythian-Adams, 'Rutland', pp. 76–8. Cf. *PNWo*, p. xv; Hart, 'Tribal Hidage', p. 138, n. 8; Thorpe, 'Growth of Settlement', pp. 96 and 102; Meaney, *Gazetteer*, p. 223; Copley, *Anglian Regions*, p. 110.

[66] 'Hwicce', pp. 60–2; *PNGl* IV, 42.

[67] *PNGl* IV, 33, n. 2; 'Hwicce', p. 60 (map; cf. maps by Bassett, 'Search', pp. 12 and 16). On the nature of charters see below, p. 96. Bassett ('Winchcombe', p. 84 and n. 16, and 'Search', pp. 7–17 and 26) offers a more complex thesis: that the Hwiccian rulers' most ancient allodial lands were based in the Winchcombe area and that they therefore retained independent rights longest there, up to the 720s. This is partly based on an interpretation of Coenwulf of Mercia's 'hereditary land belonging to Winchcombe' in S 1442 (cf. below, p. 166, n. 109), and partly on the negative evidence that before this period grants in the area were made neither by the Hwiccian kings (because it was all their patrimony, to be kept intact), nor by the Mercian kings (because they had no rights there). Against this, note that Æthelred of Mercia was involved in the grant of Withington before 704 (below, p. 96, n. 34), and that Æthelbald of Mercia granted Bredon in 716×717 (below, p. 153) and Daylesford probably in 718 (below, p. 151, n. 45). Even supposing all the recipients were Hwiccian royalty (cf. below, p. 153,

advent of documentation *c.* 675, when all the indications are that the kingdom of the Hwicce was as extensive as the diocese of Worcester known from later records;[68] one of the first extant charters issued by a king of the Hwicce (Osric, with the Mercian king's consent) is the foundation charter for Bath monastery, which lay in the valley not of the Warwickshire but of the southern (Bristol) Avon, on the West Saxon border.[69]

The kings of the Hwicce ruled a very diverse population. This may be seen from casual references in early charters to minor peoples such as the *Pencersætan* in the north (south-west of Birmingham),[70] or the **Weogoran*, who gave their name to Worcester itself and to an area called *Weogorena leag* to its west.[71] Such peoples may have been unimportant from the Mercian point of view – the only minor people in the area included in the *Tribal Hidage* is the *Arosætan* (600 hides), if these are to be located in the valley of the Warwickshire Arrow, which is far from certain[72] – but they may have retained considerable local significance. When one considers the possible social contexts of the smaller monastic ventures, for instance, it may be as well to bear in mind the existence of such peoples as the *Usmere* of the Stour valley, around the monastery of Stour in Ismere,[73] and the *Stoppingas* of the Alne valley, near Wootton Wawen, probably the site of a monastery.[74]

n. 55), these grants show that Mercian overlordship is recognized in the Winchcombe area already when we have a fair spread of charters.

[68] See above, p. 5, and below, pp. 369–94.   [69] See below, p. 94.

[70] S 1272; *PNWa*, p. xvii and n. 4; Thorpe, 'Growth of Settlement', p. 108; Stenton, *Anglo-Saxon England*, p. 44; Hooke, *Staffordshire*, pp. 12–13 and 16. For recent attempts to map some of the minor peoples of Mercia see Hart, 'Kingdom of Mercia', pp. 50–1; Hooke, *Hwicce*, p. 7.

[71] **Weogoran* is a tribal name derived from **Wigora*, a British river-name found in *Wyre* Forest north-west of Worcester and in *Wyre* Piddle near Pershore, possibly denoting the River Piddle. Cf. *PNWo*, pp. 20, 155 and 222; Jackson, *Language and History*, p. 459; *DEPN*, pp. 534 and 541; Gelling, 'Note on the Name Worcester', and *Signposts*, pp. 92 and 152; Hooke, *Hwicce*, pp. 34, 80 and 166. For *Weogorena leag* see below, p. 393.

[72] BCS 297. Cf. *PNWa*, p. xviii, n. 2.

[73] See references to their *prouincia* in S 89 and 1411; Grundy, *Worcestershire*, p. 274 and n. 5; and cf. *Worcester Cartulary*, ed. Darlington, pp. xx, n. 4, and 19, no. 23 ('flumina que uocatur Usmere'). Cf. *PNWo*, pp. 248 and 278–9; *CP*, p. 78; *DEPN*, p. 267; Gelling, 'New Look', p. 69. The location of the monastery is obscure, *pace PNWo* (cf. *VCH Wo* III, 158; Dyer, *Lords and Peasants*, pp. 15, n. 20, and 22), but was doubtless near Ismere House. See also below, p. 376 and n. 69.

[74] See the reference to their *regio* in S 94. Cf. *CP*, p. 79; *PNWa*, p. xvii; Cox, 'Place-Names of the Earliest Records', p. 42; Hooke, *Hwicce*, p. 37; Gelling, 'New Look', p. 69; Bassett, 'Search', pp. 18–19 and 21.

Some of these minor folk may have had no corporate identity before reaching the area; this is especially likely in the case of those with names in -*sætan* /-*sæte* like *Pencersætan*.[75] On the other hand a number of places are clearly named from outsiders. There must have been a group of Kentishmen (*Cantware*) at Conderton (*Cantuaretun*) near the monastery of Beckford, an area of ancient settlement in the lee of Bredon Hill's Iron Age hillfort.[76] The Whitsun Brook (*Wixenabroc*) between Fladbury and Inkberrow may take its name from an offshoot of the *Wixan* (< *Wihsan 'villagers?', cf. Gothic *weihs* 'village', Latin *uicus*), a people of 900 hides apparently placed in the Fenlands by the *Tribal Hidage*; another offshoot settled at *Ux*bridge and *Ux*endon in Middlesex. The wooded area around the Whitsun Brook may have been under-developed and have given an opportunity to such settlers from outside the area.[77] This may also have been true of the nearby *Fepsæte* of Phepson (*Fepsetna-tun*), if these were connected with the Middle Anglian *Feppingas* listed in the *Tribal Hidage* (as gen. pl. *Færpinga* [*sic*], 300 hides) after the *Arosætan*; Bede, mentioning the death of Diuma, bishop of the Middle Angles, 'in regione quae uocatur *Infeppingum*', possibly meant Charlbury on the Evenlode, near Wychwood, Oxfordshire, although that was not necessarily the main area of *Feppingas* settlement.[78] There was probably also an Irish settlement near Stratford on the Shottery Brook (*Scotta rið* 699×709(?), *Scotbroc* 1016).[79] A traveller on

---

[75] Cf. above, p. 17 and n. 6. For example, the eleventh-century bounds of Mickleton (S 911; Grundy, *Gloucestershire* II, 171) refer to the *Campsætena* (gen. pl.), but Smith regards this as merely elipsis for 'people of [Chipping] Campden' (*PNGl* I, 237–8, and IV, 49). Cf. similarly *Bradsetena* at Broadwas, *PNWo*, p. 103.

[76] *DEPN*, p. 120; *PNWo*, pp. xix and 115–16; Gelling, 'New Look', p. 71. For cropmarks in Conderton see Webster and Hobley, 'Aerial Reconnaissance', p. 12, and for the Iron Age hillfort see Millward and Robinson, *West Midlands*, p. 32.

[77] Thus Hooke, *Hwicce*, p. 164. See *PNWo*, pp. xix and 16; *CP*, p. 269; *DEPN*, pp. 488 and 514; Davies and Vierck, 'Contexts', pp. 231–2 (disagreeing with Hart, 'Tribal Hidage', pp. 143–4). Wainwright, *Archaeology and Place-Names and History*, p. 121, adds *Waxlow* (Middlesex), which is not in *DEPN*.

[78] *PNWo*, pp. xviii–xix and 137–8; BCS 297; *HE* III.22 (with p. 280, n. 1); Hart, 'Tribal Hidage', p. 152; Davies and Vierck, 'Contexts', p. 233. But cf. Gelling, 'New Look', pp. 70–1.

[79] S 64 (cf. below, n. 99) and 1388; *DEPN*, p. 420; *PNE* II, 113; Campbell, 'Debt to Ireland', p. 334, n. 19. (Differently *PNWa*, pp. 239–40; Cox, 'Place-Names of the Earliest Records', p. 26.) There was a *Scotta pæð* at the monastery of Acton Beauchamp (S 786; Grundy, *Worcestershire*, p. 8).

the saltway from Droitwich to Stratford[80] would pass through the territory of both *Fepsæte* and *Scotti*.

The existence of these other peoples in the kingdom of the Hwicce makes us see the position of its kings vis-à-vis those of Mercia in a true light. Historians have tended to stress the decline in their status from the 670s, when Osric is styled *rex*, to a century later, when Ealdred is described in a charter of Offa as 'my underking, that is to say ealdorman of his own people the Hwicce' ('subregulo meo Aldredo uidelicet duce propriæ gentis Huicciorum'), and his brother Uhtred is described rather pathetically as 'holding a certain degree of rule (*aliquod regimen*) over his own people the Hwicce'.[81] In fact, however, the Hwiccian kings may have gained more than they lost from Mercian overlordship. Possibly the Mercians helped them to establish their kingship over the minor peoples of the area (as Penda set his son Peada over the Middle Anglian peoples);[82] certainly their rule for more than a century would have been impossible without Mercian support. Their changing royal styles do not necessarily indicate a dramatic loss of real power. They may be superficially similar to the treatment meted out to the kings of Kent and Sussex by draughtsmen reflecting Offa's claims,[83] but the background was different, since the Hwicce can have had no such long history of independence from Mercia. There is no reason, on the other hand, to think that the Hwiccian dynasty was foisted on the kingdom by the Mercians. Its origins are indeed obscure. The connection with the Northumbrian royal family asserted in some later medieval sources, despite the silence of Bede on the matter, is implausible and was probably inspired by no more than a similarity of personal names.[84]

The evidence is not complete enough to justify attempts to draw up a family tree for the kings of the Hwicce,[85] but the recurrence of certain name-elements and the uniform alliteration of their names (in any vowel,

80 *PNWo*, p. 7; Houghton, 'Salt-Ways', Route F.
81 *HE* IV. 23; S 113 and 57. See Stenton, *Anglo-Saxon England*, pp. 45–6; Loyn, 'Gesiths and Thegns', p. 549; H. Vollrath-Reichelt, *Königsgedanke und Königtum bei den Angelsachsen bis zur Mitte des 9. Jahrhunderts* (Cologne, 1971), pp. 131–4 (cf. review by E. John, *EHR* 89 (1974), 613); Campbell, *Essays*, p. 92; Scharer, 'Intitulationes', p. 36. The latter part of S 113 (also quoted by Stenton) is probably spurious; see Scharer, *Königsurkunde*, p. 243 (and see p. 257 on S 57). Finberg, *Lucerna*, p. 76, speculates on the role of a '*comes* of the Hwicce', but see Sims-Williams, 'Cuthswith', p. 10, n. 5.
82 See above, p. 26, n. 46.   83 Brooks, *Canterbury*, pp. 112–15.
84 See Sims-Williams, 'People and Places'. I agree with Bassett, 'Search', p. 6.
85 Cf. Searle, *Bishops, Kings, and Nobles*, pp. 361–7; *ECWM*, p. 179.

which was allowable in Old English verse) make it certain that they were all somehow related.[86]

The first known members of the dynasty, the brothers Eanfrith and Eanhere, are mentioned in passing by Bede in his account of Wilfrid's conversion of the South Saxons in 680 or 681:

Porro regina, nomine Eabae, in sua, id est Huicciorum prouincia fuerat baptizata. Erat autem filia Eanfridi fratris Eanheri, qui ambo cum suo populo Christiani fuere.[87]

This is usually assumed to mean that the two brothers ruled jointly,[88] but Bede's words could equally well signify that Eanhere was sole ruler. The marriage alliance between the kingdoms of Sussex and Hwicce was an appropriate one, for both were assessed at 7,000 hides in the *Tribal Hidage*,[89] and both kingdoms must have been under threat from the West Saxons. We are also indebted to Bede for the name of another Hwiccian ruler: in passing he remarks (unfortunately without exact chronological precision) that Oftfor, who later became bishop of the Hwicce, went 'to the province of the Hwicce, which King Osric then ruled' ('ad prouinciam Huicciorum, cui tunc rex Osric praefuit').[90] A *floruit* of *c.* 675 for this Osric is provided by his probable attestation among Wulfhere of Mercia's *subreguli* in a Surrey charter of 672×674, and by the charter for the foundation of Bath monastery in 675, granted by Osric *rex* with the consent of Æthelred of Mercia.[91] Osric was still active in 679, if this is the correct date of the Gloucester foundation charter, according to which Æthelred granted the lands for Gloucester and Pershore monasteries respectively to 'my two servants of noble family in the province of the

---

[86] A normal state of affairs in this sort of research: F. Irsigler, 'On the Aristocratic Character of Early Frankish Society', in *Medieval Nobility*, ed. Reuter, pp. 150–1.

[87] 'The queen, whose name was Eaba, had been baptized in her own province, that is, that of the Hwicce. She was the daughter of Eanfrith the brother of Eanhere, who were both Christians, together with their people': *HE* IV.23. Colgrave renders *Eaba* as *Eafe*, but Rollason, *Mildrith*, p. 151, n. 7, notes that the Old English *Bede* renders *Eaba* as *Æbbe*. For the possibility that she became abbess of Gloucester see below, p. 123.

[88] Stenton, *Anglo-Saxon England*, p. 45. On multiple kingship see Sawyer, *Roman Britain to Norman England*, p. 49, and above, p. 27, n. 49.

[89] See above, p. 17; cf. *HE* IV.13 for the South Saxon hidage.

[90] *HE* IV.23. Cf. Wallace-Hadrill, *Commentary*, p. 164. See below, pp. 102–3.

[91] S 1165 and 51. On S 1165 cf. Scharer, *Königsurkunde*, p. 136 (misleading on Osric) and Wormald, *Bede and the Conversion*, p. 9.

Hwicce, Osric and his brother Oswald' ('duobus ministris meis, nobilis generis, in prouincia huicciorum, Osrico scilicet & Oswaldo fratre eius').[92] Osric's brother may be the Oswald whose name appears second in the column of lay witnesses in the Bath charter,[93] and also the father of an Æthelmund son of Oswald, whom Æthelbald of Mercia was to slay, afterwards making reparation to Gloucester monastery.[94]

Osric was evidently succeeded as king of the Hwicce by Oshere.[95] To the latter, late Worcester sources ascribe the foundation of the see of Worcester, which they date to 679,[96] and charters of Oshere *rex* survive for 680 and 693×?699.[97] An Evesham charter dated 706 and referring to Oshere as *quondam rex* is a forgery;[98] but probably he was 'the late king' by about this date, for by 709 his four sons, Æthelheard, Æthelweard, Æthelberht and Æthelric, were attesting charters without him.[99] The first three do not

---

[92] Text in *ECWM*, pp. 158 and 160. On *ministri* see Stenton, *Anglo-Saxon England*, p. 45 (cf. John, *Orbis*, pp. 83–5), and Thacker, 'Noblemen', p. 202. Finberg deduced the date 679 from the regnal year (*ECWM*, p. 163). The AD date 671 is surely a slip (perhaps by the s. xiv scribe) for 681, as in the Gloucester *Historia* (see Hart's edition, I, lxxii, n. 1) and other sources (*ECWM*, p. 163, n. 4; Liebermann, *Geschichtsquellen*, p. 18), including the Gloucester Chronicle by Gregory of Caerwent (*c.* 1290), of which Lawrence Nowell's transcript survives as BL, Cotton Vespasian A. v, 195r–203v, at 202r (see Brooke, *Church*, p. 52, n. 9, on this source). Cf. 682 in the late forgery printed in *ECWM*, p. 241.

[93] S 51 (Cambridge, Corpus Christi College 111, p. 60). Cf. *ECWM*, p. 163, n. 4, and 173 and n. 1. Æthelmod, in the Bath witness list and in S 1167, may be another of the family; cf. Sims-Williams, 'Wilfrid', pp. 165, nn. 9 and 11, and 178, n. 69.

[94] BCS 535; *Historia et Cartularium*, ed. Hart I, lxxii (MS 'Orwardi'). In 'cognatum ejus' the latter word probably refers to Abbess Eafe not to Æthelbald. For Æthelmund cf. below, n. 99.

[95] Oshere's relationship to Osric is unknown and there is no evidence that they ruled jointly for a while, *pace ECWM*, pp. 174–5. Finberg suggests that Os*here* was the son of Ean*here* (*ibid.*, p. 172).

[96] Sims-Williams, 'Wilfrid', p. 168.

[97] S 52 and 53. On the dates see Sims-Williams, 'Wilfrid', pp. 174–83, and 'Cuthswith', p. 9, n. 1. A synod of 736×737 looks back on Oshere as *comes* of Æthelred of Mercia and *subregula* (*sic*) *Huicciorum* (S 1429). Similarly he is recalled as *subregulus Huicciorum* in 774 (S 1255).

[98] S 54. The reference to Oshere as 'quondam rex' was probably imitated from S 94. Cf. Sims-Williams, 'Cuthswith', p. 9, n. 2.

[99] S 1177 (in 704×709) and S 64 (either in 699×709 or, following a suggestion by Professor Whitelock, in her copy of *ECWM*, that Offa of Mercia is an error for Coenred of Mercia rather than Offa of Essex, in 704×709). Only Æthelheard and Æthelric are specifically stated to be Oshere's sons in genuine charters (S 53 and 94) but the same

make a certain appearance after this date,[100] but Æthelric is better evidenced and is also the only brother to be given titles: he attests a grandiloquent charter of Æthelbald in 736 as 'subregulus atque comes gloriosissimi principis Æthilbal[di]'.[101] In a similar charter of about the same date Æthelbald, styling himself king 'not only of the Mercians but also of all the provinces generally called the Southern Angles', while, perhaps deliberately, avoiding Æthelric's royal title, calls him 'my most esteemed and beloved thegn, son of the former king of the Hwicce, Oshere' ('reuerentissimo comiti meo mihique satis caro, filio quondam Huicciorum regis Oosheræs, Æthelricæ').[102] As Æthelric was active as early as 693×?699,[103] he may have succeeded Oshere directly; but it is equally possible that one or more of his three brothers reigned first.

Another member of the family whose relations with Æthelbald were described in terms of service was Osred, who received lands in Gloucester- shire by a charter in which he is addressed as 'my most faithful servant who is of the not ignoble royal stock of the Hwiccian people' ('ministro meo ualde fideli qui est de stirpe non ignobili prosapia regali gentis Huiccio- rum').[104] The witness list that follows belongs to 737×740, but the charter may have been issued early in Æthelbald's reign (716–57). Osred is conceivably the same person as the Osred who attests an Æthelbald charter of 718, along with Æthelric and a certain Ælfred (see below), among others.[105] Whether Osred was a ruler of the Hwicce is not known. There is in fact a gap in the record of *reguli* between Æthelric and the appearance together, in charters of 757 and 759, of three brothers, Eanberht, Uhtred and Ealdred, each styled *regulus* – the first unequivocal evidence of joint

relationship may be assumed for the other two from their positions in witness lists (on Æthelweard cf. Sims-Williams, 'Cuthswith', p. 9, n. 2). In S 64 an Æthelmund attests (cf. S 79), possibly a fifth brother; but see above, p. 35, on Æthelmund son of Oswald.

100 However, S 1252 could be as late as 717.

101 S 89. There is no evidence to support the titles *rex* and *subregulus* given to Æthelheard and Æthelweard in spurious Evesham charters (S 79 and 54).

102 S 94; on the date see below, p. 149. On the terms *comes*, etc. cf. above, p. 2, n. 2. Of course, the claims made by Æthelbald were made on his behalf, perhaps under the instigation of a cleric in his service (Abbot Ibe?); see Scharer, 'Intitulationes', pp. 57–60 (cf. below, p. 227, n. 53).

103 S 53. Cf. above, n. 97.

104 S 99: a poorly transmitted charter; cf. Brooks, 'Military Obligations', p. 77, n. 1; Scharer, *Königsurkunde*, pp. 169–72, and 'Intitulationes', p. 56; and below, p. 148.

105 S 84. Cf. *ECWM*, p. 178, n. 3. On the date of this charter see below, p. 151, n. 45.

rule among the Hwicce.[106] In the former charter the brothers refer to the church of St Peter at Worcester, 'where the bodies of our *parentes* rest'; if this passage is authentic, it indicates a change in policy, for Osric is said to have been buried at Gloucester.[107] Eanberht is absent from a third charter, a grant by Uhtred *regulus Huicciorum* in 770, attested by Ealdred *subregulus*, with Offa's consent to 'donationem subreguli mei'; presumably Eanberht was dead by this time.[108] His two brothers were active at least until 777, but there is no certain evidence for them after this.[109]

Regrettably, we are not told who the *parentes* of Eanberht, Uhtred and Ealdred were. Nevertheless some connection with the family of Oshere can be traced through charters concerning Fladbury monastery.[110] At the beginning of the eighth century Bishop Ecgwine had entrusted Fladbury to Oshere's son Æthelheard.[111] In 777×780 Ealdred, *subregulus Huicciorum*, leased the monastery to his own relative (*propinqua*), the Abbess Æthelburg, for her to hold with a reversion to the episcopal see, 'just as it had been stipulated by Ælfred, and Æthelheard, and Bishop Ecgwine'.[112] She was clearly identical with the Abbess Æthelburg who was in possession of Withington and Twyning monasteries in 774 and was described as daughter of the thegn (*comes*) Ælfred.[113] Assuming, as we should, that the

---

[106] S 55 and 56. The former charter is suspicious, the latter an original. Cf. Scharer, *Königsurkunde*, pp. 214–15.

[107] See below, p. 124. But Osric may have died before the see was established. See also Uhtred's reference to 'corpora patrum meorum' at St Mary's, Worcester, in the fabricated S 61. (Only forgeries pretend St Mary's existed so early: see John, 'St. Oswald', p. 160 and n. 3.) Another forgery, S 126, calls Ealdred 'subregulus Wignornæ ciuitatis'.

[108] S 59 (supposedly an original, but cf. below, p. 155, n. 61). Cf. S 58, dated 767.

[109] S 57 (false according to Scharer, *Königsurkunde*, p. 257); S 62 (which could, of course, be as late as 780, when Bishop Tilhere dies; cf. below, p. 139, n. 110).

[110] Cf. *ECWM*, p. 178 (the Evesham forgeries there should be ignored).

[111] S 1252.

[112] S 62. On the date see above, n. 109. There is no reference to Offa, perhaps because this is a lease, not an outright grant.

[113] S 1255; note the *sicut præceptum* formula applied to Ælfred, as in S 62. I take the epithet *comes* and the reading *ad Tuueoneaum* (for scribal *Uueogernacestre!*, cf. *EHD*, p. 504, n. 3) from the twelfth-century abstract in Dugdale, *Monasticon* I, 608 (cf. *ECWM*, p. 38). One cannot easily associate this Ælfred with the other Twyning charter abstracted in *Monasticon* I, 608, by which 'Ælfredus dux regis Offani' gives Twyning to Worcester, for this has to belong to 780×796 (if genuine) and Ælfred, the father of Æthelburg, was evidently dead by the time of the 774 charter. *Ælfredus dux* may be a later member of the same family. See below, p. 132, n. 81. On the identity of the Fladbury

two Ælfreds are the same, it follows that the *subregulus* Ealdred was related in some way to Ælfred, the former owner of Fladbury. Although a relationship between this Ælfred and the earlier sub-king Æthelheard is not stated, it seems likely in view of their common interest in Fladbury. In nomenclature the *Osred* mentioned above and *Ælfred* and his daughter *Æthel*burg provide a link between the *Osric, Oshere, Æthel*heard, etc., of the early period and the later *subreguli* Uht*red* and Eald*red*.

No children of Eanberht, Uhtred and Ealdred are known. Uhtred and Ealdred seem to be the last to hold a vestige of royal power ('aliquod regimen') in the kingdom. Their place was taken by ealdormen; Offa's charter of *c.* 777 describing Ealdred both as *subregulus* and as *dux* (that is, *ealdorman*) is symptomatic of the change.[114] The first known *ealdorman* of the Hwicce, without any hint of royalty, is the Æthelmund who was slain attacking the people of Wiltshire at Kempsford in 802, apparently taking advantage of, or reacting to, a change of king in Wessex. He had been a person of importance for some while, if he may be identified with the person of the same name mentioned in several charters.[115] Nothing but his alliterating name would associate him with the Hwiccian royal dynasty. Judging by the charters, he may have been no more than an official of theirs and the Mercians: Uhtred makes a grant in 770 to 'my faithful servant Æthelmund son of the Ingeld who was ealdorman of Æthelbald king of the Mercians' ('fideli meo ministro Æthelmundo uidelicet filio Ingeldi qui fuit dux et præfectus Æthelbaldi regis Merciorum'),[116] Offa likewise grants him land in 793×796 as 'fideli meo minis-

Æthelburg I agree with Whitelock in *Asser*, ed. Stevenson, p. cxl, and *EHD*, p. 494, against Levison, *England and the Continent*, p. 251, n. 2.

[114] See above, p. 33.

[115] See Searle, *Bishops, Kings and Nobles*, p. 367. *ASC* 802 does not specifically make him 'ealdorman of the Hwicce', but probably implies that status. I am assuming that we do not have to do with more than one Æthelmund. Cf. *EHD*, p. 512; Scharer, *Königsurkunde*, p. 276; and below, p. 174, n. 146.

[116] S 59; note the lack of reference to blood relationship. On this charter see below, p. 154. If Ælmund son of Ingeld was distinct from the ealdorman, the latter *might* be a member of the Hwiccian dynasty (e.g. a son of Uhtred). Taylor, 'Osric', pp. 320–2, shows that Æthelmund son of Ingeld is the 'Ælmund Ingeldinge/Ingeldinc' who gave 30 hides 'in Æeoport' to Gloucester (S 1782; BCS 535; *Historia*, ed. Hart I, lxxiii, and II, 111; and cf. Gregory of Caerwent, Vespasian A. v, 195r). If this place is Over (*Historia*, ed. Hart I, 4, and Taylor, p. 321), he is certainly the father of the Æthelric son of Æthelmund of S 1187, who gave 30 hides 'under Ofre' to Gloucester (see below, pp. 39, n. 119, and 123, n. 41).

tro',[117] and Ecgfrith, Offa's son and successor, grants him an estate as his faithful *princeps*, whereas he refers to Ealdred and Uhtred (in connection with the earlier history of the estate) as *subreguli Huicciorum*.[118]

Æthelmund's wife Ceolburg may have been the abbess of Berkeley who died in 807, and his son Æthelric refers to an extensive inheritance in the kingdom of the Hwicce in the will that he made in (?)804, returning from a pilgrimage to Rome.[119] Æthelric's wish to be buried at Deerhurst may indicate a break with the traditions of the Hwiccian kings. By the end of the eighth century the kingdom of the Hwicce, as a kingdom, was extinct.

THE KINGDOM OF THE MAGONSÆTAN

The Hwicce's western neighbours are more elusive. They are apparently omitted in the extant texts of the *Tribal Hidage*, unless the entry 'Westerna' refers to them.[120] Neither does Bede mention them by name. Listing the bishops of the Mercian area in 731 he says simply:

prouinciae Merciorum Alduini episcopus *et eis populis qui ultra amnem Sabrinam ad occidentem habitant Ualchstod episcopus*, prouinciae Huicciorum Uilfrid episcopus, prouinciae Lindisfarorum Cyniberct episcopus praeest.[121]

Bede's circumlocution and syntax may indicate that the name 'Magon-sætan' was not in general use in 731, or that the Magonsætan were no more than a Mercian overspill under an additional bishop, not a discrete people. Alternatively, he may be emphasizing that they were more ethnically

---

[117] S 139; note the absence of consenting Hwiccian *reguli*. It may be the same Æthelmund who granted land to Glastonbury in 794 with Offa's consent, according to S 1692; cf. *PNGl* II, xii and 159; *Early History of Glastonbury*, ed. Scott, pp. 107 and 143; *Chronicle of Glastonbury*, ed. Carley, pp. 41, 107 and 288, nn. 194–5.

[118] S 148. Cf. Sims-Williams, 'Bath', p. 9, n. 8. On *princeps* '[senior] ealdorman' see Thacker, 'Noblemen', p. 204.

[119] S 1187, discussed in *EHD*, p. 512. Cf. above, nn. 115–16, and below, pp. 123, n. 41, and 175.

[120] See above, p. 18.

[121] 'Ealdwine is bishop of the province of the Mercians and Walhstod is bishop of the *peoples who dwell over the river Severn to the west*, Wilfrid is bishop of the province of the Hwicce, and Cyneberht is bishop of the province of Lindsey': *HE* V.23. See also below, pp. 90–1. Dr Keynes points out that while bishops of Worcester are bishops 'of the Hwicce' in the eighth- and ninth-century conciliar records, those of Lichfield, 'Hereford', and Leicester are bishops 'of the Mercians'.

diverse than the Mercians, Hwicce and Lindsey folk, and this could perhaps reflect some claim by Bishop Walhstod, whose name (or nickname) means 'interpreter', to rule a mixed English and Welsh diocese.[122] Whatever the case, the passage shows that the area formed a single diocese, and this is confirmed by the survival of only one episcopal list for it. On the analogy of the other dioceses one would expect that Walhstod's diocese corresponded to a secular kingdom, a supposition supported by the fact that he and his two immediate predecessors were interred in the same tomb as a *regulus* Milfrith and his wife Cwenburg; we know this from an epitaph composed by his successor, Bishop Cuthbert (736–40).[123] The names of earlier members of the dynasty (attested in later sources) also alliterate in M- and Stenton curiously argued that it is no coincidence that the name 'Magonsætan' begins with the same consonant.[124] If Stenton were correct, we could deduce that the name of the kingdom was as old as the seventh century, but in fact alliteration between names of persons and names of peoples seems uncommon and is no doubt a coincidence when it does occur. This is a pity, for we have no contemporary seventh- or eighth-century evidence for the name of the kingdom, owing to the loss of early Hereford records; it is not until a few charters of 811 and later, all of them drawn up outside the kingdom, that the name 'Magonsætan' (variously spelt) is attested.[125] This is not an ancient folk-name, but probably means 'people(s) living round Maund'.[126] It is surely significant that Maund is in the centre of the old diocese of Hereford. It may have been its corresponding centrality in the secular kingdom that led to its adoption in the name of the people.

I shall use the name Magonsætan for the seventh- and eighth-century kingdom, *faute de mieux*, but it should be mentioned that some sources offer us some other, enigmatic names. The heading of the episcopal list in the

---

[122] Middle Welsh *gwalstawt* 'interpreter' was borrowed from OE *w(e)alhstōd*: T. H. Parry-Williams, *The English Element in Welsh* (London, 1923), pp. 39–40.

[123] See below, pp. 91 and 339–45.

[124] *Anglo-Saxon England*, p. 47. Cf. Finberg, *Lucerna*, p. 71.

[125] *CP*, pp. 194 and 197; Brooks *et al.*, 'New Charter of Edgar', pp. 145–6 and n. 40.

[126] *DEPN*, p. 318; *PNE* II, 94; Rennell of Rodd, 'Land of Lene', pp. 304 and 312. Maund appears as *Magana* in S 1798. The fact that the etymology of *Maund* is uncertain (cf. Gelling, *Signposts*, pp. 102–3) should not be an objection to deriving *Magonsætan* from it. Any connection between *Magonsætan* (or *Maund*) and Romano-British *Magnis* (Kenchester) is unlikely, but not impossible; cf. *ibid.*, pp. 102–5; Jackson, *Language and History*, p. 466, n. 3; Wilmott, 'Kenchester', p. 130.

earliest extant manuscript, BL, Cotton Vespasian B. vi, 108v, written in Mercia in 805×814, has been damaged by re-agents, but was read in 1884 by Maunde Thompson as 'Nomina episcoporum uesterȩhorum post sæxwulfum'. Shortly afterwards Sweet read only *'Nomina episcoporum uest.r.'* (his italics indicate re-inking). This century M. R. James read 'nomina epiš. uestor ehonū *post* sæxulf(um)', marking *ehon* as doubtful, and R. I. Page read 'N(omina Epis*coporum*) Uestor Ȩ[.] p[.] Sæx[.]', noting that 'about four letters are lost' after Ȩ and that 'the traces suggest *ponu, poru, ronu, roru'*.[127]

The related text in Cambridge, Corpus Christi College 183, 63r, written in Wessex in 934×939, has 'Nomina Epis*coporum* Uuestor Elih' *post* Seaxuulfu*m'.*[128] In both manuscripts bishops are referred to by their peoples rather than by their sees, unless there is a qualifying word after the proper name such as *ecclesia*, so 'Uest . . .' is presumably a name for the people of the diocese. Its obscurity is underlined by the fact that the later text in BL, Cotton Tiberius B. v, 21v, written in the first half of the eleventh century, probably at Christ Church, Canterbury, has simply 'NOMINA EPI*SCO*PORUM', while Rochester, Cathedral Library, A.3.5, 114r, which shares a common Christ Church source, has the conventional 'Nomina epi*scoporum* herefordensiu*m'.*[129] Finally, in the text in the early twelfth-century Appendix (so-called) to the Chronicle of 'Florence' of Worcester, the heading is 'NOMINA PRAESULUM MAGESETENSIUM', but there is also the rubric 'HECANA'. This was presumably intended as a kingdom-name, since the parallel rubrics for the other Mercian lists are 'HWICCIA', 'MERCIA', 'MIDDANGLIA', 'LINDISSIS' and 'SUTHANGLIA';[130] nevertheless a twelfth-century interpolated copy of the Winchcombe

---

[127] E. M. Thompson, *Catalogue of Ancient Manuscripts in the British Museum*, part II, *Latin* (London, 1884), p. 80; *Oldest English Texts*, ed. Sweet, p. 169; James, *Catalogue of Manuscripts in Corpus Christi College, Cambridge* I, 433; Page, 'Episcopal Lists, Parts I–II', p. 73, n. 7, and 'Part III', p. 6.

[128] *Ibid.*, p. 10; cf. Keynes, 'Athelstan's Books', pp. 180–5. On the relationship of the texts cf. Dumville, 'Anglian Collection'.

[129] Page, 'Part III', p. 15; *Eleventh-Century Miscellany*, ed. McGurk *et al.* II, 70; *Textus Roffensis*, ed. P. Sawyer, EEMF 7 and 11 (Copenhagen 1957–62) I, 114r.

[130] See the facsimile of Oxford, Corpus Christi College 157, p. 43, in Hart, 'Early Section', p. 268. Cf. *MHB*, p. 621.

foundation charter, which draws on the 'Appendix', has the attestation of a bishop of 'Hecana quæ nunc Hereford dicitur', perhaps by guesswork.[131]

A name resembling 'Hecana' appears further on in the 'Appendix' to 'Florence', in the commentary accompanying the Mercian royal genealogies. It is stated that 'Merewald', Penda's son and Peada's full brother, was 'Westanhecanorum rex'; elsewhere in the 'Appendix' he is 'rex West-Anglorum', and in the main body of the *Chronicle*, s.a. 675, he is said to have ruled 'in occidentali plaga Merciorum'.[132] In all three places 'Florence' is drawing on the 'Kentish Royal Legend' texts which tell how a niece of Eorcenberht of Kent (640–64), variously named Domneva, Eormenburga and Eormenberga, married Merewalh (or Merewald) and bore him a son, Merefin, who died in childhood, and three daughters: Mildburg, who became abbess of Wenlock, Mildthryth, who became abbess of Minster-in-Thanet (a house founded by her mother after she separated from Merewalh and returned to Kent) and Mildthryth, whose grave is in Northumbria.[133] These 'Kentish Royal Legend' texts, however, describe Merewalh simply, either as *rex Merciorum*, as in the earliest extant text, which is probably the work of the tenth-century Ramsey scholar Byrhtferth,[134] or, more commonly, as 'son of Penda, king of the Mercians'. The two exceptions are 'Florence', quoted above, and the *Vita S. Mildburgae* (composed at Wenlock, probably in the late eleventh century) which marries Domneva to 'Merwardo (*varr*. Merwaldo, Merwale) regi Westehanorum (*var*. Westhanorum) hesperie partis Merciorum'.[135] Presumably both sources were using West Midland tradition to elaborate the Kentish data, but it is impossible to say how old that tradition was and what form

---

[131] S 167. See *Asser*, ed. Stevenson, pp. 228 and 229, n. 1, for the suggestion that *Hecana* is gen. pl. of a nom. pl. **Hecan*. According to the *Vitae* of St Ethelbert, Hereford was originally called *Fernlaʒe* or *Fernlega* (see 'Two Lives', ed. James, pp. 220, 232 and 244; *DP* III, 188, 258 and 272; *ECWM*, p. 222, n. 1).

[132] *MHB*, pp. 534, 635 and 638; facsimile of genealogy in Hart, 'Early Section', p. 269. In *The Earliest Life of Gregory the Great*, ed. Colgrave, c. 16, Rædwald of East Anglia is called 'rex uuest(r)anglorum'; this is a scribal error (cf. *ibid.*, pp. 69 and 149, n. 65), but suggests that such a term existed.

[133] For discussion and references see Rollason, *Mildrith*.

[134] *Historia regum*, ed. Arnold, *Symeonis Monachi Opera* II, 11. Cf. M. Lapidge, 'Byrhtferth of Ramsey and the Early Sections of the *Historia Regum* Attributed to Symeon of Durham', *ASE* 10 (1982), 97–122, at 119–20; Rollason, *Mildrith*, pp. 15–18.

[135] BL, Add. 34633, 206r; cf. *Nova Legenda Anglie*, ed. Horstman II, 188; Leland, *Collectanea*, ed. Hearne III, 169. Leland attributed the *Vita* to Goscelin, but see Rollason, *Mildrith*, pp. 26 and 149, n. 60.

the name took in it. Modern scholars who assert that the original name of the Magonsætan was *Hecani*, Western *Hecani*, or the like, are therefore going further than present evidence allows. [136]

The diocesan bounds give some indication of the area of the kingdom of the Magonsætan, as I shall continue to call it. Bede's generalized description of Walhstod's diocese as 'beyond the Severn to the west' need not be taken literally as evidence that the Severn was the boundary. In fact, the earliest description of the diocesan boundary between Hereford and Worcester, which was drawn up by Æthelstan, bishop of Hereford 1012–56, and inserted in a gospel book, leaves the Severn at Minster-worth to skirt round Gloucester and Worcester, along the line of the Malvern hills and river Teme, and it does not rejoin the Severn until its confluence with the Dowles Brook above Bewdley – or perhaps not even until Eardington and Quatford. [137] The later medieval diocese of Worcester encroached still further westwards, for instance in taking in Acton Beauchamp (He., formerly Wo.), a monastery which we know was in the western diocese in the early eighth century. [138]

Bishop Æthelstan did not describe his bounds with Lichfield diocese, doubtless because they were not in dispute, nor those on the Welsh side of the diocese (though he implied that the Wye was the boundary from Monmouth to the Severn), perhaps because rather special arrangements with Welsh assistant bishops obtained during the latter part of his episcopate. [139] Nevertheless, it is clear that the early diocese and kingdom, like the later medieval diocese, reached at least as far into southern Shropshire as Wenlock, where there was a seventh-century royal monastery. The area round the Wrekin and Wroxeter, north of Wenlock, had been densely settled since the Iron Age and was agriculturally important in

---

136 Cf. Stevenson, *Asser*, pp. 228–9; *CP*, p. 194; *ECWM*, p. 217; Finberg, *Lucerna*, p. 71; Hart, Tribal Hidage', pp. 139–41; Davies and Vierck, 'Contexts', p. 231; Hooke, *Hwicce*, p. 18 (cf. below, p. 88, n. 2).

137 Cambridge, Pembroke College 203, 8r; S 1561; ed. and discussed by Förster, *Themse*, pp. 767–76. See especially *ECWM*, pp. 225–7; also Darlington, *Worcester Cartulary*, p. 48; *PNGl* IV, 32, n. 1; Rowley, *Shropshire Landscape*, p. 45, n. 17; and below, pp. 392, n. 148, and 394, n. 158.

138 See my map on p. xv, and cf. below p. 150, n. 38. On the evidence for the late medieval bounds see above, p. 4, n. 9.

139 See *ASC* 1055 CD (*English Historical Documents 1042–1189*, ed. D. C. Douglas and G. W. Greenaway (London, 1953), pp. 133–4), and my review of Davies, *Llandaff Charters* etc., p. 128; cf. *LL* 278.

the Romano-British period.[140] Poignant Welsh *englynion* give a graphic, but perhaps imaginary, account of its loss to the English in the time of Cynddylan, a contemporary of Penda.[141] In the period of Mercian domination and later its people were known from the name of the Wrekin as Wreocensætan. Since they were assessed at a full 7,000 hides in the *Tribal Hidage*, they presumably stretched a good distance towards the north, where the infertile lands of the Ellesmere moraine perhaps formed a natural barrier between them and the Mercians of the Dee valley.[142] Their boundary with the Magonsætan was probably Wenlock Edge, for a tenth-century charter locates Plaish, just north of Wenlock Edge (SO/5296), 'in prouincia Wrocensetna'.[143] By contrast, the late medieval boundary of Hereford diocese, though it starts south-westwards down Wenlock Edge from the Severn, then veers north to Hoar Edge, taking in Plaish. It eventually rejoins the Severn near Shrewsbury, thus including a large area of south-western Shropshire. This has an artificial appearance, suggesting that the north-western tongue of the diocese may be a later accretion. The rise of Shrewsbury perhaps disturbed earlier patterns.

The later medieval boundary is no doubt an inexact guide to the western limits of the Magonsætan, which must have depended on their varying relations with the Welsh of Powys. Staunton on Arrow is the place farthest west to be specified as 'in pago Magesætna' (in a charter of 958),[144] but presumably the kingdom extended at least as far as the line of Offa's Dyke.[145]

---

[140] Cf. I. Burrow and A. Tyler, 'Shropshire Sites and Monument Record', *WMANS* 21 (1978), 4–13; Webster, 'West Midlands in the Roman Period', pp. 53 and 55. On the other hand, Hooke, *Territorial Organization*, p. 18, argues that the Magonsætan/ Wreocensætan frontier was a 'little developed zone'.

[141] See above, p. 29.

[142] Cf. Stanford, *Welsh Marches*, pp. 30–1 and 182. On the Wreocensætan cf. above, p. 18. In 963 their territory included Church Aston, near Newport (S 723; cf. *ECWM*, p. 240, addendum).

[143] S 723. I agree here with Hart, 'Tribal Hidage', p. 139, against Davies and Vierck, 'Contexts', p. 238, who suppose that Much Wenlock was in Wreocensætan territory. Rowley, *Shropshire Landscape*, p. 120, n. 1, suggests that Hoar Edge was the Wreocensætan/Magonsætan boundary, but the Plaish charter seems to rule this out. On the diocesan boundary see also Rees, *South Wales and the Border*, NE Sheet; Croom, 'Minster *Parochiae*', p. 73 and n. 52. Plaish was probably included along with Church Preen, a dependency of Wenlock.

[144] S 677; for bounds see Hooke, *Territorial Organization*, p. 22.

[145] Or beyond it, if the Dyke ceded land to the Welsh or marked a patrol line set back from the actual frontier (cf. Noble, *Offa's Dyke Reviewed*). Stenton thought that the

In southern Herefordshire the line of Offa's Dyke is interrupted, probably because the frontier was disputed or because the river Wye was regarded as an adequate boundary. Here the Magonsætan marched with the Welsh kingdom of Ergyng (or Erging); the name derives from *Ariconium*, the Roman station at Weston under Penyard, which is east of the Wye, an indication that the centre of the British kingdom had retreated westwards under Anglo-Saxon pressure.[146] Something about Ergyng and its seventh-century Welsh kings can be learnt from seventh- and eighth-century charters preserved, in modified form, in the twelfth-century Book of Llandaf. These imply that by the seventh and eighth centuries Ergyng was bounded by the Dore and Monnow to the west and south and by the Wye to the north and east.[147] By the time of the Domesday survey the part of this area north of the Worm and Taradr brooks (the later English hundred of Webtree, called in Welsh *Anergyng* 'non-Ergyng') was anglicized, while the southern part (Archenfield) remained 'economically and ecclesiastically still Welsh';[148] in the mid-eighth century, however, northern Ergyng was

place-names Burlingjobb and Huntington pointed to English settlement further up the Arrow valley earlier than, and across the line of, Offa's Dyke (*CP*, p. 196 and *Anglo-Saxon England*, pp. 46 and 214; cf. Darby and Terrett, *Domesday Geography*, pp. 112–13), and Dodgson, 'English Arrival in Cheshire', p. 22, n. 92, held that the assibilation in Burlingjobb pointed to an archaic locative suffix *-ingī*. But there are problems: see J. McN. Dodgson, *The Place-Names of Cheshire* III, EPNS 46 (Cambridge, 1971), xvi and 288; M. Gelling, 'The *-inghope* Names of the Welsh Marches', *Nomina* 6 (1982), 31–6, and *Place-Names in the Landscape*, pp. 118–21; and V. Watts, review of the latter, *Nomina* 9 (1985), 105.

[146] Cf. *DP* III, 217 and 264–5; Charles, 'Archenfield and Oswestry', p. 88; Jackson, *Language and History*, p. 557; *PNGl* III, 192, and IV, 24.

[147] See the charters of 'Sequence I' and 'Sequence II' listed by Davies, *Llandaff Charters*, pp. 35–7 and 41–53, and the maps of grants in Davies, *Microcosm*, pp. 76–80, Hughes, 'Celtic Church', pp. 16–18, W. Davies, *Wales in the Early Middle Ages* (Leicester, 1982), p. 93, and Jones, 'Early Historic Settlement', p. 128. For a summary of my opinions on the dating and authenticity of the Llandaf charters see Sims-Williams, review of Davies, *Llandaff Charters* etc.

[148] Charles, 'Archenfield and Oswestry', p. 88. Cf. *DP* III, 265–74; Richards, *Units*, pp. 6 and 269; Rees, *South Wales and the Border*, SE Sheet; Darby and Terrett, *Domesday Geography*, p. 75; Davies, *Microcosm*, p. 26, n. 1; Freeman, 'Some Place-Names'; Jones, 'Early Historical Settlement'. On Webtree and on the Dunsæte see above, p. 9. They spanned a river (the Wye, or Worm or Taradr?) and were contiguous with the *Wentsæte* 'people of Gwent' (or 'people next to Gwent'?).

still under Welsh control, though subject to English incursions.[149] It is therefore likely that, in the absence of Offa's Dyke, the Wye formed the boundary between the kingdoms of the Magonsætan and Ergyng. To Sir John Lloyd's objection that such a boundary would have been too close for the security of Hereford[150] it may be replied that Hereford's name ('army-ford') and pre-Viking defences suggest a frontier town,[151] and furthermore that the episcopal see may originally have been sited more centrally in the kingdom rather than at Hereford.[152]

South of Ergyng lay the Welsh kingdom of Gwent (OE *Wentsæte*), which took its name from the Roman city *Venta Silurum* (Welsh *Caerwent*). The earliest plausible charters in the Book of Llandaf are those of a king of Gwent, Iddon ab Ynyr Gwent, who is said elsewhere to have been contemporary with Cadwallon of Gwynedd (d. 634),[153] and in the 880s Gwent still had its own kings Brochfael and Ffyrnfael, although to judge by the 'leading names' in Brochfael's genealogy its dynasty by that stage was closely linked with that of Glywysing to the west,[154] which had come to exercise some sort of overlordship over Gwent.[155] By about the end of

---

[149] *LL* 192, on churches lost in the time of Æthelbald (716–57) and recovered by Bishop Berthwyn (see my map in Hughes, 'Celtic Church', p. 18, and below, p. 52). The statement in the *Vita S. Oudocei* (*LL*, pp. 133–4) that Ergyng north of the Worm and Taradr was lost to the English in the time of the saint (supposedly sixth-century but really Berthwyn's predecessor, cf. *LL* 180b) seems to be based on *LL* 192 and cannot be taken very seriously. Nevertheless, the fact that northern Ergyng did not form part of the diocese claimed by Llandaf is a point in favour of the north Ergyng charters in *LL*. The ninth-century charters mentioned by Davies, *Microcosm*, p. 26 (see also pp. 29, n. 2, and 96–7), concern *southern* Ergyng; see Hughes, 'Celtic Church', p. 19, maps 5–6.

[150] *History of Wales* I, 196 and 200, n. 26; Noble, *Offa's Dyke Reviewed*, p. 18.

[151] Cf. Sawyer, *Roman Britian to Norman England*, p. 108. It is possible, however, that Hereford's immediate hinterland was under English control; cf. *DP* III, 272–3.

[152] See below, p. 91.

[153] *LL* 121, 122, (123) and 166. On the absolute chronology see Sims-Williams, review of Davies, p. 126. The Welsh *Life* of St Beuno used there is late, but was partly based on earlier charter material (cf. W. Davies, 'The Latin Charter-Tradition in Western Britain, Brittany and Ireland in the Early Mediaeval Period', in *Ireland in Early Mediaeval Europe*, ed. Whitelock *et al.*, p. 271) and is the best evidence we have.

[154] *Asser*, ed. Stevenson, c. 80; *Early Welsh Genealogical Tracts*, ed. P. C. Bartrum (Cardiff, 1966), p. 12, §29; cf. §28 and p. 45, §9. Bartrum's emendations, which would join the two dynasties directly, are questionable; cf. Hughes, 'Celtic Church', p. 10, n. 33.

[155] Thus Hywel ap Rhys of Glywysing (Asser, c. 80) makes many grants in Gwent in *LL*. Cf. Davies, *Microcosm*, p. 91.

the seventh century, Gwent seems to have taken over Ergyng, for after the reigns there of Peibio ab Erb (contemporary with Iddon), his sons Cynfyn and Gwyddgi, and grandson Gwrgan ap Cynfyn, the Llandaf charters offer no more kings of Ergyng; instead Ergyng land is granted by a king of Gwent, Athrwys ap Meurig.[156] Gwrgan ap Cynfyn's sons Morgan and Caradog issue no charters as kings, and were perhaps squeezed out between Gwent and the Magonsætan.[157]

The common boundary between Gwent and the Magonsætan was presumably the Wye from Monmouth down to its confluence with the Severn – roughly speaking, for both the course of Offa's Dyke and the Llandaf charters suggest that some land on the east bank of the Wye remained in Welsh hands until the reign of Athelstan.[158] No place south of Yarkhill (in a charter of 811) happens to be described as 'on Magonsetum', but it is reasonable to suppose that the kingdom included the territory between the Wye, Severn and Leadon, including the part annexed to Gloucestershire in the eleventh century.[159] This is supported by the inclusion of this territory in the diocese of Hereford,[160] and, in a negative way, by the scarcity of references to it in the Worcester and Llandaf charter collections.

The first known ruler of the Magonsætan is Merewalh (or Merewald). The statement in the 'Kentish Royal Legend' texts that he was a son of Penda (d. 655) is not improbable; one may compare the way in which Penda set his son Peada over the Middle Angles. Stenton doubted the relationship between Penda and Merewalh on the grounds of non-alliteration,[161] but this is not a strong objection, since the nomenclature of the Mercian royal

---

[156] *LL* 165; his father Meurig may be the grantor of *LL* 160 slightly earlier. Any connection between Athrwys ap Meurig and the kings of 'Sequence II' is doubtful. *LL* 75, a grant by 'Erb, king of Gwent and Ergyng', is suspicious.

[157] For Gwrgan's sons see *LL* 163b. It may be his daughter who in *LL* 140 is alleged to have married Meurig ap Tewdrig, founder of the royal line of Glywysing. This may have been the period when the Wentsæte (cf. above, n. 148) stretched up to the Dunsæte; see above, p. 9.

[158] Cf. *DP* III, 188, n. 3, and 267, n. 1; *PNGl* III, xiv and 265; IV, 32, n. 1; Noble, *Offa's Dyke Reviewed*, pp. 1–12.

[159] S 1264; *PNGl* IV, 43. For the Gloucestershire annexation see *ECWM*, p. 233.

[160] Bishop Æthelstan's boundary starts at Monmouth, evidently running down the Wye to the Severn, which is the next point of reference (*ECWM*, p. 225).

[161] *Anglo-Saxon England*, p. 47, n. 1, and *CP*, p. 195; similarly *HBC²*, p. 15. But see Finberg, *Lucerna*, p. 71, and *ECWM*, p. 219, n. 2.

house was more varied than that of some other Anglo-Saxon dynasties; for instance, another son of Penda's was *Wulfhere*, and *his* son was called *Coenred*. Moreover, if Mere*walh* is the correct form of the name, as Stenton maintained,[162] we can compare the name Coen*walh* borne by Penda's brother and the name Pen*walh* borne by another member of the Mercian dynasty.[163] There are two further pieces of evidence. A Thanet charter of 746 or 748 (preserved in a fifteenth-century cartulary) refers to the 'consanguinity' of Æthelbald of Mercia (Penda's great-nephew) and St Mildthryth (Merewalh's daughter); if Merewalh was Penda's son the consanguinity would be that of second cousins.[164] Secondly, in the so-called 'Testament of St Mildburg' – the collection of early Wenlock charters appended to the *Vita S. Mildburgae* in the thirteenth-century manuscript of that *Vita* – Mildburg (Merewalh's daughter) refers to

---

[162] *CP*, p. 195, n. 1. Forms without *-d* occur in the eleventh-century manuscripts of *Pa halgan þe on Angelcynne restað* (ed. Liebermann, *Die Heiligen Englands*, p. 3) and its Latin derivatives (*ibid.*, p. 4, and *Hugh Candidus*, ed. Mellows, p. 57), in the *Passio Ethelredi atque Ethelbricti* (ed. Rollason, *Mildrith*, p. 93), and in the works of Goscelin (*Vita Mildrethae*, ed. Rollason, *Mildrith*, p. 115, and *Vita Werburgae* in PL 155, 100). Forms with *-d* occur in the mid-eleventh-century manuscript of the OE *St Mildryð* (ed. Swanton, 'Mildred', p. 24), in the twelfth-century manuscripts of the *Historia regum* (ed. Arnold, *Symeonis Monachi Opera* II, 11), of 'Florence' of Worcester (*MHB*, pp. 534, 635 and 638) and of William of Malmesbury (*Gesta regum*, ed. Stubbs I, 78 and 267), and in the *Vita S. Mildburgae* (as above, p. 42, n. 135, also London, BL, Harley 2253 (s. xiv), 132r, and Lansdowne 436 (Romsey, s. xiv), 72v). For another *Meruualh* cf. Tangl, *Ep.* xxxix. The name *Merguall* / *Mergualdus* (*gu* = /w/) passed into use in Wales (see *LL* 145).

[163] For Coenwalh see Dumville, 'Anglian Collection', p. 31. See above, p. 26, for Penwalh (a variant in the mid-eleventh-century MS H is *Penwald*!). Gelling, *Signposts*, p. 95, suggests that '*Merewalh*, literally "famous Welshman", . . . adopted this name as a matter of political expediency'.

[164] S 91. Cf. Sawyer, *Roman Britain to Norman England*, p. 39; Rollason, *Mildrith*, pp. 16, 39, 44 and 147, n. 7. Scharer, *Königsurkunde*, pp. 205–6, and S. E. Kelly, 'The Pre-Conquest History and Archive of St Augustine's Abbey, Canterbury' (unpubl. PhD dissertation, Cambridge Univ., 1986), p. 176, express doubts about the reference to the translation of Mildthryth in S 91, but Schneider, 'Women', p. 282, n. 45, is inclined to accept it. For a family tree see Searle, *Bishops, Kings and Nobles*, pp. 290–1. According to the *Vita S. Mildburgae* the order of Penda's sons was: Peada, Wulfhere, Merewald, Æthelred (references as above, p. 42, n. 135). S 68 (version B), in which Wulfhere refers to his brother *Mereuuald*, is a fabrication of which the earliest manuscript is s. xii.

Æthelred of Mercia (Merewalh's brother) as her uncle (*patruus*).[165] While it is not impossible that both the Thanet and Wenlock charters have suffered from antiquarian interpolation, there are no sure grounds for scepticism.

The *Vita S. Mildburgae* dates Merewalh's conversion to 660 AD.[166] While little trust can be put in the passage, such a *floruit* for him seems reasonable, since his father Penda flourished *c.* 628–55, and his daughter Mildthryth, abbess of Thanet, appears in charters between 696 and (?)733.[167] The statement in the 'Kentish Royal Legend' texts that Merewalh and his brother Wulfhere married Kentish princesses is plausible in view of the contemporary interdynastic marriages mentioned by Bede, such as those between Peada and Oswiu of Bernicia's daughter and between Æthelwealh of Sussex and the Hwiccian princess Eaba. Their statement that Merewalh's wife separated from him for religious reasons and returned to Kent also accords with seventh-century *mores*.[168] All the texts, apart from 'Florence' and William of Malmesbury, who call her 'E(o)rmenburga' or 'Ermenberga', agree that Merewalh's wife's name was 'Domneva' or the like, and some add that she was also called 'Eormenburga' or 'Ermenberga'.[169] As *Domneva* is probably a hypocoristic form of the

[165] *ECWM*, pp. 202 and 219. The 'Testament' is printed and discussed in *ECWM*, pp. 197–216; cf. S 1798–1802; Whitelock, 'Pre-Viking Age Church', p. 12.

[166] See below, p. 55.   [167] See S 17, 86 and 87. Cf. S 26 (724 for 727).

[168] *HE* III.21 and IV.13; Lapidge, 'Debate Poem'; P. Dronke, '"Ad deum meum convertere volo" and Early Irish Evidence for Lyrical Dialogues', *CMCS* 12 (Winter 1986), 23–32. Cf. below, p. 123.

[169] The forms are: *Eormenburge/Domne Eue* in the OE texts of *Þa halgan þe on Angelcynne restað* (ed. Liebermann, *Die Heiligen Englands*, p. 3), with *Ermenburga/Domne-Eva* in one Latin derivative (*ibid.*, p. 4) and plain *Domneua* in the other (*Hugh Candidus*, ed. Mellows, p. 57); *Domne Eafe* in the OE *St Mildryð* ('Mildred', ed. Swanton, p. 24); *Eormenburga/Domneva* in the *Historia regum* (ed. Arnold, *Symeonis Monachi Opera* II, 11); *Domneua* in *Passio Ethelredi atque Ethelbricti* (ed. Rollason, *Mildrith*, p. 93); *Domneua* in Goscelin's *Vita S. Mildrethae* (*ibid.*, p. 114) and *Vita S. Werburgae* (PL 155, 100); and in the *Vita S. Mildburgae* (BL, Add. 34633, 206v); *Ermenberga/Domneua* in the text ed. by M. L. Colker, 'A Hagiographical Polemic', *MS* 39 (1977), 60–108, at 99, and discussed by Rollason, *Mildrith*, pp. 21–5. For 'Florence' and William of Malmesbury see references above, n. 162. The forms in -*berga* are probably corrupted from -*burga* (OE -*burgl*-*burh*), although cf. *Aedilberg* beside *Sexburg* in *HE* III.8. Some of the later sources (noted by Rollason, *Mildrith*, pp. 23, 39–40 and 153, n. 39) make sisters of Domneva and Eormenburga (and in many cases Ermenberga as well!), but this is implausible. The chief obstacle to the Domneva/Eormenburg identification (*ibid.*, p. 39) is 'irminburga aeaba' in the list of abbesses in S 20, but even if this document is

name *Eormenburg* preceded by the honorific title *dom(i)na*, she has plausibly been identified with an abbess called Æbbe, Æbba, Aeaba or Eabba, who appears in charters relating to Thanet and elsewhere in Kent from 678 to 699.[170] The implication is that she had separated from Merewalh by 678, having already borne him Mildburg and Mildthryth, as well as those shadowy children Merefin and Mildgyth, if they are historical. Mildburg became abbess of Wenlock some time between 674 and 690, and according to the 'Testament of St Mildburg' was still living in 727×736.[171]

The commentary on the Mercian genealogies in the 'Appendix' to 'Florence' of Worcester's *Chronicle* states that 'Merewald' was succeeded by Merchelm, his brother.[172] His name, significantly, has the name of the Mercians (*M(i)erce*) as its first element. It may be preserved in the place-name Marchamley, Shr. ('Merchelm's *lēah*', SJ/5929), implying a connection between Merchelm and northern, Mercian territory.[173] The 'Testament of St Mildburg', which styles Merchelm 'rex', states that he was Mildburg's (not Merewalh's) brother;[174] it is not possible to adjudicate between 'Florence' and the 'Testament' here. The 'Testament' quotes a charter by which Merchelm and another brother, Milfrith, with the consent of Æthelred of Mercia (674–704), granted Mildburg various estates in the kingdom.[175] This Milfrith is styled *regulus* in the epitaph composed by Bishop Cuthbert (736–40); evidently, then, he and his wife Cwenburg had died by 740, and may indeed have been dead many years when Cuthbert composed the epitaph.[176] The *Vita* of the martyr Æthelberht of Hereford, the king of East Anglia whom Offa beheaded, alleges that the minster at Hereford was built by a certain Milfrith, a far-off king (meaning one based in the north of the sub-kingdom?).[177] This may indeed

genuine and these are two separate abbesses (*et* is absent in the earliest manuscript), *Irminburga* is not necessarily the princess Eormenburg of the 'Kentish Royal Legend'.

[170] S 10, 11, 13, 14, 15, 18, 20, 1648; cf. Rollason, *Mildrith*, p. 153, n. 31. On the names see *ibid.*, pp. 34, 38 and 151, n. 7; *ECWM*, p. 218.

[171] S 1798 (cf. Whitelock, 'Pre-Viking Age Church', p. 12) and 1802.

[172] *MHB*, p. 638 ('Mercelinus'); facsimile in Hart, 'Early Section', p. 269.

[173] *DEPN*, p. 314; *ECWM*, p. 220.

[174] *ECWM*, p. 202, 210, n. 1, and 224, n. 2.

[175] S 1799.   [176] See above, p. 14, and below, p. 342.

[177] 'In longe remotis partibus terre regio coronatus diademate quidam Milferhtus nomine': Cambridge, Corpus Christi College 308 (s. xii[in]), 7r, ed. James, 'Two Lives', p. 244; cf. Roscarrock quoted *ibid.*, p. 221; Bannister, *Cathedral Church*, p. 113; C. E. Wright, *The Cultivation of Saga in Anglo-Saxon England* (Edinburgh, 1939),

have been an act of Milfrith – it would explain why Bishop Cuthbert honoured him – though, if so, the *Vita* errs in dating it as late as the aftermath of Æthelberht's martyrdom in 794.

After Milfrith we hear no more about his dynasty, nor about any other aspect of the governance of the kingdom, until a record of a certain Nothheard, *præfectus et comes regis in Magansetum*, who granted land in Archenfield (*Erekandeffeld*) to Gloucester monastery 'through' Beornwulf, king of Mercia 834–5. Stenton commented that this shows the Magon-sætan, 'after the disappearance of their own dynasty, subject to an officer connected by a very intimate tie with the Mercian king'; Thacker, however, deduces from the fact that Nothheard 'never appears among the Mercian king's ealdormen or *duces* in numerous witness lists of the period' that *praefectus* here indicates a magnate of only local importance.[178] The name of the Magonsætan remained in use even after the introduction of the shire system, and as late as 1016 and 1041, when it had become usual for each ealdorman to have more than a single shire under him, we hear once more of the Magonsætan and their *ealdorman* (1016) or *comes* (1041).[179]

Although the royal dynasty of the Magonsætan was thus ultimately eclipsed by the Mercians, it may originally have gained from the Mercian connection. As we have seen, Merewalh may have been Penda's son, put into power by his father, like his brother Peada in the Middle Anglian king-dom. The place-name Marchamley and the royal connections of Wenlock suggest, without proving, that Merewalh and Merchelm were particularly associated with the central marches; if so, the extension of Magonsætan power south to the Bristol Channel may have depended on Mercian favour. Above all, they must have relied on Mercian support in their dealings with the Welsh kingdoms along a very long frontier. No source sets out to describe the frontier wars of the seventh and eighth centuries, but scattered allusions show them to have been frequent and fierce. In the Llandaf charters, narrative sections (of uncertain veracity) refer to grants of land to

---

pp. 95–106; *DP* III, 188, 196, 258 and 272. On Æthelberht's cult see P. M. Korhammer, 'The Origin of the Bosworth Psalter', *ASE* 2 (1973), 173–87, at 187; Rollason, 'Murdered Royal Saints', p. 9.

[178] S 1782; *Historia*, ed. Hart I, lxxiii, 4 and 64 (cf. below, p. 123). See *CP*, p. 197 and n. 2; Thacker, 'Noblemen', p. 213 (comparing the Hwiccian charters S 55 and 57, both of which are suspect). On *praefectus* cf. Sims-Williams, 'Wilfrid', p. 177.

[179] See *EHD*, pp. 62, 250, 318 and 557–8; Brooks *et al.*, 'New Charter of Edgar', p. 146, n. 40.

the church in thanks for victories over the Saxons, by Iddon of Gwent and, a little later in the seventh century, by Gwrfoddw, king of Ergyng; and a further, and particularly suspicious, charter describes Tewdrig and his son Meurig, the ancestors of the kings of Glywysing, halting the Saxon advance for thirty years by a victory at Tintern on the Wye, perhaps about the beginning of the eighth century.[180] The *Vita S. Guthlaci* refers to Welsh attacks, pillage and devastation in the reign of Coenred of Mercia (705–9), and the *Annales Cambriae* list three British victories in 722: one in Cornwall, one at an unidentified 'Pencon' (Pencoed?) in south Wales, and the third at 'Gart Mailauc', possibly the present Caerfaelog in Llanbister (Radnorshire, SO/1174) or Garth Maelog in Llanharan (Glamorgan, ST/0283), both places deep inside Welsh territory.[181] In 743, according to the *Anglo-Saxon Chronicle*, Æthelbald of Mercia and Cuthred of Wessex fought against the 'Walas'. This war, or some other in Æthelbald's long reign (716–57), is alluded to in a plausible and circumstantial document in the Book of Llandaf about 'great tribulations and devastations' on the Anglo-Welsh border, especially on either side of the Wye near Hereford, in the time of Æthelbald and the Welsh king Ithel: when peace was restored Ithel reinstated the surviving landholders, including his bishop Berthwyn, who recovered eleven or twelve churches or estates throughout Ergyng.[182] Another Llandaf charter, recording Bishop Berthwyn's receipt of an estate which a layman had bought 'in the presence of King Ithel and the noble elders of Ergyng' for a price which included 'a *Saxon woman*, a

---

180 *LL* 123, 161 and 141. We do not know whether Gwrfoddw and his son Erfig were related to the Ergyng dynasty mentioned earlier. The dates in Davies, *Llandaff Charters*, pp. 85, 97 and 103, may be too early; see my review, pp. 126–7. Morris, *Age of Arthur*, pp. 126–32, 228–9 and 561, gives a very fantastic account of Tewdrig. Even if the name Tewdrig is Germanic, as Morris claims, that does not make him a Goth, for the name *Theuderic* was in use in the Brittonic world already in the sixth century: *HF* v. 16.

181 *Life of Guthlac*, ed. Colgrave, pp. 1–2, 108–10 and 185–6; *CP*, pp. 361–2; *AC* s.a. 722; Lloyd, *History of Wales* i, 197 and n. 15; Richards, *Units*, pp. 25 and 72. Cf. the variant *Annales Cambriae* in *The Itinerary of John Leland* iv, ed. L. Toulmin Smith (London, 1909), p. 169; *DP* iii, 226, n. 1; *Brut y Tywysogyon: Peniarth MS. 20 Version*, trans. Jones, p. 131.

182 *LL* 192 (*circa* = Welsh *am* 'on either side of'); cf. *DP* iii, 271–4; Davies, *Microcosm*, p. 176, and *Llandaff Charters*, pp. 113–14; Hughes, 'Celtic Church', pp. 7, n. 21, 8, 14, n. 52, and 18 (map 3); and above, n. 149.

precious sword and a valuable horse', is symptomatic of the times.[183] The *Annales Cambriae* record a battle of Hereford in 760 between Welsh and English and, later in Offa's reign, his devastation of south Wales in 778, of Wales in the summer of 784, and of *Rienuch* (probably Brycheiniog and surroundings – if the reading is correct) in 795.[184] Finally, for what it is worth, Matthew Paris in his *Vitae Offarum* tells of a long war between Offa and a Welsh king 'Marmodius', presumably Maredudd of Dyfed who died (like Offa) in 796.[185] In all these sources, it will be noticed, the English leaders, where named, are kings of Mercia rather than of the Magonsætan; and it was the name of a Mercian king that was preserved in the name of Offa's Dyke, 'the rearing of which at enormous cost' – probably late in Offa's reign – must, in Sir John Lloyd's words, 'be looked on as a deliberate closing of the era of conquest'.[186]

[183] *LL* 185. Cf. Davies, *Microcosm*, p. 43, and on sales see my review, p. 129, and below, p. 96, n. 36.

[184] *AC* s.aa.; but for *Rienuch/Rienneth* see *Annales Cambriae*, ed. J. Williams ab Ithel, RS (London, 1860), p. 11, and Leland (as above, n. 181), and P. C. Bartrum, 'Rhieinwg and Rheinwg', *BBCS* 24 (1970–2), 23–7. This may be an error for *Rechru* in Ireland: *Brut y Tywysogyon: Peniarth MS. 20 Version*, trans. Jones, pp. 133–4; K. Grabowski and D. Dumville, *Chronicles and Annals of Mediaeval Ireland and Wales* (Woodbridge, 1984), p. 219. Cf. *DP* III, 259–61 and 271–2; Lloyd, *History of Wales* I, 197–8; *CP*, p. 359. In *AC apud/ab/cum* represent Welsh *gan* 'by'.

[185] *Vitae duorum Offarum per Mathaeum Parisiensem*, ed. W. Wats (London, 1639), pp. 16–19. Cf. R. Vaughan, *Matthew Paris*, 2nd ed. (Cambridge, 1979), p. 193.

[186] *History of Wales* I, 198; cf. *CP*, pp. 196 and 359; Hill, *Atlas*, p. 75.

3

Paganism and Christianity

The pagan Hwicce and Magonsætan are effectively prehistoric; the main evidence for them and their beliefs lies buried with them in their cemeteries, which are almost confined to the east of the kingdom of the Hwicce, along the Cotswolds and the Avon valley.[1] Modern knowledge of Anglo-Saxon paganism from non-archaeological sources is scanty, for Christians had little reason to record memories and survivals of pagan belief and custom.[2] Yet there are occasional exceptions. An eighth-century prayer book from Worcester contains a number of charm-like texts – Christian equivalents of the amulets with which some Hwicce were still being buried in the seventh century, and of the pagan *fylacteria* and *incantationes* forbidden by the Council of *Clofesho* in 747.[3] One page of this prayer book begins with a prayer asking Christ's protection on every limb of the body. Then, after a doxology in garbled Greek, it concludes:

I adjure thee, Satan, devil, elf (*satanae diabulus aelfae*), by the Living and True God, and by the terrible Day of Judgment, that it may flee from the man who goes about with this writing with him, in the name of the Father, Son and Holy Ghost.[4]

The word for the pagan Germanic sprite may be included to explain or reinforce the Christian demonology. The Christian writers of documents

[1] Meaney's *Gazetteer* may be supplemented by Pretty, 'Welsh Border', which I found most helpful when starting work on this chapter, and by more recent reports in *WMA* and elsewhere. For maps of sites, see above, p. 19, n. 15 and p. 21, n. 21.

[2] R. I. Page, *Life in Anglo-Saxon England* (London, 1970), pp. 27–44.

[3] H&S III, 364. Note e.g. the amulets at Lechlade: Miles and Palmer, *Invested in Mother Earth*, p. 18.

[4] BL, Royal 2. A. XX, 45v, ed. Kuypers, *Cerne*, p. 221 (on the manuscript see below, pp. 279–80). Cf. Grattan and Singer, *Magic and Medicine*, p. 50. On the prayer to protect the limbs see below, p. 283.

recorded further memories of paganism in the form of place-names alluding to Germanic gods, like Tiw and Woden, or to pagan shrines and sanctuaries (*wēoh*, *hearg*); but it is not easy to say how and when the places were associated with the gods, nor when the pagan shrines may have ceased to be used. Some of these names may already have been fossils in the seventh century, and others may allude to pagan practices that continued for centuries. At Tysoe ('Tiw's hill-spur'), a great Red Horse, carved into the side of Edge Hill, was still being renewed annually in the seventeenth century by 'a Free-holder in this Lordship, who holds certain lands there by that service'.[5]

WRITTEN ACCOUNTS OF THE CONVERSION

The written sources are almost silent about the date and nature of the conversion to Christianity, perhaps because they include no early hagiography from the area. There are only two local records of the conversion, one from the kingdom of the Magonsætan and the other from that of the Hwicce. Neither provides a trustworthy basis from which one might reconstruct the conversion on the analogy of evidence from elsewhere in England and abroad.[6]

The author of the *Vita S. Mildburgae*, probably writing at Wenlock in the late eleventh century, recounts an ancient story (*uetus historia*), learnt partly from written and partly from oral sources. According to this, Merewalh ('Merwaldus rex Merciorum') was a pagan (*paganismo deditus*) until a priest called Eadfrith (*Edfridus*) came from Northumbria and converted him in 660 AD.[7] In itself this is not incredible, if we compare what was happening in Mercia: Penda (Merewalh's alleged father), like all the Mercians, was an

---

[5] Thus Dugdale; see below, p. 74 and n. 74. This ceremony was done on Palm Sunday, but is not likely to have been started in the fifteenth century (when the place-name was meaningless), despite Samuel Lewis, *A Topographical Dictionary of England*, 3rd ed., 5 vols. (London, 1885) IV, s.n. 'Tysoe'.

[6] For such evidence see especially Mayr-Harting, 'Wilfrid in Sussex'; I. N. Wood, 'The Conversion of the Barbarian Peoples', in *The Christian World*, ed. G. Barraclough (London, 1981), pp. 85–98 and 314; *Irland und die Christenheit*, ed. Ní Chatháin and Richter, pp. 311–76.

[7] BL, Add. 34633, 207r–208r. On this *Vita* cf. above, p. 42, n. 135. The *Legenda de sancto Etfrido presbitero de Leoministria* appears separately in BL, Harley 2253 (s. xiv), 132r–133r; see *Facsimile of British Museum MS. Harley 2253*, ed. N. R. Ker, EETS 255 (London, 1965). See also *Nova Legenda Anglie*, ed. Horstman II, 189–90.

idolator (*idolis deditus*) in the 630s, according to Bede, and Penda himself was to remain a pagan to the end, although he allowed Northumbrian missionaries from Middle Anglia to preach in his kingdom after his son Peada and many of Peada's Middle Anglian subjects had accepted baptism from Fínán, bishop of Lindisfarne, in 653; then, when Penda died in 655, the Northumbrian Oswiu took over the Mercian throne, established a joint Middle Anglian and Mercian bishopric under Northumbrian influence, and 'the Mercians became Christians'.[8] This would be about the period of Merewalh's alleged conversion. On the other hand, it is curious that Bede knows nothing of the Northumbrian Eadfrith; and the assertion in the *Vita S. Mildburgae* that Merewalh founded the monastery of St Peter at *Leo*minster to commemorate a vision of himself in the form of a lion (*leo*), vouchsafed to Eadfrith on his way south, arouses the suspicion that there was more story than history in the *uetus historia*. Moreover, the hagiographer's assumption that Merewalh's people were also pagans and that Eadfrith was the first to preach 'in the western plain of the Mercians'[9] is hard to reconcile with the lack of archaeological evidence for pagan burial rites in the kingdom of the Magonsætan.

The other source for the conversion is the proem to a charter of Osric, king of the Hwicce, of 675, in the twelfth-century cartulary of Bath abbey. Osric begins as though the abandonment of paganism occurred only shortly before the Synod of Hertford in 672 or 673 (when the creation of new sees was decided in principle):

Cum nobis euangelica et apostolica dogmata post baptismi sacramentum Deo suffragante fuissent delata, et omnia simulachrorum figmenta ridiculosa funditus diruta, tum primitus ad augmentum catholicę et orthodoxę fidei pontificalem dumtaxat cathedram erigentes iuxta sinodalia decreta [*coenubia*] construere censuimus.[10]

[8] *HE* II.20; III.21; V.24.

[9] BL, Add. 34633, 207v–208r. The name of Leominster is thought to derive from the Welsh *Llanllieni*: Charles, 'Archenfield and Oswestry', p. 87.

[10] 'When the evangelic and apostolic dogmas were brought to us after the sacrament of baptism, by the grace of God, and all foolish figments of idols had been razed to the ground, then for the first time, for the increase of the catholic and orthodox faith, at least setting up an episcopal see in accordance with synodal decisions, we proposed to establish [monasteries]': S 51. For the emendation and for what follows see Sims-Williams, 'Wilfrid', pp. 167–74. On the problem whether to destroy or re-use pagan shrines, see R. A. Markus, 'Gregory the Great and a Papal Missionary Strategy', in *The Mission of the Church and the Propagation of the Faith*, ed. G. J. Cuming, Studies in Church History 6 (Cambridge, 1970), 29–38; Wallace-Hadrill, *Commentary*, pp. 44–5.

This Bath foundation charter probably has a genuine basis, but the authenticity of the above proem is uncertain. Certainly it is difficult to take it literally, since Bede (quoted below) would seem to imply that the Hwiccian royal dynasty and their people were Christian earlier than the proem seems to imply. Moreover, it is verbally reminiscent of passages in Aldhelm's prose *De uirginitate* about St Benedict and St Martin destroying Roman idols and temples and replacing them with Christian churches; this suggests that the writer, whatever his date, was thinking more about the conspicuous remains of *Roman* paganism to be seen at the Temple of Minerva site in Bath, than about *Anglo-Saxon* paganism.

The slightness of the local sources makes Bede's silence about the conversion of these distant kingdoms particularly frustrating. When they appear in his narrative they are already Christian. In the case of the Magonsætan this is not until the date of writing, 731, when Walhstod is named as 'bishop of the peoples who dwell over the river Severn to the west'.[11] Bede's first reference to the Christian Hwicce comes in the context of Wilfrid's exile in pagan Sussex *c.* 680.[12] Here Bede differs from Stephen's *Vita S. Wilfridi*, normally his main source. Stephen had told the Old Testament-like story of Wilfrid's running aground in Sussex in 666, when the pagan South Saxons tried to loot his ship and the 'chief of the pagan priests' (*princeps sacerdotum idolatriae*) cursed the Christians from a high *tumulus* until a sling shot brought this *magus* to the same end as Goliath. Now, many years later, in 680 or 681, Wilfrid returns as an exile to the South Saxons, who are persevering in paganism, and is received by their king, Æthelwealh. He preaches first to the king and queen, and then to their people, who have never heard the Word of God, and many thousands of pagans abandon idolatry, some voluntarily, others at Æthelwealh's command.[13] Bede omits Wilfrid's earlier encounter with the South Saxons and shortens Stephen's account of the later one, nevertheless adding important details, notably that Æthelwealh and his queen were already

---

[11] See above, p. 39.

[12] *HE* IV.13. On the date and on Wilfrid in Sussex, see Sims-Williams, 'Wilfrid', pp. 176–9, and below, pp. 105–7. Cf. M. G. Welch, *Anglo-Saxon Sussex* I, 260–5, and 'Early Anglo-Saxon Sussex: From Civitas to Shire', in *The South Saxons*, ed. P. Brandon (Chichester, 1978), pp. 13–35 and 227–31, at 29–32; D. P. Kirby, 'The Church in Saxon Sussex', in *The South Saxons*, ed. Brandon, pp. 160–73 and 240–5, at 166–70; Mayr-Harting, 'Wilfrid in Sussex'. Kirby, 'Bede, Eddius Stephanus', emphasizes the independence of Stephen and Bede.

[13] *VW*, cc. 13 and 41–2.

baptized Christians when Wilfrid arrived, although their thegns and common folk were all ignorant of Christianity. Æthelwealh had been baptized 'not long before' in Mercia, in the presence of and at the suggestion of King Wulfhere (d. 674×675), who became his godfather. His queen, Eaba, 'had been baptized in her own province, that of the Hwicce; she was the daughter of Eanfrith, Eanhere's brother, who were both Christians, together with their people'. These Hwiccian princes evidently flourished earlier than Osric (*fl.* 674–9) and Oshere (*fl.* 679–93).[14] Quite probably Æthelwealh's marriage to the Christian princess and his baptism were connected and were both due to his acceptance of Wulfhere's overlordship. Be this as it may, the passage shows that the Hwicce were Christian at the latest by the early 670s and quite possibly a generation earlier. Yet Bede says nothing about their conversion, probably because he had no information on the subject.

It is unlikely that Bede intends us to assume that the Hwiccian conversion was part of that of the Middle Angles and Mercians in the 650s, for he is scrupulous in distinguishing the Hwicce from these peoples.[15] Admittedly, when speaking of church organization before the creation of new bishoprics under Archbishop Theodore in the 670s, Bede is sometimes vague. For instance, in *Historia ecclesiastica* III.21, he says that Diuma was 'bishop of the Middle Angles and the Mercians, since a shortage of bishops made it necessary for one bishop to be set over both nations', but in ch. 24 we learn that Diuma was also bishop of Lindsey, a kingdom which was comparable in size to that of the Hwicce and which did not have a see of its own till 678.[16] Nevertheless, Bede does not intend us to gather that Lindsey was converted along with the Middle Angles and Mercians; in fact he tells us that Paulinus had preached there successfully as early as *c.* 630.[17] In the same way, while Bede may intend us to understand that the diocese of Diuma and his successors included the Hwicce, he can hardly be held to imply that the conversion of the Hwicce was contemporary with that of their Mercian overlords. Indeed, it remains historically undatable; we are *not* entitled to assume, with A. H. Smith, that it 'can hardly have preceded the baptism of the West Saxon king

---

[14] See above, pp. 34–5. On the relationship between overlordship, godparentage and baptism see A. Angenendt, 'The Conversion of the Anglo-Saxons Considered Against the Background of the Early Medieval Mission', *Settimane* 32 (1986), 747–81.

[15] Cf. *CP*, p. 184, n. 2.　　[16] Cf. *HE* IV.12. On Lindsey see *CP*, pp. 127–35.

[17] *HE* II.16. On the date see *BOH* II, 108.

Cynegils in 635, perhaps not even the death of the heathen Mercian Penda'.[18]

The dearth of local sources and Bede's silence, which is doubtless due to the geographical limitations of his sources,[19] compel the historian to rely on the archaeological evidence for religion before *c.* 675; but this is difficult to assess. Archaeology has provided little unequivocal evidence for seventh-century Christianity. No seventh- or eighth-century British or Anglo-Saxon churches have been identified for certain in the area; this is hardly surprising in view of the tiny number of (presumed) secular buildings that are known,[20] and the probability that many early churches were either wooden and easily dismantled or else formed the foundations for later churches which obliterate them.[21] Nor are there any 'Early Christian' memorial stones of the type found on the Atlantic seaboard; their distribution does not extend even to the east of Wales, presumably for cultural rather than religious reasons.[22] Nor, finally, can seventh-century burials unaccompanied by elaborate grave-goods and oriented with feet to the east be regarded as necessarily Christian, in the absence of correlation with contemporary Christian structures.[23] Such correlation is lacking so far, even in the case of the careful and suggestive excavations at Deerhurst, Hereford and Worcester. The earliest burials at Deerhurst were recognized as such precisely because they had been disturbed by the foundations of the first stone church, and it was not ascertained whether these burials, or the

[18] *PNGl* IV, 36. The date 635 is of doubtful precision; see Plummer, *Two Chronicles* II, 20. On the state of the church in the mid-seventh century see Brooks, *Canterbury*, pp. 63–71, and Hunter Blair, 'Whitby', pp. 15–17.

[19] See above, p. 16, n. 2.   [20] See below, pp. 361–3.

[21] See Theodore's *Penitential* II. i. 3 (H&S III, 190) for wooden churches. In the other category, Wenlock seems a tempting possibility. See below, p. 81.

[22] S. Victory, *The Celtic Church in Wales* (London, 1977), pp. 37 and 46; Morris, *Church*, pp. 28–33. The nearest monument (sixth-century?), at Llanveynoe, He. (see fig. 2) is lost. See V. E. Nash-Williams, *The Early Christian Monuments of Wales* (Cardiff, 1950), pp. 218, fig. 254, and 221, no. 409 (on the formula [IA]CIT IN HOC TVMVLO, cf. Jackson, *Language and History*, pp. 158, 163 and 166). Nos. 410–11, also from Llanveynoe, are much later (see also J. R. Allen, 'Early Inscribed Cross-Slab at Llanveynoe, Herefordshire', *Archaeologia Cambrensis* 6th ser. 2 (1902), 239).

[23] For discussion of recent work see Morris, *Church*; Bullough, 'Burial' (with my review of *Ideal and Reality*, pp. 115–16).

stone church, were related to any earlier building or to an oriented rectangle of charcoal, radiocarbon dated to about the seventh century and possibly a burnt part of a building or a charcoal-lined grave.[24] On the site of the late Anglo-Saxon collegiate church of St Guthlac in Hereford, on the other hand, the earliest of the burials discovered in 1960 and 1973 were associated with two contemporary or earlier oriented buildings, one wooden and the other of stone, and both apparently religious; however, the radiocarbon dating of a bone, upon which the dating of the whole assemblage depends, leaves open the possibility of an eighth-century date, well after the conversion period – and a pre-Anglo-Saxon date in the sixth or seventh centuries cannot be excluded either.[25] The latter possibility is rather more attractive in the case of two radiocarbon-dated burials under Worcester Cathedral refectory. Both graves were oriented and there were some indications that they had been placed inside a building (also oriented?). One man had traces of gold brocade round his neck, possibly part of a priest's stole, and the other skeleton (of unknown sex) was unaccompanied.[26] If these are indeed Christian burials they may provide evidence for the survival of a British Christian community rather than for the conversion of the Anglo-Saxons – although these two issues may be not unconnected, as we shall see.

Burial at churches is attested in the literary sources. King Osric of the Hwicce, who probably died *c.* 679, was buried, along with various female relatives, in the church of his own monastic foundation at Gloucester, according to the late medieval Chronicle of that house.[27] In the late eleventh century people said ('ut fertur') that Merewalh, his near con-

---

24 Rahtz, *Excavations at St Mary's*, pp. 7, 12, 34–5 and 37; Morris, *Church*, p. 26. Cf. below, p. 175, n. 149. Charcoal burials are typically late Anglo-Saxon (Shoesmith, *Hereford* I, 49), but the Deerhurst rectangle recalls certain Roman cremations: Clarke, *Lankhills*, pp. 77, 350, n. 13, and 351; McWhirr *et al.*, *Romano-British Cemeteries at Cirencester*, pp. 99–100. Layers of charcoal were found in some Bidford-on-Avon graves.

25 Shoesmith, *Hereford* I, 25. A link between St Guthlac's and King Æthelbald, the saint's patron, has been suggested: *ibid.*, pp. 1–3; Thacker, 'Pre-Viking Mercia', pp. 5–6.

26 P. A. Barker *et al.*, 'Two Burials under the Refectory of Worcester Cathedral', *MA* 18 (1974), 146–51, at 146, gave uncalibrated radiocarbon dates for two bone samples from the accompanied skeleton as 536±107 and 585±102. See also *Medieval Worcester*, ed. Carver, pp. 3, 26 and 33, and Bond, 'Church and Parish', pp. 130–2, for the suggestion that St Helen's, Worcester, may be a Romano-British foundation. With the 'stole' compare perhaps the reference to *sacra infula* in the epitaph quoted below, p. 342.

27 See below, p. 124.

temporary in the kingdom of the Magonsætan, was buried at Repton, the mausoleum of the Mercian kings; though it should be added that in the sixteenth century Leland heard a report of his body being discovered at Wenlock.[28] More reliable are the mid-eighth-century allusions to the ancestors of the Hwiccian *reguli* being buried at St Peter's, Worcester, and, in the western diocese, to the tomb constructed by Bishop Cuthbert for his predecessors, for the *regulus* Milfrith and his wife and for an unidentified Osfrith son of Oshelm.[29] These references are all to the burial of important people, and it cannot be assumed that ordinary folk were buried in or even beside churches in the seventh and early eighth centuries. Indeed, it has been argued that churchyard burial did not become general until the mid-eighth century in England;[30] presumably, on this view, earlier Anglo-Saxon Christians had been buried in a manner which cannot now be distinguished from that of pagans, perhaps in the type of cemetery known as 'Final Phase' (or, more tendentiously, 'early Christian') – these are characterized by 'Christian' orientation and an absence of elaborate grave-goods[31] – or even (at least in some parts of the country, such as the Peak District in Mercia) in barrows, the lavish grave-goods of which may indicate conspicuous waste intended to mark the status rather than the paganism of the deceased.[32] Certainly a lost text, of unknown date, asserts

[28] *Vita S. Mildburgae*, BL, Add. 34633, 210r; Dugdale, *Monasticon* IV, 55. On Repton see M. Biddle and B. Kjølbye-Biddle, 'The Repton Stone', *ASE* 14 (1985), 233–92, at 235; Stafford, *East Midlands*, pp. 106–8; H. M. Taylor, 'St Wystan's Church, Repton, Derbyshire: A Reconstruction Essay', *ArchJ* 144 (1987), 205–45; Biddle, 'Archaeology', pp. 14–22.

[29] See above, p. 37, and below, p. 342. Cf. the reference in S 1185 to tombs at St Peter's, Worcester, discussed by Bassett, 'Winchcombe', p. 91.

[30] Cf. Biddle, 'Widening Horizon', p. 69; Morris, *Church*, pp. 50 and 54; Bullough, 'Burial', p. 185; Thomas, *Christianity*, p. 236; Bruce-Mitford, *Sutton Hoo* I, 711–12.

[31] Leeds, *Art and Archaeology*, pp. 96–113; Hyslop, 'Leighton Buzzard'; Meaney and Hawkes, *Winnall*; Campbell, *Essays*, pp. 79–80; Biddle, 'Widening Horizon', pp. 68–9; Rahtz, 'Late Roman Cemeteries', p. 53; Morris, *Church*, pp. 53–8; Bullough, 'Burial', p. 198; Hawkes, 'Early Saxon Period', pp. 92–3. This sort of rite agrees quite well with 'early Christian' burial as known in the Mediterranean, Gallo-Roman and late Romano-British worlds; cf. Green, 'Plaster Burials'; Thomas, *Christianity*, pp. 228–39.

[32] Ozanne, 'Peak Dwellers'; Bruce-Mitford, *Sutton Hoo* I, 712. Cf. James, 'Cemeteries', and 'Merovingian Cemetery Studies', pp. 38–9; also Dickinson, 'Present State', p. 23; Hawkes, 'Orientation at Finglesham', pp. 37–8; Bullough, 'Burial', pp. 193–4; and Sims-Williams, review of *Ideal and Reality*, pp. 115–16.

that Cuthbert, archbishop of Canterbury 740–60 (probably identical with the bishop of the Magonsætan mentioned above), was inspired by the sight of cemeteries within towns on a visit to Rome to institute cemeteries throughout England.[33] What lies behind this assertion is uncertain, however, and it may not have any relevance to the establishment of *rural* Christian cemeteries. Moreover, other evidence suggests that burial in or near churches had long been sought after. Gildas's allusion to the graves and places of martyrdom of martyrs like St Alban, some of them in Anglo-Saxon hands by the sixth century, and the survival of the element *merthyr* < *martyrium* in Welsh place-names both suggest the psychological conditions that led to the combination of church and cemetery on the Continent, for example at Xanten (< *Ad Sanctos*) and Bonn. This is relevant since there was clearly some British substratum to Anglo-Saxon Christianity; we know, for example, that Augustine encountered the cult of a martyr, St Sixtus, in Kent.[34] Æthelwald, king of Deira in the 650s, established a monastery 'where he should be buried' and Ecgfrith, king of Northumbria 670–85, had a *praefectus* who wished his wife to be buried in holy ground (*in locis sanctis*). In Theodore's *Penitential* it is assumed that even pagans might contrive to be buried in churches.[35] The church would not have been slow to realize that in return for providing the deceased with resting-places in holy ground it could divert some of their wealth from kinsmen and from the conspicuous waste of 'pagan' rites, in the direction of soul-scot or more

[33] J. Weever, *Ancient Funerall Monuments* (London, 1631), p. 214, citing 'Appendix Cron. Roffen. in bib. Cot.': 'Cutbertus Archiepiscopus Cant. xi ab Augustino cum Rome uideret plures intra Ciuitates sepeliri, rogauit Papam ut sibi liceret cemiteria facere, quod Papa annuit, reuersus itaque cemiteria ubique in Anglia fieri constituit'. Similar statements are found in the sixteenth-century manuscripts, Cambridge, Corpus Christi College 111, p. 307 (ed. Dugdale, *Monasticon* I, 128), and 298, p. 5 (ed. A. H. Allcroft, 'Archbishop Cuthbert and the Churchyards', *ArchJ* 85 (1928), 147–8). They look like mere embellishments of the earlier Canterbury sources discussed below, p. 344. Cf. Meaney and Hawkes, *Winnall*, p. 51; Brooks, *Canterbury*, pp. 81–3; and in general see Bullough, 'Burial', p. 180.

[34] *DEB*, c. 10. Cf. Thomas, *Early Christian Archaeology*, pp. 48–74, 89, 137–41, 168, and throughout; Biddle, 'Towns', pp. 110–11, and 'Archaeology', pp. 3–6; Green, 'Plaster Burials', pp. 49–50; Morris, *Church*, p. 25; Sims-Williams, 'Gildas and the Anglo-Saxons', pp. 5–6 and 27. For Sixtus see Brooks, *Canterbury*, p. 20.

[35] See *HE* III.23 (cf. Wallace–Hadrill, *Commentary*, p. 120); Bede's prose *Vita S. Cuthberti*, c. 15, ed. Colgrave, *Two Lives of Saint Cuthbert*, pp. 204–5; and H&S III, 190–1 (discussed in my review of *Ideal and Reality*, p. 116; cf. differently Blair, 'Minster Churches in the Landscape', p. 52); Morris, *Church*, p. 50; Bullough, 'Burial', p. 192.

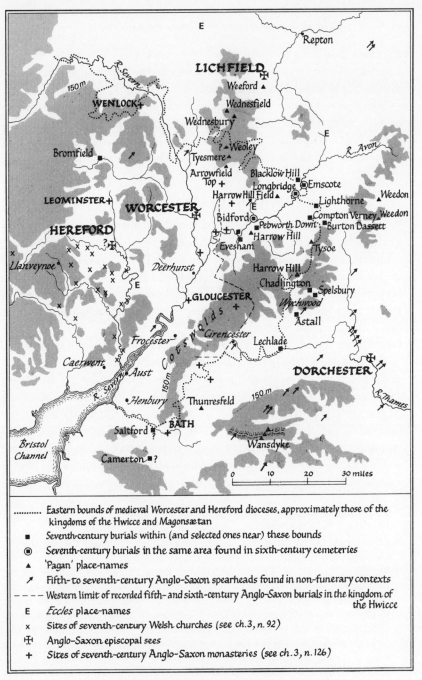

E

Repton

LICHFIELD ✠
Weeford ▲
Wednesfield ▲
Wednesbury
? ▲ Weoley E
Tyesmere ▲ R. Avon
WENLOCK ✠
150 m R. Severn
Bromfield ▪
Arrowfield Blacklow Hill
Top + Longbridge ⊚ Emscote ⊚ Weedon ▲
Harrow Hill Field ▲ Lighthorne
LEOMINSTER ✠ WORCESTER ✠ + + E Compton Verney Weedon
Bidford ⊚ Pebworth Down Burton Dassett
HEREFORD ? ✠ + + ▪ Harrow Hill
Evesham Tysoe ▲
Llanveynoe x x x x Deerhurst Harrow Hill ▪
x x x E Chadlington
x GLOUCESTER ✠ + Wychwood Spelsbury
x Cirencester ▪ Astall
Frocester Lechlade
Caerwent Cotswolds DORCHESTER ✠
Aust 150 m R. Thames
+
Henbury Thunresfeld 150 m
BATH
Saltford ▪ ?
Bristol Wansdyke
Channel Camerton ▪ ?

0   10   20   30 miles

.... Eastern bounds of medieval Worcester and Hereford dioceses, approximately those of the
kingdoms of the Hwicce and Magonsætan
▪ Seventh-century burials within (and selected ones near) these bounds
⊚ Seventh-century burials in the same area found in sixth-century cemeteries
▲ 'Pagan' place-names
↗ Fifth- to seventh-century Anglo-Saxon spearheads found in non-funerary contexts
- - - - Western limit of recorded fifth- and sixth-century Anglo-Saxon burials in the kingdom of
the Hwicce
E Eccles place-names
x Sites of seventh-century Welsh churches (see ch.3, n.92)
✠ Anglo-Saxon episcopal sees
+ Sites of seventh-century Anglo-Saxon monasteries (see ch.3, n.126)

FIG. 2 Selected archaeological and place-name evidence

63

elaborate burial fees. In or about 804 the Hwiccian noble Æthelric bequeathed four estates to the community at Deerhurst on the strict condition that he should be buried there.[36]

Burial in and beside churches may, then, go back well into the seventh century, at least for the very religious or very important; but this cannot yet be verified or quantified, owing to the scarcity of archaeological data and, in particular, to the lack of identified church buildings in the area.

CHANGES IN FUNERARY PRACTICE

While archaeology provides little indisputable evidence of seventh-century Christianity, it also provides little indisputable evidence for paganism. Inhumations with eccentric orientations and rich grave-goods can no longer be assumed to be pagan.[37] Cremation, on the other hand, was probably always non-Christian, but it was always a minority rite in the area and its abandonment could reflect competition from alternative pagan, as much as Christian, inhumation rites.[38] Nevertheless, if the funerary evidence for the area is taken as a whole, a suggestive pattern emerges.

The first point to be noted is the scarcity of inhumations accompanied by grave-goods which can be assigned to the seventh century. In the Severn valley and further west this might be explained by the small size of the Anglo-Saxon population, but such an explanation would hardly hold in the Cotswolds and the Avon valley which have yielded many hundreds of inhumations with sixth-century Anglo-Saxon grave-goods.[39] The most credible explanation is that for some reason accompanied burial was largely abandoned throughout the area in the seventh century. One can hardly

---

[36] S 1187. See above, p. 8. Cf. Bullough, 'Burial', pp. 195–7.

[37] Cf. Young, 'Paganisme'; Morris, *Church*, p. 17; Bullough, 'Burial'.

[38] Cf. above, p. 21, nn. 21–2. For possible interpretations of funerary rites see Meaney, *Gazetteer*, pp. 15–21.

[39] See above, pp. 19, n. 15, and 23, n. 33. Pretty, whose area included all our sixth-century cemeteries (except Fairford, on which cf. below, n. 62) noted from them only a possibly seventh-century coin-like pendant in Grave 13 at Bidford (see below, p. 68), and described Baginton (which is outside our area) as 'one of the few early cemeteries which may contain seventh-century material' ('Welsh Border', pp. 89–90). Typically seventh-century material is identified, for instance, in Åberg, *Anglo-Saxons in England*; Leeds, *Square-Headed Brooches*; Harden, 'Glass Vessels'; Leeds and Pocock, 'Cruciform Brooches'; Evison, 'Shield Bosses'; Ozanne, 'Peak Dwellers'; Hyslop, 'Leighton Buzzard'; Meaney and Hawkes, *Winnall*; etc.

argue that distance from Kent and other centres of production and importation prevented seventh-century objects reaching the area in view of the seventh-century riches of the equally remote Peak District.[40] Nor is it likely that in the seventh century accompanied burials moved to new, less easily detectable sites; there is only one possible instance of an accompanied burial in a churchyard,[41] and little evidence for a shift to barrow burials[42] –

[40] Ozanne, 'Peak Dwellers'. Moreover, *pre*-seventh-century glass reached Longbridge and Fairford (Harden, 'Glass Vessels', pp. 145 and 163; cf. Arnold, *Archaeology*, pp. 64–5 and 110) and sixth-century(?) Rhineland cauldrons reached Kempsford, Fairford, Bidford and even Flintshire: F. H. Thompson, 'Anglo-Saxon Sites in Lincolnshire', *AntJ* 36 (1956), 181–99, at 193–9, and R. D. Abbott, 'An Anglo-Saxon Cauldron from Kempsford, Glos.', *TBGAS* 81 (1962), 196–7; an early date for these cauldrons is assumed by Swanton, *Spearheads*, pp. 79 and 105 – cf. below, p. 68, n. 49.

[41] Wyre Piddle, where the inhumations accompanied by weapons (still kept in the church) may antedate Christian use of the site. See [W. J.] Hopkins, 'Wyre Piddle Church, Worcestershire', *Associated Architectural Societies' Reports and Papers* 19 (1887–8), 424–35, at 427–8; *VCH Wo* III, 362; Baldwin Brown, *Arts* III, 119–20; Morris, *Church*, p. 60. Copley, *Anglian Regions*, p. 128, refers to 'a shield-boss of the 7th cent.'; however, Canon J. O. C. Champion, rector of Fladbury, kindly gave me his impression that the bosses are in the earlier category (*d*) of Evison, 'Shield Bosses', p. 40. For the hypothesis of a shift of 'pagan' burials into churchyards see above, p. 62 and n. 35; Ozanne, 'Peak Dwellers', p. 47. Cf. Bruce-Mitford, *Sutton Hoo* I, 712, n. 2. Continuity between pagan cemeteries and Christian churchyards, and accompanied burial in churchyards, both seem unusual; cf. Morris, *Church*, pp. 53 and 61; Bullough, 'Burial', p. 197.

[42] Cf. below, p. 67 and n. 48. Despite the destruction of many prehistoric barrows which may have been used for secondary barrow burial, many still survive along the middle and upper Severn, along the Avon, and above all throughout the Cotswolds (see Hooke, 'Burial Features', figs. 3–5, with Smith, 'Ring-Ditches', p. 158, fig. 15), and many have been excavated (statistics in J. Drinkwater, 'Barrows in Gloucestershire: Patterns of Destruction', in *Archaeology and the Landscape*, ed. Fowler, pp. 129–56). *Sixth*-century secondary burials are found over a long stretch of the Cotswolds – at Chavenage, Hampnett, Swell and Oddington (though admittedly not in the area of the Avon valley cemeteries, where ploughing and a comparative lack of ready prehistoric barrows may be negative factors), but significantly only late fifth- and early sixth-century objects accompanied the 35 or so burials at these four sites; this suggests that while secondary barrow burial was not untraditional in the area, it did not flourish into the seventh century, unlike the Peak District and Wiltshire. For references see Meaney, *Gazetteer*, pp. 90–3; a fifth site at Temple Guiting is doubtful (O'Neil, 'Bevan's Quarry'). Dodgson, 'English Arrival in Cheshire', p. 12, Gelling, *Signposts*, p. 156, and Hooke, *Hwicce*, pp. 42–3, suggest that place-names in *hlaw*, references to 'heathen burials', etc. may extend the distribution of Anglo-Saxon barrows westwards; but see Sims-Williams, 'Settlement', p. 4, n. 11, and 'People and Places'.

and in any case it is debatable whether accompanied inhumations in churchyards and barrows stand less chance of detection than those in flat cemeteries of the sixth-century types.[43] Most probably, then, accompanied burial was more or less given up in the area in the seventh century. Seventh-century unaccompanied Anglo-Saxon (and British) burials, especially if oriented in the 'Christian' (solar) manner and detached from the old 'pagan' cemeteries, are less likely than accompanied burials to have been recognized by antiquaries and archaeologists. The earlier group of burials on the St Guthlac's site at Hereford are instructive: those found in 1960 were assumed to be eleventh-century or later and it was not until a radiocarbon test was applied to one discovered in 1973 that this was disproved. Again, a cemetery without grave-goods and with east–west orientation found near Winchcombe Abbey appeared to be 'either late/sub-Roman or mid-late Saxon', but radiocarbon determinations on two graves produced results of *c.* 560–650 and *c.* 770–980.[44]

The shortage in *funerary* contexts throughout the area of artefacts regarded as 'seventh-century Anglo-Saxon' contrasts significantly with the survival of such objects in *non-funerary* contexts: thus Swanton records sixth- to seventh-century Anglo-Saxon spearheads in non-funerary contexts as far afield as at Gloucester, Blakeney, Gl., Alcester, Wo., Puxton near Kidderminster, Wo., and Titterstone Clee, Shr. These (*and* earlier non-funerary spearheads) are shown in fig. 2. They imply that the Anglo-Saxons were present further west than the distribution of their accompanied burials.[45]

---

[43] On churchyards cf. Meaney and Hawkes, *Winnall*, pp. 51–2; Morris, *Church*, p. 61; G. Fellows Jensen, 'The Vikings in England: A Review', *ASE* 4 (1975), 181–206, at 188; and the reconsiderations by Graham-Campbell, 'Scandinavian Viking-Age Burials', and Biddle, 'Widening Horizon', p. 69. For the theory of the destruction of barrows in lowland areas see Ozanne, 'Peak Dwellers', also Taylor, *Village and Farmstead*, pp. 48–9; and cf. Sims-Williams, review of *Ideal and Reality*, p. 116, and Arnold, *Archaeology*, p. 131.

[44] Shoesmith, *Hereford* 1, 25 and 45–8; Saville, 'North Street, Winchcombe', p. 137.

[45] Unless some other explanation can be found for why no graves were recorded with these spearheads in the west. The non-funerary spearheads in fig. 2 are taken from Swanton, *Corpus*, with the addition of the KI type at Cirencester noted by D. Brown, 'Archaeological Evidence for the Anglo-Saxon Period', in *Studies in the Archaeology and History of Cirencester*, ed. A. McWhirr, BAR 30 (Oxford, 1976), 19–45, at 24. Copley, *Place-Names and Archaeology*, p. 112, seems to be in error in associating the Alcester spear with the cemetery (Meaney, *Gazetteer*, p. 257) and so dating the latter to the seventh century with J. Morris. See also below, n. 65. Compare the distribution of

The distribution of seventh-century accompanied burials forms a pattern. West of the Severn the practice seems never to have taken root. So far the only possible exception is at Bromfield. S. C. Stanford, excavating within a ditched Iron Age or Romano-British enclosure in 1978–9, discovered three rows of oriented graves, some with coffins. Two of the twenty-three graves were unused, and the only grave-goods recovered from the rest were an iron buckle and two 'scramasax' knives, which are characteristic of seventh-century and later Anglo-Saxon sites. Nearby was the ring-ditch of a ploughed-out barrow which was presumed to be Anglo-Saxon since it lay within a Roman marching camp; it was unlikely to be earlier than the seventh century, in view of the chronology of primary barrow burial. Stanford suggested that it was an element in a 'pagan' cemetery, 'dating to the conquest period in the early seventh century', which was replaced first by the oriented 'Christian' cemetery in the late seventh century and then by burial at the priory church in Bromfield village.[46] The religious labels and the sequence are hypothetical, of course, but Stanford's interpretation can be supported from elsewhere in England.[47] No doubt there were other Bromfields in the kingdom of the Magonsætan. Nevertheless the fact remains that the discovery of only one cemetery with accompanied burials and only one (presumed) barrow burial contrasts strikingly with most other seventh-century English kingdoms.[48] This negative evidence should surely be taken at face value rather than explained away by factors such as failure to investigate, excessive (or

grass-tempered pottery *beyond* the area of 'pagan' burials, mapped by Heighway, 'Anglo-Saxon Gloucestershire', p. 230. On this, however, see A. Vince, 'Did They Use Pottery in the Welsh Marches and the West Midlands between the 5th and 12th Centuries AD', in *From Roman Town to Norman Castle: Papers in Honour of Philip Barker*, ed. A. Burl (Birmingham, 1988), pp. 40–55.

[46] S. C. Stanford, 'Bromfield, Salop SO 483 766', *WMANS* 21 (1978), 45–6; 'Bromfield, Salop – Excavations in 1979', *ibid.*, 22 (1979), 41–2; *Welsh Marches*, pp. xv, 68 and 178–9; and 'Bromfield Excavations – From Neolithic to Saxon Times', *TSAS* 64 (1983–4), 1–7. On scramasaxes see Leeds, *Art and Archaeology*, p. 101, n. 2; Wilson, *Archaeology of Anglo-Saxon England*, p. 15; Meaney and Hawkes, *Winnall*, p. 43; and on the dating of primary barrows cf. Meaney, *Gazetteer*, p. 19.

[47] See above, n. 31.

[48] Cf. the map of non-churchyard cemeteries of the seventh and eighth centuries in Sawyer, *Roman Britain to Norman England*, p. 24. Primary barrow burials (O.S. *Britain in the Dark Ages*, pp. 42–3) are generally rare, however, presumably because of the labour involved. The only other instance in our area listed (Compton Verney, *ibid.*, p. 42) is a mistake: see below, n. 58.

minimal) soil disturbance by ploughing and gravel digging, or adverse soil conditions.

In the Avon valley and Cotswold areas of the kingdom of the Hwicce many hundreds of graves with sixth-century goods have been found, many of them in large cemeteries. Yet seventh-century artefacts are dramatically absent from these cemeteries. Even in the great Bidford-on-Avon cemetery only *possible* exceptions have been noted: two serpentine open-work mounts in Grave 81[49] and a coin-like pendant with a circlet of white shell in Grave 13.[50] These two female graves were laid out with feet to the north and are in the west and south of the cemetery. It is a reasonable guess that more typical seventh-century inhumations in the cemetery may be seen on the other side, most distant from the area of mixed cremation and inhumation, in a long orderly row of almost unaccompanied skeletons along the edge of the cemetery; these all face east, in contrast to the rest of the cemetery.[51] Apart from Bidford, the only other sixth-century cemeteries with seventh-century accompanied burials are (perhaps) Emscote near Warwick, from which comes an arguably late square-headed brooch,[52] Longbridge, also near Warwick, which produced what Leeds deplored as an 'execrable brooch . . . perhaps . . . the latest cruciform brooch that has

---

[49] Humphreys *et al.*, 'Bidford', pp. 104 (nos. 33–4, pl. XV, nos. 2–3) and 114; Speake, *Animal Art*, p. 70 and n. 33 and fig. 12(a). A shield-boss in Grave 182 (Humphreys *et al.*, pp. 276–7, 287 and pl. LVII, no. 2) was regarded as seventh-century by Åberg, *Anglo-Saxons*, pp. 166–7 (cf. also pp. 137 and 219 on a garnet in Grave 51, Humphreys *et al.*, pp. 103, 113 and pl. XIV, no. 3), but his art-historical argument is out of date (cf. Speake, *Animal Art*, p. 19, fig. xvi). I am grateful to Dr Nicholas Webb for advice here. The shield-boss was found with one of the cauldrons mentioned above, p. 65, n. 40.

[50] See above, p. 64, n. 39.

[51] Plans in Humphreys *et al.*, 'Bidford'; Hirst, 'Bidford'; T. Yarnell, 'Bidford-on-Avon, Warwickshire', *WMA* 26 (1983), 82–3. Cf. Meaney, *Gazetteer*, p. 258. A similar pattern at Abingdon is noted by Hawkes, 'Early Saxon Period', p. 93.

[52] Listed under Myton (cf. Meaney, *Gazetteer*, p. 260) by Leeds, *Square-Headed Brooches*, no. 109. His other brooches from our area (nos. 71, 80–1, 93, 97, 116 and 121, cf. above, p. 19) are probably all sixth-century. On the dating of nos. 93, 116 and 121 see *ibid.*, pp. 61, 71 (cf. Speake, *Animal Art*, p. 93, n. 3, and Hines, *Scandinavian Character*, pp. 111 and 181) and 74; T. M. Dickinson, 'On the Origin and Chronology of the Early Anglo-Saxon Disc Brooch', *ASSAH* 1 (1979), 39–80, at 45–6 and 48. Indeed, Hines (*Scandinavian Character*, pp. 127–8, 180 and 197) dates all the square-headed brooches, including Myton, to *c*. 500–70; but cf. review by G. Speake, *MA* 30 (1986), 203–4.

come down to us',[53] and Lechlade, which is unusual among the sixth-century Thames valley cemeteries in containing a group of mid- to later seventh-century graves, some of them richly furnished.[54] The Lechlade burials are oriented, unlike the sixth-century north–south graves which they cut through, and one of them includes a cross, which suggested a semi-Christianized community to the excavators.[55] All three sites are near the edge of the Hwiccian kingdom, as known from the diocesan boundary.

Similarly the few burials on new sites with seventh-century grave-goods tend to lie on the peripheries of the kingdom rather than spreading westwards towards the Severn. On the crest of the east-facing spur of Blacklow Hill ('black mound' or 'Blæca's mound') in Leek Wootton, which overlooks the Avon just north of Warwick on the Worcester/Lichfield diocesan boundary, excavation revealed two oriented inhumations, one accompanied by a short scramasax, which were enclosed in a double circle of pits possibly intended for planting trees, and an outer ring of post holes; the hypothesis of a pagan sanctuary suggested itself.[56] Farther south down the diocesan boundary, early seventh-century enamelled hanging-bowl escutcheons are thought to have accompanied inhumations at Lighthorne,[57] and three inhumations 'dug out of a bank' at Compton Verney on the Fosse Way in 1774 were accompanied by seventh-century pendants.[58]

---

[53] Leeds and Pocock, 'Cruciform Brooches', p. 21 (type Vk). The examples of type Va from Upton Snodsbury and possibly Bidford are presumably sixth-century (*ibid.*, pp. 13, 17 and 30, n. 78). On the other grave-goods with the Longbridge brooch see Meaney, *Gazetteer*, p. 261; Åberg, *Anglo-Saxons*, pp. 100, 102 and 207; Hines, *Scandinavian Character*, pp. 213–14 and 233. (Hines thinks the Longbridge grave is pre-600.)

[54] Miles and Palmer, *Invested in Mother Earth*, p. 8. But see now below, n. 127.

[55] *Ibid.*, pp. 12 and 19. See also summary in *MA* 30 (1986), 136.

[56] For references and a personal communication from Dr W. J. Ford see Sims-Williams, 'Wilfrid', p. 173 and n. 46. (On dating scramasaxes see above, p. 67, n. 46.) Cf. *PNWa*, p. 191; Hooke, 'Burial Features', p. 21. Gaveston was beheaded here in 1312: a curious throwback? See *Chronicles of Edward I and Edward II*, ed. Stubbs II, 44, 180 and 298. Pretty, 'Welsh Border', fig. 7, assigned a seventh-century date to Blacklow and the sites at Compton Verney, Burton Dassett and Little Hampton noted below, but not to Lighthorne and the Evesham site mentioned below, n. 65. (Those on the eastern and southern peripheries were not covered by her dissertation.)

[57] Meaney, *Gazetteer*, p. 217; Baldwin Brown, *Arts* IV, xvii and pl. CVII, no. 2.

[58] S. Pegge, 'Observations on Two Jewels in the Possession of Sir Charles Mordaunt, Bart', *Archaeologia* 3 (1786), 371–5 (note that no barrow is mentioned); Meaney, *Gazetteer*, p. 260; Ozanne, 'Peak Dwellers', p. 47; *VCH Wa* I, 264–5; Åberg, *Anglo-Saxons*, pp. 132, 153 and 217; Hines, *Scandinavian Character*, pp. 234 and 338. I owe the broad dating to Prof. P. Grierson, who would reject the usual sceatta comparison for one pendant (of which Mr David Brown kindly provided a slide).

These sites' closeness to the old borders of the Hwicce is borne out by the nearby field-name Martimow (*Mercna mere*, 'boundary of the Mercians') in Radway, on the diocesan boundary next to Kineton ('the [Mercian?] king's vill').[59] Rather farther east (outside the kingdom) a solitary inhumation at Burton Dassett was accompanied by a pot and a seventh-century scramasax.[60] Farther south, there is a rich spread of seventh-century accompanied burials in north-west Oxfordshire, in the Wychwood area; this was near the kingdom of the Hwicce, as the name *Wych*wood implies, but probably not inside it, and the burials may be those of Mercian or Middle Anglian nobles.[61] The three sites closest to the medieval diocesan boundary are the inhumations at Chadlington (an oriented cemetery) and near Spelsbury church and the lavishly furnished cremation in Asthall barrow, where the Roman road to Cirencester fords the Windrush. In the south of the kingdom almost no seventh-century grave-goods have been found, even though the Hwicce are known to have extended to the Avon at Bath by 675 at the latest.[62] Just south of the Avon, however, there is a group of oriented inhumations at Saltford, one of them accompanied by an iron knife similar to some found in the seventh-century graves at Camerton, eight miles to the south. Camerton has been regarded as a classic example of an Anglo-Saxon cemetery of the 'early Christian' or 'Final Phase' type, but it is also possible that it is a cemetery of seventh-century Britons who used 'Anglo-Saxon' artefacts; indeed the same may be true of Saltford and other supposedly English cemeteries in Somerset, where Britons may have remained in power to a late date.[63]

---

[59] For Martimow see S 773 and below, p. 388, n. 130. For Kineton see below, p. 164, n. 98. See Meaney, *Gazetteer*, p. 217, for an undated inhumation cemetery there.

[60] Myres, *Pottery and the Settlement*, pp. 164–5; Meaney, *Gazetteer*, p. 259. Late weapons have also been found, still further eastwards, at Napton Hill, Wa. (SP/455613): *ibid.*, p. 261.

[61] Hawkes, 'Early Saxon Period', pp. 91–4 (probably mistaken in thinking the area lay within Hwiccian territory). On Wychwood see below, p. 386, n. 117.

[62] When Osric of the Hwicce founded Bath monastery; see above, p. 31. Dickinson, 'Present State', p. 20, does not accept a seventh-century date for any of the burials at Hampnett and Fairford. The 'possibly' seventh-century date assigned by Copley, *Place-Names and Archaeology*, p. 104, to Kempsford, which lay on the border (*ASC* 802), is unlikely; see above, n. 40. See now below, n. 127.

[63] Meaney, *Gazetteer*, pp. 218–19; Rahtz and Fowler, 'Somerset', pp. 200–1 and references; Leeds, *Art and Archaeology*, pp. 36 and 111–13; Rahtz, 'Late Roman Cemeteries'; Morris, *Church*, p. 55. See also below, p. 82. On British independence in Somerset see P. A. Rahtz, 'Celtic Society in Somerset A.D. 400–700', *BBCS* 30 (1981–2), 176–200, at 185.

There is only one clear exception to this tendency for seventh-century accompanied burials on new (or apparently new) sites to lie on the peripheries: the group of inhumations, of unknown number, found by navvies 'on the right bank of the river Avon between a place called Little Hampton and the Oxford and Worcester Railway where it runs into Evesham'; these were accompanied by a scramasax and other weapons and a fine golden linked-pin set (often on display in the British Museum).[64] A saucer-brooch of Kentish inspiration found with an oriented inhumation on the other side of the river may be seventh-century too, and so may a spear of Kentish type found in a grave further to the east, on Pebworth Down.[65] All these objects could conceivably be associated with the eponymous Kentishmen of nearby Conderton.[66]

The overall impression is that the practice of accompanied burial never established itself in the seventh century outside the area of sixth-century settlement (insofar as this area is revealed by the distribution of cemeteries) and that within this area it tended to disappear, except on the peripheries, much earlier than in the neighbouring Middle Anglian and Mercian regions, and perhaps early in the seventh century – the typologies upon which the dating of grave-goods rests do not allow precise absolute dating.

We cannot automatically attribute the cessation of accompanied burial to Christianization, nor label the few accompanied burials 'pagan' (though the 'sanctuary' at Blacklow Hill is suggestive). Elsewhere in England and France such cessation seems to reflect the influence not of Christian ideals as such, but rather the influence of Mediterranean and local Late Roman burial customs and the spread of educated Roman rationalism – rationalism, be it said, largely mediated by Christian

---

[64] C. K. Watson, [Report], *Proceedings of the Society of Antiquaries of London* 2nd ser. 2 (1861–4), 163–4 (misquoted in *VCH Wo* I, 229, and assigned a wrong Grid Reference by Meaney, *Gazetteer*, p. 281); Baldwin Brown, *Arts* III, 372 and pl. LXXXI, no. 1, and IV, 428 and 667–8; Åberg, *Anglo-Saxons*, p. 219. Cf. Meaney and Hawkes, *Winnall*, pp. 36–7 and 47–9; Leeds, *Art and Archaeology*, pp. 108–9.

[65] T. J. S. Baylis, 'Anglo-Saxon Burial Site', *TWAS* ns 31 (1954), 39–42; Meaney, *Gazetteer*, p. 281 (SP/0403); Swanton, *Corpus*, p. 72 (cf. Swanton, *Spearheads*, pp. 61–4 and 144, type C5). It is not possible to cite spears that are definitely seventh- rather than late sixth-century in graves in the area, but late types occur in graves at Bidford, Wa. (C2–4), Broadwell, Gl. (C3), Fairford, Gl. (C2), Longbridge, Wa. (C2, G2) and Stratford, Wa. (C2–4); see Swanton, *Corpus*, s.nn.

[66] See above, p. 32.

clerics, however.[67] It might be argued, too, that the absence of the tools of war from 'Final Phase' cemeteries merely reflects a decline in the warrior ethos after a period of successful conquest.[68] Nor is the solar orientation of graves like those at Bromfield, Bidford and Lechlade a sure symptom of Christianity, which seems to have borrowed it from paganism originally; in fact it is the dominant orientation in most of the early Anglo-Saxon kingdoms, including those like Sussex which are known from historical sources to have been pagan.[69]

Nevertheless, all things considered, the cultural changes seen in the funerary evidence are most plausibly associated with a change in religion. Having honoured their dead with grave-goods for a century, the Anglo-Saxons are unlikely to have abandoned the practice simply out of deference for the customs of a defeated Romano-British population, or out of poverty or parsimony. Nor is a decline in 'warrior ethos' leading to a cessation of weapon burial likely in an area which was probably caught between contending Anglo-Saxon and Welsh kingdoms. Solar orientation of unaccompanied burials is particularly significant in the Hwiccian area (unlike, say, eastern England), since a north–south axis had previously been the norm for inhumations in this kingdom; and while the sequence of burials at Bromfield and Bidford suggested above is hypothetical, as is their Christian interpretation, there are plausible parallels, for instance at Lechlade and, elsewhere in England, at Winnall near Winchester and Finglesham in Kent.[70]

---

[67] Cf. Young, 'Paganisme', pp. 45, 61–2, etc.; also Rahtz, 'Late Roman Cemeteries', p. 54.

[68] Note that such cemeteries are concentrated in the areas where the Anglo-Saxons had been settled longest; see list in Morris, *Church*, pp. 55–6.

[69] Baldwin Brown, *Arts* III, 158–69; Meaney and Hawkes, *Winnall*, p. 53; Rahtz, 'Orientation'; Faull, 'British Survival', pp. 7–8, 31, 33–4, 37–9 and 46, nn. 7 and 10; Welch, *Sussex* I, 209–11.

[70] Hawkes, 'Orientation at Finglesham' (cf. Rahtz, 'Orientation', p. 6); Dickinson, 'British Antiquity 1977–78', p. 341; Bullough, 'Burial', pp. 190–4; Sims-Williams, review of *Ideal and Reality*, p. 116; Meaney and Hawkes, *Winnall*; Biddle, 'Widening Horizon', p. 69. See also Young, 'Paganisme', on Winnall and the complex continental examples of changes in orientation and grave-goods, and cf. the similar Romano-British problem discussed by J. L. Macdonald in Clarke, *Lankhills*, pp. 404–33. On orientation in the Hwiccian area see above, p. 19 and n. 16. Orientation with head at the north/north-east was a British Iron Age practice which lasted into the post-Roman period in some areas (Faull, 'British Survival', p. 5), but the pagan Hwiccian orientation is probably not indigenous British since there seems little evidence for it in the latest Romano-British

THE EVIDENCE OF PLACE-NAMES

A religious interpretation of the peripheral distribution of seventh-century accompanied burials is supported by the distribution of place-names which refer to Germanic gods and heathen shrines. The evidence of these so-called 'pagan place-names' is hazardous: a name like Wansdyke ('Woden's dyke') may reflect mere folklore, and some 'harrow' (*hearg*) names may refer to extinct *Romano-British* pagan shrines like those mentioned by Gildas.[71] Nevertheless, the 'pagan place-names' mapped by Dr Gelling form an interesting pattern.[72] There are a number around the southern, eastern and northern borders of the Hwicce, but none to the west nor in the kingdom of the Magonsætan. To the south are *Thunresfeld* near Chippenham and the *Woden* names near Wansdyke; to the east the two Northamptonshire places called Weedon ('sanctuary hill', from *wēo(h)* and *dūn*); and to the north Wednesfield, Wednesbury and Weeford in Staffordshire. Within the borders of the Hwicce her map includes only three places, all on the peripheries: Weoley (doubtful), *Tyesmere* and Tysoe. Weoley lies in Northfield, so-called because it lay at the extreme north of the medieval diocese of Worcester. If Weoley indeed contains the element *wēoh*, *wīh*, it may be grouped with the Wednesbury cluster of names. *Tyesmere*, 'Tiw's pool', mentioned in a charter boundary, was apparently on a ridge of high ground south of King's Norton, Birmingham.[73] At Tysoe, 'Tiw's hill-

cemeteries of the area, where the 'Christian' orientation had become the norm (see below, p. 82). A late Roman date has been proposed for inhumations 'orientated north–south' with hobnails at Fladbury (Peacock, 'Fladbury', p. 123; Bond, 'Discoveries in Fladbury', p. 19), and several of the fourth-century (?) graves at Gloucester were similar (Hurst, *Kingsholm*, p. 17). North–south burials were also found in the late Romano-British cemetery at Claydon Pike, where the earliest burial was east–west (Miles, 'Romano-British Settlement', p. 202). In the Gloucester area orientation was arbitrary, according to C. M. Heighway, 'Roman Cemeteries in Gloucester District', *TBGAS* 98 (1980), 57–72, at 57.

71 *PNGl* IV, 22–3, 36, n. 5, and 58–9; Sims-Williams, 'Settlement', p. 28, n. 121 (on Wansdyke); L. J. Bronnenkant, 'Place-Names and Anglo-Saxon Paganism', *Nomina* 8 (1984), 72 (cf. Wilson, 'A Note', p. 179); *DEB*, c. 4; cf. Sims-Williams, 'Wilfrid', p. 174, n. 47, and below, n. 97.

72 Gelling, 'Further Thoughts' (map reproduced in *Signposts*, p. 160). Cf. the less critical map in *CP*, p. 283, and, for our area, the maps in Smith, 'Hwicce', p. 57, and Ford, 'Settlement Patterns', p. 276. Willey (*PNWa*, pp. xviii and 121) is rejected by Gelling, 'Notes', pp. 63, n. 6, 67 and 73–4; cf. Wilson, 'A Note', p. 183, n. 18.

73 S 1272; Gelling, 'Further Thoughts', p. 109.

spur', it can hardly be a coincidence that there was a large Red Horse, annually 'scoured' out of the side of Edge Hill, south-east of St Mary's church.[74] It is also significant that Tysoe is on the boundary of the Hwicce (near Martimow and *Which*ford) and at the meeting of the later medieval dioceses of Worcester, Lichfield and Lincoln. It may be a very ancient site which was chosen as a boundary mark, or it may have been sited on an ancient boundary.

A name which should probably be added to Gelling's map, though not recorded before last century, is Harrow Hill in Cleeve Prior (north-east of Evesham); this was also a suitable place for a *hearg* ('[communal] heathen sanctuary [sited on a hill]'), for it lay at the meeting not only of three Anglo-Saxon estate bounds (which refer to 'turf mounds') but also of three hundreds and three shires.[75] Perhaps there was a structure there like the one excavated at Blacklow Hill. The other possible examples of *hearg* in Warwickshire are both on the peripheries of the Hwicce: Harrow Hill in Long Compton, near Whichford ('the ford [into the territory] of the Hwicce'), and Harrow Hill Field in Langley. There are none in Gloucestershire, and the sole example in Worcestershire, which should perhaps be rehabilitated as a 'pagan place-name', is Arrowfield Top (*Harewmede* c. 1300, *Harrowfield* c. 1830), near *Tyesmere* and about five miles from Weoley.[76]

Dr Gelling has argued that 'pagan place-names' tended to be coined in the seventh century, when places where the heathen religion lingered were felt to be exceptional.[77] If so, the distribution of such names in our area implies that paganism survived mainly on the peripheries, with some

[74] First recorded by William Dugdale, *The Antiquities of Warwickshire* (London, 1656), p. 422; see also Samuel Lewis, cited above, n. 5; *CP*, p. 293; *PNWa*, pp. xviii, 284 and 286; Gelling, 'Further Thoughts', p. 109, and 'Notes', p. 63. Cf. Mayr-Harting, *Coming of Christianity*, p. 28. A spring from the hill, which is now half covered with larch, runs through the village.

[75] Hooke, 'Burial Features', p. 19, *West Midlands*, pp. 299 and 365, and *Hwicce*, p. 40; S 222, 751 and 1591a; *PNWa*, pp. 201, n. 2, and 202, n. 1. Note the place-name Three Shire Elms. On *hearg* see Wilson, 'A Note'.

[76] *PNWa*, pp. xix, 300 and 369; *PNGl* iv, 36, n. 5; *PNWo*, pp. xiii, n. 1, and 333 (cf. Gelling, 'Further Thoughts', p. 103). For Whichford see Smith, 'Hwicce', p. 59; *PNGl* iv, 32; *DEPN*, p. 512; Hooke, *Hwicce*, p. 15 (differently *PNWa*, p. 302); and below, p. 386.

[77] 'Further Thoughts', pp. 104–5; 'Evidence', pp. 205 and 207; *Signposts*, p. 159; cf. *PNWo*, p. xiii, n. 1. Gelling, 'Notes', p. 63, admits that the argument need not apply to a striking monument like the Tysoe horse.

possible exceptions near Evesham, where it may be significant that the monastery is said to be a comparatively late foundation, by Bishop Ecgwine.[78] It can be seen from fig. 2 that the distribution of 'pagan place-names' correlates well with that of seventh-century burials accompanied with grave-goods, and that both correlate inversely with the distribution of ecclesiastical centres attested before 700. The obvious explanation for the peripheral distribution of the names and burials is that the areas in question were less open to influence from the centre of the kingdom and further west. (For, although it might be argued that the pagan Hwicce deliberately sited their sanctuaries on the boundaries of their kingdom,[79] it can hardly be maintained that they turned their borders into a linear necropolis.) The pattern of distribution, if due to central influence or concerted communal innovation, has obvious implications for the antiquity of the kingdom of the Hwicce and its boundaries: they may already have been some fifty years old in 675.[80]

THE CONVERSION OF THE HWICCE AND MAGONSÆTAN: A HYPOTHESIS

The remarkable lack of seventh-century accompanied burials by comparison with, for example, Kent, is best explained by the hypothesis that as early as about 630 there were Christian clerics in the kingdom of the Hwicce encouraging a rational attitude to grave-goods (and doubtless diverting them to the church) more vigorously than was the case in Kent or Mercia even fifty years later, when the royal family of the Hwicce were already 'Christian, with their people'.[81] It is hardly profitable to speculate whether the funerary changes were due to the mass conversion of the Anglo-Saxon population, perhaps in response to plague or famine or more

[78] See below, p. 141. Cf. the 'pagan place-names' round Farnham monastery, which 'may have been founded with a view to mopping up an obstinate enclave of paganism' (Gelling, 'Further Thoughts', pp. 104–5).

[79] The possibility of boundary shrines is mentioned by Phythian-Adams, 'Rutland', p. 75, and Everitt, *Continuity and Colonization*, p. 146. For 'pagan place-names' on *estate* boundaries see Gelling, *Signposts*, p. 161; and for burial on such minor boundaries (variously explained) see Morris, *Church*, p. 53; Bullough, 'Burial', pp. 184, 193 and 194, n. 42 (but cf. Arnold, *Archaeology*, p. 37); Stafford, *East Midlands*, p. 172. For the *hearg* as a conspicuous 'communal place of worship for a specific group of people, a tribe or folk group, perhaps at particular times of year', see Wilson, 'A Note', p. 181.

[80] Cf. above, p. 31.   [81] *HE* IV.13 (above, p. 34).

subtle persuasion, or whether they were enforced by a central authority. Yet there is nothing necessarily anachronistic in the supposition that the Paderborn Capitulary of 785, forbidding cremation and ordering that 'the bodies of Christian Saxons shall be taken to the church's cemeteries and not to pagan burial mounds', could have been anticipated in England by a century and a half.[82] Theodore's *Penitential* shows that legislation against some pagan funerary practices was possible in the seventh century, and it is unwise to argue from its silence on accompanied burial and orientation that these were matters of indifference.[83]

In the kingdom of the Magonsætan there is no contrast to explain between accompanied burial in the sixth century and unaccompanied burial in the seventh,[84] and it might be argued that even in the seventh century the Anglo-Saxon settlers formed a warrior aristocracy too small for their accompanied burials to stand a fair chance of detection. Comparison with the kingdom of Bernicia suggests that such an argument would be incomplete. Bernicia was apparently established in the mid-sixth century[85] and was converted in the 620s and 630s. Its known accompanied burials are few but rich, implying that the Anglian Bernicians were a small aristocracy dominating a native British population.[86] By contrast, the Severn valley, where a similar political situation may have obtained, is archaeologically more impoverished, despite more favourable soil conditions for the preservation of accompanied burials, so factors other than numbers are probably involved. The absence of ostensibly 'pagan' burials, with the possible exception of the putative barrow at Bromfield, also contrasts strikingly with the Peak District of Mercia, which can never have supported a large population, despite its numerous barrows.[87] I would argue, from the analogy of the kingdom of the Hwicce, that, while Merewalh himself may have been a pagan for much of his life (as was his

---

[82] Cf. differently Morris, *Church*, p. 50.

[83] H&S III, 190 (I. xv. 3) and 194 (II. v. 1). Cf. differently Bullough, 'Burial', pp. 189 and 191–2 (see my review of *Ideal and Reality*, p. 116).

[84] Cf. Dodgson, 'English Arrival in Cheshire', pp. 9–12 and 34.

[85] But see Sims-Williams, 'Settlement', p. 25.

[86] L. Alcock, 'Quantity or Quality: The Anglian Graves of Bernicia', in *Angles, Saxons, and Jutes: Essays presented to J. N. L. Myres*, ed. V. I. Evison (Oxford, 1981), pp. 168–86. Cf. Faull, 'British Survival'.

[87] Ozanne, 'Peak Dwellers'. The Bromfield barrow is ploughed out, but other barrows survive in the area and no Anglo-Saxon secondary burials have been found when excavating them; cf. Stanford, *Welsh Marches*, pp. 68–9.

father), the Magonsætan, like his wife, were, for the most part, already Christian; and that they had taken to burying their dead without grave-goods in cemeteries of the 'early Christian' type (as at Bromfield perhaps), in churchyards (as perhaps at the St Guthlac's site in Hertford), and at *loca sancta* which they had taken over from the Britons in the manner described by Wilfrid's biographer – Wenlock (cf. Welsh *gwyn, gwen* 'white, holy' and *llog* 'monastery' < *locus*) may be one such.[88]

The hypothesis that the Hwicce and Magonsætan (as we may call them for convenience, despite the possible anachronism) were converted early in the seventh century, perhaps more than a century before Bede wrote his *Historia ecclesiastica*, makes his silence understandable. It seems unlikely that missionaries from other Anglo-Saxon kingdoms played an important part in the conversion, in view of Bede's lack of information and the fact that the Hwicce and Magonsætan had no episcopate recognized by Canterbury at the time of the Synod of Hertford in 672 or 673.[89] Moreover it is difficult to attribute the rapid disappearance of accompanied burial to the influence of Anglo-Saxon missionaries, in view of the slowness with which grave-goods were abandoned in the other Anglo-Saxon kingdoms, including Kent. Christian influence from Wales is possible, perhaps in the wake of alliances like that between Penda and Cadwallon, especially if these were accompanied by inter-dynastic marriages. Yet Welsh sources are silent on the subject; Rhygyfarch's assertion in his *Vita S. Dauidis* that the saint founded monasteries at Bath, Repton, Leominster and elsewhere cannot be taken seriously.[90] Strong ecclesiastical influence from western Wales would have revealed itself in the distribution of 'Early Christian' monuments.[91] This objection does not apply to the hypothesis of influence from the church in the adjacent part of Wales, the existence of which is attested in the references to churches under episcopal and abbatial control west of the Wye in the 'First Sequence' of charters in the Book of Llandaf,

[88] *VW*, c. 17; Sims-Williams, 'Wilfrid', pp. 180 and 182. On the name Wenlock see *DEPN*, p. 506; Charles, 'Archenfield and Oswestry', pp. 86–7; and for *locus* see O. J. Padel, *Cornish Place-Name Elements*, EPNS 56/7 (Nottingham, 1985), 151. For the archaeology see below, p. 81, n. 106.

[89] *HE* IV. 5.

[90] *Rhigyfarch's Life of St David*, ed. J. W. James (Cardiff, 1967), c. 13. The number of foundations (twelve) recalls the popular model of St Benedict; cf. Sims-Williams, 'Wilfrid', pp. 170–3. D. A. Whitehead, *apud* Shoesmith, *Hereford* I, 3–4, takes Rhygyfarch seriously, along with the forgeries of Iolo Morganwg.

[91] Cf. above, p. 59, n. 22.

which roughly span the seventh century; these churches are plotted in
fig. 2.[92] To postulate missionary work from this quarter, however, runs
counter to Bede's categorical assertion that the Britons never preached to
the Anglo-Saxons.[93] Bede wrote at a great distance, to be sure, but form-
criticism suggests that his story about Augustine's meeting with the
British bishops at 'Augustine's Oak', on the borders of the Hwicce and
West Saxons, had originated locally, perhaps partly as an aetiology of the
name of Aust on the Severn crossing (< *Augusta*, but spelt *æt Austin*
691×699), and had passed through the hands of Welsh and English re-
dactors; and this story assumes that as early as *c.* 600 the British hierarchy
not only refused to co-operate with the Gregorian church, as we know
from elsewhere, but also themselves refused to preach to the pagan
English.[94] The *Sitz im Leben* in which this story was told was no doubt the
mutual excommunication about which we learn from Theodore's *Penitential* and from a letter written by Aldhelm, abbot of Malmesbury, as well
as from Bede,[95] and this background will have coloured it; nevertheless,
the story would have strained credulity had the Welsh bishops been
known to have preached to their neighbours across the Severn in a concerted manner.

The most attractive possibility is that the Hwicce and Magonsætan
were converted in an unobtrusive and ultimately unmemorable way by the

[92] The 'Sequence I' charters are listed by Davies, *Llandaff Charters*, pp. 35–7 (LL 77 is
to be omitted); on their ordering and dating see my review, p. 126. The churches (or, in
some cases, possibly church estates) shown on the map are: Llangoed(?), Llan-arth,
Llandeilo Bertholau, Welsh Bicknor, Madley, Dorstone, Llandinabo, Valley Dore,
Llancillo, Bellimoor, *Lann Guorboe* = Garway (but cf. Hughes, 'Celtic Church', p. 14,
n. 52, and Freeman, 'Some Place-Names', p. 69), Llanlowdy, Ballingham, Chepstow,
Dewchurch, *Lann Guoruoe* = St Devereux(?); Pencoed(?); and (with abbots as witnesses)
Doward, Moccas, Lancaut and Llandogo.

[93] *HE* I.22; II.2; V.22. I do not believe that Bede suppressed information out of bias; for
example, he records the missionary activities of Ninian, a Briton (*HE* III.4). See further
T. M. Charles-Edwards, 'Bede, the Irish and the Britons', *Celtica* 15 (1983), 42–52.

[94] *HE* II.2: S 77; *PNGl* III, 127–8. Cf. Wallace-Hadrill, *Commentary*, pp. 52–4 and
218–19, and above, p. 10. Whitelock, *Beginnings*, p. 155, remarks that 'Church
dedications in Somerset suggest . . . that unknown to Bede, a certain amount of
missionary work was carried on by the Welsh across the Bristol Channel'. The evidence is
late, however, and the only such dedication in our area, at St Briavels (SO/5504), is of
dubious relevance. I intend discussing all this elsewhere.

[95] H&S III, 197; *Aldhelmi Opera*, ed. Ehwald, p. 484. Cf. Warren, *Liturgy and Ritual*, ed.
Stevenson, p. xxiv; Loyn, 'Conversion of the English', pp. 10–12.

Britons among them.[96] There can be little doubt that the latter were Christian, even if some memories of rural paganism lingered on in places like *Nymps*field, Gl. (cf. British *nemeton* 'sanctuary'). In the sixth century even Gildas did not regard paganism as a living threat, and there is no solid evidence for the idea that pagan cults survived into that century, for instance at Blaise Castle in Henbury, Gl.[97] Continental analogies remind us that relations between the barbarian invaders and the native population need not always have been implacably hostile;[98] there may well have been intermarriage.

AN INDIGENOUS BRITISH CHURCH?

Gildas had lamented that the partition (*diuortium*) with the barbarians was cutting off the Britons from many Christian *martyria*.[99] One may speculate that the barbarians themselves may have benefited from their access to them: the instance of the survival of St Sixtus's cult in Kent has already been mentioned. Christian belief and practice could certainly survive a partial breakdown of ecclesiastical organization, as *mutatis mutandis* in some areas of ninth-century Danish settlement in England, and the case of Wales as a whole shows that Christianity did not depend on the survival of urban life. The continuing existence of British church buildings or places of organized worship seems to be indicated when Primitive Welsh *eglēs* < British

---

[96] Cf. Dodgson, 'English Arrival in Cheshire', pp. 34–7; J. Gould, 'Letocetum, Christianity and Lichfield (Staffs.)', *TLSSAHS* 5 (1963–4), 30–1; Gelling, *Signposts*, p. 159; Loyn, 'Conversion of the English', p. 8.

[97] *DEPN*, p. 346; *DEB*, c. 4; cf. Jackson, *Language and History*, p. 114; L. Alcock, *Arthur's Britain*, rev. ed. (Harmondsworth, 1973), p. 195. The interpretation of Blaise Castle as a pagan centre in the sixth century is speculative: see P. Rahtz and L. Watts, 'The End of Roman Temples in the West of Britain', in *The End of Roman Britain*, ed. Casey, pp. 183–210, at 194 and 201; Rahtz, 'Late Roman Cemeteries', pp. 55 and 60. As Rahtz and Watts say, the evidence for sixth-century pagan shrines 'is thin, to say the least' (p. 198); but historical evidence for continuing Christianity is *not* 'to say the least ambiguous' (p. 184). As Alcock says, the positive literary evidence (Gildas, the *Vita S. Germani*, etc.) 'must count for more than the negative argument from archaeology' (p. 132). Cf. E. A. Thompson, *Saint Germanus of Auxerre and the End of Roman Britain* (Woodbridge, 1984), pp. 15–25. Note also Venantius Fortunatus, *Carmina*, app. II. 31–2: 'currit ad extremas fidei pia fabula gentes / et trans Oceanum terra Britanna fauet' (ed. Leo, p. 276).

[98] Sims-Williams, 'Gildas and the Anglo-Saxons', pp. 28–9.

[99] *DEB*, c. 10. Cf. above, p. 23, n. 34.

Latin *eclēsiā* is borrowed in English place-names, as at Eccleswall, He. (where the second element is *wælle*, 'spring') and Exhall, Wa. (where the second element is *halh*, 'nook, corner of land, river-meadow, etc.'). The close proximity of these two places to *Ariconium* and Alcester suggests that religious life continued semi-rurally after the collapse of town life. Compare also Exhall (Coventry), which is near Mancetter and various Romano-British industrial sites.[100] These *eglēs* names, marked on fig. 2, help to dispel the misleading impression, given by the selection of charters in the Book of Llandaf, that British churches were concentrated west of the Wye. There must have been many outside the scope of that collection; for instance, the *Vita prima S. Samsonis* mentions an oratory established by the saint (before 556×573) in a *castellum* by the Severn, which still flourished at the date of writing, apparently early in the seventh century.[101] The Welsh had no reason to preserve charters relating to churches permanently lost to the English.

The British clergy may have deserted their *ecclesiae* when the English settled our area, just as they were to desert their *loca sancta* during the Northumbrian (and possibly the Mercian) advances of the mid-seventh century,[102] but the *eglēs* place-names at least show either that the English recognized the ecclesiastical nature of the sites and applied Old English *ecles* to them, as a meaningful loan-word from British, or else that sufficient Britons remained to pass on the appellation '*eglēs*' to the newcomers. In many more instances the English may have preferred their own word *cirice* (> *church*); moreover, various apparent instances of Old

[100] K. Cameron, 'Eccles in English Place-Names', in *Place-Name Evidence*, ed. Cameron, pp. 1–7; M. Gelling, 'Latin Loan-Words in Old English Place-Names', *ASE* 6 (1977), 1–13, at 11–12, and *Signposts*, pp. 82–3 and 96–9 (cf. Dickinson, 'British Antiquity 1977–78', p. 339); Sawyer, *Roman Britain to Norman England*, pp. 24 and 92; Thomas, *Christianity*, pp. 262–4 and 269; Morris, *Church*, pp. 45–6. See Gelling, 'Notes', pp. 62 and 75–6, and *Signposts*, p. 97. Note the position of both *Exhalls* in relation to Webster's map of 'The Avon Valley' ('West Midlands in the Roman Period', fig. 1). On *Ariconium*, see above, p. 45. The place at the north of fig. 2 is Eccleshall.

[101] *Vita S. Samsonis* I. 40–1, ed. R. Fawtier, *La vie de Saint Samson: essai de critique hagiographique*, Bibliothèque de l'École des Hautes Études 197 (Paris, 1912). But see J. K. Knight, 'Sources for the Early History of Morgannwg', in *Glamorgan County History* II, *Early Glamorgan*, ed. H. N. Savory (Cardiff, 1984), pp. 365–409, at 375. On the date and dating cf. Hughes, 'Celtic Church', p. 4; R. Sharpe, 'Gildas as a Father of the Church', in *Gildas: New Approaches*, ed. Lapidge and Dumville, pp. 193–205, at 199, n. 25.

[102] See above, p. 77, n. 88.

English *loca* 'enclosure' and *land* could conceal the ancestors of Welsh *llog* and *llan*.[103] It is difficult to imagine that all the population that frequented the British churches fled with their clergy. William of Malmesbury's surmise that a British *ecclesiola* survived at Evesham, like similar modern speculations about Deerhurst and elsewhere, cannot be regarded as an informed comment; nevertheless, since churches survived in a usable or restorable condition in Kent until the late sixth century, surely churches, and perhaps even church communities, stood a good chance of survival in the two western kingdoms, which were settled so much later than Kent?[104] The putative British cleric buried at Worcester has already been mentioned, and a Romano-British Christian 'plaster burial' may have been found under the nave of Lichfield Cathedral.[105] Several important parish churches in Gloucestershire, such as Frocester and St Mary de Lode, Gloucester, were built over Roman houses which conceivably had some Christian function. At Wenlock a Roman building with an apse-like niche in one wall, which underlies the post-Conquest church, may have been used as a church in the seventh century, when part of the Roman wall seems to have been re-rendered with plaster – perhaps giving rise to the name Wenlock 'white *llog*'.[106]

Like those of the seventh-century English, the burials of the sixth- and seventh-century Britons are hard to detect. Some may have been buried at churches, but such structures have yet to be recognized.[107] To judge by evidence from other areas, however, the mass of the Romano-British population may have been buried in cemeteries which were not exclusively Christian, being used both when the majority were pagan and when they were presumably Christian, even if there was a pagan shrine in the vicinity

---

[103] Morris, *Church*, pp. 45–6; *DEPN*, pp. 302 and 506, s.n. 'Wenlock'; cf. *PNE* II, 13–14 and 25–6.

[104] *GP*, p. 296; *HE* 1.26 and 33; Wallace-Hadrill, *Commentary*, p. 37; Brooks, *Canterbury*, pp. 17, 20 and 50.

[105] See above, p. 60; Morris, *Church*, p. 17.

[106] Heighway, 'Anglo-Saxon Gloucestershire', pp. 232–3; Woods, 'Excavations at Wenlock'. Cf. S. Pearce, 'Estates and Church Sites in Dorset and Gloucestershire: The Emergence of a Christian Society', in *The Early Church in Western Britain and Ireland: Studies presented to C. A. Ralegh Radford*, ed. S. M. Pearce, BAR British Series 102 (Oxford, 1982), 117–38; Blair, 'Minster Churches in the Landscape', pp. 44–6.

[107] See above, p. 62, on Gildas; and on 'undeveloped' and 'developed' cemeteries see Thomas, *Early Christian Archaeology*, pp. 48–90, and *Christianity*, p. 236.

(possibly disused, possibly Christianized).[108] The best studied examples in the vicinity are the great oriented cemeteries of Somerset, some of which continued in use throughout the seventh century, possibly being patronized by Anglo-Saxons as well as Britons; Camerton has already been suggested as an example,[109] but there are some possible parallels, on a much smaller scale, in our area.[110] Numismatic evidence shows that some of these cemeteries (Blaise Castle in Henbury, and Cirencester) lasted into the fifth century, but cannot of course show when they went out of use; radiocarbon dating at Stretton-on-Fosse indicates that one of the Romano-British cemeteries overlaps in time with the Anglo-Saxon cemetery, and such overlap probably occurred at Wasperton as well.[111] In much of our area, as in Somerset, solar orientation seems to be the norm from the Late Roman period onwards, and it was also found across the Welsh border in the post-Roman cemetery at Caerwent.[112] At Stretton, the superimposition of burials demonstrates a change from accompanied burial with feet to the south to unaccompanied burial with feet to the east.[113] In the Kingsholm cemetery at Gloucester, where non-solar orientation may have occurred as late as the fourth century, an important late fourth- or early

[108] My interpretation of the data referred to by Rahtz, 'Late Roman Cemeteries'; Thomas, *Christianity*, pp. 229–39. Cf. Bullough, 'Burial', pp. 186–7.

[109] See Rahtz, 'Late Roman Cemeteries' and Thomas, *Christianity*, pp. 229–39; also Rahtz, 'Orientation'; Rahtz and Fowler, 'Somerset', pp. 199–201; Bullough, 'Burial', p. 182. See above, p. 70.

[110] References are given by Rahtz, 'Late Roman Cemeteries', pp. 60–3; Clarke, *Lankhills*, pp. 348–9; *RCHM Gl* I, xlix–l and 75. See also D. Hurst, 'Droitwich, Vines Lane Roman Cemetery', *WMA* 30 (1987), 2.

[111] See above, p. 22 and nn. 27 and 29.

[112] M. Farley, 'A Six Hundred Metre Long Section through Caerwent', *BBCS* 31 (1984), 209–50, at 229–30 and 246–7.

[113] Ford, 'Stretton-on-Fosse'; and above, n. 109. Romano-British Christian influence probably explains the same change in English cemeteries like Bidford, Wasperton and Lechlade (above, pp. 22, 68 and 69). Cf. M. Todd, 'Germanic Burials in the Roman Iron Age', in *Burial*, ed. Reece, pp. 39–43, at 39 and 41; Rahtz, 'Late Roman Cemeteries', p. 54; Young, 'Paganisme', pp. 16–24 and 59. Clarke, *Lankhills*, p. 352 shows that solar orientation was widespread in the fourth century. His words seem to imply that it is lacking in the fifth century at the Kingsholm Close site at Gloucester and the Cirencester amphitheatre site, but note that the only possibly datable Kingsholm grave (see below, n. 114) did have it, and that the chronology of the various orientations at Cirencester is uncertain (McWhirr *et al.*, *Romano-British Cemeteries at Cirencester*, pp. 76, 100–1 and 106); at the latter the predominant north–south axis may have been influenced by the line of the Fosse Way.

fifth-century East Germanic man was buried facing east in an oriented stone building (a pagan or Christian mausoleum?), which possibly contained pedestals to receive other coffins laid east–west.[114] As far as the Celtic world was concerned, Adomnán of Iona, in the late seventh century, was perhaps right to assume that east was the universal direction of burial.[115]

It is not surprising that such British cemeteries are hard to identify. The only objects discovered with any frequency are boot-nails, which may easily have been mistaken for coffin-nails. The Britons of the area, being under Anglo-Saxon domination, are even less likely than their Somerset cousins to have had jewellery to bury with them, and many of them may lie unrecognized in 'Anglo-Saxon' cemeteries, any small objects accompanying them being of 'Anglo-Saxon' type, as is apparently the case at Stretton and Wasperton.[116] If we also take into account the elusive Romano-British habit of burying some dead in the corners of fields or estates,[117] then the archaeological near-invisibility of the British Christians becomes explicable. In the seventh century the Hwicce and Magonsætan put on the same cloak of invisibility. I should attribute this not to wholesale cultural assimilation – for they retained Germanic characteristics in language, anthroponymy, institutions and art – but specifically to their adopting the religious rites of the indigenous Britons.

THE MID-SEVENTH-CENTURY CHURCH

The organization of our hypothetical mid-seventh-century church is as obscure to us as it was to Bede, who says nothing about it. If emissaries of the Gregorian mission did reach the borders of the Hwicce, as his 'Augustine's Oak' story maintains, they made no lasting impact, for at the time of the Synod of Hertford in 672 or 673 Canterbury clearly recognized

---

[114] Hurst, *Kingsholm*, pp. 15–17, 35 and 131. For the ethnic identification (by H. W. Böhme) and dating see a forthcoming note by C. Hills and H. Hurst in *AntJ*.

[115] *Adamnan's De locis sanctis*, ed. D. Meehan, Scriptores Latini Hiberniae 3 (Dublin, 1958), 80.

[116] See above, p. 22.

[117] J. Collis, 'Owlesbury (Hants) and the Problem of Burials on Rural Settlements', in *Burial*, ed. Reece, pp. 26–34; Faull, 'British Survival', p. 29 (no. 36); *RCHM Gl* I, xlix–l (where it is pointed out that the Broadwell and Foxcote burials of Meaney, *Gazetteer*, pp. 90–1, may be Romano-British, though identified as English because, unusually, they have grave-goods; cf. Morris, *Church*, p. 56, s.n. 'Stow-on-the-Wold').

no bishoprics nearer to the kingdom than those of Wessex, which was less than fifty years old, and of Mercia, which was less than twenty. Christian life did not, however, depend on recognition by Canterbury. Eaba, the Christian princess of the Hwicce, lived in pagan Sussex without access to any canonically consecrated bishop until Wilfrid arrived in 680×681.[118] In her native kingdom there could well have been British, Irish or English bishops active, not necessarily as mere *episcopi vagantes*, about whom Bede and his informants knew, or preferred to know, nothing. Bede's apologetic remarks about Chad's consecration in 664 are symptomatic: after Archbishop Deusdedit's death there was not a single canonically ordained bishop in Britain except for Wine of Wessex, who performed Chad's consecration with the assistance of two bishops of the schismatic British race.[119] There was evidently more co-operation 'at the grass roots' than Theodore of Canterbury or the south Welsh clergy would have countenanced.[120]

CONCLUSION

The silence of Bede and later writers about the conversion of the Hwicce and Magonsætan is best explained by the hypothesis – and that is all it is – that their conversion was both early and the result of a complex mixture of influences, predominantly local ones, which would soon have become difficult to unravel and interpret. The rather swift conversion of the Danes who settled in eastern England from the 870s onwards provides a possible parallel. Literary and archaeological evidence, mostly of a negative character, shows that they were largely Christian by the end of the first decade of the tenth century,[121] but the local religious communities preserved no contemporary records of the conversion,[122] and a variety of factors have been suggested to fill their silence: the influence of the native English priesthood; missionaries from elsewhere in England or even from Germany; diplomatic pressure, as in the conversion of Guthrum in 878;

---

[118] *HE* IV.5 and 13.   [119] *HE* III.28 and V.24; cf. IV.2–3.

[120] This consecration 'suggests improved Anglo-British relations in the south-west' (Wallace-Hadrill, *Commentary*, p. 133). Cf. above, p. 78, n. 95.

[121] Whitelock, 'Conversion of the Eastern Danelaw', cited with agreement by Graham-Campbell, 'Scandinavian Viking-Age Burials', p. 380.

[122] Partly because of the disruption caused by the Danish settlements, but this may be overstated by Whitelock, *Beginnings*, pp. 180–1.

and 'the example of the Christian social order of Wessex and English Mercia'.[123] If such a mixture of factors was indeed involved, one may wonder whether a second Bede, writing in the early eleventh century in a remote place (say Exeter), would have been able to say much at all about the conversion of some areas of the eastern Danelaw. The real Bede may have been in a similar predicament with regard to the Hwicce and Magonsætan.

Institutions tend to preserve information about their own origins. Thus, in the case of the eastern Danelaw the historian's sources become more specific when he moves from the conversion to the establishment and re-establishment of the bishoprics and monasteries that were to dominate the ecclesiastical scene. The same appears to be true for the kingdoms of the Hwicce and Magonsætan in the late seventh century, when from *c.* 675 onwards we have a rich series of documents relating to the sees and monasteries of the area. There may be some element of illusion here, however, for while it is clear that there were notable ecclesiastical developments in the last quarter of the century – such as the foundation of sees at Worcester, and perhaps at Hereford, *c.* 679[124] – the monastic horizon of *c.* 675 may reflect the recent promotion, by clerics such as Theodore and Wilfrid,[125] of the charter as a written record of donations to the church, rather than indicate a sudden upsurge in English monasticism *c.* 675. In fact, some of the monasteries with 'foundation charters' later than 675 may have long been in existence at the date when their charters were obtained from the Mercian king or his sub-kings. The inclusion of monasteries recorded in 675–700 in fig. 2 is therefore not necessarily anachronistic in a map dealing with the seventh century as a whole.[126] It will be seen that they form an interesting pattern: they are concentrated in the blank area between the seventh-century Welsh churches and the 'pagan

---

[123] Stenton, *Anglo-Saxon England*, p. 434 (cf. the possible implications of the name Merewalh, above, p. 48, n. 163; Whitelock, 'Conversion of the Eastern Danelaw', and *Beginnings*, pp. 181–2.

[124] See below, pp. 87–91.

[125] A 'case for Augustine' has been made out (see references in Wallace-Hadrill, *Commentary*, p. 61), but it is hypothetical and hardly relevant to the area. On charters see below, pp. 92–7. The lack of early hagiography limits our knowledge about pre-charter foundations.

[126] For further details see below, pp. 92–6 on Hanbury, Leominster, Wenlock, Bath, Tetbury, Gloucester, Ripple, Pershore (?), Inkberrow (?), Withington, and Fladbury. I have also marked Malmesbury and the sees at Dorchester and Lichfield, but not other centres outside the Worcester and Hereford dioceses.

place-names' and seventh-century 'pagan' burials. This distribution is not due to the nature of the recording – quite the reverse, in fact, since the diocese of Hereford is much less well documented than that of Worcester. [127] The map tends to support the hypothesis of conversion from within.

[127] See above, p. 3. To the seventh-century graves shown in fig. 2 must now be added two recently discovered at Kemble (ST/98879759), 200 metres from the sixth-century cemetery found in 1856. See D. Wilkinson, 'Two Anglo-Saxon Graves at Kemble', *TBGAS* 106 (1988), 198–201. Kemble was on the Hwicce's southern border (see fig. 1 and below, p. 384), so the discovery confirms the pattern described above.

4

Early influences on the church

THE FOUNDATION OF THE EPISCOPAL SEES

When Theodore of Tarsus arrived in England as archbishop of Canterbury in 669 the Hwicce and Magonsætan were presumably under the nominal authority of the bishop of Lichfield, as were their Mercian overlords and the peoples of Middle Anglia and Lindsey. Such provision was obviously inadequate, especially since Bishop Chad insisted on travelling round his diocese on foot, following Irish custom. The impatient Greek is said to have lifted him bodily onto a horse. More conventionally, after Chad's death Theodore summoned a synod at Hertford in 672 and 673 which recognized in principle the need for more bishops; there were only the seven sees of Canterbury, Rochester, London, Dunwich, Winchester, Lichfield and York.[1] By 679 Theodore's main reorganization may have been completed, if we may rely on Canterbury's record of a papal council, which decreed, apparently in response to a dispute between Theodore and his bishops over the division of dioceses, that there should be an archbishop and twelve bishops.[2] To make up this number we should have to include

---

[1] *HE* III.21; IV.3 and 5. On the date of the synod see Poole, *Studies*, p. 41 and n. 4; Levison, *England and the Continent*, p. 266; Harrison, *Framework*, pp. 84–5; Brooks, 'Anglo-Saxon Charters', p. 226; Vollrath, *Synoden*, p. 69; Wood, 'Bede's Northumbrian Dates', pp. 285–7; and references. On Theodore's policy and its context see Brooks, *Canterbury*, pp. 71–6, and for a sombre sketch of the Church in the 660s see Hunter Blair, 'Whitby', pp. 15–17.

[2] 'Die Akten der römischen Synode von 679', ed. W. Levison, *Zeitschrift der Savigny-Stiftung für Rechtsgeschichte* 33, Kanonistiche Abteilung 2 (1912), 249–82, and 50, Kan. Abt. 19 (1930), 672–4, at (1912), p. 280, §6 = H&S III, 133 (cf. pp. 135 and 153); Stenton, *Anglo-Saxon England*, pp. 136–7. Gibbs, 'Decrees of Agatho', pp. 217–18, 224, n. 44, and 229–30, thinks that the relevant clause is a Canterbury interpolation,

the dioceses of the Hwicce and Magonsætan, and indeed their bishops, Bosel and Putta, attest an authentic charter already in 680, alongside their spiritual and temporal overlords, Theodore and Æthelred of Mercia.[3] According to the episcopal lists for the two sees, Bosel and Putta were their first bishops 'after Seaxwulf', the bishop of the great Mercian diocese whom Theodore had consecrated in place of Bishop Wynfrith, Chad's successor, whom he had deposed in 675 or a little earlier, for 'some act of disobedience', perhaps opposition to Theodore's plan to divide his diocese.[4] On this evidence the creation of the dioceses of the Hwicce and Magonsætan can be placed between *c.* 675 and 680.

Early twelfth-century Worcester sources attribute the foundation to Oshere in 679 and imply that Bishop Wulfstan II (d. 1095) had documents associating it with that king and his Mercian overlord, Æthelred.[5] On the other hand, the foundation charter for Bath monastery of 675 indicates that the foundation of the see had recently been accomplished by King Osric, or was at least in progress. No bishop of Worcester attests this charter, but that may fit in with Bede's statement that Tatfrith, who was chosen as the first bishop, died before his consecration.[6] Perhaps Tatfrith fell ill in 675 and was not replaced with Bosel until 679. Oftfor, Bosel's successor, who is known to have been active in the kingdom much earlier, in the reign of Osric,[7] could have provided quasi-episcopal leadership during an inter-regnum from 675 to 679.

It is unclear why Worcester was chosen for the Hwiccian see. Theodore placed his bishops in *locis oportunis*, in accordance with the papal policy of siting sees in *ciuitates*, rather than *uillulae* and *modicae ciuitates*, 'lest the name of bishop be brought into contempt'; yet Worcester, though

---

but Brooks, *Canterbury*, p. 74, treats it as genuine; see further Poole, *Studies*, pp. 51–3; Vollrath, *Synoden*, pp. 77, n. 152, 86, n. 175, and 415–16. The evidence for the seventh-century bishoprics needs re-examination (cf. *HBC*³, p. 212). The statement in many modern works that the West Midland sees were founded as a result of the Synod of Hatfield stems from a spurious document, H&S III, 152–3.

[3] S 1167; cf. below, n. 104. Hillaby's theory ('Origins', pp. 19–21) that the attesting *Putta gratia Dei episcopus* is the ex-bishop of Rochester is unconvincing; see below, n. 43.

[4] 'Episcopal Lists Part III', ed. Page, pp. 6 and 10; *HE* IV.6; Sims-Williams, 'Wilfrid', pp. 168, n. 28, and 175, n. 52. Cf. Wallace-Hadrill, *Commentary*, p. 145.

[5] Sims-Williams, 'Wilfrid', p. 168.

[6] *Ibid.*, pp. 168–9; S 51 (quoted above, p. 56); *HE* IV.23.

[7] *HE* IV.23. On Osric and Oshere see above, pp. 34–5.

recognizably a *cæster*, had been but a 'small town' in the Roman period.[8] Gloucester would seem a more obvious choice, but Osric's foundation of a monastery there, allegedly with a vast endowment of three hundred hides, may have ruled it out – an early illustration of Bede's complaint that royal generosity to monasteries made it hard to find *loci* (presumably estates) for new sees.[9] Worcester, which lies outside the area of 'pagan' burials, may have long been a Christian centre; and it would also have been an important trading centre – coins down to the time of Phocas (602–10) were discovered on Castle Hill early last century – and defensible crossing of the Severn.[10] A charter of 718×745 calls Worcester the *metropolis Huicciorum*. If this is more than a flourish by the eleventh-century copyist, it may mean that Worcester was a royal secular centre, if not a tribal 'capital'.[11] An early twelfth-century Worcester writer claims that the see was at first intended to serve both the Hwicce and the

---

[8] *HE* IV. 2 (cf. Wallace-Hadrill, *Commentary*, p. 139); *Ep.* xxviii (Tangl, p. 50 and n. 1) and *Ep.* li (Tangl, p. 87 and n. 1; cf. Reuter, 'Boniface and Europe', pp. 92, n. 72, and 94, n. 96); Todd, '*Vici*', pp. 114–15; cf. Rahtz, 'Archaeology of West Mercian Towns', pp. 114–15; Barker *et al.*, 'Origins of Worcester'; Dyer, *Lords and Peasants*, p. 21; *Medieval Worcester*, ed. Carver, pp. 2–3 and 26.

[9] *BOH* I, 413; *EHD*, p. 804; cf. Campbell, *Essays*, p. 140. Finberg suggested that Gloucester's endowment of three hundred *tributarii* (S 70) might reflect the city's *territorium* in Roman times and prefigure the three Gloucestershire hundreds of Berkeley, Whitstone and King's Barton. See *Gloucestershire Studies*, pp. 14–15 and 55 and n. 2; *ECWM*, p. 163; *PNGl* IV, 28; Thacker, 'Chester and Gloucester', p. 207; Hooke, *Hwicce*, p. 105. Dudstone, King's Barton and Gloucester itself are favoured by Heighway, 'Saxon Gloucester', pp. 375 and 381, n. 24. The size of Gloucester's *territorium* is unknown, however, and it is debatable whether it could have remained unaltered for centuries; cf. Collingwood and Myres, *Roman Britain and the English Settlements*, p. 433, n. 1; H. Hurst, 'Gloucester (Glevum): A *Colonia* in the West Country', in *The Roman West Country*, ed. Branigan and Fowler, pp. 63–80, at 76–7 and 80, not absolutely rejecting Finberg's theory; Biddle, 'Towns', pp. 106 and 112; and below, p. 94 and n. 28. On the possible survival of large administrative units cf. Taylor, *Village and Farmstead*, pp. 104–6; Sims-Williams, 'Settlement', p. 32; D. Hooke, 'Territorial Organisation in the Anglo-Saxon West Midlands: Central Places, Central Areas', in *Central Places: Archaeology and History*, ed. E. Grant (Sheffield, 1986), pp. 79–93.

[10] See above, p. 60; Barker *et al.*, 'Origins of Worcester', pp. 39 and 112; *Medieval Worcester*, ed. Carver, pp. 3, 26, 33 and 298.

[11] S 1254. Cf. Campbell, *Essays*, pp. 108 and 140; J. H. Williams, 'From "Palace" to "Town": Northampton and Urban Origins', *ASE* 13 (1984), 113–36, at 129. As to whether there were secular 'capitals' at the time see the literature cited by Sawyer, 'Royal *tun*', p. 273.

Magonsætan.[12] This is probably patriotic invention, but it is true that from that point of view it is well sited.

There were no important Roman centres in the kingdom of the Magonsætan, apart from Kenchester (*Magnis*), which was rather far west.[13] Hereford, where Roman masonry was visible, may have been regarded as a suitable site, *faute de mieux*, though it was not called a *cæster*; it takes its name *here-ford* from the 'army ford' which was probably the chief attraction of the site.[14] Yet Hereford may not have been the original location of the see. Bede does not mention it. He simply calls his contemporary, Walhstod (the fourth bishop in the extant episcopal list), 'bishop of the peoples who dwell over the river Severn to the west', true to his custom of referring to the newer bishoprics by the peoples they served rather than by their sees.[15] The first plausible document found to name Hereford is the profession of obedience to Canterbury in 801 by Wulf-heard, *Herefordensis ęcclesię episcopus*.[16] Wulfheard attended a synod in 803 as *Her[e]fordensis ciuitatis* [var. *ecclesiæ*] *episcopus*, and he referred in discussion

---

12 Dugdale, *Monasticon* I, 607 (cf. *MHB*, p. 622 and Liebermann, *Geschichtsquellen*, p. 17): 'Et quia ciuitas Wigorna, tempore quo regnabant Brytones, uel Romani in Brytannia, et tunc et nunc totius Huuicciæ, uel Magesetaniæ, metropolis extitit famosa, cathedram erexit [Theodorus] pontificalem digniter in ea, parochiarum jam diuisarum primam constituens Huuicciam' [Hereford has no part in this fivefold division! cf. H&S III, 129–30]. Cf. Sims-Williams, 'Wilfrid', p. 168, n. 25; Hooke, *Hwicce*, p. 18 and n. 82; Asser, ed. Stevenson, p. 229, n. 2.

13 See Stanford, *Welsh Marches*, pp. 156–9; Shoesmith, *Hereford* II, 4–6; cf. above, p. 40, n. 126.

14 The masonry was re-used for corn-drying ovens in the seventh or eighth centuries. See P. Rahtz, 'Hereford', *CA* 9 (1968), 242–6, and 'Archaeology of West Mercian Towns', pp. 110–11 and 117; Fowler, 'Farming', p. 276; Davies, 'Roman Settlements', pp. 153 and 166; Wilmott, 'Kenchester', pp. 127 and 130; Shoesmith, *Hereford* II, 3, 11, 30–1, 70–1 and 72–3, and III, 14. Campbell, *Essays*, p. 105, notes that S 154 calls Hereford *locus*, not *ciuitas*, but the reference is probably to Harvington, not Hereford.

15 *HE* V. 23; cf. Poole, *Studies*, p. 63, and above, p. 39. The inferences that 'Bede had never heard the name of Hereford in connection with the bishopric' (Bannister, *Cathedral Church*, p. 15), and that 'the bishops at first were merely *chorepiscopi* of Lichfield or court prelates with no fixed see of their own' (*ECWM*, p. 223), are thus wrong; Bede never names Worcester either.

16 *Canterbury Professions*, ed. M. Richter, Canterbury and York Soc. 67 ([ptd. Torquay], 1973), no. 4 (= BCS 298, cited by Bannister, *Cathedral Church*, p. 16; *ECWM*, p. 223, n. 1; Hillaby, 'Origins', p. 44). Richter's doubts about its authenticity (p. xlii) are not shared by Brooks, *Canterbury*, p. 125 (cf. p. 351, n. 57).

then to monasteries given (*præstita*) to the *ecclesia* of Hereford more than thirty years before.[17] Stenton, reasonably enough, deduced that the see of Hereford was of some antiquity in 803; yet it is not impossible that the monasteries had pertained to the church of Hereford before it became the see. Such extreme caution is necessary because of an apparent allusion to an alternative site, in a letter of Gilbert Foliot of 1173–4 (or 1163): Foliot, a former bishop of Hereford himself, asks the bishop-elect of Hereford to confirm the rights of *Lidebiri* church (Ledbury, He. or Lydbury North, Shr.), as he and his predecessors had done, 'for the sake of the episcopal see which it held long since and out of reverence for the holy bishops whose bodies lie there'.[18] If *Lidebiri* was the original see for the Magonsætan, it may have remained so at least up to and including the time of Bishop Cuthbert (736–40), who composed an epitaph, extant in manuscript copies, upon a tomb he constructed for the bodies of all his predecessors save Putta;[19] this tomb may have been known to Foliot. In that case, there could even be something in the legend that the church of Hereford was not built until after Offa's 'martyrdom' of Æthelbert in 794.[20] On the other hand, Foliot does not state specifically that the bishops of *Lidebiri* were his own predecessors, so it may have been a former Welsh see near English territory, similar to those at Dewstow (Monmouthshire), Welsh Bicknor (He.), and Glasbury (Breconshire);[21] geographically this would be more likely in the case of Lydbury than Ledbury. Thus the location of the see of the bishops of the Magonsætan in the seventh and eighth centuries remains uncertain.

[17] BCS 312 (texts B and C) and 309 (for the latter (S 1431) see below, p. 138); cf. *CP*, p. 193.

[18] *The Letters and Charters of Gilbert Foliot*, ed. Z. N. Brooke, A. Morey and C. N. L. Brooke (Cambridge, 1967), p. 300, no. 227. They suggest (n. 1) a connection with the *Lydas* of S 1798, formerly identified with Lyde near Hereford (*Luda* in the *Vita S. Ethelberti*, ed. James, 'Two Lives', p. 243); the form *Lydas* suits Lydbury and/or nearby Lydham better than Ledbury (cf. *DEPN*, s.nn.). Cf. below, n. 53. Both Ledbury and Lydbury North were episcopal manors and of Domesday 'minster' status.

[19] See above, pp. 40 and 61 and below, p. 342. William of Malmesbury is unlikely to have seen the inscription *in situ* (Sims-Williams, 'William', p. 13), so his mention of Hereford is of little value.

[20] See above, p. 50. In this case Milfrith could not have been involved.

[21] For Bicknor see Davies, *Welsh Microcosm*, p. 150, and for the others my review, p. 128.

THE FOUNDATION OF MONASTERIES BEFORE 716

Monasticism had already taken root before the sees were founded. When it began cannot be known, since charters, the main evidence, only begin in the 670s. Moreover, the monasteries named in some of the extant 'foundation charters' may have been in existence before these charters were granted: a royal grant of land 'to establish[22] a monastery' (*ad construendum monasterium*) in a given year may indicate only that royal assent was then obtained for removing from the sphere of secular law and custom an estate which was already in the possession of the recipient of the charter, and perhaps even already used to support a monastery.[23]

Charters were already being drawn up for monasteries in the reign of Wulfhere, the first Christian king of Mercia (657 – 674×675). Wulfhere granted a large estate at Hanbury, north-west of Worcester, to an abbot Colmán, and he may have granted St Wilfrid estates in western Mercia, as did his successor, King Æthelred. Æthelred granted Fladbury to Bishop Oftfor, 'for the forgiveness of my sins and those of my late wife Osthryth', so that the bishop might re-establish monastic life there, and he is said to have granted Evesham to Oftfor's successor, Ecgwine, as a site for a monastery. The previous foundation at Fladbury (*Fledanburg*) may have been that of an abbess Flæde (short for Æthelflæd, Eanflæd, etc.), to judge solely by the name 'Flæde's *burg*'; *burg* is especially likely to mean 'monastery' when combined with a female name: another example is Tetbury ('Tette's *burg*'), which is called *Tettan monasterium* in a charter ostensibly of 681, and *Tettanminster* by William of Malmesbury. Tette's identity is unknown (the sister of Ine of Wessex flourished too late), but Dr Hooke suggests that Fladbury, and the nearby area of *Flæferth* ('Flæd's(?) woodland') and *Æflæde tun* in Flyford Flavell, took their names from Ælfflæd (*c.* 654–*c.* 714), the sister of Æthelred's Northumbrian queen Osthryth; Osthryth was the heir to Fladbury, according to Evesham sources, and her death (in 697) is mentioned in the Fladbury charter.

---

[22] On *construere* see Sims-Williams, 'Wilfrid', p. 169, n. 31.

[23] See *ibid.* and above, p. 85. On the nature of charters see Stenton, *Latin Charters*, pp. 31 and 55–65, and *Anglo-Saxon England*, p. 308; Brooks, 'Anglo-Saxon Charters', p. 222; Keynes, *Diplomas*, pp. 28–39; S. Keynes and M. Lapidge, *Alfred the Great: Asser's 'Life of Alfred' and Other Contemporary Sources* (Harmondsworth, 1983), pp. 308–9; P. Wormald in *The Anglo-Saxons*, ed. Campbell, pp. 95–8, and *Bede and the Conversion of England*.

Hooke's hypothesis might be developed further: Ælfflæd, having received her education from Hild at Whitby, will have come south and founded Fladbury when her sister married Æthelred (before 679), but she will soon have returned to Northumbria, where she helped her mother Eanflæd to govern Whitby, probably when Hild died in 680 and certainly by 685. Monastic life will then have lapsed at Fladbury, perhaps because of the unpopularity of Osthryth; her promotion of the cult of her Northumbrian relative, St Oswald, was resented, and she was finally murdered by her own Mercian nobles in 697. This is a large hypothesis to hang on the common name *Ælfflæd*, especially in the face of Bede's silence. On the other hand, the exactly contemporary connection between Oftfor of Whitby and Osric of the Hwicce provides a plausible context for Ælfflæd to have come down to Osric's kingdom.[24]

Æthelred resigned in 704. His successor, Coenred, who resigned five years later, in 709, granted a nun called 'Feleburg' eight hides at Lingen, in the kingdom of the Magonsætan, either for a monastery there, or perhaps

[24] See below, pp. 106, 96, 103, 105, 140, 141, 103 and 184 respectively. For Fladbury see *PNWo*, pp. xxi and 126; *DEPN*, p. 181; Cox, 'Place-Names of the Earliest Records', pp. 32–3; Gelling, 'New Look', p. 72; Hooke, *Hwicce*, pp. 11, 84–5, 134, 136 and 220 (cf. *DEPN*, p. 183 and Gelling, *Place-Names in the Landscape*, pp. 191–2). On Ælfflæd see *HE* III.24 and IV.26; *VW*, c. 43; Hunter-Blair, 'Whitby', pp. 8, 14 and 29–30; and below, p. 185. On Osthryth see *HE* III.11, IV.21 and V.24 (cf. Thacker, 'Pre-Viking Mercia', pp. 2–3); S 76 (cf. below, p. 140, n. 119); and *Chronicon de Evesham*, ed. Macray, pp. 18 and 73 (used in *ECWM*, p. 170; but cf. Sims-Williams, 'People and Places' and below, p. 141, nn. 121 and 123). For Tetbury see S 73 (cf. S 71 and *ECWM*, p. 237); *GP*, p. 388. Cf. *CP*, p. 320; *DEPN*, p. 463; *PNGl* I, 109–10, and IV, 41 and 51; Hahn, *Bonifaz und Lul*, p. 134, n. 4; and below, p. 146, n. 13. For *burg* as 'monastery' when compounded with a female name, see *CP*, pp. 320–1, on the strength of which I have tentatively marked Alberbury on fig. 1 (the '*burg* of *Aluburg* or *Ealhburg*', *DEPN*, p. 4) and Bibury (named from an eighth-century grantee called Beage, below, p. 152); Smith, *PNE* I, 59 and 62, and Gelling, *Signposts*, p. 182, in assigning the meaning 'manor house', are too sceptical. On *burg* 'monastery' see also Campbell, *Essays*, pp. 107–8; Cox, 'Aspects', pp. 36 and 41–2; Hooke, *Hwicce*, p. 38; and below, pp. 108, 139, n. 110, and 356. Alvechurch ('Ælfgyth's church', *CP*, p. 321, n. 3) might be included because it is said to have been given to Bredon in Offa's day (Dugdale, *Monasticon* I, 608; cf. BCS 1320, where Athelstan is said to have given it to Worcester), but this may be based on a marginal annotation in MS 4 of S 117 (cf. Ker, *Books, Collectors and Libraries*, p. 54, n. 3, and Dyer, *Lords and Peasants*, pp. 11, n. 6, and 22). Alvechurch may have been founded long after 800; see M. Gelling, 'Recent Work on Anglo-Saxon Charters', *LH* 13 (1978), 209–16, at 212, and 'New Look', pp. 72–3; Hooke, *Hwicce*, pp. 139 and 229; Bond, 'Church and Parish', p. 137.

for the endowment of some other monastery, such as Wenlock, which preserved the charter.[25]

The sub-kings were also active in granting lands for monasteries. The *Vita S. Mildburgae* says that Merewalh founded Leominster after his conversion in 660. This statement cannot be checked since the history of the monastery is obscure until *c*. 1000 when a will records a layman's bequest of four bullocks to Leominster, among other West Midland religious establishments.[26] A better documented foundation in Merewalh's kingdom is Much Wenlock. According to the charters abstracted in the so-called 'Testament of St Mildburg', Wenlock was founded on land originally bought from Merewalh by an East Anglian abbot and was further endowed by grants by Merchelm and Milfrith, with the consent of Æthelred of Mercia (that is, before 704).[27] In the kingdom of the Hwicce Æthelred also gave his consent to King Osric's grant of land at Bath 'to establish a monastery of holy virgins' in 675. The Gloucester foundation charter says that Osric was granted the *ciuitas* of Gloucester 'with its land (*ager*)' by Æthelred, whom he had paid both for the right to establish a monastery in the *ciuitas* and for the right to bequeath it to his heirs, and that Osric then granted it to his sister for a monastery.[28] There may be an authentic kernel here, though the manuscript is fourteenth-century. The charter also says in passing that just as Æthelred granted Osric three hundred hides (*tributarii*) at Gloucester, so he granted Osric's brother

---

[25] S 1801. E. J. Dobson, *The Origins of 'Ancrene Wisse'* (Oxford, 1976), pp. 391–2, thinks that Hughley, 4 miles WSW of Wenlock, is the place meant. The spelling *Feleburg* is odd, but is *sic* in the manuscript.

[26] Above, p. 56; S 1534. Whitelock, *Wills*, p. 166, notes that the bequest could be to a church, rather than a religious community, at Leominster. The bequest is not so comprehensive as S 1482, by which a reeve leaves money to every priest and monk in Kent, but it does provide a useful list of West Midland houses. On such evidence from wills see Blair, *Minsters and Parish Churches*, pp. 3–5; Dyer, *Lords and Peasants*, p. 360; and above, p. 8. For maps of Leominster estates see Rennell of Rodd, 'Land of Lene', p. 309; Darby and Terrett, *Domesday Geography*, p. 61; Hooke, *Territorial Organization*, pp. 17 and 24. For the *parochia* of Leominster see Lennard, *Rural England*, pp. 400–1; B. Kemp, 'Some Aspects of the *Parochia* of Leominster in the 12th Century', in *Minsters and Parish Churches*, ed. Blair, pp. 83–95. See also below, p. 118, n. 19.

[27] See below, pp. 98–9 and S 1799. On Merchelm and Milfrith see above, pp. 50–1.

[28] See above, p. 35 and nn. 92–3. On the terminology of the Gloucester grant see *ECWM*, pp. 158–9 and 240; Grosjean, 'Saints des marches', p. 169, n. 2; Morris, *Age of Arthur*, pp. 497 and 617; and above, n. 9. See also Scharer, *Königsurkunde*, pp. 135, n. 46, and 147–8.

Oswald another three hundred hides (*cassati*) at Pershore. The allusion is doubtless to Oswald's foundation of Pershore, which is noted explicitly, and in wording related to the charter, under the year 683 in the mid-twelfth-century *Cronica de Anglia* from Worcester diocese, and, dated *c.* 689, in a set of annals seen by Leland and thought by him to come from Evesham, or more probably Pershore.[29] The reference to Pershore's three hundred hides is suspicious. The allusion is surely to the triple hundred of Pershore, which consisted of three hundred hides which were included in Edgar's confirmation to Pershore in 972 (a charter of doubtful authenticity), but which by the time of Domesday Book had been partly alienated to Westminster Abbey, although they still owed church-scot to Pershore.[30] It is difficult to accept that three hundred hides was also the endowment of Pershore in the seventh century, for the Worcestershire computation of three hundred hides for a triple hundred is agreed to be late and artificial, perhaps for the purposes of shipsoke.[31] One would therefore be tempted to agree with William of Malmesbury that Pershore was merely a foundation of the reign of Edgar,[32] were it not that the 972 charter refers to an earlier privilege granted by Coenwulf of Mercia (796–821) at the request of his ealdorman Beornnoth (a historical personage). Quite probably Pershore's early records were destroyed in the fires of 1002 and 1223,[33] and the

---

[29] *ECWM*, p. 158; Liebermann, *Geschichtsquellen*, p. 18; Leland, *Collectanea*, ed. Hearne I, 240–1. On Oswald, see above, p. 35. John, *Orbis*, pp. 200–1, thinks that the 883 (*sic*) entry for St Oswald's introduction of monks at Pershore (and elsewhere) given in the *Annales de Wigornia* (*Annales Monastici*, ed. Luard IV, 369) really refers to the 683 foundation; but this seems unlikely when one looks at the context and compares the entry in Liebermann, p. 20. On the dating in the *Annales* see Luard IV, 367, n. 2.

[30] S 786 (on authenticity cf. Brooks, 'Anglo-Saxon Charters', p. 23, and Keynes, *Diplomas*, pp. 98–100); *PNWo*, pp. 183–4; Taylor, 'Deerhurst, Pershore, and Westminster', pp. 237–41; Finberg, *Lucerna*, pp. 62–4; Grundy, *Worcestershire*, pp. 196–8; Cox, 'Vale Estates', p. 39; Bond and Hunt, 'Archaeological Work in Pershore', p. 9.

[31] See Stenton, *Anglo-Saxon England*, pp. 293, 298 and 431; H. M. Cam, *Liberties and Communities in Medieval England* (Cambridge, 1944), pp. 84 and 93–4; *EHD*, p. 429; H. R. Loyn, 'The Hundred in England in the Tenth and Early Eleventh Centuries', in *British Government and Administration: Studies presented to S. B. Chrimes*, ed. H. Hearder and H. R. Loyn (Cardiff, 1974), pp. 1–15; Darlington, *Worcester Cartulary*, pp. xiii–xv; Cox, 'Vale Estates', pp. 34–40; Hooke, *Hwicce*, p. 105.

[32] *GP*, p. 298. Cf. the later sources cited by L. Braswell, 'Saint Edburga of Winchester: A Study of Her Cult', *MS* 33 (1971), 292–333, at 294–6. Leland maintains, on the other hand, 'Alwardus non erat primus fundator Persoren: monaster: sed ueteris, à Danis destructi, reparator' (*Collectanea* I, 278).

[33] *ECWM*, pp. 11 and 98, no. 236.

alleged foundation by Oswald depends on some undocumented domestic tradition. We return to safer ground with Oshere's grant of Ripple to a monk Frithowald in 680, his grant of *Penintanham* (probably Inkberrow) to an abbess Cuthswith 'to establish a monastery' between 693 and ?699, and his grant, with the consent or participation of Æthelred, of Withington to two nuns 'to establish a monastery there' before 704.[34]

All these monasteries were founded before the accession of Æthelbald in 716 eclipsed the line of Penda. The prominence of kings in the catalogue of foundations may be misleading. In this early period charters seem to have been intended to establish a lasting record that the church had been granted land which was thereby freed from the necessity of paying food-rent and most other taxes to the king, unlike secular lands that were passed down within families or were granted by the king to his loyal retainers on a reversionary basis; hence charters had to be issued by kings.[35] The places granted in the charters were not all royal vills, though some of them may have been, and the kings may have been paid for their good offices more often than their charters reveal.[36] On the other hand, the royal support for monasticism indicated by the above account may have been genuine enough. Æthelred of Mercia became a monk in 704 and died an abbot in 716, while Coenred went to Rome to become a monk in 709.[37] Significantly, their successor, Ceolred (709–16), a notorious 'violator of nuns and infringer of ecclesiastical privileges', issued no known charters; we are told only that St Wilfrid, near the end of his life in 709 or 710, was persuaded by two of his abbots to go and confer with Ceolred 'for the sake of the position of our monasteries in his kingdom, for he promises to order his

---

[34] On these three grants see below, pp. 104–5, 191–2 and 131 respectively (consent according to S 1255, participation according to S 1429).

[35] Cf. above, n. 23.

[36] Sawyer, 'Royal *tun*', p. 279; Scharer, *Königsurkunde*, p. 46; Keynes, *Diplomas*, p. 33. But in the case of the *Penintanham* grant there is an interesting contrast between its wording '*pro remedio animæ meæ* ... dabo terram quæ dicitur Penintanham ...' (S 53) and that of a specific purchase by Cuthswith: 'dabimus tibi Cudsuidæ terram quæ dicitur Ingin . v manentium *quam tu a nobis proprio prætio redimisti* id est DC solidis ut in tua potestate sit habendi et donandi cuicumque uolueris' (S 1177).

[37] *HE* v. 19 and 24. Æthelred was buried at Bardney, Lincs. (*ASC* 716) and according to the Old English Bede and William of Malmesbury he had been abbot there (*BOH* II, 154 and 327). On him and other monk-kings see Wallace-Hadrill, *Early Germanic Kingship*, pp. 87–91; Hunter Blair, 'Bede to Alcuin', pp. 239–40; Harrison, *Framework*, p. 70; C. Stancliffe, 'Kings who Opted Out', in *Ideal and Reality*, ed. Wormald *et al.*, pp. 154–76.

whole life after my instruction'.[38] There is a possible exception in favour of Wenlock, but this charter did little for his reputation even there: a brother of the monastery foresaw how Ceolred would be tormented in hell, and when Ceolred went mad at a feast and died cursing the priesthood churchmen had no doubt that hell was his destination.[39]

EARLY EXTERNAL INFLUENCES

By the time Æthelbald ascended the Mercian throne in 716 the church was evidently well established in the dioceses of the Hwicce and Magonsætan. Under what formative influences from outside had it come?

Kentish influence, if we leave aside Bede's story of Augustine's meeting with the British bishops 'on the borders of the Hwicce and the West Saxons', begins with Theodore's reassertion of Canterbury's metropolitan authority in the 670s. The sees of the Hwicce and Magonsætan were the most lasting of his creations, for the pattern of dioceses in the area changed little before the diocese of Gloucester was formed in the sixteenth century.[40] The extent of Theodore's influence in Mercia can be gauged from his replacement of Chad's successor at Lichfield, Wynfrith, who retired to Chad's foundation at Barrow in Lindsey, by Seaxwulf, the founder-abbot of Peterborough (*Medeshamstede*).[41] What influence he exercised in the appointment of the bishops of the Hwicce and Magonsætan is less clear, though it may be noted that Oftfor, who was consecrated bishop of Worcester soon after Theodore's death in 690, had studied at Theodore's famous school at Canterbury.[42] Putta, the first bishop in the Hereford episcopal list, cannot be identified with Theodore's protégé of the same, not uncommon, name, Bishop Putta of Rochester who resigned after Æthelred of Mercia's devastation of Rochester in 676 and found refuge

---

[38] Boniface, *Ep.* lxxiii (Tangl, pp. 152–3), but quoting an additional clause from William of Malmesbury's text, *Gesta regum*, ed. Stubbs I, 81 (cf. *EHD*, pp. 816 and 820, n. 2; *BOH* II, 306 and 314); *VW*, c. 64 (on the date see Harrison, *Framework*, pp. 90–2 and 94). As noted in *BOH* II, 314, Ceolred does attest S 65; but this charter may have been tampered with in the later eighth century (cf. Harrison, *Framework*, p. 70, n. 16; Scharer, *Königsurkunde*, pp. 53, n. 175, 93, n. 47, and 149).

[39] S 1800 (cf. John, *Land Tenure*, pp. 5–6 and 6, n. 1). Cf. below, p. 269.

[40] See above, pp. 5 and 78. On the changing influence of Canterbury see Brooks, *Canterbury*, pp. 63–76.

[41] *HE* IV.3 and 6. Cf. above, n. 4.   [42] *HE* IV.23 (below, p. 102).

with Seaxwulf as a peripatetic music teacher.[43] On the other hand, Tyrhtil, who succeeded Putta as bishop of the Magonsætan in 688, may have had Home County connections; he is recorded selling fifty hides at Fulham, Middlesex, to the bishop of London during the reign of Coenred (704–9).[44] More specific links between the Magonsætan and Kent emerge in the 'Kentish Royal Legend' texts. Merewalh's queen is said to have returned to Kent and founded Minster-in-Thanet. Under her and her daughter Mildthryth (*fl.* 696–?733), Minster may have had close ties with the monastery at Wenlock where her other daughter, Mildburg (*fl.* 690–727), was abbess.[45] Wenlock was not isolated from the outside world, for in about 716 a brother in the monastery was in touch both with the abbess of Barking (Essex) and with the West Saxon, St Boniface.[46]

The monastery of Wenlock was also linked with the distinguished East Anglian monastery of *Icanho*. This had been founded in 654 by Botulf, whose life and learning were of such repute that the Northumbrian Ceolfrith, having initially set out to study monastic practice in Kent *c.* 669, then proceeded to East Anglia.[47] According to the 'Testament of St Mildburg' and the foundation charter of 674×690 incorporated in it, Æthelheah, abbot of Botulf's monastery at *Icheanog*, gave Mildburg Wenlock and other estates totalling 144 hides, both 'on condition that the aforesaid *locus* [Wenlock] shall by the grace of God remain unalterably

---

43 *HE* IV.2 and 12. See *BOH* II, 222; *CP*, p. 193, n. 3; Hillaby, 'Origins', pp. 16–19; Wallace-Hadrill, *Commentary*, p. 150. The same objections apply, though less strongly, to the suggestion in H&S III, 130 that Putta administered Hereford as Seaxwulf's deputy, before it was constituted as a separate see. Gibbs's idea that Putta's name in the episcopal lists is a Lichfield interpolation ('Decrees of Agatho', pp. 223, n. 42, and 224, n. 44) seems to depend on a misinterpretation of Cuthbert's poem, discussed above, p. 91, and below, p. 342. Hillaby (p. 28) thinks that Putta's name was inserted by a Mercian reader of *HE* IV.12 and that the only bishop of the name was at Rochester; but cf. above, n. 3. Which Bishop Putta is meant at *VW*, c. 14?

44 S 1785. Cf. Whitelock, *Bishops of London*, p. 11, n. 6; *EHD*, p. 488. For the date 688 see 'Florence', *MHB*, p. 538, n. 3.

45 See above, pp. 42 and 48. For Mildthryth's dates see above, p. 49, n. 167. There can be little doubt about the authenticity of the connection between Mildburg and Wenlock, especially in view of the reference to *monasterium Milburge abbatissę* in Boniface, *Ep.* x (Tangl, pp. 7–15), for which there is no other candidate, and the reference in 901 in S 221. On remains at Wenlock see above, p. 81, and below, p. 122, n. 39.

46 Boniface, *Ep.* x (Tangl, pp. 7–15). See below, p. 243.

47 *ASC* 654; *Vita Ceolfridi*, c. 4 (*BOH* I, 389). See Whitelock, 'Pre-Viking Age Church', pp. 10–11.

under the tutelage of the church of the worshipful abbot Botulf' and in exchange for 60 hides at *Homtun* (possibly the Hamptons east of Leominster), which Mildburg gave to 'the two parties to whom authority over the *locus* [Wenlock] belonged', namely Abbot Æthelheah and an abbess *Liobsynda* whose role is not clarified.[48] Æthelheah and his community are said to have purchased Wenlock and its estates from King Merewalh. Despite the present tense *emitur* referring to this purchase, the abbot of *Icanho* is unlikely to have been a mere middle-man between Mildburg and her own father. The most plausible interpretation is that Botulf's community had earlier acquired Wenlock and its estates from Merewalh, perhaps as a daughter house under the abbess *Liobsynda*, and subsequently made it over to Mildburg, while preserving some spiritual authority over it, perhaps as head of a monastic federation. A parallel case of an eastern monastery with lands in the west may be the pre-Viking *Medeshamstede* (Peterborough), which seems to have possessed five estates in the vicinity of Wenlock, and partly in the territory of the Wreocensætan: Shifnal (which adjoined Wenlock's estate of Madeley), Cosford in Albrighton, Strefford, Wattlesborough and Lizard Hill.[49] These holdings could be connected with the fact that Seaxwulf, the founder of *Medeshamstede*, was the bishop of Mercia in the 670s and 680s.

A letter from Osbert of Clare to the monks of Ely may reveal further East Anglian influence in the kingdom of the Magonsætan. He says that a pious nursemaid in the household of the Domesday holder of Corfton had seen a vision of Ely's foundress, St Æthelthryth (d. 679 or 680), in an ancient little church dedicated to her on the border of the Britons and the English – presumably Hyssington, the only known church of St Æthelthryth in the region.[50] Osbert learnt from another Osbert, a canon of Bromfield

---

[48] S 1798. Cf. Whitelock, 'Pre-Viking Age Church', p. 12; on *Homtun* see *ECWM*, p. 208, n. 2. On *Liobsynda* see below, p. 111. For Wenlock's estates see Hooke, *Territorial Organization*, pp. 17 and 25–30; Thacker, 'Pre-Viking Mercia', p. 5.

[49] S 68; *ECWM*, p. 147, no. 427 (the exact location of Wattlesborough, on Watling Street, is lost according to E. W. Bowcock, *Shropshire Place Names* (Shrewsbury, 1923), pp. 240–1; for Strefford see *DEPN*, p. 450). See *CP*, pp. 180–1; Whitelock, 'Pre-Viking Age Church', pp. 12–13. Cf. Gibbs, 'Decrees of Agatho', p. 228, n. 59; Whitelock, *Bishops of London*, p. 8, n. 5. On Madeley see S 1802; Croom, 'Minster Parochiae', p. 73 and n. 52.

[50] Edited from the two manuscripts by E. W. Williamson, *The Letters of Osbert of Clare, Prior of Westminster* (London, 1929), *Ep.* xxxiii (see p. 219 for the Corfton and Hyssington identifications), and by Blake, *Liber Eliensis*, pp. 281–3, respectively. For

(*fl.* 1115–32),[51] who used to recount the story of the vision while distributing alms at Wenlock Priory, that the little church of St Æthelthryth had been founded by her father, Anna, king of the East Angles (d. 654). This seems unlikely in view of the enmity between Anna and the Mercians[52] and may be a false deduction from the dedication to Anna's daughter. Nevertheless, the tradition that the church was early is interesting. As the monks of Ely were apparently ignorant of its existence, to judge by Osbert of Clare's letter and the absence of any other reference in *Liber Eliensis*, its dedication may well go back to the period before the Viking settlements eclipsed Ely's influence. It may reflect direct influence from Ely, similar to, and perhaps connected with, that from *Icanho* on Wenlock nearby.[53] On the other hand, the cult could have come via Mercia; the Mercian abbess, St Werburg, King Wulfhere's daughter, is said to have been trained at her aunt Æthelthryth's monastery at Ely, and St Wilfrid, who propagated Æthelthryth's cult, was active in Mercian territory.[54] Another possible intermediary is Seaxburg, Æthelthryth's elder sister and successor as abbess, who was clearly the chief mover behind the translation

Osbert's devotion to St Æthelthryth cf. *Ep.* xlii, cited by Barlow, *Edward the Confessor*, p. 280, n. 6.

[51] 'Brommiensis campi . . . ecclesia', identified with Bromfield by Whitelock, 'Pre-Viking Age Church', p. 12, n. 3. Williamson, like D. Knowles, C. N. L. Brooke and V. C. M. London, *Heads of Religious Houses: England and Wales 940–1216* (Cambridge, 1972), p. 117, had thought Bromholm, Norfolk, was meant; but note that the vision took place 'in confinio' of the canon's church. In addition to the charters mentioned *ibid.*, p. 86, and by Whitelock, note that Osbert (of Bromfield) attests *Charters and Records of Hereford Cathedral*, ed. W. W. Capes (Hereford, 1908), no. 12 (p. 7) in 1132. On Bromfield minster see Lennard, *Rural England*, pp. 396–7; Blair, 'Secular Minster Churches', pp. 128–31; Hooke, *Territorial Organization*, pp. 17 and 30.

[52] Whitelock, 'Pre-Viking Age Church', p. 10, n. 3.

[53] If 'in regione que appellatur Lydas' in S 1798 refers to the Lydham district, rather than to Lyde, as Finberg supposed (cf. above, n. 18), Wenlock possessed lands near Hyssington.

[54] Cf. Whitelock, 'Pre-Viking Age Church', p. 13, n. 7; Hardy, *Descriptive Catalogue* I, nos. 948–9; Thacker, 'Pre-Viking Mercia', p. 4; *HE* IV.19; and below, pp. 103–5. On the early cult of St Æthelthryth see P. Grosjean, 'Un fragment d'obituaire anglo-saxon du VIIIe siècle naguère conservé à Munich', *AB* 79 (1961), 320–45. The Kalendar discussed (and misunderstood) by Grosjean is to be dated 729×754. See Gerchow, *Gedenküberlieferung*, pp. 213–15 and 329. The addition of Boniface's name is no indication of provenance since interest in him was early and widespread: see e.g. Willibald's letter in *Epistolae Aevi Karolini* II, ed. Duemmler, 501, and below, p. 234.

of her body in (?)695 and the promulgation of her cult. By her marriage to Eorcenberht of Kent (640–64) Seaxburg was connected with the Magonsætan dynasty, for Eorcenberht's brother Eormenred was Mildburg's maternal grandfather.[55] Such complicated relationships between royal dynasties must have played an important role in the development of the church at a time when monasticism and distant marriage alliances were both chiefly the pursuit of the nobility.

There is evidence of Northumbrian influence, especially in the kingdom of the Hwicce. From the kingdom of the Magonsætan we have only the late and unverifiable story of the mission of the priest Eadfrith (*Edfridus*) from Northumbria (*a Northanhimbrorum partibus*) to convert Merewalh and his people in 660.[56] According to the *Life* of Eadfrith summarized in the *Vita S. Mildburgae*, his memory was celebrated at Leominster, but there is no other trace of his cult there. The tract on 'The Resting-Places of the English Saints' says merely that a St Ethelred rests at Leominster, and he has not been identified.[57] Eadfrith could conceivably be equated with the confessor *Eata* to whom Atcham church was dedicated already in 1075, when Orderic Vitalis was baptized there. The traditional view, however, equates this Eata with the bishop of Lindisfarne (d. 687) of the same (common) name, one of the twelve English boys trained by Aídán, and this is more likely. Whether the dedication testifies to very early Northumbrian influence is doubtful; *Atcham* means 'the *hām* or *hamm* of Eata's people', and there is a real possibility that the church's dedication was due to an Anglo-Saxon re-interpretation of a secular place-name.[58] We cannot pursue the alluring theory, put forward when crop-marks indicated two very large halls on the gravel ridge at Atcham, that Eata or a follower conducted a mission at Atcham, baptizing the

---

[55] *HE* III.8 and IV.19 (cf. Poole, *Studies*, p. 73 on the date). On Eormenred see Rollason, *Mildrith*, pp. 9, 45 and throughout. Late sources associate Seaxburg with a monastery on the Isle of Sheppey: see *ibid.*, pp. 13, 30–1, 37, 46 and throughout; *BOH* II, 239; Hardy, *Descriptive Catalogue* I, no. 845.

[56] BL, Add. 34633, 207r–208r. See above, pp. 55 and 94.

[57] Add. 34633, 208r; thus *CP*, p. 201, n. 3; Rollason, 'Resting-Places', p. 63. Differently and unconvincingly *ECWM*, p. 220.

[58] F. Arnold-Forster, *Studies in Church Dedications, or, England's Patron Saints*, 3 vols. (London, 1899) I, 400–1 (cf. *BOH* II, 193; Redin, *Uncompounded Personal Names*, p. 64); Rahtz, 'Atcham Timber Halls', pp. 54 and 58; Gelling, *Signposts*, pp. 115 and 187, and *Place-Names in the Landscape*, pp. 49 and 120. The silence of Bede, who was well-informed about Eata, is significant.

Wreocensætan in the Tern or Severn, just as Paulinus had baptized the Northumbrians in the River Glen by the royal palace at Yeavering.[59]

The Northumbrian monastery at Whitby, founded in 657 by Hild (d. 680), was a notable nursery of bishops.[60] A monk of Whitby named Tatfrith, whom Bede describes as 'a most energetic and learned man of great ability' (*uir strenuissimus ac doctissimus atque excellentis ingenii*), was chosen as the first bishop of the Hwicce, but died before his consecration, and was replaced by Bosel, whose origin is not related.[61] The latter was succeeded by another of Hild's protégés, Oftfor (*c.* 691–?699), who had long been resident in the Hwiccian kingdom, apparently since before 680, for Bede says that he was there in King Osric's day. The possibility has already been mentioned that Ælfflæd, the future abbess of Whitby, founded Fladbury monastery *c.* 678 under Oftfor's aegis. That is speculation, of course, and is not mentioned in Bede's detailed account of Oftfor:[62]

After he had devoted himself to the reading and observance of the Scriptures in both of Hild's monasteries,[63] being anxious to reach still greater heights, he went to Kent to join Archbishop Theodore of blessed memory. After he had spent some further time in sacred studies there, he decided to go to Rome too, which in those

---

[59] Rahtz, 'Atcham Timber Halls', p. 60 (see *HE* II.14). Cf. below, p. 363. On Atcham church see Taylor and Taylor, *Anglo-Saxon Architecture* I, 31–2; Rahtz, 'Atcham Timber Halls', p. 58.

[60] Hunter Blair, 'Whitby', p. 25. See *HE* IV.23. C. S. Taylor, 'Early Christianity in Gloucestershire', *TBGAS* 15 (1890–1), 120–38, at 133, suggested that the dedication to St Peter of the see of Worcester and of other early monasteries in its diocese was modelled on the dedication of Whitby.

[61] Cf. above, p. 88, and below, p. 185. I am grateful to Mr P. A. Bibire for confirming that the name *Bosel/Boisil* is Anglo-Saxon, despite C. A. Ireland, 'Boisil: An Irishman Hidden in the Works of Bede', *Peritia* 5 (1986), 400–3.

[62] *HE* IV.23. Gibbs, 'Decrees of Agatho', p. 236, speculates that Tatfrith and Oftfor were selected as anti-Canterbury candidates. On Osric's and Oshere's dates see above, pp. 34–5. The date 691 for Oftfor depends on 'Florence' (*MHB*, p. 538) but must be more or less right, as Theodore's successor was elected on 1 July 692 and consecrated on 29 June 693 (*HE* V.8). On the Canterbury succession cf. Brooks, 'Anglo-Saxon Charters', p. 225, n. 1, and *Canterbury*, p. 77. The obit of 692 for Oftfor in 'Florence' (*MHB*, p. 539) is wrong, as S 76 shows: see Sims-Williams, 'Cuthswith', p. 9, n. 1 (cf. Brooks, 'Military Obligations', p. 75, n. 1). *ECWM*, p. 32 suggests the admittedly uncertain obit of 699; see below, p. 142, n. 124.

[63] Whitby and Hartlepool, not (*pace* Hunter Blair, 'Whitby', p. 8) Hackness, which was not founded till the last year of Hild's life, when Oftfor will already have been among the Hwicce 'cui tunc rex Osric praefuit'.

days was considered to be an act of great merit.[64] After his return to Britain he went to the kingdom of the Hwicce of which Osric was then king; there he remained for a long time, preaching the word of faith and setting an example of holy life to all who saw and heard him. At that time the bishop of the kingdom, whose name was Bosel, was greatly troubled by ill-health so that he could not carry out his episcopal duties himself; so Oftfor was appointed bishop in his place with universal approval and was consecrated at Æthelred's command by Bishop Wilfrid of blessed memory, who was at that time acting as bishop of the Middle Angles; for Archbishop Theodore was now dead [d. 690] and no-one had been appointed bishop in his place.

St Wilfrid, the powerful Northumbrian churchman mentioned here, probably played a part in church affairs on other occasions. Although his activities may have been centred on his monastery at Ripon, he involved himself in the ecclesiastical life and politics of many kingdoms. His disciple and biographer, the priest Stephen, who may have had a special interest in Mercia, portrays him as the personal friend of the successive Mercian kings Wulfhere and Æthelred.[65] He says that Wulfhere frequently invited Wilfrid to Mercia to perform various episcopal functions, and adds that the king 'for the good of his soul granted our bishop many tracts of land in various places where he soon established monasteries'.[66] Æthelred may have had little direct contact with Wilfrid during the first years of his long reign (674–704), because from 678 onwards Wilfrid was exiled from Northumbria by King Ecgfrith (d. 685), with whom Æthelred allied himself. Soon after Ecgfrith's death, however, Æthelred was reconciled to Wilfrid and returned many monasteries and lands to him to possess in his own right. He endowed him with more monasteries and estates and, in a later period of exile from Northumbria, maintained him honourably as bishop to the Middle Angles, from 691 or 692 until 702 or 703.[67] As such, Wilfrid consecrated Oftfor bishop of the Hwicce, as we have just seen. Wilfrid was still in possession of monasteries in Mercia at the time of his death in 709 or 710, and was negotiating with the infamous King Ceolred in order to safeguard them.[68]

[64] See below, p. 193.

[65] *VW*, cc. 14–15, 43, 48 and 57. On Stephen and Mercia see Kirby, 'Bede, Eddius Stephanus'.

[66] *VW*, c. 14 (referring especially to 666–9; cf. *BOH* II, 317); cf. c. 51.

[67] *VW*, cc. 40–1, 43–5 and 51. On the chronology see *BOH* II, 318–19; cf. Poole, *Studies*, pp. 72–6.

[68] *VW*, cc. 64–5. Cf. above, pp. 96–7 and n. 38.

Stephen is geographically vague and names very few of Wilfrid's monasteries and estates, but charter evidence adds some precision to his narrative. Genuine charters dated by the *annus Domini* only become usual after the death of Bede, the earliest such charter of which the original is extant being a Hwiccian grant of Æthelbald of Mercia, dated 736 AD. Nevertheless, Wilfrid, who championed the Dionysian reckoning at the Synod of Whitby in 664, probably inspired the precocious use of AD dating in a few seventh-century charters which seem to have an authentic basis although only copies are extant.[69] Two are from the kingdom of the Hwicce. The earlier is the Bath foundation charter in the abbey's twelfth-century cartulary. This is dated 'anno recapitulationis Dionisii, id est, ab incarnatione domini nostri Iesu Christi sexcentesimo septuagesimo sexto, indictione iiii^{ta}, mense Nouembrio, uiii° idus Nouembris', that is (reckoning from the beginning of an indictional year in September), 6 November 675.[70] Wilfrid attests this charter, and is the only one of the clerical witnesses known to attest reputable documents dated by the *annus Domini*, apart from Bishops Eorcenwald and Hædddi, who only do so in conjunction with him. While Wilfrid may have merely chanced to be in the south when Osric and Æthelred granted the Bath charter – perhaps attending Eorcenwald's consecration as bishop of London – he could have played a more active role in the foundation of the monastery, which fell during one of the most successful periods of his career (671–8), when he built and dedicated his great churches at Ripon and Hexham.[71]

The other Hwiccian charter, extant in the early eleventh-century Worcester cartulary, concerns Ripple and is dated 'anno recapitulationis Dionisi, id est ab incarnatione Christi sexcentessimo octuagessimo, indictione sexta reuoluta'.[72] 680 was a less prosperous year for Wilfrid. Driven from Northumbria by Ecgfrith, he took temporary refuge with Æthelred's nephew Berhtwald, who was probably sub-king of a Mercian dependency in northern Wessex, where he granted Somerford Keynes to Aldhelm, abbot of Malmesbury, at a synod at *Bregford*, which seems to have lain on

---

[69] Poole, *Studies*, pp. 32–4; Harrison, '*Annus Domini*', and *Framework*, pp. 66–75; Brooks, 'Anglo-Saxon Charters', p. 225; Wallace-Hadrill, *Commentary*, pp. 125, 192–3 and 235; Sims-Williams, 'Wilfrid'. The 736 charter is S 89; see below, p. 148.

[70] S 51. See discussion and references in Sims-Williams, 'Wilfrid', pp. 165–7.

[71] *VW*, cc. 17 and 22; Taylor and Taylor, *Anglo-Saxon Architecture* I, 297–312, and II, 516–18; *BOH* II, 318. On Bath see further below, pp. 111 and 204.

[72] S 52. *Sexta* is probably an error for *octaua*. For what follows see Sims-Williams, 'Wilfrid', pp. 174–83.

the Mercian and West Saxon border. Berhtwald also gave Wilfrid land for a little monastery which 'his monks', Stephen says, 'possess to this day'. The diplomatic pressure which Ecgfrith put upon Æthelred and the West Saxon king Centwine soon forced Wilfrid himself to move on, first into Wessex and then to pagan Sussex, leaving his monks behind at the unnamed little monastery – perhaps this occasioned Aldhelm's letter to Wilfrid's monks, urging them to follow him into exile.[73] Wilfrid probably reached Sussex by the end of 680 or early in 681. The facts that the king of the South Saxons had been baptized at the instigation of Wilfrid's old friend Wulfhere, while his queen was a princess of the Christian Hwicce, would seem to have been the sole attractions of Sussex, and these facts are not mentioned by Stephen, who represents it as a desperate time for his hero.[74] The Ripple charter dated 680 AD fits the events of the year very well, with one simple emendation. It records Oshere's grant of Ripple (*Rippell*), with the consent of Æthelred, to a certain Frithowald, 'Bishop Wynfrith's monk' (*monacho Uuinfridi episcopi*), on condition that Frithowald maintain monastic life there. The only Bishop Wynfrith at the time was the ex-bishop of Lichfield who was living in retirement at his predecessor Chad's monastery at Barrow in the kingdom of Lindsey, having been deposed by Theodore five or more years previously.[75] Yet, as it happens, Stephen tells an anecdote about Wilfrid (OE *Wilfrith*) and Wynfrith being confused 'by the error of one syllable' in their own lifetimes. This provokes the conjectures that *Uuinfridi* in the eleventh-century, and much rewritten, text of the Ripple charter should be emended to *Uuilfridi*, and that Ripple is the *Rippel* in the list of his royal grants which Wilfrid read out at the dedication of his church at Ripon.[76] On this hypothesis, we may suppose that Æthelred, when expelling Wilfrid from the southern Mercian sub-kingdoms in 680 and depriving him of his lands and monasteries, nevertheless consented to a proposal from Oshere that Ripple should remain in the hands of one of Wilfrid's monks. The charter recording this may have been drawn up by Wilfrid himself or by one of his followers; this would explain its Dionysian dating clause, which is remarkably similar to that in the Bath foundation charter.

Consideration of Northumbrian influence naturally leads to the question

[73] *VW*, c. 40 (for *praefectus* read *perfectus*, with both manuscripts); S 1169; *Aldhelmi Opera*, ed. Ehwald, pp. 500–2.
[74] See above, pp. 57–8. [75] *HE* IV. 3 and 6. See above, p. 88.
[76] *VW*, cc. 17 and 25; Sims-Williams, 'Wilfrid', pp. 175–6 and 180–3.

of Irish influence. Surprisingly, there is only one trace of this in the sources: a lost charter of Wulfhere concerning Hanbury, near Droitwich, which Patrick Young and William Dugdale saw at Worcester in the seventeenth century. Dugdale listed it as 'a charter of Wulfhere about land of fifty hides which is called Hanbury' (*carta Wlfari de terra L manentium quod Hamburg dicitur* – *quod* could refer to the unrecorded neuter antecedent *monasterium*), but Young's summary is more informative:

Charta Wulfarii, Merciorum regis, qua terram .50. manentium de Heanburg Colmanno Abbati, cum omnibus pratis, syluis, puteis salis ad eam pertinentibus, ut habeat, possideat et cuicunque uoluerit derelinquat.[77]

Colmán is such a common Irish name that there is no chance of identifying this abbot.[78] It is tempting to guess that he came from Northumbria, in view of the strong Irish element in the Northumbrian church and its missions: the first bishops of the Middle Angles and Mercians were all either Irish or, like Chad, trained in Ireland. On the other hand, there were Irish monks and scholars preaching and studying in many parts of England.[79] For instance, Wilfrid encountered an Irish monastery among the South Saxons:

There was in their midst a certain Irish monk named Dícuill who had a very small monastery in a place called Bosham surrounded by woods and sea, in which five or six brothers served the Lord in humility and poverty; but none of the natives cared to follow their way of life or listen to their preaching.[80]

[77] S 1822. 'Charter of Wulfhere, king of the Mercians, by which he grants fifty hides at Hanbury to Abbot Colmán, with all pertinent meadows, woods and salt-pits, so that he may have, hold and bequeath it to whomsoever he wishes.' See Grosjean, 'Date du Colloque de Whitby', p. 272 and n. 1, quoting from the manuscripts of Dugdale (cf. G. Hickes, *Institutiones Grammaticae Anglo-Saxonicae et Moeso-Gothicae*, 2 pts (Oxford, 1688–9) II, 169, no. 16) and Young (cf. Hearne, *Hemingi Chartularium* II, 567).

[78] *Pace ECWM*, p. 12 and Hooke, *Hwicce*, p. 11. See Grosjean, 'Saints des marches', p. 166, n. 1; Hughes, 'Evidence for Contacts', p. 50 and n. 9, and 'Irish Influence', p. 61, n. 3. Hughes's comment 'Here is an Irish abbot and his *comarba*' (*ibid.*, p. 61) reads too much Irishness into the conventional English phraseology of Young's abstract (cf. above, n. 36). On Colmán see also below, p. 356.

[79] *HE* III. 21 and IV. 3; Hughes, 'Evidence for Contacts'; Campbell, *Essays*, pp. 51–2, and 'Debt to Ireland'.

[80] *HE* IV.13. But see Campbell, 'Debt to Ireland', p. 338.

Colmán's establishment was much larger than Dícuill's, to judge by its hidage, and is rather to be compared with Chad's monastery at Barrow in Lindsey, which Wulfhere also established with fifty hides of bookland, and where, says Bede, 'the traces of the rule of life established by Chad have lasted down to this day'.[81]

Although Young and Dugdale do not specify that a monastery at Hanbury was the purpose of Wulfhere's grant, this may be inferred from an original charter of Wiglaf of Mercia in 836 freeing 'the *monastery* at Hanbury, complete with the wood belonging to it and with fields and meadows, and with all appurtenances, and with salt-pits and lead-furnaces, and villages and all things belonging thereto, from small and from great causes, specified and unspecified, except the construction of ramparts and bridges', in return for gifts to king and ealdormen from the bishop of Worcester, into whose hands Hanbury had evidently passed.[82]

Hanbury parish church is post-Conquest, but is believed to stand on the site of the Anglo-Saxon monastery. In view of Colmán's Irish name, the siting of the church is interesting. It stands within a Romano-British hill-fort on a very steep hill that falls away sharply on three sides of the church, in a commanding position over an area of considerable Roman settlement round the intersection of two Roman roads; hence the name Hanbury, meaning 'high fort'.[83] An Irish abbot would feel at home in such a setting. The typical monasteries of early Ireland were situated within enclosing walls or earthworks, often those of pre-existing ring-forts presented by local landowners, and there are traces of a similar practice in the Brittonic Celtic world: the *Lives* of St Samson and St Pol de Léon speak

---

[81] *HE* IV.3.

[82] S 190; *EHD*, no. 85. There is no reason to suspect the authenticity of the charter seen by Young and Dugdale. They record no anachronistic features like an AD date (which they would certainly have noted) or an immunity clause. The 836 charter provided all the immunities for the property that could be desired. If Colmán's charter was forged before this, it is likely at least to have preserved a genuine tradition about Colmán. The fact that the charter was not copied into the Worcester cartularies is a point in its favour; it was, as the later medieval archivists would say, 'inutilis'.

[83] S. R. Bassett and C. C. Dyer, 'Hanbury: Documentary and Field-Survey (SO 9664)', *WMA* 23 (1980), 88–91; 24 (1981), 73–8; 25 (1982), 68–70; Hooke, *Hwicce*, p. 91; Blair, 'Minster Churches in the Landscape', p. 45, pl. V; and below, p. 390. The churchyard seems originally to have been circular, and at the west end of the church is an old well, as at Breedon-on-the-Hill; cf. A. Dornier, 'The Anglo-Saxon Monastery at Breedon-on-the-Hill, Leicestershire', in *Mercian Studies*, ed. Dornier, pp. 155–72; Stafford, *East Midlands*, p. 90.

of monasteries set up in *castella* by the Severn and in Brittany.[84] The Irish brought these customs with them to England: Fursa built a monastery inside the *castrum* of *Cnobheresburg*, given him by Sigeberht of East Anglia in the 630s or soon after, and during Sigeberht's reign Cedd, a Middle Angle sent by the Northumbrian church, established another church in the Roman fort at Bradwell-on-Sea.[85] Forts were not, of course, exclusively occupied by Celtic or Celtic-influenced monks,[86] but they do appear to have shown a preference for such sites.

The history and topography of Hanbury recall those of Malmesbury, which lay just to the south of the kingdom of the Hwicce.[87] Malmesbury stands on a steep, narrow-necked promontory between the Avon and one of its tributaries, probably the site of an Iron Age hill-fort.[88] The earliest form of the name is given by Bede, who describes Aldhelm as priest and abbot of the monastery 'which they call *Maildubi urbs*'; there can be little doubt, then, that Malmesbury took its name from someone with the Irish name Maíldub.[89] The *-burg* part of the name, which Bede translates by *urbs* and an eighth-century alumnus of Malmesbury translates by *ciuitas*, may simply refer to fortifications, but may also be an instance of *burg* in the sense 'monastery',[90] or even, in view of the Irish context, 'monastic city'. As a centre of cross-country traffic, a meeting-place of Hwicce and

84 Norman and St Joseph, *Early Development of Irish Society*, pp. 95–6 and pls.; above, p. 80; 'Vie de saint Paul de Léon', ed. C. Cuissard, *RC* 5 (1881–3), 413–59 (c. 15).

85 *HE* III.19 and 22; Taylor and Taylor, *Anglo-Saxon Architecture* I, 91–3 and 117–18; cf. Campbell, *Essays*, p. 101 and n. 6. On Sigeberht's chronology see *BOH* II, 173; Whitelock, 'Pre-Viking Age Church', p. 6.

86 Cf. the priest to whom Egbert of Kent gave Reculver for a monastery: *ASC* 669; Taylor and Taylor, *Anglo-Saxon Architecture* II, 503–9. On monasteries within enclosures see Cramp, 'Monastic Sites', p. 204. Finberg, *Gloucestershire Landscape*, p. 51, notes that 'the parish churches of Ozleworth, Hewelsfield, and Oldbury-on-Severn stand to this day in their primitive circular churchyards, and the name Oldbury, referring to the earthwork that surrounds the church, proves that the English builders consciously occupied a known place of ancient sanctity'. Cf. *ibid.*, p. 73, n. 1; *PNGl* III, 8 and IV, 21.

87 Cf. Sims-Williams, 'Wilfrid', p. 178, n. 67.

88 J. Haslam and A. Edwards, *Wiltshire Towns: The Archaeological Potential* (Devizes, 1976), pp. 35 and 82; J. Haslam, 'Towns of Wiltshire', pp. 113–15 and 139.

89 *HE* V.18. See Plummer's discussion of the name in *BOH* II, 310–11. Forms containing *-dun-* may be the result of misreading *-duu-* (= *-duv-*) or due to contamination with OE *dūn*.

90 See above, n. 24; *Ep.* cxxxv (Tangl, pp. 273–4) ('in Maldubia ciuitate'), discussed below, p. 227.

Wilsætan, and a stopping-place for travellers on the Fosse Way and scholars on the Bristol Channel route across England from Ireland, Malmesbury may be compared to an Irish 'monastic city' like Clonmacnoise, which is sited where a major highway meets the Shannon.[91] The eponymous Maíldub is as shadowy a figure as Colmán, and one cannot uncritically accept the standard accounts of Aldhelm's life, based on William of Malmesbury and later writers, that state that Aldhelm was trained by Maíldub at Malmesbury before going to Hadrian and Theodore's school at Canterbury and returning to Malmesbury, where he became abbot in 675.[92] Recent scholarship has questioned both the Irishness of Aldhelm's education and Maíldub's role in it.[93] On the other hand, it must be noted that Aldhelm maintained contact with Irish as well as English and continental scholars, and that one of his correspondents, who can probably be identified as Irish on internal evidence and by a process of elimination, says that Aldhelm was 'nourished by a certain holy man of our race'.[94] One cannot be certain that this holy man was Maíldub, but, unless Irishmen are to be multiplied *praeter necessitatem*, it is likely enough that he was. If so, Maíldub of Malmesbury will have been roughly contemporary with Colmán of Hanbury.

Bede's *Historia ecclesiastica* has conditioned generations of historians to see the development of the English church in terms of rivalry between the Roman and Irish missions from Canterbury and Lindisfarne, with the conversion of the monks of Iona to the Roman Easter in 716 forming a climax.[95] Such an emphasis was only natural for Bede, seeing that the British and English churches were still divided on the Easter question

---

91 K. Hughes, *Early Christian Ireland: Introduction to the Sources* (London, 1972), p. 21; Norman and St Joseph, *Early Development of Irish Society*, pp. 119–20; and further literature in Blair, 'Minster Churches in the Landscape', p. 48. On Welsh ecclesiastical use of *urbs* and *ciuitas* see Davies, *Microcosm*, pp. 32, n. 1, 61, 122 and 147. Cf. Haslam, 'Towns of Wiltshire', pp. 115 and 139.

92 E.g. Duckett, *Saints and Scholars*, pp. 1–97 and 460–77.

93 J. Marenbon, 'Les sources du vocabulaire d'Aldhelm', *Archivum Latinitatis Medii Aevi (Bulletin Du Cange)* 41 (1979), 75–90 and references; Edwards, 'Two Documents', pp. 10 and 14. Bede's failure to mention Maíldub is explained by Campbell, *Essays*, p. 52. See also Campbell, 'Debt to Ireland', p. 338.

94 *Aldhelmi Opera*, ed. Ehwald, p. 494, *Ep.* vi; *Aldhelm*, trans. Lapidge and Herren, p. 164. Cf. *ibid.*, pp. 6 and 146–7; *Aldhelm*, trans. Lapidge and Rosier, pp. 6–7 and 222, n. 17; Smyth, 'Isidore', p. 71.

95 *HE* v.22.

109

when he wrote. Yet recent historians have rightly emphasized the influence of the Frankish church of northern Gaul as well. Campbell, for example, points out that in the second half of the seventh century the English church took a new turn, with missionary bishops becoming wealthy, powerful members of the establishment, and monasteries, especially large double monasteries of monks and nuns, multiplying and producing imposing buildings and manuscripts – and that the contemporary Frankish church shared the same transformations; he argues that there was a direct connection across the Channel.[96]

Bede himself, referring to the reign of Eorcenberht of Kent (640–64), mentions that,

because there were not yet many monasteries founded in England, numbers of people from Britain used to enter the monasteries of the Franks or Gauls to practise the monastic life; they also sent their daughters to be taught in them and to be wedded to the heavenly bridegroom. They mostly went to the monasteries at Brie, Chelles and Andelys-sur-Seine.

He also names some Kentish, East Anglian and Northumbrian noblewomen who were associated with these monasteries in the Seine and Marne valleys.[97] A reverse traffic, not mentioned by Bede, is revealed in the *vita* of Bertila, abbess of Chelles (*c.* 660–*c.* 710):

Faithful kings from the parts of Saxondom across the seas [i.e. England] would ask her through trusty messengers to send them some of her followers for teaching or sacred instruction (which they had heard that she possessed to a marvellous degree), or even those who might establish monasteries of men and women in that region. For the good of their souls, she did not refuse this religious request; rather, with the counsel of the elders and the encouragement of the brothers did she send, with a thankful heart, chosen women and very devout men thither with great diligence, with both saints' relics and many volumes of books, so that through her the yield of souls increased even in that people and, by the grace of God, was multiplied.[98]

Some onomastic evidence from Wenlock and Bath can plausibly be understood in terms of these passages.

Before Mildburg became abbess (in 674×690), authority over Wenlock

---

[96] Campbell, *Essays*, pp. 49–67; Wallace-Hadrill, *Commentary*, pp. xxxiii–xxxiv, 101 and 232.

[97] *HE* III.8 and IV.23 (cf. below, n. 101). See also Hunter Blair, 'Whitby', pp. 6–7.

[98] 'Vita Bertilae', ed. Levison, c. 6. Cf. Guerout, 'Origines', p. 48 and n. 9.

belonged to Æthelheah, abbot of St Botulf's monastery at *Icanho*, and a certain abbess *Liobsynda*, whose name is Frankish: *Liobsind*. Finberg suggested that Liobsind was the first abbess of Wenlock, brought there to prepare the way for Mildburg, and he hazarded a guess that she came from Chelles, where Mildburg's sister Mildthryth is said to have been educated.[99] Although this is quite possible, it may be that Liobsind had no personal link with Wenlock and was rather associated in some way with Æthelheah in East Anglia. The East Anglian church had close ties with the Continent. Sigeberht, who came to the throne in 630 or 631, had been converted during his exile in Gaul and tried to imitate Gaulish educational institutions in his own kingdom, assisted by a Burgundian bishop.[100] King Anna's daughter Æthelberg, stepdaughter Sæthryth, and grand-daughter Eorcengota (Seaxburg's daughter) all attended the monastery of Faremoutiers-en-Brie, the first two becoming abbesses; while his sister-in-law Hereswith, the wife of Anna's brother Æthelric, retired as a nun at Chelles.[101] (Folcard's fictitious *Vita S. Botulfi* even has Botulf himself study abroad, but in Old Saxony, which had not been converted at that time!)[102]

Two names in two consecutive charters in the twelfth-century Bath cartulary provide stronger evidence of Frankish influence there.[103] The first

---

[99] See above, p. 99; Finberg, *ECWM*, pp. 202 and 208–9 and *Lucerna*, p. 74; Campbell, *Essays*, p. 58. Wenlock was settled by Cluniac monks after the Conquest and the *Testament* is preserved in a single thirteenth-century manuscript, so a possible OE name **Leofsith* (or **Leofswith*) may have been innocently 'normalized' by a French scribe (cf. Sims-Williams, 'Anglo-Latin Letter', p. 8). The earliest account of Mildthryth's life (cf. above, p. 42, n. 134) merely says that she was educated abroad (*Symeonis Monachi Opera*, ed. Arnold II, 12), and Chelles is first mentioned in eleventh-century texts: see Rollason, *Mildrith*, pp. 11, 60, 76, 78, 85, 98, 120 and 163, n. 54. The abbess of Chelles is here called *Vuilcume/Wilcoma*. This name appears in the list of queens and abbesses in the Lindisfarne *Liber vitae* (*Oldest English Texts*, ed. Sweet, p. 154, lines 20 and 24); cf. Gerchow, *Gedenküberlieferung*, p. 144.

[100] *HE* II.15 and III.18.

[101] *HE* III.8 and IV.23 (for doubts whether Chelles is correct see Wallace-Hadrill, *Commentary*, p. 232). For the relationship of Anna and Hereswith see *CP*, p. 399; *Bede*, ed. Colgrave and Mynors, p. 190, n. 3. Whitelock, 'Pre-Viking Age Church', p. 8, describes Hereswith as a widow, but she may have separated from Æthelric before his death. She was already in the monastic life in 647.

[102] *Acta Sanctorum Ordinis Sancti Benedicti*, ed. J. Mabillon, 6 vols. (Paris, 1668–1701) III, pt 1 (1672), 3–7 (c. 2); Mabillon corrects 'Old Saxony' to 'Gaul' (p. 4, n. *a*) to agree with *HE* III.8, etc. On this *vita* see Whitelock, 'Pre-Viking Age Church', p. 11, n. 1. *ECWM*, p. 209 wrongly states that Botulf studied at Chelles.

[103] S 51 and 1167. For what follows see Sims-Williams, 'Bath', and 'Wilfrid', pp. 165–7.

is the foundation charter of 675, by which Osric grants a hundred hides for a 'monastery of holy virgins' at Bath to an abbess with the continental name Berta (dative *Bertanę*). The second charter belongs to 680, and presumably relates to Bath, though this is not specifically stated: with Æthelred of Mercia's consent, a certain Æthelmod – probably the Æthelmod who attested the foundation charter – grants twenty hides by the river Cherwell, in Middle Anglia, 'Bernguidi uenerabili abbatissę et Folcburgi, et per uos monasterio uestro'. [104] The name of the abbess is English, *Beorngyth* (in an archaic spelling), but the name of the second recipient, *Folcburg*, though not impossible as an Old English formation, is only attested on the Continent. We see, then, a monastery founded at Bath by a Frankish abbess, who is succeeded by an English abbess, while the continental element continues in the person of Folcburg, who would appear to be second in command. This recalls rather strongly the missionary role of contemporary Chelles under Abbess Bertila.

In view of Bath's position on the Hwicce's West Saxon border, it may be significant that in 675 the West Saxon bishopric had been held for a quarter-century by three bishops of whom the first and third, Agilbert and Leutherius, were Franks, while the second, Wine, had been consecrated in Gaul, whereas the Hwicce had no bishop of their own, to judge by the Bath witness list. [105] In fact Leutherius (670–6) appears second after Archbishop Theodore in the column of episcopal witnesses, using the (authorial?) style of humility *acsi indignus episcopus*. Leutherius may well have drawn up the charter, for there is a close similarity between its diplomatic and that of a Dorset charter which was probably drawn up by him or one of his circle, to judge by a Frankish formula in it. [106] Little is known about Leutherius, but one can gather the sort of background and contacts he had from the life of his uncle and predecessor, Agilbert. The latter was the cousin of the founder of the monastery of Jouarre and the brother of its first abbess. After

---

[104] S 1167. On this charter and on Æthelmod see Sims-Williams, 'Wilfrid', pp. 165, n. 11 and 178, n. 69; and above, p. 35, n. 93, and below, p. 384. On its date and on S 1164 (below, n. 106) see now H. Edwards, *The Charters of the Early West Saxon Kingdom*, BAR British Series 198 (Oxford, 1988), 213, 215 and 229–33. I regard as unnecessary her theory (pp. 214 and 222) that, because Bath was all-male in 758, S 51 and S 1167 relate to two houses other than Bath (but both connected with Francia, with Æthelmod, and with cross-border witnesses); cf. below, pp. 121 and 145.

[105] *HE* III.7; cf. above, p. 88.

[106] S 1164. See Sims-Williams, 'Bath', pp. 5–6, and 'Wilfrid', pp. 165–6.

a long period in Ireland, probably in the south in view of his 'Roman' stance at the synod of Whitby in 664, Agilbert came to England. He was bishop of the West Saxons from 649 or 650 until 664, when he quarrelled with King Cenwealh, who had decided to divide the diocese, wanting an English-speaking bishop, Wine, at Winchester. Agilbert returned to Gaul, becoming bishop of Paris. Cenwealh invited him to return, but he sent his nephew Leutherius instead. Agilbert was buried in the magnificent crypt of St Paul at Jouarre, which he himself is thought to have built. [107] Jouarre is less than twenty miles from Chelles, whose influence on English monasticism has already been mentioned. The two monasteries must have been more than geographically close. Both were double monasteries and Columbanan in character. Balthild, Clovis II's English widow, had introduced the abbess Bertila and the other nuns from Jouarre in the course of founding or refounding Chelles *c.* 660, and herself lived at Chelles until her death (after 677). [108] Her presence may have encouraged an English orientation of Chelles and Jouarre. Leutherius must surely have been familiar with both houses. His part in the foundation of Berta's monastery at Bath, outside his own diocese, may plausibly be connected with this background, and it may be conjectured that the nuns Berta and Folcburg came from Chelles or Jouarre, or one of the neighbouring monasteries mentioned by Bede.

Wilfrid attested the Bath foundation charter next after Leutherius and may have inspired its Dionysian dating clause, as noted above. Quite possibly he and Leutherius collaborated in the foundation, for Wilfrid had been ordained and consecrated by Leutherius's uncle Agilbert, and collabo-rated with him at the Synod of Whitby. [109] – Such are the personal complexities of the seventh-century church whenever the sources let us see it at close range.

CONCLUSION

Taken together, these fragments of evidence give an impression of a complex interplay of external influences on the churches of the Hwicce and Magonsætan in the later seventh century. There are traces of early Irish influence at Hanbury, and at Malmesbury to the south; of Northumbrian

[107] Sims-Williams, 'Bath', pp. 6–8, and below, p. 209.
[108] Sims-Williams, 'Bath', p. 7; Wallace-Hadrill, *Commentary*, pp. 101, 193 and 232.
[109] See above, p. 104; Sims-Williams, 'Wilfrid', p. 167.

influence through the first Mercian, Middle Anglian and Hwiccian bishops, at the foundations connected with Wilfrid and, perhaps, at Leominster; of East Anglian and perhaps Kentish influence at Wenlock; and of Frankish influence at Bath and possibly at Wenlock too; and the episcopal framework was the creation of Theodore of Canterbury. These diverse influences must have produced a patchwork of contrasting types of Christian practice and culture – or, possibly, a synthesis of them, for it is clear that the practice of the regions from which influence came cannot be characterized as purely 'Roman', 'Irish', or the like. Northumbria is a good instance. A rule similar to that of Lindisfarne may have been observed at the monasteries of Hild, whence Tatfrith and Oftfor came. Yet Hild herself had originally planned to follow her sister Hereswith to Gaul, Oftfor is known to have visited Canterbury and Rome before coming to the Hwicce, and the great Northumbrian, Wilfrid, was familiar with Italian and Frankish churchmen and fiercely pro-Roman, though hardly pro-Canterbury: 'Was I not the first, after the death of the first elders who were sent by St Gregory, to root out the poisonous weeds planted by the Irish?'[110] Again, East Anglia was the meeting-place of Romano-Kentish, Frankish and Irish influences, though it can at least be said that *Icanho*, Wenlock's mother-house, was probably not a 'Celtic' type of monastery.[111] Such ethnic labels, however, are of limited use: it is easy to slip into thinking of Maíldub and Colmán in the mould of Aídán or Chad, but it must be remembered that one of the most virulent opponents of the 'Celtic' party on the Easter question was Rónán, an Irishman trained in Gaul and Italy.[112] With this qualification, the evidence from the kingdoms of the Hwicce and Magonsætan fully bears out Stenton's conclusion that 'the strands of Irish and continental influence were interwoven in every kingdom, and at every stage of the process by which England became Christian'.[113] Only the influence of the neighbouring Welsh church is conspicuous by its absence.

---

[110] Hunter Blair, 'Whitby', pp. 6–7 and 12; *HE* IV.23; *VW*, c. 47.

[111] Whitelock, 'Pre-Viking Age Church', p. 11.

[112] *HE* III. 25; Hunter Blair, 'Whitby', p. 21; Ó Cróinín, 'Irish Provenance', pp. 321–2.

[113] *Anglo-Saxon England*, p. 125. On the cross-Channel dimension see now *La Neustrie: les pays au nord de la Loire de 650 à 850*, ed. H. Atsma, 2 vols., Beihefte der Francia 16 (Sigmaringen, 1989) II, 371–432.

5

Varieties of monasticism

'Monasteries' have often been referred to in the preceding chapters. But what were they like? In the seventh and eighth centuries, the Latin word *monasterium*, and its Old English derivative *mynster*, covered a wide range of religious communities that supported themselves from the surplus produce of estates free from most royal taxes and obligations, lived by some common rule under an abbot or abbess, worshipped in a common church within the monastery, and probably provided the surrounding laity with the services of a priest or priests.[1] The broad usage of the terms *monasterium* and *abbas* was attacked at the time by Bede, in his polemical *Epistola ad Ecgbertum*:

There are innumerable places, as we all know, allowed the name of *monasteries* by a most foolish manner of speaking, but having nothing at all of a monastic way of life . . . Numberless people have been found who call themselves *abbots* and at the same time reeves or thegns or servants of the king.[2]

Moreover, when a monastic community moved elsewhere (or disbanded), but provided a priest to minister to its former monastic church,[3] no doubt

---

[1] For the monastery's church see e.g. the grant by Offa and Ealdred of the Hwicce 'ad monasterium quod proprie nuncupatur aet Clife et ad ecclesiam beati Michahelis archangeli quæ inibi fundata est' (S 141). Such monastic churches may have had a pastoral role from the first (cf. Constable, 'Monasteries, Rural Churches and the *Cura Animarum*'), although direct evidence is scarce in England; cf. Brooks, *Canterbury*, p. 187; Blair, 'Minster Churches in the Landscape', pp. 36–8, and 'Secular Minster Churches', p. 115.

[2] *EHD*, pp. 804 and 806 (*BOH* I, 413–14 and 416). Cf. Blair, *Minsters and Parish Churches*, p. 1. Compare the Council of *Clofesho* in 747: 'monasteria, si tamen ea fas est ita nominare' (H&S III, 364).

[3] As laid down in Theodore's *Penitential* VI.7 (H&S III, 195).

laymen continued to call the church – the most important element from their point of view – the *mynster*, broadening the usage still further.

Some students of the early period distinguish 'monasteries' from 'minsters' in the sense of major churches served by groups of secular clergy living a communal life though not under Benedictine monastic vows.[4] Such a distinction is anachronistic before the late Anglo-Saxon period. The apologists of the tenth-century monastic reform distinguished between regular (that is, Benedictine) houses and irregular houses, and described their unreformed predecessors as *clerici* or *canonici* (a term not heard before papal legates used it in 786);[5] the latter, however, if they had found a spokesman, might well have described themselves as monks and their institutions as monasteries. Bede's complaints about the loose use of the terms *monasterium* and *abbas* appear to have had no influence on terminology; in the ninth century Asser, even when contrasting regular and irregular communities, uses the term *monasterium* for both,[6] and there are many examples of the heads of 'secular' houses being called *abbas*[7] and the members of their communities *monachi*, even ones who dwelt in their own private houses.[8]

Contemporaries evidently saw sufficient similarity between the diverse seventh- and eighth-century communities studied here as to call them all

[4] E.g. M. Deanesly, 'Early English and Gallic Minsters', *TRHS* 4th ser. 23 (1941), 25–69, at 36. Cf. Stenton, *Anglo-Saxon England*, pp. 148–9; Brooks, *Canterbury*, pp. 187–8. For later 'minsters' see Stenton, *Anglo-Saxon England*, pp. 152–6 and 668; Barlow, *English Church 1000–1066*, pp. 169–70, 179, 184, 245, 252 and 296; M. Franklin, 'The Identification of Minsters in the Midlands', in *Anglo-Norman Studies VII: Proceedings of the Battle Conference 1984*, ed. R. Allen Brown (Woodbridge, 1985), pp. 69–88; Blair, 'Secular Minster Churches'. In many cases these 'minsters' will have been earlier monasteries which fell into the possession of sees or escaped the tenth-century monastic reform. They should not be assumed to be 'devolved' or 'degraded' monasteries, as Blair notes (*ibid.*, p. 115). They may have stayed the same while the church outside changed. Cf. below, n. 86.

[5] D. J. V. Fisher, 'The Early Biographers of St Ethelwold', *EHR* 67 (1952), 381–91, at 383–4. An isolated early instance of the *monachi / canonici* dichotomy, probably deriving from Chrodegang's Rule, appears in the papal legates' statutes of 786: Duemmler, *Ep.* iii, p. 22; H&S III, 450 and 461; cf. Levison, *England and the Continent*, pp. 105–6; Blair, 'Secular Minster Churches', p. 117; Vollrath, *Synoden*, pp. 167–8.

[6] *Asser*, ed. Stevenson, c. 93.

[7] D. Knowles, *The Monastic Order in England: A History of its Development from the Times of St Dunstan to the Fourth Lateran Council, 940–1216*, 2nd ed. (Cambridge, 1963), pp. 35 and 592.

[8] For examples, see John, 'St. Oswald', p. 171, nn. 3 and 4.

'monasteries', and they make no attempt in charters and other documents to make the polemical distinctions of later Benedictine writers. I shall follow them in using a single term.[9] The Latinate word *monastery*, being international, seems preferable to the vernacular *minster*, but both are potentially misleading, the former suggesting a degree of separation from pastoral cares that is unlikely before the secular parish ministry grew up, the latter suggesting a degree of pastoral involvement unattested in the sources.

The tenth-century shibboleth for distinguishing true monasteries – whether they observed the Rule of St Benedict – can hardly be applied in the seventh and eighth centuries, when it was normal for individual abbots to compile their own rules from a variety of sources, which might or might not include the Benedictine Rule.[10] The only person whom we can closely associate with the Rule of St Benedict in England is St Wilfrid, who was the first to introduce it into Northumbria, according to his biographer.[11] A more typical case is Ceolfrith: after training under Wilfrid at Ripon and thereby escaping Irish customs at Gilling, he went first to Kent and then to Botulf's monastery at *Icanho* to study monastic practice, before returning to Northumbria to found Wearmouth with Benedict Biscop, who had formulated his own rule on the basis of the usages of seventeen ancient continental monasteries.[12] It is a pity that we do not know what rule was followed at *Icanho*, as this might have been a useful clue to the practice at its daughter-house at Wenlock. We can say, however, that Wenlock did not conform fully to later Benedictine norms. From a letter of St Boniface *c.* 717 we learn not only about some elements of the round of monastic observance that Wenlock monks were expected to follow – obedience to superiors, religious study, attendance in church, early rising for prayer, fasting, ministering to the sick, singing psalms as a penance – but also that a monk owned a slave-girl (*ancilla*) jointly with his own brother, who was presumably a layman.[13] In this respect the rule observed in Mildburg's

---

[9] I also follow the precedent of Ferrari, *Early Roman Monasteries*, p. xix and n. 19.

[10] See Wormald, 'Bede and Benedict Biscop'; Hunter Blair, *World of Bede*, pp. 125, 147, 153, 163 and 197–209.

[11] *VW*, cc. 14 and 47. See further Sims-Williams, 'Anglo-Latin Letter', pp. 9–10 and nn. 86–7.

[12] *Vita Ceolfridi*, chs. 3–6 (*BOH* I, 389–90; *EHD*, pp. 759–60). See also Alcuin: Duemmler, *Ep.* xix (p. 54).

[13] Boniface, *Ep.* x (Tangl, p. 13), cf. below, p. 269. Compare the case of Lull, who freed two boys: below, p. 240.

monastery was laxer than that in Hild's at Whitby, where private property was forbidden. [14] On the other hand, it is noteworthy that the oldest extant copy of the *Regula S. Benedicti* (Oxford, Bodleian Library, Hatton 48) is of Worcester provenance – it was already there in the eleventh century – and may have been written in the diocese in the early eighth century, perhaps for use at one of the monasteries connected with St Wilfrid, such as Bath, which was apparently dedicated to St Peter and St Benedict. [15] The splendour of the manuscript suggests an initial veneration of the Benedictine Rule, though the absence of signs of wear may indicate lack of actual use. [16]

By later standards women were prominent in the monastic life, particularly in the later seventh and early eighth centuries, when abbesses ruled communities at Wenlock, Bath, Gloucester, *Penintanham* (probably Inkberrow) and Withington. [17] Mildburg's community at Wenlock certainly included monks, as we have seen, and probably most or all of the others did, too, for men and women were not so segregated as in later times. On the other hand, mixed communities ruled by abbots are unattested, as in the rest of Anglo-Saxon England. Communities such as Eadfrith's at Leominster, Colmán's at Hanbury, and Frithowald's at Ripple may therefore best be pictured as exclusively male. [18] Even such monasteries as these may have included nuns at some stage. In 1046 and 1086 we hear of an abbess of Leominster, and in 1086 provision was still being made for the maintenance of nuns there; conceivably Leominster had been ruled by abbesses for centuries, for its history after its foundation is quite obscure. [19] Again, the name of Fladbury monastery suggests that it may

[14] *HE* IV.23. On property-owning see Schneider, 'Women', pp. 55–7.

[15] Sims-Williams, 'Wilfrid', p. 171.

[16] Cf. below, p. 205, n. 127.

[17] See above, pp. 94–6 and references. In general, Schneider, 'Women', is fundamental.

[18] Cf. *ibid.*, pp. 24–5, for possible exceptions. The following passage may mean that monasteries ruled by a man and a woman jointly were regarded as an abuse but presumably existed: 'quidem nonnulli propria habentes monasteria, ita ea inconsulte disponunt, ut, post obitum illorum, duo simul utriusque sexus unum possideant monasterium' (H&S III, 408; trans. Taylor, 'Berkeley Minster', pp. 73–4). On the authenticity of Ecgberht's *Dialogus* see references below, p. 320, n. 197. Berkeley had an abbot *c.* 778 and in 883, but apparently an abbess in 807; see below, pp. 172 and 176.

[19] See Dugdale, *Monasticon* IV, 51 nn.; Lennard, *Rural England*, p. 400, n. 5; Barlow, *Edward the Confessor*, p. 91 and n. 2; Whitelock, *Wills*, p. 166; B. R. Kemp, 'The Monastic Dean of Leominster', *EHR* 83 (1968), 505–15, at 505–6. Leominster, *olim*

have been ruled by an abbess Flæde, though the charter re-establishing monastic life *c.* 697 speaks of 'the most proper life of monks living in it under the rule of an abbot . . . just as when the land was first handed over'.[20] Similarly, although Æthelbald granted Daylesford in 718 to a monk called Bæg(i)a 'so that a monastery may be established there and may be a dwelling place of the servants of God' (*seruorum Dei*), the later bounds attached to the extant, eleventh-century copy of the charter refer to 'the nuns' hills' (*nunnena beorgas*) as well as to 'Bæga's spring' (*bæganwella*), now Baywell [Wood].[21] Whether these eponymous nuns flourished earlier or later than Bæg(i)a is unknown.

Female monasticism was a new development in late seventh-century England. In the mid-seventh century the nobility still sent their daughters to Frankish monasteries. Only subsequently were they normally provided for at home. Hild (d. 680), the daughter of a nephew of Edwin of Northumbria, is the first notable example. In 647, intending to follow her sister to Gaul, she spent a year in East Anglia, but Aídán, bishop of Lindisfarne, recalled her to Northumbria, where she practised the monastic life for a further year on a hide of land beside the Wear. She then became abbess of Hartlepool, which had been founded 'not long before' by Heiu, 'who is said to have been the first woman in the Northumbrian kingdom to take the vows and habit of a nun, having been ordained by Bishop Aídán'.[22] Hild's monastery was a 'double monastery', that is to say, one with sections for both men and women. Such monasteries had begun to appear in rural Gaul under the influence of the monastic movement associated with St Columbanus, and the first double monastery to be headed by an abbess – a specifically Frankish development – was Luxeuil's daughter-house, Faremoutiers (*c.* 617), one of the monasteries to which the English sent their daughters.[23] In all probability, then, Anglo-Saxon noblewomen such as Hild and Mildburg were following Frankish models when they established themselves as abbesses of mixed communities.[24] The

---

dirutum (*GP*, p. 193), was joined to Reading in 1121×1123. See also above, pp. 56 and 94.

[20] See above, p. 92, and below, p. 140.   [21] S 84. Cf. *PNGl* I, 212 and 217; II, 207.

[22] *HE* III.8 and IV.23.

[23] Guerout, 'Origines', pp. 34–6, who adds the qualification: 'En Gaule, il exista dès le VIe siècle des institutions qu'on peut assimiler, à la rigueur, à des monastères doubles; mais il s'agissait de monastères urbains' (p. 35). And for double monasteries in Spain, see Hunter Blair, *World of Bede*, pp. 135–6.

[24] Campbell, *Essays*, pp. 61–2.

double monastery was swiftly naturalized, however: according to the *Penitential* attributed to him, Archbishop Theodore (668–90) decided not to follow Greek legislation and abolish double monasteries, because they were already the 'custom' in England.[25] In the ninth century Alfred's policy of establishing separate monasteries for men and women at Athelney and Shaftesbury seems not to have been imitated, whereas witness-lists show that Wenlock and Winchcombe were still flourishing as double monasteries in his day.[26]

Wenlock happens to be the only seventh- or eighth-century monastery in the region here studied for which we have direct evidence that it was double,[27] but this was probably also the case in the other communities headed by abbesses, for in early Anglo-Saxon England as a whole these turn out to be double monasteries rather than nunneries whenever there is detailed evidence.[28] A possible exception is Bath. The dispositive clause of Osric's 675 charter for Abbess Berta refers to it as a *monasterium sanctarum uirginum*, and its proem refers to his plan to set up monasteries 'sparsim uirorum sparsimque uirginum deo famulantium'.[29] Conceivably, as Harrison suggested, this reflects the preference for separate establishments for men and women expressed by Theodore, who attests the charter. On the other hand, as Harrison also saw, Bede's usage shows how natural it would be to speak of a double monastery as a *monasterium uirginum* at a time when

---

[25] H&S III, 195: 'Non licet [var. *Apud Grecos non est consuetudo*] uiris feminas habere monachas neque feminis uiros; tamen nos non destruamus illud quod consuetudo est in hac terra [var. *tamen consuetudinam istius prouinciæ non destruamus*]'. Legislation of Justinian is cited by J. Godfrey, 'The Place of the Double Monastery in the Anglo-Saxon Minster System', in *Famulus Christi*, ed. Bonner, pp. 344–50, at 349, n. 9. On the question of the authenticity of Theodore's *Penitential* see Constable, *Monastic Tithes*, pp. 25–7.

[26] *Asser*, ed. Stevenson, cc. 92 and 98; S 221 (in 901) and 1442 (in 897). Professor Whitelock drew attention to these witness-lists in an undergraduate course in 1975. See also *ECWM*, p. 198, n. 1; *Minsters and Parish Churches*, ed. Blair, pp. 3, 71 and 75.

[27] Boniface refers to a man who was clearly a monk 'in monasterio Milburge abbatissę' in the time of Ceolred (d. 716); see below, p. 243.

[28] *CP*, p. 228; *ECWM*, p. 173; P. Schmitz, *Histoire de l'ordre de Saint Benoît*, 7 vols. (Maredsous, 1942–56) VII, 47–8. On double monasteries in general, see *ibid.* I, 298–300. For England earlier surveys are superseded by Schneider, 'Women'. She is not prepared to rule out the existence of nunneries (pp. 25–6), but finds no positive evidence.

[29] S 51. On this charter, see above, pp. 56–7, 104 and 111–13.

nunneries were exceptional or unheard of.[30] Certainly, if Bath originally included some monks, it is easier to understand how it came about that it had become an all-male community by 758.[31] Moreover, Jouarre and Chelles, the two Frankish houses which may have had a particular influence on the foundation of Bath, were both double monasteries headed by abbesses in the second half of the seventh century.[32]

The Anglo-Saxon double monasteries often resembled those of Gaul in their close association with ruling dynasties. Jouarre, on the evidence of the tombs in its seventh-century crypt and its *Généalogie des fondateurs*, is a good example.[33] The emergence of aristocratic dynasties of abbesses here and elsewhere has been attributed to the way in which communities were effectively obliged to choose their abbess from among their founding family, owing to a confluence of a Germanic tendency towards treating monasteries as hereditary estates and an Irish tendency towards kings and others imposing heads on monasteries from without.[34] Germanic and Celtic influences were, of course, felt independently in England, to the virtual exclusion of St Benedict's rule about freedom of election,[35] but the similarity between the dynastic character of Frankish and English double monasteries goes further. In England, as on the Continent, many of them were power-bases for the royal families which sustained them, providing kings and would-be-kings with spiritual and cultural prestige. They served as meeting-places for their councils, as temporary or permanent retreats from the world where their daughters and widows could exercise the power traditionally exercised by women in Germanic societies, and as royal burial centres where the memorial cult of their predecessors, themselves and their progeny could be tended in perpetuity.[36] In Dr Schneider's words, 'it is obvious that the government of these monastic institutions could only be entrusted to members of the founders' families themselves'. One wonders

---

[30] Harrison, *Framework*, p. 68, and *'Annus Domini'*, p. 554, citing *HE* IV.6.

[31] S 265; for problems cf. Sims-Williams, 'Bath', p. 8 and n. 10, and 'Wilfrid', p. 171, n. 42. Cf. Stenton's similar argument in the case of St Frideswide's, *CP*, p. 229.

[32] See above, pp. 110–13; Sims-Williams, 'Bath', p. 7.   [33] *Ibid.*, pp. 6–8.

[34] Guerout, 'Origines', p. 45.

[35] See *BOH* I, xxxv and II, 262–3; Levison, *England and the Continent*, pp. 27–9; Stenton, *Anglo-Saxon England*, p. 163; Colgrave and Mynors, *Bede*, p. 460, n. 2; John, 'Problems', pp. 60–1; Wormald, 'Bede and Benedict Biscop', pp. 144, 153 and 158, n. 19.

[36] Schneider, 'Women', pp. 272–3 and literature there cited. My quotation is from p. 273, n. 3. Cf. Stafford, *East Midlands*, p. 101; Thacker, 'Pre-Viking Mercia'.

whether any 'pastoral dimension' is really needed 'to understand this frenetic minster-building'.[37]

In the kingdom of the Magonsætan the double monastery of Wenlock was closely linked with the royal dynasty. Although authority over Wenlock seems originally to have been invested in the East Anglian abbot Æthelheah, who bought the land from Merewalh, it soon came to be known as *monasterium Milburge abbatissę* after Mildburg, Merewalh's daughter, who became abbess sometime between 674 and 690 and was granted extensive estates throughout the sub-kingdom by her brothers and others, according to the so-called 'Testament of St Mildburg'.[38] Traces of an Anglo-Saxon cult of St Mildburg were found after the Norman Conquest, including an Old English memorandum by a priest Ælfstan concerning the saint's burial place in Holy Trinity church, and in the sixteenth century John Leland heard that the tomb of Merewalh himself had been discovered at Wenlock.[39]

A comparable, but better documented, dynastic monastery in the kingdom of the Hwicce was Gloucester. Its early history is summed up in a very corrupt passage in its so-called 'foundation charter':

Osricus prefatus tradidit sorori sua Kyneburge hanc terram, et ciuitatem, in liberam abbatisse potestatem, habendum, & post illa Eadburt (*sic*) abbatissa, cognata eius, accipit eam, que fuit Regina ante Wlfheri regis merciorum, & sic post eam eafe abbatissa monasterium illud (cum bona castitate) sub ecclesiastica regula bene custodiebat xxxiij. annis, et liberabat illud omnipotentis dei in celis, & sanctam Mariam uirginis, & libellum terrarum super altare sancti Petri deposuit, & familie precipiebat ut pro dei nomine liberi essent domini electione semper in eternum pro se & suis qui hereditatem sibi dederunt.[40]

---

[37] Blair, 'Minster Churches in the Landscape', p. 38. Cf. *idem*, *Minsters and Parish Churches*, pp. 1–2: 'their public rôle helps to explain the speed and efficiency of their creation'. Cf. above, n. 1.

[38] Boniface, *Ep.* x (Tangl, pp. 7–15); above, pp. 98 and 111.

[39] *ECWM*, pp. 198–9 and 207; A. J. M. Edwards, 'An Early Twelfth Century Account of the Translation of St. Milburga of Much Wenlock', *TSAS* 57 (1961–4), 134–51, at 144; above, p. 61. It is now doubted whether any Anglo-Saxon work can be seen in the extant Holy Trinity church: Woods, 'Excavations at Wenlock', p. 63.

[40] I quote the text from *ECWM*, p. 160 (cf. BCS 535 and *Historia*, ed. Hart I, lxxii). This passage is corrupt and difficult to translate accurately; on the possible meaning, see below p. 124. Has 'in nomine' been lost before 'omnipotentis dei in celis & sanct[ae] Mari[ae] uirginis'? *Eadburt* appears as *E(a)dburga* in the *Historia* (*ibid.* I, 4, 6 and 67) and in Gregory of Caerwent (for whom see above, p. 35, n. 92). For twelfth-century ideas

The charter then goes on to list the properties acquired by Abbess Eafe and those granted by Æthelbald of Mercia, Ealdred *subregulus* of the Hwicce, Æthelmund son of Ingeld (probably ealdorman of the Hwicce), and Nothheard (ealdorman of the Magonsætan), down to the reign of Burgred of Mercia (852–74), in whose time the 'foundation charter' was perhaps compiled.[41] The charter implies that Cyneburg, sister of the Hwiccian king, Osric, became the first abbess of Gloucester, and was succeeded by her kinswoman Eadburg, who had been the queen of Wulfhere of Mercia (d. 674×675). It was common for queens to return to their native kingdom and enter the religious life, after separating from their husbands[42] or being widowed: an obvious function of the double monasteries was to provide for such women. In fact Wulfhere is also said to have been married to a Kentish princess called Eormenhild, who returned to Kent to become a nun (as did her sister, Merewalh's queen).[43] Presumably either the Hwiccian or the Kentish princess had separated from Wulfhere, enabling him to marry the other. Eafe, the third and final abbess mentioned in the Gloucester 'foundation charter', was presumably another member of the Hwiccian royal dynasty, to judge by her alliterating name. Indeed, the charter says that Æthelbald of Mercia relinquished seven years of his royal refection in the city of Gloucester in recompense for killing 'her kinsman' Æthelmund son of Oswald, and the latter was doubtless Osric's brother Oswald.[44] Dr Schneider has plausibly identified Abbess Eafe with the Hwiccian princess *Eabae* (genitive) who had been married to Æthelwealh, king of the South Saxons, and may well have returned home when Cædwalla killed her consort (before 685).[45] The chronology,

about the history of the house see the letters in *Historia*, ed. Hart II, 110–11 and 115; Sims-Williams, 'People and Places'.

[41] S 1782 (BCS 535). In the Gloucester *Historia* (ed. Hart I, 4) Æthelmund is described as *subregulus Wicciorum*. Note the bequest by Æthelric son of Æthelmund to Gloucester in S 1187 (above, p. 39); in the *Historia*'s account of this his father is styled *rex* (p. 104). The lands granted to Gloucester according to S 1782 are discussed by Taylor, 'Osric', pp. 320–1 (cf. above, p. 38, n. 116); Finberg, *Gloucestershire Studies*, pp. 12–14; and *ECWM*, pp. 161, 162, n. 2, and 165. See also below, p. 145, nn. 8–9.

[42] See above, p. 49 and n. 168.

[43] 'Mildred', ed. Swanton, pp. 23 and 27; Rollason, *Mildrith*, pp. 81 and 87.

[44] See above, p. 35.

[45] Schneider, 'Women', p. 248, n. 19; *HE* IV.13 and 15. She may be the *famula Dei* Eafe to whom Æthelbald granted part of a building with two salt-furnaces at Droitwich according to a lost charter seen at Worcester by Young and Dugdale (S 1824). The Gloucester abbess is *Eua* in Gregory of Caerwent and the *Historia*, ed. Hart I, 7.

though not impossible if she was a very young girl when Æthelwealh married her, is strained, for Eadburg was still abbess in the reign of Coenred (704–9), according to a lost charter cited in the late medieval Gloucester *Historia*; and Gregory of Caerwent, the *Historia* and the 'foundation charter' claim that Eafe followed her as abbess for thirty-three years.[46]

Evidently St Peter's, Gloucester, was intimately associated with the Hwiccian royal dynasty in its heyday. Presided over by some of the most powerful women of the family, it probably served as a focus and symbol of Hwiccian independence. The *Historia* says that Cyneburg was buried beside her brother Osric in front of the altar of St Petronilla, and that Eadburg and Eafe were each buried beside their predecessor and sister.[47] If this is a correct account of their relationship and burial, we have a striking parallel with Jouarre's dynastic crypt and *Généalogie des fondateurs*. It is probably a symptom of the declining prestige of the royal dynasties of the Hwicce and Magonsætan that by the middle of the eighth century both were burying their *reguli* at their episcopal sees, rather than at their royal proprietary monasteries at Wenlock and Gloucester.[48] In 909, when the next royal burial occurred at Gloucester, it was not to St Peter's that Æthelred and Æthelflæd of Mercia translated the body of St Oswald of Northumbria but to their own foundation, St Oswald's, and in all likelihood it was there that they themselves were buried.[49]

As I understand it, the passage of the Gloucester 'foundation charter' quoted above means that Eafe obtained freedoms from royal taxation for the monastic estate – or, if one may take *liberabat* more literally, 'freed' it herself, presumably in her royal capacity. She placed her charter on the altar of St Peter and announced to her community that after her abbacy

---

[46] *Ibid.* 1, 7 and 67; *ECWM*, p. 33 (no. 9); BL, Cotton Vespasian A. v, 195r. On Eadburg see also below, p. 223.

[47] *Historia*, ed. Hart 1, 6–7. On a very late effigy of 'Osricus rex primus fundator hujus monasterii' see Canon Bazeley and M. L. Bazeley, 'Effigies in Gloucester Cathedral', *TBGAS* 27 (1904), 289–326, at 304 and 306. On the question of the identity of Abbess Cyneburg and her connection with a St Cyneburg of Gloucester, see the references in Sims-Williams, 'Cuthswith', pp. 10, n. 3, and 18, n. 3; also Hart, *Historia* 1, lxiv–lxviii; *PNGl* 11, 135; Heighway, 'Saxon Gloucester', p. 376; and 'Anglo-Saxon Gloucester to A.D. 1000', p. 48.

[48] See above, p. 61.

[49] Heighway, 'Anglo-Saxon Gloucester to A.D. 1000', pp. 45–6 and 51, n. 8.

they were to be allowed to elect their head freely.[50] Eafe's concession recalls the vow of Benedict Biscop (d. 689) that no kinsman should succeed him as abbot of Wearmouth and Jarrow. That had been a deliberate and extraordinary break with tradition,[51] and Osric of the Hwicce was truer to the norms of the time in obtaining the right to bequeath Gloucester within his own family ('sibi in perpetuam heredi- tatem possidendum & adhabendum, & post se in suam genelogiam qualicunque manu uoluerit donandam').[52] The Benedictine principle of free election, with its assumption of a community of equals controlling a common endowment, would subvert the dynastic purposes of great foun- dations such as Gloucester, since it could allow them to pass out of their founders' family's control. It is perhaps significant that after the time of Eafe, who promised free elections, the history of St Peter's becomes obscure; the (unreliable) *Historia* says simply that after her death (which it places in 767!) 'abbesses ceased'.[53]

Although a dynastic foundation like Gloucester might well be described as a 'family monastery', this appellation is usually restricted to smaller monasteries. Such a 'family monastery' was created when the head of a family turned his or her household into a monastic community, to be supported by income either from newly given land or from existing family estates (a distinction often blurred in the charters).[54] By virtue of their royal charters these communities enjoyed ecclesiastical tax-immunities, so there was a danger that secular men and women would set themselves up as abbots and abbesses to avoid taxation, possibly with the connivance of kings for whom the granting of charters was an economical way of rewarding supporters. Moreover, even when the intention behind the original foundation was religious, a 'family monastery' would be in peril of being secularized when later generations inherited it; this was sometimes safeguarded in the foundation charter by a clause which stipulated that the

---

50 *Domini* may imply a male head (*dominus*) but could stand for *dominii* from *dominium* 'rule'. *ECWM*, p. 161 thinks that here Eafe 'asks for the prayers of the community'.

51 Bede, *Historia abbatum*, c. 11 (*BOH* I, 375). Cf. above, n. 35. Note, however, Theodore's *Penitential*, VI.1–4 (H&S III, 195).

52 Text in *ECWM*, p. 158 (cf. BCS 60 and *Historia*, ed. Hart I, lxxi–lxxii); discussed by John, *Orbis*, pp. 83–5. Cf. 'in mea genealogia' in S 1413.

53 *Historia*, ed. Hart I, 7. On the inaccuracy of its chronology see *ECWM*, p. 165, n. 2. It certainly exaggerates the desolation of Gloucester after 767: Thacker, 'Chester and Gloucester', p. 208.

54 On the ambiguity of charters, see above, pp. 92 and 96.

estate was eventually to pass to the episcopal see. The bishops, no doubt, did their best to have such clauses included.

Stubbs's survey of 'family monasteries' in the diocese of Worcester, published in 1862, has set the tone for later scholars:

These family monasteries were not intended to be permanent; they were founded plainly for the cheap support of a member of the connexion, and the reversion of them to the Mother Church [of Worcester] in many cases is provided for: possibly it was a condition on which their immunities were purchased from the pious princes, a cheap way of making the best of both worlds.[55]

This appreciation may be unnecessarily grudging. Stubbs's subjective interpretation of the dry facts of the Worcester charters, only one of which refers to a clear scandal (at Withington), is coloured by Bede's categories in his attack on Northumbrian pseudo-monasteries in his *Epistola ad Ecgbertum* of 734.[56] Bede's letter should not, however, be taken at face value. Historians have insufficiently realized that the *Epistola* belongs to a tradition of monastic polemic that goes back at least as far as Cassian, who in his *Conlatio* on the Three Sorts of Monks attempted to distinguish between coenobites, hermits, and 'Sarabaites' (that is, 'persons who have deserted their communities and live each to himself'), and proposed a distinction between the terms *coenobium* and *monasterium* on the grounds that the latter 'is also used to describe the groups of Sarabaites'.[57] Moreover, Bede was writing within a particular political context and, as so often, we have only the polemics of one side. His main theme was the need for more Northumbrian bishops and the difficulty of establishing a new see since kings had already granted laymen so much land for monasteries

---

[55] Stubbs, 'Cathedral, Diocese, and Monasteries', p. 249. Cf. the more balanced assessment by P. Wormald, 'Bede, "Beowulf" and the Conversion of the Anglo-Saxon Aristocracy', in *Bede and Anglo-Saxon England*, ed. R. T. Farrell, BAR 46 (Oxford, 1978), 32–95, at 53–4.

[56] *BOH* I, 413–4; *EHD*, pp. 804–6. See also above, p. 115, and below, p. 147. For parallels in Bede's other writings and elsewhere in England, see *BOH* II, 385–6; A. T. Thacker, 'Bede's Ideal of Reform', in *Ideal and Reality*, ed. Wormald *et al.*, pp. 130–53, at 133 and 150–2, and my review, p. 115.

[57] *Conlationes* XVIII. 7 and 10 (ed. Petschenig, pp. 513–17; trans. Chadwick, *Western Asceticism*, pp. 268 and 270). Cf. Chadwick, *Cassian*, pp. 49–50. Compare the similar attack on 'remnuoth' in Jerome, *Ep.* xxii. 34 (ed. and trans. Wright, *Select Letters*, pp. 134–7); cf. Lorenz, 'Anfänge', p. 8, and Kelly, *Jerome*, p. 102. Like Cassian in *Conlationes* XVIII. 5 (ed. Petschenig, p. 509; trans. Chadwick, *Western Asceticism*, p. 266), Bede found the first coenobites in Acts IV. 32; see *BOH* II, 245 and 388.

which were free from secular taxation and 'ascribed to them in hereditary right' by charters. He therefore gives reasons to justify shutting down irregular monasteries and rescinding their charters. He presses into service what must have been commonplace secular arguments against church land-owning in general: that it took land from the aristocracy and diminished the supplies of fighting men. Thus in Gaul, Chilperic had exclaimed,

look how the *fiscus* is impoverished and how all our wealth is in the hands of churches; only bishops reign nowadays and our honour is dead![58]

And in Spain St Fructuosus had been attacked for having so many estates and monks that soon there would be no one left to 'set out on a public expedition'.[59] Such arguments could be levelled against regular communities just as much as against irregular ones.[60] No doubt they were heard when Bishop Ecgberht and his brother King Eadberht confiscated three monasteries, which an abbess had left to a 'religious abbot Forthred', and gave them to Forthred's brother, a lay magnate.[61] Bede also objects to the sinfulness and lack of a proper rule in the pseudo-monasteries, accusing the false monks of professing a monastic life for reasons of hypocrisy and to indulge in licentiousness (such as marriage). These sorts of objections, however, have always arisen whenever stricter and less strict forms of monasticism have existed side by side,[62] and may say as much about the intolerance of the 'regulars' as about the sinfulness of the 'irregulars'. Such literature has its own rhetorical traditions and we have to read between the lines. Cassian's denunciation of 'Sarabaites' begins with the statement that they 'are descended from Ananias and Sapphira' (Acts V. 1–11), a jibe also

---

[58] *HF* VI. 46, quoted by Wallace-Hadrill, *Early Germanic Kingship*, p. 65.

[59] *Vita S. Fructuosi*, cited by E. A. Thompson, *The Goths in Spain* (Oxford, 1969), p. 263; Hunter Blair, *World of Bede*, pp. 135–6; Brooks, 'Military Obligations', p. 74, n. 2. Cf. Edwards, 'Two Documents', p. 14.

[60] This was realized by Wallace-Hadrill, *Early Germanic Kingship*, pp. 65 and 91, and Roper, 'Wilfrid's Landholdings', pp. 70–1, but they did not draw out the implications for a critique of Bede's polemic.

[61] See the papal rebuke of 757×758; *EHD*, no. 184.

[62] E.g. Jerome, *Ep.* xxii (above, n. 57); Isidore's six classes of monk (discussed by W. S. Porter, 'Early Spanish Monasticism', *Laudate* 10 (1932), 67, who points to sources in Cassian and Augustine); the *Dicta de genere monachorum* (discussed by C. M. Aherne, *Valerio of Bierzo: An Ascetic of the Late Visigothic Period* (Washington, 1949), pp. 51–6); the polemics of the English tenth-century reform; the twelfth-century controversy over the status of Augustinian canons; etc.

used by Bede, and, like Bede, Cassian accuses them of being hypocritical imitators of true monks:

They make a public profession of renunciation, and acquire the credit of the title, and then go on living in their homes just as before, carrying on the same work; or they build cells for themselves, call them 'monasteries' and live in them as they please . . . They toil, not to offer their produce or earnings to the steward of the community, but to save money for themselves.

Yet, after expatiating on their extravagance and hoarding, Cassian continues with a revealing concessive clause:

Even granting that their ill-gotten earnings are sometimes distributed in better ways than these, it is still true that they are not aspiring after goodness.[63]

In the seventh-century Spanish *Regula monastica communis* attributed to Fructuosus there is another revealing clause, which admits that the founders of 'family monasteries' might have pious motives:

It is the custom of some *out of fear of hell* to form monasteries in their own homes, and with their wives, children, servants and neighbours, to unite themselves under a sacramental vow and, as we have said, in their very own vills both dedicate churches with the name of the martyrs and call them 'monasteries' by a false name. We nevertheless do not call these 'monasteries' but the perdition of souls and the ruin of the church . . . When you come across such men as these, you may believe them to be not monks but hypocrites and heretics . . . And because they live by their own whim, they do not wish to be subject to any of the elders, and they give none of their own substance to the poor but rush like paupers to seize other people's goods in order to make more profit with their wives and children than when they were in the world.[64]

The very similar polemics of Cassian, Fructuosus and Bede are best regarded as part of a dialectic of the larger, more regimented monasteries, with which the future of Western monasticism lay, against surviving manifestations of a smaller, more informal monasticism, out of which it

---

[63] *Conlationes* XVIII. 7 (ed. Petschenig, pp. 513–16; trans. Chadwick, *Western Asceticism*, pp. 268–70). But for ascetic criticism of almsgiving as worldly see Rousseau, *Ascetics*, pp. 138 and 209.

[64] PL 87, 1110. This passage has been compared with Bede's account of spurious monasteries by Hunter Blair, *World of Bede*, p. 136, and J. N. Hillgarth, 'Popular Religion in Visigothic Spain', in *Visigothic Spain: New Approaches*, ed. E. James (Oxford, 1980), pp. 3–60, at 47.

had itself grown and which it wished to stabilize or discredit.[65] The inability of monastic writers to comprehend the historical development of institutions and their tendency to regard anomalies as recent abuses and aberrations prevented them from seeing the 'family monastery' in a sympathetic historical perspective. Had they done so, they might have traced the ideal behind the 'family monastery' back to the beginnings of Western monasticism in the fourth century. We hear from Jerome, for instance, of his Roman friend Marcella who turned her villa into a sort of convent and was joined by many pious Roman women in this undertaking, which was a transitional stage between the custom of the individual consecrated virgin living with her family and the fully constituted nunnery of later times.[66] Jerome refers to a comparable group of virgins gathered round his friend Paula as her *domestica ecclesia* and describes Lea, another such friend, as *monasterii princeps*.[67] These manifestations of the monastic ideal fitted so easily into the structure of secular society as hardly to be recognizable as 'monastic' by later standards. As in the 'false' monasteries denounced by Cassian, Fructuosus and Bede, the leader was the proprietor of the *villa* and naturally, therefore, in charge of recruitment. One may contrast Jerome, complacently implying that Marcella has her servants living the religious life under her authority, with Bede, denouncing 'lay' abbots for assuming authority over 'those of their own followers whom they can persuade to promise them the obedience of a monk and receive the tonsure'.[68]

---

[65] Lorenz, 'Anfänge'; Rousseau, *Ascetics*, pp. 185 and 223. Cf. Stancliffe, *Martin*, p. 272: 'It was the ascetics *praised* by Sulpicius who were the innovators, the oddity, while those whom he criticized were leading a way of life which had been highly regarded earlier in the church's history.'

[66] Ferrari, *Early Roman Monasteries*, pp. xiv–xv and references; Metz, *Consécration des vierges*, pp. 41–93, esp. 82–3; Lorenz, 'Anfänge', pp. 3–8, 27–8, etc; and Kelly, *Jerome*, pp. 91–103. See also Rousseau, *Ascetics*, pp. 80–1, 106, n. 30 and 143–4; Stancliffe, *Martin*, pp. 29 and 145. Meyer, *Athanasius: Life of St Antony*, p. 107, n. 17, notes the ambiguity of the first reference to *parthenon* in a Christian sense (c. 3), which may refer either to a house or to a group of virgins.

[67] See respectively Jerome, *Epp.* xxx. 14 and xxiii. 2 (ed. Hilberg 1, 248 and 212), cited by Kelly, *Jerome*, pp. 97 and 93. See also Rousseau, *Ascetics*, pp. 112 and 123–4; Stancliffe, *Martin*, p. 299, n. 13.

[68] 'Si quae ancillae sunt comites propositi tui, ne erigaris aduersus eas, ne inferis ut domina. Unum sponsum habere coepistis, simul psallitis Christo, simul corpus accipitis, cur mensa diuersa sit?' (*Ep.* xxii. 29, ed. Wright, *Select Letters*, p. 122). Cf. Lorenz, 'Anfänge', pp. 6, 27 and 35, n. 70; *BOH* 1, 416; *EHD*, p. 806. On *satellites* 'followers' see Stevenson, *Asser*, p. 337.

Some historical connection between the early Roman and Anglo-Saxon 'family monastery' is not impossible. The tradition of the domestic monastery probably persisted at Rome down to the time of Gregory the Great, whose family lived in the same district as Paula. Gregory is known to have turned over patricians' houses to abbots and abbesses for them to gather their communities in, very much in the earlier tradition, and he himself says that three of his aunts, though consecrated, continued to live in their own home.[69] A similar monastic policy may therefore have been favoured by the Gregorian mission in Kent and have spread thence into the rest of southern England. On the other hand, 'family monasteries' may equally well have appeared independently in England as individual priests and missionaries were received into noble households. It was not uncommon for pious laymen to build churches (*ecclesiae*) on their estates and have them consecrated by bishops,[70] and the setting up of a monastery would be an easy next step; bishops were ready to give their approval to the 'false' lay monasteries, as Bede admitted to Ecgberht, and the Council of *Clofesho* in 747 regarded them tolerantly and pragmatically.[71] Because of the pressure of the kindred system, a pious layman and prospective abbot might have no choice but either to allow the abbacy to descend through his kin or not to establish a monastery at all. It is therefore not surprising that hereditary 'family monasteries' sprang up with the support of bishops and kings, despite the formal pronouncements in favour of freedom of election in texts such as Theodore's *Penitential*.[72]

Whether or not there is any connection between them, the comparison between the early Roman and early Anglo-Saxon 'family monasteries' is sufficient to disprove Stubbs's assumption, inherited from Bede, that they were necessarily bogus or second-rate. Indeed, there is only one case of scandal among the early 'family monasteries' of the Hwicce and Magonsæ-tan and here, at Withington on the *Tillath* (upper Coln), the impropriety

---

[69] Petersen, *Dialogues*, pp. 67–8 and 159; Ferrari, *Early Roman Monasteries*, pp. 11 and 176–8 (cf. *ibid.*, pp. 19–20, for Gregory II turning his own house into a monastery); Metz, *Consécration des vierges*, pp. 86–8 (citing PL 76, 1290–1). One of Gregory I's aunts later abandoned her vows and married 'conductor agrorum suorum' (*ibid.*, col. 1292). On the early Canterbury community see Brooks, *Canterbury*, pp. 87–91.

[70] *HE* v. 4–5 (cf. Bede's prose *Vita S. Cuthberti*, c. 34 (ed. Colgrave, *Two Lives*, p. 262)). But Blair minimizes the importance of 'private' churches served by a single resident priest: 'Minster Churches in the Landscape', pp. 56–7; 'Local Churches', pp. 267–8. For consecrations see below, p. 351, n. 90.

[71] H&S III, 364, c. 5; Taylor, 'Berkeley Minster', p. 75.   [72] See above, n. 51.

seems to have been due to a laywoman, not a self-styled abbess. Moreover, our source, a report of a synod in 736 or 737 – the very period of Bede's letter to Ecgberht – indicates no episcopal disapproval of the constitution of the 'family monastery' itself:

Æthelred, the most glorious king of the Mercians [resigned 704], with his companion, Oshere, sub-king of the Hwicce, having been asked by him, conferred into ecclesiastical right with free possession land of 20 hides by the river whose name is *Tillath* to two nuns namely Dunne and her daughter Bucge, for the establishment[73] of a monastery on it, for the forgiveness of his sins, and strengthened this their donation with the subscription of his own hand. But the aforesaid handmaid of God, Dunne, granted indisputably [with the knowledge and permission of the most reverend Bishop Ecgwine[74]] the monastery which had been built on the aforesaid estate, with its lands and also the charter descriptive of the land, over which she at that time alone presided [i.e. without Bucge], into the possession of her daughter's daughter, when herself on the point of death. But because this grand-daughter [Hrothwaru] was still young in age, she [Dunne] entrusted the keeping of the charter of the enrolled land, and also all the charge of the monastery until she should reach a riper age, to the girl's mother, a married woman. When the grand-daughter asked that the charter should be given back, her mother, not wishing to give it back, replied that it had been stolen. When at length the whole business was brought to the holy synod of the sacerdotal council, the whole venerable council decreed, along with the most reverend Archbishop Nothhelm, that the charter of donation, either of the kings or of the above-mentioned handmaid of God, Dunne, was to be most clearly written out and given to the aforesaid abbess, Hrothwaru, and that her possession of the monastery was to be most secure; the person who presumed to withdraw that original charter of the assignment of the land, either by theft or by fraudulently removing it by any means whatever, having been undoubtedly condemned and accursed by the decree of the most holy synod. And the holy synod decrees this, that after her death, this deed with the land is to be given back to the episcopal see of the city of Worcester, as it was settled before by her ancestors.[75]

Abbess Dunne, perhaps the eponym of Donnington (SP/1928) near Stow

73 *Ad construendum*; Whitelock translates 'construction', but cf. Sims-Williams, 'Wilfrid', p. 169, n. 31.
74 This clause is from S 1255.
75 S 1429; *EHD*, no. 68. On Withington see Finberg, *Lucerna*, pp. 21–65; *Gloucestershire Studies*, pp. 11–14; *Gloucestershire Landscape*, pp. 57–8; Millward and Robinson, *West Midlands*, pp. 183–92.

on the Wold,[76] was presumably a widow, and her daughter Bucge probably predeceased her (unless she left the monastery). There is no reason to identify Bucge with Dunne's unnamed married daughter, the mother of Abbess Hrothwaru.[77] It is this married daughter alone who is criticized by the council, and no disapproval of Dunne's bequest of the monastery to her own grand-daughter is expressed; this was doubtless taken for granted,[78] and it evidently had the approval of Ecgwine, bishop of Worcester.

The final clause – assuming it is genuine, for the text is from Worcester's own cartulary – shows that a reversion to Worcester had been agreed from the first precisely in order to avoid secularization of the estate by parties such as Hrothwaru's mother. This was successful. By 774 Hrothwaru had made over Withington to Bishop Milred and in that year he gave it to Æthelburg, abbess of Twyning, on condition that both monasteries reverted to Worcester after her death.[79] This Abbess Æthelburg was clearly the member of the Hwiccian royal family of this name who soon afterwards leased Fladbury monastery on similar terms.[80] She thus controlled a very considerable federation of monasteries. All three duly reverted to the see. Between 780 and 796 Twyning was handed in by Offa's *dux* Ælfred, who was presumably Æthelburg's heir,[81] and in 814 Bishop Deneberht was able to give the three hides of Twyning with its ten hides west of the Severn to King Coenwulf in return for tax relief on Worcester and its dependent *monasteria*.[82] Fladbury seems to have come back to the see via Coenwulf, for some unknown reason, for, to complete the bargain of

---

76 *DEPN*, p. 148; Sims-Williams, 'Cuthswith', p. 18, n. 3; B. Cox, 'The Significance of the Distribution of English Place-Names in *hām* in the Midlands and East Anglia', in *Place-Name Evidence*, ed. Cameron, pp. 55–98, at 73, n. 13; cf. Gelling, *Signposts*, pp. 178–9.

77 I agree here with Lapidge, 'Remnants', p. 816, but the identification of Dunne's daughter with Centwine of Wessex's daughter Bugga, on whose church Aldhelm composed a poem, is rightly rejected by Duckett, *Saints and Scholars*, p. 67, n. 171, and *EHD*, p. 494. Note also that Aldhelm makes no mention of Dunne, though she is more prominent in the charters than Bucge, whom S 1255 omits altogether.

78 Cf. *HE* v. 3 for an abbess whose daughter was abbess-elect.

79 S 1255 (*EHD*, no. 75), corrected from a twelfth-century abstract (see above, p. 37, n. 113).

80 See above, p. 37. Fladbury seems to be an episcopal manor in 780 in S 118, but this is a forgery; cf. below, p. 163, n. 94.

81 Dugdale, *Monasticon* I, 608, dated between the beginning of Heathored's episcopate (see below, n. 110) and Offa's death. See above, p. 37, n. 113.

82 S 172.

814, Coenwulf promised that after his death (which occurred in 821) the see should have Fladbury together with half the lands of Twyning, which were then to be used for the support of the church (*æcclesia*) at Fladbury.[83] Two of Æthelburg's monastic estates were thereby partially recombined for the support of a single church, at Fladbury, and the latter became a permanent part of the medieval Worcester estate – to the lasting chagrin of the neighbouring monastery at Evesham.[84] Withington likewise reverted to Worcester, though there is no record of the transaction, and it was at the centre of a large Worcester estate of about 15 square miles, described in bounds of the early eleventh century or earlier; the bounds show that the Withington estate also embraced the former monastery at Dowdeswell.[85] Like many other early monasteries, Withington was an important parish church in the later Middle Ages, with ancient rights over neighbouring churches. At what point it ceased to be a 'monastery' and became a 'minster' is impossible to say, and in any case would depend on one's definition of those terms.[86]

The Withington affair 'shows the limitations of this kind of monastery-making', according to Eric John, and 'shows the system at its worst'.[87]

---

[83] S 185. As pointed out in *ECWM*, p. 99, this is the continuation of S 172, which precedes it in the cartulary. The calendar of grants in Dugdale, *Monasticon* I, 608, col. 2, wrongly supposes that Coenwulf returned the *whole* of Twyning to Worcester. In fact the 3 hides of Twyning formed part of the Domesday estates of Winchcombe Abbey, Coenwulf's own foundation (or refoundation). See Dugdale, *Monasticon* II, 298 and 300; and below, p. 166. C. S. Taylor pointed out (see *Gloucestershire Studies*, ed. Finberg, p. 43) that the Avon only divided Gloucestershire and Worcestershire where it ran between the cathedral estate of Bredon and the Winchcombe estate of Twyning, in the two shires respectively; if Twyning had formed part of the cathedral estate, it would have been in Worcestershire, not an anomalous tongue of Gloucestershire. See *PNGl* II, 71; *PNWo*, map.

[84] The Evesham claim that Ecgwine acquired Fladbury for Evesham from Æthelred (e.g. S 1250–1; *Chronicon de Evesham*, ed. Macray, p. 71) may be rejected, but possibly some of the genuine history of Fladbury was known at Evesham: see above, p. 92.

[85] S 1556. Cf. Finberg, *ECWM*, p. 84 and *Lucerna*, pp. 22–3. Some of the territory was lost by 1066.

[86] *Ibid.*, p. 24; F. S. Hockaday, 'Withington Peculiar', *TBGAS* 40 (1917), 89–113. On such churches in western Mercia in general see Blair, 'Secular Minster Churches', p. 116, and 'Minster Churches in the Landscape', p. 40; Bond, 'Church and Parish', p. 134. Since, as Blair notes (*Minster Churches and Parish Churches*, p. 2), not all later '"old-style" minsters' were 'primary', I have resisted the temptation to argue back to before 800 from unsupported later evidence.

[87] John, *Orbis*, p. 86, and 'Problems', p. 61.

This 'worst' is hardly scandalous, however. Nothing emerges to impugn either the motives of the bishops and the abbesses concerned, or the quality of religious life at Withington, about which we have no information whatsoever. If Dunne's bequest of Withington monastery to her own grand-daughter seems irregular by the standards of Benedict Biscop and Theodore, it is no more irregular than the bishops' later transactions involving this and other monasteries that reverted to the see. The 'family monastery' cannot be said to have been discredited. The attempts by Stubbs and others to distinguish between 'family monasteries', founded out of worldly policy, and larger monasteries, founded out of devotion, seem quite anachronistic when one considers the mixed functions of great dynastic monasteries such as Gloucester.

The tax advantages of holding ecclesiastical land were only relative, both in theory and even more in practice. For example, in 699 Wihtred, king of Kent, issued a general privilege to the churches and monasteries in his kingdom, granting them freedom 'from every exaction of public tribute'; yet the 'honour and obedience' he expected from them in return may well have involved substantial expenditure,[88] and a charter of 732 still speaks of the 'royal right . . . which is known to be general in all church lands in Kent'.[89] This *ius regium* probably included, at the bare minimum, an obligation to provide men for army service, fortress-work and bridge-work (or payment in lieu), and may also have included various food-rents.[90] In a letter to St Boniface, *c.* 720, a Kentish abbess and her daughter describe how the service (*seruitium*) of the king and others added to the problems of governing their double monastery:

To thee alone have we wished to tell how we are weighed down by a crushing load of misery, and by the distraction of worldly affairs . . . It is not so much thought on our own souls, but, what is more difficult and serious, thought on the souls of all those of different sex and age committed to us . . . And to the care of souls are added difficulties with household affairs and the disputes and discords which the enemy of all goodness sows . . . Besides, poverty and the scarcity of temporal things grind us and the barrenness of our land; and the hostility of the king before

---

[88] S 20, discussed by Brooks, 'Military Obligations', pp. 75 and 79, and *Canterbury*, pp. 78, 183–4 and 192; Scharer, *Königsurkunde*, pp. 97–100. Cf. Edwards, 'Two Documents', pp. 1–9 and 13–14.

[89] S 23, discussed by Brooks, 'Military Obligations', pp. 75, 78 and 82, and Scharer, *Königsurkunde*, pp. 106–10.

[90] See the whole discussion by Brooks, 'Military Obligations'.

whom we are accused by those who envy us . . . So, too, the service of the king and queen, of the bishop and the *prefectus*, the *potestates* and the *comites* . . . Added to all these sorrows is the loss of our friends and the band of our relatives and kinsfolk. Neither son nor brother, father nor uncle have we, but an only daughter, almost destitute of everything valued in this life, an aged mother, her sister and their brother's son. He is very unfortunate, because of his own disposition and the hatred which the king bears his race. There is no one else of our kin, for in divers ways God has removed them.[91]

The monasteries of the Hwicce and Magonsætan were probably similarly placed. Before the mid-eighth century there are only a few immunity clauses, in the Hwiccian charters, and these are of doubtful authenticity.[92] This lack may well be because the early charters were all ostensibly for ecclesiastical purposes and were therefore assumed to convey such privileges implicitly – at least in theory.[93] Royal practice was another matter, as we can see from the letters which Boniface sent from the safety of Germany *c.* 747; he protests against Æthelbald of Mercia violating the privileges of churches and monasteries, appropriating their revenues, allowing his reeves and gesiths to impose 'greater violence and servitude on monks and priests than any other Christian kings before', and compelling monks to join work-parties on royal halls and vills.[94] The king seems to have admitted some of these accusations at the so-called Synod of Gumley in 749, when he issued a privilege which was similar to that of Wihtred of Kent fifty years before, but also echoed Boniface. By this privilege Æthelbald forbade the consumption of food-rents at monasteries and churches, unless given voluntarily, granted them immunity from royal works other than bridge-building and the defence of fortifications, and ordered his *principes* to remove all the tribulations which could harm the church.[95] This privilege may not have applied outside Mercia proper, but similar ones were probably issued in the sub-kingdoms, to judge by the

---

91 *Ep.* xiv (Tangl, pp. 22–3); trans. Kylie, *English Correspondence*, pp. 62–3 (the letter of Eangyth and her daughter Haeaburg *cognomento* Bucge; on their identity cf. Sims-Williams, 'Recension'). On the terminology see Thacker, 'Some Terms for Noblemen', p. 213.

92 Brooks, 'Military Obligations', p. 77, n. 1; Scharer, *Königsurkunde*, p. 45.

93 *Ibid.*, pp. 45–7.

94 Boniface, *Epp.* lxxiii and lxxviii (Tangl, pp. 146–55 and 161–70, respectively); Brooks, 'Military Obligations', p. 77. See also below, p. 271.

95 S 92, discussed by Brooks, 'Military Obligations', pp. 76–8; Scharer, *Königsurkunde*, pp. 188–95, and 'Intitulationes', pp. 49 and 61–2; Vollrath, *Synoden*, p. 145, n. 70.

wording of charters issued by the Hwiccian sub-king Uhtred in 767 and 770.[96] Even so, such privileges are unlikely to have removed all the troubles which burdened the monasteries of the Hwicce and Magonsætan, especially when massive royal expenditure like the construction of Offa's Dyke was in progress. Significantly, in the second half of the century a scribe, who was perhaps from western Mercia – for he or she wrote an awkward Anglo-Saxon half uncial with 'a distinct Celtic flavour'[97] – found it necessary to copy one of Boniface's letters of protest together with the record of the Synod of Gumley.[98]

A charter of Offa, granting land in Gloucestershire to his thegn Æthelmund in 793×796, shows that he regarded army-service as well as work on bridges and the defence of fortresses as an obligation on all his people without exception.[99] In 814 Bishop Deneberht of Worcester had to pay King Coenwulf to relieve the *monasteria* of his diocese from food-rents,[100] evidence that such renders were not quite as 'voluntary' as Æthelbald had maintained at Gumley. Indeed, two years later, when he granted an estate to Deneberht, Coenwulf was still excepting food-rent (*pascua regis et principis uel subditorum eorum*) from the attached privileges.[101] Later bishops were obliged to obtain exemptions from other burdens for the *monasteria* under their control: exemption from feeding royal huntsmen,

[96] See Brooks, 'Military Obligations', pp. 76 and 77, n. 1; Scharer, *Königsurkunde*, pp. 46, 171 n. 54, and 194–5.

[97] *CLA* II, no. 229. William of Malmesbury quotes all three of the English documents in the manuscript, and H&S III, 376 suggest that he may have used this very manuscript. Cf. Levison, *England and the Continent*, pp. 280–1; Thomson, *William of Malmesbury*, p. 44.

[98] Oxford, Bodleian Library, Arch. Selden B. 26, fol. 34 + BL, Cotton Otho A.i. The other contents were the decrees of the 747 Council of *Clofesho* and extracts from Gregory's *Regula pastoralis*. See *CLA* II, nos. 188 and 229; N. R. Ker, 'Membra Disiecta, Second Series', *British Museum Quarterly* 14 (1939–40), 79–86, at 79–80; Brooks, 'Military Obligations', pp. 76, n. 1, and 77, n. 3; Scharer, *Königsurkunde*, pp. 188–9 and 194–5; Vollrath, *Synoden*, p. 151, n. 84. One wonders whether the eighth-century *Regula pastoralis* fragment, Worcester Cathedral Library, Add. 3 (*CLA* II, no. 264), was of similar origin? It is of Welsh or Border provenance (Atkins and Ker, *Catalogus*, p. 70), and Brown, 'Irish Element', p. 108, cites it as evidence of the diffusion of Lindisfarne-style 'Phase II half-uncial' to the Midlands.

[99] S 139, discussed by Stenton, *Latin Charters*, p. 58, and Brooks, 'Military Obligations', pp. 73, n. 3, and 78. Whitelock, 'Pre-Viking Age Church', pp. 21–2, dates this charter to 793×795. On Æthelmund see above, p. 38.

[100] See above, pp. 132–3. Cf. Stenton, *Anglo-Saxon England*, p. 289.   [101] S 180.

horsemen and 'boys who lead hounds' for Stratford in 844; exemption from feeding emissaries such as the Welsh border patrol (if that is the meaning of *Walhfæreld*) for Blockley, in exchange for 300 shillings, in 855 (a year when 'the pagans were in the province of Wreocensætan', stretching King Burgred's finances); and, in 875, exemption, for the whole of the diocese of the Hwicce, from feeding the king's horses 'and those who lead them'.[102]

The independent monasteries also had to buy such privileges. We do not know the nature of the privilege which Ealdorman Beornnoth obtained from Coenwulf for Pershore, but in 836 Wiglaf released Hanbury from duties such as constructing royal vills and supporting *fæstingmen* (royal officers),[103] in 862(?) Gloucester ceded Burgred ten hides at Fairford 'for freedom from his horses', and in 883 Æthelred, ealdorman of the Mercians, granted the abbot and community of Berkeley 'remission for ever of the tribute that they are still obliged to pay to the king, namely from the portion of the king's *feorm* which was still left unexempted, in clear ale, and in beer, in honey, in bullocks, swine and sheep'.[104] For a rough idea of the original size and nature of the king's *feorm* on a community like Berkeley we may compare the dues which a nearby estate of sixty hides at Westbury-on-Trym was expected to render to Offa's royal *tun* in 793×796:

Two tuns full of pure ale and a coomb full of mild ale and a coomb full of Welsh ale, and seven oxen and six wethers and 40 cheeses and six long *peru* and 30 ambers of unground corn and four ambers of meal.[105]

Dyer notes that, although the corn and meal would be perhaps only seventeen acres' produce judging by later medieval yields, the animals alone 'represent a heavier burden of taxation than was demanded by kings from church estates in the later middle ages'.[106]

---

[102] S 198 (dated by Whitelock, 'Pre-Viking Age Church', p. 18, n. 1), 207 and 215. For the pagans (Danes) see S 206.

[103] For Pershore see above, p. 95. For Hanbury see S 190. The similar Bredon privilege (S 193) probably refers to Breedon-on-the-Hill (cf. S 197); see Sims-Williams, 'People and Places'.

[104] S 1782 (cf. *ECWM*, p. 162, n. 2) and S 218.

[105] S 146. Cf. Stenton, *Anglo-Saxon England*, p. 288; Sawyer, 'Royal *tun*', pp. 275 and n. 12 and 280; Scharer, *Königsurkunde*, pp. 277–8. Compare the *feorm* on 10 hides in the Laws of Ine, §70.1 (*EHD*, p. 406). Cf. Harmer, *Documents*, p. 104.

[106] Dyer, *Lords and Peasants*, pp. 16 and 29. See also Hooke, *Hwicce*, pp. 90–1.

Bishops, as well as kings, made fiscal and other demands on the monasteries. The Kentish abbess, in her letter quoted above, complains to Boniface about the *seruitium episcopi*. Bede writes to Ecgberht that everyone had to pay *tributa* to a bishop, even in remote hamlets where no one saw him from one year to the next;[107] his stress on exemplary poor bishops in the *Historia ecclesiastica* may be a reaction against the wealth of the bishops of his own day.[108] We know that bishops of Worcester could demand yearly food-rent by 'episcopal right' from the monasteries in their diocese,[109] perhaps as they moved round on their diocesan visitation. This emerges clearly in a dispute in 803 between the bishops of Hereford and Worcester over two (otherwise unknown) monasteries in Worcester diocese, Cheltenham (at Prestbury, the 'priests' *burg*'?) and Beckford:

In the year of our Lord's incarnation 803, indiction 11 – that is, the seventh year of the reign of Cenwulf, pious king of the Mercians – a synodal council was held at *Clovesho*, Archbishop Æthelheard presiding . . . There, among several other matters, a dispute arose between Deneberht, bishop of the church at Worcester, and Wulfheard, bishop of Hereford. Now, Cheltenham and Beckford are monasteries in the diocese of Deneberht, which formerly, in old times, were given to the church of Hereford. In these, Deneberht demanded that his right of refection (*suam pastum*), which belonged to him by episcopal right, should be restored to him. Wulfheard, on the other hand, said he ought not to give him any refection, nor had his predecessors ever had any refection there; and, if it was ever so, now for thirty years and more no-one had ever either demanded or received such refection from him or his predecessors. Then Deneberht narrated with his witness how Bishop Wermund [of Worcester, 775–c. 778] received refection at Beckford, and Hathored [780–99], in the same way, at Cheltenham; how, moreover, Wulfheard himself gave money (*pecuniam*) to him, instead of the refection; and these things he proved with witness. When, in this way, they asserted many things on this side and on that, it came to speech that the archbishop asked Deneberht to give up, for his sake, half of this right of refection, so that he should receive his refection always, one year at Beckford, and the second at Cheltenham. Then he replied that he wished and ought in all things to obey his precepts, yet with this limitation, in the witness of the whole synod, to give it for his life only and no longer; and to confirm this in writing, that all his successors may know that

---

[107] *BOH* I, 410; *EHD*, p. 802.   [108] Campbell, *Essays*, pp. 49–51.

[109] Cf. Stenton *CP*, p. 187, n. 1. I do not have any evidence for monasteries distributing tithes to the poor themselves instead of paying them to the bishop. Cf. Constable, *Monastic Tithes*, p. 201.

he never neglects any thing which rightly pertains to the advantage of the church at Worcester . . .[110]

The episcopal rights claimed here by Deneberht may be the *seruitium episcopi* that the Kentish abbess lamented. They must certainly be distinguished from the illegitimate confiscation of monastic properties by bishops that was forbidden at the Synod of Hertford and elsewhere.[111]

Bishops sought more than the right of refection from monasteries. Some monasteries, like Beckford and Cheltenham, became episcopal estates. Over others the diocesan bishops exercised wide-ranging influence, with the evident aim of eliminating a rival source of religious authority.[112] Nevertheless, there is little evidence of fundamental conflict between monastic and episcopal interests in the period.[113] Bede was a monk, but his *Epistola ad Ecgbertum* 'shows how far [he] was from later monastic opinion on episcopal interference'.[114] The situation in early Anglo-Saxon England differed greatly from that which gave rise to the conflicts between bishops and monasteries in Columbanus's Gaul or post-Conquest England. Monasticism did not intrude upon an ancient episcopate in seventh-century England; both grew up together and needed to make common cause against lay power. Ecclesiastical legislation such as Theodore's *Penitential* was intended to limit gross episcopal interference with monasteries, yet equally it was intended to encourage bishops to exercise their canonical

---

110 S 1431; trans. H. Adams *et al.*, *Essays in Anglo-Saxon Law* (Boston, Mass., 1876), pp. 320–1. 'For his sake' (*sibi*) may mean Wulfheard, rather than the archbishop as Birch understood it. For Wermund's obit cf. below, p. 158, n. 75. Heathored's dates are given as 781–798 or ?800 in *HBC*[3], p. 223, but S 120 belongs to December 780 (*EHD*, p. 505; Scharer, *Königsurkunde*, p. 251) and S 155 shows him still active in 799 (cf. *Worcester Cartulary*, ed. Darlington, p. 2, n. 5). The absence of a bishop of Worcester in 799 in S 154 suggests that he died that year (see below, p. 171, n. 127). According to the calendar in Dugdale, *Monasticon* I, 608, Offa exempted Beckford for Worcester; this is difficult to square with Hereford's possession. Bannister, *Cathedral Church*, pp. 18–19, and *PNGl* II, 110, note that Prestbury, in Cheltenham hundred, was a Hereford episcopal manor in Domesday Book. On the other hand, S 1283 suggests that it was a Worcester estate *c.* 900 (see below, p. 157). For *burg* 'monastery', see above, p. 93, n. 24.

111 *HE* IV. 5. Cf. Brooks, *Canterbury*, pp. 176–7.

112 Cf. Schneider, 'Women', p. 304: 'Independent monasteries which acted in concord with the royal family, promoting saints and working politically hand in hand with the secular powers, excluding the representatives of the unfolding church hierarchy, were unacceptable to the bishops'.

113 See Stenton, *Anglo-Saxon England*, p. 165. 114 *EHD*, p. 799.

rights of withholding consecration from unsuitable abbots and abbesses and of passing judgement on inadequate monastic observances.[115] Bishops were assumed to be there to counterbalance lay control. They were, as Bede remarks, without disagreement,

in the habit of saying that what is done in the various monasteries does not belong to the charge of kings, nor to the jurisdiction of any secular rulers, but solely to [their] episcopal enquiry and investigation, unless it happen that anyone in the monasteries is found to have offended against those very rulers.[116]

This attitude also received papal backing. In 748, for example, Pope Zacharias wrote to certain Frankish nobles:

As to monasteries built by you or erected by the devotion of the faithful: it is ordered that if a monk or nun, who happens to be a member of the founder's family, be set to preside there, whether as abbot or as abbess, he or she shall be consecrated by the bishop of the city. And when the monastic community has been established there, if after the death of the abbot or abbess a successor is chosen by the community, he or she is nevertheless to be consecrated by the bishop and not inducted by the founder of the cloister; for what has once been offered to God should remain fixed and inviolate under the rule of the bishop.[117]

Numerous documents from the Worcester archive show the influence that the bishops had on the development of monasticism, overseeing abbatial succession, eliminating lay control by securing reversions to the see, and enlisting royal support for such policies. Bishop Ecgwine's involvement with the monasteries at Withington and Fladbury is typical. Æthelred and Oshere had granted Withington to Dunne and her daughter on condition that it reverted to the see eventually, and when Dunne wished to bequeath the monastery to her grand-daughter she had to obtain Bishop Ecgwine's permission.[118] The forty-four hides of Fladbury had been entrusted by Æthelred to Bishop Oftfor in 697 or a little later,

so that just as when the land was first handed over, so again through his diligence the most proper life of monks living on it under the rule of an abbot may be recovered.[119]

[115] H&S III, 195. Cf. Brooks, *Canterbury*, pp. 175–80.
[116] *BOH* I, 418; *EHD*, p. 807.
[117] *Ep.* lxxxiii (Tangl, pp. 186–7); trans. Emerton, *Letters of Boniface*, p. 154.
[118] See above, pp. 96 and 131–2.
[119] S 76. Cf. above, p. 92. On the date cf. Sims-Williams, 'Cuthswith', pp. 9, n. 1, and 16, n. 1. For discussion of authenticity see Scharer, *Königsurkunde*, pp. 153–4.

Apparently, then, some earlier monastery (founded perhaps by an eponymous abbess Flæde?)[120] had come to an end, and Æthelred was now
looking to his bishop to see to its revival and to consecrate an abbot for it.
The role of overseer passed to Ecgwine, Oftfor's successor, who leased the
monastery to Æthelheard, one of the Hwiccian princes, in return for
twenty hides at Stratford held by ecclesiastical law (*in ius æcclesiasticum*),
provided that the rules of monastic life (*coenobialis uitæ statuta*) were kept at
Fladbury and that it reverted to the episcopal see at Worcester after
Æthelheard's death.[121]

Such documentation of the bishops' role tends to come from their own
archives, but the general impression seems consistent and accurate.
Indeed, these records of Ecgwine's transactions over Withington and
Fladbury are much more plausible than the hagiographical accounts of 'St
Ecgwine' in later Evesham tradition.[122] The early eleventh-century *Vita
S. Ecgwini*, which was partly based on charters fabricated at Evesham,
describes how Bishop Ecgwine founded Evesham monastery on a remote
and backward estate provided by Æthelred (resigned 704) and became its
first abbot.[123] Yet the relationship between monarch, bishop and mon-

---

[120] See above, pp. 92 and 118–19.

[121] S 1252. This is witnessed by Æthelheard's three brothers (see above, p. 36) and by
Omolincg abbas, presumably the prospective abbot of Fladbury (cf. Sims-Williams,
'Cuthswith', p. 9, n. 2, and 'Wilfrid', p. 169, n. 31). Its basic authenticity is
confirmed by S 62. On the later history of Fladbury, see above, pp. 37–8 and 132–3.
The documents about Fladbury which emanated from Evesham can be disregarded (cf.
Hart, *Charters of Northern England*, p. 75). Cf. above, p. 92.

[122] Other genuine charters in which Ecgwine appears are S 1177 (in Birch's edition *Signum
manus Ecuuini* is among the lay-witnesses, but he is in a separate column of his own in
the manuscript) and S 102. M. Lapidge went too far in stating that nothing is known of
the saint from 'early or contemporary records': 'Hagiography of St. Ecgwine', p. 77,
and 'Dominic of Evesham "Vita S. Ecgwini Episcopi et Confessoris"', *AB* 96 (1978),
65–104, at 65. Cf. his 'Byrhtferth and the *Vita S. Ecgwini*', *MS* 41 (1979), 331–53, at
331, n. 3.

[123] *Vita Quorundum Anglo-Saxonum* [sic], ed. Giles, p. 363. The first writer to give an exact
date appears to be the Evesham chronicler Thomas of Marleberge (d. 1236), who says
that Æthelred gave Ecgwine the site in 701 and that the latter spent six years
establishing the monastery (*Chronicon de Evesham*, ed. Macray, pp. 70–1). On the
charters and Lives of Ecgwine, see H&S III, 279–81; *PNWo*, p. xxv; *BOH* II, 246;
and the articles by Lapidge cited above, n. 122. There is room for a full study of the
'pseudo-history characteristic of the Evesham fabrications'; cf. Sims-Williams, 'Cuthswith', p. 10, n. 5; Hart, *Charters of Northern England*, pp. 63 and 75; J. Sayers,
'"Original", Cartulary and Chronicle: The Case of the Abbey of Evesham', in

astery seen in the Worcester documents about Withington and Fladbury suggests the alternative hypothesis that nothing more occurred than that Æthelred delegated the task of establishing monastic life at Evesham, as at nearby Fladbury, to Bishop Ecgwine (699?–717);[124] the inventive Evesham forgers would have been quite capable of working up these bare data into the story of St Ecgwine's devotion to Evesham, his friendship with King Æthelred, and his retirement from his see to Evesham. There may, of course, be more to the Evesham tradition than this; perhaps Ecgwine really did combine the roles of bishop and abbot. The long-standing archetype for this combination was St Martin of Tours, a saint well represented in early English church dedications.[125]

Unlike most monasteries, many of the Anglo-Saxon sees were founded on ancient Roman urban sites.[126] Eric John has seen here a symbol of their relative importance:

The vitality of the English Church depended on its monasteries: the diocese, especially where associated with these decayed urban remains, is not likely to have been of much real value.[127]

This judgement hardly tallies with the evidence. Some sees may have been rather poor,[128] but, by and large, bishops seem to have been becoming wealthier and more powerful, and the extant charters and synodical records show many of them to have been very active, not least in the promotion of

Fälschungen im Mittelalter IV, *Diplomatische Fälschungen* II, MGH Schriften 33/IV (Hannover, 1988), pp. 371–95, at 374. The most important Evesham record may prove to be the list of abbots printed in *Chronicon de Evesham*, ed. Macray, pp. 76–7; see Sims-Williams, 'People and Places'.

[124] The date 717 comes from 'Florence' (see below, p. 328, n. 4). In view of S 102 Ecgwine must have been active as bishop at least until 716. The date 699 is given in *ECWM*, p. 32 on the basis of the statement in *Chronicon de Evesham*, ed. Macray, p. 70, that Ecgwine retired to Evesham in the sixteenth year of his episcopate. In view of S 76 (above, n. 119), Ecgwine cannot have succeeded Oftfor before 697 at the earliest. Thus 'Florence' is in error in stating that Ecgwine succeeded Oftfor in 692 and began establishing Evesham 'after a few years' (*MHB*, p. 539), though he is followed here by the later annals ed. by Liebermann, *Geschichtsquellen*, p. 18, and by Luard, *Annales Monastici* IV, 365–6. Cf. Sims-Williams, 'Cuthswith', p. 9, n. 1.

[125] Levison, *England and the Continent*, p. 259; Wallace-Hadrill, *Commentary*, pp. 36–7 and 159; Everitt, *Continuity*, pp. 231 and 241.

[126] See above, p. 88.   [127] John, 'Problems', p. 58.

[128] Rochester, which Bishop Cwichelm left soon after his appointment, 'prae inopia rerum' (*HE* IV.12), was a special case, having recently been devastated by Æthelred of Mercia.

monasticism. Certainly there is no evidence to suggest that the sees of Worcester and Hereford, both of them on Roman urban sites, were less vital, materially or spiritually, than the monasteries they increasingly controlled and dominated.

6

The eighth-century church

By 716, when Æthelbald returned from exile to become king of Mercia, at least thirteen monasteries had been founded in the dioceses of the Hwicce and Magonsætan: Hanbury, Evesham, Fladbury, Tetbury, Lingen(?), Leominster, Wenlock, Bath, Gloucester, Pershore, Ripple, *Penintanham* and Withington.[1] All of these may have continued in existence in his reign (716–57), though some of them disappear from the record; the monastery of Hanbury, for example, only resurfaces in 836, by which time it was in the hands of the bishop of Worcester.[2] Often it is easier to trace the histories of the monasteries which were absorbed into the well-documented episcopal estate of Worcester than those of the 'big names' which escaped episcopal control. Knowledge of eighth-century Evesham, for instance, is limited to a thirteenth-century list of abbots[3] and a mass of late forged charters. Leominster is lost to view, and the same may be said of Pershore, though later on the monks claimed to have received a privilege from Coenwulf of Mercia (796–821).[4] The fortunes of the other 'big names' – Wenlock, Bath and Gloucester – are slightly better recorded. Wenlock's continued existence is shown by Boniface's allusion, at the very beginning of Æthelbald's reign, to 'monasterium Milburge abbatissę', and by the latest grant, of 727×736, in the so-called 'Testament of St Mildburg':

I [Mildburg] also bought a property from the king's *comes* Sigward. To him I gave a large sum of money, and he gave me an estate of three hides, with its charter, called Madeley. This purchase was witnessed and attested by King Æthelbald,

---

[1] Listed in the order of the discussion above, pp. 92–6.
[2] See above, pp. 107 and 137.
[3] Cf. above, p. 142, n. 123.   [4] See above, pp. 94–6 and 101.

Bishop Walhstod [of the Magonsætan], Bishop Wilfrith [of the Hwicce], Abbot Ova, and the *dux* Cynric.[5]

After this we hear no more of the double monastery until an original charter of 901.[6] Abbess Berta's monastery at Bath also survived, though it seems to have become a male community by the end of Æthelbald's reign.[7] About the same time, according to its unreliable *Historia*, Gloucester ceased to be headed by an abbess. The Gloucester community survived, however, as we know not only from its own list of grants from Hwiccian and Mercian notables down to *c.* 862, but also from an early ninth-century will preserved at Worcester.[8] The lands allegedly granted to Gloucester included not only nearby places, such as Pinswell in the Cotswolds (SO/9815), which Abbess Eafe 'acquired to drive her sheep there' – perhaps so that the sheep could be brought down towards Gloucester along the Green Way to Badgeworth, an estate granted by Æthelbald – but also properties on the edge of the kingdom, for instance in Wychwood (*Hwicca wudu*), and as far afield as Beaminster and Portland in Dorset.[9] According to its own records, then, Gloucester's estate was already an impressive one in the eighth century. We may add that the nun Eafe, to whom Æthelbald granted part of a building at Droitwich with two salt-furnaces, according to a Worcester charter, may be the abbess of Gloucester.[10]

As to the other monasteries founded before Æthelbald's accession, Lingen – if it was a monastery – disappears from the record, perhaps being absorbed into the estate of Wenlock, which preserved its charter,[11] and the rest – Hanbury, Fladbury, Tetbury, Ripple, *Penintanham* (if correctly

---

[5] S 1802. See *ECWM*, p. 212. For Boniface's allusion see above, p. 120, n. 27. Wenlock is Mildburg's resting-place in the earlier part of the lists discussed by Rollason, 'Resting-Places'. The passage in the 'Testament' does not prove that Mildburg was still alive in Æthelbald's reign, since the first-person narration may be a later device for presenting charters in favour of her foundation. Cf. Whitelock, 'Pre-Viking Age Church', p. 12, n. 2. The same device is used in the *Vita S. Ecgwini*; see Lapidge, 'Hagiography of St. Ecgwine', pp. 79–80.

[6] S 221. See above, p. 120.   [7] See above, p. 121 and n. 31.

[8] See above, p. 123. The will is S 1187. See discussion above, pp. 39 and n. 119, and 123, n. 41.

[9] For Gloucester's list of grants see S 1782 and *ECWM*, nos. 9, 20, 27, 40, 41, 61, 80, and 414, and pp. 161–2 and 165. On Pinswell see Finberg, *Gloucestershire Studies*, pp. 12–13; *Lucerna*, p. 41; *Gloucestershire Landscape*, pp. 57–8; *PNGl* IV, 6 and n. 4; Hooke, *Hwicce*, p. 235.

[10] See above, p. 123, n. 45.   [11] See above, p. 93.

identified with Inkberrow[12]) and Withington – all passed eventually into the possession of the see of Worcester. Tetbury and Ripple were already in the bishop's hands in the reign of Offa (757–96), according to late Worcester sources; William of Malmesbury maintains that Offa had seized the former from Malmesbury.[13] Fladbury and Withington kept their independence, more or less, during much of the eighth century, but eventually reverted to the see.[14] Abbess Cuthswith's monastery at *Penintanham* survived into Æthelbald's reign, if the Cyneburg to whom he granted Bradley near Inkberrow was Cuthswith's successor; but by the mid-eighth century Bradley and Inkberrow were in the hands of laymen, who bequeathed them to the see.[15] Many other, unknown monasteries may have been permanently secularized and so have disappeared from the record completely.

Churchmen regarded Æthelbald's rule as a mixed blessing. His accession fulfilled the prophecies of his spiritual supporter in his years of exile, St Guthlac, who was to be rewarded posthumously by the dedication St Guthlac's collegiate church in Hereford, which may have been founded as early as Æthelbald's reign.[16] On the other hand, Boniface attacked the king for appropriating church funds, forcing monks to labour on royal works, and for seducing nuns and conniving in their infanticide. Lull was to preserve an account of a vision of Æthelbald in hell.[17] The Welsh church remembered him as the devastator of churches between the Monnow and the Wye.[18] Some English archives seem to tell a more favourable story. Gloucester, for example, received land from Æthelbald,[19] and he granted the see of Worcester estates at Batsford, Woodchester and Aust in Gloucestershire.[20] He also exempted Bishop Milred from

---

[12] See below, p. 191, n. 63, and note in any case that the *Penintanham* charter was preserved at Worcester.

[13] Dugdale, *Monasticon* I, 608. For Ripple see Sims-Williams, 'Wilfrid', p. 174. According to BCS 1320 (*ECWM*, p. 39, no. 36) Offa granted (*gebecte*, but cf. *liberauit*, Dugdale, *Monasticon* I, 608) Tetbury to Worcester (cf. S 145, rejected by Scharer, *Königsurkunde*, pp. 239–40). William of Malmesbury, *GP*, p. 388, says he first seized Tetbury from Malmesbury. Cf. Finberg, *Early Charters of Wessex*, p. 218, n. 5. By *c.* 903 it was a Worcester episcopal estate; see below, pp. 157 and 160.

[14] See above, pp. 37–8, 132–3 and 140–1.   [15] See below, pp. 237–9.

[16] Cf. above, p. 60, n. 25, and below, pp. 245 and 247.

[17] *Epp.* lxxiii, lxxviii and cxv (Tangl, pp. 146–55, 161–70 and 247–50, respectively).

[18] Above, p. 52, n. 182.

[19] S 1782 (but the syntax is so confused that the donor is not entirely certain).

[20] S 101, 103 and 137. Aust had earlier been granted by Æthelred according to S 77.

paying tolls on two ships at London, which suggests that 'the bishop (together with other churchmen at the time who received similar privileges) was buying and selling in the port'.[21] In this connection it is interesting to note that Æthelbald had granted Milred's predecessor a messuage (*curtis*) in London, and that there are numismatic links between London and the kingdom of the Hwicce, possibly reflecting trade.[22] Yet Æthelbald may have been paid for all these benefactions or have had more than pious motives for them. Indeed, we are told that some of his munificence to Gloucester was in recompense for the slaying of Æthelmund son of Oswald, and that his grant to Worcester of land in Droitwich, for the construction of six furnaces and three salt-houses, was in exchange for similar property nearby.[23]

The most striking development in monasticism seen in Æthelbald's reign is a series of charters by which he rewarded or pensioned off his faithful thegns with land for monastic use. The recipients may be compared with the thegn-abbots of Northumbrian 'family monasteries' whom Bede condemned, perhaps too sweepingly, in 734:

For about thirty years . . . there has hardly been one of the reeves (*praefecti*) . . . who has not procured for himself during his time of office a monastery of this kind and involved his wife with him in the guilt of this hateful traffic; and with the prevalence of this worst of customs, the king's thegns (*ministri*) and servants (*famuli*) also have exerted themselves to do the same; and thus by a perverse state of affairs, numberless people have been found who call themselves abbots and at the same time reeves (*praefecti*) or thegns (*ministri*) or servants (*famuli*) of the king, and who, although as laymen they could have learnt something of the monastic life, not by experience but by hearsay, are yet absolutely without the character and profession which should teach it . . . Such persons suddenly receive the tonsure at

---

[21] S 98; Dyer, *Lords and Peasants*, p. 32. Cf. Barker *et al.*, 'Origins of Worcester', p. 28; Metcalf, 'Sceattas from the Territory of the Hwicce', pp. 68–9; Scharer, *Königsurkunde*, pp. 201–2.

[22] Dugdale, *Monasticon* I, 607: 'curtem [= OE *haga*] unam in Lundonia inter duas stratas, quæ Tiddbertistret et Savinstret [nominantur]'. For later such acquisitions in London by bishops of Worcester see S 208 and 346 (cf. *Monasticon* I, 609); Dyer, *Lords and Peasants*, pp. 32 and 59–60; and Brooks, *Canterbury*, p. 154; Hooke, *Hwicce*, pp. 117 and 199. On the coin evidence see above, p. 13.

[23] For Æthelmund see above, p. 35. For the Droitwich grant see S 102; *ECWM*, p. 238 (addendum). Worcester claimed to have been granted a saltworks at Droitwich already by Æthelred: *ibid.*, p. 86 no. 197. See also above, p. 123, n. 45.

their pleasure, and at their own judgment are made from laymen not into monks, but abbots.[24]

In interpreting the Æthelbald charters it has to be remembered that their dates are not necessarily those when the properties first came into the thegns' hands, but the dates when the king formally made them over as permanent, hereditable 'bookland'; they may already have held them from Æthelbald on a temporary basis as 'loanland',[25] and may indeed already have instituted some sort of monastic life on them. It is also sometimes uncertain whether the religious formulae used in the charters can be taken at face value, not so much because of the doubts raised by Bede, as because the charter was on the point of becoming a convenient medium for purely secular conveyancing.[26] For example, a corrupt charter of Æthelbald in the early eleventh-century Worcester cartulary granting estates in Gloucestershire to his loyal *minister* Osred, a member of the Hwiccian royal family, with freedom to bequeath them as he wished, may disguise a merely secular pension beneath the religious formula 'in possessionem iuris æcclesiastici pro redemptione animae meae'.[27] Fortunately other charters are more explicit and less corrupt.

The clearest is Æthelbald's charter of 736 granting Stour in Ismere to his *dux* and *comes* Cyneberht 'to establish a monastery'.[28] (By an endorsement on this original charter, Cyneberht also received an estate at *Brochyl* in Morfe Forest.[29]) In view of Bede's remarks about people who styled themselves both abbot and thegn, it is tempting to identify Cyneberht with a witness of the same name who attested Æthelbald's charters in the 740s among the laity;[30] it was, however, a common name. He is more

---

[24] *BOH* I, 416; *EHD*, p. 806. Cf. above, p. 126.

[25] Cf. Stenton, *Latin Charters*, p. 61.

[26] See *ibid.*, pp. 59–61; Scharer, *Königsurkunde*, pp. 46 and 178.

[27] S 99; the clauses 'ut ab omni tributo uectigalium operum onerumque sæcularium sit libera' and 'statuo tantum ut Deo omnipotenti ex eodem agello æcclesiasticæ seruitutis famulatum inpendat' may have been added during transmission. See the discussions by Scharer, *Königsurkunde*, pp. 169–72. Cf. above, p. 36, n. 104, and below, n. 119.

[28] S 89 (cf. below, p. 192, n. 68), most recently discussed, by P. Wormald in *The Anglo-Saxons*, ed. Campbell, pp. 95–7 (with facsimile), and by Scharer, 'Intitulationes', pp. 31–2 and 56–60. The exact position of Stour in Ismere cannot be determined; see above, p. 31, n. 73.

[29] S 89. Cf. below, p. 376, n. 71.

[30] S 90, 91 and 92. He, rather than our abbot, may be the recipient of S 1823.

certainly to be equated with the *Cyneberht abbas* who attested a charter of
757, in the last year of Æthelbald's reign.[31] In Offa's reign Cyneberht's
son, Ceolfrith, similarly styled himself *abbas* when he granted his inheritance at Stour (and also at Henbury, Gl.) to Milred, bishop of Worcester
(d. 774×775).[32] Stour in Ismere was, then, a 'family monastery', founded
by a 'thegn-abbot', which lasted only two generations. There is no reason,
however, to suppose that it existed simply for the benefit of the family;
indeed, in his charter Ceolfrith expressed fears that his kindred might
intervene to thwart his bequest to the see. The see did, however, secure
Stour, despite attempts by Offa to claim it in 781, and held it until 816,
when Bishop Deneberht ceded it to King Coenwulf in return for privileges
for other estates. This does not necessarily mean that it had ceased to be a
monastery; compare the case of Twyning, which was still styled *monasterium* when Deneberht had handed it over to Coenwulf in similar circum-
stances two years earlier.[33]

Æthelbald's grant to Cyneberht in 736 was made with the consent of
another *comes*, Æthelric, the *subregulus* of the Hwicce. About the same
time, to judge by the witness-list and diplomatic, Æthelric himself
received from his overlord a charter granting Wootton Wawen in the
region of the *Stoppingas*.[34] This grant comes at the end of Æthelric's
appearances in charters, which stretch back into the seventh century, and it
may signal his retirement from public life. Its religious formulae ('in
possessionem æcclesiasticæ rationis atque regulæ' and 'in ius monasticæ
rationis') may plausibly be understood to signify a grant for the support of a
monastery under Æthelric's auspices, quite likely at Wootton itself,
although the Anglo-Saxon fabric of the present church is probably much

---

[31] S 96. See below, pp. 225–7.
[32] S 1411. 'Henbury' rather than 'Hanbury', not only for the reasons given in *ECWM* at
no. 28, but also because the hidage (20) agrees with S 146 (BCS 273), which obviously
relates to Henbury, a member of the Domesday manor of Westbury. Cf. Taylor,
'Pre-Domesday Hide', pp. 297–302. The history of Henbury is confusing: it was
granted with Aust to Worcester by Æthelred (S 77, of doubtful authenticity), to Offa's
grandfather by Æthelbald (S 146, cf. Dugdale, *Monasticon* I, 607: 'Æthelbaldus . . .
Suthhaenburh et Austan liberauit'), to Worcester by Ceolfrith (S 1411), and later on to
Worcester again by Offa (S 146). See below, p. 153.
[33] S 180 and 172. See above, pp. 132–3.
[34] S 94. Cf. Scharer, *Königsurkunde*, pp. 176–9, and 'Intitulationes', p. 57.

later.[35] Wootton's subsequent history cannot be traced, but it came sooner or later to the see, which preserved Æthelbald's charter. According to a twelfth-century list of grants to Worcester, Beorhtwulf of Mercia 'freed' Wootton in 844 and Stratford in 845, 'both of which his predecessors had freed'.[36] The charter of exemption for Stratford survives,[37] but not the one for Wootton.

Two more of Æthelbald's charters specifically refer to minor mon-asteries, at Acton Beauchamp in the diocese of the Magonsætan, and at Daylesford in the diocese of the Hwicce. Both are dated 718, with the incompatible tenth indiction, and display many other similarities; but these features may be original, rather than the result of imitation, since the charters emanate from different archives.

A twelfth-century Evesham cartulary preserves the charter by which Æthelbald, with the consent of the bishops of the Mercians and Magon-sætan, grants three hides at Acton (*Aactune*) to his *comes* Buca 'so that it may be a perpetual habitation of the servants of God'.[38] This dubious prov-enance, and the knowledge that in the eleventh century Worcester and Evesham were in dispute over Acton, where Pershore also claimed three hides,[39] makes one suspicious of the 718 charter. Yet its formulae and spelling of names are in its favour,[40] and it says nothing about Evesham, unlike the forged Acton charter in the other twelfth-century Evesham cartu-lary.[41] It may be that for once a genuine charter had found its way into the

---

[35] See above, p. 36 and references at n. 26 above; Bassett, 'Wootton Wawen Project'; and below, p. 391. Like some other minsters, Wootton later emerged as an alien priory: Blair, 'Secular Minster Churches', p. 133.

[36] Dugdale, *Monasticon* I, 608. The reference to a *Wudutun* charter on p. 607 is doubtless to S 94 (cf. BCS 1320). See also S 1855.

[37] S 198, *recte* of 844; see above, p. 137, n. 102.

[38] S 85. Kemble is wrong in stating that the witnesses will not fit the AD date. The absence of the bishop of Worcester confirms that Acton was not then in his diocese; cf. above, p. 43.

[39] See *ECWM*, p. 146 on S 1479; Darlington, 'Æthelwig', pp. 6 and n. 2, 20, and 188 and n. 2. For Pershore see S 786. Note that the bounds of Acton in the Pershore charter (a dubious document, cf. above, p. 95, n. 30) were also preserved in the s. xi² Worcester cartulary (see S 786).

[40] *PNWo*, pp. xxv, n. 2, and 25; Scharer, *Königsurkunde*, pp. 172–4. An original charter which was preserved at Evesham is S 114; see *Chartae*, ed. Bruckner and Marichal III, no. 184, and below, n. 61. It is apparently genuine, but there is a lack of dated contemporary manuscripts for comparison.

[41] S 83. Cf. *Chronicon de Evesham*, ed. Macray, p. 72; Scharer, *Königsurkunde*, p. 161.

Evesham archive: A possible route is suggested by the fact that in the mid-eleventh century Acton was in the hands of the thegn Ordwig, whose son Æthelwig became abbot of Evesham and secured the land for his own monastery, against the counter-claim of Worcester.[42]

The chance survival of Buca's charter is a valuable indication that Æthelbald's thegn-abbots were to be found in the western diocese as well as in the better documented diocese of the Hwicce. How long did Buca's monastery last? Some early ninth-century(?) sculpture in Acton church may reflect its continuing existence. The anomaly that Acton, though in the early diocese of Hereford, was on a tongue of Worcestershire projecting into Herefordshire, suggests that it was already held by one of the Worcestershire religious houses when the shire-boundary was established.[43] The very close similarity between the stone carving at Acton and a cross-shaft at Cropthorne, an episcopal property between Pershore and Evesham, may be an early symptom of such dependency. One wonders whether the stone employed at Acton, which came from Taynton, Oxfordshire, was imported, possibly already carved, through the good offices of a Hwiccian mother-house.[44]

Bægia, the recipient of the other charter dated 718, which is preserved in the early eleventh-century Worcester cartulary, is not described as *comes* but as *seruus Dei*.[45] Æthelbald grants him six hides at Daylesford 'so that he may establish a monastery in it and it may become a habitation of the servants of God'. There is no other reference to this monastery, but allusions to 'Bæga's spring' and 'the nuns' hills' in the bounds appended to the charter in the cartulary confirm its existence.[46] It must have passed to the see by the ninth century, when privileges were obtained for the six

---

[42] See J. H. Round in *VCH Wo* I, 253 and 308 n. 2; Darlington, 'Æthelwig', p. 6, nn. 1–2; *The Vita Wulfstani of William of Malmesbury*, ed. R. R. Darlington, Camden Ser. 40 (London, 1928), p. xxiv and n. 4. Cf. S 1479.

[43] Houghton, *Worcestershire*, pp. 1–2; cf. above, pp. 5–6 and 43, n. 138.

[44] R. Cramp, 'Schools of Mercian Sculpture', in *Mercian Studies*, ed. Dornier, pp. 191–233, at 225, 227 and 230; E. M. Jope, 'The Saxon Building-Stone Industry in Southern and Midland England', *MA* 8 (1964), 91–118, at 106 and 108: the stone used at Cropthorne was probably more local, from Bredon Hill. On Cropthorne see Scharer, *Königsurkunde*, p. 250.

[45] S 84. On the date see Scharer, *Königsurkunde*, pp. 166, n. 33, and 173. The members of the episcopal *familia* are *serui Dei* in the time of Bishop Milred: Atkins, 'Church of Worcester, Part I', p. 379 and n. 3.

[46] See above, p. 119. The bounds also occur in KCD 623.

hides from the Mercian kings Ceolwulf I (821–2) and Beorhtwulf (in 841).[47] They were leased by Bishop Werferth to Ceolwulf II in 875 in return for a diocesan exemption; and late in the following century the estate was again being leased out on easy terms, the only obligation on the lessee – Bishop Oswald's own brother – being the payment of church dues, perhaps to a church at Daylesford itself.[48]

A rather different instance of a monastery on land granted to a thegn may be seen in the history of Bibury (*Beagan byrig*), if the second element of this place-name is correctly interpreted as 'monastery'.[49] The see of Worcester owned fifteen hides by the river Coln here, and Bishop Wilfrith (718–743×745) leased five of them, apparently at Ablington in Bibury, to the *comes* Leppa 'on account of the old friendship between us', for the duration of Leppa's life and that of his daughter Beage. (Æthelbald attested the charter, but was not otherwise involved.) As the daughter gave her name to Bibury, she presumably acquired the remaining ten hides, including Bibury itself.[50] What happened to the monastery – if such it was – on her death is unknown, but Bibury came back to the see eventually, forming one of the demesne manors of the bishopric. The see purchased immunities for Ablington in 855, and Bishop Werferth's lease of this member of the estate in 899 to the priest Werwulf (one of King Alfred's literary assistants, like Werferth himself), on condition that church-scot and soul-scot went to Bibury, probably implies that Bibury was a major church with ancient rights, an 'old minster'.[51]

Of all Æthelbald's thegns, the most intriguing is his first cousin, Eanwulf, Offa's grandfather. Several charters associate Eanwulf with the kingdom of the Hwicce, especially with Bredon monastery and with lands in the far south of the kingdom, and there seems to have been a tradition at Worcester, reflected in a forgery in the early eleventh-century cartulary,

---

[47] Dugdale, *Monasticon* I, 608; S 194. On the relationship between S 84 and S 194 see Scharer, *Königsurkunde*, pp. 164–6.

[48] S 215 and 1340. On church-scot, etc., see below, n. 124. Evesham later acquired Daylesford: Darlington, 'Æthelwig', pp. 6, and n. 3, and 20.

[49] See above, p. 93, n. 24; cf. Sawyer, *Roman Britain to Norman England*, pp. 155–6.

[50] S 1254. See below, p. 379.

[51] S 206 (significantly BCS 1320 deals with this as 'Beaganbyrig') and S 1279. Cf. the arrangement for church-scot for Cleeve, below, p. 157. For Bibury's later *parochia* see Blair, *Minsters and Parish Churches*, pp. 11–12.

that Offa himself dwelt in the kingdom before he came to power in 757.[52] In a questionable charter of 793×796, by which Offa promises sixty hides at Westbury and twenty at Henbury to the see after his and his son's death, Offa states that Æthelbald had granted these lands to Eanwulf.[53] Æthelbald is also said to have granted Eanwulf the nearby church of Yate, an estate allegedly transferred to the see by Offa.[54] These traditions may well be authentic.

Eanwulf probably died early in Æthelbald's reign, since he does not attest any of his charters. An early *floruit* is also suggested by the fact that Æthelbald's lost charter allowing Eanwulf to found Bredon monastery belonged to the time of Bishop Ecgwine (d. 717):

Æthelbaldus rex Merciorum terram quæ uocatur Breodun, propinquo suo, comiti Eanulfo, ad monasterium construendum, Ecguino pontificante dedit; et excepta pontis et arcis constructione, liberauit.[55]

The immunity and reservation clause in this twelfth-century summary is suspiciously anachronistic, but the substance is confirmed by a charter Offa issued at Brentford in September 780, granting properties in Gloucestershire to Bredon monastery and its church of 'the blessed Peter, prince of the apostles, which my grandfather Eanwulf erected to the praise and glory of God'.[56] In the latter charter, which is attested by Tilhere, bishop of

[52] S 55. C. Fox, *Offa's Dyke* (London, 1955), p. 289, quotes Bruce Dickins's suggestion that *puer indolis* represents OE *æpeling*. Scharer, *Königsurkunde*, pp. 214 and 232, suggests that the sub-kingdom was Offa's power base. Cf. below, n. 55.

[53] S 146. The history of these estates is complex (cf. Taylor, 'Pre-Domesday Hide', pp. 297–302). A contemporary original has Offa granting 55 hides at Westbury to his thegn Æthelmund (S 139); this might be regarded as an interim grant (cf. *EHD*, p. 512). On the other hand, the grant to Worcester may be a forgery, perhaps quite a late one; cf. Scharer, *Königsurkunde*, pp. 277–8; Wormald, 'Settlement of Disputes', pp. 155–6. On the Westbury hides, see below, p. 175. On Henbury, see above, n. 32, and below, p. 162.

[54] S 147 (as it stands, a forgery based on S 141).

[55] 'Æthelbald, king of the Mercians, gave the land which is called Bredon to his relative, the thegn Eanwulf, to establish a monastery, during Ecgwine's episcopate; and he exempted it, except for bridge- and fortress-construction': Dugdale, *Monasticon* I, 607. For the anachronism of the final clause see Brooks, 'Military Obligations', pp. 76–7 and 77, n. 1. Bassett, 'Search', p. 241, n. 35, suggests that Eanwulf was also a member of the Hwiccian royal family; there is no direct evidence.

[56] S 116. The authenticity is discussed by Scharer, *Königsurkunde*, pp. 247–9. On the date see Harrison, *Framework*, p. 116. There is a similar reference to Bredon in S 117; cf. Scharer, *Königsurkunde*, pp. 249–50. The reference to Worcester here is obviously

Worcester, Offa insists that the Gloucestershire properties should remain in his kindred's control for ever, perhaps anticipating the moves made by Tilhere's successor to dispute Offa's possession of Bredon at a second council at Brentford the following year.[57] It may have been on such grounds of kinship that Beorhtwulf, 'instructed by hostile men', reappropriated some of the Bredon estates from Worcester on his accession to the Mercian throne in 840.[58]

THE REIGN OF OFFA

In 757 Æthelbald was murdered by his bodyguard. By the end of that year civil war had driven his obscure successor, Beornred, from the kingdom of Mercia, and Offa began his thirty-nine-year reign.[59] As far as the diocese of the Hwicce is concerned (for the diocese of the Magonsætan the sources are non-existent), no immediate change in royal policy towards the church can be detected, perhaps because of the shortage of charters in the first ten years of Offa's rule – unless this lack is itself significant. Nevertheless, two trends become apparent during Offa's reign.

One is the disappearance of the thegn-abbot. This may be because Milred, bishop of Worcester from 743×745 to 774×775, succeeded in enforcing the church's opposition to the lay control of the monasteries, as voiced, in a muted and pragmatic way, by the Council of *Clofesho* which he attended in 747.[60] Yet thegn-abbots may really disappear because royal grants of bookland to laymen for purely secular purposes became socially acceptable, removing the need for the ruse deplored by Bede. We see the latter change in two extant, apparently original, charters: by a charter of 770, preserved at Worcester and perhaps written there, Uhtred, sub-king of the Hwicce, with the consent of Offa (and his queen and children), grants land in Stoke Prior by the river Salwarpe, Wo., to his faithful *minister* Æthelmund son of Ingeld, a former *dux* and *præfectus* of King Æthelbald; and by another of 779, formerly preserved at Evesham but perhaps drafted by the abbot of Peterborough, Offa grants land near Salmonsbury by the river Windrush, Gl., to his faithful *minister* Duddo.

---

interpolated. It is found both in the extant pseudo-original and in the lost Somers charter
printed by Smith; note that the latter refers only to 20 hides at *Wersðylle* and Cofton (cf.
BCS 847).

[57] See below, p. 163. [58] S 192; *EHD*, p. 520. [59] *EHD*, pp. 176 and 266.
[60] H&S III, 364. Cf. Brooks, *Canterbury*, pp. 177–80.

Both kings make the grants 'for my soul's sake' and state that the estates are to have ecclesiastical immunities; but there is no suggestion that Æthelmund and Duddo are to become abbots, or even to found churches.[61]

The other development of Offa's reign is that, despite some grants by him or his sub-kings to the see and to monasteries such as Bredon and Gloucester,[62] Offa seems to have reacted against too much land falling into ecclesiastical hands, in particular into the hands of the bishops of Worcester, who had already accumulated a large estate out of monasteries that came under episcopal control and lands granted directly by earlier kings.[63] Matters came to a head at the Synod of Brentford in 781, which will be a convenient point at which to divide Offa's long reign.

Before the Synod of Brentford

A good many monasteries founded in previous reigns were still in existence in the first part of Offa's reign, up to 781. They probably included Wenlock, Bath, Gloucester, Hanbury, Evesham, Fladbury, Withington, Stour in Ismere and his grandfather Eanwulf's foundation at Bredon. A few others, though possibly founded earlier, appear in the record for the first time in this period: Dowdeswell, Bishop's Cleeve, Twyning and Berkeley.

Dowdeswell surfaces in 759, when the Hwiccian sub-kings Eanberht, Uhtred and Ealdred, with Offa's consent, granted to an abbot Headda an estate of ten hides at Andoversford, the bounds of which included

---

[61] S 59 and 114 (cf. above, n. 40). See Scharer, *Königsurkunde*, pp. 245–6, 253, 255–6 and 258, and 'Intitulationes', pp. 32 and 67–8. M. P. Brown, 'Bibliothèque Nationale, lat. 10861', p. 132, n. 54, has raised some palaeographical doubts about both charters; these developed alongside the diplomatic criticism of S 59 by Wormald, 'Settlement of Disputes', pp. 155–6. It is not impossible, however, that S 59 is a revised copy, not necessarily forged, issued late in Offa's reign with the added consent of his heirs (as seen on the dorse), of a lost charter of 770, just as the latter would have been an updated version (with mechanical adjustment of the indiction) of the charter issued in 767 (S 58). I am indebted here to the discussion by Mr Wormald and others following a version of his paper given in Cambridge in February 1986.

[62] See S 55–63 and 104–47; also Dugdale, *Monasticon* I, 607–8; BCS 1320. A number of the grants are inauthentic; cf. Scharer, *Königsurkunde*, pp. 212–78.

[63] See Dyer, *Lords and Peasants*, pp. 9–16; Brooks, *Canterbury*, pp. 179–80. But, as Dyer remarks (p. 15), 'the long-term interests of the monarchy would have been best served by a strongly based episcopate'; though cf. above, p. 139, n. 112.

Dowdeswell.[64] Abbot Headda's monastery or church (no term is used) seems to have been at Dowdeswell, for some years later, for the sake of his soul and the soul of his relative Bishop Heathored (780–99), Headda promised that his 'inheritance' at Dowdeswell and *æt Tyreltune*, together with an upland estate (*prediolum*) on the eastern edge of the Andoversford estate, should pass to the see of Worcester when no member of his family in holy orders could be found to maintain the monastic rule, in order to avoid lay control. Headda himself is described as 'priest and abbot' and as an *alumnus* of the *familia* of the church of Worcester, where he had been brought up.[65] Headda may insist on his successors being in orders in the belief that his church, monastery or 'minster' had a duty to administer the sacraments to the surrounding population, like the continental baptismal churches, or in the spirit of the insistence of the Council of *Clofesho* in 747 that bishops should ensure that monasteries under lay lords should at least have the ministry of a priest.[66] Headda's charters mark a step on the way to the later organization of the diocese, with 'old minsters' served by priests from the episcopal *familia*. Evidently his lands did revert to the see, for by the early eleventh century they formed part of a large episcopal estate based on the former monastery at Withington.[67] His stipulations can usefully be compared with those governing the episcopal estate at Old Sodbury. Bishop Milred gave Sodbury to a certain Eanbald (who is not styled 'abbot'), on condition that

---

[64] S 56. On the bounds of this original charter see Finberg, *Lucerna*, p. 22, n. 4. Headda may already have been an abbot, or may be called *abbas* in anticipation of the founding of his monastery (cf. Sims-Williams, 'Wilfrid', p. 169, n. 31).

[65] S 1413 (on the date cf. below, n. 128). On Heathored's dates see above, p. 139, n. 110. (*Æt*) *Tyreltune* has been assumed to be near Dowdeswell, possibly Whittington (Finberg, *Lucerna*, p. 23), but perhaps it was between Tewkesbury and Cheltenham, where the element *tyrl* is attested. Cf. *PNGl* I, 13. Finberg makes a perhaps unnecessary distinction between Upper Dowdeswell, granted by the *reguli*, and Lower Dowdeswell, Headda's *hereditas* (*Lucerna*, p. 22). Headda may be the *presbyter* who attests S 55 in 757, but the text is unreliable and another Headda may be intended.

[66] See above, p. 130, n. 71; Brooks, *Canterbury*, pp. 178 and 187–8. On priest-abbots in Kent, see *ibid.*, pp. 87–8, 155, 161, 163–4 and 187–8, and for the rising number of ordained monks on the Continent see Constable, 'Monasteries, Rural Churches and the *Cura Animarum*', pp. 358–65. There is an even division between priest-abbots and plain abbots in the Lindisfarne *Liber vitae* (ed. Sweet, *Oldest English Texts*, pp. 155–6); deacon-abbots are a smaller group.

[67] Finberg, *Lucerna*, pp. 22–3 and 37 (where the reference in n. 1 should be to KCD 631, not KCD 681). See above, p. 133.

so long as there was any man in [his] family who who was willing to take holy orders, and qualified to do so, he should succeed to the estate at Sodbury; but that if it turned out otherwise, the estate should never pass to a layman, but should subsequently revert to the bishop's see at Worcester.

On the same terms, Eanbald passed Sodbury on to Eastmund (possibly the 'Eastmund presbiter' who attended the Council of *Clofesho* in 824), and Eastmund repeated Eanbald's conditions in his will. After his death, however, their family appropriated the estate, refusing to surrender it to the bishops, and eventually Bishop Werferth sought satisfaction at a Mercian council at Droitwich:

Then Eadnoth and Ælfred and Ælfstan gave me security that they would either give me back the estate or find within their family a man who would take holy orders with the estate, and be obedient to me in both ecclesiastical and secular concerns. When Eadnoth, who had the estate, said that he would give it to any member of the family who might be willing to acquire it on this condition, each replied that he would rather forego the property than take orders.

The council settled that the family should keep the land and its charters in return for an annual rent to the bishop at Tetbury (which was now an episcopal estate).[68] Whether the religious life at Sodbury had ever been monastic to the extent of being ruled by an abbot is unclear, though the parallel with Dowdeswell is suggestive.

The monastery at Bishop's Cleeve 'and the church of the blessed Michael which is established in it' first come into view in 777×779 when they received from Offa and his sub-king Ealdred a *uicus* of fifteen hides called *Timbingctun*, which lay under the Cotswold scarp (*Uuendlesclif*) north of the *Tyrl* (the Hyde Brook?). The appended bounds of *Wendlesclif*, if correctly joined to the charter, suggest that *Timbingctun* enclosed the whole of Bishop's Cleeve and the surrounding parishes.[69] Bishop's Cleeve, as this modern name indicates, was to become an episcopal manor. It must have passed to the see of Worcester by 899, when his *familia* granted Bishop Werferth certain lands 'which formerly belonged to the monastery at Cleeve', on condition that church-scot was paid to Cleeve each year. Werferth soon leased part of these lands to a kinswoman, on the same condition, and attached the remainder to Prestbury (presumably an

---

[68] S 1446. Cf. S 1433.
[69] S 141. Cf. Grundy, *Gloucestershire*, pp. 71–90; *PNGl* II, 86; Gelling, *Place-Names in the Landscape*, pp. 131 and 136. On the date see Scharer, *Königsurkunde*, p. 243.

episcopal manor).[70] Here again we see a monastery and its estates being absorbed by the see. This outcome was not envisaged by Offa and Ealdred in their charter, and might not have met with their approval.

The monastery at Twyning is first mentioned in 774, when Bishop Milred confirmed a grant of Withington monastery to Abbess Æthelburg, daughter of the *comes* Ælfred, on condition

that Æthelburg shall also return the monastery at [Twyning] with all the goods that are there, after her day to the church of Worcester, as was the injunction of her father, Ælfred.[71]

Apparently, then, Twyning monastery was already in existence in Æthelburg's father's day, perhaps during the reign of Æthelbald.[72] Æthelburg was evidently a pluralist (like Hild of Whitby herself), for she also held a lease of Fladbury from her relative, the sub-king Ealdred, with a reversion to the see; that monastery seems to have been a possession of her father's as well. All three of her monasteries came to the see in due course. Twyning was handed in between 780 and 796 by another Ælfred, a *dux* of Offa's and presumably Æthelburg's heir, and for a while it, too, was absorbed into the episcopal estate.[73]

Another monastery which emerges before the Synod of Brentford is Berkeley, which is thought to have stood at Oldminster in Hinton, north of Berkeley itself.[74] We only hear of this important monastery because Tilhere, who became bishop of Worcester *c.* 778, had been its abbot, since 759 at least.[75] It was to enjoy a long, independent life, often in conflict

---

[70] S 1415 and 1283. On Prestbury see above, p. 139, n. 110.

[71] S 1255, corrected as noted above, p. 37, n. 113.

[72] On Ælfred see above, pp. 37–8.   [73] See above, pp. 37 and 132–3.

[74] See below, p. 381, n. 95.

[75] 'Florence' s.a. 778 (possibly a year too early or late, cf. *ASC* entries) calls him simply *abbas* (*MHB*, p. 545), but the early fourteenth-century Worcester annals have 'abbas de Beorclea': *Annales Monastici*, ed. Luard IV, 366. He attests as *abbas* in 759 (S 56) and *c.* 770 (S 63; cf. *ECWM*, p. 37 on the date), and as *episcopus* (!) in a forged charter variously dated 758 (BCS 216, cf. S 104 and Scharer, *Königsurkunde*, pp. 234–5) and 760 (Dugdale, *Monasticon* I, 607; cf. BCS 1320). 'Florence' seems to have used a lost, not quite accurate, list of Worcester episcopal dates: Darlington and McGurk, 'The "Chronicon ex Chronicis"', p. 188.

with the see, and provided another of its abbots, Æthelhun, as bishop of Worcester in 914 or 915.[76]

The Synod of Brentford in 781

Tilhere's successor, Bishop Heathored, summed up his dispute with Offa at the Synod of Brentford in 781 as follows:

We have had a dispute with Offa, king of the Mercians, our most beloved lord, about certain estates. For he said that we were wrongly holding in our power without hereditary right the inheritance of his kinsman, to wit King Æthelbald, *i.e.* 90 hides in the place which is called Bath, and in many other places, namely 30 hides at Stratford, 38 at Stour, also 14 hides at a place of like name, Stour in Ismere, 12 at Bredon, 17 hides at Hampton. But the aforesaid cause of dissension being settled in the synodal council at the place which is called Brentford, we restored also to the already mentioned King Offa that most famous monastery at Bath, without any hindrance or objection, for him to possess or even to deliver to whom he should consider fit, and we conceded it most willingly to his lawful heirs to enjoy for ever; and we added 30 hides nearby on the south side of the river which is called Avon, which land we bought at a proper price from Cynewulf, king of the West Saxons. On that account, the aforesaid King Offa, as a payment of compensation, and for the concord of a very firm peace, willingly conceded the aforesaid places at Stratford, Stour, Bredon, Hampton, Stour in Ismere, without any cause of controversy or exaction, to our aforesaid church, that is, in Worcester, with this liberty that these lands were to be subjected to no greater payment of any kind than the aforementioned episcopal see. Also he willingly conceded and bestowed the food-rents for three years belonging to him, that is, six 'entertainments'.[77]

As far as Bishop Heathored was concerned, the point at issue was the see's possession of Bath and the other 'places', of which most, perhaps all, were monasteries; but Offa, whose claims are hard to substantiate, may have seen Bath as his primary objective and have claimed more than he expected to get as a matter of strategy.[78] Having defeated Cynewulf at Bensington in 779, Offa may have wished to secure royal control of Bath because of its strategic position on the West Saxon border; this would explain his interest in acquiring the 30 hides on the West Saxon side of the

[76] See 'Florence' s.a. 915 (*MHB*, p. 570), but cf. *ASC* 914 entry; *Annales Monastici*, ed. Luard IV, 369 (s.a. 917!); O'Donovan, 'Episcopal Dates, Part II', pp. 112–13; Robinson, *Times of Saint Dunstan*, pp. 46–7; and below, p. 176.

[77] S 1257; trans. *EHD*, no. 77.

[78] Stubbs, 'Cathedral, Diocese and Monasteries', p. 250.

Avon, which Cynewulf perhaps sold under compulsion.[79] Moreover, the Bath estate included 5 hides at North Stoke on the north side of the Avon, where stood Little Down Camp, a promontory fort with obvious military potential; these hides had been granted to Bath monastery in 758 by Cynewulf, doubtless under pressure from his then overlord, Offa, who confirmed the grant.[80]

Bath was not the only monastery caught up in the struggle between Mercia and Wessex. In the disputed upper Thames valley, Cookham monastery in Berkshire was in turn possessed by Æthelbald, who granted it to Christ Church, Canterbury, then appropriated by Cynewulf, and then seized from the latter by Offa, along with many other *urbes*, all of which he brought under Mercian rule. (One of these *urbes* may have been Tetbury, which Offa is said to have taken from Malmesbury.) Offa kept Cookham as long as he lived, without any supporting documents, and left it to his heirs, including an abbess Cynethryth, who was probably his widow, despite the attempts which archbishops made at 'various synods' to recover it.[81] The 781 Synod of Brentford, over which Archbishop Jænberht and Offa presided, may have been one such synod.

In claiming Cookham Offa might at least maintain that Æthelbald had once possessed it, but it is difficult to find even this much justification in the case of most of the 'places' Offa claimed from Worcester. Bath, for instance, seems to have been an independent community when Cynewulf made his 758 grant 'to the brothers in St Peter's monastery', and there is no evidence that Æthelbald had any claim to it. On the other hand, neither is there any evidence about how it had passed to the see by 781, and Offa may have found some objection to the transaction which cannot now be ascertained. Eric John's suggestion that Offa wished to protect Bath's independence is hard to accept, since the effect of the decision at Brentford was to make Bath a royal *Eigenkloster*.[82] John has also argued that Offa objected to Bath's foundation charter on the grounds that it had been issued by the Hwiccian king Osric. It is difficult to square this further

---

[79] Taylor, 'Bath', pp. 138–9; *EHD*, pp. 21 and 506. Taylor, 'Pre-Domesday Hide', p. 310, identifies the 30 hides.

[80] S 265; Sims-Williams, 'Bath', pp. 8 and n. 10 and 9 and n. 7 (cf. below, p. 385, n. 111). The date 808 is probably a misreading of 758. On the political situation *c*. 758 see also below, p. 225 and n. 42.

[81] S 1258; Brooks, *Canterbury*, pp. 103–4, 116 and 131; Sims-Williams, 'Settlement', pp. 32–3. On Tetbury see above, n. 13.

[82] John, *Orbis*, pp. 88–9. See below, pp. 174 and 205–6.

suggestion with the facts that Offa had consented to Cynewulf's grant to the monastery, and that the foundation charter for Stour in Ismere monastery, another of the disputed 'places', had been issued by a Mercian, not a Hwiccian king. One certainly has the impression, as Wormald says, that 'Offa was less concerned with legal niceties than with securing land on any pretext'.[83] On the face of it, Offa's claim to Bath appears to be a high-handed response to the political situation on the West Saxon border.

The claim to Bath should also be seen in the wider context of Offa's acquisition of monasteries over which he claimed exclusive proprietary rights – a principle which Bishop Heathored conceded, however reluctantly, in his record of the synod. Offa even obtained a privilege from Hadrian I (772–95) by which the pope consented that the many monasteries founded or 'justly acquired' by Offa and consecrated in the name of his patron saint Peter should remain under the control (*sub dicione*) of the king, Queen Cynethryth, and their descendants for ever.[84] Bath's dedication to St Peter[85] was perhaps a happy coincidence for Offa in his dealings with the papacy, during which he emphasized his devotion to Peter, the 'standard bearer and comrade' who led him to victory, and even issued a coin inscribed *s. petrvs*, probably to send as alms to Rome. This devotion to Peter may have been more than mere policy; Offa's grandfather's foundation at Bredon was dedicated to Peter, *princeps apostolorum*.[86]

Worcester's claim to the other four disputed 'places' can be partially documented. Early in the century Æthelheard son of Oshere had granted Stratford, assessed at 20 hides, to Bishop Ecgwine to hold 'by ecclesi-

[83] *The Anglo-Saxons*, ed. Campbell, p. 123 (cf. p. 126). Cf. John, *Orbis*, pp. 88–9. In suggesting that the name of the grantor of the Stour in Ismere charter (S 89) has been 'altered' (p. 89), John forgets that 'it is a charter surviving in a contemporary text' (p. 84).

[84] *Liber diurnus Romanorum pontificum*, ed. T. E. Sickel (Vienna, 1889), pp. xxviii and 122–3, no. 93; Levison, *England and the Continent*, pp. 29–31; Brooks, *Canterbury*, p. 184.

[85] S 265. Cf. Sims-Williams, 'Wilfrid', p. 171, n. 42. Of course, despite the transmitted text of the 758 charter, the dedication to St Peter could be a re-dedication of Offa's reign, especially if, as William of Malmesbury and Leland state, Offa (re)founded Bath: *GP*, p. 194; *Collectanea*, ed. Hearne 1, 84. Cf. Taylor, 'Bath', p. 138. See also above, p. 102, n. 60.

[86] Duemmler, *Ep.* cxxvii, pp. 188–9; *EHD*, no. 205; C. E. Blunt, 'The Coinage of Offa', in *Anglo-Saxon Coins: Studies presented to F. M. Stenton*, ed. R. H. M. Dolley (London, 1961), pp. 39–62, at 44–6. For Bredon, see above, p. 153.

astical law'.[87] It may already have been a monastery then; certainly it became one: at Tamworth on Christmas Day 844 King Beorhtwulf sold Bishop Heahberht immunities for 'that monastery on the Avon which is called Stratford, whose size is 20 hides';[88] and in 782 Bishop Werferth, being obliged to lease a Warwickshire estate to raise cash to pay off the Danes then encamped in London, insisted that the estate should revert 'to that monastery which is called Stratford'.[89]

The 38 hides at Stour (*æt Sture*), which presumably lay on the river Stour that flows into the Avon near Stratford, may be identical with the episcopal estate of Shottery, assessed elsewhere at 33 hides plus 6 hides of detached land. This estate seems to have been granted to the see by Offa, king of Essex, at the beginning of the century; Offa of Mercia might well dispute the East Saxon king's authority to make a grant within the Hwiccian sub-kingdom.[90] Another possibility is that *æt Sture* consisted of Alderminster (which is possibly the *æt Sture* possessed by the bishop in 855) and the adjacent 30 hides at Tredington 'by the river which is called *Stuur*', which were formerly held by the eponymous Tyrdda *comes*, but were given to the see by the Hwiccian sub-kings in 757, by another grant whose validity Offa might dispute.[91]

In the case of the other Stour, Stour in Ismere, there was no questioning the royal authority of Æthelbald's grant of the monastery to his thegn Cyneberht, by the extant original charter of 736; but Offa may have questioned the charter by which Cyneberht's son, Abbot Ceolfrith, granted his inheritance at Henbury and Stour in Ismere to the see, even though Offa himself had consented to the grant (according to the transmitted text of the charter).[92] Ceolfrith's fears, expressed in his charter's anathema, that his kindred might object to his grant are perhaps relevant. Offa himself seems to have had a personal interest in the Henbury estate, which, he said, Æthelbald had granted by charter to his grandfather Eanwulf,[93] and he may have raised some similar objection over Stour in Ismere.

---

[87] S 1252. See above, p. 141. The assessment of Stratford as 30 hides in the report of the Brentford synod may be a scribal error for 20.

[88] S 198 (cf. above, p. 137, n. 102). Cf. BCS 1320. For alleged earlier privileges see Dugdale, *Monasticon* I, 608.

[89] S 1278. Cf. *ASC* 872; O'Donovan, 'Episcopal Dates, Part II', p. 112. See below, p. 373.

[90] S 64. See further Sims-Williams, 'People and Places'.

[91] S 1273 and 55. See further Sims-Williams, 'People and Places'.

[92] See above, p. 149.   [93] S 146; cf. above, pp. 149 and 153.

As we have seen, Bredon had been founded by Offa's grandfather on land granted by Æthelbald. Only just before the 781 synod Offa clearly expected it to remain a family monastery: in 777 he had granted land at Evenlode to his *minister* Ridda, stipulating that the land should pass to Bredon monastery after the deaths of Ridda and his wife and daughter; and as recently as September 780, in the last days of Tilhere's episcopate, Offa had granted properties to Bredon monastery on condition that they remained within his kindred's control for ever.[94] The basis for the new bishop's counter-claim cannot now be divined. It is clear, however, that it succeeded: 'the 12 hides of Bredon monastery' were among the properties of the see in the 840s, along with some of the lands Offa had granted to Bredon, and were to form the nucleus of an important episcopal estate, many of whose members derived from the estate of the eighth-century monastery.[95]

The disputed seventeen hides at Hampton, near Stratford (later called Hampton Episcopi and now Hampton Lucy) had formed the subject of a charter of Offa's on 26 December 780.[96] This had granted ecclesiastical privileges to these lands, which Bishop Heathored and his *familia* leased to Offa's relative (*propinqua*), an abbess Eanburg, for the duration of her life – quite likely her monastery was at Hampton, though this cannot be assumed.[97] On the face of it, Offa would seem to have conceded his 781 claims already in December 780. It must be remembered, however, that we depend on episcopal archives for the exact wording of his charter. Moreover, Offa may have regarded the lease to his relative as merely a pragmatic interim solution to a continuing dispute with the see over its title to Hampton. The basis of his claim is again obscure. In view of the

[94] S 109 (on the date see Scharer, *Königsurkunde*, p. 236) and S 116 (cf. above, p. 153). Good relations between Offa and Tilhere are suggested by his gift of lands and a bible at the bishop's *conuiuium* at Fladbury in 780, but the charter (S 118) is unreliable; cf. below, p. 182, nn. 28 and 30.

[95] Sims-Williams, 'People and Places'. See S 117 and 1272; Dugdale, *Monasticon* I, 608.

[96] S 120. This specified them as 12 hides at Hampton itself and 5 hides at *Fæhha leag*, and in fact a twelfth-century summary of the Synod of Brentford (Dugdale, *Monasticon* I, 608) names both *Hamtun* and *Feccanlea*. The latter appears to have lain towards Tiddington; see Hart, *Charters of Northern England*, p. 81, citing S 1310 and 1318. Johansson, *Lēah*, pp. 72 and 74, separates *Fæhha*- from *Faccan*-, but the equation is accepted by Gelling, *Signposts*, p. 14. See also *DEPN*, p. 172.

[97] S 120. On the date see above, p. 139, n. 110. She may be styled 'abbess' before the foundation of her monastery; cf. above, n. 64.

involvement of Eanburg (whose name suggests a connection with *Ean*wulf) and of Hampton's proximity to Mercian royal centres at Wellesbourne and (arguably) at Kineton,[98] we may speculate that Offa's interest was connected with his family's property rights in the area. Alveston (*Eanulfestun*), on the opposite side of the Avon, conceivably takes its name from Offa's grandfather Eanwulf, the timber halls at Hatton Rock in Hampton Lucy itself may indicate an eighth-century royal palace, and Dugdale reports a tradition that Offa had another palace at Offchurch, to the north-east.[99]

It will be seen that Offa's position at the Synod of Brentford can be explained only tentatively. In some cases (perhaps Stratford and *æt Sture*) he may have maintained that grants by sub-kings were invalid, as he is known to have done in Kent;[100] John notes the interesting coincidence that charters issued by the Hwiccian sub-kings cease in or shortly before 780.[101] In other cases (such as Stour in Ismere) he may have questioned the right of an heir to leave land as he wished, even though it was held as bookland. He may also have had some reasons to question the (unrecorded) transactions by which some of the 'places' came to the see (Bath, *æt Sture*, Bredon and Hampton). Yet these hypotheses do not fully explain the situation, and it may be better to see Offa's claims in the context of tactical bargaining for the strategic site of Bath, or in a wider context of, on the one hand, opposition to episcopal monopolization of church land, and, on the other, ecclesiastical self-aggrandizement, symptoms of which are Offa's 'acquisition' of *Eigenklöster* under papal privilege, his plan to have his son and heir 'hallowed' (perhaps, Brooks suggests, by the pope in imitation of Charlemagne's action in 781) and his promotion of a Mercian archbishopric at Lichfield in 787.[102]

Yet attention should also be paid to the stress laid on heredity and on Offa's relationship to Æthelbald (really no closer than first cousin twice

---

98 S 192 and 209; *PNWa*, p. 282; Phythian-Adams, 'Rutland', p. 76; Sawyer, 'Royal *tun*', pp. 278, n. 30, and 297.

99 Of course, there are many other possibilities for Alveston (*PNWa*, p. 231), e.g. the Eanwulf who was granted Nuthurst by S 1278. For Hatton Rock see below, p. 362; a ninth-century *episcopal* palace has also been suggested as a possibility. On Offchurch see *PNWa*, pp. 177–8.

100 *EHD*, p. 510; Brooks, *Canterbury*, pp. 112–15.

101 John, *Orbis*, pp. 88–9; Scharer, *Königsurkunde*, p. 259; and above, p. 37, and nn. 109 and 112.

102 Above, p. 161; *ASC* 787; Brooks, *Canterbury*, pp. 117–18.

removed): Offa claimed that the see was holding 'without hereditary right the inheritance of his kinsman, to wit King Æthelbald'. He may have been objecting to the 'places' having been allowed to pass out of royal control during Æthelbald's reign (or even earlier, for *Æðelbaldi hereditas* may include what Æthelbald *should* have inherited, but had not). There is a partial parallel in the case of Cookham monastery, a spoil of war which Æthelbald had granted to Christ Church by charters which Offa, treating Cookham as his private monastery, refused to recognize.[103] Without regarding the 'places' held by Worcester as in any sense 'inalienable family land',[104] Offa may have felt that Æthelbald had been too free in alienating lands to the church. We have noted that Offa's grandfather Eanwulf had some connection with Bredon and perhaps others of the 'places'. Now it is striking that while Eanwulf disappears from history at the very beginning of Æthelbald's reign, Offa's father, Thingfrith, makes no appearance in the record at all. Perhaps Æthelbald passed over Offa's branch of the royal family, not least when making grants to churches and 'thegn-abbots'. Offa's claims at Brentford in 781 may reflect his resentment rather than his legal entitlement.

After the Synod of Brentford

It is significant that the only known monastic foundation in the diocese of Worcester in Offa's reign after the 781 synod is his royal Mercian *Eigenkloster* at Winchcombe. According to the late twelfth-century Winchcombe annals in London, BL, Cotton Tiberius E. iv, Offa founded a monastery (*monasterium*) at Winchcombe in 787 and installed nuns there – the annalist probably envisaged a nunnery, but it may really have been a double monastery.[105] No pre-twelfth-century source mentions Offa's role, but the foundation fits in well with the rest of his monastic policy: his acquisition of Cookham and Bath, and his papal privilege for the monasteries dedicated to St Peter which he founded or 'justly acquired'. Winchcombe may be among these, for its old church of St Peter, with its

---

103 See above, p. 160. The circumstance of Offa's feud with Jænberht makes this a special case.

104 See John, *Orbis*, p. 87.

105 Dugdale, *Monasticon* II, 300. On these annals see R. R. Darlington, 'Winchcombe Annals 1049–1181', in *A Medieval Miscellany for Doris Mary Stenton*, ed. P. M. Barnes and C. F. Slade, PPRS ns 36 (1960), 111–37. See also the Worcester-diocese *Cronica de Anglia* in BL, Cotton Vitellius C. viii, 9v, ed. Liebermann, *Geschichtsquellen*, p. 19. Cf. above, p. 120, on double monasteries.

upper floor (*solarium*) at the west end, is mentioned in the eleventh-century *Vita S. Kenelmi*.[106] The originally private nature of the foundation would be confirmed if we could be sure that it was Offa's widow, Cynethryth (abbess of Cookham in 798), who is recorded as abbess of Winchcombe sometime in the ninth century; the Winchcombe abbess may, however, be another Cynethryth, recorded as the queen of Wiglaf (827–40) in the 830s.[107] The Tiberius E. iv annalist ascribes to Coenwulf the foundation in 798 of a monastery (*coenubium*) for three hundred monks at Winchcombe, and says that the church was dedicated to the Virgin in 811, quoting the foundation charter.[108] This charter is spurious as it stands, and the annalist's separate foundations by Offa and Coenwulf look like the result of a late misunderstanding of an originally double monastery. Nevertheless, Coenwulf may well have added the church of St Mary, in which he was buried. He was clearly a major benefactor, granting Winchcombe properties which probably included the monastery of Twyning.[109] Like Offa, he

---

[106] *Vita S. Kenelmi*, ed. Antropoff, *Entwicklung*, p. xiv. See Levison, *England and the Continent*, pp. 31 and 257–8; Bassett, 'Winchcombe', pp. 87–9.

[107] *Kynedrip abbatissa* also attests in 797 as a member of the royal house, but the charter (S 152) is unreliable. As the name Cynethryth was not uncommon, neither the Cookham nor the Winchcombe identification is certain. For Cookham see *EHD*, p. 508 and Brooks, *Canterbury*, pp. 116 and 131, on S 1258. For Winchcombe see S 1442 – but perhaps this Cynethryth flourished too late to be Offa's widow. For Wiglaf's queen see S 188 and 190; Rollason, 'Murdered Royal Saints', p. 8. Levison, *England and the Continent*, p. 252, needlessly supposes that 'Cyneðryð' in S 1442 is an error for 'Quoenðryð', Coenwulf of Mercia's daughter, who attests in 811 (S 165) and who was abbess of Minster-in-Thanet *c.* 824–5 (S 1434 and 1436; cf. H&S III, 586–7). Quoenthryth is the villain of the *Vita S. Kenelmi* and was doubtless connected with Winchcombe, like her father – note the reference in S 1436 to charters at Winchcombe and to her being 'in prouincia Hwicciorum' – but there is no evidence that she was abbess of Winchcombe. The evil Quendrytha of the Kenelm legend may be a conflation of Offa's queen, Coenwulf's daughter, and the Thryth of *Beowulf*: E. Rickert, 'The Old English Offa Saga', *Modern Philology* 2 (1904–5), 29–76 and 321–76; E. S. Hartland, 'The Legend of St Kenelm', *TBGAS* 39 (1916), 13–65.

[108] Dugdale, *Monasticon* II, 300–1, and BCS 337; S 167. See also *Landboc*, ed. Royce I, 17–21. On the foundation charter (S 167), see also above, pp. 41–2. William of Malmesbury's story about Eadberht Præn's release in 811 may imply that Winchcombe already existed in 798 (*Gesta regum*, ed. Stubbs I, 95; *GP*, p. 294; cf. Brooks, *Canterbury*, pp. 124–5).

[109] For Coenwulf's burial see *Vita S. Kenelmi*, ed. Antropoff, *Entwicklung*, p. xii. There is no independent evidence as to how much older than the eleventh century St Mary's church was; cf. Bassett, 'Winchcombe', pp. 87–8. Levison, *England and the Continent*,

obtained papal privileges, from Leo III (795–816) and Paschal I (in 817), which confirmed his proprietary rights over Winchcombe and the other monasteries he had inherited from his kinsfolk or 'justly acquired'. These and other royal documents were kept at Winchcombe – as was the mutilated and blinded captive Eadberht Præn, in punishment for his seizure of the Kentish throne in 796–8.[110] Evidently Coenwulf, carrying on where Offa left off, made Winchcombe his chief royal monastery in the diocese of Worcester. The eleventh-century legend that Coenwulf's young son, Cynehelm (St Kenelm), murdered at Clent upon his father's death in 821, was buried at Winchcombe is thus quite plausible.[111]

After Cynethryth, Coenwulf's relative Ælfflæd ruled Winchcombe. According to later sources she was a daughter of Ceolwulf I (821–3) who married Wiglaf's son Wigmund (*fl.* 830), and bore him a son called Wigstan (St Wystan) who was murdered in another dynastic bloodbath in 849; like Cynehelm, Wigstan was culted as a saint, and was entombed at that other great Mercian royal monastery, Repton. In 897 Winchcombe

pp. 258–9, argues that it was very late, but with his p. 259, n. 1, cf. Bishop, *Liturgica*, p. 247. For Twyning, see above, p. 133, n. 83. For other grants see S 1861 (an original) and S 1442 on 'hereditatem Cenuulfi quæ pertinet ad Wincelcumbe'. Bassett, 'Search', p. 239, n. 29, speculates that this phrase refers to Winchcombeshire, that Coenwulf was of Hwiccian royal descent, and that he had inherited the region from Hwiccian ancestors.

[110] The papal privileges, although not naming Winchcombe, are found in Tiberius E. iv, and Leo's refers to the 'monasteria uicique ac prædia ad illum monasterium pertinentia ubi corpus tuum sepultum fuerit'. See BCS 337 and 363; *Landboc*, ed. Royce I, 21–3; and on their authenticity, Levison, *England and the Continent*, pp. 30–2 and 255–7; Brooks, 'Anglo-Saxon Charters', p. 220, and *Canterbury*, pp. 185–6; Edwards, 'Two Documents', pp. 9–15. For documents at Winchcombe see S 1436. A surviving example is S 1861 (cf. Brooks, *Canterbury*, p. 360, n. 68; Scharer, *Königsurkunde*, p. 278). For Eadberht see above, n. 108.

[111] Bassett, 'Winchcombe', shows that the probable site was a chapel dedicated to the boy martyr St Pancras. On St Kenelm see Rollason, 'Murdered Royal Saints', pp. 9–10; Thacker, 'Pre-Viking Mercia', pp. 8–12. The unneccessary, but widely accepted, theory of Rickert, Hartland, Robinson and Levison (*England and the Continent*, pp. 32 and 249) that a Cynehelm who attests various of Coenwulf's charters is his son is most unlikely (cf. *Glastonbury*, ed. Scott, pp. 110–11 and 200, n. 100). The forgery S 156 is, of course, an exception; see Brooks, *Canterbury*, p. 102. Cynehelm was a common name.

was still in existence as a double monastery, though by then it was losing some of its power and prestige to Worcester in the age of Alfred.[112]

The present study, however, concludes at the end of the eighth century. What were the salient points then?

THE CHURCH *c.* 800

Offa's short-lived archdiocese of Lichfield was being suppressed, with Coenwulf's agreement. Deneberht, bishop of Worcester, and Wulfheard, bishop of Hereford, had made, or were about to make, professions of obedience to Æthelheard, archbishop of Canterbury.[113] In other words, within the southern English church normal relations were being restored.

More striking is the lack of evidence for any kind of relations with the Welsh church, despite the fact that the 'man of God' (*homo Dei*) Elfoddw, who died in 809 as 'chief bishop (*archiepiscopus*) in the land of Gwynedd', had led the Welsh to conform over the ostensible cause of friction, the date of Easter, as far back as 768.[114] One of the arguments Offa had used to persuade Hadrian I to allow the creation of a new archdiocese was the 'extension' of the English (or Mercian?) realm, presumably in the direction of Wales; but after a papal legate's fact-finding mission to Mercia and 'parts of Wales' (*Britannię partes*) in 786, no more is heard of the latter.[115] No doubt the ruthlessness with which the Mercian kings had extended their kingdom westwards made all relations across Offa's Dyke difficult for generations: the Book of Llandaf's catalogue of churches and estates laid waste by Æthelbald may be the tip of an iceberg. The same source's records of episcopal estates, churches and monasteries west of the Wye give the impression of a prosperous Welsh church cheek by jowl with that of the Magonsætan,[116] but the only suggestion of personal contact is the

---

[112] See S 1442; Rollason, 'Murdered Royal Saints', pp. 7–8; Thacker, 'Pre-Viking Mercia', pp. 12–14. Cf. above, p. 120.

[113] Brooks, *Canterbury*, pp. 125–6; cf. above, p. 90, n. 16.

[114] *AC* s.aa. 768 and 809. Cf. Lloyd, *History* I, 203 (the 'Gwentian *Brut*' in H&S I, 204 is a forgery).

[115] Duemmler, *Epp.* cxxvii and iii; *EHD*, nos. 205 (p. 861) and 191 (p. 837). Cf. the misleading comments by D. A. Whitehead, in Shoesmith, *Hereford* II, 14.

[116] See above, p. 52, for Æthelbald's devastation. The charters of Sequence II in Davies, *Llandaff Charters*, pp. 41–53, are approximately eighth-century; cf. my review, p. 126. See maps 2–4 in Hughes, 'Celtic Church', pp. 17–18 and fig. 1 above, p. xv.

occurrence of a prayer by someone with the Old Welsh name Moucan (Modern Welsh *Meugan*) in a late eighth-century prayer book from Worcester.[117] No English names appear in the eighth-century charters in the Book of Llandaf.[118]

Within the two English dioceses the most notable development by *c.* 800 was the number of monasteries which had come under the direct control of the bishop of Worcester, through the wishes of their founders and abbots or abbesses, through the intermittent piety of Hwiccian or Mercian rulers and through tenacious episcopal litigation. The following can probably be numbered among them: Stour in Ismere, Hanbury, *Penintanham* (probably Inkberrow), Wootton Wawen, Hampton Lucy, Stratford, Fladbury, Ripple, Twyning, Bredon, Daylesford, Dowdeswell, Withington, Bibury, Tetbury, Old Sodbury(?) and perhaps already Bishop's Cleeve. We hear, too, of two monasteries in the diocese of Worcester, Cheltenham and Beckford, which had long belonged to the church of Hereford.[119] No doubt the bishop of Hereford (his see was by now certainly fixed at Hereford) possessed many more such monasteries in his own diocese, but the scarcity of Hereford records prevents their identification; Bromyard monastery, already in the hands of the bishop and his 'congregation' at Hereford when it is first recorded in the mid-ninth century, may be one such.[120] It is only because of the rich Worcester archive that we know about Cheltenham and Beckford.

The absorption of monasteries into the episcopal estate did not necessarily signify the end of religious observance in them. Cheltenham and Beckford were still called *monasteria* in 803 and so were Hanbury, Stratford and others later in the ninth century. This was more than a nominal description of secularized estates: in 875, when Ceolwulf II freed the whole

The churches (or, in some cases, possibly church estates) shown on fig. 1 are those of Sequence II, plus LL 159a, 167 and 192. For seventh-century churches see fig. 2, above p. 63.

[117] See below, p. 280.

[118] Whereas they are common from the late tenth century onwards: Davies, *Llandaff Charters*, p. 145.

[119] See above, pp. 138–9. Utel, bishop of Hereford, seems to have acquired estates at Aston Blank and Notgrove in Gloucestershire (*ECWM*, p. 36), but it is doubtful whether they were monastic; see above, p. 148 and n. 27, on S 99.

[120] S 1270. The later Hereford manors may provide a clue to others; see W. Page, 'Some Remarks on the Churches of the Domesday Survey', *Archaeologia* 66 (1915), 61–102, at 94.

of Werferth's diocese (*parrochia Hwicciorum*) from the obligation of feeding the king's horses and horsemen, the bishop promised that 'in those *monasteria* in which the aforementioned charge should have been rendered, commemoration and the Lord's Prayer were daily to be raised to heaven as long as the Christian faith should be observed in this race'. [121]

Yet it is a moot point what *monasterium* signifies in these contexts. Is one to picture a monastic community under an abbot, who might or might not also be a priest ordained by the bishop, or a pastoral 'minster' under a priest, with or without a community? The looseness with which the terms *monasterium* and *mynster* were used suggests that such distinctions mattered less to contemporaries than they have done to their Benedictine successors of later centuries. [122] Nevertheless, there does seem to have been a tendency to stress the priestly rather than the abbatial status of the rulers of *monasteria*, as in the case of Abbot Headda at Dowdeswell. [123] Such a change of emphasis was in the bishops' interests: priests would be more answerable to the see and, when the monastic founder's family died out or refused to take orders, priests could be appointed centrally, often from among the *alumni* of the episcopal *familia*. The estates dependent on presumed monasteries like Bibury or Bishop's Cleeve continued paying church-scot to their 'old minster', probably a horse-load of grain per hide, and this would contribute to its upkeep and the support of its priest or priests. [124] If the see leased out monastic lands, the 'old minster' might also benefit. There is an instance in 847, which is also interesting since it implies a division between the property of the bishop and that of his *familia*: the Worcester *familia*, leasing Kempsey and the twelve hides of Bredon monastery to Bishop Ealhhun for two lifetimes, specify, in addition to dues to the *familia*, such as English and Welsh ale, meat and bread, that his heir should provide oil for all the monastery's lamps. [125] 'Such was the conservatism of medieval ecclesiastical life', remarks Dyer in his economic

---

[121] S 190, 1278, 215; translation from *EHD*, no. 95.   [122] See above, pp. 115–17.
[123] See above, p. 156.
[124] S 1279, 1415 and 1283. Cf. also perhaps S 1340 (Daylesford). See Stenton, *Anglo-Saxon England*, pp. 152–4, 473–4 and 485; Robertson, *Charters*, pp. 290–1; Barlow, *English Church 1000–1066*, pp. 145, 160–2, 179, 195 and 198.
[125] Dugdale, *Monasticon* I, 608; *ECWM*, p. 103 no. 253. (Cf. S 1833, for the date of which see O'Donovan, 'Episcopal Dates Part II', p. 112.) I take *monasterium* to refer to Bredon, but Kempsey or Worcester could be meant. Cf. Dyer, *Lords and Peasants*, pp. 28–9. On light-dues see Barlow, *English Church 1000–1066*, p. 162. On the 'division of the *mensa*' see Brooks, *Canterbury*, pp. 157–9.

history of the bishopric of Worcester, 'that even at the end of the middle ages the rectories which succeeded the minsters still stand out in comparison with other churches because of the great wealth of their livings'.[126]

Kempsey is a monastery whose history well illustrates the relations between the see and the monasteries. It is first recorded in 799. In that year an abbot Balthun purchased freedoms for the monastery from King Coenwulf, with the right to bequeath it as he chose.[127] Abbot Balthun can probably be identified with a priest of the same unusual name to whom Bishop Deneberht (799–822), with the consent of his *familia*, granted land, describing him as an *alumnus* of Worcester and 'a dear and faithful friend of that congregation'.[128] Deneberht's *familia* included at least nine priests, four deacons, two *clerici* and three others, to judge by his charter's witness list.[129] Like that earlier *alumnus*, Abbot Headda of Dowdeswell, Balthun seems to have bequeathed his monastery to Worcester, for Coenwulf granted the see privileges for Kempsey monastery,[130] and the *familia* leased it for two lifetimes to Bishop Deneberht.[131] They leased it again in 847, to Bishop Ealhhun, who in 868 erected and dedicated a new church there to St Andrew; it was presumably intended to serve the episcopal manor, where the bishops of the Hwicce sometimes stayed.[132]

---

[126] Dyer, *Lords and Peasants*, p. 30. Cf. Blair, 'Secular Minster Churches', pp. 138–9.

[127] S 154. I accept the date (falling between Heathored's and Deneberht's episcopates, cf. above, p. 139, n. 110) and reject the historical allusion to the peace treaty as an antiquarian addition.

[128] S 1262; also Dugdale, *Monasticon* I, 608 (where 'Kemesigensi abbati Balthuno' shows that the identification was already made in the twelfth century) and BCS 1320. Cf. below, pp. 356–7. The date of S 1262 is not as certain as Robinson, *St Oswald*, pp. 8–9, supposes, as S 1413, with which he compares it, cannot be dated accurately – it is not even clear whether S 1413 belongs to Heathored's or Deneberht's episcopate, though it is unlikely to be late in the latter's as the grantor appears already in 759 (S 56). See above, p. 156 and n. 65.

[129] See also, in 814, S 1261. The use of the term *clerici* may be due to the cartulary scribe (cf. Atkins, 'Church of Worcester', Part II, pp. 4–8). On the size and composition of the Worcester *familia* see Robinson, *St Oswald*, and *Times of Saint Dunstan*, p. 126; Atkins, 'Church of Worcester'; P. H. Sawyer, 'Charters of the Reform Movement: The Worcester Archive', in *Tenth-Century Studies*, ed. D. Parsons (Chichester, 1975), pp. 84–93 and 228. Cf. possibly S 1433, discussed by P. Wormald in *The Anglo-Saxons*, ed. Campbell, pp. 123 and 125, and 'Settlement of Disputes', pp. 152–4.

[130] Dugdale, *Monasticon* I, 608 (possibly a misinterpretation of S 154, however; cf. Finberg, *Gloucestershire Studies*, p. 10).

[131] Dugdale, *Monasticon* I, 608.

[132] Above, n. 125; 'Florence', s.aa. 868 and 1033 (*MHB*, pp. 554 and 597); S 1332.

Oratorium is the word used for this church of St Andrew founded by Ealhhun. There is no evidence for bishops of the Hwicce or Magonsætan establishing *monasteria* to meet the spiritual needs of their manors, as is sometimes assumed. It has, for example, been supposed that a *monasterium* at Blockley, which is known to have been in Bishop Ealhhun's possession in 855, had been built by the bishop to serve his Dorn-Batsford-Blockley estate.[133] Yet it is just as likely that Blockley had originally been an independent foundation, perhaps dependent on Winchcombe monastery, which owned Upton in Blockley in the mid-ninth century.[134] In this diocese at least, the late Anglo-Saxon pastoral network of episcopal minster churches seems to have been assembled gradually from independent components of diverse origin; there is no obviously ancient planned matrix behind it.

Relations between the bishops and the monasteries *c.* 800 were varied but often harmonious. Since the seventh century bishops had been set in charge of particular monasteries. Some bishops had been abbots themselves, such as Tilhere of Berkeley at Worcester *c.* 778, and, at Hereford, Utel *c.* 795 and possibly his successor, Wulfheard, in 801; and Bishop Ecgwine of Worcester was remembered at Evesham primarily as abbot of that monastery.[135] Again, bishops such as Heathored of Worcester had

---

[133] S 207. Thus Finberg, *Lucerna*, p. 19 = *Agrarian History*, p. 394; cf. his further discussion in *Gloucestershire Studies*, pp. 5–11. On Blockley see J. K. West, 'Architectural Sculpture in Parish Churches of the 11th- and 12th-Century West Midlands: Some Problems in Assessing the Evidence', in *Minsters and Parish Churches*, ed. Blair, pp. 159–67, at 164.

[134] S 1442. Cf. below, pp. 380 and 387. For Worcester's Batsford and Dorn estates see S 101; Dugdale, *Monasticon* I, 608 (*ECWM*, pp. 43–4, no. 54); *Worcester Cartulary*, ed. Darlington, p. xiv.

[135] See above, pp. 140–2 and 158, n. 75. For Utel see Searle, *Onomasticon*, p. 470; H&S III, 461–2; Duemmler, *Ep.* iii (p. 29). For Wulfheard (much less certain) see the Inkberrow charter, S 1430 (attesting, soon after *Utel abbas*, as *abbas* in the cartulary copies only, but perhaps really the layman who possessed Inkberrow *c.* 789–822; cf. S 1260 and 1432); Duemmler, *Ep.* lxx; T. Sickel, 'Alcuinstudien I', *Sitzungsberichte der phil.-hist. Classe der kais. Akademie der Wissenschaften* 79 (Vienna, 1875), 461–550, at 509, n. 1, and 519, n. 3. The odd name of Alcuin's correspondent's monastery, *Hoddahelm* (Duemmler, p. 113, n.), is of little help in localizing it, although Bullough, 'Albuinus Deliciosus', p. 77, n. 14, notes that an element *helm* 'shelter for cattle' occurs in He. and Gl. (cf. *PNE* I, 242, *PNGl* IV, 138, and *DEPN*, p. 232) – and, it may be added, as a loanword in Welsh; I find no early evidence for this sense of *helm*. Wormald suggests identifying the Abbot Wilfrith of the Prologue to the *Vita S. Guthlaci* with Bishop Wilfrith of Worcester (718–743×745), but this would require a

relatives among the abbots of their dioceses, and some of these abbots were educated at the episcopal see.[136]

Nevertheless, there is evidence of friction between the bishops and those monasteries which escaped direct episcopal control. The number of independent monasteries known to have existed *c.* 800 is fewer than in the heyday of the mid-eighth century, but some which remained were powerful institutions, some of them, like Gloucester and Winchcombe, having lesser *monasteriola* dependent upon them.[137] There may have been further independent monasteries which are unknown precisely because their independence resulted in their existence not being recorded in the Worcester archive. For instance, although C. S. Taylor remarked that 'there can be little doubt that Tewkesbury, like Berkeley, had been the estate of a great minster', the only written evidence is a legend about its foundation in 715 on a site occupied by an eponymous hermit Theokus.[138] In Hereford diocese the only monastery whose existence *c.* 800 is fairly certain is Wenlock, where there was still a double monastery in 901.[139] Poor recording compared to Worcester can be blamed for the apparent disparity between the dioceses, but it may indeed have been the case that the richer, and militarily less exposed, lands to the east supported more monasteries. The bishops of Hereford needed to lease lands in Worcester diocese, as we have seen, whereas the bishops of Worcester had less need to reciprocate.[140] Perhaps it is significant that only one abbot accompanied the bishop of Hereford to the Council of *Clofesho* in 803, whereas four came with the bishop of Worcester.[141]

Evesham and Pershore are shadowy at this date, but the former seems to

very early date for the *Vita: The Anglo-Saxons*, ed. Campbell, pp. 94–5, 99 and 251 (cf. Whitelock, 'Pre-Viking Age Church', p. 15). Like *Wulfheard*, it was a common name. For a suggestion that Bishop Walhstod had been abbot of Glastonbury see below, p. 343.

[136] See above, p. 156. For the ninth and tenth centuries see above, pp. 152 and 157.

[137] S 209 (Gloucester); for Winchcombe see above, p. 166.

[138] C. S. Taylor in *Gloucestershire Studies*, ed. Finberg, p. 39. Cf. Darby and Terrett, *Domesday Geography*, pp. 4–5. For the Theokus legend see Dugdale, *Monasticon* II, 59–60; on the name cf. *CP*, p. 75; *PNGl* II, 62; von Feilitzen and Blunt, 'Coinage of Edgar', p. 204.

[139] See above, p. 120. See also above, p. 169, on Bromyard.

[140] See above, n. 119. For Worcester estates in the shire (but not necessarily diocese) of Hereford see *ECWM*, pp. 140–1, and for a Gloucester estate in Archenfield(?) see above, p. 51, and *Settlement and Society in Wales*, ed. D. H. Owen (Cardiff, 1989), p. 189.

[141] BCS 312. Cf. Whitelock, 'Pre-Viking Age Church', p. 17.

have sent its abbot, Thingferth, to the Council of 803, and Pershore is said to have obtained a privilege from Coenwulf.[142] Gloucester was continuing to receive pious donations and was to be granted a privilege in 862 by Burgred, the last effective king of Mercia.[143] Two years later Burgred held a council at Bath, at a safe distance from the Danes, and may have disposed of some of that monastery's estates. Nevertheless, Bath monastery seems to have had a continuous history; in 796 King Ecgfrith issued a charter in the 'famous monastery' that his father Offa had seized at Brentford, and even after Bath was transferred from Mercia to Wessex in the tenth century, its monastery remained a royal *Eigenkloster*, though now a West Saxon one.[144] At Winchcombe and Berkeley, powerful monastic communities flourished *c.* 800 and had increasingly litigious relations with the see.[145]

Two more independent monasteries, at Deerhurst and Westbury-on-Trym, come to light for the first time in a will made by Æthelric son of Æthelmund in (?)804. This Æthelric seems to be the son of the ealdorman of the Hwicce who was killed by the Wilsætan in 802.[146] In his will Æthelric recalls how a synod at *Clofesho* had allowed him the right to bequeath freely the estate at 'Westminster' (that is, Westbury) which his kinsmen had handed over to him, and how he had gone on pilgrimage to Rome afterwards. Now, a few years after his return, he bequeaths his inheritance at a synod at *Aclea*.[147] To Deerhurst, for his own and his father's sake, 'if it befall me that my body shall be buried there', he leaves

---

[142] *Chronicon de Evesham*, ed. Macray, p. 76. See above, p. 144.

[143] *ECWM*, pp. 153–66; Thacker, 'Chester and Gloucester', p. 208.

[144] See Sims-Williams, 'Bath', pp. 3, n. 2, and 9–10; Keynes, 'Athelstan's Books', p. 161.

[145] S 1442; Thacker, 'Pre-Viking Mercia', p. 9; Taylor, 'Berkeley Minster'; cf. B. R. Kemp, 'The Churches of Berkeley Hernesse', *TBGAS* 87 (1968), 96–110; Brooke, *Church*, pp. 67–8.

[146] See above, pp. 38–9. A solution to the problem that Æthelric seems to have come into his inheritance a 'few years' before 804 and clearly earlier than 802 (cf. Moore, *Saxon Pilgrims*, p. 89; Scharer, *Königsurkunde*, pp. 276–7) is presented by Wormald, 'Settlement of Disputes', p. 154, n. 26: 804 would be the date of the first synod at *Clofesho*, and that at *Aclea* would follow after a 'few years'. This runs into some difficulty at the other end, as *Aclea* could not be after 807, if the identification of Ceolburg is accepted (and this name is less common than Æthelmund). Were the 'few years' 804–7 precisely?

[147] S 1187; trans. *EHD*, no. 81. Cf. P. Wormald in *The Anglo-Saxons*, ed. Campbell, pp. 123–4; Scharer, 'Intitulationes', pp. 37–8. It is possible, but not proven, that Worcester forged charters in the ninth century in support of its claim; cf. Wormald, 'Settlement of Disputes', pp. 152–7; and above, nn. 53 and 61.

estates in the north(?) and east of the diocese,[148] 'on condition that that congregation carries out their vows as they have promised me'. Documents have nothing to add about this early community at Deerhurst, but architectural investigations in the 1970s, while not providing precise dates for the earliest stone church, revealed a long sequence of building phases that can be taken to imply that some parts of the surviving fabric could go back at least as far as Æthelric's will.[149]

Æthelric next bequeaths to Worcester a reversion on estates in the north of the diocese, and grants land near Gloucester to that monastery.[150] Finally, he leaves

> to my mother, Ceolburg, if she live longer than I, the land at 'Westminster' [Westbury-on-Trym] and at Stoke, that she may have it for her life and afterwards give it to the church of Worcester; that on this account she may while she lives have there protection and defence against the claims of the Berkeley people. And if any man in any dispute decrees from her an oath against the Berkeley people, she will be most free to give it with the true counsel of my kinsfolk, who granted me the inheritance, and with mine, with which I will give it to her. And if she does not get protection in the city of Worcester, she is afterwards first to seek it from the archbishop in Kent, and if she does not get it there, she is to be free with her deeds and estates to choose protection where it shall please her. If it should happen otherwise – as I hope it will not – that any man contends dishonourably against my title-deeds and inheritance, then Bishop Ealdwulf has in Lichfield the duplicate of this charter, and my close and most faithful friends have others, namely Eadberht, son of Edgar, and Æthelheah, son of Esne, in confirmation of this matter.

Offa had granted 55 hides at Westbury (*Uuestburg*) to Æthelmund, Æthelric's father, between 793 and 796,[151] and 'Stoke' was probably Stoke

---

148 Below, p. 375.

149 Personal communication from Dr H. M. Taylor (4 November 1981). See also above, pp. 59–60; and Butler *et al.*, 'Deerhurst 1971–1974'; H. M. Taylor, *Deerhurst Studies* I, *The Anglo-Saxon Fabric 1971–76* ([Cambridge], 1977). On the later history see C. S. Taylor, 'Deerhurst, Pershore and Westminster'.

150 On Bromsgrove see Robertson, *Charters*, p. 264. On 'under Over' see above, p. 38, n. 116.

151 S 139 (*HBC*³ suggests the date 794). By S 146 Offa had promised that Westbury (60 hides) and Henbury (10 hides) would ultimately go to Worcester; see above, p. 153 and n. 53. Sawyer, *Roman Britain to Norman England*, p. 145, notes that Westbury is assessed at 50 hides in Domesday Book.

Bishop (near Bristol), a member of the Westbury estate.[152] When the monastery at Westbury had been founded is unknown, but it was evidently before the above description of it as 'Wæst *mynster*'. Eventually the see did secure it, but not without opposition from the community of Berkeley monastery, just as Æthelric had feared. The abbess Ceolburg whose death in 807 is recorded in the *Anglo-Saxon Chronicle* may be Æthelric's mother. 'Florence' of Worcester adds that she was abbess of Berkeley.[153] If this addition is not a mistake due to a hazy memory of Æthelric's will, it implies that Æthelric feared that his mother's own monastic community at Berkeley would try to dispossess her of Westbury – but perhaps there were two Ceolburgs. In 824 a dispute between the see and Berkeley monastery about Westbury monastery was settled in favour of the bishop, who 'had the land with its charters, just as Æthelric had ordered that it was to revert to the church of Worcester'. Twelve hides at Stoke Bishop, however, were still in the hands of Æthelhun, abbot of Berkeley, in 883, when their return to the see after three lifetimes was arranged by Æthelred, ealdorman of the Mercians.[154] As Westbury proper was assessed at 43 hides,[155] the promise of the 12 hides at Stoke meant that Worcester stood to recover all 55 of the hides which Offa had granted to Æthelmund.

The 883 settlement may mark the end of conflict between Berkeley and the see, for in 914 or 915 Abbot Æthelhun was to succeed Werferth, Alfred's assistant, as bishop of Worcester.[156] By this time, after the eclipse of the old Mercian royal line, the position of the see of Worcester vis-à-vis the monasteries was stronger than *c.* 800. Situated in a city fortified by the West Saxon power, it enjoyed the full support of the new rulers of Mercia and was playing an important role in the Alfredian revival of education and learning. Not until the Benedictine revival reached houses such as Evesham and Pershore in the late tenth century did a potentially serious challenge to the bishop's authority appear.

---

[152] Rather than Stoke Prior, Wo., in which Uhtred of the Hwicce had granted Æthelmund 5 hides at Aston by S 58–9; cf. above, pp. 37 and 155, n. 61. See Taylor, 'Pre-Domesday Hide', pp. 298–9 (differently, Wormald, 'Settlement of Disputes', pp. 155–6). Westbury and Stoke [Bishop] are a single unit: *terram illam* (OE *hit* in BCS 1320).

[153] *MHB*, p. 547 and n. 1. Cf. above, p. 118, n. 18. Worcester is also our source for other information about Berkeley; see above, n. 75.

[154] S 1433 and 218. On the bounds of S 218, cf. S. Everett, 'A Reinterpretation of the Anglo-Saxon Survey of Stoke Bishop', *TBGAS* 80 (1961), 175–8.

[155] BCS 313 (p. 439, n. 1); though the wording is ambiguous.

[156] See above, n. 76.

7

Biblical study

For the Anglo-Saxons the study of the bible was the fundamental literary activity. Aldhelm's letter to an unknown woman called Sigegyth 'begging that you do not cease to occupy your mind with close contemplation of the Scriptures' is typical of many such exhortations.[1] In the monastic tradition reading and meditation on Scripture were well established sources of *gnosis* or, in the Latin terminology popularized by Cassian, *spiritalis scientia*, 'spiritual knowledge'. The monasteries of the Hwicce and Magonsætan would have tried to continue this tradition; a monk of Wenlock told Boniface that among the personified sins that had confronted him in a vision, one cried out 'I am sloth and sluggishness in neglecting holy reading', while another shouted 'I am the negligence and carelessness through which you have been held back from and careless about studying divine reading'.[2]

It is unlikely that such a monk would study the bible unaided. One obvious aid was a patristic commentary, 'because the spiritual treatise is the recognized teacher of those who read the sacred words', as Boniface observed, writing to England from Germany for commentaries in 735.[3] Another was a good teacher, learned in the patristic tradition; here one may instance Boniface himself, whose teaching activities before he left Wessex for his continental missions are described by his biographer Willibald:

His fame reached many in monasteries both of men and of women, far and wide. Many of these of the stronger sex, impelled by an urgent desire to study, flocked to him to drink the wholesome spring of knowledge and read through many volumes of the Scriptures. Those of the weaker sex, denied the strength for constant travel

[1] *Aldhelmi Opera*, ed. Ehwald, p. 497.
[2] Chadwick, *Cassian*, pp. 151–2; Boniface, *Ep.* x (Tangl, p. 10).
[3] *Ep.* xxxiv (Tangl, p. 59).

but inspired by the spirit of holy love, caused this man of such wisdom to be present with them and, traversing page after page, engaged closely in sacred scrutiny and contemplated arcane sacraments and hidden mysteries without cease.[4]

These words remind one of de Lubac's description of early patristic exegesis, as exemplified by Origen:

Les comparaisons de textes sont incessantes ... Méditant nuit et jour la loi du Seigneur, sans négliger aucun des livres qui la composent, le 'diligent lecteur' doit perpétuellement unir en son esprit les faits présents et passés, et rassembler les mots de toute part.[5]

Boniface's older contemporaries frequently speak of biblical study in terms of rigorous scrutiny, reminiscent on the one hand of the patristic tradition – *diligenter scrutari singula loca*, in Origen's phrase[6] – and on the other of the 'close reading' that modern literary critics advocate: Aldhelm speaks of 'Catholic Fathers winkling out the spiritual marrow of words and scrutinizing the meaning hidden in letters' and of those who 'exercise the wisest industry of their minds and the quality of lively wit in closely attentive reading',[7] and Bede refers to 'stripping off the bark of the letter to find a deeper and more sacred meaning in the pith of the spiritual sense'.[8] In view of all early medieval commentators' dependence on the Fathers,[9] it is tempting to dismiss this 'close reading' as merely a matter of inherited phraseology; but the thoughtful sense of selection or of style evinced by commentators such as Bede and Boniface (and later on by Ælfric and by creative writers such as Cynewulf) shows, when they repeat earlier exegesis, that they are not doing so mechanically and unreflectively. Bede, for instance, 'had not only read widely; he had digested and thought through what he had studied. The result was that his works, though their thought is so largely derivative, nevertheless bear the imprint of his own mind and personality'.[10]

---

[4] Willibald, *Vita S. Bonifatii*, c. 2, ed. Levison, *Vitae S. Bonifatii*, pp. 10–11.

[5] De Lubac, *Histoire et esprit*, pp. 309–10.

[6] *Ibid.*, p. 301, n. 44 (cf. p. 327, quoting Augustine, and p. 329).

[7] *Aldhelmi Opera*, ed. Ehwald, pp. 74 and 231.

[8] PL 91, 808, quoted by Laistner, *Thought and Letters*, p. 106.

[9] Cf. Levison, *England and the Continent*, p. 149; McNally, *Bible in the Early Middle Ages*, pp. 11, 29, etc.

[10] Laistner, 'Study of Jerome', p. 240. On exegesis attributable to Boniface see Parkes, 'Handwriting of St Boniface'.

References to the use of commentaries are legion. Aldhelm, for instance, speaks of 'libraries in which the commentaries of the most wise Jerome are read' and supposes that these commentaries are known to Abbess Hildelith of Barking and her companions 'racing curiously through the open fields of books' – another traditional metaphor for biblical study.[11] He imagines them investigating the mysteries of the Old Testament and analysing the fourfold sense of the Gospels as expounded in patristic commentaries, as well as reading histories and chronographies, grammars and metrical treatises.[12] A century later Alcuin recommends St John's Gospel to the nuns of Chelles as devotional reading because of the *altiora mysteria* which it contains, and in their reply they say that they have Augustine's homiletic explanations of the Gospel, and complain of their difficulty, causing Alcuin to write his own abbreviated commentary.[13] What was looked for in the patristic commentaries can be seen from the form taken by the commentaries of Bede, Alcuin and the other early medieval exegetes. These largely eschew controversy or the posing of original problems, being written rather 'to interpret the *sacra pagina* in such wise as to make it more easily a subject of contemplation'.[14] The Fathers' interpretations are accepted reverently and the attractive tentativeness with which an Augustine would temper the caprice of his exegesis is discarded;[15] 'exegesis became almost synonymous with tradition, for the good commentator was the scholar who handed on faithfully what he had received'.[16] For the early Anglo-Saxons patristic commentaries seem above all to have been aids to searching out those *altiora mysteria* which, though present in the whole of Creation, as Aldhelm's *Enigmata* attest, were felt to be most inexhaustibly present in the bible; its patristic exegesis could indeed rival the riddle and

---

11 *Aldhelmi Opera*, ed. Ehwald, pp. 303–4. For the metaphor cf. *ibid.*, pp. 231 and 232; de Lubac, *Histoire et esprit*, p. 326; also *Apponii Expositio*, ed. de Vregille and Neyrand, p. 86 ('coniuncta ergo anima Dei Verbo, introducta intellegentia legis, *discurrendo per singulos apices scripturae, et saepe dictum est . . .*' (italics mine)); Jerome, *Ep.* lxv.2 (ed. Hilberg I, 619: 'per prata uirentia et uarios diuinorum uoluminum flores . . .') and *Ep.* cxxii. 4 (ed. Hilberg III, 69: 'quasi per pulcherrima scripturarum prata discurrens . . .').

12 *Aldhelmi Opera*, ed. Ehwald, p. 232.

13 Duemmler, *Epp.* cxcv (Lent 800) and cxcvi (reply).

14 McNally, *Bible in the Early Middle Ages*, pp. 10 and 63.

15 I discuss Augustine's tentativeness and the elimination of his caution by later exegetes in a note (in preparation) on the exegesis of the *Spiritus bis ueniens*. Cf. below, p. 218, n. 19.

16 McNally, *Bible in the Early Middle Ages*, p. 29.

acrostic in intellectual excitement and aesthetic satisfaction.[17] Biblical study was probably a three-way conversation – between the biblical text, the 'ruminating reader' (another favourite image, used by Bede of Cædmon of Whitby),[18] and the author of a patristic commentary – in which the Anglo-Saxon student read each verse in conjunction with the commentary and considered each exegetical problem carefully enough to make the patristic train of thought and conclusion a personal rediscovery.

Unlike the modern 'close-reading' literary critic, the Anglo-Saxon student would not have regarded his books as 'machines for thinking', in I. A. Richards's phrase, but rather, according to the old idea expressed by Milton in *Areopagitica*, as things 'not absolutely dead' that 'do contain a potency of life in them to be as active as that soul was whose progeny they are, nay . . . do preserve as in a vial the purest efficacy and extraction of that living intellect that bred them'.[19] A student of Aldhelm's at Malmesbury called Æthilwald described the books which two Anglo-Saxons brought back from Rome as follows:

> En uehebant uolumina
> Numerosa per agmina
> Multimodis et mysticis
> Elucubrata normulis,
> Quorum auctori aius
> Adesse constat alitus;
> Quae profetae, apostoli
> Doctiloqui oraculi
> Indiderunt pergaminae
> Almo inflati flamine.[20]

The books of the bible itself were inexhaustible, quasi-sacramental entities

---

[17] Cf. Brown, *Augustine of Hippo*, pp. 253–4. Aldhelm's riddles are discussed by Lapidge and Rosier, *Aldhelm*, pp. 61–9. Cf. below, n. 21.

[18] See J. E. Cross, 'The Literate Anglo-Saxon – On Sources and Disseminations', *PBA* 58 (1972), 1–36, at 28–9; A. Crépin, 'Bede and the Vernacular', in *Famulus Christi*, ed. Bonner, pp. 170–92, at 171–2, 181–2 and 187–9; also *Aldhelmi Opera*, ed. Ehwald, p. 695, s.v. *rumino*.

[19] For earlier examples of this theme see Curtius, *European Literature*, p. 313, and Lesne, *Livres, scriptoria et bibliothèques*, p. 24.

[20] *Aldhelmi Opera*, ed. Ehwald, p. 531: 'Lo, they brought back many rows of volumes composed by manifold and mystic rules, whose author is known to have been aided by the Holy Spirit, volumes which prophets and apostles of the wise-speaking oracle, inspired by the Holy Spirit, set down on parchment.'

whose meaning went deeper than even their authors themselves had realized.[21] Their manuscript decoration was not just an enrichment of the books themselves, as in late antiquity, but 'a medium for emphasizing the sacred text – clothing the word as it were in a precious garb in the same manner as a relic was encased in a casket of gold and precious stones'.[22]

Two surviving eighth-century gospel books in Hereford and Worcester Cathedral Libraries are possibly of local origin, but this is still uncertain. The Hereford gospel book (Cathedral Library, P. I. 2) must somehow have been saved when the cathedral was destroyed in 1055, for it was already there in the reign of Cnut (1016–35), when details of a land dispute between the wife and son of a certain *Enneawn* (Welsh *Einiawn*) were entered on its penultimate leaf (fol. 134), perhaps out of deference for the Welsh custom of entering such marginalia in gospels.[23] Its late eighth-century script, spelling and abbreviations are un-English, however, and possibly it was written in Wales itself and not simply in an English scriptorium under Welsh influence, such as one might expect to find in Hereford diocese.[24] Another gospel book of the second half of the eighth century survives only in fragments from book bindings from Worcester and Dymock parish church, Gloucestershire: Worcester Cathedral Library, Add. 1 + Oxford, Bodleian Library, Lat. Bibl. d. 1 (P). Its script suggests Canterbury influence and its biblical text is of Canterbury type; but it may have been written in the Worcester scriptorium and have remained there until split up for binding books.[25]

---

[21] On the inexhaustibility of Scripture see de Lubac, *Histoire et esprit*, pp. 325, 336, etc.

[22] C. Nordenfalk, 'Before the Book of Durrow', *Acta Archaeologica* 18 (1947), 141–74, at 165. Contrast Stephen's account of the lost Ripon Gospels (below, n. 74) with Jerome, *Ep.* cvii. 12, cited below, n. 149.

[23] Sims-Williams, 'William', p. 13, n. 24; Jenkins and Owen, 'Lichfield Gospels, Part I', pp. 61–2 and 65. This custom was, however, naturalized in England by this stage: Keynes, 'Athelstan's Books', p. 189, n. 216.

[24] Cf. Jenkins and Owen, 'Lichfield Gospels, Part I', pp. 42 and 45–6, citing opinions of B. Bischoff and W. Stein; W. M. Lindsay, *Early Welsh Script* (Oxford, 1912), pp. 41–3; *CLA* II, no. 157. McGurk, 'Gospel Book in Celtic Lands', p. 174, is non-committal.

[25] *CLA* II, nos. 245 and 262; Turner, *Early Worcester MSS*, p. x (on text); Jenkins and Owen, 'Lichfield Gospels, Part I', p. 45, citing Stein. T. J. Brown also suggested Worcester origin in his unpublished Lyell Lectures (1977). Lowe compares the Royal Bible (*CLA* II, no. 214), but manuscripts with affinities with this are also found in Mercia; cf. Brown, 'Bibliothèque Nationale, lat. 10861', p. 135. In this connection,

A bible of which only a few leaves survive (BL, Add. 37777 + 45025 + Loan 81) is more clearly of eighth-century Worcester provenance (though not origin).[26] This great bible was in Worcester in the eleventh century when a cartulary in the same unusually large format was drawn up (now BL, Add. 46204 + Cotton Nero E. i, pt 2, fols. 181–4), clearly so as to be bound with it in accordance with Bishop Wulfstan II's command that the Worcester charters should be transcribed in the church's bible (*in bibliotheca sanctę ecclesię*).[27] It was presumably the bible which Worcester writers say was given to the church by Offa, and describe variously as 'a best bible with two clasps (*armillae*) made of purest gold', 'a great bible', and 'a bible written at Rome'.[28] The Roman attribution was a remarkably good guess, for the surviving leaves show that the 'Offa' Bible, although not actually Roman, was one of the three massive complete bibles which Ceolfrith, abbot of Wearmouth and Jarrow (690–716), caused to be written in a close imitation of late sixth-century Roman uncial. The most sumptuous of these bibles, the surviving Codex Amiatinus (Florence, Biblioteca Medicea Laurenziana, Amiatino 1), was for Ceolfrith to present to St Peter's, Rome, and the other two were intended for his own twin monasteries.[29] How Offa came by one of the latter copies is unknown. Some interest in the Codex Amiatinus at Worcester in Offa's time may be indicated by the inclusion in a collection of epigrams owned by Bishop Milred of the Amiatinus's dedicatory inscription by 'Ceolfrith, abbot at the extreme bounds of the English'; this was copied from the *Vita S. Ceolfridi*.[30] Milred's collection also included two couplets known otherwise

the Salisbury biblical fragments should perhaps be mentioned; see below, p. 275, n. 11.

26 *CLA* II, no. 177; Lowe, *Uncial*, pl. x. On Loan 81 see Parkes, *Wearmouth-Jarrow*, p. 3; Watson, *Medieval Libraries: Supplement*, p. 40.

27 Atkins, 'Church of Worcester, Part II', pp. 3 and 220–2; Atkins and Ker, *Catalogus*, pp. 77–9; Ker, *Books, Collectors and Libraries*, pp. 49–51. For a Eusebius fragment conceivably transmitted with the bible and cartulary leaves via Middleton Hall, see G. Norman, 'Turning over the Oldest Leaf of All?', *The Times*, 25 June 1985.

28 Respectively in S 118 (a charter of 780, forged in s. xi²; cf. Scharer, *Königsurkunde*, p. 250); in *Annales Monastici*, ed. Luard IV, 366; and in a letter of Senatus of Worcester edited by Turner, *Early Worcester MSS*, pp. xli and xlvii. For a doubtful fourteenth-century allusion see *ibid.* pp. xli–xlii.

29 *CLA* III, no. 299; Parkes, *Wearmouth-Jarrow*, pp. 3, 17 and 21.

30 See below, p. 348. Milred died before 780, the alleged date of Offa's gift of the bible to Bishop Tilhere (S 118), but no reliance can be placed on the latter date (cf. above, p. 163, n. 94), although the gift itself need not be doubted. Turner, *Early Worcester MSS*,

only from the Codex Amiatinus (in which only the first appears, written in silver on 8r):

> Eloquium domini quaecunque uolumina fundunt,
> spiritus hoc sancto fudit ab ore deus.
> Esaias domini cecinit miracula uates
> atque euangelicis concinit ore tubis.[31]

These elegiacs, perhaps by Bede himself, convey the attitude to the sacred text that led to a majestic bible like the Worcester bible being produced, being adorned with gold clasps, and being presented, probably as a prestigious gift, by a king such as Offa.

The Cathedral Libraries at Worcester and Hereford also contain remnants of three seventh- and eighth-century uncial manuscripts of biblical commentaries. The fly-leaves of Hereford, P. II. 10, are an eighth-century uncial fragment of an Irish (or Irish-influenced) commentary on Matthew, thought by Lowe to have been copied in Northumbria because of a similarity to the above-mentioned 'Offa' Bible.[32] Worcester, Add. 2, from the binding of a twelfth-century Worcester book, is a seventh-century Spanish fragment of Jerome's commentary on Matthew, and Add. 4 is a bifolium of an eighth-century English manuscript, with some Northumbrian features, of Paterius's extracts from Gregory the Great's writings on the Old and New Testaments. Unfortunately we have no means of knowing whether these commentaries reached the area at an early date. This is also true of a late eighth-century Northumbrian(?) fragment of Jerome on Matthew, which was found in 1960 in a house in Coalbrookdale, not far from Wenlock: Shrewsbury, County Record Office, Fragm. 1–2.[33]

---

p. xlii, suggested 'the occasion of the marriage of Offa's daughter with the king of Northumbria in 792'.

[31] Lapidge, 'Remnants', p. 819 (no. 27): 'Whatever volumes display [translating *pandunt* from the Amiatinus] the Lord's eloquence, God the Spirit has poured this forth from his holy mouth. Isaiah the prophet sang the Lord's miracles and sounded forth from his mouth with evangelic trumpets'. Cf. Bruce-Mitford, 'Codex Amiatinus', pl. X; K. Corsano, 'The First Quire of the Codex Amiatinus and the *Institutiones* of Cassiodorus', *Scriptorium* 41 (1987), 3–34, at 29; Sims-Williams, 'William', pp. 24–5.

[32] *CLA* II, no. 158 (Lowe's Cirencester provenance was rejected by Ker, *Medieval Libraries*, p. 52); Lowe, *Uncial*, pl. XV; Bischoff, *Studien* I, 245; J. F. Kelly, 'Frigulus: An Hiberno-Latin Commentator on Matthew', *RB* 91 (1981), 363–73, at 371.

[33] *CLA* II, nos. 263 and 265, and Suppl. 1760; Lowe, *Uncial*, pl. XXXVI. Turner, *Early Worcester MSS*, p. xii, thought that the Jerome reached Worcester 'while uncial MSS were still used and read, within a century, say, after the date when it was written'. On this and the Shrewsbury fragment see Ker, *Books, Collectors and Libraries*, pp. 113–20.

The first known biblical student in the region is Oftfor, bishop of Worcester. Bede tells us that after Oftfor had devoted himself to studying and observing the Scriptures in both of Hild's monasteries (Whitby and Hartlepool) he went to Theodore in Kent seeking 'more perfect things' (*perfectiora*), and spent some more time there in biblical studies (*lectiones sacrae*).[34] No denigration of the standards of Hild's monasteries is implied, for the school of Theodore at Canterbury was unique. Theodore was a native of Tarsus and had received a full Greek literary education.[35] Bede says that he was 'trained in secular and divine literature, both Greek and Latin' and describes his assistant Hadrian, who had been abbot of a monastery near Naples, as 'a man of African race and well versed in the holy Scriptures, trained both in monastic and ecclesiastical ways and equally skilled in the Greek and Latin tongues':

Because both of them were extremely learned in sacred and secular literature, they attracted a crowd of students into whose minds they daily poured the streams of wholesome learning. They gave their hearers instruction not only in the books of holy Scripture but also in the art of metre, astronomy, and ecclesiastical computation. As evidence of this, some of their students still survive who know Latin and Greek just as well as their native tongue.[36]

One of this 'crowd of students' was Aldhelm of Malmesbury, who in his letters confirms Bede's description (except in the matter of Greek) and gives us a vivid picture of the intellectual excitement of Theodore's classes: if Theodore were to be 'hemmed in by a mass of Irish students, like a savage wild boar checked by a snarling pack of hounds, with the filed tooth of the grammarian – nimbly and with no loss of time – he would disband the rebel phalanxes'.[37] Aldhelm alludes to Theodore and Hadrian as 'teachers who are citizens of Greece and Rome ... who are able to unlock and unravel the murky mysteries of the heavenly library to the scholars who are eager to study them'.[38] Something of the nature of this teaching is indicated by the biblical glosses attributed to Theodore and Hadrian, which are marked by realistic explanations of the biblical text, based on

---

[34] *HE* IV.23, quoted above, p. 102.

[35] *Ep.* lxxx (Tangl, p. 173); cf. Lapidge, 'Theodore and Hadrian', p. 45, n. 1.

[36] *HE* IV.1–2. Cf. Brooks, *Canterbury*, pp. 94–8; Lapidge, 'Theodore and Hadrian'.

[37] *Aldhelmi Opera*, ed. Ehwald, p. 493; cf. *Aldhelm*, trans. Lapidge and Herren, p. 163. The relevant letters are nos. 1, 2 and 5. See *ibid.*, pp. 8, 137–9, and 146.

[38] *Ibid.*, p. 163; *Aldhelmi Opera*, ed. Ehwald, p. 492.

direct knowledge of the Orient, and by the use of Greek commentaries of the literal, Antiochene (rather than the allegorical, Alexandrian) school.[39]

Clearly, the biblical studies which Oftfor found in Canterbury would have been *perfectiora*, but Whitby itself was a centre of such studies. Hild 'compelled those under her direction to devote so much time to the study of the holy Scriptures and so much time to the performance of good works, that there might be no difficulty in finding many there who were fitted for holy orders, that is, for the service of the altar'. To prove this point Bede names four Whitby monks who became bishops in addition to Bishop Oftfor and the monk Tatfrith, who died before he could be consecrated bishop of the Hwicce.[40] Tatfrith, like Oftfor, may have travelled in search of learning, if he is the Tatfrith referred to in a gloss in some manuscripts of Aldhelm's *Epistula ad Ehfridum*, which was composed perhaps *c.* 675 and at any rate before 690. The gloss 'tunning tatfrið' is added where Aldhelm refers to 'a mass of ravenous scholars and an avid throng of sagacious students' travelling to and fro between the schools of Ireland and England. This may be a miscopying, through the easy confusion of c and t, of *cunning tatfrið*, 'Tatfrith's experience'.[41]

The styli and book-clasps found in the excavations at Whitby indicate that much writing went on there, in an opulent environment rich in imported luxuries.[42] Unfortunately only two literary works survive which can be attributed to either of Hild's monasteries: an anonymous *Vita* of Gregory the Great, which was written at Whitby in the early eighth century; and a letter to the abbess of Pfalzel near Trier, asking her to look after an English abbess on pilgrimage to Rome. The letter was written by Hild's successor, Ælfflæd (d. *c.* 714), whose possible connection with

---

[39] Bischoff, *Studien* I, 206–9; Lapidge, 'Theodore and Hadrian'. An edition by these two scholars is forthcoming: *The Milan Biblical Glosses from the School of Canterbury*, Cambridge Studies in Anglo-Saxon England (Cambridge).

[40] *HE* IV.23; see Hunter Blair, 'Whitby', pp. 25–9.

[41] *Aldhelmi Opera*, ed. Ehwald, p. 490 and n. *c*; *Aldhelm*, trans. Lapidge and Herren, pp. 161 and 201, n. 30. On the date see *ibid.*, pp. 15 and 143–4 (cf. Sims-Williams, 'Wilfrid', p. 171). Sweet, *Oldest English Texts*, p. 501, cites four instances of the name from the Lindisfarne *Liber vitae*; there are no more in Searle, *Onomasticon*. On Tatfrith see above, p. 102.

[42] Campbell, *Essays*, p. 63; Cramp, 'Monastic Sites', pp. 228 and 456, and 'Monkwearmouth and Jarrow', pp. 8, 10 and 17; *Anglo-Saxons*, ed. Campbell, p. 79, fig. 78; Fell, 'Hild', p. 84.

Fladbury has already been discussed.[43] The thoughtful author of the *Vita S. Gregorii* had imperfect Latin, but he (or she) displays a detailed knowledge of the bible and a profound admiration for Gregory's exegetical works, which were evidently available at Whitby. Colgrave's argument that Hild 'probably felt that the scriptures alone sufficed for instruction' and that 'the Whitby monastery would not be strong in books other than those strictly bearing upon the scriptures and that the instruction was consequently limited'[44] depends upon the lack of any parade of sources in the *Vita* and upon the silence of Bede. Yet Bede's emphasis on the place of *lectio diuinarum scripturarum* in Hild's monasteries does *not* imply that this was the sole literary activity in them, for biblical study was both the ground and apex of all other studies. As Aldhelm reminded Æthilwald, the aim of secular studies was to reach the 'deepest and most sacred meanings' of Scripture through a better understanding of language, since the *lex diuina* itself follows the rules of grammar nearly everywhere.[45] Similarly Boniface, in his *Ars grammatica*, emphasized the importance of grammatical study for those who would scrutinize the sacred text in search of its deeper meaning (*in sacrosancto scrutinio laborantibus ad subtiliorem intellectum*), and his biographer Willibald outlined the ideal course of study when he referred to grammar, metrics, the historical exposition of the bible, and its threefold spiritual interpretation.[46] In Geoffrey Shepherd's words, 'in reading the Bible one learned all that needed to be learned, just as one needed to learn about everything to understand the Bible'.[47]

Oftfor may conceivably be the link between Whitby and Worcester which explains how two unusual details about Gregory the Great, reflected in the Whitby *Vita*, surface again much later in Worcester. In ch. 24 the Whitby writer asserts that the Romans called Gregory 'golden mouth' (*os*

---

[43] *Ep.* viii (Tangl, pp. 3–4). On Ælfflæd and Fladbury see above, pp. 92–3.

[44] B. Colgrave, 'The Earliest Life of St Gregory the Great, Written by a Whitby Monk', in *Celt and Saxon: Studies in the Early British Border*, ed. N. K. Chadwick *et al.*, corrected reprint (Cambridge, 1964), pp. 119–37, at 130. Cf. *Life of Gregory*, ed. Colgrave, pp. 36–7. Dr Lapidge tells me that Colgrave's conclusion needs further modification in the light of Siân Mosford's unpublished D.Phil. dissertation (Oxford University, 1989).

[45] *Opera*, ed. Ehwald, p. 500. Cf. Riché, *Education and Culture*, pp. 391–2; Sawyer, *Roman Britain to Norman England*, p. 7.

[46] *Bonifatii (Vynfreth) ars grammatica*, ed. G. J. Gebauer and B. Löfstedt, CCSL 133B (Turnhout, 1980), 11 (cf. Leclercq, *Love of Learning*, pp. 46 and 292); *Vita S. Bonifatii*, c. 2 (ed. Levison, *Vitae Sancti Bonifatii*, p. 9).

[47] 'Scriptural Poetry', p. 2.

aureum) because of the eloquence that flowed from his mouth.[48] In fact, of course, the Romans called Gregory no such thing – 'golden mouth' was rather the epithet of St John Chrysostom – and the writer is probably drawing, directly or indirectly, on an Irish source. In Ireland, as early as *c*. 632, Gregory was commonly styled *os aureum*; in vernacular texts this is *bél óir* or *gin óir* which suggests that the epithet had its origin in an etymological interpretation of the termination of *Grigoir*, the Irish form of *Gregorius*, which might be associated both with Latin *os, oris* 'mouth' and with Irish *óir* 'of gold, golden'.[49] In Anglo-Saxon England, however, the epithet only reappears in the Old English version of Gregory's *Dialogi* by Alfred's assistant, Werferth, bishop of Worcester *c*. 873–*c*. 915, who similarly speaks of a stream of eloquence issuing from Gregory's 'golden mouth' (*gyldenmuþ*) and says that the Romans call him *Os Aureum*, the Greeks *Crysosthomas*.[50] Werferth is clearly following something like the passage in the Whitby *Vita* here, though, as he is more detailed and as the *Vita* seems never to have been widely available,[51] he is probably not using

---

[48] 'Ut a gente Romana quę pre ceteris mundo intonat sublimius proprię (*sic*) de aurea oris eius gratia, os aureum appellatur' (*Life of Gregory*, ed. Colgrave, pp. 116–18). Colgrave translates: 'therefore he was called the "golden mouthed" by the Romans because of the golden eloquence which issued from his mouth in a very special way, far more sublimely and beyond all others in the world'. Cf. *ibid*., p. 155, n. 99.

[49] Cummian's letter to Ségéne *De controuersia paschali* (PL 87, 975): 'Ad Gregorii papae, urbis Romae episcopi (a nobis in commune suscepti, et oris aurei appellatione donati) uerba me conuerti.' For some later references see Bischoff, *Studien* I, 214, n. 40, and 221, n. 70; J. Vendryes, 'Betha Grighora', *RC* 42 (1925), 119–53, at 123; P. Grosjean, 'Quelques textes irlandais sur saint Grégoire le Grand', *RC* 46 (1929), 223–51, at 225; P. O'Neill, 'A Middle Irish Poem on the Maledictory Psalms', *Journal of Celtic Studies* 3 (1981), 40–58, at 57–8.

[50] *Bischofs Wærferth von Worcester Übersetzung der Dialoge Gregors des Grossen*, ed. H. Hecht, 2 vols. (Leipzig, 1900–7) I, 179 (introduction to Book III): 'Her onginneð se þridda flod of ðam neorxnawanglican wylle, þe þurh þone gyldenan muþ forð aarn þæs halgan papan 7 biscopes sancte Gregories, þone Romane for þære fægran worda gyfe Os Aureum nemniað'; cf. I, 94 (introduction to Book II): 'se mid Grecum Crysosthomas is gehaten'. For Werferth's authorship see *Asser*, ed. Stevenson, c. 77, and William of Malmesbury, *Gesta regum*, ed. Stubbs I, 131. Cf. Whitelock, 'Prose of Alfred's Reign', pp. 77–8. As R. Torkar showed in a paper on 'King Alfred's Preface to his *Soliloquies*' at the conference of the International Society of Anglo-Saxonists in 1985, Werferth's stream imagery is typically Alfredian. On the other hand, it is quite conventional in praising eloquence, e.g. Venantius Fortunatus, *Carmina* IV.viii.15–16 and VIII.xviii.1–4 (ed. Leo, pp. 85 and 199).

[51] Only the ninth-century manuscript from St Gallen survives. Even Bede may not have known it.

the *Vita* itself but some lost source used by the Whitby author and also available at Worcester.

A common source is certainly the probable explanation for the second unusual item in the Whitby *Vita* that surfaces at Worcester. Ch. 28 tells, or rather alludes to, a story about a 'certain pope' who, by expelling St Jerome, extinguished a lamp which God had lit, for 'Jerome was a light upon the lampstand in Rome, not only for the Romans but for the whole world; for Rome is the chief of cities and mistress of the world'; this pope 'rightly merited that his own light should be put out by St Gregory'. The full story is only to be found in early twelfth-century dress, in John of Worcester's marginal annotations to the Lives of Popes Siricius and Gregory in the Worcester copy of William of Malmesbury's recension of the *Liber pontificalis*.[52] The story, a fiction based on the historical coolness between Jerome and Pope Siricius, tells how Siricius despised Jerome when he came in rough skins bringing his Vulgate, but honoured him when he came expensively dressed. Jerome rebuked the Pope and was driven from Rome ('a mundi capite lux mundi pellitur urbe'). Gregory later avenged Jerome by breaking the lamp which burned over Siricius's tomb, uttering a *bon mot*:

> Tumba tegit papam, qui mundi lumen ab Urbe
> expulerat dudum, quod replet dogmate mundum.[53]

This anecdote cannot derive from the brief allusion in the Whitby *Vita S. Gregorii*, but it could be based on its lost source. John of Worcester states

[52] Cambridge, University Library, Kk. 4. 6, 233r and 244v, printed by W. Levison, 'Aus Englischen Bibliotheken II: Englische Handschriften des Liber Pontificalis', *NA* 35 (1910), 333–431, at 425–6, and summarized by Colgrave, *Life of Gregory*, p. 159, n. 120. The mixture of prose and verse and the use of occasionally bisyllabic leonine rhymes point to redaction in the twelfth century; cf. references in Brooke, *Church*, p. 85. We must therefore suppose that the text is a reworking of a story in the *Dicta Alfredi* – perhaps inspired by the fashion for anti-Roman satire (see J. Benzinger, *Invectiva in Romam: Romkritik im Mittelalter vom 9. bis zum 12. Jahrhundert* (Lübeck and Hamburg, 1968); Thomson, *William of Malmesbury*, p. 30). Whitelock, 'Prose of Alfred's Reign', p. 72, was mistaken in dating the marginalia late twelfth-century; the hand is the one attributed to William of Malmesbury by M. R. James, *Two Ancient English Scholars: St. Aldhelm and William of Malmesbury* (Glasgow, 1931), p. 21, but now assigned to John of Worcester; see Ker, *Books, Collectors and Libraries*, pp. 65–6; Thomson, *William of Malmesbury*, pp. 75, 122 and 172; Brett, 'John of Worcester', p. 105, n. 2; Darlington and McGurk, 'The "Chronicon ex Chronicis"', p. 185.

[53] 'A tomb covers the pope, who had once expelled from the City the light of the world which fills the world with learning.' On Jerome and Siricius cf. Rousseau, *Ascetics*, pp. 129–30.

that the story could be read in the 'authentic sayings of King Alfred' ('quod in angulsaxonum regis Aelfredi ueridicis dictis legitur'). These *dicta regis Alfredi* are also cited for the seventh-century succession of the kings of Wessex in the so-called Appendix to 'Florence' of Worcester, which may also be John's work.[54] There was thus a book at Worcester in the twelfth century known as the *Dicta Ælfredi*.[55] Its attribution as a whole to Alfred cannot be trusted in view of the well-established tendency to ascribe any ninth-century work with vernacular elements to that king,[56] but one may at least say that it was probably a ninth-century manuscript, and of southern English provenance in view of the details about seventh-century West Saxon kings which it contained.

Werferth's 'golden mouth' passage and John's anecdote look as if they come from the same stable; both concern Gregory and Rome, and both pontificate mistakenly about Roman matters ('erat Rome mos antiquitus institutus . . .'). If this Gregorian material was already at Worcester in some shape or form in the Alfredian period, that is still two centuries after Oftfor's episcopate; hence it is highly speculative to suggest that it was brought from Whitby, or sent to Whitby, in Oftfor's time. Yet bearing in mind that the material in question is peculiar to Whitby and Worcester and that Oftfor is the only known link between the two (apart from Tatfrith, who died before his consecration, and Ælfflæd, whose connection with Fladbury is very doubtful), the possibility seems worth mentioning.

One might wonder, finally, seeing that Rome is prominent in this Gregorian material, whether there is any significance in the fact that Oftfor

[54] *MHB*, p. 641. Cf. *HBC*[2], p. 23; Brett, 'John of Worcester', p. 111.

[55] Whitelock, 'Prose of Alfred's Reign', pp. 71–3, and 'William of Malmesbury on the Works of Alfred', pp. 90–2, suggested that it may have been identical with the *manualis liber* or *Enchiridion (Handboc)* of Alfred, from which William quotes on the subject of Aldhelm's life and his kinship to the West Saxon kings (*GP*, pp. 332–3 and 336; also *Gesta regum*, ed. Stubbs I, 132), and she pointed out that the Alfredian attribution may reflect an erroneous identification with *enchiridion suum, id est manualem librum* described by Asser. The book used by William may have been inscribed with the words *enchiridion* and *manualis liber*, copied from Asser, especially if it was at Worcester, where there was a copy of Asser (used in the compilation of 'Florence'); this would explain the agreement in wording between William and Asser (on the vexed question of William's knowledge of Asser, cf. Whitelock, 'William of Malmesbury on the Works of Alfred', pp. 91–3, and Thomson, *William of Malmesbury*, pp. 69, 151, n. 59, and 199). Certainly William had close connections with Worcester and John of Worcester (Brett, 'John of Worcester'), and could have used the *Dicta Ælfredi* there.

[56] See *The Proverbs of Alfred*, ed. O. S. Arngart, 2 vols. (Lund, 1942–55) II, 4–5.

had been to Rome before coming to the kingdom of the Hwicce;[57] could he have brought the Roman stories in the *Vita S. Gregorii* to England and transmitted them to Whitby? This does not seem very likely. As we have seen, the idea that the Romans called Gregory 'golden mouth' probably came from Ireland. Moreover, although the author of the *Vita* tends to be vague about the sources of the 'ancient stories' set in Rome which are related in cc. 20–3, 26, and 28–9, in the case of c. 29 he (or she) makes it clear that the story was already current in Northumbria – 'some of our people (*quidam de nostris*) also tell a story related by the Romans . . .' – and in fact the story in question was to be accepted only with difficulty in Rome.[58]

As a prominent biblical student and as the only known direct link between Rome and the Hwicce in the seventh century, Oftfor comes to mind as a possible owner of a fifth-century Italian manuscript of Jerome's commentary on Ecclesiastes: Würzburg, Universitätsbibliothek, M. p. th. q. 2.[59] Although this manuscript was already in Germany and

---

[57] *HE* IV.23, quoted above, p. 103. Oftfor is not the only known link between Whitby and Rome: note the letter of Ælfflæd, above p. 185. If 'what [Bede] knew of the see of Worcester appears to have come through Whitby and Wilfridian sources' (Kirby, 'Bede's Native Sources', p. 368), some Worcester material will have reached Whitby in or after Oftfor's day.

[58] This story has been supposed to be of Irish origin, but see L. Bieler, 'Ancient Hagiography and the Lives of St. Patrick', in *Forma futuri: studi in onore del Cardinale Michele Pellegrino* (Turin, 1975), pp. 650–5; J. F. Nagy, 'Close Encounters of the Traditional Kind in Medieval Irish Literature', in *Celtic Folklore and Christianity: Studies in Memory of William W. Heist*, ed. P. K. Ford (Santa Barbara and Los Angeles, 1983), pp. 129–49, at 137, n. 18. Cf. *Life of Gregory*, ed. Colgrave, pp. 52 and 161, n. 122; G. Whatley, 'The Uses of Hagiography: The Legend of Pope Gregory and the Emperor Trajan in the Middle Ages', *Viator* 15 (1984), 25–63.

[59] *CLA* IX, no. 1430. See the fuller discussion in Sims-Williams, 'Cuthswith'. The Würzburg manuscript is the base of the edition by Adriaen. His other main text is Paris, Bibliothèque Nationale, lat. 13349 (northern France, s. viii^med, Corbie provenance: *CLA* V, no. 657). Baesecke, *Vocabularius*, p. 90, asked whether the text in Kassel, Landesbibliothek, Theol. Fol. 21 (?Northumbria, s. viii, Fulda provenance: *CLA* VIII, no. 1134) derives from that in the Würzburg manuscript, but this cannot be tested from Adriaen's limited apparatus. The same applies to any possible connection with St Paul in Carinthia, Stiftsbibliothek, 3 i (25. 2. 36) (Luxeuil, *c.* 700: *CLA* X, nos. 1454–6), which may be the text used by Angelomus of Luxeuil (PL 115, 555–6) and the exemplar of Épinal, Bibl. Munic. 78 (Murbach, s. ix^med); cf. Laistner, 'Early Medieval Commentaries', pp. 41 and 44–5; *Apponii Expositio*, ed. de Vregille and Neyrand, pp. xiii–xv. The next English manuscript known to me is s. xii, from Ely: see N. Ker, 'MS. Bodley 582', *Bodleian Library Record* 1 (1938–41), 241–2.

probably at Würzburg by the last quarter of the eighth century,[60] it came there via England, as is shown by an inscription on 1r in Anglo-Saxon, which Lowe, Bischoff and Thurn date *c.* 700:

> Cuthsuuithae. boec.
> thaerae abbatissan.[61]

This Abbess Cuthswith was very probably the abbess of the same unusual name who is mentioned in two charters which were preserved at Worcester until the seventeenth century; no-one else of this name at any period is known.[62] By the first charter (of 693×?699) Oshere, king of the Hwicce, and his son Æthelheard granted Abbess Cuthswith the fifteen hides of *Penintanham* (probably Inkberrow) to establish a monastery.[63] The second charter (of 704×709) concerned Cuthswith's purchase of the five hides of *Ingin(n)* (probably Ingon, a dozen miles from Inkberrow) from Æthelheard and his brother Æthelweard, in exchange for 600 shillings (*solidi*).[64] Abbess Cuthswith conceivably belonged to the Mercian royal family, where female names in *C-* are common, or to the Hwiccian dynasty, a member of which named *C*yneburg occurs among the early Gloucester abbesses.[65] On the other hand, she may have been related to a *comes* of Oshere named *Cuth*bert; the latter does not normally appear in Hwiccian charters yet consents to the first grant and attests the second one – rather

---

[60] To judge by the similarity of certain pen trials on 1r to those in another Würzburg manuscript (Universitätsbibliothek, M. p. th. f. 27, 90v): Sims-Williams, 'Cuthswith', pp. 3–4.

[61] 'A book of Cuthswith the abbess', *CLA* IX, no. 1430a; Lowe, *Uncial*, pl. 1b; Bischoff and Hofmann, *Libri Sancti Kyliani*, p. 88 and pl. 13; Thurn, *Pergamenthandschriften*, p. 86. Cf. below, n. 67.

[62] Cf. Searle, *Onomasticon*, p. 150. The identification was first proposed by Chroust, *Monumenta Palaeographica* I.5, commentary on pl. 2; Brandl, 'Chrousts Fund'. On the s. xvii transcripts of the charters see Sims-Williams, 'Cuthswith', pp. 6–10 ('H' is in the hand of William Hopkins; see Sims-Williams, 'People and Places').

[63] S 53. On the date see Sims-Williams, 'Cuthswith', p. 9, n. 1. It depends on the date of Oftfor's death; cf. above, p. 142, n. 124. The macron above the *t* of *Penitanham* was noted and expanded to *Penintanham* by Finberg, *ECWM* (2nd ed.), p. 239. On his identification of *Penintanham* '?Inta's *hām* by the hill' with Inkberrow (*Intanbeorgas* 'Inta's hills') see Sims-Williams, 'Cuthswith', pp. 11–13, and 'People and Places'.

[64] S 1177. On the identification with Ingon (SP/2157) see Sims-Williams, 'Cuthswith', p. 12; Cox, 'Place-Names of the Earliest Records', p. 23. Ingon adjoins Hatton Rock and Hampton Lucy, on which cf. above, p. 164, and below, p. 362.

[65] See above, p. 122.

conspicuously, since the only other witnesses are Coenred of Mercia, Bishop Ecgwine and the two grantors. Cuthswith's purchase of the further five hides at *Ingin(n)* shows that her monastery had prospered, and that she was a wealthy woman and so not unlikely to own an Italian manuscript of Jerome, which must have been valuable. It is clear that considerable wealth was needed to acquire manuscripts. Benedict Biscop, for instance, received eight hides from King Aldfrith in exchange for a particularly fine manuscript 'of the Cosmographers' that he had bought in Rome, and these eight hides later were later exchanged for twenty by Ceolfrith.[66]

The Hwiccian identification of the *Cuthsuuitha abbatissa* of the Würzburg manuscript is strengthened by Engelbert's remarks on the script of some pen trials in English uncial on 1r (*adonai dñe dĩ meus*) and 113v (*omnium inimicorum suorum dominabitur* and *dñs tamquam*).[67] He noted a similarity to the script of the charter of 736 by which Æthelbald of Mercia granted land for the monastery at Stour in Ismere, in the north of Worcester diocese, and pointed out a particular similarity with the script of the endorsement (which must have been added before 757 at the latest), especially in the form of the N in *donaui*, with its long left tail turning to the left.[68] The pen trials suggest, then, that Cuthswith's Jerome was still in the diocese of Worcester in the first third of the eighth century, and arrived in Germany during the period when the English missionaries were importing large numbers of commentaries and other books from their homeland.[69] It may have been taken to the Continent by Burghard, an

---

[66] Bede, *Historia abbatum*, c. 15 (*BOH* I, 380). See Levison, *England and the Continent*, p. 42 (cf. Bischoff, *Studien* I, 208–9). On the value of manuscripts in general cf. Lesne, *Livres, scriptoria et bibliothèques*, pp. 24–7.

[67] Engelbert, 'Bemerkungen', pp. 410–11. These comparisons are questioned by Scharer, *Königsurkunde*, p. 179, n. 94, but were accepted by T. J. Brown in his unpublished Lyell Lectures (1977). For facsimiles of 1r see Brandl, 'Chrousts Fund', Bischoff and Hofmann, *Libri Sancti Kyliani*, pl. 13, or G. Mältzer and H. Thurn, *Universitätsbibliothek Würzburg: Kostbare Handschriften* (Wiesbaden, 1982), pl. 4. None is available for 113v. On the endorsement of the charter see also *Vespasian Psalter*, ed. Wright, p. 56.

[68] London, BL, Cotton Augustus ii. 3; S 89. Facsimiles in Lowe, *Uncial*, pl. XXIII; Bruckner and Marichal, *Chartae* III, no. 183. The charter and its endorsement may well have been drawn up at Worcester. Worcester is in fact its s. xi² provenance (Ker, *Catalogue*, pp. 266–7, and *Books, Collectors and Libraries*, p. 49) but it may have come there later in the eighth century, when the monastery at Stour in Ismere reverted to the see. Cf. above, pp. 148 and 159.

[69] See Levison, *England and the Continent*, pp. 139–48; Baesecke, *Vocabularius*, pp. 84–110; Riché, *Education and Culture*, pp. 435–7; Tangl, p. 308, s.v. *libri*. On

Anglo-Saxon who became bishop of Würzburg in 741×742, and was in correspondence *c.* 740 with an Abbess Cyneburg, possibly Cuthswith's successor; or it may have been presented to the missionaries by Milred, bishop of Worcester, around the time of his visit to Germany in 753.[70]

To understand how a fifth-century Italian manuscript could have come to Cuthswith's monastery, one looks for some seventh-century book collector and traveller: a Benedict Biscop with Hwiccian connections.[71] Two possibilities are Wilfrid and Oftfor, both of whom attested the *Penintanham* foundation charter.[72] Wilfrid had been active in the area rather earlier, *c.* 675 and *c.* 680, and it was he who consecrated Oftfor as bishop of the Hwicce (before 693).[73] Nothing connects him with Cuthswith, however, and the early sources say remarkably little about him as a collector and donor of manuscripts, with the exception of his gift to Ripon of the four Gospels 'written out in purest gold on purpled parchment and illuminated'.[74] In any case, there would have been many calls on his munificence among his own monasteries. Oftfor is the more likely possibility. This scholar-pilgrim must have appeared an even more important figure in the narrower confines of the Worcester diocese than he appeared to Bede in the broad stream of English church history. Bede's comment on Oftfor, that 'he decided to go to Rome too, which in those days was considered to be an act of great merit' ('etiam Romam adire curauit, quod eo tempore magnae uirtutis aestimabatur'), may reflect doubts about the value of pilgrimages to Rome,[75] but in the eulogistic context Bede's

the growth of the Würzburg library in particular see Bischoff and Hofmann, *Libri Sancti Kyliani*, p. 160. An instance of Boniface writing home for commentaries was cited above, n. 3.

[70] See below, p. 241.

[71] See Bede's *Historia abbatum* and the *Vita S. Ceolfridi*, both in *BOH* I; Lowe, *Uncial*; Wormald, 'Bede and Benedict Biscop'; Bullough, 'Roman Books', pp. 27–8.

[72] As noted by J. Hofmann, 'Angelsächsische Handschriften in der Würzburger Dombibliothek', in *Heiliges Franken: Festchronik zum Jahr der Frankenapostel 1952* (Würzburg, 1952), pp. 172–6, at 173. This paper was not available to me when writing 'Cuthswith'; I am grateful to Dr Hans Thurn for a copy.

[73] See above, pp. 103–5.

[74] *Life of Wilfrid*, ed. Colgrave, c. 17. Cf. *HE* v.19. See Roper, 'Wilfrid's Landholdings', pp. 68–9; Bruce-Mitford, 'Codex Amiatinus', p. 15. Peter of Blois, a canon of Ripon, adds *pluresque libros noui ac uet: testamenti* (Leland, *Collectanea*, ed. Hearne IV, 110); cf. Sims-Williams, 'Wilfrid', p. 182.

[75] *HE* IV.23 (quoted above, p. 103); Sims-Williams, 'Cuthswith', p. 15, nn. 1–2; Constable, 'Opposition to Pilgrimage', p. 127; Wallace-Hadrill, *Commentary*, p. 164.

primary meaning is surely that such a pilgrimage was much rarer in Oftfor's day than in 731, when many English pilgrims of all classes were going to Rome.[76] In the seventh century, by contrast, contacts appear to have been prized but infrequent: when Wilfrid first wished to go to Rome, 'a road hitherto untrodden by any of our race', he had to wait a whole year in Kent (652–3) before a suitable fellow-traveller, Benedict Biscop, appeared.[77] Biscop and Wilfrid, indeed, appear exceptional in respect of their travels, and most of the seventh-century journeys to Rome had some connection with one or other of these Northumbrian pioneers.[78] Oftfor, whose very name (surely a nickname) 'the much journeyed' (*oft-for*) is significant, stands out as the most important known link between Worcester and Italy in the seventh century. Considering his interest in biblical studies, Oftfor is bound to have acquired books in Italy; Rome was the pre-eminent source of manuscripts and a pilgrimage that did not bring back items such as books or relics was 'empty and useless', as Bede makes clear.[79] Abbess Cuthswith must have known Oftfor. He had long been resident in the kingdom of the Hwicce, apparently under the patronage of King Osric, and was bishop at the time of the foundation of her monastery. While no special connection between Oftfor and *Penintanham* is evident, except that he attested the foundation charter *propria manu*, it may have been the first foundation of his episcopate, and we know that he was concerned to build up monasticism in his diocese from the fact that Æthelred of Mercia put him in charge of restoration of monastic life at Fladbury.[80] If *Penintanham* is correctly identified with Inkberrow, it was only ten miles east of his see at Worcester.

The fifth-century Italian script of Cuthswith's Jerome was described by Lowe as 'a beautiful bold uncial of the oldest type'.[81] Uncial must have

---

[76] Sims-Williams, 'Cuthswith', p. 15, n. 3.   [77] *Life of Wilfrid*, ed. Colgrave, c. 3.

[78] See the references in Sims-Williams, 'Cuthswith', p. 15, n. 6 (but that to Saint-Bertin, cited from W. J. Moore, is inaccurate; cf. Grierson, 'Relations Between England and Flanders', p. 94, n. 6).

[79] Levison, *England and the Continent*, pp. 132–4; Riché, *Education and Culture*, pp. 351–2; Wormald, 'Bede and Benedict Biscop', pp. 149–50. Bede, *Homelia* I.13 (ed. Hurst, p. 93), is quoted by Constable, 'Opposition to Pilgrimage', p. 127.

[80] See above, pp. 103 and 140. On *manu propria* cf. Chaplais, 'Letter from Wealdhere', p. 17, n. 26.

[81] *CLA* IX, no. 1430a. Facsimiles of 4v, 5r, 12v and 64r are published by Chroust, *Monumenta* I.5, pls. 2–3; and Lowe, *Uncial*, pl. 1a.

been the script of the great majority of the Italian manuscripts brought to England in the seventh century, where it competed with the established Insular scripts.[82] The adoption of uncial, which was not used in Ireland, probably expressed allegiance to the Gregorian, Roman tradition in the seventh-century English church.[83] Cuthswith's Jerome is important in this connection, for it is the oldest *extant* uncial manuscript that could have served as a model for the development of 'English uncial' in an English scriptorium.[84] Furthermore, six thicker leaves (three bifolia) of the manuscript's original 114 leaves are replacements inserted in England in the seventh century, presumably because of loss or damage to these pages (fols. 10, 13, 63, 68, 81 and 82).[85] D. H. Wright observed that the English scribe merely did 'his unequal best to reproduce the unfamiliar letter forms', so his work is simply imitative and not a good illustration of the development of English uncial from Italian models, while Lowe remarked that the supply leaves were 'written, if one may judge from the syllable-by-syllable copying, by a scribe for whom Latin was an alien tongue and who was not completely sure of his uncial characters'.[86] Parkes takes a more positive view and treats these supply leaves as an example of the way in which the Anglo-Saxons, writing in the uncial tradition where *scriptura continua* was the norm, delicately introduced the practice of word-separation, as understood by ancient grammarians and transmitted by Irish teachers:

In the supply leaves to the Jerome manuscript, as well as instances of copying syllable by syllable, word-separation is more frequent [than in the uncial supply leaves of the Burghard Gospels], although there are numerous instances of the confusion between free and bound morphemes commonly found in early examples of word-separation: for example, in the treatment of prefixes and prepositions such as *in* in 'inueniet' and 'inscripturis', and *de* in 'detraxisti' and 'defestuca'. This

---

[82] *Ibid.*, p. 7; Parkes, 'Legibility', p. 24.

[83] Cf. Brown, 'Irish Element', p. 102; Parkes, *Wearmouth-Jarrow*, pp. 17 and 21; Parkes, 'Legibility', p. 25.

[84] Lowe, *Uncial*, p. 18.

[85] *Ibid.*, p. 18; Bischoff and Hofmann, *Libri Sancti Kyliani*, p. 88. The appearance of the added leaves can be seen from the facsimiles of 63r and 63v published by Chroust, *Monumenta* I.5, pl. 3, and Lowe, *Uncial*, pl. v. The apparatus to Adriaen's edition of the commentary is not full enough to answer the question whether the text on the added leaves was copied from the damaged original leaves or taken from some other source.

[86] Wright, 'Notes on English Uncial', p. 450; Lowe, *Uncial*, p. 18.

confusion arose because ancient grammarians had failed to recognize a division below that of a word, and had themselves confused free and bound morphemes.[87]

The basic purpose of word-separation was, of course, to make the text more readily intelligible for study.

Jerome's preface to his commentary on Ecclesiastes – missing in Cuthswith's copy – shows that it was intended to encourage women ascetics. It was addressed to Paula, one of the Roman noble women who had turned her house into a monastery, and to her daughter Eustochium:

I remember that, about five years ago, when I was still living at Rome, I read Ecclesiastes to the saintly Blesilla [Paula's daughter, d. 384] so that I might provoke her to the contempt of this earthly scene, and to count as nothing all that she saw in the world; and that she asked me to throw my remarks upon all the more obscure passages into the form of a short commentary, so that, when I was absent, she might still understand what she read. She was withdrawn from us by her sudden death, while girding herself for our work; we were not counted worthy to have such an one as the partner of our life; and, therefore, Paula and Eustochium, I kept silence under the stroke of such a wound. But now, living as I do in the smaller community of Bethlehem, I pay what I owe to her memory and to you.[88]

In a letter to Laeta, another daughter of Paula – a letter whose curriculum for female education made it very popular in the early Middle Ages – Jerome recommended that Laeta's daughter should study Ecclesiastes next after the psalter and the Proverbs of Solomon: 'in reading Ecclesiastes let her become accustomed to tread underfoot the things of this world'.[89] It is fitting, then, that the earliest extant copy of Jerome's commentary on Ecclesiastes should have been owned three centuries later by an abbess. The distance between Jerome's Rome and seventh-century England may not have seemed very great. The monastic ideal expressed in Paula's monastery was not so distant from that expressed in the English 'family monasteries',

---

[87] Parkes, 'Legibility', pp. 18 and 24–6. The Burghard leaves were supplied in Northumbria according to Parkes, *Wearmouth-Jarrow*, pp. 4 and 25, n. 11; cf. below, p. 290, n. 74.

[88] *Commentarius*, ed. Adriaen, p. 249; trans. (Preface only) Fremantle *et al.*, *Letters and Select Works*, p. 487. Cf. Kelly, *Jerome*, pp. 98–9, 110–11, 145, 150 and 152.

[89] *Ep.* cvii.12, trans. Wright, *Select Letters*, p. 365. The popularity of *Epp.* cvii and cxxviii is noted by Laistner, 'Study of Jerome', p. 252, and *Thought and Letters*, p. 48; cf. Schneider, 'Women', pp. 150–1.

among which Cuthswith's monastery must probably be counted.[90] Nor
had the needs of exegesis changed much, as is shown by the fact that
Alcuin's commentary on Ecclesiastes is little more than an abridgement of
Jerome's.[91] The relationship between Jerome and the Roman women
whom he instructed seems to be repeated in Boniface's teaching activities
in Wessex, as described by Willibald; Aldhelm, addressing Hildelith of
Barking and other nuns in his prose *De uirginitate*, often seems to take on
the mantle of Jerome; and the nuns of Chelles, writing to ask Alcuin to
compose a commentary at Tours and send it to Paris, specifically compare
him with Jerome writing in Bethlehem at the behest of women in Rome.[92]

The value of Jerome's commentary lay in its achievement in reconciling
with Christian belief the nihilism and epicureanism of Ecclesiastes, which
had nearly led to its exclusion from the Jewish canon, as Jerome himself
notes.[93] He reconciles the two both on a literal and on an allegorical level
with impressive success, granted his premise that a reconciliation is
possible. For example, here he explains the text 'Vanity of vanities, said the
preacher, vanity of vanities, all is vanity' (Ecclesiastes I.2) by comparing
the figure of speech in II Corinthians III.10:

We read in Exodus that Moses's face was glorified so greatly that the sons of Israel
could not look upon it. That glory, says the apostle Paul, in comparison with the
glory of the gospel, is no glory: 'for even that which was made glorious', he says,
'had no glory in this respect, by reason of the glory that excelleth'. Thus we ourselves can say that the heaven, earth, seas and everything that is contained in this
circle, are good in themselves, yet, compared to God, are as nothing. And in the
same way, if I see the glimmer of a lantern, I may be content with its light, but
afterwards, when the sun rises, I may not be able to perceive what used to shine,
and I see, too, the lights of the stars made invisible by the radiance of the sun.
Perceiving thus the elements and the complex variety of things, I wonder at the
magnitude of creation; yet, remembering that all things are passing away, and that
the world is growing old as it nears its end, while God alone remains what he has
been, I am compelled to say, not once but twice: 'vanity of vanities, all is vanity'.[94]

90 See above, p. 130 and on *Penintanham*, below, p. 238.
91 Laistner, 'Study of Jerome', p. 243; 'Early Medieval Commentaries', p. 41; PL 100,
719 note *a*.
92 Duemmler, *Ep.* cxcvi. For Boniface and Aldhelm see above, p. 177, and below, n. 96.
93 *Commentarius*, ed. Adriaen, p. 360. See the discussion by Kelly, *Jerome*, pp. 149–52.
Gregory, *Dialogi* IV.4 (ed. de Vogüé III, 26), says that Ecclesiastes contains vulgar
untruths spoken *in persona*.
94 Ed. Adriaen, pp. 252–3.

Even Anglo-Saxon readers who found Jerome's philological discussions and classical allusions beyond them could not be unimpressed by such passages. Again, in discussing the text beginning 'There is nothing better for a man, than that he should eat and drink, and that he should make his soul enjoy good in his labour' (Ecclesiastes II.24), Jerome concludes his literal interpretation: 'thus far we have followed the letter, lest we should seem to forget the simple meaning completely and despise the poor historical sense in our pursuit of spiritual riches'; but then he gives a spiritual interpretation of the 'good' which a man should enjoy – not the fruit of his own greed or of others' forced labour, but the truths of Scripture:

Thus it is good to consume the true food and true drink of the Lamb's flesh and blood which we find in the divine books.[95]

Nothing could be better attuned to the Anglo-Saxons' sacramental understanding of the richness of the bible than this double metaphor. One can see why Bede, in an epigram preserved in Milred of Worcester's collection, praises Jerome for unpicking the mystic locks of the prophets and displaying the Hebrew treasure-houses to the Latin world, for stealing into Isaiah's arcane places and bringing forth the gospel light.[96]

At the beginning of this commentary Jerome repeated Origen's theory, later to be adopted from Jerome by Alcuin, Angelomus of Luxeuil and the Irish *céili Dé*, that Solomon wrote Proverbs for the instruction of children, Ecclesiastes to remind adults of the transitoriness of worldly things, and the Song of Songs for those approaching death.[97] Similarly, in his letter to Laeta, mentioned above, Jerome prescribed that a girl should read the Song of Songs last of all, lest 'if she were to read it at the beginning, she might be harmed by not perceiving that it was the song of a spiritual bridal expressed in fleshly language'.[98] Despite – or perhaps because of – such warnings, the Song of Songs was eagerly studied; Dom Jean Leclercq goes so far as to say that it was that book of the bible 'most read, and most frequently

---

[95] *Ibid.*, p. 272. Cf. p. 278 on Ecclesiastes III.12–13, discussed by Kelly, *Jerome*, p. 151.

[96] Lapidge, 'Remnants', p. 802 (no. 2). Cf. Sims-Williams, 'Milred', pp. 33–4, and 'William', p. 24. Compare Aldhelm's account of Jerome: *Aldhelmi Opera*, ed. Ehwald, pp. 303 and 441.

[97] Ed. Adriaen, p. 250. Cf. PL 100, 668–9; 115, 556; McNamara, 'Early Irish Exegesis', pp. 71 and 73. See Kelly, *Jerome*, p. 150, and Laistner, 'Early Medieval Commentaries', p. 41 and n. 36.

[98] *Ep.* cvii. 12, trans. Wright, *Select Letters*, p. 365.

commented in the medieval cloister'.[99] The diocese of Worcester may be the source of Boulogne-sur-Mer, Bibliothèque Municipale, 74 (82), an eighth-century English copy of a commentary on the Song of Songs by a certain 'holy abbot Apponius', to which is appended a letter by a woman named Burginda.[100] This mysterious author Apponius composed his voluminous twelve-book commentary in the early fifth century, probably at Rome in view of his stress on the role of the bishop of Rome as Christ's vicar.[101] Its difficult Latin and exotic preoccupations, including Origenist speculation about Christ's soul, set it outside the mainstream of medieval Western exegesis, and Bede's apparent disdain for it is easy to understand.[102] Nevertheless, although few complete manuscripts survive, it was used quite widely in various forms in the Western churches between the eighth and twelfth centuries.[103] Its attraction for Anglo-Saxons less attuned than Bede to the perils of non-patristic commentaries may have been Apponius's supreme confidence in his own ability to guide the reader through the *mysteria* of the biblical text to the *arcana intelligentia legis diuinae*. In the Song of Songs the Holy Spirit speaks in riddles (*aenigmata*), never literally, Apponius says; in it the *amatoria Verbi Dei et animae* are sung in the form of a bridal song. In part, he thinks, the Song is an allegory of the soul being introduced by Christ to the figural understanding of the Old Testament.[104] Apponius's exegesis proceeds by an exceptionally random association of ideas: for instance the verse 'When the king sitteth at his table, my spikenard sendeth forth the smell thereof' (1.11) reminds him of

---

99 Leclercq, *Love of Learning*, p. 90. On the influence of the Song of Songs see also below, p. 309.

100 *CLA* VI, no. 738. See my fuller discussion in Sims-Williams, 'Anglo-Latin Letter', where I draw on personal communications from the late Professor T. J. Brown. The author is called *apponi sancti abbatis* in the explicit.

101 *Apponii Expositio*, ed. de Vregille and Neyrand, pp. xcv and cviii–cxiii.

102 See *ibid.*, pp. xciii–xciv; A. Grillmeier, *Christ in Christian Tradition* I, *From the Apostolic Age to Chalcedon (451)*, trans. J. Bowden, 2nd ed. (London, 1975), pp. 384–8; M. L. W. Laistner, 'The Library of the Venerable Bede', in *Bede, His Life, Times and Writings*, ed. A. H. Thompson (Oxford, 1935), pp. 237–66, at 252.

103 See *Apponii Expositio*, ed. de Vregille and Neyrand, pp. vi–xliii; Sims-Williams, 'Anglo-Latin Letter', pp. 5–6; M. McNamara, 'Plan and Source Analysis of *Das Bibelwerk*, Old Testament', in *Irland und die Christenheit*, ed. Ní Chatháin and Richter, pp. 84–123, at 104–5, and 'Early Irish Exegesis', pp. 71–3.

104 Ed. de Vregille and Neyrand, pp. 80, 47 (cf. 307), 80 and 82–3 respectively. On *arcana mysteria* in the thought of Apponius see J. Witte, *Der Kommentar des Aponius zum Hohenliede* (Inaugural-Dissertation (theol.), Erlangen, 1903), p. 62.

Jesus being anointed by Mary in Simon the Leper's house, and he interprets the latter house as the fallen world entered by Christ in the Incarnation, and now filled by the odours of penitence and good works.[105]

Boulogne 74 is a unique copy of an abbreviated version of Apponius, distinct both from the original full text preserved in other manuscripts and quoted by Bede and by Angelomus of Luxeuil,[106] and from another abridgement, usually circulating under the name of Jerome, which is found in many manuscripts of the late eighth century onwards, mostly from monasteries in western Belgium and north-eastern France.[107] The text of Apponius from which the Boulogne abridgement was made is related to the text abbreviated by Pseudo-Jerome and to a text circulating in the ninth century in the Vosges, where it was used by Angelomus.[108]

Through later damage, Boulogne 74 lacks the first two books and part of the third book of Apponius, and for the rest its text is careless; Apponius's plea to copyists that they would check their transcriptions, 'lest the effort put into so great a labour should be marred by the somnolence of scribes', went unheeded by the Anglo-Saxon scribe. Many of the latter's textual errors may, of course, have been taken over mechanically from an exemplar; on several pages he or she fails to fill the final line, which suggests page-by-page copying from an exemplar.[109]

[105] Ed. de Vregille and Neyrand, pp. 63–5.

[106] Sims-Williams, 'Anglo-Latin Letter', pp. 5–6; *Apponii Expositio*, ed. de Vregille and Neyrand, pp. xxx–xxxiv; M. Didone, 'L'explanatio di Apponio in relazione all' "Expositio" di Beda ed all' "Enarrationes in Cantica" di Angelomus', *Civiltà classica e cristiana* 7 (1986), 77–119.

[107] They are listed and discussed in *Apponii Expositio*, ed. de Vregille and Neyrand, pp. xvii–xxvii and lvii–lviii. The combined evidence of manuscripts V (Saint-Amand) and Bo (Arras) points to a north-east Frankish archetype for the Pseudo-Jerome, although the editors show that it was also known in Irish and Anglo-Saxon circles on the Continent (pp. xxxviii–xlii). In 'Anglo-Latin Letter', pp. 5–6 and nn., I suggested that the two abridgements were derived from some lost abridgement, but this is denied by de Vregille and Neyrand (pp. xxvii, n. 94, xli and xliii), who show that the textual similarities are due to similar texts of Apponius being abridged, and presumably regard the shared omissions as coincidental. They print the full text of both abridgements (pp. 313–463). A. Vaccari, 'Notulae Patristicae, I. Apponii in Canticum Canticorum', *Gregorianum* 42 (1961), 725–8, suggested that the abridgements were Irish, but see Sims-Williams, 'Anglo-Latin Letter', p. 6; cf. de Vregille and Neyrand, pp. xvii and xli.

[108] See *ibid.*, pp. xiii–xv, xlii–xliii and liv–lviii.

[109] *Ibid.*, p. 2 (cf. pp. xxviii, lviii and lxvi). Cf. E. A. Lowe on the Bobbio Missal, in his *Palaeographical Papers 1907–1965*, ed. L. Bieler, 2 vols. (Oxford, 1972) I, 172–3.

The immediate provenance of the Boulogne manuscript is the monastery of Saint-Bertin at Saint-Omer. The entry 'Appodii (*sic*) liber in Cantica Canticorum' in the lost Saint-Bertin catalogue printed in 1788, and said then to belong to *c.* 1104, gives a terminus ante quem of *c.* 1104 for its arrival at Saint-Bertin, presumably through one of the many early medieval contacts between England and Flanders.[110]

Boulogne 74 was probably written somewhere in southern England (including Mercia), and probably as early as the first half, or perhaps the first quarter, of the eighth century. Some care was taken over the decorated initials, but parts of the manuscript have an informal, even hasty and scrappy, appearance. The mixing of formal and informal scripts seen here is a southern English trait, and a similar capriciousness may be found in eighth-century manuscripts from Würzburg, which had southern English connections, as we have already seen.[111]

The most striking feature of the manuscript is its ornamentation, described by Lowe as follows: 'initials in bold black or outline occasionally filled in with red, and surrounded with red dots; occasionally dotted red lines traverse the inner space of the initial horizontally'. Lowe, followed by Wright and Farmer, noted a resemblance to the initials in Oxford, Bodleian Library, Hatton 48, a copy of the *Regula S. Benedicti* dated *c.* 700 by Lowe and others, but s. viii[med] by Wright, partly on the basis of his similarly late dating of the Apponius.[112] The scribe of the Apponius was eclectic, drawing on a wide variety of styles only one of which can fairly be compared with the stately and consistent style of the Hatton initials; but, with the important exception that the Apponius initials lack the character-istic Hatton 'ribbon-like sweep' and wedge-shaped triangular finials, the similarities between the comparable initials in the two manuscripts are striking.[113] In the use of red dots, as in other respects, Lowe's description of the Hatton 48 initials will apply equally well to the Apponius: 'they are outlined in black, filled with red, and surrounded by red dots; here and

---

110 Sims-Williams, 'Anglo-Latin Letter', p. 4; Berthod, 'Notice', p. 228. Cf. Grierson, 'Relations Between England and Flanders'.

111 *CLA* VI, no. 738; Sims-Williams, 'Anglo-Latin Letter', pp. 1–2.

112 Wright, 'Notes on English Uncial', p. 449. Cf. *CLA* II, no. 240; Bischoff, *Studien* II, 332; Farmer, *Rule*, pp. 22–3; and the reviews of Farmer by G. Storms, *English Studies* 53 (1972), 153–4, E. Manning, *Scriptorium* 24 (1970), 445–6, and Engelbert, 'Bemerkungen'.

113 See my detailed discussion in 'Anglo-Latin Letter', p. 2 and n. 13. In addition to the complete facsimile in *Rule*, ed. Farmer, see *Anglo-Saxons*, ed. Campbell, p. 87, fig. 85.

there little groups of three red dots are used; occasionally lines of red dots traverse the inner space of the initial horizontally or delimit it vertically and horizontally – a feature recalling the Blickling Psalter' (a mid-eighth-century, possibly Midland, manuscript).[114] A more unusual similarity between the Apponius and Hatton 48 is the use of bands of triple black lines, the middle one thicker, crossing the interior of the outlined stems of the letter at right angles, with the two outer and thinner lines often delimiting the colouring-in of the outline. This type of banded decoration is of foreign, perhaps Italian, origin,[115] but the use, at the mid-point of the stems of a letter, of triple lines with a thick middle band is very unusual: among early English manuscripts it seems to occur only in the Apponius, in Hatton 48 and in Paris, Bibliothèque Nationale, lat. 17177, 8r. This last is a fragment of Theodore of Mopsuestia from Corbie, unfortunately of unknown origin: Lowe judged that it was written s. viii-xi, 'presumably in a Continental centre with Anglo-Saxon connections' (which would explain its 'initials of Insular type'), but T. J. Brown thought that it could have been written in England itself and belong to the first half of the eighth century.[116] Finally, we may add that, as Professor Brown pointed out in his unpublished Lyell lectures, the A on IV of Würzburg, Universitätsbibliothek, M. p. th. f. 79, a southern or Mercian copy of Isidore's *Synonyma* in a mixture of scripts, is similar to those in Hatton 48 in its clean outlines and 'ribbon-like sweep', even though the stems of the letter are not occupied with banding. This manuscript probably reached Germany in the last quarter of the eighth century, perhaps through Mainz.[117] Bischoff now dates it before the middle of the eighth century, and Professor Brown, who regarded it as a manuscript of similar sort and age to the Apponius, favoured the first

---

[114] *CLA* II, no. 240. On the Blickling Psalter (*CLA* XI, no. 1661), cf. Brown, 'Irish Element', p. 108; Sims-Williams, 'Anglo-Latin Letter', p. 17, n. 16.

[115] M. Schapiro, 'The Decoration of the Leningrad Manuscript of Bede', *Scriptorium* 12 (1958), 191–207 (at 197–8, discussed in detail by Sims-Williams, 'Anglo-Latin Letter', p. 3 and nn. 24–6). See further the mass of relevant material in Nordenfalk, *Spätantiken Zierbuchstaben*. Curiously, the same motif occurs on Anglo-Saxon pottery dated before *c.* 500 by Myres, *Pottery and the Settlement*, p. 30.

[116] *CLA* V, no. 4 (p. 42); cf. Farmer, *Rule*, p. 13; Sims-Williams, 'Anglo-Latin Letter', p. 3 and nn. 17 and 19.

[117] *CLA* IX, no. 1426; J. Hofmann, 'Altenglische und althochdeutsche Glossen aus Würzburg und dem weiteren angelsächsischen Missionsgebiet', *BGDSL* 85 (1963), 27–131, at 59.

quarter of the century, and noted a similarity between its uncial and that of the Stour in Ismere charter of 736 discussed above.[118]

Of the manuscripts compared with the Apponius, only Hatton 48 has a localization: it is a southern production, possibly from the orbit of Worcester where the manuscript was in the second half of the eleventh century.[119] While it could have been brought in from outside the diocese, one more naturally supposes that it was written either at Worcester itself, or else at one of the many early monasteries that were absorbed into the Worcester estate. Engelbert's comparisons with the script of the Stour in Ismere charter and with the uncial pen-trials in the Cuthswith Codex have given some plausibility to an origin for Hatton 48 in Worcester diocese.[120]

It would be unwise to assign Boulogne 74 to Worcester diocese merely on the basis of its similarities with Hatton 48 and various southern or Midland manuscripts. Instead, some converging evidence which points towards an English centre with Frankish connections must be taken into account. Its text of Apponius is of the same family as the one used in an abridgement in circulation in north-eastern Gaul. Its decoration is related to that in the Theodore of Mopsuestia fragment, whose provenance is Corbie in Picardy, a house founded in the mid-seventh century by Clovis II's English queen Balthild, 'whose influence', Lowe thought, 'may partly account for the relations of the abbey with England, as seen in extant manuscripts'.[121] Again, Professor Brown observed that a small minuscule of the same type as in the Apponius occurs in another manuscript at Boulogne, Bibliothèque Municipale, 58 (63 and 64), together with a 'hybrid minuscule' which recalls that of the Apponius. This manuscript contains Augustine's letters, and like the Apponius, its immediate provenance is Saint-Bertin; it may be the 'Augustini liber Epistolarum' listed along with the 'Appodius' in the Saint-Bertin catalogue of *c.* 1104. Its origin is problematic, however, for the membranes are prepared partly in the Insular and partly in the continental manner. Lowe attributed it to

[118] Bischoff, *Studien* II, 333 (cf. Bischoff and Hofmann, *Libri Sancti Kyliani*, p. 95; Lowe, *CLA* IX, no. 1426 and *Uncial*, pl. XXXIII); Sims-Williams, 'Anglo-Latin Letter', pp. 1 and 3–4. On the charter cf. above, p. 192.

[119] See Farmer, *Rule*, pp. 21–2; Ker, *Books, Collectors and Libraries*, pp. 131–3.

[120] Engelbert, 'Bemerkungen', pp. 410–11; Sims-Williams, 'Cuthswith', pp. 4–5. See above, p. 192.

[121] *CLA* VI, p. xxii. Cf. Bischoff, *Studien* II, 326. On the Corbie library see the references given by Wormald, 'Bede and Benedict Biscop', p. 150 and n. 70, and forthcoming work by D. Ganz. On Balthild see above, p. 113.

'Anglo-Saxon scribes, perhaps on the Continent'. (He dated it s. viii² but Professor Brown saw no reason to date it after the middle of the century.)[122] A final pointer to the Apponius manuscript's semi-continental background is the presence on the last folio (62r) of a copy of a letter to an unnamed youth from a woman with the otherwise unattested name *Burginda*. The first part of this name is the non-diagnostic Common Germanic element *Burg-*. The second part, however, is the rare continental hypocoristic suffix *-inta*, or the rare West Frankish element *-gind*, or else a spelling, under continental influence, of the common Old English element *-gȳth* (cf. Frankish *-gundis*, etc.). The letter, which is in the same hand as the Apponius, is not Burginda's (or Burgyth's) holograph, to judge by an apparent lacuna, but the scribe or patron of the manuscript probably had some connection with her, for the letter is not of the quality to be preserved merely as a stylistic model. She may, indeed, have been the patron of the manuscript. [123]

This converging evidence suggests that the Boulogne manuscript is from some centre in southern England with Frankish connections in the early eighth century. As we saw in ch. 4, there is a good deal of evidence for English ecclesiastics who went to Gaul in the seventh century, but little is known about the traffic in the reverse direction mentioned in the *Vita* of Bertila, abbess of Chelles (*c.* 660–*c.* 710), which describes her sending over followers with 'many volumes of books' to establish monasteries for men and for women. As far as I know, the only examples of such monasteries in southern England are Bath and the more doubtful case of Wenlock. We have already seen that the first abbess of Bath bore a Frankish name, *Berta*, and that Leutherius, the Frankish bishop of Wessex, can be associated with the diplomatic of her foundation charter of 675. [124] I would suggest that the continental connections of the Boulogne Apponius can be explained by the hypothesis – and that is all it is – that it was written at Bath.

We can also entertain the possibility that the Hatton 48 copy of the *Regula S. Benedicti* was written in early eighth-century Bath and passed to Worcester, perhaps when Bath was temporarily absorbed into the Worcester estate later in the century, before the Synod of Brentford. [125] A relevant consideration is that it is a unique, and at that a *de luxe*, copy of the Benedictine Rule from a time when this Rule was not widely accorded

---

[122] *CLA* VI, no. 737 (cf. Suppl., no. 1678); Sims-Williams, 'Anglo-Latin Letter', pp. 1–2.
[123] *Ibid.*, pp. 7–8, and below, pp. 212–15.   [124] See above, pp. 110–13.
[125] See above, p. 159.

pre-eminence in England.[126] It must have been produced at a house where this Rule was held in especial esteem; a further indication of this is the fact that the scribe's own revisions reveal knowledge of more than one text.[127] Scholars have argued for connections with Wilfrid (whose support for the Benedictine Rule is well known), or with Wessex (because of the place accorded to the Rule by Boniface and supposedly by Aldhelm), or with Frankish influences (because of the importance of the 'Columbanan' monasteries in the diffusion of the Rule).[128] Bath origin would happily reconcile these views: Wilfrid was active in the kingdom of the Hwicce and on the West Saxon border in 675 and 680, and he attested the Bath foundation charter, for whose Dionysian dating clause he may have been responsible; Leutherius, bishop of Wessex, and nephew of Agilbert, Wilfrid's Frankish ally at the Synod of Whitby, took part in its foundation; there was a continental element in the monastery's personnel; and already in the reign of Athelstan (before the tenth-century Benedictine revival) Bath seems to have been dedicated to St Benedict as well as St Peter.[129] Certainly, Bath seems a more attractive possibility than Evesham, which was suggested by Farmer; Wilfrid is not linked with Evesham by any source earlier than Byrhtferth's historically worthless *Vita S. Ecgwini*, where he is merely introduced as archbishop of York. Moreover, as Evesham, unlike Bath, never came under the control of the see it is not easy to see how Hatton 48 might have reached Worcester.[130]

The Apponius manuscript could have reached Saint-Bertin *c.* 933 among the 'many alms' sent by that famous dealer in manuscripts, King Athelstan, who probably controlled Bath as a royal proprietary monastery;[131] or it could be one of the many books with which Sæwold, abbot

---

[126] Cf. above, p. 117.

[127] Farmer, *Rule*, pp. 19 and 23; cf. Lapidge, 'Theodore and Hadrian', p. 63, n. 104. Engelbert, 'Bemerkungen', p. 411, rather perversely argues for origin in a non-Benedictine centre, because of the absence of signs of wear on the manuscript; but early transference from its original home to Worcester might explain this.

[128] See Sims-Williams, 'Anglo-Latin Letter', pp. 9–10 and nn. 86–8. Cf. Holdsworth, 'Boniface the Monk', esp. p. 66, n. 44. On the rule observed at Jouarre and Chelles see Guerout, 'Origines', p. 44, and Levison, 'Vita Bertilae', p. 96.

[129] See above, pp. 104–5, 111–13 and 118; Sims-Williams, 'Wilfrid', p. 171.

[130] From the latter point of view the monastery at Ripple is a more promising candidate; see above, pp. 104–5. Cf. Farmer, *Rule*, p. 25; *Vita Quorundum Anglo-Saxonum* [sic], ed. Giles, pp. 379–80. On the *Vita* see above, p. 141.

[131] *EHD*, no. 26; Grierson, 'Relations Between England and Flanders', p. 88. For Athelstan and Bath see Sims-Williams, 'Bath', p. 10, and Keynes, 'Athelstan's Books', p. 161. Cf. above, p. 174.

of Bath, fled to Flanders after the Norman Conquest.[132] We only have a list of the books which Sæwold gave to the monastery of Saint-Vaast at Arras, none of which is known to have reached Saint-Bertin. However, a late tenth-century volume of continental and Anglo-Saxon saints' lives and sermons from the Saint-Bertin library (Boulogne, Bibliothèque Municipale, 106 (127), fols. 1–92 and 119–71), written in a number of continental hands,[133] is closely related in script and contents to Arras, Bibliothèque Municipale, 1029 (812), which was one of the manuscripts which Sæwold of Bath presented to Saint-Vaast.[134] The Arras book was written in a mixture of English and continental hands, probably reflecting the fact that Bath monastery had been settled in 944 by Flemish monks from Saint-Bertin, refugees from the monastic reforms of Gérard de Brogne.[135] The similarity in contents between the Arras and Saint-Bertin manuscripts is obvious; moreover, Colgrave noted that the continental hands which wrote the *Vita S. Guthlaci* in each are similar, though not identical, and that the texts they wrote are 'so closely connected that it is clear that either one was a copy of the other, or, what is more likely, that both are from the same exemplar', in all probability 'an English original at

---

132 See Grierson, 'Livres de l'abbé Seiwold' and 'Relations Between England and Flanders', p. 108; Lapidge, 'Booklists', pp. 58–9.

133 Described by Colgrave, *Life of Guthlac*, pp. 35–9 (dating it *c.* 1000, but giving wrong shelf-mark) and by Wilmart, 'Livres de l'abbé Odbert', p. 180. The description by Van der Straeten, *Manuscrits hagiographiques*, pp. 129 and 137, is very inadequate. Note that Wilmart dates the relevant hands later than Colgrave (to s. xi²), but that *CLA* Suppl., no. 1678 says s. x. Cf. Gneuss, 'Preliminary List', p. 50, no. 804.

134 Colgrave, *Life of Guthlac*, pp. 34–5. Cf. Grierson, 'Livres de l'abbé Seiwold', pp. 103–5 and 109; Lapidge, 'Booklists', p. 61, no. 19; Gneuss, 'Preliminary List', p. 49, no. 780. Cf. the inadequate description by Van der Straeten, *Manuscrits hagiographiques*, pp. 62–3. Boulogne 106 at first contained the *vitae* of Walaric (abbot of Saint-Valéry-sur-Somme), Filibert, Aycadre (both abbots of Jumièges in the seventh century), Bavo and Guthlac. Arras 1029 contains the *vitae* of Cuthbert, Guthlac, Dunstan, Filibert and Aycadre. It seems likely that some *vitae* in Arras 573 (462) (Saint-Vaast, s. xiii; Van der Straeten, *Manuscrits hagiographiques*, pp. 42–7) are copied from Arras 1029; cf. the relationship of the texts of the *Vita S. Filiberti* in each manuscript (Levison, 'Vita Filiberti', pp. 575–6).

135 Grierson, 'Livres de l'abbé Seiwold', pp. 103–5; Colgrave, *Life of Guthlac*, p. 35. Cf. *EHD*, no. 26; Grierson, 'Relations Between England and Flanders', pp. 89–90 and 108; Keynes, 'Athelstan's Books', p. 161. It is an interesting question whether King Edmund, who gave them Bath, realized that he was thereby *restoring* Bath into continental hands; cf. above, p. 112, on Berta and Folcburg.

Bath'.[136] It is not clear when or how Boulogne 106 came to Saint-Bertin. The Bath monks, having left Saint-Bertin in protest in 944, are not likely to have sent manuscripts there; but the manuscript may have reached Saint-Bertin indirectly, for example via Saint-Vaast (as an unwanted duplicate of Arras 1029?). The important point is that Boulogne 106 shows that some Bath books did come to Saint-Bertin somehow or other, so that the Apponius could have travelled the same route – perhaps via Saint-Vaast, where it would have been an unwanted duplicate of a late eighth-century copy of the Pseudo-Jerome abridgement, now Boulogne, Bibliothèque Municipale, 42 (47).[137] Boulogne 106 was clearly at Saint-Bertin by the fifteenth century, but was apparently already there in the twelfth or even the eleventh century, for a figure bearing a crook and book in an eleventh-century illustration of Christ in Majesty on lv is labelled 'bertinus abbas' in a twelfth-century hand.[138]

Another aspect of Boulogne 106 is of further interest in connection with my hypothesis about the Apponius. The seventeenth-century binding of Boulogne 106 is that of Benoît de Béthune, abbot of Saint-Bertin. Bound in at the front is a leaf of Gregory's *Homelia in euangelia*, described by Lowe as written 's. viii–ix' in 'Anglo-Saxon minuscule still retaining some majuscule features' (that is, in T. J. Brown's 'hybrid minuscule'), 'in an Anglo-Saxon scriptorium, possibly on the Continent, to judge by a certain similarity to one hand of Boulogne 58 (63 and 64), foll. 20^{v}–21'.[139] We have already seen that the scripts of the latter manuscript – Augustine,

136 Colgrave, *Life of Guthlac*, pp. 46–7. Levison, 'Vita Filiberti', p. 575, notes the similarity between the texts of the *Vita S. Filiberti* in the two manuscripts.

137 *CLA* VI, no. 736 (where the commentary, starting at 162r, is not mentioned). The provenance is Arras: P. Grierson, 'La Bibliothèque de St-Vaast d'Arras au XIIe siècle', *RB* 52 (1940), 117–40, at 136, no. 218. Cf. *Apponii Expositio*, ed. de Vregille and Neyrand, pp. xvii-xviii and lvii-lviii.

138 S. xv is shown by the *ex libris* and by a list of contents which includes the items in the inserted gatherings, fols. 93–118, which were written at Saint-Bertin: Wilmart, 'Livres de l'abbé Odbert', p. 180; Colgrave, *Life of Guthlac*, pp. 36–7. Colgrave, *ibid.*, pp. 37–9, assumes that the figure was intended to be St Bertin by the artist, and that this, and another Christ in Majesty on 1r, were added at Saint-Bertin in the eleventh century, after the book had come there from Bath. It is worth noting that the manuscript is not referred to in the Saint-Bertin catalogue of *c.* 1104 (see Berthod, 'Notice').

139 *CLA* Suppl., no. 1678. The binding fragment at the other end of the manuscript is late medieval, and worm holes show it to have been re-used; is it from a rebinding of the fifteenth century? Cf. above, n. 138.

Epistulae – are of the same type as the Apponius, and that it, too, could have been written at an English centre with continental connections, such as Bath. It is therefore very interesting to find a leaf in a similar hand turning up in the binding of a book which went from Bath to Saint-Bertin. While it is not proven that the Gregory leaf had formed part of the original Bath binding of Boulogne 106, its presence is very suggestive. [140]

No early Anglo-Saxon manuscripts from Bath have been identified with certainty. [141] But in assessing the hypothesis that the Boulogne 74 Apponius and the Hatton 48 *Regula S. Benedicti* were produced there the potential of Bath monastery should not be underestimated. Considerable learning and discipline could flourish in the English double monasteries, as we know from Bede's and Rudolf of Fulda's accounts of Whitby, Barking and Wimborne. [142] Many double monasteries must also have been places of considerable ostentation, as Aldhelm's vivid invective against the aristocratic taste in clothing cultivated by some nuns attests – and the 'wealth of personal knick-knacks' from the Whitby excavations shows that Aldhelm was not merely following a literary convention. [143] On either count, one would expect that they were centres for manuscript production. There is

---

[140] See above, p. 203. One may compare another Saint-Bertin book which was rebound for Abbot Benoît, the twelfth-century Boulogne, Bibliothèque Municipale, 27 (32), the binding of which includes a strip of an uncial Augustine (s. vi-vii) inside the back cover; Wilmart's hypothesis that this strip had formed part of the original twelfth-century binding which was re-used by Benoît's binder, is confirmed by the fact that further pieces of the same Augustine had been used, probably in the twelfth century, to repair a tenth-century Saint-Bertin manuscript (Saint-Omer, Bibliothèque Municipale, 150). See Wilmart, 'Restes d'un très ancien manuscrit', pp. 289 and 293–4; *CLA* VI, no. 734. Unlike the more modern fragments used in binding Boulogne 27, the uncial fragments have clearly been re-used from some earlier binding.

[141] See Ker, *Medieval Libraries*, p. 7. Looking for early Bath books I have examined Saint-Vaast books known to have been given by Sæwold and Saint-Bertin books with Insular connections, but without any definite results. (See also below, p. 275, n. 11.) I regret to say that there is no similarity in script between the bibulous scribbles (noted by Ker, *Catalogue*, nos. 4 and 327) in Hatton 48 and Arras, Bibl. Munic. 764 (739) (one of Sæwold's books, cf. Gneuss, 'Preliminary List', p. 49, no. 780).

[142] *HE* IV.7–11 and 23–4; *EHD*, no. 159. On Barking see also above, pp. 179 and 197. In general, see Schneider, 'Women'.

[143] *Aldhelmi Opera*, ed. Ehwald, pp. 317–18; Cramp, 'Monkwearmouth and Jarrow', p. 17; Sawyer, *Roman Britain to Norman England*, p. 238. For the literary background to Aldhelm's satire, cf. e.g. Jerome, *Epp.* xxii.13 and 32 and cvii (trans. Wright, *Select Letters*); Leander of Seville's Rule for nuns in PL 72, 881 (citing I Peter III.3 and I Timothy II.9); and especially R. B. Domra, 'Notes on Cyprian's *De Habitu Virginum*, its Source and Influence', *Traditio* 4 (1946), 399–407. Cf. E. Crowfoot and S. C.

evidence that this was the case; for example, in 735 Boniface wrote to Eadburg, who may have been abbess of Wimborne, asking her to copy St Peter's Epistles in letters of gold and thanked her for other gifts of books and vestments.[144] In view of Bath's probable Frankish connections, it should also be noted that Chelles was a source of books and teachers in Bertila's time and continued in importance for manuscript production and biblical study into Carolingian times;[145] and that, while Jouarre's history immediately after the early eighth century is obscure, yet for the earlier period we can refer not only to Agilbert's visit to Ireland to study the bible (*legendarum gratia scripturarum*), at a time when the school of exegesis around Lismore was at its apogée, and to his standing with churchmen such as Wilfrid, Alhfrith and Theodore,[146] but also to the magnificence of Jouarre's crypt of St Paul and its tombs, if these are rightly assigned in part to the Merovingian period. Some scholars have compared the remarkable relief work on Agilbert's own tomb with the sculptured crosses he could have seen in the British Isles, though most would prefer to regard both as manifestations of a common renaissance, of which the Anglo-Frankish links mentioned by Bede are a part.[147]

One may wonder whether the Anglo-Saxons' biblical study led to activity in the practical sphere – *in opere intellegens*, as Jerome recommended to the virgin Principia – or whether, in the words of his celebrated letter to Eustochium criticizing false virgins, 'parchments are dyed purple, gold is melted for lettering, manuscripts are decked with jewels: and Christ lies at their door naked and dying'.[148] The decoration of manuscripts like the Hatton *Regula S. Benedicti* or the Boulogne Apponius, both of which have inaccurate texts, would probably have been reproved by Jerome; 'instead of jewels or silk', he wrote to Laeta, 'let her love the manuscripts of the Holy

Hawkes, 'Early Anglo-Saxon Gold Braids', *MA* 11 (1967), 42–86; H&S III, 369, §§ 19–20 (cf. *EHD*, p. 84); Alcuin, *Ep.* xv, ed. Duemmler, p. 41.

[144] Boniface, *Ep.* xxxv (Tangl, p. 60), in 735. On the identification see Sims-Williams, 'Recension'.

[145] Levison, 'Vita Bertilae', pp. 96–7; Bischoff, *Studien* I, 15–32; *CLA* VI, p. xxii; and above, p. 179.

[146] Grosjean, 'Date du Colloque de Whitby', p. 270; Ó Cróinín, 'Irish Provenance', p. 245; *HE* III.7 and 25, and IV.1.

[147] Cf. Sims-Williams, 'Bath', p. 7, n. 3, and p. 8, nn. 6–8; E. Fletcher, 'The Merovingian Crypt of Jouarre', *JBAA* 131 (1978), 113–18 and pl. XX.

[148] *Epp.* cxxvii.4 and xxii.32 (trans. Wright, *Select Letters*, pp. 447 and 131–3). Cf. Laistner, 'Study of Jerome', p. 252, on the fame of *Ep.* xxii. Aldhelm praises it: *Opera*, ed. Ehwald, p. 304.

Scriptures, and in them let her prefer correctness and accurate arrangement to gilding and Babylonian parchment with elaborate decorations'.[149] Yet manuscripts such as Cuthswith's Jerome and the Worcester gospels are plain, though elegant, and give the text priority. In any case, the decoration of Insular books may often express a quasi-sacramental reverence for the sacred word, rather than being an end in itself.[150] This reverence could deteriorate, it is true, into a magical evaluation of the bible, as in a Worcester prayer book where the gospel *initia*, so often highlighted in Insular gospel books, are isolated like amulets.[151] On the other hand, we should recall that Hild made those, like Oftfor and Tatfrith, who studied under her divide their time between 'study of the Scriptures' (*lectio diuinarum scripturarum*) and 'works of righteousness' (*opera iustitiae*). Gregory II, interpreting Boniface's career in 719, rightly saw his biblical study not as an end in itself, but as the discovery of the *uerbum diuinum*, which could naturally lead to a missionary vocation:

Your pious purpose, as it has been declared to us, and your well-proved sincerity of faith demand of us that we make use of you as our co-worker in spreading the divine words, which by the grace of God is our special care. Knowing, therefore, that you have been from childhood a student of sacred literature and that you now wish, for the love of God, to extend the talent divinely entrusted to you, by dedicating yourself ceaselessly to missionary work and the teaching of the mystery of faith among the heathen, carrying to them the saving knowledge of the divine oracle, we rejoice in your loyalty and desire to further the work of grace vouchsafed to you.[152]

Similarly, after Boniface's martyrdom in 754, Cuthbert, archbishop of Canterbury – arguably a former bishop of the Magonsætan – 'makes no distinction between Boniface's role of Christian missionary and that of an exponent of the traditional Anglo-Saxon religious culture of his age', when he described him, in the letter to be discussed in the following chapter, as 'a famous investigator of the divine books and a splendid soldier of Christ'.[153]

[149] *Ep.* cvii.12, trans. Wright, *Select Letters*, p. 365. Cf above, n. 89.

[150] See above, p. 181. In the letter cited above, n. 144, Boniface says that the manuscript decoration is 'ad honorem et reuerentiam sanctarum scripturarum ante oculos carnalium in predicando'.

[151] See below, p. 293.

[152] *HE* IV.23; *Ep.* xii (Tangl, pp. 17–18), trans. Emerton, *Letters of Boniface*, pp. 32–3.

[153] *Ep.* cxi (Tangl, pp. 238–43); see below, p. 233; G. W. Greenaway, 'Saint Boniface as a Man of Letters', in *The Greatest Englishman*, ed. Reuter, pp. 33–46, at 34. Parkes, 'Handwriting of St Boniface', pp. 172–5, argues that Boniface's belief in the bible's practical relevance in the mission field emerges from the glosses to the Epistle of James in the Codex Fuldensis.

8

Letter-writing

Anglo-Saxons played a full part in continuing the ancient literary tradition of letter-writing and letter-collecting.[1] Seventh- and eighth-century England already displays all the main medieval types of letter. There are purely practical communications, such as the letter of Wealdhere, bishop of London, to Archbishop Berhtwald in 704×705, and semi-public treatises in epistolary form, such as Bede's *Epistola ad Ecgbertum*.[2] There are also numerous letters of friendship, congratulation, exhortation, encouragement, or condolence, notably in the collected correspondence of Aldhelm, Boniface and Lull.[3] The originals of even practical letters stood little chance of being preserved, since they had no value as legal instruments, unlike charters. Indeed, a twelfth-century Canterbury archivist endorsed 'Epistola inutilis' on Wealdhere's letter, and it is a happy accident that it has survived; it is the oldest extant letter on vellum or parchment in Western Europe.[4] Fortunately, however, letter-collections in book form were sometimes made, either because of the writers' importance or because of their letters' value as models of style.[5] Education in letter-writing was clearly based on imitation. This is well conveyed by a letter which Boniface received soon after 732 from Leofgyth, a nun at Wimborne in Dorset. She concludes by asking Boniface to correct her rustic style and to send one of his own letters as a model (*exempli gratia*); she

[1] See G. Constable, *Letters and Letter-Collections*, Typologie des sources du moyen âge occidental 17 (Turnhout, 1976); Gerchow, *Gedenküberlieferung*, pp. 25–59.
[2] Chaplais, 'Letter from Wealdhere'; *BOH* I, 405–23; *EHD*, nos. 164 and 170.
[3] See *Aldhelmi Opera*, ed. Ehwald; Tangl.
[4] Chaplais, 'Letter from Wealdhere', pp. 5–7, 19 and 21 (this excludes epistolary title deeds and public letters).
[5] Cf. *ibid.*, p. 6. For a possible reason for preserving Wealdhere's letter see *EHD*, p. 792, n. 1.

then adds four lines of halting verse (in formulae culled from Aldhelm), which she had

> tried . . . to compose according to the rules of the poetic tradition, not trusting in my own boldness, but desiring to practise the first steps of a meagre and feeble talent, and wanting your help. I have learnt this art from the teaching of Eadburg, who continues unceasingly to search into the divine law.[6]

Here we see a pupil labouring over letter-writing and versification while her teacher is deep in more abstruse biblical studies.

In this chapter the correspondence of Burginda, Ecgburg, Bishop Milred and Cyneburg is discussed. It must be admitted at once that the identification and localization of the three women writers is provisional – inevitably so, since no exhaustive lists of women religious were compiled, unlike bishops and kings. The temptation to make identifications on the basis of slight evidence has to be resisted; the desire to put human faces to bare names has been a fundamental attraction of antiquarian studies. (F. S. Scott, in his comparison of the BERCHTGYD stone at Hartlepool with a letter in the Boniface correspondence, is unusually restrained in saying that 'it would certainly be *pleasant* if one could think that it was our Berchtgyd who wrote from Hartlepool to her brother, in the mission field in Germany, this pathetic appeal . . .')[7] One justification for discussing some letters whose connection with the Hwicce or Magonsætan is uncertain is that the evidence needs to be set out as dispassionately as possible. In any case, even if one or other of the letters discussed below eventually proves to belong to another part of England, no great damage will have been done, since it is not being claimed that the area had a peculiar, individual literary culture. Indeed, this was probably not the case, so that even such a letter might nevertheless illustrate important facets of the literary activity that would undoubtedly have been pursued among the Hwicce and the Magonsætan.

I begin with a letter whose localization is uncertain: the letter from 'Burginda' (*Burgyth?*) to an unnamed 'youth', copied by the main scribe of

---

[6] *Ep.* xxix (Tangl, pp. 52–3); *EHD*, no. 169. Cf. Lapidge, 'Aldhelm's Latin Poetry', pp. 230–1. On Eadburg see Sims-Williams, 'Anglo-Latin Letter', p. 22, n. 119, and 'Recension', also below, p. 243; I deduce from this letter that she was at Wimborne, not Thanet.

[7] 'The Hildithryth Stone and the Other Hartlepool Name-Stones', *AAe* 4th ser. 34 (1956), 196–212, at 209; cf. below, n. 103. For a possible letter of Alcuin to a bishop of Hereford, see above, p. 172, n. 135.

Boulogne-sur-Mer, Bibliothèque Municipale, 74 (82), at the end of Apponius's commentary on the Song of Songs. In the previous chapter I suggested that this manuscript may have been written at Bath. It is possible that Burginda belonged to another centre, since she herself seems unlikely to have been the scribe, to judge by the apparently inaccurate transcription of her letter. On the other hand, seeing that her letter is hardly of sufficient quality as to be preserved as a model of style, the scribe or patron of the manuscript presumably had some special interest in or connection with her. The continental nature or spelling of the name *Burginda* argues for a close connection with the scriptorium which produced the manuscript. It is even possible either that the manuscript was copied under Burginda's patronage and that she provided her epistle as an epilogue for it, and failed to notice that her scribe had mangled it, or that the whole manuscript is a copy of a lost manuscript written by Burginda or under her patronage. In either case the omission of the youth's name could be explained by supposing that the lost opening folios of the manuscript contained a dedication naming him. On the other hand, in the surviving collections of eighth-century English correspondence one often finds that the compilers have omitted the name of sender or recipient, presumably because they were interested in only one of the two;[8] that may also be the case here.

Burginda writes as follows (I leave the Insular orthography unaltered):

O inclite iuuenis uenturique eui inscius – utrum gloriosa Felicitas tibi uehat sub astris dilicias saeculi, an spumas agit ore cruento Miseria – et ideo totis contendere uiribus, ut tibi clara lux nitet in caelo, spiretque salubrior aura aeternasque dies atque inmutabile tempus, et secreta Deo regnaris ditissima campis beata nimis, sereno in cardine sedis. 'Solus, agius sanctusque Deus', uox omnibus una est.

Accipe animoque tuo quod Spiritus alme bis ueniens per corda creat, ut duo iusa colas tabulis conscripta lapideis: 'Dilegite mente Deum feruenti plenus amore'; rursum ait: 'Carus sit tibi quoque proximus ut tu'. Hoc pactum ius omne tene, et semper quandocumque ad Deum uiuentem in excelso animum funderis in praces (*sic*), et nimius rorarent lumina fletu, [*memoria*] mei nominis Burgindae digna tuis meritis, ut digna sit oratio uotis.

This is obscure, and probably corrupt, but might be translated somewhat as follows:

---

[8] E.g. Boniface, *Ep.* xxxi (Tangl, p. 55). Both names might be omitted from letters preserved solely as stylistic models.

O illustrious youth, (as you are) ignorant of the age to come – whether glorious Felicity may bring to you the delights of the world beneath the stars, or Misery foam at her gory mouth – strive, therefore, with all your strength, so that the clear light may shine in heaven for you, and a more wholesome breeze blow for eternal days and immutable Time, and you may reign over the (places) secret to God, most rich and blest in fields, in the serene apex of (his) abode. 'Alone, Holy, Holy God', there is one voice to all (there).

Receive in your soul that which the twice-coming Spirit kindly creates in (men's) hearts, so that you may observe the two commandments written on the tables of stone: 'Love God with your mind, full of fervent love'; (and) again, it says: 'May your neighbour also be as dear to you as yourself'. Keep all this Covenant, and always, whensoever you pour out your soul to the Living God on high in prayers, and your eyes become very moist with weeping, may [the remembrance] of my name Burginda be as worthy of your good offices as prayer is worthy of (your) vows.

When I first edited this letter, I conjecturally filled the apparent lacuna after *fletu* by supplying *memoria*, which the careless scribe could easily have omitted by haplography before *mei nominis*. For the formula, one may compare a letter of Cyneheard, bishop of Winchester, sending gifts *c.* 754, 'quae te suscipere pro tua humilitate obnixae precamur habereque ad *memoriam mei nominis* saltim aliquot spatium temporis', a letter of Ælfwald, king of East Anglia, promising Boniface *c.* 748 '*memoriaque nominis uestri* in septenis monasteriorum nostrorum sinaxis perpetua lege censeri debet', and a letter of Alcuin in 800: 'nunc uero in presenti deprecor, ut *nostri nominis* habeatis *memoriam* in sanctis sacris orationibus uestris'.[9] The restoration of *memoria* was questioned by Peter Dronke, for whom 'the letter would seem to be an autograph, hence . . . the diplomatic text . . . should probably be accepted without emendation, assuming only the

---

[9] *Epp.* cxiv and lxxxi (Tangl, pp. 246–7 and 181–2, respectively), cf. below, n. 38; Duemmler, *Ep.* cxcv. Cf. *Ep.* vii (Tangl, p. 2), Archbishop Berhtwald *c.* 710: 'obsecro, ut, cum tui [*tui mei*! MS – a significant error for us] memoriam in crebris orationibus feceris, mei nihilhominus [*sic*] meminisse digneris'. My emendation is accepted by Gerchow, *Gedenküberlieferung*, p. 49. De Vregille and Neyrand, *Apponii Expositio*, p. xxviii, endorse my view that the Boulogne manuscript, 'oeuvre de scribes [*sic*] peu lettrés', is not the autograph either of the Apponius abridgement or of Burginda's letter. For haplography in the main text cf. *ibid.*, pp. 421 and 431: *mobilitatem* (30v) < *immobilem bonitatem*; *uetestamenti* (40r) < *ueteris testamenti*.

word-division "fle tu".[10] This attractive solution is difficult to accept. It may readily be granted that the scribe might not signal the word-division in *fle tu mei*; for instance, *proximusut* is written as one word. What the scribe originally wrote, however, was *fletusmei* and the *s* has been erased,[11] either by the scribe or by some later reader (who was perhaps also trying to save the sense by supposing *fle tu* plus genitive of respect). While such a careless copyist might easily make a declensional error and add an *s* to *fletu*, it seems implausible that the author herself could have miswritten *fletus* when she had the imperative *fle tu* in mind.

The composition's scarcely fulfilled ambition and imperfections reflect Burginda's education. She has been taught grammar, but not thoroughly, as the confusions of tense, mood and voice show;[12] these errors cannot be blamed solely on the copyist, for they occur most noticeably when Burginda is not following a model (so far as I have discovered) or is adapting the syntax of one to her own purposes. Burginda has obviously been introduced to models for letter-writing; the *memoria mei nominis* formula shared with Cyneheard, Ælfwald and Alcuin is an indication of this, if the emendation is correct. Indeed, her composition is essentially a combination of two common forms of letter: an exhortation to strive for the heavenly reward, and a request for prayers. Above all, Burginda's words show something of her reading. This was fitting in a letter; Aldhelm, thanking Hildelith and her fellow-nuns for their letters, remarked:

In your writing there shone richly forth the holy compact of promised prayers, which you pledged with trustworthy avowals, but also there was revealed, in the wise course of your remarks, the honeyed study of the holy Scriptures.[13]

---

[10] Dronke, *Women Writers*, p. 322. He kindly explains by letter that he interprets the conclusion as follows, taking the genitives after *fle tu* as genitives of respect: '. . . and always, whenever you pour your spirit into prayers to the God living on high and your eyes shed their dew abundantly (*nimius = nimis*), then weep (*fle tu*) over my name, Burginda [i.e. in respect of my name – meaning, pray for me too], who deserves your good offices, so that your prayer may deserve to obtain what it asks'. The proposed reading disturbs the metrical cadence *rorarent lumina fletu(s)*, and *flere* with genitive is not attested in the *Thesaurus Linguae Latinae*, nor in J. B. Hofmann, *Lateinische Syntax und Stilistik*, rev. A. Szantýr (Munich, 1965), pp. 32, 116 and 358.

[11] Cf. Sims-Williams, 'Anglo-Latin Letter', pp. 7, 10 and 19, n. 64. In this article I printed a diplomatic text; see also *Apponii Expositio*, ed. de Vregille and Neyrand, p. 463.

[12] Sims-Williams, 'Anglo-Latin Letter', p. 10.

[13] *Aldhelmi Opera*, ed. Ehwald, p. 229.

In Burginda's case reading of the poets is more evident than biblical study. In fact, the greater part of what she writes is adapted, with varying success, from earlier hexameter verse.

Of the pagan poets she seems to quote only Vergil, the most widely-read in Anglo-Saxon England, but here it is not easy to decide whether she may not have drawn her Vergilian phrases from intermediaries. The clearest case of direct borrowing is her personified *Miseria* 'ore cruento', who is reminiscent of *Furor*, who rages, 'ore cruento', in the closed temple of war in *Aeneid* I.295, but is blended with an echo of the eager race-horse in *Georgics* III.203, which 'will foam bloody flecks from its mouth' (*spumas aget* [var. *agit*] *ore cruentas*) – a subconscious image for the 'illustrious youth' himself? This young horse, 'still ignorant of life' (*etiam inscius aeui*, line 189), may have reminded Burginda of Vergil's description of Vulcan in *Aeneid* VIII.627 as 'not unaware of seers nor ignorant of the age to come' (*haud uatum ignarus uenturique inscius aeui*). Yet the direct source for her 'uenturique eui inscius' may have been the Christian adaptation of Vergil's cadence in line 41 of the anonymous North African *Carmen ad Flauium Felicem de resurrectione mortuorum et de iudicio Domini*, written between 496 and 523:

> si qui uellit poenas aeternae euadere flammae
> ignarusque die *uenturique inscius aeui*,
> et iustae potius adipisci praemia uitae:
> hunc unum meminisse Deum solumque precandum . . .[14]

Similarly her 'Accipe animoque tuo' may either echo the Vergilian formula (*Aeneid* III.250 and X.104)

> *accipite ergo animis* atque haec mea figite dicta

or may, more likely, echo Juvencus's application of it to Christ, introducing the Parable of the Sower:

---

[14] Ed. Waszink. 'Whoever wishes to escape the punishments of everlasting flames, ignorant of (the time of) the Day (of Judgment) and unaware of the age to come, and wishes to obtain instead the rewards of righteous life, (must) remember that this one and only God is to be prayed to.' The elliptical syntax is discussed by L. Eizenhöfer, 'Totenpräfation aus einem altchristlichen Gedicht', *Archiv für Liturgiewissenschaft* I (1950), 102–6, at 104. For English knowledge of the *Carmen* see Sims-Williams, 'Anglo-Latin Letter', pp. 13–14 and n. 107; N. Wright, 'Imitation of the Poems of Paulinus of Nola in Early Anglo-Latin Verse', *Peritia* 4 (1985), 134–51, at 143.

accipite ergo animis, qui sit de semine sensus.[15]

Burginda's description of heaven is adapted from the description of Paradise in the *Carmen ad Flauium Felicem*, lines 194–7:

> lux ubi clara nitet spiratque salubrior aura,
> aeternaque dies atque inmutabile tempus
> et secreta Deo regio ditissima campis
> beataque nimis sereno in cardine sedes.

Her confusion of subjunctive and indicative ('ut nit*et* . . . spiretque') may be due to faulty adaptation from this source. The syntax of the last three lines is turned upside down by her substitution of *regnaris* 'you may reign' for *regio* 'realm', but she makes the necessary consequential changes of *aeternaque* to *aeternasque* (without manuscript authority) and *sedes* to *sedis* (on which see below). Burginda's next sentence is taken from an earlier line (185) in the *Carmen*, which describes heaven on the Day of Judgment:

> 'solus agius sanctusque Deus' uox omnibus una est.[16]

It is interesting to compare Burginda's texts of the *Carmen* with the (now acephalous) text in the tenth-century manuscript Paris, BN, lat. 8318, 73r–74v, which contains a heavily emended version of lines 108–290, followed by the *Carmina ecclesiastica* of Aldhelm – the scribe concludes the relevant gathering (fols. 73–80) with 'expł. opuscula aldhelmi' (80v). It is probably significant that this reworking omits lines 186–92, with the result that the descriptions of heaven and Paradise are merged, just as in Burginda's letter, only in the reverse order. Moreover, we find the reading *sedis* instead of *sedes*:

> solusque agius sanctusque Deus uox omnibus una est
> aeternaque dies atque inmutabile tempus
> lux ubi clara lucet spirat salubrior aura

---

[15] *Euangelia* II.775 (ed. Huemer, p. 76). '*Take to heart therefore*, and fix (there) these words of mine / what meaning there may be concerning the seed [see below, p. 219].' On the formulaic approach to hexameters, see Lapidge, 'Aldhelm's Latin Poetry'.

[16] '[There is a place] where clear light shines and a more wholesome breeze blows, and (there is) eternal day and immutable Time, and a realm secret to God, most rich in fields, and a most blest abode in the serene apex (of the world)'; 'Alone, Holy [*hagios*], Holy God, there is one (unison) voice to all there'. On the source and significance of line 185 see Sims-Williams, 'Anglo-Latin Letter', pp. 12–13.

> et secreta Deo regio ditissima campis
> beataque nimis sereno in cardine sedis.[17]

Burginda's text of the *Carmen* cannot have been identical with this (note its *solusque*, its reversal of the second and third lines, and its *lucet spirat* for *nitet spiratque*), but it may well derive from a text similar to the one she used. In view of its transmission with the poems of Aldhelm (who certainly knew the *Carmen*), one wonders whether it is of English provenance, and even whether it had passed through Aldhelm's hands. The proximity of Bath to Malmesbury may be borne in mind.

The second part of Burginda's letter is adapted from the epic version of the Acts of the Apostles by Arator (*c.* 544), a work much quoted by Aldhelm and Bede. Arator explains why the bible describes the Spirit being given to the disciples on two different occasions (John xx.22 and Acts II):

> *Ut duo iussa colant tabulis conscripta duabus:*
> *'Dilige mente Deum feruenti plenus amore',*
> *Rurus ait: 'Carus tibi sit quoque proximus ut tu'.*
> *Hoc pactum ius omne tenet, quod Spiritus almus*
> *Bis ueniens per corda creat:* semel hunc dedit Auctor
> In terris, ut ametur homo; post misit ab astris,
> Ut flagrent humana Deum.[18]

Burginda shows no knowledge of Arator's source for this allegorical exegesis, Augustine's fifth sermon for Ascension Day,[19] nor of the other examples of it in Augustine and Gregory, but she does allude to the same biblical texts as Augustine and Arator, which suggests that she may have used Arator's work as a companion to reading the bible; her 'Accipe . . .

---

[17] Cf. the inaccurate edition by J. A. Giles, *Sancti Aldhelmi Opera* (Oxford, 1844), p. 132. Modern scholars of course reject the seventeenth-century attribution 'Aldhelmus' on 73r: *Aldhelmi Opera*, ed. Ehwald, pp. xvi and 9–10; *Carmen ad Flauium Felicem*, ed. Waszink, pp. 15–16.

[18] *Aratoris de actibus apostolorum* I.229–35 (ed. A. P. McKinlay, CSEL 72 (Vienna, 1951), 25): '. . . so that they should observe the two commandments written on two tables: "Love God with your mind, full of fervent love"; (and) again, it says: "May your neighbour also be as dear to you as yourself". This Covenant contains all the law, which the kindly twice-coming Spirit creates in (men's) hearts: the Author (Jesus) gave this once on earth, so that man should be loved; afterwards he sent it from heaven, so that humankind should love God.' On Aldhelm and Bede, see *ibid.*, pp. xxvi–xxviii.

[19] PL 38, 1222–3. Cf. Sims-Williams, 'Anglo-Latin Letter', p. 22, n. 112. I discuss this exegesis in a paper in preparation. Cf. above, p. 179, n. 15.

quod Spiritus alme bis ueniens per corda creat' appears to be a conflation of two texts quoted by Augustine: 'insufflauit et dixit eis: *"Accipite* Spiritum sanctum"' (John XX.22) and 'caritas Dei diffusa est in cordibus nostris per Spiritum sanctum, qui datus est nobis' (Romans V.5). She seems to use Arator's 'quod Spiritus . . . per corda creat' to refer either to Charity or else to the 'word of the Kingdom' which is 'sown in the heart' (*quod seminatum est in corde*) according to the above-mentioned Parable of the Sower (Matt. XIII.19). By changing Arator's *tenet* 'contains' to *tene* 'observe' she radically alters the sense of her original, as in the case of her alteration of *regio* to *regnaris* in the *Carmen ad Flauium Felicem.* As in her treatment of that passage, she rearranges the order of her model. By substituting *lapideis* 'of stone' for *duabus* 'two' she reinforces Arator's equation of the two tables of stone, on which Moses received the Ten Commandments and the Covenant (*pactum*), with Christ's two-fold new commandment given by Christ on which 'hang all the law and the prophets' (*uniuersa lex pendet, et prophetae*). This equation was presumably due, not to ignorance, but to a figural understanding of the Old Testament. Indeed Apponius tantalizes his readers by listing 'the law received on the two tables written by God's finger' (*in duabus tabulis legem susceptam digito Dei scriptis*) among the various arcane types and figures of the Old Testament into whose interpretation the Christian soul is to be initiated, apparently through coming to understand Christ's law of Charity (*ordo caritatis*).[20] Unfortunately, however, it is not at all clear that Apponius influenced Burginda here, since she follows Arator so closely.

Burginda's line of thought is not very clearly expressed, and any literary merits in her letter are entirely due to her use of Vergil, Arator and the *Carmen ad Flauium Felicem.* She is clearly less learned than many of Boniface's female correspondents, and her composition would hardly have been preserved had it not formed part of the Apponius codex. Yet for us it is an illuminating indication of the education one woman received; it may be compared with the evidence of Leofgyth's letter, quoted above.

Burginda's composition shows that poetic images were appropriate in a letter.[21] In this respect it is comparable to a letter which Boniface received

[20] Exodus XXIV.12; XXXI.18; XXXII.15–19; XXXIV.1, 4 and 28–9; Deut. IV.13; IX.9–11 and 15–X.5; Matt. XXII.37–40; Mark XII.29–31; *Apponii Expositio,* ed. de Vregille and Neyrand, p. 80 (cf. pp. 83 and 328).

[21] Indeed Boniface and Lull break into verse in order to exhort their correspondents. See *Epp.* ix, ciii and cxl (Tangl, pp. 4–7, 225–7 and 279–80, respectively). Cf. M. Roger,

in 716×718 from a certain Ecgburg, who has often been identified as a member of the royal house of the Hwicce.[22] In her highly poetic letter – unfortunately too long to quote – Ecgburg, like Burginda, expresses her admiration for her correspondent, though in much more fulsome terms, reminiscent of the heightened language of early Christian letter-writers such as Jerome and Paulinus of Nola. Ecgburg also resembles Burginda in drawing on Vergilian personifications:

> crudelis ubique
> luctus, ubique pauor et plurima mortis imago,

Aeneas's account of Troy in ruins, serves to express her feelings upon separation from her sister Wethburg, who has gone to Rome:

Iesum testor: ubique dolor, ubique pauor, ubique mortis imago.[23]

The use of poetic phrases throughout this letter is reminiscent of the style of some of Jerome's letters, and indeed she makes a couple of direct borrowings from what Kelly has described as 'one of the most beautiful and emotionally uninhibited of his letters'. There, echoing Horace's simile of the mother who 'from the curving shore turns not her face' (*curuo nec faciem litore demouet*, *Carmina* IV.v.14), Jerome expressed his longing to see Rufinus:

Credas mihi uelim, frater, non sic tempestate iactatus portum nauta prospectat, non sic sitientia imbres arua desiderant, non sic curuo adsidens litori anxia filium mater expectat.[24]

L'enseignement des lettres classiques d'Ausone à Alcuin (Paris, 1905), pp. 311–12. The first poem appended to *Ep.* cxl is perhaps re-used or adapted from an earlier poem, for the last line (*Crede mihi, quia te summo conplector amore*) occurs already in Ecgburg's letter, discussed below (*Ep.* xiii): *Idcirco crede mihi Deo teste, quia te summo conplector amore.*

[22] *Ep.* xiii (Tangl, pp. 18–21); trans. Kylie, *English Correspondence*, pp. 57–60, and Emerton, *Letters of Boniface*, pp. 34–6. See Hahn, *Bonifaz und Lul*, pp. 101–3; Taylor, 'Osric', p. 324; *ECWM*, p. 176; D. N. Dumville in *HBC*³, p. 11.

[23] 'Everywhere cruel grief, everywhere sorrow and many a form of death' (*Aeneid* II.368–9); 'I call on Jesus as witness, that everywhere (was) sorrow, everywhere grief, everywhere a form of death' (*Ep.* xiii (Tangl, p. 19)). For Vergilian and other sources see Tangl's notes.

[24] *Ep.* iii.2, ed. Hilberg, I, 14; trans. Fremantle *et al.*, *Letters and Select Works*, p. 5: 'Believe me, brother, I look forward to seeing you more than the storm-tossed mariner looks for his haven, more than the thirsty fields long for the showers, more than the anxious mother sitting on the curving shore expects her son.' Cf. Kelly, *Jerome*, p. 45.

Ecgburg takes over Jerome's similes intact to express 'how much I desire to enjoy your sight':

Quapropter, crede mihi, non sic tempestate iactatus portum nauta desiderat, non sic sitientia imbres arua desiderant, non sic curuo litore anxia filium mater expectat, quam ut ego uisibus uestris frui [*var.* fruere] cupio.

It is to Ecgburg's credit that she retains the crucially evocative adjective *curuus*. Undoubtedly she carries the legitimate practice of literary allusion too far, using Jerome as a prop for her own Latin. On the other hand originality was not at a premium; 'nothing has been said which has not been said before', as she might have read in Jerome's exposition of 'there is nothing new under the sun' (Ecclesiastes 1.10) in Cuthswith's manuscript.[25] Questions of sincerity hardly arise: after all the similes were not original in Jerome's letter either. The verbatim borrowings in Ecgburg's letter, like those in Burginda's, undeniably reflect a strongly derivative element in Anglo-Latin culture. Yet her predilection for sea-imagery, which is evident in the quotations in many other Anglo-Latin letters, probably corresponds to a real element in the Anglo-Saxon poetic sensibility, to judge by numerous vernacular poems:

> Scip sceal genægled,   scyld gebunden,
> leoht linden bord.   Leof wilcuma
> Frysan wife,   þonne flota stondeð . . .
> Lida biþ longe on siþe,   a mon sceal seþeah leofes wenan,
> gebidan þæs he gebædan ne mæg.   Hwonne him eft gebyre
>   weorðe,
> ham cymeð, gif he hal leofað,   nefne him holm gestyreð,
> mere hafað mundum   mægðegsan wyn.[26]

On the influence of Jerome's letters see the all too slight remarks of Laistner, 'Study of Jerome', pp. 251–2; cf. J. N. Hritzu, *The Style of the Letters of St Jerome* (Washington, 1939). The 'importance du sentiment' in early Christian letters is stressed by Favez, *Consolation*, pp. 130–9; cf. Dronke, *Women Writers*, p. 30.

[25] *Commentarius*, ed. Adriaen, p. 257: *nihil est dictum, quod non sit dictum prius* (a quotation from Terence, as commented on by 'my teacher Donatus'). Cf. Kelly, *Jerome*, p. 11.

[26] *Maxims I*, ed. and trans. T. A. Shippey, *Poems of Wisdom and Learning in Old English* (Cambridge, 1976), pp. 68–9: 'A ship is riveted, a shield, the bright linden wood, is lashed with hides. The Frisian's wife is glad to see the arrival she has wished for, when his ship is drawn up . . . A seaman is away for a long time, but still one must always look for the one you love to return, wait for what cannot be hurried. When he gets an opportunity again, he will come home, if he is alive and safe, unless the sea prevents

The localization of Ecgburg in the kingdom of the Hwicce, mentioned above, hinges on an identification of Oshere, sub-king of the Hwicce, with Ecgburg's brother of the same name, who is mentioned in the first part of her letter:

Since I tasted the bond of your love in my inner self, I confess, its savour pervades my body like some thing of honeyed sweetness. And although I find I am now robbed of the sight of you in the flesh, I shall ever hang about your neck with a sister's embraces. Thus, my beloved, you, who have been a brother, are now to be called both father and brother in the Lord of Lords, for, after cruel, bitter Death separated from me him that I loved above all others, my blood-brother Oshere, I used to esteem you with a charitable love beyond almost all your sex. And, not to spin out words too long, no day unrolls nor night slips by without some recollection of your teaching. Therefore believe me, as God is my witness, I embrace you with the noblest kind of love.[27] And I am confident that you never forget that friendship with my brother on which you could always rely. I too, though slower in learning and lower in merits than he, am not behind him in concern for your loving self. And, though decreasing with the swift passage of the seasons, the black cloud of my grief has never left me; the increasing length of time has rather added increasing injuries, as it is written: 'the love of man brings sorrow, but the love of Christ illumines the heart'.

Ecgburg's use of tenses and conjunctions is idiosyncratic, but she certainly gives the impression that Oshere had died some time before the date of writing (716×718); this would agree with the identification with Oshere of the Hwicce who appears to have died (or retired to a monastery?) by 709 at the latest.[28] Finberg, who accepted the identification, interpreted *amara mors et crudelis* as referring to a 'tragic' death, in the journalistic sense of a violent death, and attempted to associate it with the mysterious assassination of the Mercian queen Osthryth in 697; but such an interpretation is very forced.[29] We know nothing about the learning or merits of Oshere of

him, the ocean has his ship, the raider's joy, in its grasp'. For examples of the image of life as a voyage etc. see G. V. Smithers, 'The Meaning of *The Seafarer* and *The Wanderer*', *MÆ* 26 (1957), 137–53, and 28 (1959), 1–22. Cf. Dronke, *Women Writers*, p. 31, on resemblances between Latin letters and vernacular poetry. Poetic sea-imagery is particularly striking in a letter by Lull: *Ep.* xcviii (Tangl, pp. 218–22) (cf. below, n. 95).

[27] Cf. above, n. 21. The quotation at the end of this passage has not been traced.

[28] See above, p. 35.

[29] *ECWM*, pp. 176–7; cf. above, p. 93. Finberg's statement that Osthryth was Oshere's kinswoman rests on treacherous Evesham authority.

the Hwicce, but there is no reason why he should not have known Boniface. Ecgburg's description of herself as Boniface's pupil (*ultima discipulorum seu discipularum tuarum*) is not incompatible with her belonging to the kingdom of the Hwicce, rather than Wessex, in view of Willibald's statement that Boniface's fame as a teacher spread far and wide, so that women who could not travel to study with him caused him to come to them.[30]

In her letter Ecgburg also mentions her sister Wethburg, who was in prison in Rome. It is not recorded that King Oshere had sisters called Ecgburg and Wethburg, but, in view of Anglo-Saxon naming customs, it is relevant that two other members of his family with names in *-burg* are recorded, as successive abbesses of Gloucester: Cyneburg, sister of Osric (Oshere's predecessor), and her relative Eadburg, who was said to be the widow of Wulfhere of Mercia (d. 674×675) and to have survived at least to the reign of Coenred (704–9).[31] It has indeed been suggested that Ecgburg was the same person as this Eadburg of Gloucester.[32] The equation is unsatisfactory in so far as *Ecgburg* and *Eadburg* are distinct names, but cannot be ruled out in view of the very late date of the Gloucester sources, which could have corrupted *Ec(g)burg* into *E(a)dburg*. We can compare Goscelin's comment, in the eleventh century, that the name *Æthelburg* might be corrupted to *Eadburg*.[33] More closely still, we can compare the case of the sister of Ælfwald, king of the East Angles (d. 749), who is called *Ecgburg* in the early manuscripts of the contemporary *Vita S. Guthlaci*, but *Eadburg* in two later manuscripts and in the *Liber Eliensis*.[34] The corruption was natural, for *Eadburg* was a very common name and *Ecgburg* an unusual one; the only other known bearers of it are two in the list of 'queens and abbesses' in the Lindisfarne *Liber vitae* (who may be Boniface's correspondent and the East Anglian abbess) and one in a ninth-century charter.[35] Nevertheless, there can be no certainty that the Gloucester abbess 'Eadburg' was really called Ecgburg.

---

30 See above, p. 177.   31 See above, pp. 122–4.

32 W. Smith and H. Wace, *A Dictionary of Christian Biography*, 4 vols. (London, 1877–87) IV, 160; Taylor, 'Osric', p. 324.

33 Rollason, *Mildrith*, pp. 62–3.

34 *Life of Guthlac*, cc. 48 and 50, ed. Colgrave, pp. 146 and 156; *Liber Eliensis*, ed. Blake, p. 19 (*Ædburga*).

35 *Oldest English Texts*, ed. Sweet, pp. 154–5, lines 27 and 47, and 460, line 24 (= S 1436); Gerchow, *Gedenküberlieferung*, pp. 142–3; Searle, *Onomasticon*, p. 218 (Searle's Domesday example on p. 551 is a mistake).

Boniface's correspondent has sometimes been identified with the above-mentioned Abbess Ecgburg, the sister of King Ælfwald,[36] but only the identity of name supports the identification; we hear nothing of this East Anglian abbess having a sister named Wethburg[37] or a brother Oshere, and no contacts between Boniface and East Anglia are known, other than his formal exchange of prayers with King Ælfwald's monks.[38] Moreover in Ecgburg's letter itself there is an indication that she came from somewhere in the west. It ends with a postscript by a certain Ealdbeorht, addressed to Boniface:

Ego autem similiter Ealdbeorcth pauperculus Christi in Domino cum omni affectu saluto te. Deprecor te, ut illius amicitiae, quam olim spopondisti, in tuis deificatis orationibus recorderis, et licet corpore separemur, tamen recordatione iungamur.

If we can localize the writer of this postscript, we shall have a clue to Ecgburg's own locality. Now a person of the same name adds a postscript to a letter sent to Lull, Boniface's successor as bishop of Mainz (754–86), by a certain Tyccea:

Ego quoque minimus ecclesiae seruus supplici pro Domino deprecatione rogito, ut mihi cum mea familia domino Deo cuncta dispensanti ac rite regenti inter ceteros fideles uestros amicos in commune benigne suscipiatis, qui proprio dicor nomine Aldbercht diaconatus officio fungens, licet indignus, ut sancti gradus ministerium

---

[36] Haigh, 'Monasteries of Heiu and Hild', p. 375. This article is justly criticized by Whitelock, 'Pre-Viking Age Church', p. 15, n. 8.

[37] Later Anglo-Saxon sources mentioned a daughter of King Anna called Wihtburg who was buried at East Dereham (*CP*, pp. 395–6 and 396 n. 1; Whitelock, 'Pre-Viking Age Church', p. 8, n. 8; S 1486). She was thus Ecgburg's cousin, not her sister (cf. the table in *CP*, p. 399). The suggestion by Hahn, *Bonifaz und Lul*, p. 103 and n. 4, that she may be the Wethburg in the letter and that the place of her burial may have been Dyrham near Bath is very unlikely. The Wethburg mentioned in the letter is probably the one who was in Rome at the time of Boniface, *Ep.* xxvii (Tangl, pp. 47–9; *EHD*, no. 168), which gives no help in localizing her in England. It is uncertain which *Uichtburg* is mentioned in the Lindisfarne *Liber vitae* (cf. Gerchow, *Gedenküberlieferung*, p. 143).

[38] *Ep.* lxxxi (Tangl, pp. 181–2; Kylie, *English Correspondence*, pp. 152–3). Colgrave, *Life of Guthlac*, pp. 15–16, and Whitelock, 'Pre-Viking Age Church', p. 16, misinterpret the phrase quoted above, p. 214, as referring to seven *monasteries* in East Anglia rather than the seven canonical offices, recently re-endorsed by the Council of *Clofesho* (cf. *Aldhelmi Opera*, ed. Ehwald, p. 71; *BOH* II, 238–9; H&S III, 367).

olim acceptum uestris saluberrimis intercessionibus meliorando de die in diem proficiam.[39]

Such postscripts are uncommon in eighth-century English correspondence, so probably the same Ealdbeorht wrote both; he was perhaps the scribe of the letters.[40] The identity of the Tyccea who sent the later letter is not stated, but a reasonable guess may be made at localizing him, as this is an uncommon name. Apart from a layman *Ticcea*, who attests a spurious charter of Ine in the Malmesbury cartularies with a witness-list based (at least in part) on a genuine list for 705×709, there is only an abbot *Tyccęa*, who attests a charter of Æthelbald of Mercia of 757: BL, Cotton Charter viii. 3. Since only one other instance of the name *Ticcea/Tyccęa* is recorded[41] – in the Northamptonshire place-name Titchmarsh (*Ticceanmersc*) – there is a good chance that Lull's correspondent was the abbot who attests Æthelbald's charter, which is of just the right date.

Cotton Charter viii. 3 grants land by 'the wood which they call *Toccan sceaga*' to an abbot Eanberht. Stenton showed that, as Cynewulf of Wessex consents and several of his known *prefecti* attest, *Toccan sceaga* was in West Saxon territory and the grant reflects Æthelbald's overlordship in Wessex.[42] Wallenberg later associated *Toccan sceaga* with Tockenham in northern Wiltshire, and this has been generally accepted, for Tockenham

---

[39] *Ep.* xiii, to Boniface: 'But I, too, Ealdbeorht, a pauper of Christ, greet you in the Lord with all affection. I beg you to remember in your holy prayers that friendship which you once pledged, so that although we are separated in the body, yet we may be joined in remembrance' (Tangl, pp. 18–21). *Ep.* cxxix, to Lull: 'I also, the least servant of the church, beg for suppliant prayers to the Lord, so that, with God dispensing and duly ruling all things, you may kindly receive, in communion among your other faithful friends, me, with my *familia*, who am called by the proper name Ealdbeorht, discharging the office of deacon, although unworthy, so that I may perform the long-since accepted ministry of this holy grade, improving from day to day with help of your health-giving intercessions' (Tangl, pp. 266–7).

[40] As rightly observed by Haigh, 'Monasteries of Heiu and Hild', pp. 375–6 and 380, though his further deductions are worthless. Hahn, *Bonifaz und Lul*, p. 104, leaves the question open.

[41] S 245 and 96 (for the date of the latter see *EHD*, p. 19; it may be a copy of *c.* 800 or later: Bruckner and Marichal, *Chartae* III, no. 193; Scharer, *Königsurkunde*, pp. 182–4); Searle, *Onomasticon*, p. 451; *DEPN*, p. 475 (cf. below, n. 58). But see below, n. 57.

[42] *CP*, pp. 57–8. Cf. Scharer, 'Intitulationes', pp. 57 and 60. On the political situation on the Mercia–Wessex border see also Stenton, *Abingdon*, pp. 22–5 and 50; *EHD*, pp. 19–21, 498, 506 and 508; Finberg, *Early Charters of Wessex*, p. 218; and above, p. 160.

and *Tocan stan* nearby appear to be the only West Saxon place-names that contain the personal name *Toc(c)a*.[43] Despite Stenton's statement that 'the recipient of the charter, an abbot named Eanberht, is otherwise unknown',[44] he is surely likely to be the same person as the *Æambriht* listed as the fourth abbot of Malmesbury after Aldhelm in the twelfth- or thirteenth-century Malmesbury manuscript BL, Cotton Vitellius A. x, fols. 158–60,[45] and as the *Cambrithus* listed as the sixth in Hearne's transcript of a lost Malmesbury manuscript of the fourteenth century or later.[46] The identification is supported by the fact that Malmesbury possessed Tockenham.[47] This suggests that Cotton Charter viii. 3 is of Malmesbury provenance, if not origin. The lists of Malmesbury abbots were probably put together from William of Malmesbury's *Gesta pontificum*, supplemented by charters and other documents,[48] so possibly their compilers took Eanberht's name from the charter itself. If so, it is also possible that they made a wrong deduction, and that Eanberht belonged to some other monastery in the region, whose property at *Toccan sceaga* was later absorbed by Malmesbury, together with what we call Cotton Charter viii. 3. Thus we have to reckon with the possibility that the grant attested by Abbot

---

[43] See S 96; also *CP*, p. 58, n. 1; *DEPN*, p. 476; and Finberg, *Early Charters of Wessex*, pp. 70–1 (who connects *sceaga* with *Shaw* Farm in Lyneham near Tockenham; cf. *PNWilts*, p. 272). For the name *Toc(c)a* see Searle, *Onomasticon*, pp. 455 and 579; Redin, *Uncompounded Personal Names*, p. 110; *PNGl* I, 133; *DEPN*, s.n. *Tockholes*, etc.

[44] *CP*, p. 58, n. 1. Two abbots named Eanbercht appear in the Lindisfarne *Liber vitae* (ed. Sweet, *Oldest English Texts*, pp. 155–6, lines 69 and 87).

[45] Ed. Birch, 'Succession of the Abbots of Malmesbury', p. 342. Cf. Ker, *Medieval Libraries*, p. 128. The list is assigned to the ?tenth century by Edwards, 'Two Documents', p. 10. Compare the spelling of *Eanberht* as *Æanberht* in S 23 and as *Æmbriht* in S 756 (bounds).

[46] *Chronicles of Edward I and Edward II*, ed. Stubbs II, cxviii. (This list has two extra abbots after Aldhelm.) On the date and provenance of Hearne's source see *ibid.*, pp. xlii and xliv.

[47] See S 306, by which Æthelwulf of Wessex grants five hides at Tockenham to Malmesbury in 854. O'Donovan, 'Episcopal Dates, Part II', p. 108, thinks that this charter may have a genuine base. In any case it establishes that Tockenham was a Malmesbury estate. Finberg, *Early Charters of Wessex*, p. 71, points out that in Domesday Book Tockenham (a Malmesbury estate) is assessed at 10 hides, which agrees with the 757 *Toccan sceaga* charter. Cf. William of Malmesbury's interlineation in *GP*, p. 391 in his account of S 322 (= *Gesta regum*, ed. Stubbs I, 119–20), noted by Finberg, *Early Charters of Wessex*, pp. 73, 200, n. 1, and 208, n. 5.

[48] Cf. Birch, 'Succession of the Abbots of Malmesbury', pp. 314–15.

Tyccęa was not to Malmesbury itself but to some other house in the vicinity.

Besides Tyccęa, two other abbots attest Cotton Charter viii.3:

> Manus. Tyccęaan abb*atis*
> Manus Herecan. abb*atis*
> Manus Cyneberhti. abb*atis*
> Manus Bęgloci. b*resb*iteri
> Manus Ecggan. b*resb*iteri.[49]

Cyneberht may be the ageing abbot of Stour in Ismere, as Dorothy Whitelock suggested, for he is the only known abbot at this period bearing this (not uncommon) name; he may have been in attendance on Bishop Milred of Worcester, the only non-West-Saxon bishop to attest the charter.[50] *Hereca* was undoubtedly the abbot of that unique name who attested a grant to Malmesbury from Cynewulf of Wessex in 758[51] and he must also be the *Hereca abbas* whose greetings were conveyed to Bishop Lull (754–86) in an anonymous letter preserved in the ninth-century collection of Lull's correspondence.[52] The anonymous writer of this letter reminds Lull of their former friendship at Malmesbury, when Abbot Eaba was educating Lull and used to call him *Lytel*, 'little one'. Perhaps he was still a monk at Malmesbury, though this is not made clear; he was certainly closely connected with Hereca, who also signs the letter, and the letter strongly suggests that he was a member of Hereca's community. Hereca may even have been abbot of Malmesbury,[53] in which case Abbot Eanberht, to whom

---

[49] S 96. I quote from Bruckner and Marichal, *Chartae* III, no. 193; Birch (BCS 181) misunderstood the abbreviation *bb*.

[50] *EHD*, p. 492. On Cyneberht and Stour in Ismere see above, pp. 148–9 and 192. The other bishops are Herewald of Sherborne and Cyneheard of Winchester, Lull's relative.

[51] S 260. This is a purely West Saxon document. One cannot assume that one or other of Hereca and Beorn (the other abbatial witness) was abbot of Malmesbury; note that Abbot Eanberht did not attest the grant to himself of *Toccan scaega*.

[52] *Ep.* cxxxv (Tangl, pp. 273–4). On stylistic grounds it is probable that *Ep.* lxxix (of 747×748) is by the same writer (Hahn, 'Ueber einige Briefe', pp. 394–6, and *Bonifaz und Lul*, p. 235; Tangl, p. 171, n. 1, and p. 274, n. 1). The latter letter contains a clear quotation from Aldhelm, perhaps a relic of the writer's education at Malmesbury.

[53] The fact that Hereca is not mentioned in William of Malmesbury or in the lists of Malmesbury abbots mentioned above is no argument against him having been abbot of Malmesbury, for (unless *Eanberht* could be equated with *Eaba*) they are also ignorant of the abbot Eaba mentioned in *Ep.* cxxxv (Tangl, pp. 273–4). Hahn, 'Ueber einige Briefe', p. 396, and *Bonifaz und Lul*, p. 239, n. 4, suggested that the latter was the *Eobe*

Toccan sceaga was granted, must have ruled some other monastery, which is quite possible, as we have seen. Finally, the priest *Begloc* in the above witness-list of 757 may well be Lull's and his father's former slave-boy *Begiloc*, whom they had freed many years earlier, before *c.* 740 according to a letter sent to Cyneburg, who may have been abbess of Inkberrow.[54]

The important point for the present purpose is that Abbot Tyccea appears in a witness-list containing ecclesiastics from either side of the Hwiccian/West-Saxon border, and that therefore Ealdbeorht, who added the postscripts to the letters of both Ecgburg and Tyccea, can reasonably be assigned to the same area.

Hahn and Robinson identified the *Tyccęa abbas* who attested the 757 charter with an Abbot Tica of Glastonbury mentioned in William of Malmesbury's *De antiquitate Glastoniensis ecclesiae*, while Stenton identified the Glastonbury abbot with the Tyccea who wrote to Lull.[55] From a geographical and chronological point of view, these complementary and compatible identifications are satisfactory, for William associates Tica with a (lost) Glastonbury charter of Sigeberht of Wessex, who reigned for one year in 756.[56] A difficulty arises from the fact that the names *Ticcea* and *Tica* seem to be distinct.[57] This cannot be regarded as insuperable, however, for William's form *Tica* may be a miscopying, variant or Latinization of *Ticcea/Tyccea*; compare the variant spellings of Titchmarsh, Northamptonshire, in later medieval texts of Edgar's alleged confirmation

---

abbas who attested S 94, Æthelbald's grant of Wootton Wawen to Oshere's son Æthelric (cf. above, p. 149). See also S 89 (*Ibe*) and 103 (*Iebe*); cf. above, p. 36, n. 102.

54 See below, p. 241 and n. 102.

55 Hahn, *Bonifaz und Lul*, p. 239; Robinson, *Somerset Historical Essays*, p. 37; Stenton, *Anglo-Saxon England*, p. 174.

56 *Glastonbury*, ed. Scott, pp. 104–6 (c. 47) and 146. S 1680. William's date 754 is probably based on *ASC* which is two years behind. On Tica see further below, pp. 343 and 348.

57 Thus *DEPN*, p. 473 s.v. *ticcen*. But Redin, *Uncompounded Personal Names*, p. 110, seems to regard them as the same and adds 'When the same person (?) is called *Tyccæa* and *Tica* nothing can of course be stated as to the quantity and quality of the vowel, or the palatalization of the medial consonant.' For examples of *Tic(c)a* and *Tycca* see Searle, *Onomasticon*, pp. 451 and 462, who cites S 37 and the bounds of S 771; *PNOx* II, 316; Gelling, *Signposts*, p. 203. See also *DEPN*, p. 473, s.nn. *Tickenham, Tickford, Tickhill, Tickton*, though some or all of these may rather contain *ticcen* 'kid'; cf. *PNE* I, 182, and II, 178; A. H. Smith, *The Place-Names of the West Riding of Yorkshire*, 8 vols., EPNS, 30–7 (Cambridge, 1961–3) I, 52–3; Gelling, *Place-Names in the Landscape*, p. 317.

to Thorney: *Tutean Mersce, Tutan Mersce, Ticanmersc, Ticceanmersce*, etc.[58] In fact Robinson points out that the unique name *Wiccea* in the late tenth-century list of Glastonbury abbots in BL, Cotton Tiberius B. v, 23v (Christ Church?, s. xi¹), 'is probably a mistake for Ticcea' and refers to the abbot whom William calls *Tica*.[59]

We have now established that the Ecgburg who wrote to Boniface between 716 and 718 about her late brother Oshere could, chronologically, be a sister of King Oshere of the Hwicce and could perhaps be identical with the abbess of Gloucester, called 'Eadburg' in later sources, who was certainly related to Oshere and may have been his sister. We have seen, too, that the identification is satisfactory geographically: Ealdbeorht, who added a postscript to Ecgburg's letter, was also to add a postscript, some thirty or so years later, to a letter to Lull from Tyccea, who had West Saxon and Hwiccian connections and may have been abbot of Glastonbury. It would be quite understandable for Ealdbeorht to be active both in the kingdom of the Hwicce, perhaps at Gloucester, and in Wessex, perhaps at Glastonbury. Nevertheless, all this is very far from proving that Ecgburg belonged to the former kingdom. The crucial matter is the widely held identification of her brother Oshere with King Oshere. In favour of this identification it may be said that *Oshere* is a fairly unusual name. The only other examples of it found by Searle were an abbot in the Lindisfarne *Liber vitae*, a Kentish nobleman mentioned in five documents relating to the first half of the ninth century and a moneyer of the second half of that century; to these we must now add the OSHERE whose name is inscribed on a helmet of *c.* 700 from York.[60] More evidence will have to be found before the identification can be regarded as at all certain.

I now turn to a letter whose origin in the kingdom of the Hwicce is indisputable. In the ninth-century collection of Lull's correspondence, and of other materials gathered by him at Mainz, there is a copy of a letter of

---

[58] S 792; J. E. B. Gover *et al.*, *The Place-Names of Northamptonshire*, EPNS 10 (Cambridge, 1933), p. 221.

[59] *Somerset Historical Essays*, p. 44. The list is printed *ibid.*, pp. 41–2; cf. *Eleventh-Century Miscellany*, ed. McGurk *et al.* II, 74; Dumville, 'Anglian Collection', p. 43; Redin, *Uncompounded Personal Names*, p. 110.

[60] *Oldest English Texts*, ed. Sweet, p. 156, line 78; Searle, *Onomasticon*, pp. 374–5; P. V. Addyman *et al.*, 'The Coppergate Helmet', *Antiquity* 56 (1982), 189–94; D. Tweddle, *The Coppergate Helmet* (York, 1984); Hines, *Scandinavian Character*, p. 289. The charters, in the order given by Searle, whose dates need correction, are S 1200, 270, 271, 287, 1198; cf. Harmer, *Documents*, p. 86; Brooks, *Canterbury*, p. 148.

condolence received from Bishop Milred of Worcester on the occasion of Boniface's martyrdom in Frisia in 754 (Vienna, Nationalbibliothek, Vindobonensis 751, 50v-51r).[61] The copy concludes with the words which must have been written on the outside of Milred's letter when it was folded up and tied for the journey to Mainz:[62]

epistola.Milredi.ep̄isc offerenda Lullę ep̄isc.

We learn from his letter that Milred had visited Boniface in Germany in the year before his martyrdom and had there formed a friendship with Lull, who, by the time the letter was written, had succeeded Boniface as bishop of Mainz. It is an elegant, if syntactically involved, letter:

To Bishop Lull, most loving lord and best beloved in Christ, Milred, servant of the servants of God.[63]

After I had departed unwilling and sorrowful from your presence and from the bodily sight of the most holy pastor and most blessed father Boniface, and, with the help of your kind prayers, had reached the land of my birth through various chances and many turns of fate (*per uarios casus et multa discrimina rerum*), there, before the full circle of the year was complete, the sad news was brought to me that the most blessed father had passed from the prison-house of the flesh (*ergastulum carnis*) to the heights above – if indeed it is right to call it sad news when we have been privileged to send (*pręmittere*) such a patron before us to the heavenly kingdoms, by whose sacred intercessions we firmly believe ourselves to be sustained in all things, with God's help. Although with many and bitter tears we have lamented a lost solace of this present life (*pręsentis uitae amisum solacium*), yet he, the glory and support of all whom this fatherland has brought forth (*decus et columen omnium, quos pręsens protulit patria*), who has been consecrated a martyr to Christ through shedding his blood, greatly calms and soothes our sorrowful hearts with a greater joy, now that his best work has been accomplished in his most blessed agony and his most glorious end has been completed. We, remaining in this vale of tears, in this life full of temptations, lament our lot; he, a martyr of Christ, has completed his strenuous pilgrim's task and come to a very glorious death and dwells, as I believe (*ut credo*), if God in his goodness allows, in the

[61] *Ep.* cxii (Tangl, pp. 243–5). Facsimile edition by Unterkircher, *Sancti Bonifacii Epistolae*. On the manuscript, see Unterkircher's introduction and Lapidge and Herren, *Aldhelm*, pp. 16–18.

[62] On this feature of the Vienna manuscript, cf. Chaplais, 'Letter from Wealdhere', pp. 9–10.

[63] *Seruus seruientium Dei*; cf. Sims-Williams, 'Wilfrid', p. 166, n. 15; Edwards, 'Two Documents', pp. 4–6.

supernal city, a faithful intercessor for our sins with Christ in the heavenly Jerusalem, united with her holy citizens in their most blessed life.

That is what I have to say about our most beloved father; I desire with all my heart that you will have information sent to me about his noble life and glorious end.

It occurs to me to say something else, with regard to our mutual friendship. From the depths of my heart I beseech your most sweet Charity and humbly beg you, as if in reality prostrate before your feet, to keep in your heart, with a remembrance not transitory but steadfast, that brotherly love which Boniface, our common father of blessed and holy memory, joined and tied between us with sacred words and holy prayers, while Christ's love assented; for I know beyond all doubt that it will be of great profit to you and me if we strive to fulfil the precepts of so illustrious a teacher. May it not be irksome for you, beloved master, to instruct me in brotherly love, the least in merits of all your brothers, to strengthen me with sacred precepts, to support me with holy prayers! For I declare and vow with a true promise that I shall gladly follow your sincere commands to the limits of my strength; and, as long as the spirit governs these limbs and the breath of life dwells in these mortal members (*quamdiu spiritus hos regit artus uitalisque flatus his moribundis inhabitat membris*), I promise before God to keep a faithful friendship with you in constant affection, in intimate love, and I earnestly wish with all my strength that, if Christ permits, that which is written may come to pass: 'They had all things in common'.[64]

But I have ensured that all these things which I have said briefly will be disclosed more fully orally by the bearers of this letter, if Almighty God grants a prosperous journey. I am also sending some little gifts, which I hope you will accept with the same love as, God knows, they have been sent by me.

May Christ graciously care for Your Charity as you intercede for our sins!

I do not send the book of Porphyrius's poems because Bishop Cuthbert has so far delayed in returning it. Emmanuel![65]

The first part of this letter (especially *beatissimum patrem de ergastulo carnis ad superna migrasse*) resembles other early Christian letters of consolation. Most of the similarities are too general for sources to be identified. The way in which Milred begins by placing the coming of the sad news in the context of his own life (*Postquam a tua presentia . . .*) is vaguely reminiscent both of Ambrose's consolation *De obitu Valentiniani*, c. 26 —

Iam superabam Alpium iuga, et ecce nuntius amarus mihi et omnibus de tanti morte imperatoris

---

[64] Acts IV.32. Cf. above, p. 126, n. 57.
[65] Rustic capitals are used at the end, perhaps indicating Milred's autograph. On the *liber pyrpyri* (sic) *metri* see below, pp. 329–32.

– and of the opening of Sulpicius Severus's letter to Aurelius on the death of St Martin:

Posteaquam a me mane digressus es . . .[66]

Milred's image of the soul imprisoned in the body was as old as Socrates (Plato, *Phaedo*) and had become a consolatory commonplace.[67] Even the expression *ergastulum* (instead of the more usual *carcer*), which Milred shares with other Insular writers,[68] had already been used by Ambrose in his *De excessu fratris*, II.20:

Si caro nostra carcerem fugit . . . quanto magis anima nostra corporeum istud euadere gestit ergastulum . . .[69]

Milred's verb *migrasse* reflects another ancient theme, death as a migration of the soul (Plato, *Apology*, 40), which had shaped Christian attitudes to death: 'he departed, rather than died, and emigrated from us', wrote Ambrose (*abiit ergo, non obiit, et emigrauit a nobis*), and Jerome says of another: 'You would have thought that he was not dying, but starting on a journey' (*intellegeres illum non emori, sed migrare*).[70] Another pagan consolation, that the deceased had 'not perished but gone ahead', was frequently expressed by Christian writers such as Augustine: *non decessit sed praecessit*. 'What you suppose to be death is a setting-out', wrote Tertullian in *De patientia*, 9, 'and he who has gone ahead is not to be grieved for' (*profectio est quam putas mortem; non est lugendus qui antecedit*).[71] By a figure of

---

[66] 'I had just passed the Alps, and behold, the bitter news of the death of so great an emperor was announced to me and everyone' (*Ambrosii Opera* VII, ed. Faller, p. 342); 'After you had left me in the morning . . .' (Sulpicius, *Ep*. ii.1, ed. Fontaine, *Sulpice Sévère* I, 324).

[67] Lattimore, *Themes*, p. 23 and n. 19; Beyenka, *Consolation*, p. 20. For example, Jerome, *Ep*. cviii.23 'corpore quasi carceri' (ed. Hilberg II, 340); Fortunatus, *Carmina* IV.xiv.3 'de carcere carnis euntes' (ed. Leo, p. 89).

[68] *Columbani Opera*, ed. Walker, p. 76; *Aldhelmi Opera*, ed. Ehwald, p. 603, s.v. *ergastulum*; *HE* IV.3 (p. 342); *Ep*. cxv (Tangl, p. 248).

[69] 'If our flesh shrinks from prison . . . how much more does our soul desire to escape from that prison-house of the body . . .' (*Ambrosii Opera* VII, ed. Faller, p. 260). See also von Moos, *Consolatio* III, 175–6.

[70] Ambrose, *Ep*. xv.3 (PL 16, 996); Jerome, *Ep*. lx.13 (ed. Wright, *Select Letters*, p. 292). Cf. Beyenka, *Consolation*, p. 2; Favez, *Consolation*, pp. 54 and 156. The verb *migrare* is also used by Archbishop Cuthbert in his letter of consolation, *Ep*. cxi (Tangl, p. 239, line 27).

[71] PL 38, 90 and 528; PL 1, 1375. Cf. Beyenka, *Consolation*, pp. 13, 30, 48–9, 51, 80 and 94; von Moos, *Consolatio* III, 320.

speech, the dead could thus be said, for instance by Cyprian and Ambrose, to be 'not lost but sent ahead' (*non amitti sed praemitti*),[72] or, as Augustine puts it, in a letter of consolation:

De hac uita, unde migraturi quosdam nostros migrantes non amisimus, sed *praemisimus*.[73]

This is the expression used by Milred: 'cum talem ad caeli patronum meruimus *pręmittere* regna'. Milred also alludes to the common theme that death is an escape from the miseries of this life and that the dead are happier than the living. According to Ambrose, for instance, 'one should be grieved that [Valentinian] was snatched from us, but consoled because he has passed over to better things' (*dolendum est, quod nobis cito raptus sit, consolandum, quod ad meliora transierit*), and Jerome argues that 'we lament our own lot, not his, and the more blest he is, the more sorrowful are we' (... *non illius, sed nostram uicem dolentes; quanto ille felicior, tanto nos amplius in dolore* ...), or, in another letter of consolation, that 'it is we who are more to be grieved over ... he now, carefree and victorious, looks down upon you from on high' (*nos dolendi magis ... ille iam securus et uictor te aspicit de excelso*).[74]

Milred's letter differs from most letters of consolation, however, in that he is able to draw comfort from the fact that Boniface had become a national martyr. The same patriotic note is struck in the letter of consolation which Lull received at about the same time from Archbishop Cuthbert (the 'Bishop Cuthbert' of Milred's postscript):

Though the bitterness of this grief tears our hearts, yet a certain new and strong delight comes often to our minds to sweeten and assuage the sorrow. The more frequently we reflect thereon, the more joyously we thank the admirable, nay the ineffable goodness of God, that the race of the English settled in Britain deserved to send forth from itself openly before the eyes of all to spiritual agonies such a famous investigator of the divine books, and such a splendid soldier of Christ, together with many well-trained and instructed disciples, – through the grace of

---

[72] Cyprian, *De mortalitate*, 20 (PL 4, 618); Ambrose, *De excessu fratris* 1.71 (ed. Faller, *Ambrosii Opera* VII, 246). Cf. Favez, *Consolation*, p. 165 and n. 5; von Moos, *Consolatio* III, 320–2.

[73] 'We have not lost those who migrate from this life, from which we ourselves are to migrate, but *have sent them ahead*': *Ep.* xcii (PL 33, 318); Beyenka, *Consolation*, p. 98.

[74] *De obitu Valentiniani*, 46 (ed. Faller, *Ambrosii Opera* VII, 352); Jerome, *Epp.* lx.7 and lxxv.2 (ed. Hilberg I, 555, and II, 31). Cf. Favez, *Consolation*, pp. 67–8, 148–9 and 154.

the omnipotent God, – to the safety of many souls: that as leader and standard-bearer, going before, and with God's help, bravely overcoming opposition, through the impulse of his holy preaching, and the example of piety and goodness he might happily lead fierce nations far and wide, wandering long in by-paths, from the broad and deep pit of eternal perdition to the bright streets of the heavenly city. What has really been accomplished the outcome of events proclaims more splendidly than words, especially in those places which no teacher before him sought to visit for the purpose of preaching. Wherefore, after the choice and the number of the apostles, a mystery unequalled in the whole world, and the ministry of other disciples of Christ who preached the gospel at that time, we lovingly place this man among the splendid and glorious doctors of the orthodox faith, and praise and venerate him.

Cuthbert goes on to say that a general synod had decided to celebrate the day of the martyrdom of Boniface and his companions as an annual church festival, and that he was to be regarded as a special patron-saint (*patronus*) with St Gregory and St Augustine (who had already been adopted at the Council of *Clofesho* in 747).[75] If Milred of Worcester attended the synod in question, he would have heard others' reactions to Boniface's death, which would explain the similarities between his sentiments and Cuthbert's. Yet both bishops may have responded quite independently in similar fashion. The Fathers of the church had taught that the crown of martyrdom was a consolation,[76] but in fact the letter of consolation most similar to those of Milred and Cuthbert is Sulpicius's letter to Aurelius on the death of St Martin; Martin was not martyred, but Sulpicius had portrayed him as a patron and intercessor equal in merit to the martyrs:

Come then, I beg of you, to me without delay, that we may mourn in common him whom in common we love. And yet I am well aware that such a man ought not to be mourned over, to whom, after his victory and triumph over the world, there has at last now been given the crown of righteousness. Nevertheless, I cannot so command myself as to keep from grieving. I have, no doubt, sent on before me one who will plead my cause in heaven, but I have, at the same time, lost my great source of consolation in this present life; yet if grief would yield to the influence of reason, I certainly ought to rejoice (*praemisi quidem patronum, sed solacium uitae praesentis amisi, etsi, si rationem ullam dolor admitteret, gaudere deberem*). For he is now

---

[75] *Ep.* cxi (Tangl, pp. 238–43); trans. Kylie, *English Correspondence*, pp. 199–200 (cf. *EHD*, no. 183). Cf. H&S III, 368. On Boniface as *patronus* in Germany, see Holdsworth, 'Boniface the Monk', p. 50. See also above, p. 100, n. 54.

[76] Augustine, *Sermo* cccix, *In natale Cyprianis martyris* (PL 38, 1410), cited by Beyenka, *Consolation*, p. 54.

mingling with the Apostles and Prophets, and (with all respect for the saints on high be it said) he is second to no one in that assembly of the righteous as I firmly hope, believe, and trust (*ut spero, credo et confido*), being joined especially to those who washed their robes in the blood of the Lamb. He now follows the Lamb as his guide, free from all spot of defilement. For although the character of our times could not ensure him the honor of martyrdom, yet he will not remain destitute of the glory of a martyr, because both by vow and virtues he was alike able and willing to be a martyr.[77]

This passage may well be echoed in Milred's 'cum talem . . . *patronum* [MS *patronem*] meruimus *prǫmittere*', '*prǫsentis uitae amisum* [*sic*] *solacium*' and '*ut credo*'.

Milred's reference to his journey home from Germany 'per uarios casus et multa discrimina rerum' is an apt allusion to the wanderings of Aeneas in *Aeneid* I.204–6:

> per uarios casus, per tot discrimina rerum
> tendimus in Latium, sedes ubi fata quietas
> ostendunt.[78]

No doubt Milred (like Burginda and Ecgburg) quotes directly from Vergil, the most influential of all the pagan poets in Anglo-Saxon England – there even survives an early eighth-century fragment of an abbreviated version of Servius's commentary on the *Aeneid*, which was written somewhere in south-western England (Malmesbury has been suggested) and which was probably taken to Fulda by Boniface or one of his associates.[79] Milred quotes the *Aeneid* again near the end of his letter:

unde fateor et fida promissione spondeo . . . quamdiu *spiritus hos regit artus* uitalisque flatus his *moribundis* in*habitat membris* . . .

---

[77] Sulpicius, *Ep.* ii.7–9, ed. Fontaine, *Sulpice Sévère* I, 328 (with commentary at III, 1210–14); *The Works of Sulpitius Severus*, trans. A. Roberts, Nicene and Post-Nicene Fathers II (Oxford, 1894), 20. Cf. P. Brown, *The Cult of the Saints: Its Rise and Function in Latin Christianity* (London, 1979), pp. 55, 63 and 65; Beyenka, *Consolation*, p. 30; von Moos, *Consolatio* I, 104, and III, 328.

[78] 'Through various chances and so many turns of fate, we make for Latium, where the fates show us peaceful homes'.

[79] Spangenberg, Pfarrbibliothek, s.n. See *CLA* Suppl., no. 1806; Parkes, 'Handwriting of St Boniface'; Thomson, *William of Malmesbury*, p. 106. On Vergilian influence see, for example, Wright, 'Bede and Vergil'. The earliest extant Vergil of probable Worcester provenance is Vatican, Reg. lat. 1671 (s. x²): see T. A. M. Bishop, *English Caroline Minuscule* (Oxford, 1971), no. 19; Hunter Blair, 'From Bede to Alcuin', p. 252.

This echoes both Aeneas's promise to remember Dido 'while the spirit governs these limbs' (*dum spiritus hos regit artus*, *Aeneid* IV.336) and Vergil's philosophical discourse on the seeds of life, which would be fiery sparks if they did not 'inhabit earthly limbs and dying members' (*terrenique habitant artus moribundaque membra*, *Aeneid* VI.732). Perhaps Milred's use of Vergil was partly inspired by the following passage in Jerome's letter of consolation to Paula on the death of Blesilla, for whom he had intended the commentary on Ecclesiastes:

Itaque dum *spiritus hos artus regit*, dum uitae huius fruimur commeatu, *spondeo*, promitto, polliceor: illam mea lingua resonabit, illi mei dedicabuntur labores, illi sudabit ingenium.[80]

As Tangl notes, Milred's epithet for Boniface, *decus et columen omnium quos presens protulit patria*, echoes Horace's grandiloquent epithet for Maecenas:

> mearum
> grande decus columenque rerum.[81]

Such poetic allusion and diction was customary in *consolationes*; Ambrose, for example, commemorates his brother in *De excessu fratris* I.27 as *praedulce decus* (Vergil, *Aeneid* XI.155) and *totius patriae decus*.[82] It is unlikely, however, that Milred could have known Horace's works. Probably the epithet reached him indirectly, for it passed into the stock phraseology of Late Latin letters: Ausonius in a verse epistle refers to his correspondent as 'meum patriaeque decus columenque senati', and Sidonius addresses correspondents as 'amicitiae columen . . . Hibericarum decus inlustre regionum', 'columen decusque morum', and 'decus Getarum, / Romanae

---

[80] *Ep.* xxxix.8, ed. Hilberg I, 308; trans. Fremantle *et al.*, *Letters and Select Works*, p. 54: 'Therefore, so long as breath animates my body, so long as I continue in the enjoyment of life, I engage, declare, and promise that Blaesilla's name shall be forever on my tongue, that my labors shall be dedicated to her honor, and that my talents shall be devoted to her praise.' I have not found any close parallels to Milred's letter in Jerome's other letters of consolation.

[81] *Carmina* II.xvii.3–4: 'great glory and support of my existence'; Tangl, p. 244, n. 1. On p. 243, n. 4, Tangl notes a parallel in Aldhelm for Milred's *amaris . . . lacrimis*, but this was a commonplace phrase: A. Campbell, 'Some Linguistic Features of Early Anglo-Latin Verse and its Use of Classical Models', *TPS* 1953, 1–20, at 5.

[82] *De excessu fratris* I.27 (ed. Faller, *Ambrosii Opera* VII, 224): 'most sweet glory . . . glory of the whole fatherland'.

columen salusque gentis'.[83] A note of patriotism still clings to the epithet in Milred's English context, reminding us of his earlier use of the line about Aeneas's journey from Troy to Latium *per uarios casus, per tot discrimina rerum* to refer to his own homecoming from Germany to England.

To sum up, while Milred does not seem to depend on verbal borrowing to the same extent as Burginda and Ecgburg, he is steeped in the thought and diction of the traditional Christian *consolatio*; moreover, he alludes effectively to Latin poetry, as we would expect, judging from his postscript on Porphyrius's poetry and from other evidence for his interest in Latin verse (discussed in ch. 11 below).

Milred's letter is interesting on another score. By confirming that the missionaries in Germany had links with the Hwicce as well as the West Saxons, it helps to show how the manuscript of Jerome's commentary on Ecclesiastes which belonged to Cuthswith, abbess of *Penintanham c.* 700, may have reached Würzburg. As we saw in ch. 7, the manuscript left England for Germany sometime during the last two thirds of the eighth century. Milred himself could, then, have taken it to Germany in 753, or could have sent it later: the postscript to his letter to Lull shows that books, as well as letters and 'little gifts', were being exchanged. The fact that Cuthswith's charter was preserved at Worcester indicates that her monastery at *Penintanham* came into the possession of the see at some stage, and this may have been the occasion for its books to pass into the hands of the bishop.

If we accept Finberg's identification of *Penintanham* with Inkberrow,[84] we can be more specific about the connection between the monastery and the see. At a synod at Chelsea in 789,

some contention was made between Bishop Heathored [of Worcester] and Wulfheard son of Cussa concerning the inheritance of Hemele and Duda which they had nominated to pass to Worcester after their death, that is, Inkberrow (*Intanbeorgas*) and Bradley (*Bradanlege, Bradan læg*), wherefore Wulfheard wished,

---

[83] 'Mine and the fatherland's glory, and the senate's support': Ausonius, *Ep.* xxiv.56, ed. C. Schenkl, *D. Magni Ausonii Opuscula*, MGH, Auct. antiq. 5.2 (Berlin, 1883), 189; 'support of friendship ... illustrious glory of Spanish lands', 'support and glory of manners', 'glory of Goths, and support and salvation of the Roman race': Sidonius, *Epistulae* VIII.5 and *Carmina* XXIII.2 and 70–1, ed. A. Loyen, *Sidoine Apollinaire: poèmes [et] lettres*, 3 vols. (Paris, 1960–70) III, 91, and I, 144 and 146–7. Cf. Sims-Williams, 'Gildas and Vernacular Poetry', p. 182 and n. 92.

[84] See above, p. 191 and n. 63.

if he could, to divert that piece of land (*illum agellulum*) from the aforesaid church in Worcester, through ignorance and foolishness. Then the bishop refuted him ... and said that it would not be right for him to hand it over to any other after himself, except to the aforesaid *ciuitas*, that is, to Worcester. And because of the request of those who acquired that land and had given it to the aforesaid church, and because of their love [?for Wulfheard], the counsellors of the [episcopal] *familia* agreed that that man should have and hold it during his lifetime. Then the archbishop with all the provincial bishops made an end and reconciled them, so that Wulfheard should possess the land as long as he lived, and that after he walked the way of his fathers the lands and the charters with them should be returned without any contradiction thither, to the church of Worcester.[85]

Bradley is adjacent to Inkberrow. The reference to it makes it possible to reconstruct part of the monastery's history after Cuthswith's death, for, in the Worcester cartulary, BL, Cotton Tiberius A. xiii, 7v, just before a transcript of the above document (7v–8v), there is a transcript of a charter of Æthelbald of Mercia granting Bradley to a woman named Cyneburg, probably in 723.[86] It is clear from the account of the synod of 789 that Hemele and Duda had held Inkberrow and Bradley as a unit ('illum agellulum'). It is conceivable that they acquired Cuthswith's former estate at Inkberrow and Cyneburg's at Bradley in two separate transactions rather than as a unit, but the coincidence of two estates owned by women being adjacent, the coincidence of their being merged in subsequent records and both destined for ecclesiastical use, and the coincidence of the alliteration of the names *Cuthswith* and *Cyneburg* make it far more likely that Cyneburg had succeeded Cuthswith at Inkberrow and had enlarged the monastic estate by acquiring Bradley. *Penintanham*/Inkberrow, then, was probably a 'family monastery' and Cyneburg's acquisition of Bradley was probably a continuation of the expansion of the monastic estate that had begun with Cuthswith's purchase of Ingon. Kemerton (*Cyneburgingctun*), a little further down the Avon valley (SO/9436), may be another estate of Cyneburg's.[87] As to the two 'who acquired that land', Duda may be the Dudda *pincernus* who attests grants of land in Kemerton and Fladbury *c.*

[85] S 1430. On the texts of this document and the subsequent history of Inkberrow see Sims-Williams, 'Cuthswith', pp. 12–13. Cf. above, p. 172, n. 135.

[86] S 95. See further Sims-Williams, 'Cuthswith', p. 17, nn. 3–4; Scharer, *Königsurkunde*, pp. 167–8.

[87] See Sims-Williams, 'Cuthswith', p. 18, n. 3. Cf. Gelling, *Signposts*, p. 178. (On Donnington see further above, p. 132, n. 76.)

777–81,[88] and Hemele was very probably the thegn (*fidelis*) to whom Æthelbald of Mercia (716–57) granted a property near Stonebow, about seven miles south-west of Inkberrow.[89] By 789, therefore, local land-owners had acquired Cuthswith and Cyneburg's former monastic property and had bequeathed it back into ecclesiastical possession. Hemele and Duda were evidently well disposed towards the church of Worcester, where they were buried according to Tiberius A. xiii, 8r.[90] They could have handed over any Inkberrow books to Bishop Milred (or his predecessor) as soon as they had acquired Inkberrow; they would be of no use to most laymen. This hypothesis assumes that they acquired the monastery during (or before) Milred's episcopate, which lasted from 743×745 to 774×775;[91] that is quite plausible, since the faithful Hemele must have received his grant from Æthelbald by 757 at the latest.

Bishop Milred is thus the most likely channel by which the Jerome commentary could have reached Germany, just as Bishop Oftfor is the most likely means by which it could have come from Italy to *Penintan-ham*.[92] But another letter preserved among the correspondence of Boniface and Lull offers another possible link between Inkberrow and Würzburg. The letter in question was sent between 739 and 741 to an Abbess Cyneburg in England by three of Boniface's English assistants, Denehard, Lull and Burghard, the last of whom became the first bishop of Würzburg (742–53) soon afterwards; it is the only letter which reveals anything about Burghard's English background.[93] The contents and the elaborate and overloaded Aldhelmian style indicate that the letter was actually written by Lull.[94] In fact much of the letter may concern him exclusively, but it is not easy to tell because of the ambiguity of the 'we' forms:

[88] S 57 and 62. Cf. Sims-Williams 'Cuthswith', p. 18, n. 4. Whitelock, 'Some Charters', p. 80, would identify him with the *minister* Duddonus, granted land near Bourton-on-the-Water (SP/1620) by S 114.

[89] S 1825. See Sims-Williams, 'Cuthswith', pp. 18–19.   [90] S 1430.

[91] See below, p. 328, n. 1.

[92] See above, p. 193.

[93] *Ep.* xlix (Tangl, pp. 78–80). On the identity of 'B' see Sims-Williams, 'Cuthswith', p. 19, n. 8. Burghard's nationality is stated in the *Vita S. Burghardi prima*, c. 2, ed. O. Holder-Egger, 'Vitae Burchardi Episcopi Wirziburgensis', MGH, Scriptores 15.1 (1887), 44–62, at 47. Holder-Egger's doubts (p. 47, n. 7) were mistaken: see Tangl, p. 78, n. 4, and Moore, *Saxon Pilgrims*, p. 70, n. 4. The see at Würzburg may have been created in 741 or 742: Reuter, 'Boniface and Europe', pp. 92–3.

[94] See Tangl's notes and Hahn, 'Ueber einige Briefe', pp. 385–94.

To the most esteemed lady and most religious abbess of Christ, Cyneburg, endowed with the nobility of royal stock, Den[ehard], and L[ull] and B[urghard], your sons and fellow-countrymen, [send] the greeting of everlasting health.

Because we enclose you with love in the chamber of the heart before all others of the female sex, we wish the Clemency of Your Kindness to know that we, on account of the decease of father and mother and our other kinsmen, have gone across to the German peoples and have been received into the venerable Archbishop Boniface's rule of monastic life; and we are assistants in his work, insofar as the meanness of our poor little . . . [*lacuna*] is of use. So now from the innermost entrails of our breasts we humbly beg you to deign to keep us in communion with your sacred congregation and, with the aid of your prayers, to bring our boat, worn out by the stormy seas of this world, to the port of safety; and not to decline to defend us with the shield of your prayers against the black darts of sins, just as we too, though . . . [*lacuna*], are interceding every moment for the well-being of Your Excellence. If indeed we were present in body on bended knee begging in earnest petition with showers of salt tears, we hope that this could be obtained; now, absent, we ask the same with vehement prayers. Moreover we wish the Diligence of Your Wisdom to know that, if any of us happens to visit the realms of this British land, we will seek out the obedience and government of no man in place of subjection to your benevolence, because we have placed the firmest hope of our minds in you.

Likewise we beg you to trouble to send over, by the bearers of these letters, the two boys named Begiloc and Man whom I, Lull, and our father freed, when we were going to Rome for the good of my [*var.* your] soul, and entrusted to our uncle, if they are free to decide, and if it is their will, and if they are accessible to you (*in tua potestate sint*). And if anyone wrongly wishes to prevent them from making the journey, we beg you to be so good as to defend them. A small consignment of little gifts accompanies this letter, three in number, that is, small presents (yet indicating the heart's whole affection) of frankincense, pepper and cinnamon. We beg you not to consider the size of the gift but to pay attention to the love which is spiritual charity. We also ask you to correct the rusticity of this little letter and not to refuse to send us some words of your own sweet self, which we will be satisfied to hear eagerly and joyfully.

Fare you well, living long for God and in a happy life interceding for us.

Hahn deduced from the phrase 'quos ego Lul et pater *noster* liberos dimisimus Romam destinantes' that Denehard and Burghard may have been Lull's blood brothers.[95] That is quite possible; note also the plurals in

---

[95] *Ibid.*, p. 387, n. 5. Note, however, Lull, *Ep.* xcviii (Tangl, p. 219, trans. Kylie, *English Correspondence*, p. 99), which gives the impression that Lull alone was almost without relatives. This letter (in the first person singular) may also have been addressed to Abbess Cyneburg (cf. Tangl, p. 219, n. 9).

'genitoris et genetricis et aliorum propinquorum *nostrorum* [ob] obitum ad Germanicas gentes *transiuimus*⁹⁶ usque in uenerandi archiepiscopi Bonifatii monasticę conuersationis regula suscepti ipsiusque laboris *adiutores sumus* . . .', where the use of the plural noun *adiutores* suggests that all three writers are meant throughout. Hahn also suggested that the Cyneburg to whom the letter was addressed was identical with the Cyneburg to whom Æthelbald granted Bradley by the charter of 723 mentioned above.⁹⁷ (The interest of his suggestion was disguised by his conflating her with an abbess with the distinct name *Coenburg* and by the fact that the charter's *Bradanlæh* was mistakenly placed in Wiltshire rather than Worcestershire.)⁹⁸ If it was the Hwiccian Cyneburg who was their supporter and spiritual mother, she could have presented Cuthswith's book to Burghard or to one of the other two before they went to the Continent and joined Boniface in Germany or on their mooted return visit to England; or she could have sent it over with Milred in 753, if she was still alive then.

It must be admitted, however, that although no other Cyneburg is recorded at this period,⁹⁹ the name is not an uncommon one, so that Hahn's identification is very far from certain. On the other hand what we are told about the abbess Cyneburg in the letter is not incompatible with the identification. The letter begins with a compliment on her royal blood: we have already suggested that the Bradley Cyneburg was related to Cuthswith, and that Cuthswith may have belonged to the Mercian or Hwiccian royal line.¹⁰⁰ Similar female names occur in the former family (*Cyne*wise, *Cyneburg* and *Cyne*swith) and there is an earlier *Cyneburg* (abbess of Gloucester) in the latter.¹⁰¹ We learn from the letter that Cyneburg lived within reach of Lull's uncle. It is not known where Lull's family came from, but, as we have seen, he had been educated at Malmesbury, and the freed slave *Begiloc* mentioned in the letter may be identical with the priest *Bęgloc* who was to attest Æthelbald's grant of *Toccan sceaga* to Malmes-

---

⁹⁶ I.e. from Rome; cf. Moore, *Saxon Pilgrims*, pp. 66–7.

⁹⁷ *Bonifaz und Lul*, p. 149.

⁹⁸ See Sims-Williams, 'Cuthswith', p. 20.

⁹⁹ Searle, *Onomasticon*, p. 154. There are three persons of the name in the list 'Nomina reginarum et abbatissarum' in the Lindisfarne *Liber vitae* (ed. Sweet, *Oldest English Texts*, p. 154, lines 22, 26 and 31).

¹⁰⁰ See above, pp. 191 and 238.   ¹⁰¹ *HBC*², p. 15; and above, p. 123.

bury(?) in 757.[102] Thus Lull probably came from either the West Saxon or the Hwiccian side of the border. We know that Cyneheard, who became bishop of Winchester in 756, was related to Lull, though not how closely;[103] his origins are obscure and he cannot be assumed to have been a West Saxon, for Æthelbald of Mercia may have been strong enough to be able to secure a Mercian appointment, if he so wished, while Wessex was in anarchy in 756.[104] However this may be, even if Lull was a West Saxon, he and his two colleagues could easily have had dealings with the Hwiccian Cyneburg. We are compelled to leave the question of Cyneburg's identity open.

Like the letters of Burginda and Ecgburg, the letter to Cyneburg has an unproven connection with the Hwicce. Nevertheless, if the connection could be proved, it would only confirm what we already know for certain from Milred of Worcester's letter, that the missionaries in Germany were supported by the Hwiccian church. Milred's letter clearly reveals a sophisticated level of attainment in letter-writing, based on imitation of earlier letters and poetry. The earlier letters of Burginda and Ecgburg are less polished, but can reasonably be regarded as beginners' essays in that same tradition, and perhaps from the same diocese.

[102] See above, p. 228. The only other occurrences of the name given by Searle, *Onomasticon*, p. 82, are three clerics named *Baeglog/-lug* in the Lindisfarne *Liber vitae* (ed. Sweet, *Oldest English Texts*, pp. 158–61, lines 172, 208 and 290).

[103] *Ep.* cxiv (Tangl, pp. 246–7). Cf. Levison, *England and the Continent*, p. 238, n. 3. We also know the names of Lull's aunt *Cyne*hild and her children Bald*hard* and Berthgyth (*Epp.* lxvii, cxlvii and cxlviii (Tangl, pp. 139–40, 284–5 and 285–7, respectively), and notes; Dronke, *Women Writers*, p. 30). It is conceivable, judging from their names, that Abbess *Cyneburg*, *Burghard* and Dene*hard* were all members of the same family, though if so Lull and Berthgyth's regrets about their lack of kindred could hardly be taken literally!

[104] The year in which the infamous Sigeberht came to the throne (*ASC*). On the mid-eighth-century political situation see above, n. 42.

9

The unseen world: the monk of Wenlock's vision

An illuminating episode in the religious life of the Magonsætan is known because it came to the attention of Boniface and his correspondent Eadburg, who may have been a nun at Wimborne in Wessex.[1] The letter of Wynfrith (Boniface) to Eadburg describing the vision of a brother at Wenlock must have been written before the spring of 719, when he changed his name to Boniface on the occasion of his visit to Rome, but after the death of Ceolred, king of Mercia, in 716, for Boniface remarks that Ceolred was 'without doubt still alive' when the visionary saw him in hell. The latter phrase suggests that the vision itself fell in 715 or 716.

Eadburg had asked Boniface to send her a written account of the wonderful visions of the man 'in Abbess Mildburg's monastery who recently died and came to life again' just as he had learnt them from the venerable Abbess Hildelith. This Hildelith, abbess of Barking, was a person of considerable literary attainments, as we can see from the dedication of Aldhelm's prose *De uirginitate* and from Bede's extracts from a then widely known *libellus*, largely concerned with visions, compiled at her East Saxon monastery.[2] The extent to which the account Boniface eventually sent to Eadburg was indebted to any oral or written report from Hildelith is unclear, however, for he states that he recounts the vision as he himself, with three witnesses, heard it from the visionary's own lips 'while he [the visionary, or if *peruenit* is emended to *perueni*, Boniface] recently came to those regions from overseas'. In the context, 'those regions' (*istas*

---

[1] On Eadburg cf. above, p. 212, n. 6. Boniface's letter is *Ep.* x (Tangl, pp. 7–15). I quote the translation by Kylie, *English Correspondence*, pp. 78–89, with silent changes. For German and Italian translations see Rau, *Bonifatii Epistulae*, pp. 31–43, and Ciccarese, *Visioni*, pp. 343–61. On the text and its background see Sims-Williams, 'Recension'.
[2] *Ibid.*; HE IV.7–9

regiones) can only refer to the general vicinity of Wenlock, so we must infer that Boniface encountered the visionary in England, either before he went on his mission to Frisia in 716 or after he returned in 717 (the latter if *peruenit* is emended to *perueni*).[3]

A literary historian might classify the Wenlock vision without difficulty as a combination of three genres of vision: the vision of the world from the sky; the vision of heaven and hell;[4] and the political or propagandist vision.[5] A precedent, authority and pattern for the reaction of all three genres was set for the Latin West in the late sixth century by the *Dialogi* of Gregory the Great; Gregory's example is acknowledged explicitly by the author of the *Visio Baronti* (written in western Berry) and by Bede, and implicitly by Boniface, who echoes Gregory's wording.[6] Nevertheless it would be a grave error to assume that all medieval visions are purely literary inventions because, while that is clearly true of pseudepigrapha like the Irish *Fís Adamnáin*, there is also ample evidence for the real existence of visionaries.[7] Boniface's very circumstantial account, presented as sworn testimony to Eadburg, is a good example.

Although Boniface does not call the Wenlock brother (*frater*) a monk, the content of the vision implies that he followed the round of monastic observance, so he was probably a full member of Mildburg's community.[8] (If one may believe the 'Testament of St Mildburg', she was still living.)[9] He must have come to Wenlock as an adult, for he said that a man whom he had wounded in his secular life accused him in his vision. In this marginal position between lay and monastic life he resembles other visionaries, who were often either very religious laymen, like Dryhthelm in Ayrshire in the

[3] Sims-Williams, 'Recension'.

[4] See below, n. 40; and for general surveys see H. R. Patch, *The Other World According to Descriptions in Medieval Literature* (Cambridge, Mass., 1950); F. Neiske, 'Vision und Totengedenken', *FS* 20 (1986), 137–85; Dinzelbacher, *Vision*; Amat, *Songes*; Ciccarese, *Visioni*; Carozzi, 'Géographie de l'Au-delà'.

[5] On these see W. Levison, *Aus rheinischer und fränkischer Frühzeit* (Düsseldorf, 1948), pp. 229–46; Kamphausen, *Traum und Vision*, pp. 146–54; Dinzelbacher, *Vision*, p. 82; Ciccarese, 'Purgatorio', pp. 58–76; Holdsworth, 'Visions and Visionaries', pp. 150–1.

[6] 'Visio Baronti', ed. Levison, c. 17; *HE* v.13; below, n. 40. Cf. Ciccarese, '*Visio Baronti*', p. 26, n. 7; Carozzi, 'Géographie de l'Au-delà', pp. 425 and 430. There was a copy of 'Barontus' at Worcester *c.* 1050: Lapidge, 'Booklists', pp. 63–4.

[7] See Sims-Williams, 'Visionary Celt', p. 80, nn. 30–1. Cf. Ciccarese, 'Gregorio di Tours', p. 261, n. 30 (in general she exaggerates the element of invention and literary imitation).

[8] Sims-Williams, 'Recension'.   [9] *ECWM*, p. 220.

690s, or monastic *conuersi*, like Barontus, who had entered the monastery of Longoretus (Lonrey, Saint-Cyran-en-Brenne, dép. Indre) shortly before his vision in 678×679, and Guthlac, who spent nine years as a soldier, partly on the Welsh border, before entering the monastery of Repton at the age of twenty-four. After only two years at Repton, Guthlac began his solitary life in the Fens, which lasted from before 704 to shortly before the accession of Æthelbald of Mercia in 716, precisely the period of the Wenlock vision.[10]

Most visions of heaven and hell came during sickness or apparent death. This is the case with the Wenlock visionary. His fellow-brethren were already performing his obsequies when he 'returned to the body at first light, having left it at first cockcrow', and he described his sense of disgust (or, as we might say, alienation) towards his body and those who were caring for it. For a week afterwards his bloodshot eyes were blind, and he never recovered his full powers of memory. In view of many modern testimonies to such deathbed *ekstasis* we cannot dismiss the medieval ones as purely literary inventions, whatever their ultimate psychological explanation.[11]

A vision's impact depends on the visionary and on the society in which he lives. In the modern West those who recover from apparent death tend to be diffident about articulating their experiences[12] and what they say is of marginal effect, especially if it has no religious or spiritualist content. But on the lips of a charismatic leader in the right context a vision can have a powerful effect. An example is the beginning of the American Indian Shaker religion: in 1881 a member of the Squaxin tribe, Puget Sound, Washington, recovered from 'death' and began to preach a revelation, broadly similar to the Wenlock visionary's, which found immediate favour with his Christian, but residually shamanistic, audience:

---

[10] *HE* v.12; 'Visio Baronti', ed. Levison, c. 1; *Life of Guthlac*, ed. Colgrave. On laymen as visionaries cf. Holdsworth, 'Visions and Visionaries', pp. 142–3; Dinzelbacher, *Vision*, p. 225.

[11] Cf. Hampe, *To Die is to Gain*, p. 141, n. 34. On dreams/visions see *Dreaming: Anthropological and Psychological Interpretations*, ed. B. Tedlock (Cambridge, 1987). One feature that may be a literary formula is the synchronization with cockcrow and first light (Ciccarese, 'Visio Baronti', p. 38, n. 40, and *Visioni*, pp. 227, 332 and 365); on the other hand, this could be an adaptation of a folklore motif, for cockcrow traditionally marks the *end* of the time of spirits (Amat, *Songes*, pp. 323–4). For flagellation in dreams see *ibid.*, p. 220.

[12] Hampe, *To Die is to Gain*, pp. 28 and 95. Another popular collection of case studies is R. A. Moody, *Life after Death* (Covington, Georgia, 1975). Such material is assessed by C.

At night my breath was out, and I died. All at once I saw a shining light – great light – trying my soul. I looked and saw my body had no soul – looked at my own body – it was dead. I came through the first time and told my friends, 'When I die, don't cry,' and then I died again . . . Angels told me to look back and see my body. I did, and saw it lying down. When I saw it, it was pretty poor. My soul left body and went up to judgment place of God. I do not know about body after 4 oclock. I have seen a great light in my soul from that good land; I have understand all Christ wants us to do. Before I came alive I saw I was a sinner. Angel in heaven said to me, 'You must go back and turn alive again on earth.' I learned that I must be good Christian man on earth, or will be punished . . . When I came back, I told my friends, 'There is a God – there is a Christian people. My good friends, be Christian'.[13]

Similarly, the Wenlock brother's vision endowed him with a prophetic role – indeed, a political role, since he criticized King Ceolred (criticism suppressed in the Old English translation of Boniface's letter):[14]

The blessed angels instructed him . . . to return at once to his own body and not to hesitate to make everything that had been shown him known to those who believed and asked with religious intention, but to refuse to relate it to scoffers. They told him to recount all her past sins in order to a certain woman who dwelt in a far distant region . . . and to expound all those spiritual visions to a priest named Begga[15] and afterwards to proclaim them to men according to how he was instructed by him. He was to confess his own sins, which the impure spirits had imputed to him, to this priest making amends for them as he judged fit; and, as a token of the angelic instruction he was to testify to the priest that unknown to men he [the priest] had worn an iron girdle round his loins for love of God . . . And afterwards he proved from their own testimony that what the angels had revealed to him about the sinful woman and the religious priest was true. Moreover the subsequent and swift death of the wicked king proved beyond doubt that what he had seen concerning him was true.

The Wenlock brother was perhaps on the brink of a charismatic career: his vision and power of second-sight had been accepted; his reputation had

Zaleski, *Otherworld Journeys: Accounts of Near-Death Experience in Medieval and Modern Times* (New York, 1987).

[13] J. Mooney, *The Ghost-Dance Religion and the Sioux Outbreak of 1890*, Reports of the Bureau of American Ethnology 14.2 (Washington, 1896), 752; cf. Eliade, *Shamanism*, pp. 142–3 and 320–1.

[14] Sisam, *Studies*, p. 206.

[15] *Bogia* according to the Old English translation: *ibid.*, pp. 206, n. 1, and 223. Cf. von Feilitzen and Blunt, 'Coinage of Edgar', p. 189, n. 3.

spread through the monasteries of southern England, and he may have carried it overseas, [16] perhaps on pilgrimage or in flight from Ceolred; and his condemnation of Ceolred qualified him to succeed Guthlac as the confidant of Ceolred's enemy and successor, Æthelbald. [17]

But this is conjecture. We know too little about the personal qualities of the Wenlock visionary and the priest who advised him. Moreover the England of 716 was a more sophisticated country than the England that had welcomed St Fursa eighty years before when he came across from Ulster through Wales to East Anglia, preaching a vision very like the Wenlock visionary's. [18] The organized Western church was typically suspicious of charismatic 'holy men'; Headda, the bishop of Lichfield at the time of the Wenlock vision, even had a *librarius* (notary?) who claimed to be able to detect bogus prophets, 'for he said he lived among the Irish, and there had seen false hermits and pretenders of various religions, whom he found able to predict the future and perform other miracles, but he knew not by what power'. [19] Even within the ascetic tradition there was a long history of suspicion about visions and visionaries, stretching back to St Paul (II Corinthians XII.4). [20] Even in Boniface's account one can detect the visionary's lines of defence against the charge of vain-glory: angels had commanded him to reveal his vision; [21] he had taken the advice of a holy priest; and he would only narrate his vision to those it would help. [22]

As far as we know, contemporaries accepted the Wenlock visionary's integrity; but whether he acquired the authority of a Fursa or a Guthlac is not indicated. It is perhaps significant that he is never heard of again, even

---

[16] This depends on accepting the reading *peruenit* (above, p. 243).

[17] Guthlac died less than a year before Æthelbald's succession: *Life of Guthlac*, ed. Colgrave, c. 52.

[18] *Vita S. Fursei*, c. 6, ed. Krusch, 'Vita Virtutesque Fursei abbatis Latiniacensis'; *HE* III.19. For the Irish background see P. Ó Riain, 'Les vies de saint Fursy: les sources irlandaises', *Revue du nord* 68 (1986), 405–13, and 'Sanctity and Politics in Connacht *c.* 1100: The Case of St Fursa', *CMCS* 17 (Summer 1989), 1–14.

[19] *Life of Guthlac*, ed. Colgrave, c. 46; cf. P. Brown, *Society and the Holy in Late Antiquity* (London, 1982), pp. 151–2 and 185–90.

[20] Rousseau, *Ascetics*, pp. 28, 156 and 246; Amat, *Songes*, p. 21. Cf. *HF* VII.1 (p. 290).

[21] An old motif (see II Enoch XXXIII.6 and II Baruch LXXVI.5 in *Pseudepigrapha*, ed. Charlesworth I, 156 and 646) which may have occurred independently to many visionaries (cf. the American Indian example above).

[22] Another old motif (Rousseau, *Ascetics*, p. 28), also echoed by Bede in his accounts of Fursa (it is not from the *Vita S. Fursei*) and Dryhthelm, *HE* III.19 and V.12.

in Bede's *Historia ecclesiastica*, and that Boniface and Eadburg seem to have been more interested in the vision than in the visionary himself.

The priest Begga, while instructing the visionary how to proclaim his vision, may have played an important role in shaping it by asking leading questions about the topography of the hereafter and its denizens.[23] There is a close parallel in Bede's account of Dryhthelm:

> In the neighbourhood of his cell [at Old Melrose] there lived a monk named Hæmgisl, who was an eminent priest and whose good works were worthy of his rank. He is still alive, living in solitude in Ireland and supporting his declining years on a scanty supply of bread and cold water. He would often visit this man and learn from him, by repeated questionings (*repetita interrogatione*), what sort of things he saw when he was out of the body; it is from his account that these particulars which we have briefly described came to our knowledge.[24]

Like Hæmgisl, Begga was an ascetic: he had worn an iron girdle round his loins for many years – an Eastern austerity, sometimes condemned, which is known much later in the area to the author of *Ancrene Wisse*.[25] Begga may have been well-informed about visions of heaven and hell, which were widely reported in Western Europe in the sixth and seventh centuries,[26] for stories about them circulated at a sub-literary level among ascetic circles.[27]

Any investigation of the literary sources of the Wenlock vision is complicated by the probability that it had gone through several stages of evolution by the time Boniface wrote to Eadburg. What the brother actually 'saw' is irrecoverable, but we may surmise that it included universal archetypes, like the element of 'ascent', and more culturally specific elements, due for example to those popular beliefs about the fate of the soul that were inspired by biblical and apocryphal allusions, by *exempla* of the 'body and soul' type and by eschatological homilies.[28] As he

---

[23] Cf. Holdsworth, 'Visions and Visionaries', p. 149; Dinzelbacher, *Vision*, p. 231.

[24] *HE* v.12.

[25] Chadwick, *Cassian*, p. 23, n. 3; *Ancrene Wisse, Parts Six and Seven*, ed. G. Shepherd (London, 1959), p. 18. Shepherd notes (p. 15) that the later English visionary, Godric (see Shepherd, 'The Prophetic Cædmon', pp. 115–16), wore out three shirts of chain-mail.

[26] On problems of transmission see preliminary remarks in Sims-Williams, 'Visionary Celt', pp. 78–96 (cf. a more Irish interpretation by Carozzi, 'Géographie de l'Au-delà', pp. 440 and 447).

[27] Cf. Rousseau, *Ascetics*, pp. 28–9. See, for example, Hygbald and Ecgberht in *HE* iv.3.

[28] For 'body and soul' see references in M. J. B. Allen and D. G. Calder, *Sources and Analogues of Old English Poetry* (Cambridge, 1976), pp. 40–50; McNamara, *Apocrypha*,

attempted to articulate his experience it would have undergone a process analogous to what Freud called 'secondary elaboration', by which a 'dream loses the appearance of absurdity and incoherence, and approaches the pattern of an intelligible experience'.[29] The more he repeated his story, the more it would tend to conform to earlier accounts of visions known, orally or in monastic reading, to himself and to Begga and others who heard him. Finally, his vision would not have escaped literary refinement when Boniface redacted it; it may be noted that Boniface had two versions at his disposal, one via Abbess Hildelith and one from the visionary himself.[30]

Three earlier visions show fundamental similarities to the Wenlock vision, and must surely have been known in some form to the visionary as well, no doubt, as to Boniface. The earliest is the 'Long' text of the *Visio S. Pauli*, a translation of a Greek-Egyptian apocryphal *Apocalypse of St Paul*, which purported to recount the visions which St Paul had declined to utter in II Corinthians XII.[31] Condemnations by Augustine, Aldhelm, Ælfric and others reveal that this Apocalypse enjoyed a long popularity, and Aldhelm's citation of the 'Long' text shows that this was available in England by the time of the Wenlock vision;[32] later evidence for the 'Long' text is provided by an Old English translation and some Old English homilies.[33]

The second influence on the Wenlock vision is the account of Fursa's

---

pp. 109–13 and 127–8; *Vision of St Paul*, ed. Healey, pp. 97–8. For homilies (best attested in the late Anglo-Saxon period) see M. McC. Gatch, 'Eschatology in the Anonymous Old English Homilies', *Traditio* 21 (1965), 117–65, and *Preaching and Theology in Anglo-Saxon England* (Toronto and Buffalo, 1977), pp. 60–116. A *summa* of eschatology by the time of the Wenlock vision is provided by Julian of Toledo, *Prognosticum futuri saeculi* (*Opera*, ed. Hillgarth I, 9–126).

[29] Quoted in E. R. Dodds's study of the cultural conditioning of dreams: *The Greeks and the Irrational* (Berkeley and Los Angeles, 1951), p. 114 (cf. *idem, Pagan and Christian in an Age of Anxiety* (Cambridge, 1965), p. 39).

[30] Carozzi, 'Géographie de l'Au-delà', p. 449. Cf. the 'triple déformation' discussed by Dulaey, *Le rêve*, p. 160.

[31] I cite the *Visio Pauli* according to James's edition of the Fleury manuscript in *Apocrypha Anecdota* I, 11–43 (corrigenda II, 138), and his translation in *Apocryphal New Testament*, pp. 526–53. See also the edition of the St Gallen manuscript by Silverstein, *Visio Sancti Pauli*, pp. 131–47.

[32] Silverstein, *Visio Sancti Pauli*, pp. 4, 6 and 9. Cf. *Aldhelmi Opera*, ed. Ehwald, p. 256; *Catholic Homilies, Second Series*, ed. Godden, p. 190.

[33] *Vision of St Paul*, ed. Healey. Cf. Silverstein, *Visio Sancti Pauli*, pp. 7–9 and 96–7.

visions in the *Vita S. Fursei*.[34] The latter was itself influenced by the *Visio S. Pauli*, so it is not always possible to decide whether the Wenlock vision was influenced by Paul's visions or by Fursa's. The visions which Fursa recounted on his travels through Ireland, Wales, England and France were written down at Péronne in 656×657, soon after the saint's death in 649×650.[35] Knowledge of the *Vita S. Fursei* in early eighth-century England is shown by the use made of it by Bede, who speaks as if this *libellus* was readily available, and by Felix in his *Vita S. Guthlaci*.[36] Oral reports about Fursa, which reached Bede from East Anglia, could also have reached Wenlock, since the monastery was connected with the East Anglian monastery of *Icanho*, and another East Anglian house, *Medeshamstede*, possessed estates in Shropshire.[37] However, one detail in the Wenlock vision seems to derive from an ambiguity in the *Latin* text of the *Vita S. Fursei*.[38]

A third vision which influenced the Wenlock vision is that of the Northumbrian, Dryhthelm, which Bede places in the 690s. The simplest way of explaining the numerous general and verbal similarities between Boniface's account of the Wenlock vision and Bede's account of Dryhthelm in the *Historia ecclesiastica*, is to suppose that the priest Hæmgisl's lost account of Dryhthelm, which Bede used in the 730s, was already in circulation in the south a few decades earlier.[39]

Boniface reports that the Wenlock visionary,

said that, amidst the pain of a sharp sickness he had been freed from the weight of the flesh. It was much as though one seeing and awake had his eyes veiled by a thick covering; this being suddenly taken away, everything would become clear which before had been invisible, hidden and unknown. In like fashion when the covering of this mortal flesh had been thrown aside, before his gaze lay gathered the universe, so that in a single view he beheld all lands and peoples and seas.

Verbal echoes of Gregory's *Dialogi* here show that Boniface interpreted the

---

[34] 'Visioni di Fursa', ed. Ciccarese (also with trans. in her *Visioni*, pp. 190–225). The rest of the *Vita S. Fursei* was ed. Krusch (see above, n. 18).

[35] A. Dierkens, *Abbayes et chapitres entre Sambre et Meuse (VIIᵉ – XIᵉ siècles)*, Beihefte der Francia 14 (Sigmaringen, 1985), 71, n. 8, and 304, n. 147.

[36] *HE* III.19; *Life of Guthlac*, ed. Colgrave, pp. 17 and 179–80. There is a fragment from Worcester (BL, Royal 4. A. XIV, fols. 107–8 (s. viii/ix)), but this was probably written at Winchester: *CLA* II, no. 216; Ker, *Books, Collectors and Libraries*, p. 114, n. 17.

[37] See above, p. 99.   [38] See below on *mundus*.

[39] Sims-Williams, 'Recension'.

monk's vision of the world in terms of St Benedict's contemplative cosmic vision.[40] Yet the basic experience described is much more widely attested; for example, an Eskimo shaman described his 'illumination' to Rasmussen:

it is as if the house in which he is suddenly rises; he sees far ahead of him, through the mountains, exactly as if the earth were one great plain and his eyes could reach to the end of the earth. Nothing is hidden from him any longer. Not only can he see things far, far away, but he can also discover souls, stolen souls, which are either kept concealed in far, strange lands, or have been taken up or down to the Land of the Dead.[41]

Further details, however, align the monk of Wenlock's vision with Christian tradition:

As he quitted the body, angels of such dazzling brightness that he could scarcely look upon them for their splendour, bore him up. With sweet and harmonious voices they were singing: 'O Lord, rebuke me not in thy wrath: neither chasten me in thy hot displeasure' [Psalm XXXVII.2].

On his supposed deathbed the monk will have recalled the angels who take away the souls of the dying in Christian literature from the parable of Dives and Lazarus (Luke XVI.22) onwards, and the angelic songs which, according to Gregory the Great, were 'often' heard at the moment of death.[42] In particular he may have recalled how in Fursa's first vision angels sang a psalm-verse when they carried him upwards from the body and when

---

[40] *Dialogi* II.35 ('omnis etiam *mundus*, uelut *sub uno* solis radio *collectus*, ante oculos eius adductus est') and IV.8 ('quasi *sub uno* solis radio *cunctum* in suis oculis *mundum collectum* uidit'), ed. de Vogüé II, 238 and III, 42. Cf. Anon., *Ep.* cxv (Tangl, p. 248); Levison, 'Bearbeitung', p. 384, n. 1. See especially P. Courcelle, 'La vision cosmique de saint Benoît', *Revue des études augustiniennes* 13 (1967), 97–117, and D. N. Bell, 'The Vision of the World and of the Archetypes in the Latin Spirituality of the Middle Ages', *AHDLMA* 44 (1977), 7–31; also Ciccarese, 'Gregorio di Tours', p. 254, n. 9. Note that Boniface says that the vision was seen in 'spiritual contemplation' (p. 14, line 21). The phrase *mundi machina*, for which Tangl compares Aldhelm, is quite common (cf. Eugenius of Toledo, *Carmina* I.1, a text found in early prayer books: PL 101, 579 and 1397), but Rau, *Bonifatii Epistulae*, p. 33, n. 8, notes that Boniface's whole phrase *totius mundi machina* occurs in the *Oratio Moucani* discussed below, p. 320.

[41] Quoted by Eliade, *Shamanism*, p. 61. Cf. Carozzi, 'Géographie de l'Au-delà', p. 435: 'Le christianisme sort lentement de son contexte mystérique paléochrétien pour adopter, au contact des nouveaux convertis du monde barbare, le langage religieux universel, celui que connaissent les anthropologues et les historiens des religions.'

[42] Gregory, *Dialogi* IV.15 (ed. de Vogüé III, 58). Cf. Julian of Toledo, *Prognosticum* I.10 (ed. Hillgarth, pp. 24–5).

they returned him to the body.[43] Fursa's second vision is certainly recalled by the sequel in the Wenlock monk's account:

'They raised me up,' said he, 'high into the air, and circling the whole world (*mundus*) I beheld a blazing fire, the mighty flame soaring terribly aloft, as though to grasp the whole mechanism of the world (*totius machina mundi*) in its embrace, had not the holy angel calmed it with the sign of Christ's holy cross. When he had made the sign of the holy cross before the threatening flame, it gradually retired. By its terrible heat I was sorely tried, while my eyes were burned, and my sight was shattered by the brightness of the gleaming spirits until an angel, splendid to behold, touched my head with a protecting hand, and brought me safe from harm in the flames.

Compare the *Vita S. Fursei*:

The holy angel, which was at his right side, said: 'Look back at the world (*mundus*).' Then the saint looked back, and saw a dark valley in the depth below him, and saw four fires there in the air at a certain distance from each other. Then the angel said to him again: 'What are these fires?' The man of God said he did not know. The angel said: 'These are the four fires which burn up the clean man [or 'mankind' (*mundus*)] after all sins have been wiped out in baptism, after confession and renunciation of the devil and his works and pomps. Promise-breakers light the fire of mendacity. The second fire is of cupidity . . . the third, of discord . . . the fourth, of mercilessness . . .' The fires increased and became one and were approaching him. Fearing the menacing fire, the man of God said to the angel who was talking to him, 'The fire is coming near me.' The angel replied: 'What you have not kindled will not burn in you. However terrible and great the fire is, it examines individuals according to their merits . . .' Then he saw the holy angel going ahead and dividing the fire into two walls on either side; and the two holy angels defended him from the fire on each side.[44]

This part of Fursa's vision was clearly inspired by the *Visio S. Pauli* (c. 13), but the latter is less close to the Wenlock vision; Paul, for example, is a detached observer and does not need angelic protection from the static 'great cloud of fire spread over the whole world', which is identified as 'unrighteousness'. The significance of the fire has developed

---

[43] 'Visioni di Fursa', ed. Ciccarese, c. 3. The angels in the *Vita S. Guthlaci*, ed. Colgrave, c. 33, sing the same verse, with the same Gallican reading *ibunt* (cf. *BOH* II, 171). On psalmody and prophetism see Shepherd, 'Prophetic Cædmon', pp. 118–19; cf. Cassian, *Conlationes* X.11, on the use of psalms in contemplation (ed. Petschenig, pp. 303–6; trans. Chadwick, *Western Asceticism*, pp. 243–4), discussed below, p. 319.

[44] Ed. Ciccarese, c. 8.

still further in the Wenlock vision: it threatens to engulf the world. We are meant, then, to identify it with the fire that will destroy the world on the Day of Judgment (II Peter III.7 and 10).[45] This eschatological theme had appeared already in the second-century *Apocalypse of Peter*, a pendant to II Peter, but this apocalypse was little-known in the West[46] and a more likely source is the well-known *Apocalypse of Thomas*,[47] whose lurid eschatology was widely disseminated in Latin and the vernaculars through the legend of the Fifteen Signs Before Doomsday:

> Ticfa nel derg teinntide
> atuásciurd nime ninaig
> granna, gér, garb, geintide,
> lethfaid dartalmain tinaig.[48]

Fursa's four fires of sin may have been interpreted as the fire of Judgment Day because the number four had eschatological associations[49] and because St Paul had spoken of the fire of the Day of Judgment testing every man's work.[50] On the other hand, it is difficult not to suspect that

---

[45] On the destruction of the world by fire see D. S. Russell, *The Method and Message of Jewish Apocalyptic* (London, 1964), p. 216. This theme is prominent in the *Sibylline Oracles* (Charles, *Pseudepigrapha*, p. 375), and see also the prophecies of fire in IV Ezra (II Esdras) XV–XVI.

[46] James, *Apocryphal New Testament*, pp. xxi and 513 (cf. version on pp. 521–2 in the *Sibylline Oracles* and that in II Clement XIII.3, quoted by James, *Lost Apocrypha*, p. 88). Cf. Silverstein, *Visio Sancti Pauli*, p. 93, n. 10; McNamara, *Apocrypha*, pp. 102–3.

[47] 'Fumus ignis magni eruptus erit per portas celi, et cooperiet totum celum usque in sero ... Tunc in aduentum meum soluetur clausura ignis paradysi ... Haec est autem ignis perpetuus, qui consumit orbem terrarum, et uniuersa mundi elementa' ('Un texte non interpolé de l'apocalypse de Thomas', ed. P. Bihlmeyer, *RB* 28 (1911), 270–82, at 272–3). Cf. the text in F. Wilhelm, *Deutsche Legenden und Legendare* (Leipzig, 1907), p. 42* (*sic*), and the translations in James, *Apocryphal New Testament*, pp. 558–61. On the Latin texts see M. Förster, 'A New Version of the Apocalypse of Thomas in Old English', *Anglia* 73 (1955), 6–36, and McNamara, *Apocrypha*, pp. 119–21.

[48] 'A red, fiery cloud will come from the north of vaulted heaven, ugly, rough, sharp, heathen, it will spread out over the many-sided (?) earth': the Irish *Saltair na Rann*, lines 8025–8, ed. and trans. W. W. Heist, *The Fifteen Signs before Doomsday* (East Lansing, Michigan, 1952), pp. 2–3 (cf. pp. 34, 68, 81–2 and 97, n. 56). See also McNamara, *Apocrypha*, pp. 128–38.

[49] Silverstein, *Visio Sancti Pauli*, p. 73.

[50] I Corinthians III.12–15. Cf. the patristic etc. passages on 'intelligent fire' testing men's souls cited by James, *Lost Apocrypha*, pp. 90–1, and *Testament of Abraham*, pp. 147, 153

the *mundus* attacked by fire in the *Vita S. Fursei* was misunderstood as 'world, earth, universe'. Bede's summary is quite ambiguous, giving the impression that he understood *mundus* in the latter sense, and Ælfric translates it as 'earth' (*middaneard*).[51] Possibly a variant or corrupt text of the *Vita S. Fursei* circulated in England.

It was believed that souls might be intercepted by hostile demons as they left the body. For instance, a prayer in an eighth-century prayer book from Worcester, echoing liturgical prayers for the dead or dying, asks:

whensoever thou deignest to take me, that thou sendest an angel of peace who may guard my soul and take it into a place of refreshment (*in locum refrigerii*), and may make it pass without fear the principalities and powers of darkness . . . so that flying across I may be able to ascend the strait way through the aerial powers, on a prosperous course and safe journey, to the gates of Paradise and to the holy, longed for, and ever enjoyable abodes of pleasantness (*sedes amoenitatis*) . . . so that in the terrible hour of the examination of thy Latter Day, I may migrate on the heavenly journey, safe from enemies, to meet thee, eternal God.[52]

and 159–60, by Le Goff, *Purgatory*, pp. 9–10 and 53–4, and by Amat, *Songes*, pp. 149–50 (cf. below, n. 81). The point of contact can be seen from Ælfric's exegesis of the Pauline text: 'Swa eac ða ðe habbað góde weorc. ne þoliað náne pínunge. *on þam bradum fyre þe ofergǽð ealne middaneard*. ac hí farað þurh þæt fyr to criste buton ælcere dare. swilce hí on sunnan leoman faron' (*In dedicatione ecclesiae*, ed. Godden, *Catholic Homilies, Second Series*, p. 343); there is only a partial source for this in Caesarius of Arles, *Sermo* clxxix: see J. E. Cross, 'Ælfric and the Mediaeval Homiliary – Objection and Contribution', *Scripta Minora Regiae Societatis Humaniorum Litterarum Lundensis*, 1961–2, no. 4, p. 12.

51 *HE* III.19 (*audiuit hos esse ignes qui mundum succendentes essent consumturi*, which Colgrave translates, 'he was told they were the fires that were to consume the world'); *Catholic Homilies, Second Series*, ed. Godden, p. 193 ('and se engel cwæð him to; Þas feower fyr ontendað ealne middaneard. and onælað þæra manna sawla. þe heora fulluhtes andetnysse. and behát ðurh forgægednysse awægdon'). Perhaps Ælfric, who seems to translate *mundus* in both senses, was influenced by Bede here?

52 London, BL, Royal 2. A. XX, 34r, 36r and 37v, ed. Kuypers, *Cerne*, pp. 215–17 (on this abecedarian prayer see below, p. 311). On liturgical prayers see Ntedika, *Évocation de l'Au-delà*, and Sicard, *Liturgie de la mort*. Their non-Scriptural basis was noted by James, *Testament of Abraham*, pp. 129–30; cf. B. Grogan, 'Eschatological Teaching in the Early Irish Church', *PIBA* 1 (1976), 46–59, at 52–5; Le Goff, *Purgatory*, pp. 122–4. Bede remarks that unclean spirits could not harm Benedict Biscop's soul as it left the body: *BOH* I, 378; cf. Ntedika, *Évocation de l'Au-delà*, p. 64, n. 59. For many examples of the theme see A. C. Rush, 'An Echo of Christian Antiquity in Gregory the Great: Death a Struggle with the Devil', *Traditio* 3 (1945), 369–80. For struggles between angel(s) and demon(s) over men cf. Milik, '4Q visions'; Stone, 'Metamorphosis of Ezra', pp. 10–11; Amat, *Songes*, pp. 376–8.

Again, not long before the Wenlock vision, a sinful Mercian thegn of King Coenred (704–9) found his deathbed surrounded by angels and devils carrying books listing his good and bad deeds; the devils dismissed the angels, saying 'Why do you sit here since you know for certain *the man is ours?*' – This cry, *noster est ille*, was perhaps an echo of their cry, *noster est ille uir*, in an Insular(?) homily describing the struggles of angelic and demonic hosts around a sinner's deathbed.[53] Such beliefs help to explain the sequel in the Wenlock vision:

> He added that during the time while he was out of the body, such a multitude of souls leaving the body had gathered where he was as to exceed what he had thought before to be the numbers of the whole human race. An innumerable band of evil spirits and a bright choir of heavenly angels had also assembled; and there was the greatest dispute between the demons and the angels over the souls leaving the body, for the demons were accusing the dead and making heavy the burden of their sins, while the angels were excusing them and lightening their load.

This section was probably inspired above all by the *Visio S. Pauli* (cc. 11–16). There Paul, looking down on the cloud of fire spread over the world, asks to see righteous and sinful souls leaving the body. The description of the opposition which the souls encounter is abbreviated and corrupt in the Latin text, which obscures (deliberately?) the Eastern doctrine of the 'toll-stages' (*telonia*) at which souls are subjected to daemonic examination on their ascent through the heavens. Nevertheless, enough was probably known of this doctrine in the West[54] for Paul's dialogue with his angel guide to be intelligible:

> 'Is it necessary that both the righteous and the sinners meet the witnesses (*testes*) when they are dead?' – 'The way by which all pass to God is one: but the righteous having an holy helper with them are not troubled when they go to appear in the presence of God.'[55]

---

53 *HE* v. 13; see Willard, *Two Apocrypha*, pp. 95–7; C. D. Wright, 'Apocryphal Lore and Insular Tradition in St Gall, Stiftsbibliothek MS 908', in *Irland und die Christenheit*, ed. Ní Chatháin and Richter, pp. 124–45, at 134–7. Cf. *nostra est* in the homily cited below, n. 91.

54 Rivière, 'Rôle du démon'; Daniélou, 'Démons de l'air'; Ntedika, *Évocation de l'Au-delà*, pp. 259–60; Sims-Williams, 'Triad', pp. 80–1; J. Stevenson, 'Ascent through the Heavens, from Egypt to Ireland', *CMCS* 5 (Summer 1983), 21–35. See below, p. 257, for Evagrius.

55 *Visio S. Pauli*, c. 12; for the translation cf. Silverstein, *Visio Sancti Pauli*, p. 104, n. 14.

The reason for supposing the *Visio S. Pauli* to be the source, rather than the *Vita S. Fursei*, where Fursa himself is at the centre of a dispute between the angels and the demons flying in the fire, is that at this point the Wenlock visionary is still, like St Paul, a detached observer.

Immediately afterwards, however, in a section too long to quote, the monk of Wenlock is himself confronted by accusations by his own personified sins, which are backed up by the demons; he is defended by his virtues, which are supported by the angels, who make the most of them (like good Anglo-Saxon oath-helpers). His original dream-experience may have resembled the 'life panorama' reported by those who have come near to death, and the 'tribunal dreams' which trouble men of bad conscience, like the above Mercian thegn.[56] Its lengthy literary stylization, however, owes something to the elaborate lists of opposing vices and virtues in the ascetic tradition. These were imprinted on the mind by such prayers as *Mane cum surrexero*, found in both of the extant eighth-century prayer books from Worcester:

... Keep my feet, lest they frequent idle homes; but let them stand in prayer to God. Keep my hands, lest they often stretch out to take gifts; but rather let them be raised, clean and pure, in prayers to God ... Keep my mouth lest I speak vain things or tell secular fables or malign my neighbour ... but rather may it be prompt to praise God, slow to anger. Keep my ears lest they hear detraction or lying or idle speech (*uerbum otiosum*); but may they be opened daily to hear the word of the Lord so that I may pass the whole day according to thy will. Grant me, Lord, fear of thee, compunction of heart, humility of mind, a pure conscience, so that I may look towards heaven, despise the earth, hate sins, delight in justice. Take from me, Lord, worldly care, appetite for gluttony, desire of fornication ...[57]

The dramatic confrontation between the Wenlock visionary and the sins and demons recalls the opposition which the wicked soul and its guardian angel meet in the *Visio S. Pauli*, c. 16:

When therefore they were come unto the principalities, and it would now go to enter heaven, one burden was laid upon it after another: error and forgetfulness and whispering met it, and the spirit of fornication and the rest of the powers, and said unto it: Whither goest thou, wretched soul, and darest to run forward into heaven?

[56] Hampe, *To Die is to Gain*, p. 50; Dulaey, *Le rêve*, p. 174. Cf. Ciccarese, 'Visio Baronti', p. 35, n. 29; Amat, *Songes*, pp. 132–6, 210, 219 and 381–2.

[57] BL, Harley 7653, 2v–3v (ed. Warren, *Antiphonary of Bangor* II, 84–5); cf. BL, Royal 2.A. XX, fol. 22 (ed. Kuypers, *Cerne*, pp. 209–10). On this prayer see below, pp. 284 and 324.

Stay, that we may see whether we have property of ours in thee, for we see not with thee an holy helper.[58]

This soul received no angelic support at the *telonia*, unlike the Wenlock monk. That element can, however, be paralleled in Athanasius's *Life of St Antony*:

When [Antony] was about to eat and stood up to pray, about the ninth hour, he felt himself carried off in spirit, and – strange to say – as he stood he saw himself, as it were, outside himself and as though guided aloft by certain beings. Then he also saw loathsome and terrible beings standing in the air and bent on preventing him from passing through. As his guides offered resistance, the others demanded to know on what plea he was not accountable to them. Then, when they set themselves to taking an account from his birth, Antony's guides intervened, saying to them: 'As for the things dating from his birth, the Lord has erased them; but as for the time since he became a monk and promised himself to God, you can take an account.' Then, as they brought accusations but could not prove them, the way opened up to him free and unhindered; and presently he saw himself approaching, so it seemed to him, and halting with himself; and so he was the real Antony again.[59]

The demons' reeling off Antony's sins 'from his birth' (*a natiuitate*) could have suggested the intervention of the sins which the Wenlock monk had committed 'since his youth' (*a iuuentute*), for Athanasius's *Life* was well-known in Evagrius's Latin translation; it clearly inspired Guthlac's career (or, at least, his biographer's portrayal of it). On the other hand, the influence of the *Vita S. Antonii* may have been indirect, through the *Vita S. Fursei*, which seems to blend the *Vita S. Antonii* and *Visio S. Pauli* in an elaborate sequence of demonic and angelic cut and thrust. Some of the accusations are quite similar. For example, Satan accuses Fursa of idle talk (*otiosos sermones*), while the Wenlock monk is confronted by his personified idle speech (*otiosum uerbum*). Again, just as the latter sees a man whom he had wounded, so Fursa sees a man who had been involved in one of his

---

[58] Cf. the St Gallen text (Silverstein, *Visio Sancti Pauli*, p. 133). The corresponding confrontation in c. 14 is missing from the latter, and corrupt in the text printed by James. See also the personification in c. 11, and cf. Origen, quoted by James, *Testament of Abraham*, p. 19.

[59] PG 26, 933–6 (with Evagrius's translation); *Athanasius: Life of Antony*, trans. Meyer, c. 65. Cf. Rivière, 'Rôle du démon', pp. 49–50; Daniélou, 'Démons de l'air'.

sins.[60] While such similarities could be due to ascetic categories of vices and virtues working independently on two bad consciences, the general similarity of context makes it very probable that the *Vita S. Fursei* influenced the Wenlock narrative at some stage.

Where the Wenlock vision differs from the above parallels is in personifying the vices and virtues. There are only traces of this in the biblical texts on the Day of Judgment: Romans II.15–16 says 'their own thoughts argue the case on either side, against them or even for them, on the day when God judges the secrets of human hearts', and according to IV Ezra (II Esdras) VII.35 'righteous deeds shall awake and unrighteous deeds shall not sleep'.[61] The personification is more concrete in the *Apocalypse of Peter*, as extant in Ethiopic: on Judgment Day God will 'command them to enter into the river of fire while the works of every one of them shall stand before them'.[62] In the *Visio S. Pauli*, c. 14, the motif is applied to the individual judgment at the moment of death:

I looked and saw all [the righteous man's] works that he had done for the name of God, and all his desires which he remembered and which he remembered not, all of them stood before his face in the hour of necessity.[63]

While this passage may have had some influence on the Wenlock narrative, it will be noticed that these deeds do not actually speak. That unusual detail may be derived from the Greek *Beatitudes* attributed to Ephrem the Syrian, which circulated in a Latin version in the early Middle Ages: when angels come to take a dying man's soul from his body, all its good and evil deeds committed by day and night stand by; the sinful soul is frightened to hear and see them, and asks them for an hour's respite, but they reply: 'You

---

[60] 'Visioni di Fursa', ed. Ciccarese, cc. 7 and 16 (Fursa had accepted a gift from a dying sinner). Cf. Dinzelbacher, *Vision*, pp. 171–2, and Carozzi, 'Géographie de l'Au-delà', p. 449; they refer to the *psychomachia* tradition, but no link with Prudentius is evident. For *otiosa uerba*, etc. see e.g. *Columbani Opera*, ed. Walker, pp. 108, 142, 144 and 148.

[61] See Charles, *Pseudepigrapha*, p. 583, n. 35. Cf. Isaiah LIX.12. On the personification of good works cf. the speculations of C. H. Kraeling, 'The Apocalypse of Paul and the "Iranische Erlösungsmysterium"', *HThR* 24 (1931), 209–44, at 226–31, and see below, n. 64.

[62] *Apocryphal New Testament*, trans. James, p. 514.

[63] Cf. the death of the sinner in c. 15, also extant in the St Gallen text, ed. Silverstein, *Visio Sancti Pauli*, p. 133.

did us, we are your deeds, we will always accompany you; we shall go to God together with you.'[64]

In short, the first part of the vision shows the influence – probably at various levels and by various stages – of a number of Latin texts describing the experience of death or seeming-death.

The second part turns abruptly to the topography of hell and heaven. Here the similarities with Dryhthelm's vision begin. That took the form of a guided tour of unknown regions, following the pattern first set by the *Book of Enoch*. It began with Dryhthelm and his guide setting off in the direction of the rising sun, which recalls the frequent compass directions of the *Book of Enoch* and later apocalypses. Their movement was horizontal, in contrast to the vertical movement in Fursa's vision and the first part of the Wenlock vision. The angel showed Dryhthelm in turn the provisional hell, the eternal hell, the provisional heaven and the eternal heaven. The same fourfold pattern appears in the brother of Wenlock's vision. Boniface gives his description of the two hells as follows:

He told, too, how he had seen, as it were in the depths of this earth many fiery pits (*puteos*), belching forth terrible flames, and as the black flame (*tetra flamma*) burst forth, the souls of the miserable men (*hominum spiritus*), in the form of birds, flew through the flames lamenting and bemoaning, with human cries, their deserts and their present punishment. They rested, hanging for a little time on the edges of the pits, and then screaming, fell into the depths (*cecidisse in puteos*). One of the angels said, 'This moment of rest shows that the Almighty God means, on the Day of Judgment to come, to grant these souls relief from punishment and eternal rest.'

But under these pits in the lowest depths, as if in a deeper hell (*infernus inferior*), he heard the awful weeping and wailing of sorrowing souls, terrible, beyond the power of words to describe. And the angel said to him, 'The lamentations and

---

[64] Sims-Williams, 'Ephrem', p. 209, n. 15 (on the Graeco-Latin Ephrem see also Pattie, 'Ephraem'); with the last phrase cf. 'Visio Baronti', ed. Levison, c. 3. For personified deeds in genuine Ephrem and their background see 'Ephrem's Letter to Publius', ed. and trans. S. P. Brock, *Le Muséon* 89 (1976), 261–305 (cc. 5 and 9 and p. 297), a reference I owe to Dr Brock. A later, vaguer parallel to the Wenlock personification is cited by Dinzelbacher, *Vision*, p. 171, n. 817. Cf. also *Vita S. Ioannis Eleemosynarii*, PL 73, 374–5. There is also a vague similarity to the 'Ego . . . ' speeches of the patriarchs in the Pelagian *Epistula ad Claudiam de ultimo iudicio* (Lapidge and Sharpe, *Bibliography of Celtic-Latin Literature*, no. 1244). James, *Testament of Abraham*, p. 68, cites an Islamic passage rather like the Wenlock vision, but it seems to be an independent development of the tradition of the difficulty of extracting a righteous man's soul; see Charlesworth, *Pseudepigrapha* I, 565 and 577–8; Stone, 'Metamorphosis of Ezra', pp. 10–11. Silverstein, 'Dante', pp. 108–9, denies Islamic influence on the personification motif.

weeping which you hear in the depths come from those souls to whom the mercy of God will never come. But everlasting flame will torture them without end.'

The idea of two hells, as found here and in Dryhthelm's vision, was an important stage in the development of Purgatory and Hell as distinct 'places'.[65] It originated, presumably, through applying to mankind (and telescoping the chronology of) what the *Book of Enoch*, followed by Jude 6 and II Peter II.4, says about the fallen angels being imprisoned in a 'waste place' ('dark pits of hell' in II Peter) next to the fiery abyss where they will finally be consigned on the Day of Judgment.[66] Although such a doctrinal development is not clear in the *Visio S. Pauli*, this has a suggestive passage which might easily be interpreted in terms of the two hells whose existence Augustine deduced from the reference to *infernus inferior* in Psalm LXXXV.13.[67] After showing Paul many lesser places of torture, including torment-pits, a fiery river and a place of ice and snow, the angel leads him to an abyss sealed with seven seals (obviously reminiscent of the sealed abyss into which Satan is cast in Revelation XX; cf. also Revelation IX):

When therefore the well (*puteus*) was opened, straightway there arose out of it a stench hard and evil exceedingly, which surpassed all the torments: and I [Paul] looked into the well and saw masses (lumps) of fire burning on every side, and

---

[65] Ciccarese, 'Purgatorio', pp. 46–56. Cf. Le Goff, *Purgatory*, pp. 110, 115 and 370; Carozzi, 'Géographie de l'Au-delà', pp. 478–80 and 483–5. For precursors of the provisional hell (Tertullian, Ambrose, Jerome) see Amat, *Songes*, pp. 150–1, 386–7 and 402.

[66] 1 Enoch X.4–6 and 11–14; XVIII.11–XIX.1; XXI; and LIV.1–7; also the Slavonic II Enoch XVIII.6 and XL.12. (Both are translated in *Pseudepigrapha*, ed. Charlesworth I, 5–213.) Cf. Charles, *Pseudepigrapha*, p. 180. 1 Enoch was little known in the Latin West (Charlesworth, *Pseudepigrapha* I, 8; H. J. Lawlor, 'Early Citations from the Book of Enoch', *Journal of Philology* 25 (1897), 164–225). The fragment from Worcester, BL, Royal 5. E. XIII (s. ix^med), ed. James, *Apocrypha Anecdota* I, 146–50, probably came there in the tenth century from Brittany, where there is other evidence for 1 Enoch: D. N. Dumville, 'Biblical Apocrypha and the Early Irish: A Preliminary Investigation', *PRIA* 73 C (1973), 299–338, at 319 and 331; Frantzen, 'Tradition of Penitentials', pp. 37–8. The early Fathers often mention that hellfire lies ahead for the fallen angels (see Meyer's note, *Athanasius: Life of Antony*, p. 117), and the parallel with mankind is manifest in Matthew XXV.41 (quoted below, p. 268); cf. Augustine, *De ciuitate Dei* XXI.24 (CCSL 48, 789–92); Haymo, PL 118, 574.

[67] *Enarrationes in Psalmis* LXXXV.17–18 (CCSL 39, 1190–1), followed by Gregory, *Dialogi* IV.44 (ed. de Vogüé, III, 156–8 and n.) and *Moralia in Iob* XII.13 (CCSL 143A, 636), and by Julian of Toledo, *Prognosticum* II.4 (ed. Hillgarth, pp. 45–7). Cf. Silverstein, *Visio Sancti Pauli*, pp. 56 and 115–16; Dinzelbacher, *Vision*, pp. 92–3. Augustine also

anguish, and there was straightness in the mouth of the pit (*puteus*) so as to take but one man in. And the angel answered and said unto me: If any be cast into the well of the abyss (*puteus abyssi*), and it be sealed over him, there shall never be any remembrance made of him in the presence of the Father and the Son and the Holy Ghost or of the holy angels.[68]

This passage in the *Visio S. Pauli* may well have influenced the Wenlock visionary's arrangement of *provisional* fiery pits above and eternal *infernus inferior* below. Its sinking *puteus abyssi* probably influenced Dryhthelm's *eternal* hell as well:

As we [Dryhthelm and the angel] went on 'through the shades in the lone night', there suddenly appeared before us masses of black flame (*flammarum tetrarum*), constantly rising up as if from a great pit (*puteo*) and falling into it again (*decidentes in eundem*). When my guide had brought me to this place, he suddenly disappeared and left me alone in the midst of the darkness and of the horrible scene. I saw, as the globes of fire now shot up and now fell back again ceaselessly into the bottom of the pit, that the tips of the flames as they ascended, were full of human souls (*spiritibus hominum*), which like sparks flying upward with the smoke, were now tossed on high and now, as the vaporous flames fell back, were sucked down into the depths. Furthermore, an indescribable stench which rose up with these vapours filled all these abodes of darkness.[69]

This description of the *eternal* hell influenced the conception and even, in the italicized passages, the wording of the Wenlock *provisional* hell. Presumably the details were transferred to the latter's lesser hell because

distinguishes the fire that torments Dives from the eternal fire of Judgment Day: *Enarrationes in Psalmis* LVII.17 (CCSL 39, 722–3). Cf. Julian of Toledo, *Prognosticum* II.20–1 (ed. Hillgarth, pp. 56–9).

68 *Visio S. Pauli*, c. 41. Its relevance to the Dryhthelm and Wenlock visions is noted by Silverstein, *Visio Sancti Pauli*, pp. 87–8 and 127, n. 34. Cf. Kamphausen, *Traum und Vision*, pp. 73, n. 31, and 110, n. 68. Cf. the *inferior puteus abyssi* of the seventh-century Vision of Bonellus recounted by Valerius of Bierzo: PL 87, 435; *Visioni*, ed. Ciccarese, p. 290.

69 *HE* v.12. Cf. *BOH* II, 296. The quotation is from *Aeneid* VI.268, and *flammarum globi* recalls Vergil on Etna; cf. Fontaine, *Suplice Sévère* II, 770 and n. 3, and III, 1223, n. 1. Compare the description of Gehenna ('eructantibus flammis . . . globus ignium . . .') in Pseudo-Cyprian, *De laude martyrii* (ed. G. Hartel, *S. Thasci Caecili Cypriani Opera Omnia*, 3 vols., CSEL 3 (Vienna, 1868–71) III, 43), discussed by Amat, *Songes*, pp. 154–5. The darkness of, or lack of light from, the flames of hell is stressed in Gregory's *Moralia in Iob*, e.g. IX.95 and 100–2 (CCSL 143, 523–4 and 528–30); cf. M. Dando, 'The Moralia in Job of Gregory the Great as a Source for the Old Saxon Genesis B', *Classica et Mediaevalia* 30 (1969), 420–39, at 421–4 and 435–6.

the monk, or Boniface, associated the rising and falling of Dryhthelm's souls with the idea of a recurrent respite in anticipation of eventual salvation. This idea was probably suggested by the passage in the *Visio S. Pauli* where Christ granted the inhabitants of hell periodic refreshment for ever; this was shortly after the episode of the sealed abyss.[70]

The Wenlock vision thus shows the influence of the *Visio S. Pauli* both directly and through the vision of Dryhthelm (presumably in Hæmgisl's lost version). As we shall see, the same applies to its provisional and eternal places of the blessed, which symmetrically balance the two hells:

He saw, too, a place of wonderful pleasantness (*mire amoenitatis locum*), in which a glorious multitude of beauteous men rejoiced with exceeding joy; and they invited him to come and share their happiness, if it were permitted him. There came thence a fragrance of a wonderful sweetness (*mirę dulcedinis flagrantia*), because it was the gathering of the blessed in their bliss. And this place, the holy angels told him, was the renowned Paradise of God.

He beheld also a river of fiery pitch, boiling and blazing, wonderful and terrible to behold. Across it a beam was set for a bridge, to which the holy and glorious souls hastened as they left the assembly, eager to cross to the other bank. And some crossed with certain step. But others slipped from the beam and fell into the hellish stream. Of these some were entirely immersed, while others were only partially covered, it might be to the knees, or to the waist, or even to the armpits (*uero usque ad ascellas*).[71] And yet each one of those who fell climbed from the river upon the other bank brighter and more beautiful than he was before he had fallen into the river of pitch. And one of the blessed angels said of the souls who fell: 'These are the souls who, after the end of their mortal lives, had a few trivial faults not entirely washed away, and needed bountiful castigation from a merciful God, that they might be worthily offered unto him.'

Beyond the river he saw, shining with great splendour, walls (*muros*) of astounding length (*longitudinis*) and immeasurable height (*altitudinis*). And the holy angels said: 'This is the holy and renowned city, the heavenly Jerusalem, in which these holy souls will find joy for ever.' He said that these souls and the walls of the glorious city to which they hurried after crossing the river, were resplendent

[70] *Visio S. Pauli*, cc. 43–4. Cf. Silverstein, *Visio Sancti Pauli*, pp. 79–81, 87 and 108, n. 74. On the theme in general see *ibid.*, pp. 126–7; Ntedika, *Évocation de l'Au-delà*, pp. 95–6 and 135; James, *Apocrypha Anecdota* I, 111–12; R. Willard, 'The Address of the Soul to the Body', *PMLA* 50 (1935), 957–83, at 966–73; Silverstein, 'Dante', p. 107; *Vision of St Paul*, ed. Healey, pp. 48–50.

[71] Classical Latin *axillas* (cf. *Ep.* cxv (Tangl, p. 248, line 32)); not 'merely to the ankles' (Kylie).

with such a flood of dazzling light, that the pupils of his eyes were shaken by the exceeding splendour, and he could no longer look upon them.

Jesus's words 'Today thou shalt be with me in Paradise' were believed to imply a provisional paradisal location for the righteous until the final Judgment: 'by this text to the penitent thief', wrote Cassian, 'he shows that the souls of the dead do not lose their senses or their affections like hope and melancholy, joy and fear, and that they begin to experience a foretaste of what they will receive in the Last Judgement'.[72] In one of his homilies Bede teaches that some of the elect await the resurrection in Paradise, while others suffer purgatorial flames and reach this Paradise more slowly, sometimes helped by the prayers of the living.[73] Unfortunately, no early English texts of requiem masses survive, though prayers for the departed were recommended by Theodore of Canterbury and by the Council of *Clofesho* in 747.[74] Yet, in an eighth-century eastern French sacramentary, a requiem mass refers unambiguously to a provisional Paradise in a prayer that the deceased should receive 'remission of all sins, and should rest until the Day of Resurrection in a pleasant place of light (*usque ad resurrectionis diem in lucis amoenitate*)'.[75] That similar prayers were known in England is suggested by a private prayer in the early ninth-century Book of Cerne:

I beg thee, Lord, give me after my death a prosperous journey to reach the gentleness of the everlasting Paradise, and allow me to rest there with the holy souls until the time of the Resurrection (*usque ad tempus resurrectionis*); and afterwards allow me, Father, to have some share of eternal blessedness with the saints and elect and to see thy glorious face for ever, with the blessed and perfect, world without end.[76]

In the Wenlock vision the conception of the provisional *amoenitatis locus* differs from these texts theologically, since the resurrection of the body is ignored: each soul passes in its own time from the provisional Paradise to

---

[72] *Conlationes* I.14 (ed. Petschenig, p. 23; trans. Chadwick, *Western Asceticism*, p. 205). See also Ntedika, *Évocation de l'Au-delà*, pp. 158, 161, 166, 176 and 222.

[73] *Homelia* I.2, ed. Hurst, pp. 12–13.

[74] H&S III, 194 and 373; Willis, *Further Essays*, pp. 208 and 221; Sicard, *Liturgie de la mort*, p. 77.

[75] *Ibid.*, pp. 340, 353–4 and 413, citing the Phillipps Sacramentary.

[76] *Ibid.*, p. 354; *Cerne*, ed. Kuypers, no. 3 = no. 52. For more ambiguous references to the *amoenitas paradisi* in the Worcester prayer books see above, p. 254 and below, p. 288. On this expression see E. Bishop's 'Liturgical Note', *ibid.*, p. 240, and

the heavenly Jerusalem (rather than from purgatorial fire to *provisional* Paradise, as in Bede's homily). One influence here could have been an antiphon sung in funeral processions, which might be understood in terms of a two-stage journey, first to Paradise and then to the Heavenly City:

> In paradisum deducant te angeli,
> in tuo aduentu suscipiant te martyres
> et perducant te in ciuitatem sanctam Hierusalem.[77]

A more certain influence on the celestial geography of the Wenlock vision is the *Visio S. Pauli*. Paul is taken to the Land of Promise, flowing with milk and honey, where righteous souls are sent temporarily (*interim*) after leaving the body; Christ is to reign here during the Millennium. Beyond this *terra repromissionis* is a river called Lake Acherusa, in which St Michael washes the souls of penitent sinners before bringing them to the city of Christ beyond. Paul crosses the river on a golden ship – an episode quoted with disapproval by Aldhelm.[78] On the other side he comes to the city of Christ:

They that dwelt in the city of Christ rejoiced greatly over me as I came unto them, and I entered and saw the city of Christ. [And its light was greater than the light of the air, far greater in quantity and intensity than the light of this world.] And it was all of gold, and twelve walls compassed it about, and there were twelve towers within, and every wall had a furlong between them round about.[79]

Inside, Paul is greeted by patriarchs and prophets, as is the brother of Wenlock in the provisional Paradise.

The *Visio S. Pauli* also influenced Dryhthelm's vision, but the latter differs both from the *Visio S. Pauli* and from the Wenlock vision in that the walled city comes before the Paradisal country, and is not cut off by a river;

Ntedika, *Évocation de l'Au-delà*, p. 172. Cf. Amat, *Songes*, pp. 117–19, 124–8 and 398–401.

[77] 'May angels lead you into Paradise; at your coming may the martyrs receive you and bring you into the holy city of Jerusalem'. See Sicard, *Liturgie de la mort*, pp. 134–5 and 215–20; Ntedika, *Évocation de l'Au-delà*, pp. 163–7 and 257–8.

[78] *Visio S. Pauli*, cc. 21–3; *Aldhelmi Opera*, ed. Ehwald, p. 256. Cf. E. Peterson, 'Die Taufe im Acherusischen See', *Vigiliae Christianae* 9 (1955), 1–20.

[79] *Visio S. Pauli*, c. 23. The added clause is from the St Gallen fragment, ed. Silverstein, *Visio Sancti Pauli*, p. 138. This may have inspired the light in Dryhthelm's vision, though this is a commonplace: see Ciccarese, 'Visio Baronti', p. 46, n. 56, and 'Purgatorio', p. 55, n. 46; Ntedika, *Évocation de l'Au-delà*, pp. 185–93; and Burginda's letter, above, p. 213.

nor is Dryhthelm greeted by a company of men.[80] This shows that the *Visio
S. Pauli*'s influence on the Wenlock vision was not simply via Dryhthelm's
vision. Nevertheless, the latter certainly had its influence on the wording
of the Wenlock vision:

I [Dryhthelm] saw a very great wall (*murum*) in front of us which seemed to be of
endless length (*longitudini*) and height (*altitudini*). I began to wonder why we were
approaching this wall, since I could nowhere see any gate or window or steps to it.
When we had reached the wall we suddenly found ourselves on top of it, by what
means I know not. There was a very broad and pleasant plain, full of such a
fragrance of growing flowers that the marvellous sweetness of the scent quickly
dispelled the foul stench of the gloomy furnace which had hung around me. So
great was the light that flooded all this place that it seemed to be clearer than the
brightness of daylight or the rays of the noontide sun. In this meadow there were
innumerable bands of men in white robes, and many companies of happy people
sat around; as he led me through the midst of the troops of joyful inhabitants, I
began to think that this might perhaps be the kingdom of heaven of which I had
often heard tell. But he answered my thoughts: 'No', he said, 'this is not the
kingdom of heaven as you imagine'.

When we had passed through these abodes of the blessed spirits, I saw in front of
us a much more gracious light than before; and amidst it I heard the sweetest
sound of people singing. So great a fragrance of wonderful scent (*odoris flagrantia
miri*) spread from this place that the scent which I had thought superlative before,
when I savoured it, now seemed to me a very ordinary fragrance; and the wondrous
light which shone over the flowery field, in comparison with the light which now
appeared, seemed feeble and weak. When I began to hope that we should enter this
delightful place, my guide suddenly stood still; and turning round immediately,
he led me back the way we had come.

Lake Acherusa, although it had purgatorial qualities for the souls washed
in it, was not a fiery river. A river of fire appears elsewhere in the *Visio S.
Pauli*, however; moreover, sinners are sunk in it up to (*usque ad*) the knees,
navel, lips, or hair in accordance with the degree of their guilt.[81] Yet there

---

[80] Compare *Visio S. Pauli*, c. 25 etc. and the greetings received by Fursa. For celestial
welcomes see Amat, *Songes*, pp. 393–4. Gregory says that everyone can recognize
everyone else in heaven: *Dialogi* IV.34–5 (ed. de Vogüé III, 112–16), followed by Julian
of Toledo, *Prognosticum* II.24 (ed. Hillgarth, p. 61).

[81] *Visio S. Pauli* c. 31. Graduated immersions are discussed by T. Silverstein, *Visio Sancti
Pauli*, pp. 12–13, and '*Inferno*, XII, 100–126, and the *Visio Karoli Crassi*', *MLN* 51
(1936), 449–52. Cf. also the example in the *Falasha Book of Ezra* (trans. J. Halévy,
Tĕʿĕzâza Sanbat (Commandements du sabbat) (Paris, 1902), p. 180), a work discussed by

is no exact correspondence with the Wenlock *usque ad* sequence, and the important detail of the bridge is missing. The most obvious source for the latter is the bridge leading to Paradise, seen in a vision by a soldier at Rome in 590 and related three years later by Gregory the Great in his *Dialogi*, a work certainly known to Boniface.[82] Gregory's river was not purgatorial and the motif of graduated immersions was absent. Nevertheless, the brother of Wenlock could perhaps have read or heard this well known source and have combined it with the *Visio S. Pauli*'s river;[83] one might compare the case of a dream of Leofric, earl of Mercia, as related in an eleventh-century Worcester manuscript, which was clearly inspired by a memory of Gregory's bridge.[84] On the other hand, a closer analogue occurs in the vision of Sunniulf, abbot of Randan near Clermont-Ferrand (apparently *c.* 571), told by Gregory of Tours:

[Sunniulf] himself used to tell how once he was shown in a vision a certain river of fire, into which men, assembling together on one part of the bank, were plunging like so many bees entering a hive. Some were submerged up to the waist, some up to the armpits (*usque ad ascellas*), some even up to the chin, and all were shouting

Stone, 'Metamorphosis of Ezra', pp. 4–5 and 13–14. From a doctrinal point of view they are equivalent to the river of 'intelligent' fire through which all men pass in, for example, the *Apocalypse of Peter* (James, *Apocryphal New Testament*, pp. 507, 514, 517 and 523); cf. above, n. 50.

82 *Dialogi* IV.37 (ed. de Vogüé III, 130–2). Gregory's story left its traces on the wording of Dryhthelm's vision (e.g. Bede's *hominum albatorum conuenticula*). Plummer, *BOH* II, 297, compares Dryhthelm's provisional Paradise with the *Apocalypse of Peter* but the resemblance is not close; see James, *Apocryphal New Testament*, p. 508. For the fragrance see e.g. I Enoch XXIV–XXV and XXXII, and Amat, *Songes*, pp. 300, n. 224, 398, n. 136, 400, 402 and 468, s.v. *parfum*. On the walled Paradise, cf. Silverstein, 'Dante', pp. 98 and 101–2. According to Tertullian, saints have a provisional location in Paradise, hidden behind 'a sort of wall formed by the fiery zone' (*maceria quadam igneae illius zonae*), while ordinary sinners wait in a lower 'prison': Amat, *Songes*, pp. 118 and n. 5, 150 and 272.

83 Just as in about the eleventh century the bridge was added from Gregory the Great to the graduated immersions passage in Redaction IV of the *Visio S. Pauli* (ed. H. Brandes, *Visio S. Pauli: Ein Beitrag zur Visionslitteratur* (Halle, 1885), p. 76). Cf. T. Silverstein, *Visio Sancti Pauli*, pp. 52, 78 and 97, n. 54, 'Dante', pp. 95–6, 98 and 106, n. 87, and 'The Vision of Saint Paul: New Links and Patterns in the Western Tradition', *AHDLMA* 26 (1959), 199–248, at 218, at 220–1 and 224; *Vision of St. Paul*, ed. Healey, p. 53. (Redaction IV may of course have been influenced by Gregory of Tours and/or Boniface.)

84 'An Old English Vision of Leofric, Earl of Mercia', ed. A. S. Napier, *TPS* 1908, 180–8; H. T. Silverstein, 'The *Vision of Leofric* and Gregory's *Dialogues*', *RES* ns 9 (1933), 186–8.

out that they were being burned very severely. A bridge led over the river, so narrow that only one man could cross at a time, and on the other side was a large house all painted white.

Sunniulf's monks provided the interpretation that anyone who failed to exercise proper discipline would fail to cross the bridge and fall headlong.[85] The immersion *usque ad ascellas* makes it tempting to suppose that this story influenced the Wenlock vision; on the other hand the *Historia Francorum* was not so widely available as the *Dialogi*. In any case, the fact that the two Gregorys almost certainly wrote independently suggests that already in the sixth century stories of the otherworld bridge, which perhaps derived ultimately from the Zoroastrians' Činvat bridge, were circulating orally in the West;[86] the Wenlock visionary may, then, have heard yet another independent account of it.

To sum up: the second part of the vision, describing a journey through heaven and hell, seems to have been inspired principally by the *Visio S. Pauli* and by Hæmgisl's lost account of Dryhthelm's vision, although probably there was also influence from the liturgy and from orally circulating ideas about the topography of the otherworld.

The literary inspiration of the third and final section of the vision is less clear. This is hardly surprising, since it deals with the fate of a number of individuals and the emphasis is prophetic rather than apocalyptic. The fact that Boniface does not transmit the names of the individuals, apart from King Ceolred, probably weakens the force of this section of the visionary's narrative. We can only guess whether Boniface omitted the names of the others because they were local Magonsætan whose names would have meant nothing to his correspondent, Eadburg, or because he wished to protect them.

The first personage to be described was a deceased abbot. His fate is

---

[85] *HF* IV.33.

[86] On the independence of the two see Petersen, *Dialogues*, pp. 76 and 130; D. N. Dumville, 'Towards an Interpretation of *Fís Adamnán*', *Studia Celtica* 12/13 (1977–8), 62–77, at 71–3. Cf. Ciccarese, 'Gregorio di Tours', pp. 261–6, and 'Purgatorio', pp. 46–7. Even as late as the Irish text discussed by Dumville new input from Eastern tradition can perhaps be seen in the detail that the bridge widens for the good and narrows for sinners (cf. Eliade, *Shamanism*, pp. 395 and n. 91 and 482–6). From the eleventh century this detail also appears in manuscripts of the *Visio beati Esdrae*, c. 36 (cf. Charlesworth, *Pseudepigrapha* I, 588, n. 23, and I. P. Culianu, '"Pons subtilis": significato di un simbolo', *Aevum* 53 (1979), 301–12).

decided in 'that assembly' (*illum conuentum*), presumably the assembly of departed souls, angels and demons witnessed earlier. The abbot's fair soul is seized by the demons, but rescued by the angels, supported by a great band of white souls, former members of the abbot's community, who praise his rule. This vaguely recalls the *Visio S. Pauli*, where Paul is praised by the souls of those whom he directed on earth.[87] Finally, an angel, echoing Christ's words at the Day of Judgment (Matthew XXV.41), 'Depart from me, ye cursed, into everlasting fire, prepared for the devil and his angels' ('Discedite a me, maledicti, in ignem aeternum qui paratus est diabolo et angelis eius'), drives the wailing demons into the 'aforesaid' pits of fire, saying: 'Discedite, miserrimi spiritus, in ignem aeternum.' Nevertheless, they soon re-emerge from the 'eternal' fire to take part in the assembly again.

The monk had also been able to see the merits of living people. The virtuous were watched over by guardian angels, but the wicked were accompanied by familiar devils who would persuade them to commit a sin and then immediately report it to their confrères. If his vision still depends on the *Visio S. Pauli* here, this could be a reminiscence of the episode where two groups of guardian angels gather in heaven twice a day to adore God and, respectively, to report the deeds of the good and the sinful;[88] although no *demons* report, that detail is found in an Old English homily which derives from the *Visio S. Pauli*, and is a predictable elaboration and schematization.[89] However, the doctrine that every man is accompanied by a good and bad angel was well known in the West, having been transmitted from the *Shepherd of Hermas* by Cassian and others.[90] For example, in a homily which is extant in Latin and Old English, a demon

---

[87] C. 46. For the motif of the righteous man rescued from demons see e.g. James, *Lost Apocrypha*, pp. 36–8.

[88] *Visio S. Pauli*, cc. 7–10; cf. III Baruch XII–XVI (Charlesworth, *Pseudepigrapha* I, 674–9).

[89] *Wulfstan: Sammlung der ihm zugeschriebenen Homilien*, ed. A. Napier (Berlin, 1883), no. XLVI, p. 233 (cf. no. XLVIII, p. 248); cf. Silverstein, *Visio S. Pauli*, p. 7; *Vision of St. Paul*, ed. Healey, p. 43. For later examples, see 'Les deux chagrins du royaume du ciel', ed. and trans. G. Dottin, *RC* 21 (1900), 349–87, at 380–1; *Selections from Early Middle English*, ed. J. Hall, 2 vols. (Oxford, 1920) I, 34–7; A. B. van Os, *Religious Visions: The Development of the Eschatological Elements in Mediaeval English Religious Literature* (Amsterdam, 1932), p. 249.

[90] Chadwick, *Cassian*, p. 131 and n. 1; P. Dronke, 'St Patrick's Reading', *CMCS* 1 (Summer 1981), 21–38, at 38, n. 39; James, *Testament of Abraham*, p. 14; Milik, '4Q visions', p. 87; Amat, *Songes*, p. 163.

reassures other demons gathered around a deathbed: 'Fear not, he is ours (*nostra est*); I know all his works, I was always with him by day and by night.'[91] The naive dramatization of the Wenlock devils is especially reminiscent of a monastic folktale, told in various forms by Cassian, Gregory the Great, and the *Vitae patrum*, about someone overhearing troops of demons reporting to their chief about their varying success at tempting individuals to sin.[92]

Among the living sinners seen by the Wenlock visionary was a certain girl 'grinding at a mill' (*molentem in mola*). She saw someone else's new sieve, decorated with carvings, found it attractive, and stole it: five hideous demons gleefully reported the theft to the aforementioned assembly. This circumstantial vignette seems to take us to the heart of the realities and values of rural society: but perhaps the visionary was really recalling Christ's vivid prophecy of the *parousia*: 'Two women shall be grinding at the mill; the one shall be taken, and the other left' ('Duae molentes in mola: una assumetur, et una relinquetur').[93] Another unnamed person seen in the vision was clearly no imaginary person, but another monk at Wenlock:

I saw there the sad soul of a brother who had died a short time before. I attended him in his last illness and performed the burial rites; when dying he bade me relying on his word to ask his brother to manumit, for his soul's sake, a slave girl whom they owned in common. But the kinsman, bound by avarice, did not fulfil the request. And with deep sighs the soul kept accusing the unfaithful brother and making bitter complaint.

We may compare the happier case of the two slave boys freed by Lull and his late father, who are mentioned in his letter to Abbess Cyneburg, which I discussed in the previous chapter.[94]

The last individual to be described, prophetically suffering torment, was Ceolred himself, 'who, there is no doubt, was still in the flesh when this vision was seen':

---

91 Pseudo-Augustine, *Sermo lxix ad fratres in eremo*, ed. with other versions in parallel by L. Dudley, 'An Early Homily on the "Body and Soul" Theme', *JEGP* 8 (1909), 225–53, at 228, c. 4.

92 Gregory, *Dialogi* III.7 (ed. de Vogüé II, 280); Cassian, *Conlationes* VIII.16 (ed. Petschenig, p. 232); *Vitae patrum* v.v.39 (PL 73, 885–6).

93 Matt. XXIV.41 (note the influence of XXV.41 above). Cf. C. H. Dodd, *The Parables of the Kingdom*, rev. ed. (London, 1969), p. 66.

94 Cf. above, pp. 117 and 240.

He beheld the king protected against the onslaught of demons by a screen of angels like a great book spread out above him. But the enraged demons kept demanding of the angels that this defence be taken away and that they be permitted to work their cruel will upon him. They imputed to him a multitude of horrible and unspeakable crimes, and threatened that he must be shut in the direst dungeons of hell and there, as his sins merited, be tortured by eternal torments. Whereupon the angels, more disheartened than was their wont, said: 'Alas, that a sinner should not suffer his defence to stand, and that through his own fault we cannot afford him any aid'. And they took away the bulwark from above him. Then the demons with joy and exultation, gathering from all the universe in numbers he thought beyond all men who drew the breath of life, harassed and tore him with infinite tortures.

The simile of the book for the angelic umbrella which protected Ceolred is a vivid reminder of the impact of the book, as object, on the imagination and figural language of early medieval society.[95] There may be some particular influence here from biblical and apocryphal traditions about books of sins and virtues.[96] If so, however, there may have been some confusion (as might well occur in a dream), for one might have expected the king's sins to have filled a large book and the book of his virtues to have been a puny and useless defence. Certainly, that was the case in the vision seen by the thegn of Ceolred's predecessor, Coenred: the thegn found that angels had his good deeds in a beautiful but tiny codex, whereas demons were staggering under the weight of the vast book in which his sins were listed in a hideous script.[97] On the other hand, the visionary (or Boniface) may have been pondering on the scale of the Book of Life in Revelation xx, 'which book, if thought of literally, who could estimate its vastness or length?' – as Augustine had asked.[98]

By an ironic and curious coincidence Wenlock is the only monastery known to have claimed to have received a charter from Ceolred.[99] The vision shows us that even at Wenlock churchmen hated him. The

---

[95] Cf. Curtius, *European Literature*, pp. 310–15, and above, p. 180.

[96] Cf. Sims-Williams, 'Triad', pp. 109–10 and references. The ideas of spiritual defence and the *liber uitae* are loosely coupled in *Cerne*, ed. Kuypers, no. 36, and in early liturgies *chirographa peccatorum/delictorum* are often mentioned, e.g. *Liber sacramentorum Romanae aecclesiae*, ed. Mohlberg, § 848.

[97] *HE* v.13. Cf. Sims-Williams, 'Triad', pp. 80–2 and 109; *Vision of St. Paul*, ed. Healey, p. 44.

[98] *De ciuitate Dei* xx.14 (CCSL 48, 724).   [99] See above, p. 97, n. 39.

contemporary visionary, Guthlac, is also said to have prophesied Ceolred's demise, addressing the exiled Æthelbald:

Not as pillage nor as spoil will a kingdom be given to you, but you will be given it from the hand of the Lord. Wait for him, whose days are spent, for the hand of the Lord oppresses the man whose hope is seated in wickedness, and his days will pass away like a shadow. [100]

This may explain why Æthelbald, in his royal charters, would stress his divine legitimacy, by implied contrast with Ceolred. [101] Many years later, in a letter of warning to Æthelbald in 746×747, Boniface recalled Ceolred's death, and attributed it to the machinations of a familiar demon very like the tempting devils he had described thirty years before in his account of the Wenlock vision:

Ceolred, your venerable Highness's predecessor, feasting in splendour amid his companions was – as those who were present have testified – suddenly in his sin sent mad by a malign spirit, who had enticed him by his persuasion to the audacity of breaking the law of God; so that without repentance and confession, raging and distracted, conversing with devils and cursing the priests of God, he departed this light without a doubt to the torments of hell. [102]

This letter was to be 'preached' to Æthelbald by the priest Herefrith. (The obit of a 'Herefrith man of God' is recorded, ominously enough, in 747.)[103] Here is a further indication that the mentality revealed by the Wenlock monk's vision interacted with the visible, secular world, that it was more than literary diversion. As at Frankish feasts, [104] Anglo-Saxon kings and bishops may have swapped accounts of such visions of their predecessors in hell, each well aware of their symbolism and contemporary implications.

The vision of the monk of Wenlock – as much because of, as despite, its similarities to the visions of Fursa and Dryhthelm and to popular apocrypha like the *Visio S. Pauli* – is an invaluable guide to contemporary conceptions, hopes and fears about death, judgment and the hereafter, and about the omnipresent world of angels, demons and departed souls. Few such visions would have been written down. This one, through the chance that it was taken up and interpreted by Boniface, was disseminated far

[100] *EHD*, p. 774 (*Vita S. Guthlaci*, c. 49). [101] Scharer, 'Intitulationes', pp. 51–4.
[102] Boniface, *Ep.* lxxiii (Tangl, p. 153); *EHD*, no. 177, p. 820.
[103] Boniface, *Ep.* lxxiv (Tangl, pp. 155–6); *EHD*, nos. 5 and 178.
[104] *HF* VIII.5. Cf. Carozzi, 'Géographie de l'Au-delà', pp. 433–4, and above, n. 5.

beyond the kingdom of the Magonsætan and long after Ceolred's demise: indeed, a version of it was still being copied in Italy in the fifteenth century.[105] It allows the modern historian of the Magonsætan to participate in a view of the world in which spirits were often down-to-earth, the unseen was sometimes visible, and the ineffable could be expressed in language.[106]

[105] Levison, 'Bearbeitung', p. 385; Sims-Williams, 'Recension'.
[106] Cf. Carozzi, 'Géographie de l'Au-delà', pp. 424–5.

10

Prayer and magic

According to Ecgberht of York (d. 766), a priest ought to equip himself before his ordination with a psalter, lectionary, antiphonary, missal, baptismal order and martyrology.[1] Only miserable remnants of such books survive, which give little more than glimpses of the public worship of the early Anglo-Saxon church.[2] The surviving fragments of eighth-century Anglo-Saxon sacramentaries suggest that the liturgy then was mainly 'Eighth-century Gelasian' in character, that is, a Gallican modification of Roman usage.[3] The nature of seventh-century worship is scarcely open even to conjecture. It would be wrong, for example, to imagine a simple opposition between 'Roman' influences from Canterbury and 'Irish' influences from Northumbria, for we know that Gregory the Great had encouraged Augustine to be eclectic in his use of the available Roman and Gallican liturgies, and that Northumbria was an influential centre in the dissemination of Roman chant.[4] Churchmen and books were too mobile for simple geographical or ethnic generalizations to be viable. A case in point is Putta, bishop of Rochester, who had learnt the technique of chanting *more Romanorum* from Gregory's disciples: after the destruction of his cathedral in 676 he retired to Mercia and went about giving instruction in church music (*ecclesiae carmina*) wherever he was asked. (Some have supposed that he became bishop of the Magonsætan, which is unlikely.)[5]

---

[1] H&S III, 417; Willis, *Further Essays*, p. 227. On the problem of the authenticity of Ecgberht's *Penitential* cf. Frantzen, *Literature of Penance*, p. 74, and 'Tradition of Penitentials', pp. 30–1; H. Gneuss, 'Liturgical Books in Anglo-Saxon England and their Old English Terminology', in *Learning and Literature*, ed. Gneuss and Lapidge, pp. 91–141, at 96–7.

[2] See Willis, *Further Essays*, pp. 189–243.

[3] Cf. Bullough, 'Alcuin and the Kingdom of Heaven', p. 11, n. 26.

[4] Willis, *Further Essays*, pp. 191–9 and 201–2.   [5] *HE* IV.2 and 12. Cf. above, p. 97.

The area studied in this book was already under a variety of external influences in the seventh century.[6] These probably affected the public worship of the churches, although deductions are difficult. For example, one might imagine that Abbess Berta promoted a Gallican liturgy at Bath; on the other hand, the Roman liturgy was already making progress in Gaul in her day, and the only extant complete manuscript of the 'Old Gelasian' sacramentary was probably copied *c.* 750 at Chelles, one of the Frankish houses with English connections.[7] Again, Colmán, the Irish abbot of Hanbury, may have promoted Irish usages; yet we cannot speculate about what they might have been because the Irish churches were liturgically eclectic.[8] At Malmesbury there is a hint of possible Irish influence (to be connected with Maíldub?) in the fact that Aldhelm agrees with a rare reading in the Stowe Missal when he quotes the Canon of the mass: but is this an Irish emendation of the Roman text or a genuine early reading, conserved in Ireland?[9]

The only surviving liturgical document from the area is an exposition of the mass (incipit 'Primum in ordine . . .') in Oxford, Bodleian Library, Hatton 93 (s. viii/ix), a manuscript of twelfth(?)-century Worcester provenance, which probably originated in that general area, to judge by similarities with manuscripts such as BL, Royal 2. A. xx (discussed below).[10] According to Lowe, it was written 'probably in the same Mercian centre that produced the Salisbury Cathedral Library biblical MS. 117'; but

---

[6] See above, ch. 4.

[7] Bischoff, *Studien* I, 20, 23–4 and 31; U. Ziegler, 'Das Sakramentar Gelasianum Bibl. Vat. Reg. lat. 316 und die Schule von Chelles', *Archiv für Geschichte des Buchwesens* 16 (1976), 2–142.

[8] Warren, ed. Stevenson, *Liturgy and Ritual*.

[9] *Opera*, ed. Ehwald, p. 293; see Willis, *Further Essays*, p. 213.

[10] T. J. Brown, 'Late Antique and Early Anglo-Saxon Books', in *Manuscripts at Oxford: An Exhibition in Memory of Richard William Hunt*, ed. A. C. de la Mare and B. C. Barker-Benfield (Oxford, 1980), pp. 9–14, at 13; cf. *idem*, 'Irish Elements', p. 115. In an oral communication (25 Jan. 1980) Prof. Brown told me that he regarded Hatton 93 as a Worcester, not a south-western manuscript. It is moved firmly into the ninth century by M. P. Brown, 'Bibliothèque Nationale, lat. 10861', pp. 127 and 135, n. 67, and Morrish, 'Dated and Datable Manuscripts' (with facsimile as pl. 2). This is plausible, but there are no fixed palaeographical *comparanda* for taking it very far beyond 800: the Book of Cerne, if its AEDELVALD EPISCOPVS was the bishop of Lichfield, as seems likely, could still be as early as 818, and some relevant late eighth-century charters are not yet proven to be ninth-century forgeries (cf. above, p. 155, n. 61).

the origin of the latter is unknown.[11] The *Expositio missae* in Hatton 93 is not a holograph, for it is full of serious copying errors, especially faulty word-division, such as *ad herode cantatur* for *a clero decantatur*, 39r. Wilmart argued that it probably originated in Carolingian circles; certainly it is found in many continental manuscripts of the ninth century and later, and was employed before 822 by Hrabanus Maurus.[12] It makes some use of Augustine, Cassiodorus and Isidore, but basically seems an original work, intended to educate priests in the literal meaning and significance of the words they uttered in the Roman mass.[13] If the Hatton copy was made at Worcester during the episcopate of Deneberht (799(?)–822), as Wilmart speculated, it gives us some idea of the education which priest-abbots such as Balthun of Kempsey received in the episcopal *familia*.[14]

PRIVATE PRAYER

In contrast to the poor survival of liturgical books, early Anglo-Saxon England is rich in private prayer books. According to Lowe, four survive from the late eighth and early ninth centuries:

R = the Royal Prayer Book (BL, Royal 2. A. XX, s.viii²).
H = the Harley Fragment (BL, Harley 7653 [formerly Add. 5004], s.viii/ix).
N = the Book of Nunnaminster (BL, Harley 2965, s.viii/ix).

[11] *CLA* II, no. 241 (cf. no. 259 and Morrish, 'Dated and Datable Manuscripts', p. 527). B. Bischoff (*apud* D. H. Wright, review of *The Moore Bede*, ed. P. Hunter Blair in *Anglia* 82 (1964), 110–17, at 117) in turn compared the Salisbury fragments with New York, Pierpont Morgan Library, M. 826, a leaf of Bede's *Historia ecclesiastica* (*CLA* XI, no. 1662; *HE*, pp. xlv–xlvi). Is it relevant for the localization of all three manuscripts that the Bede may have belonged to Sæwold, abbot of Bath (Grierson, 'Seiwold', p. 110, n.22)? On Sæwold see above, p. 205. In this connection I have to report that the eleventh-century Saint-Bertin Bede, Boulogne, Bibliothèque Municipale, 103 (on which cf. *HE*, p. lxi and N. Huyghebaert, 'Un moine hagiographe: Drogon de Bergues', *SE* 20 (1971), 191–256, at 210, n. 50), is textually unrelated to the Pierpont Morgan fragment.

[12] Wilmart, 'Traité', and 'Expositio missae', col. 1023; Morrish, 'Dated and Datable Manuscripts', p. 514, n. 11. Hatton 93 corresponds roughly to the text in PL 138, 1173D–1186, but lacks the commentary on the *Pater noster* (col. 1184B–C).

[13] Wilmart, 'Expositio missae', cols. 1017 and 1019–22.

[14] Wilmart, 'Traité', p. 138; cf. above, p. 171. Morrish, 'Dated and Datable Manuscripts', pp. 513–14, has not disproved a broad dating to Deneberht's episcopate; we do not know how 'much time to allow for the transmission of the text from the Continent'.

275

C = the Book of Cerne (Cambridge, University Library, Ll. 1. 10, s. ix).[15]

There must have been many more such books in circulation, judging by the textual variation between some of the prayers in these four. On the Continent comparable private prayer books are not known until the ninth century, and then initially in areas under English influence – as in the case of a series of inter-related Carolingian prayer books which seem to owe their inspiration to Alcuin at Tours, or the so-called Fleury Prayer Book, which was written in Bavaria in 815/20–840.[16] Nothing similar survives from early Ireland, but the English books include some Irish compositions, such as the *Lorica* or 'Breastplate' of Laidcenn (d. *c.* 665); their number may have been exaggerated in the past, partly because of a former misapprehension that H was an Irish manuscript.[17] An indisputably Irish prayer-collection is not found earlier than the small collection of the late ninth or early tenth centuries which was added, probably at St Gallen, to the Graeco-Latin Psalter, Basel, Universitätsbibliothek, A. VII. 3.[18]

[15] These are Lowe's dates: *CLA* II, nos. 215, 204 and 199, and p. xiii. Morrish, 'Dated and Datable Manuscripts', proposes s. viii/ix or s. ix [in] for H (cf. below, n. 34), s. ix[1] for R and N (but see below, n. 103), and *c.* 818–30 for C (cf. above, n. 10). R is printed as an Appendix to Kuypers's edition of C, *The Book of Cerne*; H is printed by Warren, *Antiphonary* II, 83–6; N is edited by Birch, *Nunnaminster*. Various later additions to R are printed by Warren, *Antiphonary* II, 99–102, by Warner and Gilson, *Catalogue* I, 35–6, and by Storms, *Anglo-Saxon Magic*, nos. 37–8, 55, A8 and A11 (his nos. 56–61 belong to the original manuscript, not to the eleventh century as stated).

[16] See *Precum Libelli*, ed. Wilmart, and the so-called 'Officia per Ferias' in BN, lat. 1153 (Saint-Denis, s. ix[med]), printed in PL 101, 509–612 (cf. Wilmart, 'Manuel', pp. 263–5, and Barré, *Prières anciennes*, p. 10); Fleury Prayer Book in PL 101, 1383–1416 (dating by Prof. Bischoff, via Prof. D. A. Bullough). On the continental prayer books and (especially later on) psalters see Wilmart, 'Manuel'; Salmon, 'Livrets' and 'Nouvelle liste'; Bullough, 'Alcuin and the Kingdom of Heaven'. The late eighth-century dates given for some continental *livrets* in Salmon's lists are misleading: the 'collection' (of three prayers!) in Einsiedeln, Stiftsbibliothek, 199, pp. 459–61, is dated s. viii/ix in *CLA* VII, no. 875 (cf. also Barré, *Prières anciennes*, pp. 8, n. 48 and 90), and the two private prayers in Vatican, Palat. lat. 67 are tenth-century additions (cf. Salmon, *Analecta*, pp. 127–8 and 186).

[17] R and H do not contain Laidcenn's *Lorica*, but the opening of a prayer on 18r of R (= C, no. 1) seems to echo it: 'Sanctam ergo unitatem trinitatis iterum atque iterum frequenter flagitans suffragare . . .' The number of certainly Irish prayers is especially exaggerated by Godel, 'Irisches Beten'.

[18] *Psalterium Graeco-Latinum: Codex Basiliensis A. VII. 3*, ed. L. Bieler, Umbrae Codicum Occidentalium 5 (Amsterdam, 1960). Cf. Barré, *Prières anciennes*, pp. 93–5, who notes

The Latin private prayer book may have been a specifically English, or at least Insular, innovation, intended to meet the needs of people to whom Latin was a foreign language, and who could not pray spontaneously as the Fathers had urged. Private prayers in prose were certainly written in antiquity, for many of the Fathers concluded their treatises with them, and some included prayers as models of how to pray; but there seems to be no evidence for early *collections* of such literary prayers. Indeed the Eastern Fathers stressed that private prayers should be kept simple, and that even ascetics who sought to 'pray without cease' should repeat single phrases of humble petition to God.[19]

Eastern ascetical teaching on these *cris de coeur* was conveyed to the West by Cassian: 'We should pray often but shortly. If we dawdle about our prayers, the subtle enemy might be able to sow a seed in our heart.'[20] Ælfric, similarly, recommended praying 'shortly', and according to Kathleen Hughes, who rejects a magical interpretation of the requirement that the Irish *loricae* should be frequently repeated,

the habit of constant and repeated prayer belongs to the very oldest stratum of Celtic Christianity. Patrick, in his fifth-century Confession, tells us: 'My spirit was moved so that in a single day I would say as many as a hundred prayers, and almost as many in a night' [ch. 16]. It is impossible to believe that he did not repeat himself.[21]

The key to the deepest and most perpetual prayer, according to Cassian, was the repetition of the psalm-verse 'O God, make speed to save me: O Lord make haste to help me' ('Deus in adiutorium meum intende; Domine ad adiuuandum me festina', Psalm LXIX. 2 [AV LXX. 1]). Abba Isaac, Cassian's

---

that the contents are not necessarily Irish compositions; by contrast on p. 63 he wrongly describes H as Irish.

19 Hausherr, 'Comment priaient les pères'; Barré, *Prières anciennes*, p. 4; *Athanasius: Life of Antony*, ed. Meyer, p. 108, n. 22. For patristic prayers see A. Hamman, *La prière*, II. *Les trois premiers siècles* (Tournai, 1963), and *Early Christian Prayers*. The most recent survey is in the *Dizionario degli Istituti di Perfezione*, ed. G. Pelliccia and G. Rocca (Rome, 1974–) VII (1983), s.v. 'Preghiera'.

20 *Conlationes* IX. 36 (ed. Petschenig p. 283; trans. Chadwick, *Western Asceticism*, p. 233). Cf. Cassian, *Institutiones* II. 10 (PL 99, col. 99; *Cassian*, trans. Gibson, p. 209 and n. 3). Cf. Hausherr, 'Comment priaient les pères', p. 286.

21 Ælfric, *Catholic Homilies, Second Series*, ed. Godden, pp. 250–1 (quoted by D. G. Bzdyl, 'Prayer in Old English Narratives', *MÆ* 51 (1982), 135–51, at 137); Hughes, 'Irish Influence', p. 53.

interlocutor, praises this formula as an 'impenetrable breastplate (*inpenetrabilis lurica*) and shield' against demons, and exhorts him:

Meditate on it, never stop turning it over within your breast. Whatever work or ministry you are undertaking, go on praying it. While you are going to sleep, or eating, or in the last necessities of nature, think on it. It will be a saving formula in your heart, will guard you from the attacks of demons . . . You should think on it . . . going to bed or rising from bed. You should write it on the doors of your lips, the walls of your house, the sanctuary (*penetrabilibus*) of your breast.[22]

Such a recommendation, endorsed by Cassiodorus and St Benedict, led to the verse being institutionalized in the public Offices of the Church.[23] Columbanus, for example, prescribed that all his monks, at the end of every psalm, should say it silently at all the Offices of day and night, kneeling 'with equanimity' – an insistence which 'testifies to the difficulty experienced in carrying it out', as Curran remarks: 'at the long morning vigil on Saturday and Sunday mornings this practice would have entailed seventy-five genuflexions'.[24] Columbanus himself is said to have uttered it to ward off an attack by wolves.[25]

It may have been Cassian's praise of the *inpenetrabilis lurica* that led the Irish church to adopt the metaphor of the *lorica/lurica* as a term for a protective prayer,[26] as for instance when Blathmac ends his eighth-century poem to the Virgin:

> Cech oen diamba figel se
> fo lige ocus éirge

[22] *Conlationes* x.10 (ed. Petschenig, pp. 298 and 302; trans. Chadwick, *Western Asceticism*, pp. 240 and 242). Cf. Hausherr, 'Comment priaient les pères', p. 285.

[23] Chadwick, *Cassian*, pp. 172, 183 and 201. It is an antecedent of the 'Jesus Prayer' of the later Eastern church: *ibid.*, p. 143, n. 1; Cross and Livingstone, *Dictionary of the Christian Church*, s.vv. 'Hesychasm' and 'Jesus Prayer'.

[24] *Columbani Opera*, ed. Walker, p. 158; Curran, *Antiphonary of Bangor*, pp. 168 and 178. Cf. Chadwick, *Cassian*, p. 201.

[25] *Vita S. Columbani* 1.8, ed. B. Krusch, 'Vitae Columbani Abbatis Discipulorumque eius Libri Duo Auctore Iona', MGH, SS. rer. Merov. 4 (Hannover and Leipzig, 1902), 1–152, at 74.

[26] Cf. Barré, *Prières anciennes*, p. 4, n. 20. On the other hand Gougaud, 'Étude sur les *loricae*', pp. 265 and 277, speculated that the term arose from the habit of asking Christ, the Cross or an angel to be a *lorica* for the soul (e.g. below, p. 286). On *loricae* see also Godel, 'Irisches Beten', pp. 293–306; Herren, *Hisperica Famina* II, 23–31; and T. D. Hill, 'Invocation of the Trinity and the Tradition of the *Lorica* in Old English Poetry', *Speculum* 56 (1981), 259–67. Franz, *Benediktionen* II, 270, saw them as prototypes for later Western protective prayers.

ar imdídnad diänim tall
amail *lúirech* co cathbarr;

Cách nod-géba do cach deilb
i troscud aidchi Sathairnn
acht rob fo déraib cen meth,
a Maire, níb ifernach. [27]

While the image of the 'breastplate of righteousness' (*lorica iustitiae*) had been used by St Paul in his injunction to Christians to put on the armour of God (Thess. v.8; Ephes. vi.11–18; cf. Isaiah LIX.17), Paul did not specifically equate that armour with prayers. Such an interpretation is already clear, however, in a letter Columbanus sent to his disciples at Luxeuil in 610:

And do not hope that it is men alone who persecute you; there are devils in those who envy your possessions; against them take up that armour of God to which the apostle points, and make a path to heaven, hurling those arrows, as it were, of earnest prayer. [28]

The extant Irish and Irish-inspired loricae are mostly prolix, yet nevertheless retain the iterative character and protective intention of Cassian's psalmodic *inpenetrabilis lurica*.

WORCESTER AND THE ROYAL PRAYER BOOK AND HARLEY FRAGMENT

Perhaps it was the writing down of *loricae* in seventh-century Ireland that paved the way for the compilation and composition in eighth- and ninth-century England of the more varied private prayer books such as R, H, N and C. Of these prayer books, R and H – possibly the earliest of their kind in Europe – can be connected with the Hwicce. The Royal Prayer Book (R) belonged *c.* 1649 to the antiquary John Theyer, of Cooper's Hill, Brockworth, near Gloucester. [29] It was probably one of the books which

---

[27] *The Poems of Blathmac son of Cú Brettan*, ed. and trans. J. Carney, Irish Texts Society 47 (London, 1964), 48–9: 'Everyone who has this as a vigil-prayer at lying down and at rising for unblemished protection in the next world like a *breast-plate* with helmet; everyone, whatever he be, who shall say it fasting on Friday night, provided only that it be with copious tears, Mary, may he not be for Hell.'

[28] *Ep.* iv.2, ed. and trans. Walker, *Columbani Opera*, pp. 26–7.

[29] See Warner and Gilson, *Catalogue* I, 33 and 36.

Theyer acquired from Worcester Cathedral Library: Ker noted that the script of a twelfth-century addition on the final leaf (fol. 52) indicated Worcester provenance, and identified it with the 'Precationes quædam charactere saxonico 4to' in the 1622/3 Cathedral Library catalogue.[30] The prominence of St Benedict in marginal collects added by 'one hand, perhaps of the 10th cent.' suggests that it belonged to a reformed house like Worcester at that time, and the language of its Old English glosses (s. x^1) is Mercian. All these indications would suit Worcester provenance.[31] In fact R probably also originated in or near Worcester. Its hands were regarded as Mercian by Lowe, and T. J. Brown specifically compared the gospel fragment, Worcester, Cathedral Library, Add. 1.[32] Most unusually, R includes a prayer by an author with the Old Welsh name *Moucan*, implying western influence, and a metrical creed by a certain *Cuð*, an English name only otherwise attested in a collection of epigrams owned by Milred, bishop of Worcester in the third quarter of the eighth century.[33]

Ker made the interesting, if unprovable, suggestion that three lost leaves once appended to BL, Cotton Otho A.viii, may have been detached from R.[34] According to Smith and Wanley, the leaves contained: *Versus exametri et pentametri de Apostolis omnibus* (perhaps identical with the *Ymnum de apostolis* in C, no. 71);[35] *Oratio in Hebdomada majori, feria quarta*; an *Oratio Gregorii Papae*, glossed in Old English; and an *Oratio Bedae presbyteri uersibus hexametris*. Ker noted that a connection with R was supported both by the Mercian dialect of the gloss and by Wanley's description of the codex as 'in

---

30 Ker, *Catalogue*, no. 248; *Catalogus*, ed. Atkins and Ker, pp. 18, 55 and 67.

31 Warner and Gilson, *Catalogue* I, 35 (see 10v, 13v, 16r and 30v; cf. Warren, *Antiphonary* II, 99–100); A. Campbell in *Vespasian Psalter*, ed. Wright, pp. 88–9; Dumville, 'English Square Minuscule', p. 149, n. 6.

32 *CLA* II, xix and no. 215; Brown, unpublished Lyell Lectures. See above p. 181.

33 See below, pp. 321, n. 201 and 358.

34 Ker, *Catalogue*, no. 169; cf. *The Old English Life of Machutus*, ed. D. Yerkes (Toronto, 1984), pp. xxvii–xxx. In an unpublished communication to Sir Ivor Atkins of 18 May 1943 (bound in the Worcester Cathedral Library copy of Atkins and Ker, *Catalogus*, facing p. 67), Ker writes: 'There is absolutely no evidence, but it doesn't seem impossible that [H] is a detached fragment of [R]. I am pretty certain that some leaves at the end of Otho A. viii came from the Royal ms. too ... but it must be clearly understood that there is no decent proof [of either suggestion].' On the other hand, according to Morrish, 'Dated and Datable Manuscripts', p. 526, 'features in the palaeography' of H 'lack the maturity apparent in' R. H is perhaps too fragmentary for a fair comparison.

35 Cf. Ker, *Catalogue*, no. 169; Meyer, 'Poetische Nachlese', pp. 607–13.

quarto' and of the script of the *Oratio Gregorii* as 'litteris Saxonicis ualde antiquis'. To these arguments it may be added that R has lost leaves before and after fol. 39, which begins with an acephalous prayer in elegiacs, attributed by the Fleury Prayer Book (the only other copy) to Bede (*Oratio Bedae presbiteri*), and continues with a paraphrase in elegiacs of Psalm LXXXIII (AV LXXXIV), probably also by Bede;[36] thus R seems to have included verse-prayers by Bede, like the Otho fragment. Furthermore the so-called *Oratio Gregorii* (incipit 'Dominator dominus deus omnipotens') recurs in numerous early medieval prayer books, including C and N,[37] so one might expect it to have appeared in R in its complete form.

The Harley Fragment (H) probably has an origin similar to that of R. Although its format is slightly smaller and the hand is not identical with any of the hands of R, its seven leaves may conceivably be a stray gathering from R, written by a further scribe. At any rate they may have been bound or shelved with R at an early date: H contains not only a vernacular gloss, 'perhaps in the same hand' as the early tenth-century glosses in R, but also a spidery Y-like mark at the beginning of a prayer (a prayer also found on fol. 22 of R), which closely resembles such marks in similar ink towards the end of R.[38]

The fact that two prayers in R recur in H, with considerable textual differences, is not incompatible with R and H forming a single collection, for such duplication can be seen within the Book of Cerne as well, presumably as a result of mechanical compilation from several sources.[39] Mechanical compilation could also explain the fact that the prayers in H, unlike those in R, have been partially adapted for the use of a woman (*famula*), for a similar inconsistency of gender occurs in N.[40] Moreover,

---

[36] *Ibid.*, pp. 614–19; PL 101, 1397; *Bedae Opera Rhythmica*, ed. Fraipont, pp. 445–6 and 449, nos. XV and XVII. The Otho *Bedae presbyteri oratio* may have been one or other of Bede's hexameter psalm paraphrases (*ibid.*, nos. XVI and XVIII), of which one is included in the Book of Cerne (see below, p. 333). A facsimile of R, 39r is given by Morrish, 'Dated and Datable Manuscripts', plate 6.

[37] Sims-Williams, 'Ephrem', p. 210, n. 25; *Pre-Conquest Prayer Book*, ed. Muir, no. 24.

[38] *CLA* II, nos. 204 and 215; Ker, *Catalogue*, no. 244. Cf. above, n. 34.

[39] R fol. 20 = H 4v–5v, and R fol. 22 = H 2v–3v (the latter certainly from a different textual tradition, cf. Wilmart, 'Manuel', p. 275, n. 3); C, nos. 3 = 52 and 30 = 69, cf. p. xiv.

[40] *Nunnaminster*, ed. Birch, pp. 15–17. Cf. Ker, *Catalogue*, no. 244. It may be worth noting that where C (no. 1, p. 82) reads 'conseruare uirginitatem meam', R (19r) has simply 'conseruare me'.

although the masculine gender is used in R, the prominence of charms to ease bleeding that refer to Christ's healing of Beronice (the woman afflicted by the flux of blood) suggests that some of its material was drawn from a compilation made for female use. A double monastery would be an obvious context.

Nevertheless, these arguments for the unity of R and H are perhaps special pleading, and it is more likely that they are independent instances of a once common type of codex which came to be preserved together, at least by the tenth century, probably at Worcester.

DAILY DEVOTION, HEALING AND MAGIC

Unlike the Book of Cerne, which began with a (now acephalous) Old English guide to morning devotions, R and H lack any indication of how their contents should be used. For parallels we may best turn to the Carolingian prayer books which include brief treatises on how to sanctify the day, from the moment of waking, by private prayer and psalmody, evidently in imitation of the Divine Office.[41] (These ninth-century continental treatises seem more relevant to R and H than does the morning office of similar date in the Irish Book of Mulling.) For instance, the order of prayer in a mid-ninth-century Tours prayer book[42] begins: 'as soon as you arise from your bed, make the sign of the cross on your forehead and breast and say: *Auxiliatrix esto mihi Trinitas sancta*' – this is a prayer first attested in R[43] – 'and then *Domine Deus in nomine tuo leuabo manus meas*' – a prayer which Alcuin recommended Charlemagne to say 'when you arise from your bed'.[44] It continues with prayers for use when 'approaching the church door' and then 'prostrate before the altar', which suggests that it was intended for clerics, or for laymen with easy access to a church. The more primitive-looking *Commemoratio de ordine quotidianae orationis* in the Fleury Prayer Book[45] specifies recitation, from the moment of waking, of psalm-verses (including the *Deus in adiutorium meum intende . . .* , with triple

---

[41] A. Wilmart, 'Manuel', p. 263, n. 3, and 'Lettres de l'époque carolingienne', *RB* 34 (1922), 234–45, at 240–2. For the Mulling office see Nees, 'Colophon Drawing', pp. 86–7.

[42] *Precum Libelli*, ed. Wilmart, pp. 68–75.

[43] 46r; cf. Barré, *Prières anciennes*, pp. 64 and 92, on the mistaken title 'Oratio sanctae Mariae'.

[44] Duemmler, *Ep.* ccciv; re-ed. Wilmart, *Precum Libelli*, pp. 33–6.

[45] PL 101, 1412–13.

genuflection),[46] prayers and canticles, such as the *Gloria in excelsis*, *Pater noster*, *Christe audi nos* (the Litany of the Saints),[47] and *Credo in Deum*, all of which are included in R. More unusually, the *Commemoratio* specifies a ritual which involves signing all the bodily members with the cross and concludes with a prayer to the cross: *Crux mihi refugium*. This ritual helps to explain a *lorica*-like prayer in R (45v) which invokes the protection of the cross on the members in turn.[48] In fact, it supports Dom Gougaud's

[46] Cf. *Precum Libelli*, pp. 49 and 73. See above, p. 278.

[47] The text given at PL 101, 1391–5, was re-edited by M. Coens, 'Les litanies bavaroises du "libellus precum" dit de Fleury (Orléans MS. 184)', *AB* 77 (1959), 373–91. For English litanies see M. Lapidge, 'Litanies of the Saints in Anglo-Saxon Manuscripts: A Preliminary List', *Scriptorium* 40 (1986), 264–77. Bishop, *Liturgica*, pp. 137–64, showed that the framework of the Litany of the Saints probably originated in Greek in papal circles in the late seventh century (cf. Barré, *Prières anciennes*, p. 37; Badcock, 'Anatolian Prayer Book'; Lapidge, 'Theodore and Hadrian', pp. 49 and 51). Bishop (followed by Kantorowicz, *Laudes*, p. 35) also argued that the Greek and Latin texts reached England early and were disseminated on the Continent through Insular channels, chiefly on account of the Greek text occurring in the so-called 'Athelstan Psalter' (an addition, s. x[med]: Keynes, 'Athelstan's Books', p. 194) and Latin texts of this framework appearing early in England (in R fol. 26, which Bishop (p. 147) mis-dated s. viii[in]) and in Ireland (*Stowe Missal*, ed. Warner, fols. 12 and 30, and its lost congener at Fulda, ed. Pralle, 'Keltisches Missale', pp. 19–20; to this Irish evidence add St Gallen, Stiftsbibliothek, 1395, p. 427 (s. viii[2]), in J. Duft and P. Meyer, *The Irish Miniatures of the Abbey Library of St. Gall* (Olten-Berne-Lausanne, 1954), p. 76 and pl. XXVII). This picture is complicated both by the existence of bilingual texts on the Continent, emanating from St Gallen (notably St Gallen, Stiftsbibliothek, 17 (s. ix[2]), ed. P. Cagin, *L'euchologie latine étudiée dans la tradition de ses formules et de ses formulaires*, I. '*Te Deum*' ou '*Illatio*'? (Solesmes, 1906), pp. 501–5), and by the fact that the earliest continental Latin versions, at the end of the eighth century, are not really much later than R: *Gellonensis*, ed. Dumas and Deshusses I, §2313; *Ordines*, ed. Andrieu III, 249 (from a prototype of *c*. 770–90 according to Vogel, *Introduction*, pp. 123 and 145–7); *Die Glossen des Psalters von Mondsee*, ed. F. Unterkircher (Freiburg, Switz., 1974), pp. 508–12; *Palimpsest-Studien*, II. *Altertümliche Sakramentar- und Litanei-Fragmente im Cod. Lat. Monac. 6333*, ed. A. Dold (Beuron, 1957), p. 88*. See also Coens, 'Anciennes litanies', p. 8; below, n. 75; and the careless synthesis by A. Knopp, 'Sanctorum Nomina Seriatim: Die Anfänge der Allerheiligenlitanei und ihre Verbindung mit den "Laudes Regiae"', *Römische Quartalschrift für christliche Altertumskunde und Kirchengeschichte* 65 (1970), 185–231 (cf. below, n. 88). Nevertheless, there *are* early Anglo-Saxon references to the Litany of the Saints in the *Vita S. Gregorii*, c. 32 (ed. Colgrave, p. 138), and in the 747 Council of *Clofesho* (H&S III, 368). The Greek *Sanctus* and *Agnus Dei* in R 18v (see below, n. 170) and 29*r, are later (s. x?) additions. Cf. Bischoff, *Studien* II, 262–3 and references.

[48] On this prayer see Sims-Williams, 'Triad', pp. 90–1, and above, p. 54. For 'Crux mihi refugium' see Wilmart, 'Croix', p. 38, n. 7; *Precum Libelli*, ed. Wilmart, p. 55.

suggestion that each named member was signed with the cross in the recitation of *loricae* like that of Mugrón, which is apparently a tenth-century Irish translation of the prayer in R, 45v.[49] Compare, too, a medieval Welsh poem echoing the *lorica* tradition:

> Kyntaw geir a dywedaw
> y bore ban kyuodaw:
> 'croes Crist in wissc ymdanaw'.[50]

Another prayer, found in R, fol. 22 and H, 2v–3v, begins '*In the morning when I rise*, make haste to help me, O lord . . .' ('*Mane cum surrexero*, intende ad me, Domine . . .') in R, where, as in later books, it is entitled 'morning prayer'.[51] In the Book of Cerne and in the early ninth-century Troyes Prayer Book (from Tours) this morning prayer is combined with an Irish (?) hymn that also occurs in R, 25r as *Oratio matutina*; this hymn begins:

> Ambulemus in prosperis
> huius diei luminis
> in uirtute altissimi
> Dei deorum maxim[i].[52]

Under the heading *Oratio*, H contains what might be, but for the singular verbs, a companion evening hymn, in the same metre (fol. 7):

> In pace Christi dormiam
> ut nullum malum uideam

[49] Gougaud, 'Étude sur les *loricae*', p. 109. Cf. Storms, *Anglo-Saxon Magic*, pp. 222 and 226.

[50] Sims-Williams, 'Triad', p. 101, n. 135: 'The first word I say in the morning when I rise [is] "Christ's Cross [is] a garment (*lorica?*) around me".'

[51] See *ibid.*, p. 100, nn. 133–4, for references to other versions (cf. above, n. 39), to which add *Pre-Conquest Prayer Book*, ed. Muir, no. 67. A metrical adaptation is edited by W. Meyer, 'Drei Gothaer Rythmen aus dem Kreise des Alkuin', *Nachrichten von der kgl. Gesellschaft der Wissenschaften zu Göttingen*, Philol.-hist. Kl., 1916, 645–82, at 664–7 and 674–9.

[52] 'Let us walk in the good fortune of the light of this day, in the strength of the highest and greatest God of gods.' Cf. C, no. 7; *Precum Libelli*, ed. Wilmart, p. 11; *Irisch-keltische Hymnodie*, ed. Blume, no. 224. On this hymn cf. Sims-Williams, 'Triad', p. 101. It is reworked as the second part of an *Oratio pro iter agentibus* in the Fleury Prayer Book (PL 101, 1414); cf. W. Meyer, 'Gildae Oratio Rythmica', *Nachrichten von der kgl. Gesellschaft der Wissenschaften zu Göttingen*, Philol.-hist. Kl., 1912, 48–108, at 81, no. 29. For the first part see *ibid.*, p. 74, no. 4, and Wilmart, 'Manuel', p. 293, n. 4. Its use as a *Reisegebet* may be due to a literal interpretation of *ambulare*, a common metaphor in the Psalms.

a malis uisionibus
in noctibus nocentibus;
sed uisionem uideam
diuinam ac propheticam . . .

The only other copy of the latter hymn is in the fifteenth-century Irish Leabhar Breac; this, and the invocation of SS Patricius and Cyricius, suggest an Irish origin.[53]

Such texts clearly reflect the themes of such communal daily prayers as the *Orationes matutinales et uespertinales* in an eighth-century southern English liturgical fragment:

Exurgentes de cubilibus nostris *auxilium* gratiae tuae *matutinis*, domine, praecibus imploremus: ut discussis tenebris uitiorum *ambulare* mereamur in luce uirtutum: per dominum nostrum.[54]

It is likely, then, that some of the prayers in R and H were originally designed for use in a daily round of prayer, as recommended in the Carolingian prayer books. Nevertheless, they are not arranged in the manuscripts with this in mind; for instance in R the *Ambulemus in prosperis* is *preceded* by a prayer apparently intended to be said before receiving communion (24v).[55]

Unlike N and C and some of the Carolingian prayer collections, R and H show no clear plan and appear to be devotional miscellanies. Yet one theme recurs too often to be coincidental, and distinguishes them from the continental books: alongside prayers of considerable theological and literary sophistication, as advanced as anything in the Carolingian collections, R and H return again and again to the theme of protection against

---

53 'May I sleep in the peace of Christ, so that I see no evil from evil visions that bring harm by nights; but may I see a divine and prophetic dream . . .': *Irisch-keltische Hymnodie*, ed. Blume, no. 225. See Warren, *Antiphonary* II, 86 and 91–2; *Irish Litanies*, ed. Plummer, pp. 34 and 112. *Curig* was also culted in Wales, however: *DP* I, 143, n. 1.

54 'Rising from our beds, Lord, we pray for the aid of the grace of thy morning, so that, with the shadows of sins scattered, we may be worthy to walk in the light of virtues, through our Lord': BL, Add. 37518, 116r (s. viii¹), ed. Mohlberg, *Liber sacramentorum Romanae aecclesiae*, p. 267. Cf. Bullough, 'Alcuin and the Kingdom of Heaven', p. 11, n. 26.

55 The last third of the 'Oratio sancti Augustini episcopi' translated below, p. 311. Cf. *The Prayers and Meditations of St Anselm*, trans. B. Ward (Harmondsworth, 1973), pp. 30 and 100–1.

illness, death and supernatural adversity. The books themselves, as physical objects, may even have had a prophylactic function.

This aspect is clearest in the case of H. The fragment opens with an acephalous invocation of angels ('. . . be health to me, Cherubim be strength to me, Seraphin be salvation and armour to me . . . '), asking them to pray for a woman (*me Dei famula*) 'so that no unclean spirit nor adversary may ever harm me'. This is a version of a prayer ('Gabriel be a breastplate (*lurica*) to me . . . ') found only in C (no. 54) and the pseudo-Bedan *Collectanea* (Oratio v).[56] It is a *lorica* for the living; but it would also recall the angels' role as psychopomps for the dying – as in the experience of the monk of Wenlock. Thus the coffin of St Cuthbert (d. 698) was inscribed with drawings of the apostles (given in the order of the Canon of the Roman mass, as too in the litany which follows in H) and of seven named archangels. One of the latter was [R]VMIA[EL], a name found, in the West, only in Insular sources and in a mass for the dead in an eighth-century northern French manuscript (Paris, Bibliothèque Nationale, lat. 256):

Accept, Lord, the soul of this thy servant *N*. May thy seven angels stand by him. May Raphael be health to him. May Racuel be a helper to him. From all the arts of the devil may he be unafraid. May Michael be a shield of justice to him. May Rumiel be a helper to him. May Saltyel be a protector to him. May Danail be health to him. Deliver (*libera*), Lord, the soul of thy servant *N*. as (*sicut*) thou didst deliver the Israelites from Mount Gibeon, and Jonah from the belly of the whale and Daniel from the lions' den . . .[57]

Such invocations were regarded as unorthodox in Rome by the time H was copied: a synod which investigated a Frank, Aldebert, and an Irishman, Clemens, in 745 had condemned the former for composing a prayer invoking non-scriptural archangels – 'or rather demons'.[58]

[56] PL 94, 561–2 (Oratio v). On the *Collectanea* see below, p. 335, n. 29.

[57] *Missale Gallicanum Vetus*, ed. Mohlberg, pp. 97 and 167. See Sims-Williams, 'Anglo-Latin Letter', p. 13, and nn. 104–5; further, F. Combaluzier, 'Fragments de messe pro defuncto (VIIIème siècle)', *EL* 69 (1955), 31–5; Sicard, *Liturgie de la mort*, pp. 295–301; Ntedika, *Évocation de l'Au-delà*, pp. 78–80; Willard, *Two Apocrypha*, pp. 10–11; McNally, *Irische Liber de numeris*, pp. 126–7; J. Carey, 'Angelology in *Saltair na Rann*', *Celtica* 19 (1987), 1–8, at 6–7; Herren, *Hisperica Famina* II, 30 and 47; Dronke, 'Leiden Love-Spell', p. 67, n. 14. For *Saltyel* and *Danail* see E. Peterson, 'Engel- und Dämonennamen: Nomina barbara', *Rheinisches Museum für Philologie* 75 (1926), 393–421, at 400 and 413. For Eastern attestations of *Rumiel* see G. Davidson, *A Dictionary of Angels* (New York, 1967), p. 248.

[58] *Ep.* lix (Tangl, p. 117).

H continues with a litany calling upon David, Elijah, Moses, the apostles and numerous women saints to 'preserve my soul and spirit and heart and sense and all my flesh'. Further invocations begin on fol. 2, introducing a series of four charm-like texts, among which a misplaced rubric is embedded:

Whosoever has this writing with him will be frightened neither by nightly nor by noonday fear.

The first of the four texts calls for the collapse of 'my enemies through these angels . . . just as (*sicut*) Goliath collapsed before thy boy David', the second is directed against the malice of spirits and men, the third is a prayer lest 'Egyptians' do bodily harm to God's male and female servants 'by sea or river, in food or drink, in sleep or awake', and the fourth is a *Libera me* addressed to God. Evocation of Old Testament paradigms with *sicut* formulae goes back to Jewish and early Christian antiquity.[59] The martyrs, like Juliana in the Italian *Passio* known to Bede and Cynewulf, call for liberation upon God,

who didst place thy servant Moses in Egypt, and didst save him from the hand of Pharoah, and didst lead thy people through the Red Sea . . . , and didst prostrate the giant Goliath through the hands of thy servant David . . .[60]

The paradigms occurred, too, in the Pseudo-Cyprianic Prayers,[61] which spawned numerous exorcisms and magical texts, for example:

you [the Devil] were destroyed by the Egyptians' plagues, you were drowned in the

---

[59] See especially L. Gougaud, 'Étude sur les "Ordines Commendationis Animae"', *EL* 19 (1935), 3–27; P. Lundberg, *La typologie baptismale dans l'ancienne Église* (Uppsala, 1942), pp. 33–63; Franz, *Benediktionen* II, 393–8; Ntedika, *Évocation de l'Au-delà*, pp. 72–83; Sicard, *Liturgie de la mort*, pp. 300 and 361–72. A well-known but late example is the so-called *Oratio S. Brendani*, edited and discussed by Salmon *et al.*, *Testimonia*, pp. vii–xxxviii and 1–31.

[60] *Passio S. Iulianae Nicomediae*, in *Acta Sanctorum*, Feb. II, pp. 877–8. Cf. Dekkers and Gaar, *Clavis*, no. 2201; J. Wittig, 'Figural Narrative in Cynewulf's *Juliana*', *ASE* 4 (1975), 37–55, at 43, n. 3, and 52. This sixth- or seventh-century text is cited by Ntedika, *Évocation de l'Au-delà*, pp. 75–6; the similar Prayer of Severus, cited *ibid.*, p. 75, is much earlier: see *Early Christian Prayers*, ed. Hamman, no. 82.

[61] *Ibid.*, nos. 241–2; Dekkers and Gaar, *Clavis*, no. 67, Appendix. For their transmission in ninth-century prayer books (see PL 101, 567–9) see Wilmart, 'Manuel', p. 281 and n. 1.

person of Pharaoh, were destroyed in Jericho . . . , were beheaded by David in the person of Goliath . . .[62]

From the eighth century onwards *Libera . . . sicut . . .* formulae appear in the liturgy of the dead: the earliest example was quoted above from BN, lat. 256, but a version closer to H occurs in a liturgical *Oratio pro defunctis* which passed into the ninth-century continental private prayer books:

Liberate (*libera*), Lord, the soul of thy servant *N.*, just as (*sicut*) thou didst liberate the people of Israel from the hand of the Egyptians . . . , just as thou didst liberate David from the hand of the giant Goliath . . .[63]

In eighth-century liturgies death was commonly identified with the Exodus from Egypt.[64] Thus the charm-like texts in H might give protection at the hour of death as well as in daily life.

Towards the bottom of 2v of H a large initial marks the start of *Mecum esto sabaoth, mane cum surrexero*, the already mentioned 'morning prayer' of R. In view of the semi-magical context, it is interesting to note that this prayer, as arranged in H, asks God to preserve the feet, hands, mouth, ears and eyes (in that ascending order) – although ostensibly this is so that they may act virtuously and avoid sin, which sets the prayer apart from a charm or *lorica*.[65]

Another large capital at the top of 4r marks the start of a simple prayer of invocation, which also occurs in C (no. 29). The beginning in H, 'Pater et filius et spiritus sanctus *illa sancta trinitas esto mihi adiutrix*', seems to be contaminated by the prayer *Auxiliatrix esto mihi sancta Trinitas*, which is found in R, 46r and is recommended for morning use in the Tours prayer book discussed above. The main interest of the prayer is eschatological. The writer prays that the archangels will take him (or her) to Paradise:

I beseech holy and glorious Michael, Raphael and Uriel, Gabriel and Raguel, Heremiel and Azael, that they take my soul on the Latter Day (*in nouissimo die*, cf. Job XIX.25, John VI.44) with a choir of angels and lead it to the pleasance of paradise (*amoenitatem paradisi*).[66]

---

[62] *Missale Gallicanum Vetus*, ed. Mohlberg, §61.

[63] PL 101, 1390 (Fleury Prayer Book); cf. *ibid.*, col. 552 ('Officia per Ferias'); Sicard, *Liturgie de la mort*, pp. 366–7.

[64] *Ibid.*, pp. 309 and 373.   [65] See above, pp. 256 and 284, and below, p. 324.

[66] The version in C (no. 29) omits the more dubious archangels. Compare R, 18r (= C, no. 1): 'Rogo sanctum Michaelem archangelum et gloriosum qui ad custodiendas animas potestatem accipit ut animam meam suscipere dignetur a corpore meo exituram, atque

He then requests the Apostles' help on the Day of Judgment so that 'my joyful soul may see the pure Divinity'. The wording recalls the liturgy of the dead, while the conception of the afterlife recalls the vision of the monk of Wenlock.[67]

The title 'INCIPIT ORATIO' (H, 4v) introduces a sophisticated meditation on the text *Trahe me post te* from the Song of Songs, found more fully in R (fols. 20–1), and this is followed by a unique prayer, under the heading 'IN NOMINE DEI SUMMI',[68] which similarly touches on the theme of the 'fire of God's love' (*amoris tui ardor*). This runs into a shortened text of the *Te Deum*, of Irish type.[69]

The theme of death and judgment returns after the *Te Deum*. A prayer beginning 'Deus altissime . . .' (6v–7r) is excerpted from the conclusion of the treatise *De poenitentia* attributed to Ephrem the Syrian, in which 'Ephrem' pleads for mercy when he – or rather 'she', for the text is adapted for a woman – shall come before the heavenly host to be judged.[70] The 'ORATIO' which follows is the evening hymn *In pace Christi dormiam*, discussed above. Since 'In pace . . . dormiam' (Psalm IV.9) was a common metaphor for death[71] it is natural that the hymn ends with a prayer that the soul 'leaving the body' should not be left in hell. The final item, 'ORATIO SANCTI IOHANNIS', which breaks off at the foot of 7v, is the prayer 'Open the door of life to me as I knock', attributed to St John in his apocryphal *Acta*; dying, St John asks that he should not meet the Prince of Darkness, but should feast again at Christ's table.[72]

---

in amoenitatem paradisi perducere ac ibi conlocare in requiem beatorum spiritum.' Similar addresses to Michael recur in C, no. 18 (p. 113), in PL 101, 477 (cf. Wilmart, 'Manuel', p. 271, n. 8), in 'Fragmenta Liturgica I', ed. K. Gamber, *SE* 16 (1965), 428–54, at 453, and in the unpublished Würzburg Psalter: Oxford, Bodleian Library, Laud lat. 96 (Tegernsee, s. xi²), 242r. See also above, p. 286.

[67] See above, p. 263.

[68] Cf. R, 46r. An Irish symptom according to Warren, *Antiphonary* II, 35 and 87, but the invocation occurs, for instance, in the *Penintanham* and Acton charters (S 1177 and S 85) and elsewhere; cf. Scharer, *Königsurkunde*, p. 174, n. 68; E. Okasha, 'The Non-Ogam Inscriptions of Pictland', *CMCS* 9 (Summer 1985), 43–69, at 58; Storms, *Anglo-Saxon Magic*, p. 270; etc.

[69] Cf. Warren, *Antiphonary* II, 92–4; also 'Liturgical Fragments', ed. H. M. Bannister, *JTS* 9 (1907–8), 398–427, at 425–7.

[70] Sims-Williams, 'Ephrem', pp. 224–5. Cf. Pattie, 'Ephraem', p. 23, for translation.

[71] Ntedika, *Évocation de l'Au-delà*, p. 219.

[72] Warren, *Antiphonary* II, 95–6; *Acta Iohannis*, ed. Junod and Kaestli I, 312–15; II, 578–9 and 831. See Wilmart, 'Manuel', p. 297, n. 2, for other occurrences in prayer books, i.e.

The Royal Prayer Book is more clearly a miscellany than the Harley Fragment, perhaps because of its greater length (52 folios), yet here too the theme of physical and supernatural protection is prominent, particularly in the opening and closing pages, where a few texts cross the boundary from religion to magic.

R begins with ten folios of lections from the gospels. Superficially this recalls C, which opens with the Passion and Resurrection narratives from all four gospels, and N, where the Passion narratives (1–16r) precede a series of meditations on the life of Christ (fols. 19–32). The twenty-six lections in R, however, are unconnected extracts which hardly mention the central mysteries of the faith. A number of them are supplied with rubrics indicating the days of their liturgical use (for example Matthew XII.46–50 is headed De mar[tyribus]), but there is no discernible liturgical principle behind the selection. The rubrics may merely have been taken over from the gospel book which supplied the extracts. In this connection it is interesting that the unusual choice of the lection De martyribus agrees with the lections in the Lindisfarne Gospels (c. 700) and related texts, which derived from a lectionary of the Naples region, known to Bede and perhaps brought to England by Theodore and Hadrian or by Benedict Biscop.[73] It has been suggested that the so-called Burghard Gospels in Würzburg, which include a lectionary of this type, added c. 700, reached Würzburg via the Midlands, like Abbess Cuthswith's manuscript of Jerome; but unfortunately there is no firm evidence.[74]

A unity of subject matter is apparent when R's lections are read straight through. First come the beginnings and endings of the first three gospels and the beginning of John. Then there is a group of what the *Book of*

C, no. 60; the Pseudo-Bedan *Collectanea* (PL 94, 562); the 'Officia per Ferias' and Fleury Prayer Book (PL 101, 607–8 and 1383); and the Nonantola Psalter (*Thomasii Opera*, ed. Blanchinus, p. 528; cf. Salmon, *Analecta*, p. 136, no. 71).

[73] Warner and Gilson, *Catalogue* I, 33. Cf. K. Gamber, 'Die kampanische Lektionsordnung', *SE* 13 (1962), 326–52; *Bedae Opera Homiletica*, ed. Hurst, pp. ix–xvi; Levison, *England and the Continent*, pp. 142–3; Willis, *Further Essays*, pp. 214–16; Lapidge, 'Theodore and Hadrian', p. 46, n. 7. The use of this lection for 'Nat. cuiuslibet sanctae Martyris' in a ninth-century Fleury gospel book (Poitiers, Bibliothèque Municipale, 17 (65)) is listed as a 'rare usage' by W. H. Frere, *Studies in Early Roman Liturgy* II, *The Roman Gospel-Lectionary*, Alcuin Club Collections 30 (London, 1934), 111 and 238.

[74] Würzburg, Universitätsbibliothek, M. p. th. f. 68 (Thurn, *Pergamenthandschriften*, pp. 54–6); Bischoff and Hofmann, *Libri Sancti Kyliani*, p. 159, n. 270. Cf. Wright, 'Notes on English Uncial', pp. 446–7 and 455–6; and above, p. 196, n. 87.

Common Prayer calls 'comfortable words'. Thirdly come narratives of Jesus's miraculous powers, especially his miracles of healing. Finally, there are texts emphasising the power which Christ gave his saints and their special relationship to him; the conclusion of one of these texts reverts to the theme of spiritual and physical protection:

And when he had called unto him his twelve disciples, he gave them power against unclean spirits, to cast them out and to heal all manner of sickness and all manner of disease (Matthew x. 1 = R, 10v).

These second, third and fourth groups of lections clearly correlate with the prayers and charms that follow: the 'comfortable words' promising salvation to all believers are a counterpart to the prayers expressing penitence and aspiration to eternal life; the miracle stories (all of them healing miracles except the stilling of the storm) anticipate the charms and benedictions of the sick; and the texts about the powers of the saints give force to the litanies and prayers which seek their intercession and sometimes enumerate the Apostles in the order of Matthew x.2–4 (the sequel of the lection quoted above).[75] The effect of selection is such as to give the impression of an apocryphal gospel in which Jesus figures solely as a thaumaturge and personal saviour, rather than a teacher. The ease with which such texts could be used for magico-medical purposes can be seen from the employment in the Old English *Lacnunga* of the 'comfortable words': 'Come unto me all that travail and are heavy laden, and I will refresh you' (Matthew xi.28).[76]

The first group of lections – the beginnings and endings of the gospels – are more consonant with the rest than might appear. The idea of including the *initia* of the four gospels in a prayer book also occurred to the compiler

---

[75] See R, 18v, 26r, and 40v–41r. In the first two places Matthew's order, James–Thaddeus–Simon, is altered to James–Simon–Thaddeus (under the influence of the grouping James–Simon in Luke vi.15 and Acts i.13). Bishop, *Liturgica*, pp. 139–40 and 161–3, noted that this aberration (and the remarkable placing of John the Baptist 'historically' before the Virgin Mary at 26r, cf. Kantorowicz, *Laudes*, p. 51) also occurs *c*. 800 in the Stowe Missal (ed. Warner, fol. 32) and he attributed it to Irish influence. This issue is complicated by the occurrence of James–Simon–Thaddeus in the Litany in Cologne, Dombibliothek, 106 (Cologne or Werden, *c*. 805), 73r, ed. Coens, 'Anciennes litanies', pp. 11–13. (Here the Virgin precedes the Baptist and Apostles, and marginal renumbering elevates her position above the archangels; see L. W. Jones, *The Script of Cologne* (Cambridge, Mass., 1932), pl. XLV.)

[76] Grattan and Singer, *Magic and Medicine*, p. 188.

of the Prayer Book of Charles the Bald (858), and the inclusion of the endings of the first three gospels as well may be an idiosyncratic extension of this.[77] The incipits (and explicits) may stand symbolically for the gospels as a whole: in some Insular 'pocket gospel books', such as the Book of Deer, extracts from the gospels, decorated at or near the beginning, and more rarely at the end, seem intended to represent the gospels as a whole, functioning as atropaic or healing amulets rather than as texts for serious study.[78] As is well known, the opening of John, or *In principio* . . . (R, 4r), was held to have protective powers and was used in benedictions throughout the Middle Ages and beyond (for instance by Chaucer's Friar).[79] This would have been consonant with the non-Christian practice of reciting cosmology to heal the sick.[80] To some extent, however, the *initia* of the other gospels were used similarly. In eleventh- or twelfth-century Italy a wax cross inscribed with the *initia* was placed on a dead Christian's chest,[81] and from the twelfth century the *initia* were widely used in benedictions against bad weather: a synod in 1470 at Passau condemned the practice of taking the sacrament out into the fields, noting that a ritual against storms, involving reading the *initia* to the four points of the compass, was commonplace.[82] A similar conception, though not specifying the *initia*, can be seen in an Old English spell 'by which you can improve your fields': you recite 'Crux Matheus, Crux Marcus, Crux Lucas, Crux Sanctus Johannes' over hallowed sods on the four sides of your land and invoke 'Erce, mother of earth'.[83] Again, the morning-prayer ritual in

---

[77] Sims-Williams, review of Hughes, *Celtic Britain*, p. 308. In Ireland the virtue of certain protective hymns seems to have resided in their last three stanzas, which could be used alone, *pars pro toto*: Warren, *Liturgy and Ritual*, ed. Stevenson, pp. lxxxviii–lxxxix.

[78] Cf. Sims-Williams, review of Hughes, *Celtic Britain*, p. 308, and Nees, 'Colophon Drawing', p. 89, n. 73. McGurk, 'Gospel Books in Celtic Lands', pp. 167–8, discusses emphasis on Matthew 1.18 and Luke 1.5 (as in R).

[79] *Stonyhurst Gospel*, ed. Brown, pp. 30–4; Thomas, *Religion and the Decline of Magic*, p. 328. See Franz, *Benediktionen*, and Storms, *Anglo-Saxon Magic*, throughout.

[80] See M. Eliade, *Myths, Dreams and Mysteries*, trans. P. Mairet (Glasgow, 1968), p. 162; Barb, 'Survival of Magic Arts', p. 122.

[81] *North Italian Services*, ed. Lambot, p. 62; Sicard, *Liturgie de la mort*, p. 372, n. 66.

[82] Franz, *Benediktionen* II, 57, n. 2, 57–8, 88, 91–2, 97–8 and 121, n. 1. As evidence that early sources were used in some weather benedictions, note that a fifteenth-century Bavarian one (*ibid.* II, 94–5) uses C, no. 26 (see L. Gjerløw, 'Notes on the Book of Cerne and on MS Uppsala C 222', *NTBB* 47 (1960), 1–29, at 2–4).

[83] Storms, *Anglo-Saxon Magic*, pp. 172–7, no. 8 (cf. p. 182); Grattan and Singer, *Magic and Medicine*, pp. 62–3; Nees, 'Colophon Drawing', pp. 87–8; Hill, 'The *æcerbot*

the Fleury Prayer Book – from the diocese of Passau, seven and a half centuries before the 1470 synod – recommends signing all the members of the body in turn and then holding a gospel book and invoking four pairs of Evangelists and Prophets while rotating *anticlockwise* and facing the four points of the compass in turn:

> Matthaeus et Isaias intercedant pro me.
> Marcus et Jeremias intercedant pro me.
> Lucas et Ezechiel defendant me.
> Joannes et Daniel custodiant me.

The structure of this ritual can be compared with the colophon-drawing preceding the morning office at the end of the Book of Mulling, an Irish pocket gospel book of about the same date as R. The drawing evokes the plan of a monastery bounded at four points of the compass by paired crosses of the four Evangelists and Prophets, given in *anticlockwise* order.[84]

Thus the inclusion of the incipits and explicits of the gospels in R may be an extension of the symbolic use of the gospel *initia* or of the names of the Evangelists for magical or ritual purposes. Yet it may also reflect what Bede describes as a 'beautiful and ancient custom in the church', by which the mystery and symbolism of the four Evangelists were explained to catechumens, and their openings (*exordia, principia*) were recited.[85] This rite, known as *Traditio euangeliorum* or *Apertio aurium*, occurred during the most important of the weekly 'scrutinies' during Lent, which prepared those to be baptized on Easter Saturday by prayers, exorcisms and other ceremonies. This was the first time that such adults and babies were allowed to remain at mass after the reading of the Gospel. Four deacons, carrying the four gospels, processed from the sacristy, preceded by candles and censers, and placed them at the four corners of the altar. While the congregation stood in silence, the first deacon read the opening of Matthew

Charm', pp. 215–16. *Erc* is an Old Irish word for a white cow with red ears; these have magic properties in Celtic texts.

[84] PL 101, 1412; Nees, 'Colophon Drawing', p. 79 (but note that the order would be clockwise if the pre-Vulgate order Matthew–John–Luke–Mark was followed); Sims-Williams, review of Hughes, *Celtic Britain*, p. 308.

[85] *De tabernaculo* II and *In Ezram et Neemian* II, ed. D. Hurst, *Bedae opera exegetica*, CCSL 119A (Turnhout, 1969), 89 and 310–11. Cf. É. Ó Carragáin, 'A Liturgical Interpretation of the Bewcastle Cross', in *Medieval Literature and Antiquities: Studies in Honour of Basil Cottle*, ed. M. Stokes and T. L. Burton (Cambridge, 1987), pp. 15–42, at 21–3.

and the priest expounded Matthew's symbol, the Man. A similar procedure followed with Mark, Luke and John. There followed ceremonies by which the catechumens received the Creed (the *Traditio symboli*) and Lord's Prayer (the *Explanatio orationis dominicae*); then they were dismissed before communion was taken. Such, at least, was the procedure on the Continent in the eighth century,[86] and the rite admired by Bede was probably similar.

In such a ceremony the Insular illuminated gospel books would come into their own as visual aids. The *Apertio aurium* must have encouraged the veneration of the gospel *initia* and Evangelist symbols in the British Isles. That it also had some influence on the choice of lections in R is suggested by the exact passages used there (Matt. I.I and 18; Mark I.I–3; Luke I.5–6; John I.I–14), which textually seem to stand between the brief readings of the Gallican rite in the eighth-century Bobbio Missal (Matt. I.I–2 and 18a; Mark I.I–3; Luke I.5; John I.I–3) and the longer *initia* specified in the Gelasian sacramentaries (Matt. I.I–21; Mark I.I–8 [*or* I.I–11]; Luke I.5–17; John I.I–14).[87]

The association of the lections with the *Apertio aurium* is perhaps reinforced by the fact that they are followed by the Lord's Prayer and

---

[86] *Liber sacramentorum Romanae aecclesiae*, ed. Mohlberg, §§ 299–309 (the Gelasian Sacramentary); *Gellonensis*, ed. Dumas and Deshusses I, §§ 534–43 and 2262–79 (the former section representing the 'Eighth-century Gelasian', *ibid.* II, xxx–xxxii); *Liber sacramentorum Engolismensis*, ed. P. Saint-Roch, CCSL 159C (Turnhout, 1987), §§ 699–710; *Ordines*, ed. Andrieu II, 428–33. The Gelasian ritual is dated *c.* 650 by Vogel, *Introduction*, p. 139, but may be as old as the sixth century according to Chavasse, *Gélasien*, p. 168.

[87] *The Bobbio Missal: Text*, ed. E. A. Lowe, HBS 58 (London, 1920), §§ 175–82; *Liber sacramentorum Romanae aecclesiae*, ed. Mohlberg, §§ 302–8 (I assume that 'initium euangelii secundum Lucam' means I.5ff., as explicitly in *Gellonensis* §2273 etc.). In the 'Eighth-century Gelasian' sacramentaries (e.g. *Gellonensis* §538 and *Engolismensis* §705) the Marcan reading is I.I–11. The Bobbio Missal seems to give an abbreviated recension of the Gelasian rite, and is presumably Gallican since it is closely related to the northern French one in the Missale Gallicanum Vetus (which unfortunately omits the text of the *initia*): P. de Puniet, 'Les trois homélies catéchétiques du sacramentaire gélasien pour la tradition des Évangiles, du Symbole et de l'Oraison dominicale', *RHE* 5 (1904), 505–21 and 755–86; 6 (1905), 15–32 and 304–18, at (1904) 508–18; cf. A. Dondeyne, 'La discipline des scrutins dans l'église latine avant Charlemagne', *RHE* 28 (1932), 5–33 and 751–87, at 30–1. See also above, n. 78.

Apostles' Creed (11v–12r),[88] just as the *Apertio aurium* was followed by the *Traditio symboli* and *Explanatio orationis dominicae*. On the other hand, the inclusion of the Apostles' Creed and Lord's Prayer was almost inevitable. Bede remarks that he had often given ignorant priests English translations of them, and adds:

> For the holy Bishop Ambrose, when speaking of faith, advises each of the faithful to repeat the words of the Creed in the morning, and by it, as if by a spiritual antidote, to fortify themselves against the poisons of the devil which he can cast at them by day or night with malignant craft. Also the custom of assiduous prayer and genuflexion has taught us that the Lord's Prayer should often be repeated.[89]

The lections' prophylactic function is underlined by the next item, the apocryphal letter of Christ to Abgar, king of Edessa,[90] followed by a rubric to the effect that no one who carries it will be harmed by his enemies or their spells (*carmina*), by the snares of the Devil, by hail or thunder, at home or in the city, by sea or land, by day or night. Here we glimpse the background to Alcuin's complaint to Archbishop Æthelheard about people who carried the admonitions of the gospel on little scraps of parchment round their necks rather than in their hearts.[91]

---

[88] An Old Roman version of the Creed: Bullough, 'Alcuin and the Kingdom of Heaven', p. 46, n. 106; cf. Warren, *Antiphonary* II, 99, n. 1; Bishop, *Liturgica*, p. 141; Badcock, 'Anatolian Prayer Book', pp. 167–70 and 177–9; Lapidge, 'Theodore and Hadrian', p. 51. The speculations of students of the Litany such as Badcock and Knopp (above, n. 47) are marred by their ignorance that the version of this creed in the Laudian Acts is an eighth-century addition (*CLA* II, no. 251).

[89] *BOH*, I, 409 and II, 381; *EHD*, pp. 801–2.

[90] Cf. *New Testament Apocrypha*, ed. E. Hennecke and W. Schneemelcher, trans. R. McL. Wilson, 2 vols. (London, 1963–5) I, 437–44; A. Siegmund, *Die Überlieferung der griechischen christlichen Literatur in der lateinischen Kirche bis zum zwölften Jahrhundert* (Munich, 1949), p. 40, n. 2; James, *Apocryphal New Testament*, p. 477. The letter was accepted as authentic in England and Ireland: see *Ælfric's Lives of Saints*, ed. and trans. W. W. Skeat, EETS os 76, 82, 94 and 114, reprinted in 2 vols. (London, 1966), II, 60–1; *Pre-Conquest Prayer-Book*, ed. Muir, no. 18; McNamara, *Apocrypha*, no. 51. 'Incipit epistola Saluatoris domini nostri Iesu Christi ad aeuagarum [*sic*]' (followed by the apocryphal prayer of St John against poison, 'Deus meus et pater . . . ') appears in the order of prayer in Basel, A. VII. 3, 2r (cf. above, n. 18).

[91] Duemmler, *Ep.* ccxc, quoted by Brown, *Stonyhurst Gospel*, pp. 30–1. Charms and prayers might also be used in this way; an example from R was given above, p. 54. Cf. the rubric to the prayer 'Domine Deus omnipotens qui es trinus et unus' (Wilmart, *Auteurs*, pp. 575–7, and L. Gjerløw, *Adoratio Crucis: The Regularis Concordia and the Decreta Lanfranci* (Oslo, 1961), pp. 142–3) in the Würzburg Psalter (see above, n. 66):

The three-part *Oratio* which follows the *Epistola ad Abgarum* on fol. 13 of R reinforces the theme of healing:

(*a*) May Almighty God and our Lord Jesus Christ and the Holy Spirit keep me by day and night, body and soul, here and everywhere, for ever and ever.

(*b*) May the Lord bless me and keep me, and may the Lord show his[92] countenance unto me and have mercy upon me, and may he turn his face to me and give me peace and health (*pacem et sanitatem*). Amen.

(*c*) God the Father who created you heals you (*sanat te Deus pater qui te creauit*). Jesus Christ who suffered for you heals you. The Holy Spirit who is poured forth within you heals you. Your faith which has liberated you from every danger and from iniquity heals you.

I have not noticed (*a*) elsewhere, but (*b*) and (*c*) seem to be taken from rites for the visitation of the sick, adapted for personal use in the case of (*b*) by the alteration of the second person pronouns to first person.[93] Perhaps (*a*) and (*b*) were to be said by the sick person – they were both glossed in Old English – and (*c*), which was not glossed, was pronounced by the visiting priest. The Insular churches may have played an important role in the development of such rites: Bede's stress on the practice of unction was an impetus for the development of an unction liturgy on the Continent in the ninth century, and in the Gaelic-speaking world masses for the sick, mostly including unction, are already prominent both in the earliest Irish sacramentary (the ninth-century Stowe Missal) and, significantly for us, as appendages to the gospel books of Mulling, Dimma and Deer.[94] Section (*b*) of the above prayer is based on Moses's blessing 'Benedicat tibi Dominus ... et det tibi pacem' (Numbers VI.24–6). This was widely used as a benediction for all sorts of occasions, including the Irish masses for the sick and the influential order for the visitation of the sick (§ CXXXIX.29) in the tenth-century *Romano-German Pontifical*, which originated in Mainz; but

'Quicumque hanc orationem in die cantauerit, nec malus homo nec diabolus umquam in ulla causa nocere poterit. Et si de hac uita migrauit, infernus nunquam ipsam animam accipit' (245v). For further examples see Gougaud, 'Étude sur les *loricae*', pp. 110–15; Godel, 'Irisches Beten', pp. 303–4; Wilmart, 'Manuel', p. 296, no. 98; Barré, *Prières anciennes*, p. 7, n. 44; *Pre-Conquest Prayer-Book*, ed. Muir, pp. 42, n. 1, and 61.

[92] *Suam* is interlined by the scribe or a contemporary, but omitted in Kuypers's edition.

[93] Sims-Williams, 'Triad', pp. 94–5. For the gloss on (*a*) and (*b*) see J. Zupitza, 'Mercisches aus der Hs. Royal 2 A 20 im Britischen Museum', *Zeitschrift für deutsches Alterthum* 33 (1889), 47–66, at 61.

[94] Cf. P. Sims-Williams, review of Warren, *Liturgy and Ritual*, ed. Stevenson, in *JEH* 40 (1989), 594–5 and references.

the only text to add *et sanitatem* with R seems to be the mass for the sick added to the Book of Mulling *c.* 800. This suggests that (*b*) is adapted from an Irish rite for the sick.[95] That may also be true of (*c*). The next occurrences of (*c*), which is first attested in R, seem to be in a mid-ninth-century *Benedictio super infirmum* from Nonantola[96] and then, more significantly, in the *Romano-German Pontifical* § CXXXIX.27, shortly before (*b*); interestingly, the intervening item (§ CXXXIX.28) is a benediction first found in R, 19v–20r. R's version, entitled 'Deprecatio', is another adaptation for personal use, altering *te* to *me* and omitting *tecum* before *in diebus et in noctibus*:

The blessing of God the Father with his angels be upon me. The blessing of Jesus Christ with his apostles be upon me. The blessing of the Holy Spirit with the seven gifts be upon me. The blessing of St Mary with her daughters be upon me. The blessing of the catholic Church with her chosen sons be upon me. Let the merits and prayers of the saints be [with me] by day and night[.] In word, in deed, in thought, at all times I put myself under the power of the holy Trinity.[97]

The enumerative style and the prominence of the triad 'word, deed, thought' suggest that this benediction, and indeed the whole group of prayers for the sick shared by R and the *Romano-German Pontifical*, is of Irish origin. The hypothesis is supported by the fact that in Vienna, Österreichische Nationalbibliothek, lat. 1888 (Mainz, s. x^ex), which is a copy of the lost mid-tenth-century Mainz Ritual used by the compilers of the *Romano-German Pontifical*, we find that (*c*) and the above 'Deprecatio' are followed by a remarkable *Super demoniacum*, an exorcism of the devil from every conceivable part of the body, which is extant in Irish manuscripts of the seventh, eighth and ninth centuries and is closely related to the seventh-century *Lorica* of Laidcenn.[98]

R's use of the indicative *sanat te* '(God) heals thee' in (*c*), where all the continental texts have the subjunctive *sanet te* 'may (God) heal thee', betrays the quasi-magical aspect of this section of the prayer book. It

95 Sims-Williams, 'Triad', p. 94.

96 *Ibid.*, pp. 95, n. 99, and 106; also *North Italian Services*, ed. Larnbot, p. xl, n. 3.

97 Cf. Sims-Williams, 'Triad', p. 95, n. 98. The sequel in R ('Christus nos benedicat . . . ') occurs independently in Munich, Staatsbibliothek, Clm. 14128 (s. ix²), 165r, an Insular-type prayer book from St Emmeran ('Prayer Book', ed. Frost, pp. 33 and 36).

98 Sims-Williams, 'Triad', pp. 89–93 and 95; see further Smyth, 'Isidore', pp. 69–70; Herren, *Hisperica Famina* II, 25 and 39–41; H. B. Porter, 'The Origin of the Medieval Rite for Anointing the Sick or Dying', *JTS* ns 7 (1956), 211–25, at 221 and 225.

should probably not be dismissed as an example of a common Hiberno-Latin confusion in the first conjugation,[99] for the same *sanat te* recurs in a version of (*c*) in the Old English magical and medical collection *Lacnunga*, in a formula to be sung into a potion.[100] There it is combined with Matthew IV.23, a favourite ritual text in *Lacnunga*,[101] which also appears among the lections in R (7r):

And Jesus went about all Galilee, teaching in their synagogues, and preaching the gospel of the kingdom, and healing all manner of sickness and all manner of disease among the people.

The equivalent text from Matthew (*sic!*) IX.35 is quoted in a Hiberno-Latin sermon with the interesting comment that 'it was fitting that Luke, who was a physician, should narrate [thus] about Christ, who is the physician of the whole human race'.[102] *Christus medicus* indeed dominates these prayer books.[103]

The three-part *Oratio* on fol. 13 of R is followed by the Magnificat, the Benedictus and the Benedicite (in its full form, as in Daniel III.52–90, without Christian additions). The invocation of natural forces in the last of these canticles anticipates a *lorica*-like litany on fols. 46–7, which calls upon 'the seven heavens and the four creatures of the world – fire, air, water, earth – and sun, moon and shining stars'.[104] After the three

---

99 Cf. *Irish Penitentials*, ed. Bieler, pp. 38–41; Grosjean, 'Manuscrit 49 de la Reine Christine', pp. 122–3; Ó Laoghaire, 'Irish Elements', p. 155.

100 Storms, *Anglo-Saxon Magic*, pp. 240 and 245. Grattan and Singer, *Magic and Medicine*, p. 128, emend unnecessarily.

101 See also *ibid.*, p. 109, n. 4. Sedulius's versification of the text was used as a charm: Storms, *Anglo-Saxon Magic*, pp. 258–61.

102 *Analecta Reginensia*, ed. A. Wilmart, Studi e testi 59 (Vatican, 1933), 94; the Celticity of the passage is shown by the description of Luke as 'IIII scriptor euangelii': cf. Grosjean, 'Manuscrit 49 de la Reine Christine', p. 118; Ó Laoghaire, 'Irish Elements', p. 153.

103 On this theme see Sims-Williams, 'Ephrem', pp. 213–14, and below, p. 306. Morrish, Dated and Datable Manuscripts', pp. 519–21, mistakenly derives the metaphor from Alcuin's *Confessio peccatorum pura* (see below, n. 196) and uses it as a major criterion for dating R and N to the ninth century.

104 Cf. Gougaud, 'Étude sur les *loricae*', pp. 38–40; *Irish Litanies*, ed. Plummer, pp. xxiv and 102–7; G. Mac Eoin, 'Invocation of the Forces of Nature in the *Loricae*', *Studia Hibernica* 2 (1962), 212–17; Dronke, 'Leiden Love-Spell'. The four elements sometimes symbolize the four Evangelists: R. E. McNally, 'Two Hiberno-Latin Texts on the Gospels', *Traditio* 15 (1959), 387–401, at 392 and 395; Hill, 'The *æcerbot* Charm',

canticles there follows, on 16v, a charm to stop blood flowing. At this point there is a clear break in the manuscript: a leaf is missing or cancelled, and an *Oratio sancti Hygbaldi abbatis*, on the new quire (17r), begins with a major zoomorphic initial. From here on, the magical aspect of the codex is less prominent and, with one exception,[105] does not reappear until near the end of the volume, where there are two more charms against bleeding on fol. 49 (not to mention a fourth[106] added on the back flyleaf by a twelfth-century Worcester scribe). All three charms against bleeding are really variants of one another,[107] and it will be enough to describe the third. It is interspersed with the sign + (not always shown in Kuypers's edition), which probably indicates that the sign of the cross should be made.[108] The first + is followed by the rubric: 'In the name of the Holy Trinity and all the saints, to stop blood write this'; then, in corrupt Greek, 'Stop the blood from the place' – *topos* ('place') being a sexual euphemism in Greek medical texts. Then follows the solitary name *Beronice*. She, according to the apocryphal *Acta Pilati*, was the unnamed woman whom Jesus cured of the issue of blood that she had suffered for twelve years;[109] one of the gospel accounts of her (Matthew IX.20–2) occurs in a lection on fol. 9. Her name is followed by verse 16 of Psalm L : 'Deliver me from bloods, O God, thou God of my salvation.' After formulae telling the disease or demons (in corrupt Greek) to 'go away',[110] and (in Latin) asking for Christ's help, comes a quotation of the stanza about her from Caelius Sedulius's abecedarian hymn *A solis ortus cardine*:

> Riuos cruoris torridi
> contacta uestis obstruit,

p. 215; H&S III, 411 (cf. Bullough, 'Roman Books', p. 30). On the prayer in R see Meyer, 'Poetische Nachlese', pp. 624–5; Godel, 'Irisches Beten', pp. 300–426.

105 On 45v; see above, p. 54 and n. 4. The initial on 17r is shown in *CLA* II, no. 215.

106 Storms, *Anglo-Saxon Magic*, no. 55; Barb, 'Blutsegen', p. 487. Cf. Ker, *Catalogue*, p. 318.

107 See Barb, 'Blutsegen'; *Nunnaminster*, ed. Birch, pp. 110–11.

108 Cf. A. A. Barb, 'St. Zacharias the Prophet and Martyr: A Study in Charms and Incantations', *Journal of the Warburg and Courtauld Institutes* 11 (1948), 35–67, at 38.

109 See *ibid.*, pp. 42–5; James, *Apocryphal New Testament*, p. 102; Cross and Livingstone, *Dictionary of the Christian Church*, s.n. 'Veronica'; Grattan and Singer, *Magic and Medicine*, pp. 10, 34, 50 and 189, n. 2; Storms, *Anglo-Saxon Magic*, pp. 56, 226, 233, 268, 270 and 275; Birch, *Nunnaminster*, p. 111; Franz, *Benediktionen* II, 510–11, 595 and 603; Clarke, *Lankhills*, p. 433, n. 3.

110 Daly, 'Palindrome', p. 97.

fletu rigante supplicis
arent fluenta sanguinis.

Again, it can hardly be coincidence that R ends with the full text of this and another (seventh-century?) abecedarian hymn (fols. 50–1).[111] The charm concludes by repeating the name *Beronice* and the psalm-verse once more, plus a meaningless, but perhaps impressive, Greek palindrome ('Having reaped I established a lofty-roofed monument') with a Latin semi-translation.[112]

A version of the above charm occurs as a roughly contemporary addition to a copy of Isidore's *De natura rerum* made at Fulda about the turn of the eighth to ninth centuries.[113] There it follows two Old High German charms against fever and against cancer, of which the second is thought to be an imperfect translation from a lost Old English original.[114] This suggests that a version of R's charm against blood may have passed from England to the continental Anglo-Saxon centre in the eighth century, perhaps in the baggage of one of the nuns who participated in the German mission.

How the magical material reached the Worcester area is entirely obscure. The Greek phrases suggest that some of it originated in the Mediterranean world, where sorcery flourished, despite periodic opposition, and where the wearing of inscribed amulets was recommended in respectable medical treatises.[115] Even before they became fully Christian,

[111] 'By the touch of his garment he impeded streams of hot blood; by the flowing tears of the suppliant the floods of blood dry up.' Sedulius's hymn was much used in the Office; see Hesbert, *Corpus* IV, xii and 507. Cf. PL 101, 609–11. For the anonymous hymn see Schaller and Könsgen, *Initia*, no. 588.

[112] Daly, 'Palindrome' (already noted by Barb, 'Blutsegen', pp. 489–90).

[113] Basel, Universitätsbibliothek, F. III. 15a, 17v–18r. See Barb, 'Blutsegen'; P. Lehmann, *Fuldaer Studien*, Sitzungsberichte der Bayerischen Akademie der Wissenschaften, Philos.-philol. und hist. Klasse, 1925, 3. Abhandlung (Munich, 1925), pp. 47–8 (with facsimile of 17v); F. Keller, 'Bilder und Schriftzüge in den irischen Manuscripten der schweizerischen Bibliotheken', *Mittheilungen der antiquarischen Gesellschaft in Zürich* 7 (1853), 59–97, at 87; *CLA* VII, no. 842.

[114] G. Eis, *Altdeutsche Handschriften* (Munich, 1949), pp. 25–6 (with facsimile of 17r); Ker, *Catalogue*, p. 475.

[115] E.g. *Marcelli De medicamentis liber*, ed. M. Niedermann and E. Leichtenhan, trans. J. Kollesch and D. Nickel, 2 vols. (Berlin, 1968), I, 128, 196, 200 and 374; II, 438 and 554. See Barb, 'Survival of Magic Arts'; M.-Th. d'Alverny, 'Survivance de la magie antique', in *Antike und Orient im Mittelalter*, ed. P. Wilpert, Miscellanea Mediaevalia I (Berlin, 1962), 154–78; Brown, *Religion and Society*, 119–46. A sympathetic

the Hwicce may have used such texts during the syncretic phase seen in cemeteries like that at Lechlade.[116] An indigenous British magic tradition cannot be ruled out, in view of the Romano-British ritual tablets at sites such as Bath,[117] although the only possible evidence of such influence seems to be the invocation of *Garmund, Godes ðegen* – arguably the Welsh saint Garmon (< British Latin *Garmanus* < *Germanus*) – in an Old English charm.[118] Some magical texts certainly came from Ireland (though a stereotyped idea of the Irish church as 'peculiar' should not lead to their importance being exaggerated). Corrupt Old Irish formulae appear in the Old English medical books,[119] and a Latin charm in the Book of Nunnaminster, beginning 'Head of Christ, eye of Isaiah, forehead [of Elijah], nose of Noah, lip [of Job], tongue of Solomon . . .', recurs, with exactly the same lacunae, in a ninth-century Irish hand in a gospel book now at St Gallen (Stiftsbibliothek, 1395, p. 419). There an Old Irish rubric explains:

This is sung every day about your head against headache. After singing it you put your spittle into your palm, and you put it round your two temples and on the back of your head, and then you sing your paternoster thrice and you put a cross of your spittle on the crown of your head and you then make this sign five times on your head.

The uncorrupted text of the charm survives only in a late medieval Irish manuscript (Dublin, Trinity College, H. 3. 17, col. 658d), where the Irish rubric is: 'Heaven and long life and riches to him who will sing it lying down and rising up'.[120]

Although R contains the greatest amount of magical material, some is found in all four early English prayer books. It is significant that it tends to occur at the peripheries of the codices – at the beginning or end, or at the ends of quires – and that it disappears almost entirely from the ninth-

view is taken by M. L. Cameron, 'Bald's *Leechbook*: Its Sources and their Use in its Compilation', *ASE* 12 (1983), 153–82, at 177–8, and 'Anglo-Saxon Medicine and Magic', *ASE* 17 (1988), 191–215.

116 See above, pp. 54 and 69.

117 R. S. O. Tomlin, 'Was Ancient British Celtic Ever a Written Language?: Two Texts from Roman Bath', *BBCS* 34 (1987), 18–25; Herren, *Hisperica Famina* II, 28–9.

118 Grattan and Singer, *Magic and Medicine*, p. 67; Storms, *Anglo-Saxon Magic*, no. 15 and p. 316. Cf. E. P. Hamp, 'Latin *er* in British Celtic', *Études celtiques* 17 (1980), 161–3.

119 H. Meroney, 'Irish in the Old English Charms', *Speculum* 20 (1945), 172–82.

120 Sims-Williams, 'Triad', p. 91 and references; cf. Blathmac's *lúirech*, above, p. 279.

century continental prayer books. Both these facts show that the compilers were aware of a distinction between magic, even Christian magic, and religion.[121]

APOCRYPHAL AND PATRISTIC INFLUENCES

Since the authors of medieval magical texts showed a distinct preference for the apocrypha over the canonical books of the bible,[122] the presence of some apocryphal elements in H and R can be mentioned here. We have already noted the *Epistola ad Abgarum* in R and have seen that the *Oratio sancti Iohannis* in H, 'Aperi mihi pulsanti ianuam uitę ...', is St John's dying prayer in the *Acta Iohannis*. This prayer also occurs in C (no. 60). Immediately afterwards, C includes a prayer from an earlier episode in these *Acta*, uttered by the saint before he drank a poisoned cup without ill effects (no. 61). This sonorous prayer reappears in N (fol. 37), as well as in various later Anglo-Saxon and Irish sources, and was widely used in the Middle Ages both as a charm against poison and as a liturgical blessing for wine.[123] Although it does not appear in H or R, its gnostic-sounding close[124] –

Do thou quench the venom of this poison, put out the deadly workings thereof, and void it of all the strength which it hath in it: and grant in thy sight unto all these whom thou hast created, eyes that they may see, ears that they may hear, and a heart that they may understand thy greatness (*da ... oculos ut uideant, aures ut audiant, et cor ut magnitudinem tuam intelligant*)[125]

– is echoed in a prayer, first found in R (47v):

[121] The distinction is that 'religion' appeals for divine aid whereas 'magic' coerces natural or divine forces; cf. Thomas, *Religion and the Decline of Magic*, p. 46.

[122] Barb, 'Survival of Magic Arts', p. 123. C, no. 66 is St Andrew's apocryphal address to his cross (cf. p. vii), and seems to underlie the *Dream of the Rood*; cf. Shepherd, 'Scriptural Poetry', pp. 16–17.

[123] Sims-Williams, 'Triad', p. 103, nn. 148–9. James, *Apocrypha Anecdota* II, xvii, compared the Priscillianists' use of a hymn abstracted from an apocryphon.

[124] Cf. '... mind, so that we may understand Thee, speech, so that we may expound Thee, knowledge so that we may know Thee' in the Prayer of Thanksgiving: *The Nag Hammadi Library in English*, ed. J. M. Robinson (Leiden, 1977), p. 298. But see Ps. CXIII [AV CXV]. 5–6; Isaiah VI.9–10; Matthew XIII.14–15; Mark IV.12; Romans XI.8.

[125] *Apocryphal New Testament*, trans. James, p. 262; *Acta Iohannis*, ed. Junod and Kaestli II, 825.

Da cor quod te timeat, sensum qui te *intellegat, oculos* cordis qui te *uideant, aures* quae uerbum tuum *audiant*.

This formula reappears in countless later prayers, undergoing many variations and transformations as the prayer was transmitted and reworked as far afield as Spain. [126]

The above prayer from R (incipit 'Deus iustitiae . . .') is entitled *Oratio sancti Augustini*, perhaps because its rather impressive, monumental style is vaguely reminiscent of Augustine's prayers. Such erroneous ascriptions are typical of the early Insular and continental prayer books, and give the false impression that these books have the authority of the Apostles and Fathers. [127] Nevertheless, they do include some genuine patristic material, principally from such Greek treatises attributed to Ephrem the Syrian as circulated in Latin translation, from Augustine's works and from Isidore's *Synonyma de lamentatione animae peccatricis*, the 'weird and hypnotic grandeur' of which is a possible source for the iterative, pleonastic style of some Insular prayers. [128]

I have noticed no extracts from Isidore in H and R, but H's prayer 'Deus altissime, Deus misericordie, qui solus es sine peccato . . .' (6v–7r) is abstracted from the emotional peroration of the Ephremic *De poenitentia*:

O most high God, who alone art without sin, grant me, a sinner, grace in that hour [of Judgment] on account of thy great and uncountable mercies, and grant that my sinfulness, which is now hidden, appear not then before the watching angels and archangels, prophets and apostles, righteous ones and saints. But save me, a sinner, by thy grace and mercy, and bring me into the paradise of delights

---

[126] 'Give a heart that may fear thee, a mind which may understand thee, eyes of the heart which may see thee, ears which may hear thy word.' See Sims-Williams, 'Triad', pp. 101–3, and 'Ephrem', pp. 219–20.

[127] See *ibid.*, pp. 210–11, where an Irish origin is suggested for some patristic attributions. Cf. e.g. the 'Oratio Augustini', 'Oratio Gregorii', and 'Oratio Ambrosi' in the Stowe Missal, ed. Warner, 13r, 19r and fol. 31.

[128] PL 83, 825–68. The quotation is from M. Winterbottom, 'Aldhelm's Prose Style and its Origins', *ASE* 6 (1977), 39–76, at 60. See references in Sims-Williams, 'Ephrem', pp. 212 and 217–18, and 'Anglo-Latin Letter', pp. 17–18. Cf. F. di Capua, 'Lo stile commatico in alcune preghiere del periodo carolingio', in *Miscellanea liturgica in honorem L. Cuniberti Mohlberg*, 2 vols. (Rome, 1948–9) II, 209–21. The latter differs from most scholars in seeing no Irish input into the iterative style; cf. C. D. Wright, 'The Irish "Enumerative Style" in Old English Homiletic Literature, Especially Vercelli Homily IX', *CMCS* 18 (Winter 1989), 27–74.

with all the perfect. Receive thy servant's prayer, O Lord, with the prayers of all thy saints who have ever pleased thee, because to thee is due all glory and adoration, world without end. Amen.

This same extract is included as a 'prayer of Effrem the deacon' in the Troyes Prayer Book (written at Tours about the time of Alcuin's death in 804) and it recurs in several later continental books; where it was first excerpted we cannot tell.[129]

Two prayers in R are *catenae* from Augustine. An *Oratio sancti Augustini episcopi* on 23r–24r ('Deus uniuersitatis conditor . . . regni tui') is made up of excerpts from the long prayer with which Augustine began his *Soliloquia*.[130] That prayer, in Augustine's grandest theological manner, was largely a statement of the attributes of God, but the excerpter, ignoring the rhetorical structure of the original, has picked out the more personal, first-person passages, for instance:

Iam te solum amo, te solum sequor, te solum quaero. Tibi solum seruire paratus sum quia tu solus iuste dominaris. Tui iuris esse cupio. Iube quæsso atque impera quicquid uis, sed sana et aperi aures meas quibus uocem tuam audiam. Sana et aperi oculos meos quibus nutos tuos uideam. Pateat mihi pulsanti ianua tua. Quomodo ad te perueniatur doce me. Nihil aliud habeo quam uoluntatem. Nihil aliud scio nisi fluxa et caduca spernenda esse, certa et aeterna requirenda . . . [131]

This selection of sensual and liminal images tends to take us away from Augustine's intellectual quest and into the gnostic, eschatological preoccupations of the prayers from the *Acta Iohannis*. The same abridgement is found in the Fleury Prayer Book.[132] As the latter text has some superior

129 Sims-Williams, 'Ephrem', pp. 224–6. To the occurrences listed there, add the fragmentary version in Salmon, *Analecta*, p. 162, no. 369 bis. The reference to Montpellier 40 in my n. 94 should read 404 (cf. Salmon, 'Nouvelle liste', p. 148). Cf. above, n. 70.

130 PL 32, 869–72; *Augustine: Earlier Writings*, trans. J. S. Burleigh, Library of Christian Classics 6 (London, 1953), 23–6.

131 'Now thee only I love; thee only I follow; thee only I seek; thee only am I ready to serve because thou alone art justly Lord. I desire to be under thy jurisdiction. Command, I beseech thee, and order whatever thou wilt, but heal and open my ears that I may hear thy voice with them. Heal and open my eyes that I may see thy beckonings with them. Let thy door be opened to me as I knock. Teach me how to come to thee. I have nothing else but the will to come. I know nothing save that transient and dying things are to be spurned, certain and eternal things to be sought after . . . '

132 PL 101, 1397–8 (with an extraneous litany etc. added, which is related to R, 40v–42r). See also cols. 580–2 for the full text and 599D–600A for a short extract in a composite

readings, it cannot derive from R. The compiler of R must, therefore, have taken his *Oratio* from some lost earlier collection.

An untitled item on fol. 21 of R, framed between two invocations to the Trinity,[133] is freely based on Augustine's *Confessiones*. It is a fervent prayer beginning 'Thee, Lord, I ever seek; thee I love above all beauties; thee I love above [all] lovers . . . ' ('Te domine semper quaero, te diligo super omnes pulchritudines, te super amatores amo'). The debt to Augustine is most obvious in the following passage:

Bonus est ergo qui fecit me et ipse est bonum meum, fortitudo mea, et salus mea, altitudo mea et honor meus, fiducia mea et firmamentum meum, gloria mea et gaudium meum, decor meus et dulcedo mea. Sero te amaui, pulchritudo mea perpetua. Miserere mei, domine, et accende in me ignem amoris tui. Magnus es, domine, et laudabilis et ualde magna uirtus tua et sapientiae tuae non est numerus. Et laudare te uult homo aliqua portio creaturae tuae. Et tu excita (*sic*) ut laudare te delectet. Inquietum est cor meum donec requiescat in te. Ecce uulnera mea non abscondi. Medicus es et eger sum, misericors es et miser sum.

The first sentence elaborates the close of *Confessiones* I:

Bonus ergo est qui fecit me, et ipse est bonum meum . . . Gratias tibi, dulcedo mea et honor meus et fiducia mea . . .[134]

Then comes a feeble echo of a celebrated neo-Platonic passage in X.xxvii.38:

Sero te amaui, pulchritudo tam antiqua et tam noua, sero te amaui![135]

The next sentence – 'Have mercy on me, O Lord, and kindle in me the fire of your love' – may reflect the sentiment that soon follows at X.xxix.40:

prayer (cf. Constantinescu, 'Alcuin', p. 33), both from the 'Officia per ferias' (see above, n. 16). For use in these and other ninth-century sources of Augustine's prayer at the end of the *De Trinitate* (PL 42, 1097–8) see Wilmart, 'Manuel', p. 274, n. 1; PL 94, 529CD (= *Precum Libelli*, ed. Wilmart, pp. 162–3); PL 101, 491–2, 608–9 and 1395–6.

[133] 20v and 21v. With these non-Augustinian invocations cf. 24r and 27r, C, nos. 14 (p. 101) and 55; *Precum Libelli*, ed. Wilmart, p. 11.

[134] 'Good therefore is he who made me, and he is my good . . . Thanks to thee, my sweetness and my honour and my trust . . . '

[135] 'Too late did I love thee, O Beauty both so ancient and so new, too late did I love thee!' Cf. Courcelle, *Recherches*, pp. 464–78.

O amor, qui semper ardes et numquam extingueris, caritas, deus meus, accende me!¹³⁶

Then follows, almost verbatim, the opening of Book I:

Great art thou, Lord, and greatly to be praised: great is thy power, and of thy wisdoms there is no number. And man wishes to praise thee, being a part of thy creation . . . Thou provokest (*excitas*) him so that he delights to praise thee . . . our (*nostrum*) heart is restless until it may rest in thee.

The text then returns to X.xxviii.39, fastening on the image of *Christus medicus*,¹³⁷ so popular in the early prayer books:

Domine, miserere mei! ei mihi! ecce uulnera mea non abscondo: *medicus* es, aeger sum; misericors es, miser sum.¹³⁸

While the compiler omits Augustine's explicitly autobiographical sentences, and fails to convey the subtlety of his introspection, his extracts do embody some of the essence of the *Confessiones*: the *confessio laudis* and *confessio peccati*; the 'imaged lyricism'; the theme of divine love that would inspire Cistercian spiritual writers.¹³⁹ In fact, there is probably a literary descent from the Augustinian prayers of the Carolingian prayer books, through the ninth-century Italian cycle of prayers known as the *De psalmorum usu*, down to Jean de Fécamp (a native of Ravenna), whose meditations, as Courcelle has shown, heralded a revival of interest in the *Confessiones* in the eleventh century.¹⁴⁰ The prayer in R may indicate that this lineage began in England; at any rate it corrects the false impression

---

¹³⁶ 'O love, which ever burnest and art never quenched, O charity, my God, kindle me!'

¹³⁷ Cf. Sims-Williams, 'Ephrem', p. 214 (cf. above, n. 103).

¹³⁸ 'Lord, have mercy on me. Alas for me! Behold I do not hide my wounds: thou art the physician and I am sick; thou art merciful and I am miserable.' See *Sancti Aureli Augustini Confessiones*, ed. P. Knöll, CSEL 33 (Vienna, 1896), 28–9, 255, 256, 1, and 256, respectively.

¹³⁹ Cf. Mohrmann, *Études* I, 372, 376–7, and II, 260–5; J. Fontaine, 'Sens et valeur des images dans les "Confessions"', in *Augustinus Magister: Congrès international augustinien, 1954, Communications*, 3 vols. (Paris, n.d.) I, 117–26.

¹⁴⁰ Courcelle, *Tradition littéraire*, pp. 254–5 and 262–4. For use of the *Confessiones* in ninth-century prayer books see also Wilmart, 'Manuel', pp. 289, n. 5, and 290, n. 1; Barré, *Prières anciennes*, p. 7; also *Precum Libelli*, ed. Wilmart, p. 91, lines 23–9. Much of the Pseudo-Augustinian *Liber Meditationum* in PL 40, 901–42, is by Jean de Fécamp: Wilmart, *Auteurs*, pp. 127–8. For Jean's debt to the *De psalmorum usu* see Wilmart, 'Manuel', pp. 265 and 289, n. 5.

given by Courcelle's monumental studies, that the *Confessiones* were
without influence in England between the time of Bede and Aelred of
Rievaulx.[141]

As well as exploiting Augustine's works directly, composers of prayers
could learn from him how to use the bizarre, even illogical imagery of the
poetic books of the bible to express psychological or transcendental
concepts beyond the reach of classical literary and logical discourse.[142]
They could also learn the primitive form of mysticism that led Dom
Cuthbert Butler to hail Augustine as 'for me the Prince of Mystics, uniting
in himself, in a manner I do not find in any other, the two elements of
mystical experience, viz. the most penetrating intellectual vision into
things divine, and a love of God that was a consuming passion'.[143] At the
centre of Augustine's teaching on contemplation is the *desiderium* or
longing of the soul for God, 'like as the hart desireth the water-brooks' –
for later mystics this was the preliminary basis for their quest, not its
essence – and at the centre of his teaching on 'unceasing' prayer is *flagrantia
caritatis* or 'the burning of charity':

If you would pray without ceasing, do not cease too long. Your ceaseless longing is
your ceaseless voice. You will be silent if you stop loving . . . the chilling of charity
is the heart's silence: the burning of charity is the heart's clamour.[144]

An anonymous *Oratio sancta* on fol. 20 of R, just before the prayer based on
the *Confessiones*, is thus thoroughly Augustinian in spirit:

Fill me, Lord, with the spirit of thy charity,[145] that my soul may ever be filled by
the abundance of thy mercies, and that thou who art my help may thyself be my
prize (*ipse sis prǫmium*). Thine be all for which I live. Stand by me, so that I, who
cannot exist without thee, may be able to live following thee. 'Draw me: after thee
we will run', for thou hast said: 'No man cometh unto the Father but by me, and
no man can come to me, except the Father draw him.' Draw me to the high peak of
the virtues. I consider that my own strength does not suffice unless I am drawn by
thee. Draw me whether[146] through love or through sorrow; draw me through

---

[141] Cf. Courcelle, *Tradition littéraire*, pp. 254–5, and *Recherches*, pp. 464–78. For Alcuin's
knowledge, at York, of the *Confessiones*, *Soliloquia* and *De Trinitate* see Bullough,
'Alcuin and the Kingdom of Heaven', pp. 17–18.

[142] Cf. above, n. 139.   [143] *Western Mysticism*, p. 24; cf. pp. 31–2 and 35–6.

[144] *Enarrationes in Psalmis* XXXVII.14 (CCSL 38, 392); cf. Burnaby, *Amor Dei*, pp. 96–9.

[145] Cf. *Liber sacramentorum Romanae aecclesiae*, ed. Mohlberg, §1330, and parallels at §216
in *Missale Gallicanum Vetus*, ed. Mohlberg, p. 121.

[146] *Siue . . . siue* may also mean 'both . . . and': Mohrmann, *Études* II, 256, n. 25.

bitter and sweet, through adverse and prosperous, through strait and broad, through soft and hard. I know that 'it is not of him that willeth, nor of him that runneth, but of God that showeth mercy'. Draw me so that I may run in the tracks of thy commandments, as thou hast said 'Come, follow me'. Draw me through whatsoever thou wilt if only I may possess thee, the one and only hope of my life now and henceforth, so that I may never be separated from the vast fire of thy love (*ab ingenti ardore amoris tui*), because thou art all that I desire (*desidero*). Nor have I, nor seek I, anything else, neither on earth nor in heaven, save this, that I may be with thee in thy mercy, so that I shall rejoice and glory in thee, Lord. I long greatly for no earthly thing, but, with all the desire of my inward parts, desire thee, the one God, who livest and reignest, through all ages, Amen.

Versions of this *Oratio sancta* also appear in H (4v–5v), in the early ninth-century Paris Prayer Book from Tours, and in the eleventh-century Psalter of Bury St Edmunds.[147] It seems to embody the essence of Augustinianism, as defined by Gilson:

at the same time adherence of the mind to supernatural truth and humble surrender of the whole man to the grace of Christ: the mind's adherence to the authority of God implies humility, but humility in its turn implies a trust in God which is itself an act of love and charity.[148]

Despite the violent language of the prayer, the writer is not professing that disinterested love of God 'whatever he may do with us', expressed by later medieval and modern theologians. Rather, for him as for Augustine, beatitude and knowledge of God are synonymous, and he echoes a favourite Augustinian text: 'God himself is our prize' (*Deus ipse nobis praemium*).[149] Everything else is worthless, since, in Augustine's words, 'nothing that God can promise is of any worth, apart from God himself'.[150] Spiritual teachers before Augustine had defined this single-minded aspiration in terms of charity,[151] but Augustine (for example in some of the passages already quoted) exploited the more forceful, emotive – and to some profane – vocabulary of *amor* and *amare* in place of *caritas* and *diligere*.[152] The image

---

147 *Precum Libelli*, ed. Wilmart, p. 43; 'Bury Psalter', ed. Wilmart, no. II.

148 Quoted by Burnaby, *Amor Dei*, p. 79.

149 Cf. *ibid.*, pp. 243–4, 247, 256–7, 272–5 and 291–2; Hausherr, 'Comment priaient les pères', p. 47, n. 4.

150 *Sermo* clviii.7, quoted by Burnaby, *Amor Dei*, p. 246.

151 Hausherr, 'Comment priaient les pères', p. 46.

152 Burnaby, *Amor Dei*, pp. 95, and n. 4, and 99; Courcelle, *Recherches*, p. 461; *Tradition littéraire*, p. 218, n. 5. In *Confessiones* X.xxix.40 Augustine addresses God as 'amor, qui

of fire, too, was typical of Augustine, though not of course limited to him,[153] so it is significant that *ardor amoris tui* appears in the prayer – a foretaste of Richard Rolle's *Incendium amoris*.

The above *Oratio sancta* is based on the Song of Songs I.3: 'Draw me: after thee we will run' (*Trahe me: post te curremus*). This image is understood in terms of the life-journey of man, whose 'great woe', according to Augustine, is 'not to be with him without whom he cannot be' – a metaphor which he qualified by the words 'we go not by walking, but by loving' (*imus non ambulando, sed amando*).[154] Two modes of travel were implied by the scriptural text – the 'drawing' by God and the running by man – and exegetes could dwell on either. Gregory, for instance, in his commentary on the Song of Songs, stresses the striving elements in *curremus*; men pursue God by walking, running or running hard.[155] That is the literally 'ascetic' ('athletic') interpretation, found, too, in Cassian, and also in the eighth *Instructio* attributed to Columbanus, on human life as a roadway:

Let us beseech [God] ... that ... we may more closely approach, or more clearly understand, and singing on our journey let us say, *Let us run after Thee towards the odour of Thy perfumes*, and, *My soul has clung behind Thee*, and *Draw me after Thee*; that with these songs we may speedily pass through this world, and controlled from above may scorn the things of the present, and ever thinking of heavenly things may shun the things of earth ...[156]

Kathleen Hughes was tempted to see a vague echo of this passage in the *Oratio sancta* – understandably, since she was the first to show that Columbanus was used by Alchfrith the Anchorite, the author of some of

---

semper ardes et numquam extingueris, caritas, deus meus' (above, p. 306). This sort of language was traditional in exegesis of the Song of Songs: Courcelle, *Recherches*, p. 462, n. 1.

[153] It is used in connection with prayer by Gregory, e.g. *Moralia in Iob* XV.53 (CCSL 143A, 782); see Butler, *Western Mysticism*, pp. 113–15. Cassian speaks of the 'loftier state of prayer, formed by the contemplation of God alone and by a charity that burns like fire (*caritatis ardore*)' in *Conlationes* IX.18 (ed. Petschenig, p. 265; trans. Chadwick, *Western Asceticism*, p. 222). Cf. Chadwick, *Cassian*, pp. 142–7.

[154] *De Trinitate* XIV.16 and *Ep.* clv.4, quoted by Burnaby, *Amor Dei*, pp. 90, 93–4 and 156.

[155] *Expositiones in Canticum Canticorum* XXV (CCSL 144, 25).

[156] *Columbani Opera*, ed. and trans. Walker, pp. 94–5. Cf. Cassian, *Institutiones* V.17–18 (PL 49, 233–4; *Cassian*, trans. Gibson, p. 240).

the prayers in the Book of Cerne.[157] Unlike Columbanus, however, the author of the *Oratio sancta* emphasizes the verb *trahe* and neutralizes the import of *curremus* by introducing the Pauline text: 'It is not of him that willeth, nor of him that runneth, but of God that showeth mercy' (Romans IX.16). The stress is on human dependence, rather than human volition, in accordance with Augustine's teaching on Grace. Although Augustine wrote frequently of man's quest for God, this quest was originally inspired by God's Grace, and the verb *trahere* played an important role in this doctrine, generally in connection with the Johannine text used in the *Oratio sancta*: 'No man can come to me, except the Father which hath sent me draw him' (John VI.44; cf. XIV.6). The Father's 'drawing' is 'a violence done to the heart', according to Augustine, yet 'not a rough or painful violence ... It is sweet, its very sweetness draws'.[158] On the one hand it involves God's legitimate exercise of a terror inspired by love; on the other it co-operates with the innate motivation of the soul. Thus *trahere* was invested with all the complexity of Augustine's teaching on religious coercion, Grace and free will.[159] The *Oratio sancta* seems to be a meditation on this Augustinian verb. It may have been inspired by the direct study of Augustine, for, while other theologians who accepted Augustine's teaching on man's dependence on God used the Johannine text in a similar way,[160] only Augustine, so far as I have discovered, combines it with the text from the Song of Songs, in his *Tractatus in Iohannem*.[161]

LITURGICAL INFLUENCES

An *Oratio sancti Augustini episcopi* which follows the prayer from the *Soliloquia* in R (24v) vaguely recalls some Augustinian phrases and themes, but its style, and the direct address to Christ, are quite un-Augustinian:

[157] Hughes, 'Irish Influence', p. 59, n. 2. On Alchfrith see Sims-Williams, 'Ephrem', p. 209.

[158] *Sermo* cxxxi.2, quoted by Burnaby, *Amor Dei*, p. 221; cf. *ibid.*, p. 247.

[159] Cf. *ibid.*, pp. 98, 214 and 221–2; Brown, *Religion and Society*, p. 270, and *Augustine of Hippo*, pp. 374–5.

[160] E.g. Cassian, *Conlationes* XIII.3, 9 (combined with the Romans text) and 10 (ed. Petschenig, pp. 364, 372–3 and 375; *Cassian*, trans. Gibson, pp. 423 and 426–7). Cf. Chadwick, *Cassian*, pp. 127–8.

[161] *Tractatus in Iohannem* XXVI.5 (CCSL 36, 262).

Lord Jesus Christ, who didst pass (*qui transisti*) from this world to the Father and didst love thy people who were in the world, make me to pass (*fac me transire*) in mind and soul from earthly things to supernal things, to despise all transitory things and to desire only heavenly things, and to burn gently with the flaming fire of thy love and to overflow, perpetually panting. And thou, who deignest to wash the feet of thy holy apostles with thy sacrosanct (*sacrosanctis*) hands, purify my thought and heart by pouring in the radiance of the Holy Spirit. Lord God Jesus, who after thou hadst dined with thy disciples didst take the sacrosanct bread and cup in thy holy and venerable hands (*sanctis uenerabilibusque manibus tuis*), and gavest [them] to thy apostles as a symbol of thy body and blood, grant me that I, remaining continually in thee and thou in me through receiving holy communion, may be freed from the snares of enemies and be made a partaker of eternal life. [162]

This prayer illustrates two important facets of the prayers in R.

First, it is a meditation on the events of the life of Christ, a genre which apparently developed in eighth-century England. There is a whole series of such prayers further on in the manuscript, arranged in alphabetical sequence from 'Altus auctor . . .' to 'Zelotis sempiterne Deus . . .' (fols. 29–38). A similar sequence occurs in N, although only three prayers in R (its *L*-, *Q*- and *R*-prayers) actually recur in N: N's *De .vii. donis Spiritus sancti* (27v, not a close parallel), *De naribus* (29v–30r), and *De auribus* (30r). [163] The affective religion of these cycles of prayers is remarkably precocious, anticipating the prayers of St Anselm by some centuries. [164]

Secondly, the prayer illustrates the liturgical influence on some of the prayers in R. [165] Its structure, with invocations followed by relative clauses (*qui . . .*) and main-clause petitions, is that of three collects; the antithesis of 'qui transisti' and 'fac me transire' is typical of a Roman collect, [166] even if the amount of amplification introduced destroys the balance expected of a collect. There is, moreover, an explicit allusion to the solemn, sacral language of the classic Roman form of the Canon of the mass, in which

---

162 The first two 'collects' here recur in *Pre-Conquest Prayer-Book*, ed. Muir, no. 22.
163 Cf. *Nunnaminster*, ed. Birch, pp. 24–5; Sims-Williams, 'Ephrem', p. 209; Lapidge, 'Debate Poem', p. 13, n. 53; Morrish, 'Dated and Datable Manuscripts', p. 521. Compare the above prayer with the two *Orationes in caena Domini* in N, fol. 24.
164 Cf. Sims-Williams, 'Ephrem', p. 226.
165 This was discussed but exaggerated by Edmund Bishop in his celebrated 'Liturgical Note' in *Cerne*, ed. Kuypers, pp. 234–83: see Sims-Williams, 'Ephrem', pp. 213–15.
166 Cf. Mohrmann, *Liturgical Language*, p. 67. Bede's prayer at the end of *HE* v.24 is a good example of what Bishop, *Liturgica*, p. 19, called the 'soberness and sense' of Roman liturgy.

Jesus is said to take the bread not simply 'in his hands', or even *in sanctis manibus suis* (as quoted by Ambrose and found later still in Spain and Ireland), but *in sanctas ac uenerabiles manus suas*. This is also the wording known to Bede, and that given in the exposition of the mass in Hatton 93, 28v. [167]

A more subtle and unexpected allusion to the Canon, in the context of the Crucifixion, occurs in the *K*-prayer on fol. 32:

O author of charity, teacher of chastity, and lover of men, most kind God, O Christ, who didst extend thy arms on the wood of the cross, stretch out to me the hand of thy mercy. With the point of thy fear and trembling and recognition and love, pierce my very hard breast, O thou who sufferest thy *holy and venerable hands* to be pierced by nails on the cross; and cleanse my hands and breast from all wounds of sins, thou who didst permit thy innocent hands to be fixed to the cross, my Lord, Jesus Christ.

The structure of these sentences is again that of a collect, amplified with additional matter, such as the invocations 'lover of men, most kind God' (*amator hominum, benignissime deus*), which echo a prayer beginning *Philanthrope, agathe . . .* in the Graeco-Latin 'Ephrem' corpus. [168]

There is further clear liturgical allusion in a litany-like prayer on fols. 18–19 of R (no. 1 in C), which invokes the aid of angels, apostles and saints. After enumerating the nine orders of angels, from 'angels and archangels' to 'cherubin and seraphin', it adds:

Intercedite pro me, qui cotidiae ante thronum gloriae[169] laudes aeterno deo sine fine concinnant dicentes:

> Sanctus, sanctus, sanctus,[170] dominus deus sabaoth,
> Pleni sunt caeli ac terrae gloriae tuae.
> Osanna in excelsis.
> Benedictus qui uenit in nomine tui,
> Osanna in excelsis.

---

[167] See Sims-Williams, 'Ephrem', p. 213 and n. 34. Cf. PL 138, 1181. On the pre-Christian origin of this cumbrous sacral diction see Mohrmann, *Liturgical Language*, pp. 58–60 and 74, and *Études* III, 232–5 (cf. R. Schmitt, *Dichtung und Dichtersprache in indogermanischer Zeit* (Wiesbaden, 1967), pp. 207–8).

[168] Sims-Williams, 'Ephrem', p. 226.

[169] Cf. Bishop's note in *Cerne*, ed. Kuypers, p. 241, and *Irische Palimpsestsakramentar*, ed. Dold *et al.*, §57, n. 'Intercede for me, you who daily before the throne of glory sing praises to the eternal God without end, saying: Holy, Holy, Holy . . .'

[170] 'agios agios agios' is interlined in a later hand (cf. above, n. 47).

This clearly alludes to the introduction to the *Sanctus* and *Benedictus* in the Preface of the mass. For example, the Preface in an eighth-century liturgical fragment from Northumbria concludes:

Laudesque tuas, domine, fidenter intendas coniungere uocibus angelorum, qui gloriam tuam concinnunt sine fine dicentes . . .[171]

Edmund Bishop, who tended to exaggerate the Spanish influence on the Anglo-Saxon prayer books, thought that the above litany-like prayer echoed the wording of the *Illatio* (Preface) in the Mozarabic liturgy:

Tibi *cherubin ac seraphin* senarum uolatus stridore alarum *eterne* laudis trigemina concinentes incessabile uoce canticum laudis exsoluant ita dicentes . . .[172]

The resemblance was illusory, however, because the 'cherubin and seraphin' of the prayer in R are simply the tail-end of its enumeration of the nine angelic orders, and the adjective *aeternus* is applied differently in the two texts. It is significant, on the other hand, that the words following the enumeration of the saints at the end of the prayer (' . . . quorum omnium quaesumus meritis precibusque . . . ') are taken from the Canon of the Roman mass and do not appear in the Mozarabic books.[173]

The amplification of Roman collects seems to have been a normal procedure in composing private prayers. For example, in a prayer in C (no. 28) and N (34v), the *cursus* and sober, precise framework of a collect from the Leonine Sacramentary is broken down by interpolating a series of invocations between the 'Deus' and the relative 'qui' of the model:

> inmortale praesidium
> omnium postulantium
> liberatio supplicum
> pax rogantium
> uita credentium

---

[171] '[It is right and proper] faithfully to join thy praises, Lord, with the voices of the angels, who sing thy glory without end, saying . . .': *Missale Francorum*, ed. L. C. Mohlberg (Rome, 1957), Appendix, p. 76, §183.

[172] 'To thee cherubin and seraphin, with the noise of the flying of their six wings, singing threefold songs of eternal praise with unceasing voice, render a song of praise, saying thus . . .' See Bishop's 'Liturgical Note' in *Cerne*, ed. Kuypers, pp. 240 and 276 (table). Cf. lines 17–18 of the ADELVALD acrostic, *ibid.*, p. 41; and *Irische Palimpsest-sakramentar*, ed. Dold *et al.*, §30 and n. On the question of Spanish influence see Sims-Williams, 'Ephrem', pp. 215–17 (cf. Curran, *Antiphonary of Bangor*, pp. 152–4).

[173] See Bishop's 'Liturgical Note' in *Cerne*, ed. Kuypers, pp. 241 and 282.

resurrectio mortuorum
spes fidelium
gloriatio humilium
beatitudo iustorum.[174]

Insofar as the paratactic, rhyming style of this interpolation has a *liturgical* source, it can be found in the 'Gallican' liturgy, the ancient liturgy of Gaul and Spain which, in most Western European lands, including Ireland, competed with, and contaminated, the 'Roman' liturgy in the seventh and eighth centuries. The Gallican style, though vapid and pleonastic – Edmund Bishop said it would not bear the test of translation into English – was also ostentatiously literary. Gallo-Roman, Frankish and Spanish churchmen, poets and even kings (Chilperic) had striven to display their literary talents in composing masses.[175] Already in the mid-fifth century we hear of a Marseilles priest writing a great corpus of masses 'suitable in its entirety for praying to God and acknowledging (*contestandi*) his benefits', which revealed 'deep and disciplined eloquence'.[176] The use of rhyme and parataxis in such compositions may be illustrated by a *Contestatio* (the equivalent of the Roman Preface) from the earliest manuscript collection of Gallican masses, from early seventh-century Burgundy:

Dignum et iustum est, uere equum et iustum est et sanctum est nos tibi gratias agere, domine, sancte pater, omnipotens aeterne Deus: praecem fundere, te confetiri, in tuis laudibus gloriari, *qui omnem uerbum iubes, sapientia disponis, uirtutem confirmas, rationem dispensas.* Digne igitur ac iuste te laudare *quem omnis angeli cumlaudant et astra mirantur, maria benedicunt, terra ueneratur, inferna suscipiunt,* cui cyruphym et seraphym non cessant clamare dicentes: [Sanctus, Sanctus, Sanctus . . .].[177]

---

174 '[O God], immortal defence of all postulants, liberation of suppliants, peace of beseechers, life of believers, resurrection of the dead, hope of the faithful, boast of the humble, beatitude of the just, [who . . .].' See *Cerne*, ed. Kuypers, pp. xxvi–xxvii, 125, n. 19, 258 and 281; *Sacramentarium Veronense*, ed. L. C. Mohlberg (Rome, 1956), §599, Mense Iulio XXXIII. For more examples of the style of the interpolation see *Irische Palimpsestsakramentar*, ed. Dold *et al.*, pp. 166–8.

175 Bishop, *Liturgica*, p. 5. See Porter, *Gallican Rite*, pp. 47–8; P. Séjourné, 'Saint Isidore de Séville et la liturgie wisigothique', in *Miscellanea Isidoriana* (Rome, 1936), pp. 221–51, at 230–1; *HF* II.22, VI.46 and VIII.20.

176 Gennadius, *De uiris illustribus* LXXIX (PL 58, 1104), quoted by Porter, *Gallican Rite*, p. 47.

177 'It is worthy and just, it is indeed right and just and it is holy, for us to give thee thanks, Lord, holy Father, almighty eternal God; to pray, to confess thee, to glory in thy

This style is not, however, specifically liturgical; in fact the italicized phrases derive from the third-century writers Minucius Felix and Novatian.[178] For this reason it would be wrong to posit Gallican liturgical inspiration for private prayers in these styles on the basis of slight verbal parallels. Bishop, for example, described the incipit 'Deus iustitiae te deprecor, Deus misericordiae, Deus inuisibilis, inconprehensibilis, Deus inenarrabilis . . .' (*Oratio sancti Augustini*, R, 47v) as 'a possible quotation' of the opening of a prayer in the *Missale Gothicum*:

Deus iusticiae, deus misericordiae, deus inmortalitatis et uitae, deus splendoris et gloriae . . .[179]

In fact, the description of God in negative terms such as *invisible*, *incomprehensible* and *ineffable*, while ancient in Christian liturgy, was equally common in philosophical and theological genres.[180]

The most likely case of Gallican liturgical influence can be seen in an untitled prayer on fol. 27 of R, which, significantly, precedes the liturgical *Gloria in excelsis* and the beginning of the Creed of St Damasus. It is hardly a private prayer at all, since God is referred to in the third person:

. . . Ideo laudandus est a nobis, quia adest salus nostra, id est dominus noster Iesus Christus. Adest lux mundi, exspectatio sanctorum, uita credentium, resurrectio mortuorum, salus gentium. Laudent eum caeli quos fecit, terra quam ipse

> praises, who rulest everything [by thy] word, disposest with wisdom, strengthenest [with] virtue, dispensest reason; worthily and justly to praise thee, whom all the angels praise and the stars admire, the seas bless, the earth venerates, the depths receive, to whom cherubim and seraphim do not cease to cry, saying . . .'. 'Mone' Mass, in *Missale Gallicanum Vetus*, ed. Mohlberg, §318 (cf. p. 62). Porter, *Gallican Rite*, p. 48, describes the Gallican use of internal rhyme as 'probably Gothic in origin'; however, rhyme, parataxis and alliteration, although generally eschewed in Roman liturgy (cf. Chavasse, *Gélasien*, p. 147, n. 22), were widespread in other genres: Mohrmann, *Études* I, 376 and 397–8; II, 258 and 269–71; III, 97–8.

178 See Mohlberg, *Missale Gallicanum Vetus*, pp. 136–7. Bishop, *Liturgica*, pp. 176–8, argued that a stylistically similar passage in Pseudo-Ildefonsus, *Sermo* ix (PL 96, 272), was the source of a *Contestatio* in the *Missale Gothicum* (ed. Mohlberg, §98): '*Speciosus thalamus, de quo* dignus *prodit sponsus, lux gentium, spes fidelium*, praedo daemonum, confusio Iudaeorum, uasculum uitae, *tabernaculum gloriae, templum caeleste*'; but in this case the relationship was probably vice versa (cf. Sims-Williams, 'Ephrem', p. 217, n. 56).

179 *Missale Gothicum*, ed. Mohlberg, §531; Bishop in *Cerne*, ed. Kuypers, pp. 265 (no. 63) and 281. Cf. the long list of epithets for God in the Stowe Missal, ed. Warner, 22v–23r; Praell, 'Keltisches Missale', p. 20.

180 Mohrmann, *Liturgical Language*, p. 25; Chadwick, *Cassian*, p. 149.

constituit, fundamenta maria quas (*sic*) ipse dilatauit. Ipse enim et creando uniuersa constituit et melius reparando firmauit. Ipse est enim totius postestatis (*sic*) summa, festiuitas sanctorum. Ipse est rex regum et dominus dominantium, arbiter saeculi, paterfamilias caeli, uita credentium, salus dolentium, lux fugans tenebras, reuocatur (*sic*) errantium, liberator pereuntium, qui est lux de luce, fons uitae et inmortalitatis. In omnibus his laudamus et benedicamus Dominum Deum nostrum et depraecamur eum ut misericordiam eius consequi mereamur in saecula saeculorum, amen. [181]

This recalls the didactic manner and inflated style of the *Prefationes* and *Contestationes* of Gallican masses. [182] Again, however, this style was not exclusively liturgical. There are indeed striking verbal parallels in Alcuin's treatise *Aduersus Elipandum* IV.15:

Ipse est rex gloriae, et rex regum, et Dominus dominantium, et Deus deorum, et Deus magnus, et Deus omnipotens, et uerus Dei Filius. Per ipsum uniuersa creata sunt: per ipsum uniuersa restaurata sunt, quae in coelis, et quae in terris sunt . . . Ipse est conuiuum angelorum, festiuitas sanctorum, salus infirmorum . . . Hic est uita credentium, resurrectio mortuorum, redemptio captiuorum, lux indeficiens . . . [183]

Possibly Alcuin was recalling the Gallican liturgy, but this cannot be

---

[181] 'Therefore he is to be praised by us, because our salvation is at hand, that is our Lord Jesus Christ. The light of the world is at hand, the expectation of saints, the life of believers, the resurrection of the dead, the salvation of peoples. Let the heavens which he made praise him, the earth which he himself founded, the bottoms of the ocean which he himself filled. For he, creating, established all things and strengthened them by renewing them. For he himself is the height of all power, the festivity of saints. He himself is king of kings and lord of lords, judge of the world, father of heaven, life to believers, salvation to grievers, light driving darkness to flight, caller-back of wanderers, liberator of the dying, he who is light from light, fount of life and immortality. In all these things we praise and bless the Lord our God, and beg him that we may be worthy to seek his mercy for ever and ever. Amen.' The Creed of St Damasus was noted by Warner and Gilson, *Catalogue* I, 34.

[182] Cf. Porter, *Gallican Rite*, p. 50.

[183] PL 101, 298–9. Cf. H. B. Meyer, 'Alkuin zwischen Antike und Mittelalter', *ZKT* 82 (1959), 306–50, at 319–20. For two prayers in similar style in the 'Alcuinian' prayer books see *Precum Libelli*, ed. Wilmart, pp. 17–18 and 59; the second is followed by the Prayer of St Polycarp (*Early Christian Prayers*, ed. Hamman, no. 68), which was transmitted by Alcuin: Bullough, 'Alcuin and the Kingdom of Heaven', pp. 12–13, nn. 27 and 30.

proved, since the enumeration of the attributes of God or Christ is common in Christian literature.[184]

In the liturgy, collects beginning 'Te . . .' or 'Tu . . .' are chiefly Gallican (including here Spain and Ireland), and their elaboration 'in which a long row of titles can follow each other without any recognizable connection of thought' has been regarded as specifically Irish:

Tu es spes et salus. Tu es uita et uirtus. Tu es adiutor in tribulationibus. Tu es defensor animarum nostrarum, Deus Israel, in omnibus, qui regnas.

This is a relatively restrained early example from the late seventh-century Antiphonary of Bangor.[185] Such Irish collects were possibly the starting point for private prayers in which the 'tu es . . .' formula was developed at enormous length. There are two principal examples. Prayer no. 10 in C was plausibly regarded as Irish by Dom Kuypers, who pointed out that it recurs in the Irish Graeco-Latin psalter at Basel and is attributed to St Patrick in another mid-ninth-century psalter (Angers, Bibliothèque Municipale, 18).[186] The other is found in R (46r), as well as in C (no. 22) and in many later sources, generally with extreme textual variation – perhaps due to oral transmission, for, according to the Tours prayer book quoted above, the prayer was to be said daily on rising:

Auxiliatrix esto mihi Trinitas sancta. Exaudi me, exaudi me, deus meus. Tu es deus meus uiuus et uerus. Tu es pater meus. Tu es deus meus pius. Tu es rex noster magnus. Tu es iudex meus iustus. Tu es magister meus unus. Tu es adiutor meus optimus. Tu es dilectus meus pu[l]cherrimus. Tu es panis meus uiuus. Tu es sacerdos in aeternum. Tu es dux meus ad patriam. Tu es lux mea uera. Tu es dulcedo mea sancta. Tu es sapientia mea clara. Tu es simplicitas mea pura. Tu es unitas mea catholica. Tu es consolatio mea pacifica. Tu es custodia mea tota. Tu es proditio mea bona. Tu es salus mea sempiterna. Tu es misericordia mea magna. Tu

---

[184] One sees it, for example, in the prayer 'Te domine semper quaero . . .' in R (fol. 21), and that is derived from Augustine's *Confessiones*, as shown above, p. 305.

[185] 'Thou art hope and salvation. Thou art life and virtue. Thou art a helper in troubles. Thou art the defender of our souls, God of Israel, in all things, who reignest' (etc.). See *Antiphonary*, ed. Warren II, xxvii–xxviii, 22 and 24; cf. Curran, *Antiphonary of Bangor*, pp. 104–6, 113 and 155 (I quote from p. 104). For 'Tu. . .' elaboration elsewhere, note *Psalter Collects*, ed. Brou, p. 111, Africana Series no. 150 (cf. Mohrmann, *Études* III, 245–63).

[186] *Cerne*, ed. Kuypers, p. xxv; for other copies see Sims-Williams, 'Triad', p. 108, n. 179.

es sapientia mea robustissima. Saluator mundi qui sine fine uiuis et regnas in saecula saeculorum. Amen.[187]

PENITENTIAL AND ASCETIC PRAYERS

Penitential formulae are more important and pervasive than formulae from masses.[188] One needs to reckon here with influence not only from ancient liturgies of public penance, but also from forms of private confession to a 'soul friend', developed above all by the Irish church.[189] In the confessional prayers in R the main influence is obviously the Bible: the Prodigal Son and the Publican (Luke XV. 18 and XVIII. 13) from the New Testament,[190] and, from the Old Testament, the Seven Penitential Psalms.[191] Since peniten-

---

[187] For the sake of comparison I quote my hasty transcript of the unpublished text from Paris, Bibliothèque Nationale, lat. 2731A, fol. 64 (Rheims area, s. ix^ex: see Bullough, 'Alcuin and the Kingdom of Heaven', p. 13, n. 29). For other copies see: C, no. 22; *Precum Libelli*, ed. Wilmart, pp. 13 and 42; 'Prayer Book', ed. Frost, pp. 38–9; Wilmart, 'Manuel', p. 280, n. 2; and cf. above, p. 282 and n. 43. The earliest version may be Einsiedeln, Stiftsbibliothek, 27 (1195), fol. 19 (Swiss?, s. viii/ix.: *CLA* VII, no. 872); this is the 'une prière' (mis)cited by Salmon, 'Livrets', p. 226. For versions combined with other prayers see Wilmart, 'Bury Psalter', pp. 202–3, and 'Manuel', pp. 271, n. 8, 291, no. 79, and 292, n. 2; PL 40, 914; *The Portiforium of Saint Wulstan*, ed. A. Hughes, 2 vols., HBS 89–90 (London, 1958–60) II, 4.

[188] The *Confiteor* did not become part of the mass until the eleventh century, although *apologiae*, private confessions for the priest alone, appear in sacramentaries from the beginning of the eighth century onwards and influenced, and were influenced by, prayers in private prayer books. See Sims-Williams, 'Triad', pp. 107–8 and references.

[189] See especially Frantzen, *Literature of Penance* and 'Tradition of Penitentials'.

[190] R fols. 25, 28v, 40, 41v, 42v–43r. Both texts are used in the 'Oratio milite (*sic*) in templo' on fol. 25 (other copies occur in *Florilegium Frisingense*, ed. Lehner, pp. xxxi–xxxii and 38, 'Prayer Book', ed. Frost, p. 36, and 'Gebetbuch des frühen 11. Jahrhunderts', ed. Heiming, no. 8), at 41v and in the *Oratio Moucani* on 42v–43r. The title of the prayer on 40v, 'Precatio ad sanctam Mariam et sanctum Petrum et ad ceteros apostolos' (cf. Barré, *Prières anciennes*, p. 55), seems to refer to the whole composite prayer on 40r–42r, of which the first part occurs in C (no. 23) and the 'Officia per Ferias' (PL 101, 602), the middle part in the Fleury Prayer Book (*ibid.*, 1398A–C), and the last part in the eleventh-century Nonantola Psalter (*Thomasii Opera*, ed. Blanchinus, p. 523, col. a; cf. Salmon, *Analecta*, p. 133, no. 40) and in 'Manuscriptum Gertrudae filiae Mesconis II regis Poloniae', ed. W. Meysztowicz, *Antemurale* 2 (1955), 105–57, no. 73.

[191] See Cross and Livingstone, *Dictionary of the Christian Church*, s.v.; Bullough, 'Alcuin and the Kingdom of Heaven', pp. 19–20 and 67; *Precum Libelli*, ed. Wilmart, pp. 27–30, 53 and 76; PL 101, 526–31.

tials commonly prescribed the recitation of psalms as a penance for minor sins, their influence was inevitable. In any case, the recitation of the psalter, making the psalmist's thoughts one's own,[192] was fundamental to the Office and to private prayer, and many early medieval prayer collections were essentially adjuncts to the psalter.[193] Bede's abbot, Ceolfrith, was presumably exceptional in reciting the whole psalter twice or thrice daily,[194] but lesser, or busier, mortals could make a token attempt at complete recitation by using the 'breviate psalters', excerpted by others and included in prayer books such as the Book of Cerne.[195]

The apocryphal *Prayer of Manasses*, a canticle in the early church, supplied a more exotic penitential image in a prayer at R, 28v: 'my sins are multiplied like the sand on the sea shore' ('multiplicata sunt delicta mea uelut harena quae est in litore maris'). This simile, which is also echoed in the *Confessio peccatorum pura* which Alcuin composed for Charlemagne,[196] may have been transmitted to England in the Roman Antiphonary, in which it occurs as a respond.[197] A more immediate inspiration for the

---

192 Cassian, *Conlationes* X.11 (ed. Petschenig, pp. 304–5; trans. Chadwick, *Western Asceticism*, pp. 243–4). 'Psalter Collects' were introduced into the Western church, perhaps by Cassian, to help to give the psalms a Christian character; see Cross and Livingstone, *Dictionary of the Christian Church*, s.v.; Mohrmann, *Études* III, 245–63; *Psalter Collects*, ed. Brou. I have noticed no certain echoes in R and H.

193 Cf. Barré, *Prières anciennes*, pp. 9–10; Salmon, 'Livrets', p. 223.

194 Willis, *Further Essays*, p. 204.

195 *Cerne*, ed. Kuypers, pp. 174–95. Cf. Bishop, *Liturgica*, pp. 195–6; D. N. Dumville, 'Liturgical Drama and Panegyric Responsory from the Eighth Century? A Re-Examination of the Origin and Contents of the Ninth-Century Section of the Book of Cerne', *JTS*, ns 23 (1972), 374–406, at 384–5 and 399–405; *Precum Libelli*, ed. Wilmart, p. 143, n. 1; PL 101, 569–79; Bullough, 'Alcuin and the Kingdom of Heaven', p. 68, n. 158; *Bedae Opera Rhythmica*, ed. Fraipont, pp. 452–70; Salmon, *Analecta*, pp. 69–119; Salmon *et al.*, *Testimonia*, p. 42.

196 E.g. PL 101, 525D and *Precum Libelli*, ed. Wilmart, p. 23, line 21. The attribution is upheld by Wilmart, 'Manuel', p. 282, n. 5, and 'Bury Psalter', pp. 210–11, by Bullough, 'Alcuin and the Kingdom of Heaven', p. 15, and by Frantzen, *Literature of Penance*, p. 89. Cf. above, n. 103.

197 On Latin texts of the *Prayer of Manasses* see H. Schneider, 'Der Vulgata-Text der *Oratio Manasse*', *Biblische Zeitschrift*, ns 4 (1960), 277–82. The *Oratio Manasse* appears in the 'Gebetbuch des frühen 11. Jahrhunderts', ed. Heiming, no. 11, but not so far as I know in earlier private prayer books, although there is a quotation in a mid-ninth-century Tours prayer book (*Precum Libelli*, ed. Wilmart, p. 83, lines 26–8). For the antiphon (and echoes of it) see *Corpus*, ed. Hesbert IV, 343, no. 7372; PL 78, 832; Wilmart, 'Croix', p. 45 and n. 6; Barré, *Prières anciennes*, pp. 115, n. 74, and 131, n. 23.

prayer at R, 28v, however, may be an order for the reconciliation of penitents preserved in C (no. 14). It begins with the Penitential Psalm *Miserere mei* 'to the end' (Psalm L [AV LI]), followed by the *Pater noster*, the Prodigal Son's prayer, and the 'sands of the sea' passage from the *Prayer of Manasses*.[198] This *Reconciliatio penitentium* is given in C in the first person throughout so that a reader could use it for his own confession, but it may have been adapted from an order for administering the sacrament of confession. Its affinities are with the Insular rite of private penance, rather than the ancient rite of public penance; according to the Gelasian Sacramentary (Vatican, Reg. lat. 316), psalms were not to be used on the occasion of public penance, whereas that Sacramentary's order for private penance (added at the end of the eighth-century manuscript) begins with psalms, including the *Miserere mei*.[199]

Manasses's simile is also echoed in the *Oratio Moucani* (R, 42r–45r). In fact one can well imagine that the Welsh author, apart from this direct quotation (43v), modelled his alliterative parallelism on the style of the *Prayer of Manasses*. His use of rhyme, on the other hand, is more like the *apologia* (a private penitential prayer said by a priest during mass) in the eighth-century Gallican *Missale Gothicum*.[200]

Moucan's prayer is in rhyming couplets, of irregular syllabic count, and is divided into nine sections, most of them ending with the Hebrew refrain

Knowledge at York of the Antiphonary seems to be indicated by Ecgberht's *Dialogus* (H&S III, 411), but there are problems: cf. Vogel, *Introduction*, p. 330; Willis, *Further Essays*, p. 228; Bullough, 'Roman Books', pp. 30–1, and 'Alcuin and the Kingdom of Heaven', pp. 4–5; Constantinescu, 'Alcuin', p. 52. (The antiphon is not among those printed *ibid.*, pp. 38–51.)

[198] The parallel was noted by F. Cabrol, 'Le "Book of Cerne": les liturgies celtiques et gallicanes et la liturgie romaine', *Revue des questions historiques* 76 (1904), 210–22, at 218 (inaccurate in details). Note that the hexameters towards the end of C, no. 14 (p. 102, lines 1–2) recur more fully in R, 33v; see Meyer, 'Poetische Nachlese', pp. 599–600 and 619–20. The latter part of the prayer on 28v of R recurs on 48v–49r as part of the *Oratio sancti Augustini* mentioned above, p. 303; cf. also C, no. 25; 'Bury Psalter', ed. Wilmart, no. XIV; and PL 138, 1324B (cf. Vogel, *Introduction*, pp. 135–6).

[199] *Liber sacramentorum Romanae aecclesiae*, ed. Mohlberg, §§ 349 and 1701; Vogel, *Introduction*, p. 172. This view of C's *Reconciliatio penitentium* is questioned by Frantzen, *Literature of Penance*, p. 87, but cf. *ibid.*, p. 138 ('public penance was not well known in the eighth century in England'), also *idem*, 'Tradition of Penitentials', pp. 47 and 52–3 and n. 168.

[200] Ed. Mohlberg, §275. Cf. *Cerne*, ed. Kuypers, pp. xxv–xxvi, xxix, n. 1, xxxiii and 95, n. On *apologiae* cf. above, n. 188.

'eloe, sabaoth, ia, adonai eli eli laba (*sic*) sabacthani' (cf. Mark xv.34).[201]
Its style is quite unlike any other prayer in the Anglo-Saxon prayer books.
Like Manasses, Moucan begins with an imposing invocation to God the
Creator and continues with a long prayer of repentance, couched in biblical
language. He starkly juxtaposes biblical images which are stark in
themselves:

> Erue a framea animam meam,
> et de manu canis solue eam.
> Miserere mei, deus, miserere mihi;
> parce, omnipotens, quia peccaui.
> Pęnitentiam ex corde suscipe;
> pauperem de stercore erige.
> Si iniquitates meas obseruaberis,
> sicut cera liquefiam a facie ignis.
> Plumbi pondere praegrauata,
> uelut arena peccata mea.
> Verbum Dei mei semen
> suffocat in me spinarum noxium gramen.   Eloe, sabaoth.[202]

The allegorical element in Moucan's prayer is strong, and as challenging
as anything in early medieval exegesis: the idea of the disfigurement of the
spiritual temple within him leads to the idea of the removal of the historical
temple to Babylon ('The Chaldaic flame has moved the two cherubim');
that historical exile suggests the figurative exile of the Prodigal Son, upon
whose return the fatted calf was killed; that killing becomes a figure of the
blood of Christ the Lamb, and is then equated with the blood sprinkled on
their lintels by the Israelites at the first Passover, in turn equated with the
scarlet thread in the window by which the household of Rahab the harlot

---

[201] See partial edition by Meyer, 'Poetische Nachlese', pp. 621–4. The use of Hebrew here
is not mere magical verbiage (cf. Gougaud, 'Étude sur les *loricae*', p. 117, n. 3; Godel,
'Irisches Beten', p. 305, n. 354). The name *Moucan* (later *Meugan*) is distinctively Old
Welsh, not Cornish. Cf. P. Sims-Williams, review of *The Welsh Life of St David*, ed.
D. S. Evans, in *JEH* (forthcoming).

[202] 'Draw forth my soul from the spear; / and release it from the hand of the dog. / Have
mercy upon me, God, have mercy on me; / forgive, Almighty, for I have sinned. /
Accept repentance from the heart; / raise up the poor man from the dung. / If thou wilt
observe my iniquities, / I shall melt like wax before the face of fire. / My sins, like sand, /
have weighed me down with the weight of lead. / The seed of noxious thorns chokes in
me / the word of my God, the seed. / Eloe, sabaoth,' (etc.) (43v–44r).

was saved in Jericho.[203] This remarkable penitential prayer ends with a cluster of texts linked by the theme of heat: Moucan's soul panting like the hart for the Fount of Living Water; the Good Shepherd who makes his flock rest at noon (cf. Song of Songs 1.6 [AV 1.7]); the fire of God's love which should burn up Moucan's heart; the noontide demon (Psalm XC.6) from whose terrors he begs to be spared in death.[204] The *Oratio Moucani*, more than any other prayer in the early medieval prayer books, fits Cassian's description of a type of prayer that involved 'wandering haphazardly through the Bible and meditating on a variety of different texts'.[205] It would appeal to the audience of Apponius's commentary on the Song of Songs.[206]

The most prominent, and perhaps the earliest, penitential prayer in R is the *Oratio sancti Hygbaldi abbatis*,[207] which begins with large initial letters on 17r. Hygbald is almost certainly the 'very holy and continent' abbot of that name in the late seventh century, whom Bede localizes in the province of Lindsey, part of the old greater Mercian diocese. His cult, celebrated on 14 December, was probably based at Hibaldstow, Lincolnshire.[208] Describing himself as 'a miserable and unworthy homunculus', Hygbald calls for forgiveness to the Trinity, and then to Father, Son and Holy Ghost in turn. His invocation of the Father shows a mixture of two styles:

Deum omnipotentem patrem deprecor, qui creauit caelum et terram, mare et omnia quae in eis sunt [Acts IV.24, cf. Exodus XX.1], qui est in omnibus et super omnia Deus benedictus in sęcula, ut dimittat mihi omnia peccata mea atque

---

[203] fol. 42. Cf. Hughes, 'Irish Influence', pp. 57–8.

[204] Cf. J. B. Friedman, *Orpheus in the Middle Ages* (Cambridge, Mass., 1970), pp. 188–9 and 239, n. 57.

[205] *Conlationes* X.14 (ed. Petschenig, p. 308; trans. Chadwick, *Western Asceticism*, p. 246).

[206] See above, p. 199.

[207] The name is faint, but I have read most of it; the second letter seems to be y, not u. Cf. Hughes, 'Irish Influence', p. 56, n. 5. The prayer is anonymous in C (no. 34), the only other copy.

[208] See *HE* IV.3; *An Old English Martyrology*, ed. and trans. G. Herzfeld, EETS os 116 (London, 1900), 220–1. *Þa halgan þe on Angelcynne restað* says that he rests at *Ceceseg* near the river Ancholme in Lindsey, presumably meaning Hibaldstow: see Rollason, 'Resting-Places', pp. 69 and 89; *DEPN*, p. 238; cf. S 68 for *Hibaldestow*. The other pre-Conquest men noted by Searle, *Onomasticon*, p. 310, are: an abbot (perhaps the same man) and fifteen priests, clerics or monks in the Lindisfarne *Liber vitae* (listed in *Oldest English Texts*, ed. Sweet, p. 494); Hygebald in *ASC* (E) 710 (probably an error for Sigebald, cf. *EHD*, p. 170, n. 8); and Hygebald, bishop of Lindisfarne 780×781–803, who would probably have been styled *episcopus* rather than *sanctus abbas* in R if R was

crimina quae feci a conabulis iuuentutis meae usque in hanc aetatis horam, in factis, in uerbis, in cogitationibus, in uisu, in risu, in gressu, in auditu, in tacto olfactoque, uellens, nolens, sciens nesciensque, in spiritu uel in corpore, delinquens commisi.[209]

Here Hygbald begins in the style of a collect, with relative clauses (he addresses the Son and the Spirit in the same way). These establish a solemn, hieratic atmosphere; the text from Acts IV.24 was much used, presumably with this intention, in liturgies, prayers and benedictions, and it formed part of the 'sacrilegious prayer' of Aldebert, condemned in 745.[210] On the other hand, the rhythmical, rhyming style, and the exhaustiveness, of the lists that follow are typical of prayers in the Irish *lorica* tradition – although by listing sins rather than parts of the body Hygbald may deliberately modify this model.[211] In stressing 'deeds, words, thoughts' Hygbald may be influenced by Irish writers, who favoured this (originally Zoroastrian) triad, which they probably took from late patristic texts.[212] Irish influence on Hygbald is plausible, for Bede says that he went to Ireland to visit Ecgberht, with whom he discussed the lives of the early Fathers, whom they both wished to emulate.[213]

The preoccupation with minor sins in Hygbald's *Oratio* is not in itself especially Irish, but is characteristic of Western asceticism in general. Cassian, for example, had commented:

inpossibile namque est quemlibet sanctorum non in istis minutiis, quae per

written after 781 (and before 781 he would hardly be *sanctus*). Cf. Hughes, 'Irish Influence', p. 57.

[209] 'I beseech God the omnipotent Father, who created heaven and earth, sea and all that therein are, who is blessed God in all and over all for ever, that he discharge me of all my sins and misdeeds which I have done from the cradle of my youth until this hour of my life, [and which] in deeds, in words, in thoughts, in sight, in laughter, in going, in hearing, in touch and smell, willing, unwilling, knowing and unknowing, in spirit or in body, I have committed in folly.'

[210] *Ep.* lix (Tangl, p. 117); cf. above, p. 286. See Sims-Williams, 'Ephrem', p. 213, n. 33, arguing against Bishop's view that the use of Acts IV.24 is Irish. For an early example, see K. Gamber, 'Privatgebete aus der alten Kirche Ägyptens', *Heiliger Dienst* [Salzburg] 15 (1961), 81–5, at 82.

[211] Cf. Hughes, 'Irish Influence', pp. 56–7; Frantzen, *Literature of Penance*, pp. 85–7.

[212] During the eighth century it found its way into the continental liturgy of penance, apparently under Irish influence, and was eventually introduced into the mass as the *Confiteor*. See Sims-Williams, 'Triad', esp. pp. 99–100 and 105–8.

[213] *HE* IV.3. Cf. above, p. 248, n. 27.

sermonem, per cogitationem, per ignorantiam, per obliuionem, per necessitatem, per uoluntatem, per obreptionem admittuntur, incurrere.[214]

A broad ascetic tradition, perhaps sub-literary, clearly lies behind many prayers. Cassian had defined 'prayers' (as opposed to supplications, intercessions and thanksgivings; cf. 1 Timothy II.1) as vows to renounce vices and to observe virtues.[215] The 'morning prayer' in R (fol. 22) and H (2v–3v) is essentially such a prayer, except that the semi-Pelagian self-reliance of Cassian's 'vows' is replaced by more orthodox requests to God, in the old ascetic tradition of 'beggary to God'.[216]

Mane cum surrexero intende ad me, Domine, et guberna omnes actus meos et uerba mea et cogitationes meas ut tota die in tua uoluntate transeam.

Dona mihi, Domine, timorem tuum, cordis conpunctionem, mentis humilitatem, conscientiam puram, ut terram despiciam, cęlum aspiciam, peccata odiam, iustitiam diligam.

Aufer a me solicitudinem terrenam, gulae appetitum, concupiscentiam fornicationis, amorem pecuniae, pestem iracundiae, tristitiam saeculi, accidiam uanam, laetitiam terrenam.

Planta in me uirtutem abstinentium, continentiam carnis, castitatem, humilitatem, caritatem non fictam . . . [217]

Such lists of virtues introduced by *dona* or *da* are common in later prayer

---

[214] 'It is impossible for any holy man not to fall into those little sins which are incurred through speech, thought, ignorance, forgetfulness, necessity, willingly or inadvertently': Cassian, *Conlationes* XI.9 (ed. Petschenig, p. 324); cf. *Western Asceticism*, trans. Chadwick, p. 252.

[215] *Conlationes* IX.9–14 and 17 (ed. Petschenig, pp. 259–65; trans. Chadwick, *Western Asceticism*, pp. 219–22).

[216] Cf. Hausherr, 'Comment priaient les pères', pp. 46 and 296; Cassian, *Conlationes* X.11 (ed. Petschenig, p. 303; trans. Chadwick, *Western Asceticism*, p. 243). On the ascetics' presumption that Grace would aid their efforts cf. Chadwick, *Cassian*, pp. 121–2.

[217] 'In the morning when I rise, stretch out to me, Lord, and govern all my deeds and my words and my thoughts so that I may pass the whole day in thy will. Grant me, Lord, fear of thee, compunction of heart, humility of mind, a pure conscience, so that I may despise the earth, look towards heaven, hate sins, delight in justice. Take from me worldly care, appetite for gluttony, desire of fornication, love of money, the plague of wrath, the sadness of the world, vain melancholy, earthly joy. Plant in me the virtue of the abstinent, continence of the flesh, chastity, humility, unfeigned charity . . . ' (R fol. 22). For other copies see above, n. 51. The sins vary widely. Part of the version in H is translated above, p. 256.

books, but may have been spread by the Irish in particular.[218] A very early example, which distils much ascetical teaching in a few words, is a prayer of St Columbanus:

Domine deus, destrue [et] quicquid in me plantat aduersarius eradica, ut destructis iniquitatibus, in os et cor meum intellectum et opus bonum inseras, ut opere et ueritate tibi soli deseruiam, et intelligam mandata tua, et teipsum requiram. Da memoriam.[219] Da charitatem. Da castitatem. Da fidem. Da omne quod scis ad utilitatem animae meae pertinere. Domine, fac in me bonum, et presta mihi quod scis oportere, qui regnas.[220]

In the 'morning prayer' the balanced lists of *aufer* + vices and *planta* + virtues may reflect the ascetical principle of 'curing opposites by opposites' (*contraria contrariis curare*), promoted in the West by Cassian and taken up in the British and Irish penitentials and elsewhere.[221] For example, the second *Instructio* attributed to Columbanus, like the 'morning prayer', employs the Cassianic parable of the farmer and the stylistic device of homoioteleuton:

Studiamus ergo in primis uitia eradicare, uirtutesque insinuare; eradicemus

---

218 Cf. A. Wilmart *et al.*, *The Bobbio Missal: Notes and Studies*, HBS 61 (London, 1924), p. 34, arguing for the Irish nature of §§ 451 and 453; on the latter see further Wilmart, 'Bury Psalter', pp. 198 and 201–2. Cf. also C, nos. 15 (cf. above, n. 37) and 30 = 69 (cf. 'Bury Psalter', ed. Wilmart, no. XI). On the other hand, the 'demande des vertus' is inherent in the ascetic tradition (Hausherr, 'Comment priaient les pères', p. 52), and although such lists are foreign to the liturgy of the mass, they occur in other liturgical genres; see e.g. *The Benedictionals of Freising*, ed. R. Amiet *et al.*, HBS 88 (London, 1974), 66–7, nos. A II and A V. The list quoted above is borrowed in the prayer 'Domine Deus omnipotens qui es trinus et unus' (above, n. 91).

219 I.e. *spiritalis memoria* or recollectedness; see Cassian, *Conlationes* I.17 (ed. Petschenig, p. 26; trans. Chadwick, *Western Asceticism*, p. 207). Cf. Butler, *Western Mysticism*, pp. 38–9 and 99; Hausherr, 'Comment priaient les pères', pp. 55–7.

220 'O Lord God, destroy and root out whatever the adversary plants in me, that with my sins destroyed thou mayest sow understanding and good work in my mouth and heart; that in deed and truth I may serve thee only, and understand thy commandments and seek thyself. Grant memory. Grant charity. Grant chastity. Grant faith. Grant all that thou knowest to pertain to the profit of my soul. O Lord, work good in me, and provide me with what thou knowest that I need; who reignest (etc.).' I quote from the 'Officia per Ferias' in BN, lat. 1153, 92r (*et* is added *in marg.*); cf. PL 101, 604. For other copies see Wilmart, 'Manuel', p. 292 and n. 5. Walker (*Columbani Opera*, pp. lxiii and 214) knew only one eleventh-century manuscript and was unsure of the attribution.

221 *Irish Penitentials*, ed. Bieler, p. 5; *Columbani Opera*, ed. Walker, p. 171, n. 4. Cf. C, no. 15 (cf. above, n. 37).

superbiam, plantemus humiliatem, eruamus iram, fundemus patientiam, excidamus inuidiam, insinuemus beneuolentiam.[222]

A more elaborate instance occurs in a later, more certainly Irish homily, defining eightfold 'spiritual circumcision':

primo, ut a nobis abscidamus auaritiam et gulae concupiscentiam et plantemus pro ea abstinentiam; secundo, ut a nobis abscidamus fornicationem et pro ea plantemus castitatem . . .[223]

The 'morning prayer' continues the opposition of virtues and vices by listing the parts of the body that may perform good and bad deeds, a moral variation of the *lorica* tradition. This section, and the prayer, end:

Custodi pedes meos ne circumeant domus otiosas; sed sint in oratione Dei. Custodi manus meas ne porrigantur sępe ad capienda munera, sed potius eleuentur in precibus Domini munda et purae, quo possim dicere cum propheta: eleuatio manum mearum sacrificium uespertinum.[224]

The disapproval of visiting is a clear indication of the ascetic origin of the prayer,[225] and the objection to *frequent* alms-taking points in the same direction. The attribution of the prayer to Jerome in many later prayer books was probably due to its ascetic character.[226] It may be no coincidence that the prayer ends (as quoted above) with the psalm-verse with which

---

[222] 'Therefore let us seek above all to root out the vices and plant the virtues; let us root out pride and sow humility, let us pluck up wrath and lay down patience, let us prune envy and plant good will': *Columbani Opera*, ed. Walker, pp. 68–9; on the style, cf. R. E. McNally, '"Christus" in the Pseudo-Isidorian "Liber de Ortu et Obitu Patriarcharum"', *Traditio* 21 (1965), 167–83, at 172.

[223] 'First, that we may cut out avarice and desire of gluttony from ourselves and instead plant abstinence; secondly, that we may cut out fornication from ourselves and instead plant chastity . . .': Ó Laoghaire, 'Irish Elements', pp. 153–4.

[224] 'Keep my feet lest they go round visiting idle homes; but rather let them [be kneeling] in prayer to God. Keep my hands lest they stretch out often to take gifts; but rather may they be raised, clean and pure, in prayers to the Lord, whereby I may say with the prophet: "The raising of my hands is an evening sacrifice"'.

[225] Cf. Cassian, *Conlationes* 1.20 (ed. Petschenig, p. 31; trans. Chadwick, *Western Asceticism*, p. 210); *Columbani Opera*, ed. Walker, p. 154.

[226] Cf. Sims-Williams, 'Ephrem', p. 210.

Abba Isaac concludes his first Conference on prayer, as night comes on, at an evocative moment in Cassian's *Conlationes*.[227]

CONCLUSION

Although H and R are the earliest prayer books of their kind in Europe, they cannot be regarded as original works of devotion composed in the Worcester region. This is clear from the inclusion of material by Augustine, 'Ephrem', Hygbald, Bede, Moucan and others, and from the existence elsewhere of variant versions of many of the anonymous prayers. The two books may testify to receptivity rather than creativity. However this may be, they provide a varied cross-section of the region's religious culture, which, like any other sort of culture, must have been an amalgam of local and imported elements.

The texts range from personal, Augustinian devotions, which explore the theology of Grace, to medical charms, which instead bring to mind Harnack's thesis that the Gentiles understood Christianity at first as a mystery religion offering physical and spiritual healing.[228] They reveal how the Bible, the apocrypha and the works of the Fathers were understood and used. They reflect ascetic ideals. They tell us directly about the practice of private daily devotion, and indirectly about the mass, the visitation of the sick and penance.

Edmund Bishop remarked that 'the study of Liturgy, whatever else it may be, must also be a study in religious psychology'.[229] This should be even truer of the study of private prayer books, which Bishop was the first to promote.[230] The Harley Fragment and Royal Prayer Book, once they have been fully studied, should offer an insight into the religious mentality of the Hwicce fully equal to the monk of Wenlock's more sensational contribution in the kingdom of the Magonsætan.

---

[227] *Conlationes* IX.36 (ed. Petschenig, p. 283; trans. Chadwick, *Western Asceticism*, p. 233). On Irish knowledge of Cassian see P. Ó Néill, 'The Date and Authorship of *Apgitir Chrábaid*: Some Internal Evidence', in *Irland und die Christenheit*, ed. Ní Chatháin and Richter, pp. 203–15, at 207–8; Warren, *Liturgy and Ritual*, ed. Stevenson, p. xlii, n. 200.

[228] A. Harnack, *The Mission and Expansion of Christianity in the First Three Centuries*, trans. J. Moffatt, 2nd ed., 2 vols. (London, 1908) I, 101–24; cf. E. J. and L. Edelstein, *Asclepius: A Collection and Interpretation of the Testimonies*, 2 vols. (Baltimore, 1945) II, 132–8.

[229] *Liturgica*, p. 123.　　　[230] Cf. above, p. 3.

11

Milred, Cuthbert and Anglo-Latin poetry

Milred became bishop of Worcester between 743 and 745 and died in 774 or 775.[1] At the beginning of this period Æthelbald of Mercia granted him the toll due on two ships at London, where the bishops of Worcester may have been trading.[2] The other bishops attesting Æthelbald's charter were Ingwald of London (d. 745), and Milred's own predecessor, Bishop Wilfrith (d. 744×745?), so presumably Milred had been appointed to succeed Wilfrith during the latter's lifetime;[3] perhaps Wilfrith was incapacitated by illness or old age, for he had been bishop of Worcester at least since Ecgwine's death in 717, if not longer.[4] Nothing is recorded of Milred's life before he became bishop, but we know something about his activities as diocesan. For example, we see him granting episcopal land at Sodbury to a certain Eanbald, on condition that his heirs returned it to the see if they did not take holy orders,[5] and at the end of his life we find Milred

---

[1] 'Florence' s.a. 743 says 'Wilfrido Hwicciorum episcopo, de hac uita subtracto, Milredus successit' (*MHB*, p. 543), and S 98 shows that Milred was bishop by 745. Milred's obit is s.a. 772 (*recte* 774) in *ASC*, but 'Florence' (*MHB*, p. 544) puts it in 775, perhaps really the date of his successor's accession. Cf. Darlington and McGurk, 'The "Chronicon ex Chronicis"', p. 188.

[2] S 98. See above, p. 147, n. 21

[3] Robertson, *Charters*, pp. 259–60. For parallels, see Sims-Williams, 'Wilfrid', p. 167. Perhaps we should accept the date 743 for Milred's accession in 'Florence' and the 745 obit for Wilfrith in 'Simeon of Durham' (*EHD*, pp. 265 and 285, n. 9); but possibly the whole of the latter annal belongs to 744 (cf. *EHD*, p. 265, n. 5).

[4] Cf. 'Florence' s.a. 717: 'S. Ecgwinus tertius Wicciorum episcopus, transiuit ad Dominum ... Pro quo Wilfridus, religionis uir eximiæ, electus illo adhuc superstite, præsulatum suscepit Wigorniensis ecclesiæ' (*MHB*, p. 541). But the notion that Ecgwine retired from the episcopate may derive from unreliable Evesham tradition; cf. above, p. 142 and n. 124.

[5] See above, p. 156.

granting the monastery of Withington to the abbess of Twyning, on condition that both monasteries revert to Worcester after her death.[6] These were the typical everyday concerns of a bishop of Worcester. The much more unusual fact of his life, that he travelled to Germany in 753, is not noticed in extant English sources, and we would not know about it but for the preservation among Lull's correspondence of Milred's letter, discussed in ch. 8 above.

Milred's letter to Lull, with its elegant echoes of Vergil, is itself an indication of Milred's literary interests and aspirations. Moreover, in a postscript he apologizes for not sending Lull a book of poems because a Bishop Cuthbert had failed to return it:

librum pyrpyri metri ideo non misi quia gutbertus epis*copus* adhuc reddere distulit.[7]

The reading *pyrpyri* in the ninth-century Vienna manuscript was correctly emended by Kylie to *Porphyri*, which Levison then correctly identified as a reference to Publius Optatianus Porphyrius, Constantine's court-poet, who specialized in elaborate picture-poems containing acrostics in the form of crosses and so on. Levison suggested that the acrostics of Aldhelm, Boniface and Lull were inspired by Porphyrius's efforts and noted the 'metrum Porfilii' (*sic*) in the early ninth-century library catalogue of Lorsch near Mainz, and the existence of another copy at Fulda, where it was imitated by Hrabanus Maurus (d. 856), abbot of Fulda and archbishop of Mainz.[8] Earlier writers had translated 'purple book of metre', as if *pyrpyri* were for *purpureum* agreeing with *librum*.[9] Such drastic emendation was uncalled for; yet some such confusion may have been present in the mind of

---

6 See above, p. 132.

7 'I do not send the book of Porphyrius's poems because Bishop Cuthbert has so far delayed in returning it': *Sancti Bonifacii Epistolae*, ed. Unterkircher, 51r; Boniface, *Ep.* cxii (Tangl, p. 245).

8 Kylie, *English Correspondence*, p. 209; Levison, *England and the Continent*, p. 145 (also see p. 281). Cf. D. Schaller, 'Die karolingischen Figurengedichte des Cod. Bern. 212', in *Medium Aevum Vivum: Festschrift für Walther Bulst*, ed. H. R. Jauss and D. Schaller (Heidelberg, 1960), pp. 22–47. Levison refers to Bede's allusion to Porphyrius in his *De arte metrica*, but Dr N. Wright points out to me that the allusion shows that Bede had not seen the poems themselves and was merely following and misunderstanding Jerome. Cf. Wright, 'Bede and Vergil', p. 362, n. 5.

9 G. F. Browne, *Boniface of Crediton and his Companions* (London, 1910), p. 289; S. J. Crawford, *Anglo-Saxon Influence on Western Christendom 600–800* (Oxford, 1933), p. 70.

the scribe, because luxury editions of Porphyrius's *carmina figurata* were produced on purple parchment, with the pictures made by the words of the poems picked out in gold and silver.[10]

The bishop 'Gutbertus' who failed to return Milred's Porphyrius can only be Cuthbert, archbishop of Canterbury 740–60. He had corresponded with Boniface and, like Milred, he sent Lull a letter of condolence when Boniface was killed.[11] In it Cuthbert mentions that earlier letters and messengers between Boniface and himself had established that their respective communities should pray for each other's living and dead.[12] Lull may have heard that Milred had a copy of Porphyrius through this correspondence with Canterbury; but equally well, Milred himself may have mentioned it when he was in Germany.

Nordenfalk has argued that the copy of Porphyrius which Milred lent to Cuthbert may have been a Late Roman copy, perhaps as old as Porphyrius's day, and may have influenced the decoration of the gospel book known as the Codex Aureus (Stockholm, Kungliga Biblioteket, A. 135).[13] If so, failure to return a book can rarely have been better justified. The Codex Aureus was probably written at Canterbury in the mid- or late eighth century.[14] Alternate leaves were dyed purple and written in gold, silver and white, and the rest were written in red and black. Before writing certain pages, the scribe drew large figures on them, such as crosses, rectangular, diagonal, or zig-zag patterns, and then spaced his uncial letters so as to fit them, often using different inks to emphasise the design. This unique decoration of the gospel text was evidently inspired by a manuscript of Porphyrius's picture-poems, which were originally produced in gold and

---

[10] See Nordenfalk, 'Note', p. 153.

[11] *Epp.* lxxviii and cxi (Tangl, pp. 161–70 and 238–43); trans. Kylie, *English Correspondence*, pp. 176–91 and 198–205. See above, p. 233. On a further manuscript of *Ep.* lxxviii see Levison, *England and the Continent*, p. 281. On Cuthbert and Lull cf. Hahn, *Bonifaz und Lul*, pp. 218–34; Brooks, *Canterbury*, pp. 83–5; also Moore, *Saxon Pilgrims*, p. 69.

[12] Boniface, *Ep.* cxi (Tangl, p. 241).

[13] Nordenfalk, 'Note', pp. 153–5. Cf. S. M. Kuhn, 'Some Early Mercian Manuscripts', *RES* ns 8 (1957), 355–74, at 365. A relevant purple page is reproduced in colour by Nordenfalk, *Celtic and Anglo-Saxon Painting*, plate 33, and three in black and white by Alexander, *Insular Manuscripts*, pls. 157–9.

[14] *CLA* XI, no. 1642 favours s. viii^ex. See also Engelbert, 'Bemerkungen', p. 408. Nordenfalk, *Celtic and Anglo-Saxon Painting*, p. 96, thinks a date in the 750s, during Cuthbert's archiepiscopate, possible, and Alexander, *Insular Manuscripts*, p. 56, no. 30, favours s. viii^med.

silver on purple parchment or in black and red on plain parchment, as the poet himself says.[15] The similarity of the patterns is shown by Nordenfalk's parallel plates from the Codex Aureus and from a ninth-century manuscript of the figure poems of Porphyrius and Hrabanus Maurus from Saint-Denis (Paris, Bibliothèque Nationale, lat. 2421). There are differences in function, however, in tune with the Anglo-Saxon reverence for the Bible:

> Whereas the patterns in the Constantinian poems have the function of isolating distinct sentences, those in the Gospels do not fill any 'literary' function at all, since the text did not lend itself to cross-word-combinations of the letters into new words. The English scriptorium simply enjoyed the patterns for their own sakes, as a sort of visual punning ... A spirit of playfulness, even whimsicality governs the composition of the pages, and we would call it childish, if it were not evidently a solemn game for the purpose of enhancing the holiness of the sacred text.[16]

The decoration of the Codex Aureus seems designed to express the inexhaustible mystery and riddling or acrostic-like multiplicity of meanings of the holy text. This impression is enhanced by the use of different inks for the *nomina sacra*. Thus the Codex Aureus is not just another example of 'barbarous' misuse of an Antique pattern, but a convincing reinterpretation of one for new ends.

Nordenfalk suggests that Milred's Porphyrius, after inspiring the Codex Aureus at Canterbury, did reach Mainz eventually, as Milred intended, and served to inspire Hrabanus's picture-poem *De laudibus sanctae crucis*, one of the surviving copies of which is written in gold and silver on purple parchment.[17] The whole argument is persuasive, although open to the

---

[15] Nordenfalk, 'Note', p. 153. On Porphyrius, see further Nordenfalk, *Spätantiken Zierbuchstaben* I, 57–62 and references.

[16] Nordenfalk, 'Note', pp. 154 and 153. Cf. above, pp. 179–81.

[17] Vatican, Biblioteca Apostolica, Reg. lat. 124 (Nordenfalk, 'Note', p. 155). This is reproduced and discussed by P. E. Schramm and F. Mütherich, *Denkmale der deutschen Könige und Kaiser* (Munich, 1962), no. 22, and the sister-manuscript, Vienna, Nationalbibliothek, Cod. 652, 33v (also from Fulda), is reproduced and discussed by G. Henderson, *Early Medieval* (Harmondsworth, 1972), pp. 222–3 and 262. The *De laudibus* in Cambridge, Trinity College, B. 16. 3 is reproduced by E. Temple, *Anglo-Saxon Manuscripts 900–1066* (London, 1976), pls. 45–6; and that in Berne, Burgerbibliothek, 212 by Nordenfalk, *Spätantiken Zierbuchstaben* II, pls. 12–13. I have personally consulted only the Paris manuscript and Cambridge, University Library, Gg. 5. 35, 211r–225r (cf. Rigg and Wieland, 'Canterbury Classbook', p. 122).

criticism that Milred's copy was not necessarily the only *de luxe* Porphyrius in circulation.

Some further traces of Milred's literary dealings with Archbishop Cuthbert may possibly be seen in some late tenth-century additions to another Canterbury manuscript: London, BL, Cotton Vitellius A. xix (s. x^med) written (in all probability) at St Augustine's.[18] The additions in question are four epigrams and a prose note which were added to 7v–8r, 88r and 114r in an Anglo-Caroline hand, with titles in fine rustic capitals for every item except the third.[19] This third, untitled item (at 8r, preceding a blank half page) contains the fairly unusual name Milred, severed by the poetic device of tmesis:

> Hos tibi .Mil. lyrico .red. feci carmine uersus;
> Suscipe, care Deo, quæso uice muneris illos,
> Et felix inter felices uiue per aeuum.[20]

This dedication clearly refers not to the main contents of the manuscript, Bede's prose and verse *vitae* of St Cuthbert, but to the other epigrams scattered through the manuscript in the same hand, or at the least to the preceding Items I and II on 7v–8r. Whether the text means that the collection referred to was compiled *by* 'Mil-red' or *for* him depends on whether one construes this name with *feci* or with *tibi*. Although Milred of Worcester held no monopoly over the name,[21] it is extremely likely that he is the 'Mil-red' mentioned, since he is known to have collected epigrams, as we shall see. It is even tempting to conjecture that the unnamed party – whether the author or dedicatee of the poem – was Archbishop Cuthbert, and that the book from which the St Augustine's scribe copied the verses had been in Canterbury since Cuthbert and Milred's day.

Neither Milred nor Cuthbert composed all the epigrams added to the manuscript, even if they collected them, for Item II (7v–8r), 'VERSVS DE

---

[18] Bishop, 'MSS. Connected with St Augustine's', p. 93 (cf. p. 324). Cf. Ker, *Catalogue*, no. 217.

[19] Sheerin, 'Leland and Milred', pp. 178–9. He also notes 'five *Alleluia* texts with neumes', added 'at about the same time'. These are in a quite different hand. My quotations are taken from the manuscript, as Sheerin's printers let him down.

[20] 'I, ?Milred, have made these verses in lyric poetry for you, ?Milred; beloved of God, receive them, I beg you, as a gift and, fortunate among the fortunate, live for ever.'

[21] Cf. Searle, *Onomasticon*, pp. 352 and 568. But the only other ecclesiastics are an abbot and a cleric in the Lindisfarne *Liber vitae* (ed. Sweet, *Oldest English Texts*, pp. 156 (line 82) and 161 (line 279)).

ORATIONE DOMINICA', a verse paraphrase of the Lord's Prayer, is simply abstracted from Juvencus's ever-popular fourth-century versification of the gospel story. It also appears separately in some continental manuscripts, sometimes similarly entitled 'De oratione dominica', and also in the Book of Cerne.[22] Many of the variant readings agree with the Book of Cerne and may reflect a Mercian textual tradition. It may be significant that the Book of Cerne merges the Juvencus paraphrase with one of Bede's psalm paraphrases; these were probably known to Milred for one of them is transmitted in the Royal Prayer Book.[23] Item IV (fol. 88r) is otherwise unidentified, but is somewhat reminiscent of the ecclesiastical riddles popular in seventh- and eighth-century England:

DE SACRO BAPTISMATE
Fons sacer est fidei qui culpas abluit omnes
Tinguitur hoc quisque incipit esse nouus.[24]

Item I (fol. 7v), on the other hand, may, to judge by slight verbal similarities, be by the same writer as the dedicatory epigram, or at least may have influenced it; both have *care Deo* preceded by an imperative and followed in the next line by *felix* referring to the person being exhorted. In the present case *felix* comes from Vergil's famous line:

felix qui potuit rerum cognoscere causas.

Tatwine, archbishop of Canterbury 731–4, re-used this line for a riddle on Philosophy,

est felix mea qui potuerit cognoscere iura[25]

but the writer of Item I applies it to the study of the Bible:

22 *Euangelia* I.590–604 (ed. Huemer, p. 32); *Cerne*, ed. Kuypers, no. 2, lines 10–20; Meyer, 'Poetische Nachlese', pp. 598 and 619. Cf. Walther, *Initia*, nos. 18174 and 18179; Schaller and Könsgen, *Initia*, no. 15347.

23 See above, p. 281; *Bedae Opera Rhythmica*, ed. Fraipont, p. 450, no. XVIII. By contrast, the variants from Huemer's text listed by Sheerin do not agree consistently with any one manuscript in Huemer's apparatus, nor with the text printed by H. Walther, 'Versifizierte *Paternoster* und *Credo*', *Revue du moyen âge latin* 20 (1964), 45–64, at 46.

24 '*Concerning holy baptism*: There is a holy spring of faith which washes all faults away; whoever is moistened by this begins to be a new man.'

25 'Happy is he who can discover the causes of things' (*Georgics* II.490); 'Happy is he who could discover my laws' (*Collectiones Aenigmatum Merovingicae Aetatis*, ed. F. Glorie, 2 vols., CCSL 133–133A (Turnhout, 1968) I, 168).

DE QVATTVOR CLAVIBVS SAPIENTIÆ, ID EST INDVSTRIA LEGENDI, ASSIDVITAS
INTERROGANDI, CONTEMPTVS DIVITIARVM, HONORIFICENTIA DOCTORIS

[D]ilige, *care Deo*, Scripturae discere causas,
Felix ut possis rerum cognoscere causas.
Celsa tenet nam bis binas sapientia claues,
E quibus in primis industria magna legendi est.
Inde secundo loco fit percunctatio crebra;
Tertia quae sequitur contemptus diuitiarum est.
Debita doctorum fulget ueneratio quarta.
Quattuor hae claues caelestis uerba sophiæ
Rite tibi reserant, lector, si diligis illas.
Frater amate mihi idcirco te sedulus oro
Clauibus prædictis operam dare meque memento,
Vt precibus domino semper commendes in almis.[26]

The phrase *te sedulus oro* addressed to the *lector* may come from the verses
attributed to a certain Florianus prefixed to many copies of Prosper of
Aquitaine's *Epigrammata ex sententiis S. Augustini*, a favourite school text:

Vnde ego *te*, lector, relegis qui haec *sedulus, oro*
Intentas adhibere sonis caelestibus aures . . .[27]

[26] *'Concerning the Four Keys of Wisdom, i.e. industry in reading, assiduity in asking questions,
contempt of riches, respect for the teacher*: Love, beloved of God, to learn the causes of
Scripture, so that, fortunate, you can discover the causes of things. For high wisdom
comprises twice two keys, of which the first of all is great industry in reading. Then in
second place follows frequent questioning. The third which follows is contempt of
riches. Due reverence for teachers shines as the fourth. These four keys duly unlock the
words of heavenly wisdom for you, reader, if you love them. Therefore, my beloved, I
earnestly beg you to attend to the aforesaid keys and remember me so that you may ever
commend me in kindly prayers to the Lord.'

[27] 'Wherefore, reader who earnestly reads these verses, I beg you to apply attentive ears to
heavenly sounds': edited from Milan, Biblioteca Ambrosiana, C. 74 sup. (s. ix), 117r
[*sic. leg.*] by C. Pascal, *Letteratura latina medievale: nuovi saggi e note critiche* (Catania,
1909), p. 58; the verses are said to be a later addition by M. Ferrari, '"In papia
conveniant ad Dungalum"', *Italia medioevale e umanistica* 15 (1972), 1–52, at 37. See also
PL 51, 51; Walther, *Initia*, no. 7475; Schaller and Könsgen, *Initia*, no. 5836; K. A.
De Meyier, *Codices Vossiani Latini*, 3 vols. (Leiden, 1973–7) II, 198. Only inferior
parallels can be found in Schumann, *Hexameter-Lexicon* V, 84. For copies of the epigram
in tenth- and eleventh-century Canterbury schoolbooks see M. Lapidge, 'The Study of
Latin Texts in Late Anglo-Saxon England: [I] The Evidence of Latin Glosses', in *Latin
and the Vernacular Languages in Early Medieval Britain*, ed. N. Brooks (Leicester, 1982),
pp. 99–140, at 105–6; Rigg and Wieland, 'Canterbury Classbook', p. 121. On Prosper
in England see K. Toth, 'Altenglische Interlinearglossen zu Prospers *Epigrammata* und
Versus ad Coniugem', *Anglia* 102 (1984), 1–36.

The poem in the Canterbury manuscript is a version of the common medieval theme of the Five Keys of Wisdom.[28] This variant with *four* keys is rare and doubtless primitive. A version occurs in the Pseudo-Bedan *Collectanea*, which are believed to be of Insular origin and at least as old as the eighth century:

Quatuor claues sunt: sapientia uel industria legendi, assiduitas interrogandi, honor doctoris, contemptio facultatum.[29]

Another version of the Four Keys of Wisdom occurs in the *Liber de numeris* IV.25, which is believed to be an Irish compilation made in Germany in the second half of the eighth century; here the keys are 'Sedulitas legendi, adsiduitas interrogandi, honor magistri, contemptio mundi'.[30] There is a close parallel in Zürich, Zentralbibliothek, Rheinau 140, 36v, a miscellany written in the second half of the eighth century, probably at St Gallen, and closely related to Irish material of the *Liber de numeris* sort: 'industria legendi, sedulitas interrogandi, contemptio facultatum, honorificatio

[28] As Sheerin notes, 'Leland and Milred', pp. 178–9. See Lehmann, *Büchertitel* II, 51–2; R. Avesani, 'Leggesi che cinque sono le chiavi della sapienza', *Rivista di cultura classica e medioevale* 7 (1965), 62–73. Cf. the following epigram from two twelfth-century manuscripts, metrically a later composition: 'Disce libens et quere frequens; utriusque memor sis; / Dilige doctorem, simul et metuas monitorem; / Hę claves quinque tibi pandent claustra *sophię*' (ed. J. Werner, *Beiträge zur Kunde der lateinischen Literatur des Mittelalters aus Handschriften gesammelt* (Aarau, 1905), p. 20).

[29] This obviously needs emending so as to be translated: 'There are Four Keys of Wisdom: industry in reading, assiduity in asking questions, honouring the teacher, contempt of riches': Bede, *Opera* (Basel, 1563) III, 648 (PL 94, 541); cf. R. Flower, *Catalogue of Irish Manuscripts in the British Museum* II (London, 1926), p. 488. L. W. Daly and W. Suchier, *Altercatio Hadriani Augusti et Epicteti Philosophi*, Illinois Studies in Language and Literature 24 (Urbana, 1939), 36, note that this section is related to the *Ioca Monachorum*, but this seems not to apply to the passage quoted. No manuscript of the *Collectanea* survives; cf. Lapidge and Sharpe, *Bibliography of Celtic-Latin Literature*, no. 1257; M. Lapidge, 'Latin Learning in Dark Age Wales: Some Prolegomena', in *Proceedings of the Seventh International Congress of Celtic Studies, 1983*, ed. D. E. Evans *et al.* (Oxford, 1986), pp. 91–107, at 100–2. Copies of *Collectanea Bede* and his *Flores ex diversis* in mid-sixteenth-century England were noted by Bale, *Index Britanniae Scriptorum*, ed. R. L. Poole and M. Bateson (Oxford, 1902), pp. 42, 44, and 516. A 'Bede liber collectaneus' occurs in the Saint-Bertin catalogue of *c.* 1104 (ed. Berthod, 'Notice', p. 228), on which see above, p. 201.

[30] 'Zeal in reading, assiduity in asking questions, honouring the teacher, contempt of the world': quoted by McNally, *Irische Liber de numeris*, p. 83. On the *Liber* cf. Sims-Williams, 'Triad', p. 87.

magistrorum'. The Canterbury poem is clearly very similar to all three sources, but the nearest verbal parallel (with only the trivial variant 'honorificatio doctorum') appears in a miscellany copied at Freising in the second half of the eighth century by the Anglo-Saxon scribe Peregrinus.[31] As the *Four* Keys of Wisdom are very unusual,[32] I would conclude that the poem was probably based on a seventh- or eighth-century Insular source containing numerical material similar to that in the *Collectanea* and *Liber de numeris*.

This conclusion is perhaps supported by the prose note on 114r. This lists the six ages of man: *infantia* (until 7), *pueritia* (until 14), *adolescentia* (until 28), *iuuentus* (until 59, *recte* 49), *senectus* (until 77), and *senium* ('quæ nullo tempore finitur').[33] The ultimate source is clearly Isidore of Seville, *Differentiae* II.xix.74–6, but the title, 'SEX AETATES HOMINIS SUNT', agrees with the derivative in the Pseudo-Bedan *Collectanea*, and there may be a comparable passage in an unprinted section of the *Liber de numeris* (II.5).[34] The prose note is thus of similar character to the Four Keys of Wisdom poem, and the hypothesis suggests itself that both items occurred in the collection of material to which the 'Mil-red' dedication refers. Other copies of the prose note occur among other numerological material in two

[31] On Rheinau 140 cf. *ibid.*, p. 86; *CLA* VII, no. 1021; L. C. Mohlberg, *Katalog der Handschriften der Zentralbibliothek Zürich* I, *Mittelalterliche Handschriften* (Zürich, 1951), p. 229; I have used a photostat kindly supplied by Dr M. Germann. For Peregrinus see *Florilegium Frisingense*, ed. Lehner, pp. 20 and 36. Cf. *Sedulii Scotti Collectaneum Miscellaneum*, ed. D. Simpson, Corpus Christianorum, Continuatio Mediaeualis 67 (Turnhout, 1988), 11: 'Quatuor claues sunt sapientiae: industria legendi, asiduitas interrogandi, contemptus pecuniarum, honorificatio doctorum.'

[32] The only other example which I have seen cited is the 'quatuor claues sapiencie' in Mainz, Stadtbibliothek, 231 (s. xv?), cited by Lehmann, *Büchertitel* II, 52. In fact, the reading of the manuscript is 'quinque sunt claues sapiencie' (163v), as a photostat kindly supplied by Dr K. Behrens reveals.

[33] Something went wrong with the printing of the figures in Sheerin's edition, 'Leland and Milred', p. 179.

[34] Isidore in PL 83, 81 (cf. J. A. Burrow, *The Ages of Man: A Study in Medieval Writing and Thought* (Oxford, 1986), pp. 74, n. 46, 82, n. 73, and 87–8); *Collectanea* in Bede, *Opera* (Basel, 1563) III, 668 (PL 94, 556); McNally, *Irische Liber de numeris*, p. 32 (but according to McNally this last is from *Etymologiae* XI.ii.1–7). The same title appears in *The Irish Sex Aetates Mundi* (ed. D. Ó Cróinín (Dublin, 1983), p. 66, but seems to have been added by the editor; cf. H. L. C. Tristram, *Sex Aetates Mundi*, Anglistiche Forschungen 165 (Heidelberg, 1985), 211, n. 80. Eugenius of Toledo versified the *Differentiae* passage as 'Sex sunt aetates hominis . . .', and this was transmitted as a separate poem (Schaller and Könsgen, *Initia*, no. 14973 bis).

manuscripts of the Anglian Collection of genealogies and episcopal lists (London, BL, Cotton Vespasian B. vi (Mercia, 805×814), 107r, and Cambridge, Corpus Christi College 183 (Wessex, 934×939), 68v), and presumably derive from their late eighth-century Mercian archetype.[35] On the other hand, the Six Ages prose note does not come into the category of 'uersus', and may have been transmitted independently of the 'Mil-red' verses, perhaps with the Anglian Collection and/or with Bede's *Vitae S. Cuthberti* (for CCCC 183 includes texts of the *uitae* closely related to those in Vitellius A. xix).[36] The note was available at St Augustine's in Cambridge, Corpus Christi College 320, pt II (St Augustine's, s. x²), p. 98, amid other numerological material related to the Anglian Collection's,[37] and it also occurs in a later St Augustine's manuscript of Bede's metrical *Vita S. Cuthberti*: Vatican, Biblioteca Apostolica, Reg. lat. 204 (s. xi^{in}), 24v, a manuscript related to Vitellius A. xix.[38] It is tempting to suppose that the 'Mil-red' poems, Anglian Collection and *Vitae S. Cuthberti* had been transmitted together since the late eighth century, but further textual study would be needed to establish this as a probability – especially in view of the fact that the verses and prose note in Vitellius A. xix are not by the same scribe as the *vitae*.

According to William of Malmesbury (writing in 1125), 'Florence' of Worcester, and various post-Conquest Canterbury historians, Archbishop Cuthbert was translated from Hereford in 740.[39] This is quite possible

---

[35] James, *Catalogue of Manuscripts in Corpus Christi College, Cambridge* I, 439. On these manuscripts see above, p. 41. The continental derivatives of the *Differentiae* passage quoted by E. Sears, *The Ages of Man: Medieval Interpretations of the Life Cycle* (Princeton, 1986), pp. 64 and 177, nn. 43–4, seem unrelated (the one in Munich, Bayerische Staatsbibliothek, Clm. 14532 (St Emmeram, s.x), 93v, is unprinted, and I am indebted to Dr H. Hauke for a transcript).

[36] *Two Lives of Saint Cuthbert*, ed. Colgrave, p. 46; *Vita Sancti Cuthberti*, ed. Jaager, p. 33.

[37] James, *Catalogue of Manuscripts in Corpus Christi College, Cambridge* II, 137. For the provenance see Bishop, 'MSS. Connected with St Augustine's', p. 326.

[38] A. Wilmart, *Codices Reginenses Latini* (Vatican City, 1937–) I, 482–3; Ker, *Catalogue*, nos. 217 and 389; *Vita Sancti Cuthberti*, ed. Jaager, p. 33; Gneuss, 'Preliminary List', p. 58, no. 93.

[39] *GP*, pp. 8 and 298–9; 'Florence' (following William according to Darlington and McGurk, 'The "Chronicon ex Chronicis"', p. 194, n. 51) in *MHB*, p. 543 (s.a. 741); H&S III, 340; metrical *Vita Cuthberti* in Lambeth Palace, 159 (Christ Church, s. xvi), fol. 229, printed in part by Wharton, *Anglia Sacra* II, 72 (cf. Hardy, *Descriptive Catalogue* I, 483, no. 1035; James, *Catalogue of Manuscripts of Lambeth Palace*, p. 254). Brooks, *Canterbury*, p. 344, n. 52, 'would interpret [S 24] to mean that Cuthbert was

chronologically. Cuthbert, the fifth bishop in the 'Hereford' list, was consecrated in 736, and is not heard of after he attended the synod that debated the question of Withington monastery in that same year or in the following one; his successor, Podda, is first recorded in 747.[40] It is, moreover, quite plausible that three successive archbishops of Canterbury under Æthelbald of Mercia should be from areas under his sway: Tatwine, an abbot from Breedon-on-the-Hill; Nothhelm, a priest from London; and Cuthbert of the Magonsætan. Episcopal translation was uncanonical,[41] but as overlord in Kent Æthelbald would have been in a position to insist on it. If Archbishop Cuthbert had been bishop to the Magonsætan until 740, it may explain why Milred in his postscript to Lull in 754 calls him *episcopus*, rather than *archiepiscopus*; he may have slipped into using his former title.[42]

On the other hand, some doubt remains about the identification of the bishop of the Magonsætan with the archbishop, for the *Anglo-Saxon Chronicle*, the *Continuation* of Bede, and 'Simeon of Durham' all record Archbishop Cuthbert's consecration without mentioning any translation,[43] and Eadmer, too, is silent on the point in his brief account of Cuthbert in his *Vita S. Bregwini*, written in 1123–4.[44] To this argument from silence one may add that a ninth-century Canterbury forger was evidently ignorant of the identification, since he included both *Cuðberhtus archi-*

acting as abbot [of Lyminge] in 741 rather than that he had been abbot before his election as archbishop'; cf. Scharer, *Königsurkunde*, p. 113.

[40] S 1429; *EHD*, p. 264 ('Simeon of Durham'); for Podda see BCS 174. An addition to 'Florence' s.a. 741 adds Podda's succession to the annal about Cuthbert's translation (*MHB*, p. 543, n. 2; Darlington and McGurk, 'The "Chronicon ex Chronicis"', p. 194, n. 51).

[41] Professor Whitelock told me that Sir Frank Stenton thought the translation unlikely for this reason. On the other hand Mr K. Harrison referred me to the translations of Mellitus from London to Canterbury, Wine from Winchester to London, and John of Beverley from Hexham to York (*HE* II.7; III.7; V.3). Some of these precedents were arguably special cases. For other examples of canonical irregularity in England see Harrison, *Framework*, pp. 103 and 108, also Sims-Williams, 'Wilfrid', p. 167, n. 16.

[42] The avoidance of the archiepiscopal title is too early to be connected with the Mercian archiepiscopal pretensions of Offa's reign.

[43] *EHD*, pp. 174, 265 and 285. Cf. Brooks, *Canterbury*, p. 80.

[44] 'Life of Bregwine', ed. Scholz, pp. 139–40, c. 3 (also in Wharton, *Anglia Sacra* II, 185–6). The *Vita* wrongly attributed to Osbern (*ibid.* II, 75–7), is merely an epitome of Eadmer's (cf. Hardy, *Descriptive Catalogue* I, 484, no. 1037; Scholz, p. 136).

episcopus and *Cuðberht episcopus* in a witness-list intended to suit the year 742.[45]

Some further poetic material tends to tip the balance in favour of the bishop's identity with the archbishop, and sheds more light on his relations with Milred. In his discussion of the Hereford bishops in his *Gesta pontificum* of 1125, William of Malmesbury quotes two poems by Cuthbert 'which I saw recently', the one commemorating the completion of some embroidered Cross-cloths, commissioned by his predecessor Walhstod, and the other on a tomb which he constructed for the bodies of his predecessors, Bishops Tyrhtil, Torhthere and Walhstod, for the sub-king Milfrith and his queen, and for a certain Osfrith son of Oshelm.[46] Now, when John Leland visited Malmesbury in the sixteenth century he found what was almost certainly the source for the poems 'recently' seen by William in 1125: a 'very ancient book of epigrams' (*antiquissimus codex epigrammaton*), or 'very old book of sacred poems' (*uetustissimus codex sacrorum carminum*), from which Leland transcribed or cited twenty-nine poems, among them the two poems by Cuthbert.[47] This codex has not survived complete, but what is almost certainly a bifolium from it, written in mid-tenth-century Anglo-Saxon Square minuscule, annotated by Leland and re-used for a book binding, turned up in Berlin in 1934, and is now in Urbana-Champaign, University of Illinois Library, 128.[48] At the front of this 'libellus' Leland found verses, evidently composed by some contemporary of Milred's, which show that the book – or rather its eighth-century exemplar – was compiled by (or for) Bishop Milred:

> Hunc proprie librum *Milredus* possidet ipse,
> Antistes sanctus, magno qui dignus honore:
> Est etenim dapibus scripturæ plenus & actu.[49]

Here, then, is clear evidence that Bishop Cuthbert, like the archbishop who was later to borrow the Porphyrius, was interested in Latin poetry and was in literary contact with Milred.

[45] S 90. Cf. H&S III, 342; Whitelock, 'Pre-Viking Age Church', p. 20, n. 6; Brooks, *Canterbury*, pp. 317–19.

[46] *GP*, pp. 299 and 629. Cf. Sims-Williams, 'William', pp. 13–14.

[47] For references to Leland's various citations see Sims-Williams, 'Milred', pp. 22–4.

[48] *Ibid.*, pp. 24–6. Watson, *Medieval Libraries: Supplement*, p. 48, lists it as a Malmesbury manuscript, but it was probably brought there by William, or later still; cf. Sims-Williams, 'Milred', p. 24; 'William', p. 14.

[49] 'Milred himself possesses this his own book, the holy bishop who is worthy of great honour: it is truly full of the feasts and drama of Scripture': Leland, *Commentarii*, ed. Hall

Some further significant points emerge from Cuthbert's two poems in Milred's collection. The first, on the Cross-cloths, was transcribed by Leland as follows:

> Haec ueneranda crucis Christi uexilla sacratae
> cẹperat antistes uenerandus nomine Walhstod
> argenti atque auri fabricare monilibus amplis.
> sed quia cuncta cadunt mortalia [temp]ore certo
> ipse opere in medio moriens e carne recessit,
> linquit et infectum quod uult existere factum.
> ast ego successor praefati prẹsulis ipse
> pontificis, tribuente Deo, qui munere fungor,
> quique gero certum Cudbright (*sic*) de luce uocamen,
> ocyus impleui omissum hoc opus ordine cepto [var. *coeptum*].[50]

Cuthbert was probably influenced here by an inscription in the church of the Holy Apostles in Rome, commemorating John III's completion of the work begun by Pelagius I:

> Hic prior antistes uestigia parua reliquit;
> suppleuit coeptum papa Iohannes opus.[51]

The only English copy of this papal inscription is that given by William of Malmesbury in his edition of the *Liber pontificalis*, an edition enlarged by illustrative poems which William almost certainly took from the Milredian

---

1, 113. Cf. Leland's *Collectanea*, ed. Hearne III, 114, and re-edited by Lapidge, 'Remnants', p. 802, no. 1. See Sims-Williams, 'Milred', p. 22.

[50] Lapidge, 'Remnants', p. 812, no. 20. 'The venerable bishop named Walhstod began to make these venerable veils for Christ's sacred Cross with many threads of silver and gold. But because all mortal things decline at a definite time, he, dying in the midst of the work, departed the flesh, and left undone what he wished to be done. Yet I, the aforesaid bishop's successor, who am myself discharging the office of bishop by God's grace, and bear a definite name Cuth*berht*, from "light" [*be(o)rht* "bright"], have swiftly completed this abandoned work that had been duly begun.' Cf. *Collectanea*, ed. Hearne III, 116 and 265; *Commentarii*, ed. Hall I, 134–5. On variant readings (partly due to Leland's errors, emendations, and collation with William of Malmesbury) see Sims-Williams, 'Milred', pp. 23 and n. 15, and 24, n. 17; 'William', pp. 12–13. Leland's spelling 'Cud*bright*' seems intended to bring out the word-play on *lux/berht*. *Hoc* is scanned wrongly, as in the poem by Cumma, below, p. 355; I shall not comment on such metrical points henceforth.

[51] Sims-Williams, 'William', pp. 13 and 19: 'Here the former bishop left small traces; Pope John completed the work that had been begun'.

collection of epigrams.[52] Here, then, is an instance of Bishop Cuthbert (like Archbishop Cuthbert) using the same poetic sources as Milred.

Milred's collection also included some elegiacs commemorating the gift of a veil to St Peter's, Rome, by the Visigothic king Chintila (636–40): 'In uelo quod a Cintilane rege Romae directum est'.[53] Although there are no verbal correspondences between these elegiacs and Cuthbert's hexameters, they may perhaps have given Cuthbert the idea of writing a poem on a similar subject.[54] His poem has been described as the 'earliest surviving evidence of luxurious liturgical embroidery made in Anglo-Saxon England' – a forerunner of the magnificent embroideries extant at Maaseik, and of the 'stole for the divine service' designed by Dunstan 'with various figured patterns, which [the noblewoman Æthelwyn] would afterwards embellish and diversify with gold and precious stones'.[55] Cuthbert's church must have resembled the church at Bardney, where a *uexillum* of gold and purple hung over Oswald's tomb, or the church at Ripon, which Wilfrid 'clothed in gold and purple and the shining metal of the exalted Cross'.[56] May we not see here a convergence of interests between Bishop Cuthbert and the Archbishop Cuthbert who borrowed the *carmina figurata* manuscript from Milred?

Cuthbert's other poem was transcribed by Leland as follows:

> Qui quondam extiterant famosi late per orbem,
> corpora sen[a ten]et horum hic marmor adumbrans,
> tumbaque mirifico presens fabricata decore
> desuper exculpto cohibet cum culmine tecta.
> hos ego Cudbertus sacri successor honoris
> inclusi tumulis, exornauique sepulchris.

---

[52] *Ibid.*, pp. 13, n. 20, and 32–3. On William's *Liber pontificalis* see Thomson, *William of Malmesbury*, pp. 119–38.

[53] Leland, *Collectanea*, ed. Hearne III, 115; Lapidge, 'Remnants', p. 808, no. 15; Sims-Williams, 'Milred', pp. 30–1; 'William', pp. 25–6.

[54] But for other examples see G. Bernt, *Das lateinische Epigramm im Übergang von der Spätantike zum frühen Mittelalter* (Munich, 1968), p. 19. *Vexillum crucis* often means simply 'sign of the Cross', but the other meaning 'Cross-cloth' is more appropriate in the context of the poem. A poem '*Vexillum* sublime *crucis uener*are, fideles . . .' probably occurred in Milred's collection: Sims-Williams, 'William', p. 25.

[55] M. Budny and D. Tweddle, 'The Maaseik Embroideries', *ASE* 13 (1984), 54–96, at 89.

[56] *HE* III.11 and V.19; G. Henderson, *Bede and the Visual Arts*, Jarrow Lecture 1980 ([Jarrow, 1980]), p. 4.

pontifices ex his ternos sacra infula cinxit:
Torthere, Wal^hstode (*sic*) et Tyrhtil sunt nomina, quorum
quartus erat regulus[57] Milfrith, cum coniuge digna
Quenburga; exstitit e senis haec ordine quinta.
sextus praeterea est Oshelmi filius Osfrith:
en quorum claudit tumba hic corpora sena.[58]

Cuthbert obviously intended these verses to be inscribed at the place where he had entombed the bodies of the six persons mentioned, possibly at Hereford, although it is not certain that the see was already established there.[59] Tyrhtil, Torhthere and Walhstod were his immediate predecessors between 688 and 736, the second, third and fourth bishops on the 'Hereford' episcopal list. The list's first bishop, Putta, may have been buried elsewhere, for example in a monastery or at some earlier site for the see, such as *Lidebiri*, where the bodies of 'holy bishops' were said to lie in the twelfth century.[60]

The *regulus* Milfrith was later remembered at Hereford as the builder of Hereford cathedral;[61] *if* this rather confused tradition is correct, it would explain why Cuthbert honoured Milfrith and his wife and would confirm that the see was already fixed at Hereford in his day. Nothing is known about the sixth person entombed by Cuthbert. The 'tomb' (*tumba*) was evidently a large structure, containing a number of separate 'mounds'

[57] Leland originally wrote 'Quartus erat regulus' (*Collectanea*, ed. Hearne III, 117) and 'regulus est quartus' (Lapidge, 'Remnants', p. 813, no. 21) may be one of the emendations he transferred from William's 'improved' text of the poem (*GP*, p. 299). Cf. above, n. 50.

[58] 'Here overshadowing marble holds the six bodies of these people who once lived, famous far through the world, and the present tomb, made with marvellous elegance, covered with a carved roof above, confines (them). I, Cuthbert, successor to holy honour, have enclosed them in tombs and adorned them with sepulchres. Of these, the sacred stole (?) [cf. above, p. 60, n. 26] encircled three bishops. Torhthere, Walhstod and Tyrhtil are their names; the fourth of them was the sub-king Milfrith, with his worthy wife Cwenburg; she lived fifth in order of the six. The sixth besides is Osfrith son of Oshelm. Behold, a tomb shuts up six bodies here' (*Collectanea*, ed. Hearne, III, 117; Lapidge, 'Remnants', p. 813, no. 21).

[59] See above, p. 90,

[60] See above, p. 91. Hillaby, 'Origins', p. 33, argues that if Putta were a genuine Magonsætan bishop, Cuthbert would have to have included him in the translation; but note that Archbishop Cuthbert did *not* translate the bodies of his predecessors at Canterbury (see below).

[61] See above, p. 50.

(*tumuli*) or 'sepulchres' (*sepulchra*), possibly a *porticus* adjacent to the episcopal church, or an *accubitorium*.[62] It was probably an impressive work, even if we discount the reference to 'marble' as poetic licence, for the monks of Glastonbury, who were famous for their funerary 'pyramids', seem to have imitated it – or at least lines 3–4 of Cuthbert's inscription – in their tomb, 'worthy both in its size and in the artistry of its carving', for their abbot Tica (d. 756×760 ?):[63]

> Tumba hec mirifico fulget fabricata decore.
> Desuper exsculptum (*sic*) condit sub culmine Tican.[64]

The Glastonbury community would have had a particular interest in Cuthbert's monument if, as Robinson maintains, Bishop Walhstod had been abbot of Glastonbury in the 720s (a *Wealhstod* is the second abbot in the Glastonbury list).[65]

In these tomb-building activities Bishop Cuthbert again resembles the archbishop. The latter is famed in Canterbury tradition for changing the archbishops' burial-place from St Augustine's to a new church of St John, placed as close as possible to the sanctuary of Christ Church cathedral. In his Life of Cuthbert's successor, Archbishop Bregwine, Eadmer, who had himself seen St John's destroyed by fire in 1067, says:

Cuthbert . . . amongst his other good works . . . constructed a church to the east of the great church, and almost touching it, which he solemnly dedicated in honour of St John the Baptist. He fabricated this church for the following purposes: that

---

62 For the latter see *Thesaurus Linguae Latinae*, and the reference in Green, 'Plaster Burials', p. 48. Hillaby, 'Origins', p. 31, argues for a *porticus*. On tomb-chambers see Lattimore, *Themes*, p. 250.

63 Thus William of Malmesbury described it: *Glastonbury*, ed. Scott, p. 68 ('Ea est et mole structure et arte celature non ignobilis'). The tradition that Tica was a Northumbrian who escaped from the Danes with relics is anachronistic (cf. *ibid.*, p. 194, n. 55; *Chronicle of Glastonbury Abbey*, ed. Carley and Townsend, p. 291, n. 265; Fell, 'Hild', pp. 88–9). For Tica in 756 (and 757?) see above, p. 228; an abbot Guba appears in 760 (S 1684; cf. Robinson, *Somerset Historical Essays*, p. 37). On the Glastonbury 'pyramids' see A. Watkin, 'The Glastonbury "Pyramids" and St Patrick's "Companions"', *DR* 63 (1945), 30–41; Taylor and Taylor, *Anglo-Saxon Architecture* I, 255–7; Cramp, 'Monastic Sites', p. 245; *Chronicle of Glastonbury Abbey*, ed. Carley and Townsend, p. 276, n. 47.

64 'This tomb, made with marvellous elegance, shines; beneath its carved roof above, it hides Tica'; *Glastonbury*, ed. Scott, p. 106. Cf. *Chronicle of Glastonbury Abbey*, ed. Carley and Townsend, pp. 106–7.

65 Robinson, *Somerset Historical Essays*, pp. 33 and n. 4 and 34; *Eleventh-Century Miscellany*, ed. McGurk *et al.* II, 74. On Walhstod's dates see below, n. 111.

baptisms might be celebrated therein; that certain judicial trials which are wont to be held in the church might be carried on there; and lastly that the bodies of the archbishops might therein be buried, thus departing from the ordinary ancient custom of burial beyond the walls of the city in the church of the blessed apostles Peter and Paul [i.e. St Augustine's], where the bodies of all his predecessors were placed.[66]

William of Malmesbury adds a further anecdote about Cuthbert tricking the St Augustine's monks by contriving his own secret burial in his new church.[67] The later twelfth-century Christ Church historian, Gervase, apparently following a text in the main Christ Church cartulary of *c.* 1090,[68] has the same anecdote, and a further story about Cuthbert obtaining papal backing:

When Cuthbert went to Rome to receive the pallium from Pope Gregory, he obtained from him, that all future archbishops might be buried in the church of Canterbury, and that a cemetery should be made within that city. From the earliest times, the kings of Kent, the archbishops, and the monks of Christ Church, as well as the people of the city, had been buried in the atrium or churchyard of the church of the Apostles Peter and Paul [St Augustine's], beyond the walls. For the Romans, who were first sent into England, said that the city was for the living and not the dead. But now by Divine permission, and at the request of Cuthbert, it was ordained by Pope Gregory, with the consent of King Eadbrith, that the archbishops of Canterbury should be buried in their own church, to the intent that they might have their resting-place where they had ruled in honour.[69]

The later St Augustine's historians ignore this story of Cuthbert's meeting with Gregory III (731–41) or ridicule it (on inadequate chronological grounds); yet they do not dispute that it was Cuthbert who changed the

---

[66] 'Life of Bregwine', ed. Scholz, pp. 139–40, c. 3; cf. translation in Willis, *Architectural History*, p. 2, and in H. M. Taylor, 'The Anglo-Saxon Cathedral Church at Canterbury', *ArchJ* 126 (1969), 101–30, at 102, with discussion at 109–10, 112–14 and 122–3. See also Brooks, *Canterbury*, pp. 39–40, 51, 55 and 81–3; Wallace-Hadrill, *Commentary*, p. 55; Biddle, 'Archaeology', p. 13. Eadmer describes Bregwine's tomb, next to that of Cuthbert: 'Planum siquidem sepulchrum fuit, paulum a pauimento decenti opere altius structum' (c.7).

[67] *GP*, p. 15.

[68] This text was ptd Twysden, *Scriptores*, col. 2210, from Cambridge, Corpus Christi College 189. Cf. Brooks, *Canterbury*, p. 344, n. 54; *The Historical Works of Gervase of Canterbury*, ed. W. Stubbs, 2 vols., RS (London, 1879–80) II, 345, n. 1.

[69] *Ibid.* II, 344–5 (cf. I, 14); trans. Willis, *Architectural History*, p. 2. See also the metrical *Vita Cuthberti* cited above, n. 39.

archbishops' place of burial to Christ Church.[70] There may be some truth in this tradition, then, which certainly constitutes a remarkable resemblance to the Magonsætan bishop's policy of translating the bodies of his predecessors.

The most important testimony to Milred of Worcester's poetic interests is his collection of poems. The primary witness of this collection is the mid-tenth-century bifolium at Urbana, which contains sixteen poems (hereafter U1–U16). This copy was perhaps made at Worcester, perhaps elsewhere. When Leland saw it and recorded twenty-nine poems (hereafter L1–L29), it was at Malmesbury, possibly having been brought there in the 1120s by William of Malmesbury, who probably quotes from it in several of his works, as we have seen.[71] It is impossible to be sure that the tenth-century manuscript was an exact copy of Milred's codex, but since none of its contents can be proved to be later than Milred's day, and many are undoubtedly contemporary or earlier, we can assume that it underwent little or no expansion after Milred's time.

Besides these derivatives of the Milredian collection, its influence, or the influence of something very like it, seems to be felt in a short collection of epigrams preserved in a mid-ninth-century manuscript from Würzburg – conceivably drawing on material taken to Germany by Milred himself, possibly with the Cuthswith codex – and in some apparent derivatives of Alcuin's poetic *Nachlass*.[72]

Milred's collection of poems must have been extensive, and no single witness gives an adequate picture of its nature; for example, only two poems in the extant fragment (U14–15) were noted by Leland (L9–10).

---

[70] E.g. Twysden, *Scriptores*, cols. 1773–4, trans. A. H. Davis, *William Thorne's Chronicle of Saint Augustine's Abbey, Canterbury* (Oxford, 1934), pp. 26–30; Thomas of Elmham, *Historia*, ed. Hardwick, pp. 317–18. For further late(?) sources, see above, p. 62, n. 33.

[71] See above, n. 48. Dumville, 'English Square Minuscule', p. 149, n. 6, favours Worcester origin for U. U was edited by L. Wallach, 'The Urbana Anglo-Saxon Sylloge of Latin Inscriptions', in *Poetry and Poetics from Ancient Greece to the Renaissance: Studies in Honor of James Hutton*, ed. G. M. Kirkwood, Cornell Studies in Classical Philology 38 (Ithaca, 1975), 134–51, but see important corrections in Schaller, 'Bemerkungen'. L is cited according to the numbering in the edition of Lapidge, 'Remnants'; cf. also Hearne's edition of Leland's *Collectanea* III, 114–18 (on minor differences between these editions see above, n. 50 and references).

[72] For these see Schaller, 'Bemerkungen', pp. 13–17; Sims-Williams, 'Milred', pp. 35–8, and 'William', pp. 22–7.

Leland naturally concentrated on the poems of interest to an English antiquary, as did William of Malmesbury in his *Gesta regum* and *Gesta pontificum*.[73] In his edition of the *Liber pontificalis*, on the other hand, William concentrated on poems which he thought relevant to the popes under discussion; probably all or nearly all of the forty-one poems in the Cambridge manuscript of William's *Liber pontificalis* (hereafter C1–41) derive from the Milredian collection.[74] The poems in the Urbana fragment, too, are as much of Roman as of English interest, and bear witness to the well-known Anglo-Saxon devotion to Rome. On one folio (U1–9) we find two inscriptions from the church of St Peter *ad Vincula* in Rome and a couplet (on a picture from the Vatican?) headed 'uincula Petri', a couplet from Vergil (perhaps a caption for a mural), inscriptions from St Laurence without the Walls and St Mary beyond Tiber, Pope Damasus's epigram on St Felix (inscribed at Rome or Nola), and the epitaph of St Augustine's mother, Monica, from Ostia. The contents of the other (non-consecutive) folio are more diverse and less easily identified (U10–16): an inscription on St Paul from some altar; an epigram on a picture of the Four Animals/ Evangelists; an inscription from the *porticus* of a church of SS Stephen and Lawrence; a poem to the Virgin from the Lateran; a poem by an Irishman on a chapel dedicated to St Patrick (U14/L9); Bede's inscription on the cathedral built by Cyneberht, bishop of Lindsey (U15/L10); and a one-line fragment at the foot of the page.[75]

Milred's collection is to some extent comparable with other syllogae of inscriptions and epigrams which circulated in the early Middle Ages. It clearly drew on some of these, as well, perhaps, as on the notebooks of Anglo-Saxon pilgrims returning from Rome. The small mid-seventh-century Spanish sylloge known as the *Anthologia Isidoriana* probably

---

[73] Presuming that Milred's collection was his source for Bede's epitaph (L29) and for Cuthbert's poems (L20–1) in these two works respectively. See Sims-Williams, 'William', p. 12 and references. The suggestion (Lapidge and Rosier, *Aldhelm*, pp. 38–9, 44 and 232, n. 1) that Faricius and William of Malmesbury quote Aldhelm, *Carmina ecclesiastica* 1 (= L5) from U is improbable since U is unlikely to have been at Malmesbury in Faricius's day (see above, n. 48).

[74] The poems in C (Cambridge, University Library, Kk. 4. 6) are edited by A. Silvagni, 'La silloge epigrafica di Cambridge', *Revista di archeologia cristiana* 20 (1943), 49–112, and discussed by Thomson, *William of Malmesbury*, pp. 126–9, and Sims-Williams, 'William'. On the manuscript see also above, p. 188.

[75] See discussion of U by Schaller, 'Bemerkungen', and Sims-Williams, 'Milred' and 'William'.

provided Monica's epitaph (U9), the distich on a picture of St Peter (U2), the poem on the veil sent to Rome by Chintila (L15), and the epitaph of Pope Damasus (C2).[76] A second sylloge, apparently known in eighth-century England, but extant in a ninth-century French manuscript (BN, lat. 8071, fols. 60–1 – hereafter P), probably provided not only Italian texts such as Damasus's inscription on St Felix (U8/P XXI.9) and some of the papal inscriptions that surface in William's *Liber pontificalis*, but also some elegiac couplets, attributed to Bede, on Jerome's commentary on Isaiah (L2/P XXI.13).[77] A third probable source is the late seventh-century *Sylloge Laureshamensis secunda*, preserved in a ninth-century manuscript from Lorsch. This is the most likely source for the fifth- to seventh-century papal epitaphs from St Peter's, some of them very rare, which recur in William's *Liber pontificalis* and other derivatives of the Milredian collection.[78]

While some of the Roman texts in the Milredian collection may have reached Worcester by circuitous routes – via Spain in the case of those in the *Anthologia Isidoriana* – others may have been brought back to England by pilgrims returning from the Holy City who had copied inscriptions themselves or acquired *syllogae* in the way that modern travellers buy guide-books. Milred's collection would not be of practical help to such pilgrims, however; to judge by the rubrics in U, Milred was interested more in the saints themselves than in their resting-places, though (like the compiler of the *Old English Martyrology*)[79] he included such information where available in his sources. Some of these, such as the 'Epytaphia Apostolicorum in Ecclesia Beati Petri' in the *Sylloge Laureshamensis secunda*, had a topographical rationale, and others, such as the collection underlying P, were miscellaneous and topographically unspecific. Dr Rodney Thomson's attractive hypothesis that a mid-seventh-century guide to the

---

[76] *Inscriptiones*, ed. de Rossi II, 250–4, §XXII. Cf. Sims-Williams, 'Milred', pp. 29–32, and 'William', pp. 17–18.

[77] *Inscriptiones*, ed. de Rossi II, 56–7 and 242–9, §§ V and XXI. Cf. Sims-Williams, 'Milred', pp. 32–4 and 36, 'William', pp. 18–22, 23, n. 74, and 24. Mr A. Orchard has drawn my attention to parallels which suggest that a version of P was known to Aldhelm.

[78] *Inscriptiones*, ed. de Rossi II, 124–30, §XI. Cf. Sims-Williams, 'William', pp. 28–30.

[79] E.g. Eugenia: 'hyre lichama resteð wið Romebyrig on þam wege þe man nemneð Latina' (quoted and discussed by Rollason, 'Resting-Places', p. 79); that Eugenia rests in the Via Latina is also noted in William of Malmesbury's itinerary (*Gesta regum*, ed. Stubbs II, 407).

gates, streets and churches of Rome, preserved in William of Malmesbury's *Gesta regum*, derives from the Milredian collection is unfortunately unverifiable.[80]

The texts in Milred's collection were gathered together for their merits as poetry, rather than their religious significance or practical value to pilgrims; the presence of items such as 'Versus Vergilii' (U4) confirms this. Like the other *syllogae* of early medieval Europe, it was probably intended to provide models for inscriptional verses.[81] As early as Bede's day, Roman and continental models were the indispensable basis for Anglo-Latin epigraphic verse, a voluminous genre of which only a fraction survives. It is something of an understatement to describe the Roman funerary epitaphs which arguably reached York in the decades after Bede's death as 'representative examples of the distant inheritors of the antique literary tradition, tired perhaps but not dead or entirely despicable'.[82] Such material, read voraciously and imitated closely, provided the impetus for new English developments; we have already seen, for example, an inscription from the church of the Holy Apostles in Rome (P XXI.14/C29) helping Bishop Cuthbert with his verses on the work begun by Walhstod (L20), and Cuthbert's verses on the tomb of Walhstod and others (L21) in turn being imitated a few years later in Tica's epitaph at Glastonbury.[83] Epigraphy integrated the Anglo-Saxon church, for all the uncouthness of its personal names and place-names, into the Universal Church. The point is well made by the Codex Amiatinus, the pandect of the bible which Ceolfrith, abbot of Jarrow (d. 716), intended to present to St Peter's, Rome; the book was written in an imitation of Italian uncial so exact that it deceived scholars until this century, but once bore an epigram by 'Ceolfrith, abbot at the extreme bounds of the English' (L13), testifying to the fact that the distant Anglo-Saxons had caught up with Rome in the composition of verse.[84]

---

[80] *Ibid.* II, 404–8; cf. Thomson, *William of Malmesbury*, pp. 129–30; Sims-Williams, 'William', pp. 31–3.

[81] Cf. L. Wallach, *Alcuin and Charlemagne* (Ithaca, 1959), p. 197; Lapidge, 'Remnants', pp. 800–1; Lapidge and Rosier, *Aldhelm*, pp. 35–7; Keynes, 'Athelstan's Books', pp. 162–3.

[82] Bullough, 'Roman Books', p. 29. On York and *syllogae* cf. Sims-Williams, 'Milred', p. 33, n. 70, and 'William', p. 32.

[83] See above, pp. 340 and 343.

[84] Lapidge, 'Remnants', pp. 806–7, points out that Milred has the version of the epigram in the anonymous *Vita Ceolfridi* (*BOH* I, 402), not the original (for which see Lowe, *English Uncial*, pl. VIII). See above, p. 182.

While Milred's collection may not have been self-consciously intended to make the point that the Anglo-Saxon church had inherited the traditions of the older Christian churches, unlike the tract on the Resting-places of the English Saints and the *Old English Martyrology*,[85] it nevertheless shows that continuity. Verses from most parts of England are represented in it.

From the neighbouring diocese came Bishop Cuthbert's epigrams on his *uexilla crucis* and tomb (L20–1), discussed above. Cuthbert, if he was indeed translated to Canterbury, may also have supplied the epitaphs of the archbishops Berhtwald (d. 731) and Tatwine (d. 734), which are otherwise unrecorded (L17 and 19). Also from Canterbury may come the 'Sibylline verses concerning the Day of Judgment' listed by Leland (L14), if these were the sibylline verses beginning 'Iudicio tellus sudabit maesta propinquo', which are believed to have been translated from the Greek in Theodore and Hadrian's school.[86] Leland also gives an extract 'from a barbarous poem concerning the consecration of a certain basilica' (L25):

> In honorem almissimi
> ac doctoris dulcissimi
> Sancti Pauli solenniter
> ac uocati feliciter,
> Hedde, pontifex petitus
> ac cum amore accitus,
> dedicauit deicola
> atque clarus celicola.[87]

'Hedde' is probably Hæddi, bishop of Wessex 676–705, but the latter was probably not himself the author, for he would hardly have praised himself

---

[85] Discussed by Rollason, 'Resting-Places'.

[86] See Lapidge, 'Remnants', pp. 807–8; Lapidge and Rosier, *Aldhelm*, pp. 16 and 265, n. 8. Alternatively, they could be the sibylline verses 'Iudicii signum tellus sudore madescat', which were well known from Augustine, *De ciuitate Dei* XVIII.23 (CCSL 48, 613–14), and of which a version is found, for instance, in Cambridge, Corpus Christi College 173, 82v–83v (Kent, s. viii), together with the other sibylline poem. See James, *Catalogue of Manuscripts in Corpus Christi College, Cambridge* I, 400; M. B. Parkes, 'The Palaeography of the Parker Manuscript of the *Chronicle*, Laws and Sedulius, and Historiography in Winchester in the Late Ninth and Tenth Centuries', *ASE* 5 (1976), 149–71, at 151; *CLA* II, no. 123.

[87] 'In honour of the most gentle and sweet teacher, solemnly and happily called St Paul, Hæddi, the bishop, asked and lovingly summoned, a worshipper of God and famous inhabitant of heaven, dedicated . . .'

as *clarus*.[88] Now a poem addressed to Hæddi, in another form of octosyllabics, is preserved in the tenth-century St Augustine's manuscript of Theodore's *Penitential*:

> Te nunc, sancte speculator
> uerbi Dei digne dator,
> Hæddi, pie praesul, precor,
> pontificum ditum decor,
> pro me tuo peregrino
> preces funde Theodoro.[89]

This suggests that Hæddi and Theodore exchanged octosyllabics. Canterbury, then, might be Milred's source for the 'barbarous poem' naming 'Hedde'. On the other hand, it could have reached Worcester directly from Wessex, where it was presumably prominently inscribed on the church which Hæddi had dedicated. That ceremony is likely to have been an elaborate ritual, commemorated by a public inscription naming the persons involved, especially as Hæddi's predecessors Agilbert, Wine and Leutherius had probably promoted Gallican customs in Wessex. The name of 'Hedde episcopus' could still be seen on a 'pyramid' at Glastonbury in William of Malmesbury's day.[90]

---

[88] Moreover, Mr A. Orchard points out that the poem was probably written after Hæddi's death, as *caelicola* is used of the deceased by the Anglo-Latin poets. Headda of Lichfield (Hæddi's contemporary) and Headda of 'Hereford' (Milred's contemporary) are less likely subjects, for the final syllables *-a* and *-ile* were distinguished. For evidence (not clearly presented) see Searle, *Onomasticon*, pp. 276 and 281–2; Redin, *Uncompounded Personal Names*, pp. 66–7 and 126–7. No reliance can be placed on the spelling 'Hedde' in S 49, even if this does refer to the Headda of the Hereford list (for whom see Page, 'Episcopal Lists', p. 94).

[89] CCCC 320, pt II (see above, n. 37), p. 71. 'Now, holy bishop, worthy preacher of God's word, Hæddi, pious prelate, glory of splendid bishops, I beg you to pray for me, your foreigner, Theodore'. See Lapidge, 'Remnants', pp. 817–18; 'Debate Poem', pp. 11–12; 'Theodore and Hadrian', pp. 46–7; M. W. Herren, 'The Stress Systems in Insular Latin Octosyllabic Verse', *CMCS* 15 (Summer 1988), 63–84, at 82–3. The reading *Theodoro* is questioned by M. Deanesly and P. Grosjean, 'The Canterbury Edition of the Answers of Pope Gregory I to St. Augustine', *JEH* 10 (1959), 1–49, at 20.

[90] *Gesta regum*, ed. Stubbs I, 25–6; *Glastonbury*, ed. Scott, p. 84. Cf. Robinson, *Somerset Historical Essays*, p. 27, and above, n. 63. On Hæddi's predecessors see above, p. 112, and on the *ordo consecrationis basilicae nouae* and Gaulish customs see Willis, *Further Essays*, pp. 135–73 and 222; I. Wood, 'The Audience of Architecture in Post-Roman Gaul', in *The Anglo-Saxon Church*, ed. Butler and Morris, pp. 74–9.

The text of Aldhelm's dedicatory verses on his own church of Peter and Paul at Malmesbury (L5) may have reached Milred straight from Malmesbury.[91] This may also apply to two other poems which may be connected with Aldhelm, although he was not their author. The first is an epitaph for Bugga, daughter of Centwine of Wessex (L24), which is partly modelled on Aldhelm's poem on the construction of her church during the reign of Ine (688–726).[92] The other (U14/L9) is a dedicatory epigram for a chapel of St Patrick, otherwise only attested in a collection of poetry associated with the name of Aldhelm's Irish correspondent Cellanus, abbot of Péronne in Picardy (d. 706).[93] It is uncertain whether the poem refers to a chapel at a foreign centre such as Péronne, which possessed relics of St Patrick in the ninth century, or to an Insular one, such as Malmesbury or Glastonbury.[94] Leland's guess that it was by Bede is not substantiated by the heading in U, and must be rejected since the poem was clearly written by an Irishman.

Judging by Leland's extracts, Bede was the Anglo-Latin author best represented in the collection, which probably drew on Bede's lost *Liber epigrammatum*.[95] In the case of the poem commemorating a cathedral built by the bishop of Lindsey, Cyneberht (*fl.* 731), Leland's Bedan attribution

---

91 *Carmina ecclesiastica* I (ed. Ehwald, *Aldhelmi Opera*, p. 11). Cf. above, n. 73.

92 *Carmina ecclesiastica* III (*ibid.*, pp. 14–18). See Lapidge, 'Remnants', pp. 815–17; Lapidge and Rosier, *Aldhelm*, pp. 40–1, 44 and 47–9. The identification of Bugga with the daughter of Dunne, abbess of Withington, is unlikely; see above, p. 132, n. 77.

93 L. Traube, *Vorlesungen und Abhandlungen*, ed. F. Boll, 3 vols. (Munich, 1909–20) III, 95–119. See Sims-Williams, 'Milred', pp. 24–5, 'William', p. 16, and references. The poem imitates Vergil's epitaph (*Vitae Vergilianae Antiquae*, ed. C. Hardie, 2nd ed. (Oxford, 1966), p. 14), which, Dr N. Wright pointed out to me, Aldhelm seems to have known (see *Aldhelmi Opera*, ed. Ehwald, pp. 88–9). On Aldhelm and Cellanus, see Lapidge and Herren, *Aldhelm*, pp. 14–15, 18–19, 149 and 167. Traube's supposed 'eighth line' seems Aldhelmian (cf. Lapidge, 'Aldhelm's Latin Poetry', p. 226), and Mr A. Orchard points out to me that *sibi uindicat* and *dona lauacri* may both come from Aldhelm's *Carmen de uirginitate*, which was known to Cellanus.

94 For Malmesbury as an Irish foundation see above, pp. 108–9. For Glastonbury, where the cult of St Patrick is of uncertain antiquity, see Hughes, 'Evidence for Contacts', pp. 57–8; Lapidge, 'Indract'. A possible problem with assigning the poem to Péronne is that Péronne claimed to have Patrick's relics, according to the ninth-century *Virtutes S. Fursei* (ed. Krusch, p. 447), whereas the poem says that 'Scottia felix' holds his bones. A similar objection applies to Glastonbury.

95 See Lapidge, 'Remnants'; also Sims-Williams, 'Milred', p. 38, n. 106 (for 'fol. 26' read 'fol. 39'); 'William', p. 26, n. 88.

(L10) is confirmed by U15: 'Versus Beda [*sic*] in absida basilice'.[96] Leland's misattribution of the preceding poem (U14/L9) to Bede may have been due to this ascription and to the frequency of Bedan material in the manuscript. Other Bedan poems noted by Leland include riddles (L4),[97] epigrams to St Michael, and to St Mary on the consecration of a church in her honour (L6–7), and verses on the *porticus* of the church of St Mary (Hexham), built by Wilfrid, 'in which he mentions Bishop Acca' (L8); since Leland did not transcribe these, they cannot be identified with any extant poems for certain.[98] He did transcribe the elegiac couplets by Bede on Jerome's commentary of Isaiah (L2/P XXI. 13) and some anonymous, but similar and possibly Bedan, elegiacs (L27), which are otherwise known only from a single couplet quoted in Ceolfrith's Codex Amiatinus, written at Wearmouth or Jarrow in Bede's lifetime.[99] Milred's collection also included the above-mentioned dedicatory inscription from the Codex Amiatinus (L13). The final item transcribed by Leland was Bede's own four-line epitaph (L29), which William of Malmesbury regarded as 'unworthy of the tomb of so great a man'.[100] Perhaps all this material came to Worcester in a manuscript of Bede's *Liber epigrammatum*. That Bedan poetry did reach the area is shown by the presence of two of Bede's poems on fol. 39 of the Royal Prayer Book; it may have contained more, for leaves are lost before and after this leaf.[101]

With regard to the transmission of Bede's poems, Leland's penultimate epigram, which he transcribed without title or comment (L28), is of some interest:

> Hos, Albine, tibi, merito uenerabilis abba
> uersiculos scripsit uerbi celestis amator

---

[96] The poem is discussed and edited from U and L by Schaller, 'Bemerkungen', pp. 17–21.

[97] Leland is not likely to have ascribed anonymous riddles to Bede since he was aware of the work of other Anglo-Latin riddlists, whose work he saw at Glastonbury: *Commentarii*, ed. Hall I, 131.

[98] For a possible identification of L6 see Sims-Williams, 'Milred', p. 37. On early English dedications to St Michael see Levison, *England and the Continent*, p. 263; Finberg, *Lucerna*, p. 57 and n. 2; cf. Everitt, *Continuity*, p. 256.

[99] See Sims-Williams, 'Milred', p. 33, and 'William', pp. 24–5, and above, pp. 183 and 198.

[100] *Gesta regum*, ed. Stubbs I, 67. Cf. above, n. 73.

[101] See above, pp. 281 and 333.

Beda, dei famulus, mira quos carminis arte
composuit doctor, nostro qui clarus in orbe
extitit: ingenii cuius monimenta refulgent
plurima temporibus nullis abolenda per ęuum. [102]

There is a slight problem in supposing that this epigram accompanied a volume of Bede's poems sent to Bede's collaborator Albinus, Hadrian's successor as abbot of SS Peter and Paul (St Augustine's), Canterbury, since Thomas of Elmham says that this Albinus died in 732, earlier, that is, than Bede, who is spoken of in the past tense in the epigram. [103] We could, however, make the simple emendation of *scripsit* to *scripsi* and construe: 'I have written for you, Albinus, these verses which Bede composed . . .' In this case, the epigram could record the sending of Bedan verses to Alcuin, who used the name Albinus; moreover, we know that some Bedan material among Alcuin's putative *Nachlass* was probably transmitted to Alcuin via Milred's collection or a congener of it. [104] The problem here is that Alcuin did not become an abbot until the end of the century so that the poem would have to be later than Milred's day. It may be preferable, then, to look for another Albinus. *Albinus* is a natural Latinization of either *(E)al(c)hwine* (as in the case of Alcuin) or of *Hwit(t)a*, a name derived from *hwit* 'white', [105] but the only other known Albinus is Hwit(t)a, one of Boniface's Anglo-Saxon assistants in Germany, who became bishop of Büraburg, near Fritzlar, Hesse, in 741 or 742: he is called Albinus in, for

---

[102] 'Bede, servant of God, lover of the heavenly word, wrote these little verses for you, Albinus, deservedly venerable abbot – (verses) which the teacher composed, with the marvellous art of poetry, (he) who was famous through our world: the very many monuments of his learning gleam, never ever to be destroyed.'

[103] Lapidge, 'Remnants', p. 819. Lapidge suggests that the epigram was written or revised after the death of both men. The obit 732 given by Elmham, *Historia*, ed. Hardwick, pp. 301–2, is not necessarily accurate: see *BOH* II, 2.

[104] Sims-Williams, 'Milred', pp. 35–8; 'William', pp. 23–7. Mr A. Orchard has found significant parallels to L28 in Alcuin's poetry.

[105] Searle, *Onomasticon*, p. 65; Redin, *Uncompounded Personal Names*, pp. 50 and 58. Redin points out that the name *Wit(t)a* is distinct from *Hwit(t)a*, though sometimes confused with it. Compare the case of Alcuin's pupil Hwita, nicknamed Candidus: J. Marenbon, *From the Circle of Alcuin to the School of Auxerre: Logic, Theology and Philosophy in the Early Middle Ages* (Cambridge, 1981), p. 38. On Alcuin's names see Bullough, 'Albinus Deliciosus', pp. 80, n. 24, and 83.

example, a work written at Fulda in 836.[106] Presuming that Hwita was an abbot before he became bishop of Büraburg, the poem could have been addressed to him, perhaps by Milred himself, who had connections with the missionaries in Germany, as we saw in ch. 8. Some (admittedly rather conventional) similarities in content and style to Milred's verses 'Hos tibi .Mil. lyrico .red. feci carmine uersus' are the opening *Hos . . . tibi*, and the cadences *carminis arte/carmine uersus* and *per maeuum/ per ęuum*.[107]

It is difficult not to associate the above epigram with a prefatory letter to the *Epistola de obitu Bedae* at the beginning of The Hague, Koninklijke Bibliotheek, 70. H. 7, fols. 42–65 (s. x[in]). The anonymous writer tells *reuerentissimus Albinus* that he will hear below about the death of 'the aforesaid priest Bede – evidently the first part of the prefatory letter is missing – from Bede's disciple Cuthbert's letter to 'a certain fellow-disciple'.[108] This raises similar problems about the identity of the recipient Albinus,[109] but one may well imagine that both the Bedan *uersiculi* quoted above and the preface to the *Epistola de obitu Bedae* were destined for one and the same Albinus.

Other poems in Milred's collection include Anglo-Saxon names. The abbot of the *Epitaphium Widsiði abbatis* noted by Leland (L12) cannot be identified. A more promising case is Abbot Cumma, mentioned as patron in an epigram perhaps inscribed on a gold and silver vessel (L22):

---

[106] *Lupi Vita Wigberti Abbatis Friteslariensis*, c. 24 (ed. O. Holder-Egger, MGH Scriptores 15.1 (Hannover, 1887), 36–43, at 42–3: MSS *Albuinus, Albuuinus, Albewinus*). On the name cf. *Acta Sanctorum, Oct. XI*, pp. 947–9. On Hwit(t)a see *Epp.* lii, lvi and lxxiii (Tangl, pp. 92–4, 98–102 and 146–55, respectively); Levison, *England and the Continent*, pp. 80 and 236. The continental sources mostly call him Witta, but *Hwita* is confirmed by the part of *Ep.* lxxiii preserved in England; see Tangl, p. 147; *Vita Quorundam* [sic] *Anglo-Saxonum*, ed. Giles, p. 360; Levison, *England and the Continent*, pp. 280–1.

[107] See above, p. 332. With 'Hos . . . tibi . . . uersiculos . . .' cf. Schaller and Könsgen, *Initia*, s.v. *Hos*; P. C. Jacobsen, 'Carmina Columbani', in *Die Iren und Europa*, ed. Löwe I, 434–67, at 442, n. 29. For *carmin(a) uers(u)* and *per aeuum* see Schumann, *Hexameter-Lexicon* I, 285, and IV, 209. Sedulius, *Carmen paschale* 1.94, has 'nullisque abolenda per aeuum' (ed. Huemer, p. 22).

[108] N. R. Ker, 'The Hague Manuscript of the Epistola Cuthberti De Obitu Bedæ with Bede's Song', *MÆ* 8 (1939), 40–4.

[109] Cf. R. Brotanek, 'Nachlese zu den Hss. der *Epistola Cuthberti* und des *Sterbespruches Bedas*', *Anglia* 64 (1940), 159–90, at 162–4; Levison, *England and the Continent*, p. 244, n. 1; *EHD*, p. 624, n. 2.

Aurificum manibus uas hoc ego Cumma iubendo
abbas, diuini nutus moderamine, supplex
argenti atque auri perfeci pondere multo.[110]

Lapidge plausibly identifies this Cumma with the abbot of Abingdon who
received a charter from Æthelbald of Mercia before 736.[111] The charter is
an eleventh- or twelfth-century forgery, but the forger may have known
that Cumma was a genuine abbot of Abingdon or at least have taken the
name from a genuine grant to an abbot of this name at some other house.[112]
The unreliable Abingdon Annals in Cambridge, Trinity College R. 17. 7
(s. xiv), put Cumma's death in 784, which seems late but not impossible;
this would make him a contemporary of Milred.[113] The rarity of the name
is a further point in favour of the identification.[114]

An intriguing, unmetrical item (L23), perhaps extracted from several
lines of an epigram, concerns an abbot with the English name Cunneah
(i.e. *Cyneheah*) and a person with the Irish name Colmán:

---

[110] 'I, Cumma, a suppliant, abbot by the dispensation of the divine consent, completed by
my order, through the hands of goldsmiths, this vessel (made) with a great weight of
silver and gold.'

[111] Lapidge, 'Remnants', p. 814; S 93. (The charter cannot be dated closely because the
date of the accession of Bishop Walhstod (*fl.* 731) is unknown; the date 727×731 in
*HBC*³, p. 217 depends on S 85, on which see above, p. 150, n. 38.) Apart from this
charter, Cumma does not figure in the Abingdon Chronicles in BL, Cotton Claudius C.
ix and B. vi: *Chronicon Monasterii de Abingdon*, ed. J. Stevenson, 2 vols., RS (London,
1858) I, 38–40. The spelling *Conanus* in the thirteenth-century Abingdon Chronicle
in Cotton Vitellius A. xiii (*ibid.* II, 272–3) is clearly inferior. (On this Chronicle see
Stenton, *Abingdon*, pp. 1–2.) He is *Cumanus* in the Abingdon version of 'Florence' in
Lambeth Palace Library, 42 (s. xii), excerpted by Wharton, *Anglia Sacra* I, 163 (cf.
James, *Catalogue of Manuscripts of Lambeth Palace*, p. 60). On Æthelbald and Abingdon
see Stenton, *Abingdon*, pp. 10 and 22. *Cumanus* is an attested Latin name.

[112] Cf. the discussion of early Abingdon charters by Stenton, *Abingdon*, where the Cumma
charter is merely mentioned in passing on p. 22, n. 2; and Scharer, *Königsurkunde*,
p. 186.

[113] Cited by Dugdale, *Monasticon* I, 505 (not used by Stenton, *Abingdon*).

[114] Searle, *Onomasticon*, pp. 145–6; I regard *Cyma* as a distinct name (see *ibid.*, p. 152 and
Redin, *Uncompounded Personal Names*, p. 75). *Cumma* occurs among the lay witnesses of
two dubious West Saxon charters (S 242 and 256), and otherwise the only other
example is abbot *Cuman* of Glastonbury, placed in 800–22 by William of Malmesbury,
and he has been regarded as a mere mistake for *Muca(n)*, abbot in 802: *Glastonbury*, ed.
Scott, p. 110 (the date 746, *ibid.*, p. 147, is worthless); see ibid., p. 200, n. 103;
Robinson, *Somerset Historical Essays*, p. 39; Lapidge, 'Indract', p. 181.

Cunneah abbas, qui uenit huc de transmarina Scottia
hos Colmanno ciui tuo quondam uersus diximus.

This seems to mean: 'O Abbot Cyneheah, we/I spoke these verses to
Colmán, your former *ciuis*, who came here from Ireland overseas.'[115] *Ciuis*
probably means 'monk' in view of the common Hiberno-Latin use of *ciuitas*
(Old Irish *cathir*) for 'monastery'; the *ciuitas* in question may have been in
England rather than Ireland, since Cyneheah is an English name – we have
already seen that an Irish foundation in England such as Malmesbury could
be described as *ciuitas*.[116] The epigram appears to be intended to
accompany a gift to Abbot Cyneheah of a copy of some verses originally
addressed to the Irishman Colmán, a former member of Cyneheah's
community. The name Colmán is extremely common,[117] but only two
suitable persons of the name are recorded in England. Colmán, bishop of
Lindisfarne (661–4), who came from Iona, is described by Bede as 'missus a
Scottia' and 'de Scottia'.[118] In what sense, however, could he be the *ciuis* of
an abbot Cyneheah? The other possibility is the Colmán who was abbot of
Hanbury during the reign of Wulfhere of Mercia.[119] This Colmán is also a
long time before Milred, but as Hanbury is only about seven miles from
Worcester, it would be fitting if verses addressed to its abbot should be
known to Milred of Worcester a century later.

Another possibly local poem is the following epitaph (L26):

> Quarto idus Octebrium
> tertio dono dierum
> ciuis sub cęlo conditur[120]
> Balthunus, atque orditur
> sacerdotis in seculo
> functus felix officio;
> fuisse fertur florido

---

[115] Lapidge, 'Remnants', p. 814, interprets the poem as follows: 'Abbot Cunneah is
sending some verse to an unnamed Irishman, verse which he had formerly sent to one
Colmán; Cunneah has apparently come to England from Ireland itself.' This is possible,
but I prefer, in view of the 3rd sg. *uenit*, to understand the relative clause as referring to
Colmán, and get the best sense by taking *Cunneah abbas* as vocative, rather than as
subject of *diximus*. Some words are surely missing.

[116] See above, pp. 108–9. [117] See above, p. 106, n. 78.

[118] *HE* III.25 and IV.4.

[119] See above, pp. 106–8. [120] Lapidge's emendation of *cuius . . . conditor*.

Dei cum auxilio.[121]

Dr Lapidge's tentative identification of this priest with a *Bealdhun* in a West Saxon witness-list of 705×709 is implausible since the latter appears to be a lay witness – probably identical with the *Bealthun* (note the West Saxon -*ea*-) who in 708 granted land in Somerset to an abbot Froda, who also attests the other charter.[122] More likely the epitaph is that of the priest (*sacerdos*) *Balthunus*, an *alumnus* of Worcester to whom Deneberht, bishop of Worcester, granted lands near Cirencester in the early 800s.[123] This Balthun was apparently also abbot of Kempsey in 799; the lack of reference to his abbacy both in Deneberht's charter and in the epitaph is consonant with the tendency to stress the priestly rather than abbatial status of the rulers of *monasteria* at the period.[124] The identification of the subject of the epitaph with the Worcester *alumnus* is attractive, since *B(e)aldhun* is an unusual name (the only occurrence not already mentioned being a *Balðhun* in the list of clerics in the early ninth-century Lindisfarne *Liber vitae*).[125] The problem that Balthun died a generation after Milred is not insuperable, since so short a text could well have been added to Milred's manuscript at Worcester, perhaps in the margin, before the tenth-century copy seen by Leland was made.

Finally we may note another epitaph with possible Worcester connections, transcribed by Leland (L18) as follows:

> Pausantes uno pariter cubile (*sic*) tenentur
> Cð et Sigbertus, dominumque deumque colentes,
> laudibus ętheriis cęli super astra locati
> qua simul aeternis donentur in axe coronis,
> angelicosque inter cętus sine fine manentes
> perpetuam Christo laudem regique deoque
> dulcisonis iugiter modulentur uocibus una.[126]

---

[121] Lapidge translates: 'On the fourth ides of October, with the addition of three days (*i.e.* October (12 + 3) = 15), Balthunus is established as a citizen under the heavenly kingdom and begins (his celestial career), having successfully discharged the office of priest in this world; he is said to have lived with the bountiful support of God'.

[122] Lapidge, 'Remnants', p. 819; S 245 and 1176. Cf. Edwards, 'Two Documents', p. 3.

[123] See above, p. 171.   [124] See above, p. 170.

[125] *Oldest English Texts*, ed. Sweet, p. 161, line 289; Searle, *Onomasticon*, p. 84.

[126] 'Dying, Cuth and Sigberht are both contained in one bed, worshippers of their Lord and God, situated above the stars of heaven with ethereal praises, where together they may be presented with eternal crowns on high, and, dwelling without end among the

Cð is no doubt intended for *Cuð*, which would scan, and not for a bisyllabic name. Lapidge suggests that the poet intends us to understand *Cuthbertus et Sigbertus*.[127] While this is possible, there is no reason why *Cuð* should not occur as an uncompounded name, even though no example is cited in Searle's *Onomasticon*. The name of the abbot *Cudd* who attests charters during the episcopate of Milred's successor, Wermund, is a distinct formation,[128] and the only instance of *Cuð* known to me is in the heading to a versified creed in the Royal Prayer Book, on fol. 40r, immediately following the elegiacs by Bede:

> *uersus cvð de sancta trinitate*
> Mente canam domino grates laudesque rependens
> Pro cunctis tribuit quae sacra mihi gratia Christi.
> Credo deum patrem qui uerbo cuncta creauit
> Qui genitor rerum mundum sub lege cohercens
> Et nulla sub lege manet cui condere uelle est
> Quem frons nulla uidet sed totum conspicit ipse.
> Credo deum Christum passus qui cuncta nouauit
> Omnia pacificans unum qui fecit utraque
> Qui deus et homo natura perfectus utraque
> Certa salus constat uitae spes unica terris
> Qui regit aetherium princeps in principe regnum.
> Credo deum pariter summum te spiritus alme
> Qui caelo ueniens purgasti crimina mundi
> Multiplicique hominum replesti pectora dono.[129]

angelic assemblies they jointly modulate perpetual praise to Christ their king and God, with voices sounding sweetly together.'

[127] Lapidge, 'Remnants', p. 811, n. 2. St Guthlac is called *Gud* in the acrostic poem in Cambridge, Corpus Christi College 307, printed by James, *Catalogue of the Manuscripts of Corpus Christi College, Cambridge* II, 105, and discussed by Dumville, 'English Square Minuscule Script', p. 166, and Morrish, 'Dated and Datable Manuscripts', p. 536. For the syncope in *Sigbertus* see *Æthelwulf: De Abbatibus*, ed. A. Campbell (Oxford, 1967), p. xlviii.

[128] S 109 (see also S 145). Cf. Redin, *Uncompounded Personal Names*, p. 16.

[129] 'In my mind I shall sing thanks and praises to the Lord, repaying him for all that Christ's sacred Grace has paid to me. I believe in God the Father who by his Word created all things, who (is) author of things, ordering the world under his law, and remains under no law, for whom to will is to create; whom no countenance sees yet himself sees all. I believe in Christ, God, who, having suffered, renewed all things, who, making peace, made all things one, and who (as) God and man, perfect in each nature, remains both a certain salvation and the only hope of life for the earth, who rules the heavenly kingdom as the supreme prince. I believe likewise in thee, equally the

It is surely significant that this prayer book is of Worcester provenance, and was possibly written at Worcester itself, perhaps even as early as Milred's episcopate. There are two points of verbal similarities between the Milredian collection and the epitaph and creed. First, as Lapidge has noted, the unusual cadence *dominumque deumque colentes* in the epitaph echoes *dominumque deumque colendum / iussit* in the poem on St Patrick (U14/L9).[130] Secondly, the most complete parallel to the cadence *uitae spes unica terris* in *Cuð's* creed is in the fragmentary poem U16, a single line at the end of a verso:

> Hoc tibi Christe, deus uitæ spes unica terris.[131]

These echoes suggest that both the *Epitaphium Cð et Sigberti* and the *Versus cvð de sancta trinitate* may have originated in Milred's literary circle.

That circle can now be seen to have played a significant role in the transmission of Latin poetry in eighth-century England. We have found that Milred knew his Vergil, and that he sent Porphyrius's *carmina figurata*, and perhaps other *uersiculi*, to Canterbury. He owned a book of poetry that included, side by side, Roman inscriptional verses from collections assembled in Spain and elsewhere, and examples of the new Anglo-Latin poetry which had been founded upon Christian Latin models by Theodore, Aldhelm and Bede, and by poets nearer at hand, such as Cuthbert, bishop of the Magonsætan. Milred himself remains a rather shadowy personality, except in his letter to Lull. Yet the material he preserved demonstrates how closely the cultivation of Anglo-Latin poetry was intertwined with the development of schooling, architecture, and the decorative arts. In the twentieth century, when that Latin tradition has finally come to an end, we are better placed than ever to appreciate the eighth-century achievement.

> highest God, O gentle Spirit, who coming from heaven didst purge the sins of the world and didst fill men's breasts with the manifold gift': *Cerne*, ed. Kuypers, p. 218; Meyer, 'Poetische Nachlese', pp. 614–15. On the manuscript see above, ch. 10. Mr Orchard points out Cuð's deep debt to Sedulius's *Carmen paschale*, esp. IV.13–15 and 308 (ed. Huemer, pp. 92 and 112).
>
> 130 Lapidge, 'Remnants', p. 811. Schumann, *Hexameter-Lexicon*, has no good parallels.
> 131 'This to you, Christ, God, only hope of life for the earth . . .' See Sims-Williams, 'Milred', p. 26 and n. 33. There is no example of the complete cadence in Schumann, *Hexameter-Lexicon* V, 236–7.

12

The church in the landscape

How did the monasteries and dioceses fit into their environment? Most regional studies start with such questions, and work 'upwards' from physical geography to the economic and social basis of the mentalities revealed by texts. The problem with such an approach is that, in Christopher Taylor's words, 'it is still not clear what Saxon England looked like'. The varied landscape which one surveys from the Cotswolds, or from the Malvern hills, has been shaped not only by millions of years of geological and climatic change, but also by millennia of inconsistent exploitation by a fluctuating human population. In dealing with surviving artefacts, documents and manuscripts, we are dealing with specific, often tangible evidence. The surviving landscape, however, cannot yet be read like a book. Indeed, 'the age between the fifth and ninth centuries AD', to quote Taylor again, 'despite an enormous amount of new work, seems to be more dark than ever'.[1]

Nevertheless, it seems feasible to tackle two basic questions about the inter-relation of history and the environment: how were the monasteries sited in the early diocese-kingdoms; and how geographically coherent were those units?

THE DISTRIBUTION OF SETTLEMENT

The plausibility of answers to such questions depends on our impression of the disposition of settlement in the landscape. This impression is formed mainly by inference, because direct archaeological evidence of early Anglo-Saxon settlement is slight. The only relevant archaeological distri-

[1] Taylor *apud* Hoskins, *Making of the English Landscape*, p. 8.

bution which is full enough to be meaningful is that of the accompanied burials of the sixth to seventh centuries; and these burials cannot be taken to indicate the full extent of settlement, particularly in the seventh century when the rite of accompanied burial was in decline.

The paucity of archaeological evidence for domestic buildings exemplifies the shortage of data. The only urban buildings which can be securely dated to the early period are timber buildings associated with metalled tracks at Hereford, one of which was sealed between mid-seventh- to eighth-century grain-drying ovens and the mid-ninth-century western ramparts. This post-hole building was '9m long and 2.5m wide with a large central posthole and was separated into two rooms by a north–south passage'.[2] In the countryside, palisade enclosures and post-hole structures were found *c.* 1971 beside the 'pagan' Anglo-Saxon cemeteries at Alveston, near Stratford, and at Bidford-on-Avon; but these are unpublished,[3] and the best known small rural habitation is still the sunken dwelling (or '*Grubenhaus*') discovered forty years earlier at Bourton-on-the-Water, Gl. The Bourton dwelling, which E. T. Leeds dated 'not earlier than the seventh century' on the basis of the absence of decorated pottery, was found in a gravel pit at an altitude of about 450 ft, on the Fosse Way (SP/171221). It was of oval shape, 20 ft by 12 ft 6 in., and 3 ft deep in the gravel. Thirteen small post holes sloping inwards towards the middle of the hut suggested that the roof (of reeds or turf?) was supported by poles meeting at an apex about 12 ft above the floor. The entrance appeared to have been on the west side, facing the Fosse Way, but this side was destroyed before excavation. In the eastern part there was a hearth, embedded in which were potsherds, fragments of clay rings to stand vessels on, and animal bones. Accumulated broken pots, clay rings and animal bones in the north-west corner suggested that this was used for meals. The eastern end was free from rubbish and was presumably for sleeping. Close by the south wall there was a crude stone seat, which could be used when working at an upright loom about 5 ft wide, which was evidenced by two post holes 12 in. in diameter and by a pottery spindle-whorl and clay loom-weights. Part of a quern and various cooking and other pots were also found.[4] A comparable structure was found in 1967 at Fladbury Rectory in

---

[2] Shoesmith, *Hereford* II, 28–32, 48–50 and 72–3, esp. 31. Cf. above, p. 90.

[3] Rahtz, 'Buildings and Rural Settlement', pp. 408–9.

[4] G. C. Dunning, 'Bronze Age Settlements and a Saxon Hut near Bourton-on-the-Water, Gloucestershire', *AntJ* 12 (1932), 279–93; cf. Arnold, *Archaeology*, p. 113; Rahtz,

the Vale of Evesham (SO/996464), adjacent to a late Romano-British cemetery and situated in a pre-existing ditch 9 ft deep. The purpose of this *Grubenhaus* was shown by a circular bread-oven chamber about 6 ft across. The oven had finally burnt down so that much of the original woodwork was preserved as charcoal. The majority of grains were of six-row barley (*Hordeum vulgare*). Fragments of combs, loom-weights, knives and querns were found in the fill above the oven. Next to it was a small building of post-hole construction, probably contemporary. Radiocarbon dating indicated a date of 851 ± 51.[5]

These *Grubenhäuser* at Bourton and Fladbury may not be typical early dwellings but specialized artisans' huts for weaving and baking respectively. The excavator of Fladbury suggested that the size of the oven could indicate that it served the monastery of Fladbury or a 'palace' of the bishop of Worcester, which may have succeeded it.[6] Such larger seventh- or eighth-century structures have yet to be found and dated, although the evidence of literary texts and excavation elsewhere in England suggests that they once existed. Elsewhere, notably at Yeavering in Northumberland, air-photography has given the first indication of royal halls, but so far we have only the possible case of Hatton Rock (SP/237577) in Hampton Lucy, near Stratford-upon-Avon. Here aerial photographs showed the crop-marks of groups of rectangular buildings, 'too large to be those of a "normal" settlement site . . . [and] of similar scale to the great 7th century halls of Yeavering, or the 10th to 14th century halls at Cheddar'.[7] Rahtz suggested that the site might belong to Offa's reign, pointing out the royal connections of Hampton Lucy and other places in the area (Ingon, Wellesbourne and Stratford) and surmising that the whole area was originally a royal estate.[8] A trench cut through the site in 1970 confirmed that the crop-marks represent major buildings and *Grubenhäuser*, and a radiocarbon date of 875 ± 88 indicated an eighth–tenth-century date for a

'Buildings and Rural Settlement', p. 411. Compare the crop-marks of sunken dwellings at Lechlade: Miles and Palmer, *Invested in Mother Earth*, p. 20. On types of buildings see Arnold, *Archaeology*, pp. 23–35, 171–5 and 192–3.

[5] Peacock, 'Fladbury'; Bond, 'Fladbury', p. 19; Fowler, 'Farming', pp. 275–6. A ninth-century date is accepted by Rahtz, 'Buildings and Rural Settlement', pp. 65 and 419.

[6] Peacock, 'Fladbury', p. 124.

[7] P. Rahtz, 'A Possible Saxon Palace Near Stratford-upon-Avon', *Antiquity* 44 (1970), 137–43, at 142.

[8] *Ibid.*, p. 139. Cf. D. Hooke, 'Wellesbourne: A Survey', *WMA* 27 (1984), 113–16, and *Hwicce*, p. 204; and above, p. 164.

probable *Grubenhaus*, though some of the pottery could be earlier.[9] Further excavation will therefore be needed before a function, and a date as early as Offa, can be assigned to Hatton Rock. On the other hand, a rectangular timber-framed building at Stretton-on-Fosse was evidently very early, since it was cut into by 'pagan' Anglo-Saxon burials; but publication of details of its size and nature is awaited.[10]

The only other such site in the area lies outside the presumed boundaries of the kingdom of the Magonsætan, in the parish of Atcham, east of Shrewsbury. Here crop-marks on a gravel ridge (SJ/552115) indicate two very large timber halls, comparable to Yeavering.[11] In view of the proximity of the Wrekin and Wroxeter, the site may be a royal centre of the Wreocensætan; but again only excavation, 'which should not be long delayed' (St Joseph), can prove or disprove this.

Toponymics supplement the sparse archaeological record of settlement but there are problems. The geographical distribution of documents is patchy, especially outside the diocese of Worcester, and consequently the same applies to the distribution of place-names attested by 731, or even by 850.[12] If we take into account place-names attested at later periods, considering, for example, all names in -*tūn* [-*ton*] and -*lēah* [-*ley*] attested by 1086,[13] we gain a more complete coverage, though at the expense of raising the problem of the chronology of the names and of the settlements to which they refer. Even Dr Hooke's excellent detailed picture of the West Midland landscape in the Anglo-Saxon period is inevitably partial, since the charter bounds on which it is chiefly based are unevenly distributed, chronologically and topographically, being concentrated on the late

---

9 S. Hirst and P. Rahtz, with C. Dyer, 'Hatton Rock 1970', *TBWAS* 85 (1971–3), 161–77; Price and Watson, 'Sedgeberrow', p. 90. Cf. Rahtz, 'Buildings and Rural Settlement', pp. 67–8 and 422.

10 It is described as 'small' by W. J. Ford, 'Stretton-on-the-Fosse Saxon Cemetery, Warwks.', *WMANS* 12 (1969), 29–30, but as 'large' in *MA* 15 (1971), 134. Cf. Gardner *et al.*, 'Stretton 1971–76', p. 30.

11 J. K. St Joseph, 'Air Reconnaissance: Recent Results, 39', *Antiquity* 49 (1975), 293–5; Rahtz, 'Atcham Timber Halls', and 'Archaeology of West Mercian Towns', p. 111. Cf. above, p. 101.

12 See respectively Cox, 'Place-Names of the Earliest Records', and Thorpe, 'Growth of Settlement', p. 101. Cf. Everitt, *Continuity*, pp. 120–1, on Kentish records up to 850. Bassett, 'Search', p. 11, gives a map of Hwiccian grants up to 821.

13 Thorpe, 'Growth of Settlement', pp. 104–5; Hooke, *Hwicce*, pp. 48–9. For Herefordshire see below, n. 149.

Anglo-Saxon estates of the church of Worcester; moreover, the boundary clauses by definition refer to peripheral features of the landscape, often perhaps strikingly atypical ones.[14]

General deductions from the incidence of natural resources may extend the picture of the distribution of early Anglo-Saxon settlement. The distribution of land suitable for arable cultivation is most relevant here, although if one were to list all the resources of the countryside, in the manner of the Anglo-Saxon charters, one would add woodland for fuel, timber and swine-feeding, meadow for stock rearing, rivers and ponds for fishing, brine-springs and saltmarshes for salt making, and so on. Good land for cultivation can to some extent be deduced from the contours on maps, since altitude is an important factor, but it is not an over-riding one; for example, low-lying land may have a heavy, ill-drained clay soil that is hard to clear of woodland and difficult to till when cleared. Neither can we extrapolate directly from modern surveys of land suitability and utilization, which assume modern techniques of heavy ploughing, fertilization and drainage, nor even from late medieval evidence.[15] It seems safer to rely instead on estimates of the varying potential of the soils in the region, and on evidence for pre-Anglo-Saxon settlement, which tells us about the preferences of early farmers. The formation of soils depends not only upon the underlying geology, drainage, rainfall and surface evaporation (altitude being relevant here as a major influence on rainfall and temperature in the area), but also upon previous land use (in other words, upon the preferences of earlier farmers).[16] These factors can be gauged in a very general way by studying the lie of the land and its surface geology together with the

---

[14] Hooke, *West Midlands* and *Hwicce*, esp. pp. 50–1, 191 and 227.

[15] But for some interesting comments on the high quality land of the bishop's manors (many of them former monasteries), as defined by the Ministry of Agriculture, see Dyer, *Lords and Peasants*, p. 23; he gives much information on the later medieval use of these estates (e.g. p. 124). See also Copley, *Archaeology and Place-Names*, p. 14, and *Anglian Regions*, p. 19.

[16] Mackney and Burnham, *Soils*. Even in the *Agrarian History*, ed. Finberg, little attention is paid to soils, except in the Roman section and then mostly in south-east England (pp. 59–72). The 'soil associations' of the maps of the Soil Survey of England and Wales are not much help for settlement studies, and the fact that they do not distinguish soils according to drainage is a disadvantage. The Survey's series of Soil Drainage Maps is in its infancy.

evidence for prehistoric agriculture.[17] Because relatively small-scale geological maps do not show all minor deposits, there are dangers in relying on them for very detailed work on soils and settlement;[18] but they are probably adequate when characterizing large areas, or in cases where they can be supplemented from detailed surveys of particular places.

Such an 'environmental' approach to settlement history has its limitations, as Taylor has shown, pointing out numerous instances where human factors rather than 'geographical determinism' must be invoked to explain settlement on 'poor' rather than 'good' sites.[19] The limitations are particularly evident for the Roman period, when population and land-exploitation are believed to have been dense, but the environment may have been influential in the early Anglo-Saxon period, when the population is thought to have contracted dramatically, with a consequent recession of settlement and regeneration of woodland pasture in poor areas such as Wychwood.[20] For this period, the traditional assumption of a close relationship between easily cultivable soils and early settlement nuclei still seems a plausible starting-point, especially when backed up by evidence from other disciplines. For example, the probable inter-relation of geology, prehistoric archaeology and toponymy has been demonstrated by studies around Coventry. There F. W. Shotton, surveying the distribution of Neolithic, Bronze Age and Iron Age material, showed a close correlation (amply corroborated by subsequent finds) with belts of light, permeable

[17] For an overview of the Pleistocene geology of the area see Wills, *Palaeogeography*, pp. 107–42, and Arkell, *Geology of Oxford*, pp. 191–240; also the Institute of Geological Sciences' *Quaternary Map of the United Kingdom* and smaller maps and surveys.

[18] Thorpe, 'Growth of Settlement', p. 87, n. 5; Mackney and Burnham, *Soils*, p. 10; Gelling, 'Notes', p. 71; V. E. Watts, 'Comment on "The Evidence of Place-Names" by Margaret Gelling', in *Medieval Settlement*, ed. Sawyer, pp. 212–22, at 217–19; Ford, 'Settlement Patterns', p. 289; Stafford, *East Midlands*, p. 75.

[19] Taylor, *Village and Farmstead*, pp. 12, 20, 63–4, 84, 100, 117, 148, etc. Cf. Hooke, *Hwicce*, p. 248: 'both historical and environmental factors were relevant . . .' Evidence of early Anglo-Saxon preference for light soils, including river-terrace gravels, is cited by Arnold, *Archaeology*, pp. 44–7. Grundy, *Worcestershire*, pp. i–xvii, attempted to correlate place-names, geology and hidage, but many of his premises were unsound.

[20] Cf. Taylor, *Village and Farmstead*, pp. 83–4, 110 and 116, and *apud* Hoskins, *Making of the English Landscape*, p. 40; T. R. Slater, 'Professor Harry Thorpe, 1913–77: An Appreciation and Assessment', in *Field and Forest*, ed. Slater and Jarvis, pp. 9–30, at 20; Fowler, 'Lowland Landscapes', p. 6; Hooke, *Hwicce*, p. 154; B. Schumer, *The Evolution of Wychwood to 1400: Pioneers, Frontiers and Forests* (Leicester, 1984), p. 16; Everitt, *Continuity*, pp. 1–2, 95, 342, 344 and 361, n. 3.

soils associated with rivers and streams; and aerial photography sub-sequently revealed numerous crop-marks following the same pattern, which confirmed the importance of these soils around Coventry.[21] Such a correlation cannot be taken quite at face value, because crop-marks show up best on the well-drained gravels, and the settlements they reveal are especially likely to turn up fortuitously because of gravel quarrying,[22] but the pattern is not entirely illusory either: it is a general rule that 'the "Newer Drifts" give easily cultivated fertile soils, often of greater value than those which would have been derived from the "solid" formations they bury'.[23] Moreover, Dr Gelling's study of the place-names of a predominantly boulder-clay area north-east of Coventry in relation to the recent drift geology showed a clear correlation between pre-Viking settlement names and islands of sand or gravel.[24] Early Anglo-Saxon estates, then, were focussed on good soils.

CENTRES AND PERIPHERIES

To show that the kingdoms of the Hwicce and Magonsætan were geographically coherent and regionally distinct, we would at least have to show that their estate-centres and areas of densest settlement were generally distant from their boundaries. This is to assume, of course, that the Anglo-Saxons of the post-migration period had political boundaries. That is not anachronistic. Respect for territorial divisions is apparent as

[21] F. W. Shotton, 'The Distribution of Neolithic, Bronze Age and Iron Age Relics around Coventry', *Proceedings of the Coventry and District Natural History and Scientific Society* 1 no. ix (1938), 184–92; Thomas, 'Archaeological Gazetteer', pp. 41–2 and maps; Webster and Hobley, 'Aerial Reconnaissance'; Ford, 'Settlement Patterns', pp. 288–92; cf. Millward and Robinson, *West Midlands*, pp. 17–18 and 26.

[22] A map of all gravels and all known *river*-gravel crop-marks was given by RCHM, *A Matter of Time: An Archaeological Survey of the River-Gravels of England* (London, 1960), p. 11. For more recent rethinking see Taylor, *Village and Farmstead*, pp. 18–20; Webster, 'Prehistoric Settlement', pp. 42–3; Hunt, 'Archaeology in the Avon and Severn Valleys'; S. Esmonde-Cleary, 'Romans and River Gravels', *WMA* 25 (1982), 25–9; 'The Archaeology of the River Gravels', ed. J. Wills, *WMA* 28 (1985), 67–75.

[23] Wills, *Palaeogeography*, p. 126.

[24] Gelling, 'Notes', pp. 69–74 and 76–9; 'Evidence', pp. 209–11; *Signposts*, pp. 234–6 and fig. 21. These correlations do not show that unfavourable sites were not settled, since they may originally have been subsidiary members of the named settlements: cf. Gelling, 'New Look', pp. 62–3; G. Fellows-Jensen, 'Anglo-Saxons and Vikings in the British Isles: The Place-Name Evidence', *Settimane* 32 (1986), 617–39.

soon as documentary history begins, in the existence of land-grants,[25] and the compiler of the *Tribal Hidage*, too, thought of peoples in geographical terms. Poets give the same impression. A Briton is praised in the *Gododdin* because 'he fixed the boundary', and the author of *Widsith* probably intended a covert compliment to Offa of Mercia's construction of his Dyke against the Welsh when he praised his ancestor and namesake:

No-one of his age did in battle greater deeds of valour with a single sword. He marked out a boundary against the Myrgings, by *Fifeldore* (the River Eider). The English and the Swæfe have held it ever since as Offa won it.[26]

It is hard to weigh up the extent to which such boundaries were dictated by the natural divisions of water and marginal land and the extent to which they reflected ancient polities or the vagaries of territorial acquisition, military might and tribal alliance in the period of Anglo-Saxon settlement. Primitivist nineteenth-century historians certainly exaggerated the exist-ence and determining influence of impassable seas and forests, and there has been a reaction against environmental explanations and a tendency to stress the arbitrary, though possibly ancient, nature of administrative units.[27] Nevertheless, contemporaries perceived the importance of the environment; the kingdom of the South Saxons was said to have resisted attack 'because of the multitude of rocks and density of forests'.[28] We should allow for the possibility of a combination of environmental and human factors in the geographical formation of the early Anglo-Saxon kingdoms: an inhospitable upland area, for instance, might be avoided for settlement (especially if there was no demographic pressure), and woodland might be allowed to regenerate there, not simply to ward off enemies but also to provide timber, fuel and swine-pastures for more central agrarian

---

[25] P. Sawyer, 'Anglo-Saxon Settlement: The Documentary Evidence', in *Anglo-Saxon Settlement and Landscape*, ed. T. Rowley, BAR British Series 6 (Oxford, 1974), 108–19. For the *Tribal Hidage*, see above, p. 17. Contrast the view of Mayr-Harting, *Coming of Christianity*, p. 17. The assumption that 'boundaries were constantly changing' is discussed by Arnold, *Archaeology*, pp. 183–4.

[26] *Aneirin: Y Gododdin*, ed. A. O. H. Jarman (Llandysul, 1988), p. 29; D. Whitelock, *The Audience of Beowulf* (Oxford, 1951), p. 63.

[27] Cf. Sims-Williams, 'Settlement', pp. 3 and n. 7 and 32; Taylor, *Village and Farmstead*, p. 20; J. Gould, 'Primeval Woodlands, Clearance and Regeneration in the West Midlands', *WMA* 24 (1981), 153–6; Everitt, *Continuity*, p. 343; and above, pp. 89, n. 9, and 365, n. 20.

[28] *VW*, c. 41.

settlements; conversely, an unattractive belt of clay in the centre of a kingdom might nevertheless be settled and farmed, since labour and transport would present fewer problems than on the exposed peripheries.

Very broadly speaking, a glance at a contour map[29] suggests that the kingdoms of the Hwicce and Magonsætan coincided with natural geographical regions (although there were varied *pays* within those regions). The Hwicce were based on the valleys of the middle Severn and (Warwickshire) Avon and their tributaries and on the land enclosed by the surrounding watersheds. The Magonsætan were based on the territory excluded by the Hwicce to the east, by the Welsh highlands to the west, and by the fertile upper Severn valley to the north, which was probably occupied by the Wreocensætan.[30] At its centre were the slighter valleys of the Wye, Lugg and Teme – a less obvious focus than that of the Hwiccian kingdom.

The hypothesis that early Anglo-Saxon kingdoms were regionally coherent, with boundaries mainly running through lands relatively unfavourable for settlement and with their richer lands mainly in central areas, seems plausible *a priori*.[31] There were clearly exceptions, however, such as where the boundaries ran along rivers. River boundaries had to be imposed by the sword, like Offa the Angle's along the Eider;[32] this is a corollary to E. T. Leeds's observation that, because the Anglo-Saxons tended to settle along rivers to judge by their burial sites, watersheds were their natural boundaries ('without contending that the line of any watershed formed a real obstruction to expansion').[33]

In the later medieval West Midlands, centres of agrarian activity and, hence, of dense settlement formed the regional focus, playing a role equivalent to the modern Birmingham/Black Country conurbation (which has shifted the centre of gravity northwards). In the thirteenth century

[29] Note especially the 200 ft contour on the O.S. *Map of Britain in the Dark Ages*. Cf. the 150 m. contour on fig. 2, above p. 63.

[30] See above, p. 44. The situation of Wreocensætan territory suggests that it was settled earlier than that of the Magonsætan or that they obtained the upper hand in the pursuit of land.

[31] Cf. Hooke, *Hwicce*, pp. 248–50.

[32] Though rivers might form useful administrative boundaries *within* peoples, e.g. the North and South Mercians (cf. Chadwick, *Origin*, pp. 10–11; Hart, 'Tribal Hidage', p. 136) and at a very local level (cf. Hooke, *Hwicce*, pp. 58–9). It is well known that dialect boundaries and rivers rarely coincide.

[33] Leeds, *Settlements*, p. 79; cf. Hills, 'Review, p. 310.

there is a marked correlation between such central agricultural areas and
the distribution of episcopal and Benedictine monastic estates (as opposed
to those of the Augustinian and Cistercian houses, which were on more
marginal land).[34] The same appears true of the siting of the Hwiccian see
and monasteries, and their estates; they look well placed to have exercised a
centripetal function in the kingdom, and would appear, whatever the
asceticism of their bishops and monks, to have followed the pattern of
secular settlement and to have been endowed with some of the most
valuable lands in the kingdom. In the kingdom of the Magonsætan the
picture is less clear, but the sources are very inadequate.[35]

The theoretical issues raised above are best exemplified in the kingdom-
diocese of the Hwicce, since the equivalence of the Hwiccian political and
ecclesiastical boundaries, and their course, have been firmly established[36]
and because so many more monasteries are attested in this kingdom than in
that of the Magonsætan.

THE HWICCIAN CHURCH

The precise siting of the early Hwiccian monasteries and the exact extent of
their estates is generally unknown; the boundary clauses appended to the
seventh- and eighth-century charters in the later cartularies are mostly
additions of the later Anglo-Saxon period,[37] and the charters' assessment of
estates in terms of the hide (land that supported one taxable free family
with its dependent tenants) rather than the acre means that they do not
define precise areas for us. Nevertheless, when one notes the frequent
equivalence of known early bounds and later ones and bears in mind that
the whole kingdom of the Hwicce is assessed at only 7,000 hides in the
Tribal Hidage, it is clear that the early monasteries, which were sometimes
assessed in tens or scores of hides, possessed many square miles.[38]
Monasteries such as Fladbury (44 hides), Ripple (30), Kempsey (30) and
Hanbury (50) must have controlled, besides the named centre, many

---

[34] See map in Hilton, *A Medieval Society*, p. 27.
[35] On Leominster and Wenlock estates see above, pp. 94, n. 26, and 99, n. 48.
[36] See above, p. 5.   [37] Hooke, *Hwicce*, pp. 52–71.
[38] Sawyer, *Roman Britain to Norman England*, p. 143, notes that the early bounds (S 1171)
of Barking monastery (40 hides) cover more than 60 square miles. Cf. in general Scharer,
Königsurkunde, pp. 36–40; Lloyd Jones, *Wales and the Marches* I, 91–2; Loyn, *Governance*,
pp. 36–40; Wallace-Hadrill, *Commentary*, p. 33.

subsidiary estates, rarely named in charters, as in the case of the bishops' manors that succeeded them.[39] Some monastic estates are described as including appurtenances at some distance, often woodland,[40] and the records allow us to see some monasteries, like the see at Worcester itself, gradually acquiring scattered dependencies; these need to be taken into account in assessing the wealth of the total estate.[41]

The early monasteries may have been situated at the villages and towns which bear their names today, but continuity of name cannot be assumed to show continuity of site, and certainly not to show that nucleated settlements existed in the early period.[42] Nor can we assume that later parish churches mark the original nucleus of earlier monastic settlements, even though ecclesiastical topography seems to be very conservative – churches often become isolated while secular settlements drift away.[43] In many cases, however, approximate continuity of site is confirmed by topographical elements in the place-names themselves that refer to features of the landscape (e.g. Hanbury, Kempsey, Pershore, Twyning, Ripple). If, as seems reasonable, we provisionally assume such continuity where early evidence of site is lacking and examine the position of the modern successor villages and churches, it soon becomes apparent that nearly all the early monasteries were situated on outstandingly good agricultural land, on the sort of sites that might equally have attracted a royal vill. In this they resemble the early Welsh churches on the other side of the

[39] Cf. Sawyer, *Roman Britain to Norman England*, p. 144; Campbell, *Essays*, pp. 110–11; Dyer, *Lords and Peasants*, pp. 93–5 and 355–6. Hanbury's dependencies are mentioned in S 190.

[40] Hooke, *Hwicce*, p. 79. Cf. Everitt, *Continuity*, p. 336.

[41] Dyer, *Lords and Peasants*, pp. 23–5; Ford, 'Settlement Patterns', p. 281; Sawyer, *Roman Britain to Norman England*, pp. 146–7. Ford shows that later medieval linked settlements in Warwickshire group themselves in pairs on either side of, rather than across, the diocesan boundary. It is going far beyond the evidence to regard this (with Sawyer, p. 50) as showing that the boundary line existed before the creation of the kingdom of the Hwicce; the links may be seventh-century and later and need not reflect pre-existing British multiple estates.

[42] Cf. Taylor, *Village and Farmstead*, pp. 15 and 122; Price and Watson, 'Sedgeberrow', p. 91; Hooke, *Hwicce*, p. 141. As Stafford says (*East Midlands*, p. 29), 'the picture may be exaggerated because it is precisely where such drift has occurred that village sites are now available for excavation'. Cf. Fowler, 'Agriculture and Rural Settlement', p. 42.

[43] Cf. Sawyer, *Roman Britain to Norman England*, p. 164; Morris, *Church*, pp. 63–4; Taylor, *Village and Farmstead*, pp. 116, 123–4, 128 etc.

border.[44] It is exactly what one would expect from Bede's complaint that some monasteries were indistinguishable from secular estates.[45]

CENTRAL AREAS

Broadly speaking, the most attractive areas for settlement in the kingdom of the Hwicce were the sandy and gravelly terraces of the Severn from Bridgnorth to its confluence with the Avon at Tewkesbury, and of its tributaries the Stour and (especially) the Avon, and, secondly, the Cotswold hills.[46] The concentration of settlements, including monasteries, in these central areas must have had a unifying effect on the kingdom.[47]

The Severn and Avon Terraces

The Severn and Avon river terraces, which were formed by these rivers alternately accumulating debris in their flood plains and eroding down to lower channels, provide exceptionally fertile and well drained soils, above the level of the present flood plains; furthermore, they benefit from the early onset of spring due to winter warmth from the Bristol Channel.[48] An 'Aerial Reconnaissance over the Warwickshire Avon' published in 1965 revealed crop-marks of over a hundred settlement sites, closely linked with the fertile terraces, and to a lesser extent, the lighter permeable soils in the region on scattered glacial deposits. Subsequent aerial evidence accumulated rapidly, and was in full agreement with the distribution of prehistoric earthworks and objects and of Romano-British remains, so that by 1974 it could be claimed that 'the Avon valley may have a higher concentration of

---

[44] Davies, *Microcosm*, p. 28, and 'Roman Settlements', p. 156. On coincidence and non-coincidence of minsters and vills see Blair, 'Minster Churches in the Landscape', pp. 40–50.

[45] See above, pp. 126–30 and 147–8. Cf. Reece, 'Cotswolds', p. 187.

[46] Cf. Hooke, *Hwicce*, pp. 190–226.

[47] So too must the linkages noted above, n. 41. See also above, p. 7.

[48] Millward and Robinson, *West Midlands*, pp. 11, 20–4, 26–8, and 168–72; Kellaway and Welch, *Bristol and Gloucester District*, p. 80; Williams and Whittaker, *Stratford and Evesham*, pp. 60–8; B. K. Roberts, 'The Anatomy of Settlement', in *Medieval Settlement*, ed. Sawyer, pp. 296–326, at 302; Darby and Terrett, *Domesday Geography*, pp. 270–1; Hilton, *A Medieval Society*, p. 12; Dreghorn, *Geology*, pp. 54–9; Mackney and Burnham, *Soils*, pp. 67–8. Cf. Tomlinson, 'River-Terraces of the Avon', and Wills, 'Pleistocene Development'.

sites than any comparable part of Wessex'.[49] The significance of crop-marks and chance archaeological discoveries on river-gravels is now less clear,[50] but we can be certain that the Avon terraces and associated permeable soils were settled more or less continuously from Neolithic times to the advent of the Anglo-Saxons in numbers in the sixth century. The distribution of early pottery and 'pagan' burials suggests strongly that the earliest of those Anglo-Saxon settlements were along the Avon valley.[51]

The crop-marks along the Severn above Tewkesbury are more sporadic by comparison, and place-names suggest that the density of Anglo-Saxon settlement was also lower along the middle Severn.[52] One may invoke geological determinism here. The Avon was once the main river in the region and the middle Severn only a tributary, hence the former created more extensive ancient terraces. After the Severn became the main drainage system the Avon's volume declined so that it was less able to overlie its later terraces with recent alluvium, which would have given rise to ill-drained gley soils. By contrast, although the lower Severn, as the original 'lower Avon', produced important early terraces providing good high sites for settlement, it generally covered its lower terraces in recent alluvium carried by the continuing volume of water (as at Gloucester). Above Bewdley the middle Severn terraces are negligible compared to those of the Stour,

[49] Thomas, 'Archaeological Gazetteer', p. 42. See Webster and Hobley, 'Aerial Reconnaissance'; Millward and Robinson, *West Midlands*, pp. 29–30; Thorpe, 'Growth of Settlement', pp. 87–8 and 92–3; Webster, 'West Midlands in the Roman Period', pp. 50 and 55; B. G. Cox, 'Romano-British Occupation Sites in the Vale of Evesham', *VEHSRP* 1 (1967), 11–16; Bond, 'Fladbury', p. 17 and n. 2; Bond and Hunt, 'Archaeological Work in Pershore', pp. 5–7; Ford, 'Settlement Patterns', p. 275; Hunt, 'Archaeology in the Severn and Avon Valleys'.

[50] See above, n. 22.

[51] Myres, *Pottery and the Settlement*, p. 17 (map); he notes 'scarcely any certainly fifth-century pottery' in the Avon cemeteries (p. 116 and n. 2). For burials see Ford, 'Settlement Patterns', pp. 274–6; Thorpe, 'Growth of Settlement', pp. 101–3; and the more up-to-date maps in Pretty, 'Welsh Border', and cited above, p. 19, n. 15. Gelling suggests that the absence of names in *tūn* and *lēah* between Evesham and Tewkesbury may indicate that these places originated before the fashion for such names set in ('Evidence', pp. 208–9; 'Notes', p. 69); but this is hard to reconcile with the number of *tūn* names along the Avon below Stratford, which she thinks denote Romano-British sites occupied by the English in many cases ('Notes', p. 68).

[52] Webster, 'West Midlands in the Roman Period', p. 55 (for the Tewkesbury river-gravels see *Roman West Country*, ed. Branigan and Fowler, pp. 115 and 165); Hunt, 'Archaeology in the Severn and Avon Valleys'; Thorpe, 'Growth of Settlement', p. 106 (cf. map in Gelling, 'Evidence', p. 206 = 'Notes', p. 64).

because originally this part of the middle Severn was a mere tributary to a larger Stour.[53]

The distribution of seventh- and eighth-century monasteries neatly reflects the relative importance of these various river terraces.

The area round Hampton Lucy monastery (17 hides) is thick with crop-marks indicating early settlement, including the early Anglo-Saxon halls at Hatton Rock on the Avon's third terrace. Hampton itself stands on the second terrace, and there is a glimpse of the rare first terrace (elsewhere usually covered with alluvium) near Hampton Lucy mill.[54] The monastery's 17 hides were made up of 12 at Hampton and 5 nearby at *Fæhha leag*, an area towards Tiddington, perhaps of woodland (though there was open land, *feldland*, there by the tenth century).[55] At Stratford there are large stretches of the second terrace, which rises to about 30 ft above the level of the alluvium, and on the south side of the river there are vestiges of the higher terraces. The twelfth-century town was located on the gravels north of the Avon, on top of the open fields of an earlier rural community, which was perhaps the descendant of the community which used the fifth- or sixth-century cemetery south of the river.[56] The monastery (20 hides) may have had a similar focus, below the Roman river crossing that gave it its name of *Strætford*. Two hides of woodland (*rus siluaticum*) at Nuthurst, eleven miles to the north, were attached to it.[57]

Of the Avon terraces, the second is the most extensive, and between Stratford and Tewkesbury its sand and gravels, which give rise to excellently drained soils, form a flat terrace 15 to 21 ft above the alluvium, in places more than a mile wide, notably between Evesham and Pershore;

---

[53] Wills, *Palaeogeography*, pp. 131 and 136–7, and 'Pleistocene Development', pp. 163, 207–9, 217–18, 224 and 228; R. P. Beckinsale and L. Richardson, 'Recent Findings on the Physical Development of the Lower Severn Valley', *Geographical Journal* 130 (1964), 87–103.

[54] Webster and Hobley, 'Aerial Reconnaissance', pp. 17–18 and fig. 10; Millward and Robinson, *West Midlands*, p. 30; Tomlinson, 'Country North of Stratford', pp. 443–4 and pl. XXVII.

[55] S 1310. See above, p. 163 and n. 96.

[56] Tomlinson, 'Country North of Stratford', pp. 441, 443 and pl. XXVII, and 'River-Terraces of the Avon', pp. 150, 157–8 and pl. X; T. R. Slater, 'The Analysis of Burgages in Medieval Towns: Three Case Studies from the West Midlands', *WMA* 23 (1980), 52–65, at 52 and 55; Slater and Wilson, *Stratford*, pp. 1, 9–10 and 29–30. Cf. above, p. 22, n. 30.

[57] S 1278. Cf. S 64; Dyer, *Lords and Peasants*, p. 25. On Stratford monastery see above, p. 162.

hence the Vale of Evesham was known as the 'granary' of Worcestershire before the advent of modern market gardening.[58] At Evesham, which takes its name from the bend (*hamm*) in the Avon, the second and third terraces occur (and the fifth at Green Hill); the medieval town and abbey stand on the gravels of the third, which is separated from the second by a distinct rise of about ten feet and reaches about 128 ft. According to the abbey's records, its eighth-century predecessor possessed very extensive estates on both sides of the Avon – but it is impossible to distinguish fact from fiction in these records.[59] Fladbury is sited on a large, flat sandy stretch of the second terrace which reaches to Wyre Piddle. Many early Anglo-Saxon and older remains near Fladbury parish church indicate fairly continuous occupation. As the eighth-century monastery is assessed at 44 hides it probably stretched some miles northwards, like the later episcopal manor.[60] Pershore monastery, which takes its name from the bank (*ōra*) of the Avon, also stood on its second terrace, overlooked by Allesborough Hill (the fifth terrace), and in the vicinity of Romano-British and earlier sites. As in the case of Evesham, we have no reliable information about its early estates.[61]

Bredon village is sited on gravels of the third terrace, and is possibly on the site of the monastery (12 hides), which was founded by Offa's grandfather and endowed in Offa's reign with properties in the Cotswolds and in the woodland area in the north of the diocese.[62] Twyning, on the opposite side of the river, stands at about 110 ft on the edge of the fourth

---

[58] Tomlinson, 'River-Terraces of the Avon', pp. 150 and 152; Williams and Whittaker, *Stratford and Evesham*, pp. 60–8; R. W. Sidwell, 'A Short History of Commercial Horticulture in the Vale of Evesham', *VEHSRP* 2 (1969), 43–51, at 43.

[59] Tomlinson, 'River-Terraces of the Avon', pp. 140, 145, 148–9 and 158; Wills, 'Pleistocene Development', pp. 199 and 222; Millward and Robinson, *West Midlands*, p. 169. Cf. Cox, 'Vale Estates'.

[60] Tomlinson, 'River-Terraces of the Avon', p. 152; Bond, 'Fladbury' and references; cf. Dyer, *Lords and Peasants*, p. 94; Hooke, *Hwicce*, p. 134. For a coin-hoard of *c*. 400 see B. Watson, 'Fladbury, Late Roman Coinhoard', *WMA* 29 (1986), 2–3.

[61] Tomlinson, 'River-Terraces of the Avon', p. 152 and pl. x; Wills, 'Pleistocene Development', pp. 178–9; Bond and Hunt, 'Archaeological Work in Pershore', pp. 2 and 5–8; A. G. Vince and P. F. Whitehead, 'An Abandoned Flandrian River Channel at Pershore: Stratigraphy, Pottery, and Biota', *VEHSRP* 7 (1979), 9–24. Cf. above, pp. 94–6.

[62] Tomlinson, 'River-Terraces of the Avon', pp. 145 and 149; *ECWM*, p. 38, no. 31 and addendum, p. 238; S 109, 116 and 117 (cf. above, pp. 152 and 163); Dyer, *Lords and Peasants*, p. 25.

terrace, which is composed of rough-bedded gravel and seams of yellowish sand, 30 ft or more thick near the church. The monastery was cramped by its position between the Avon and Severn – hence its name *(be)twīnum ēam*, '(place) between the rivers' – and was assessed at only 3 hides; but it also possessed 10 hides on the west bank of the Severn, which must have included stretches of the Severn terraces as well as wooded country.[63]

Deerhurst stands on a small patch of the Severn's third (or Main) terrace. As remains of this terrace are rather rare downstream from Tewkesbury (either because the deposits were never laid down, owing to tidal scouring, or were eroded with the Severn's successive rejuvenations), it is clear that the siting of the Anglo-Saxon settlement on this terrace was deliberate. Moreover, the Anglo-Saxon church and the substantial Roman buildings that preceded it were positioned so as to escape the flooding of the Severn.[64] By the eleventh century numerous estates were dependent on Deerhurst. We can see an early stage in the process in a bequest to its 'congregation' in (?)804 of estates in the valley of the Warwickshire Stour (Todenham and (?)Preston) and at *Screfleh*, probably a wooded area, perhaps Shrewley in the same county (SP/2267) or Shrawley further up the Severn (SO/8065).[65] The estate of Ripple monastery (30 hides) occupies a low-lying strip (*ripel*) along the Severn, on the first extensive area of the third terrace and on the second terrace, which makes its first unequivocal appearance here, at about 10 ft above the present flood plain.[66] Downstream from Ripple this second (or 'Worcester') terrace is submerged by later alluvium, but above Ripple it becomes a striking feature of the valley up as far as the confluence with the Stour, and is the location for many settlements. Among them are the city of Worcester, which is mainly built on this terrace, and Kempsey, whose church stands within an early

---

[63] Tomlinson, 'River-Terraces of the Avon', p. 141 and pl. x; Wills, 'Pleistocene Development', pp. 182, 198 and pls. XIV and XVII; also Dreghorn, *Geology*, pp. 62–4 (on Cheltenham Sands overlying the gravels under the village); *PNGl* II, 71; and above, pp. 132–3 and n. 83; also Grundy, *Gloucestershire*, pp. 253–4.

[64] Wills, 'Pleistocene Development', pp. 163, 186–7, 206–7 and pl. xv; Rahtz, *Excavations at St Mary's*, pp. 6–7 and pl. I = Butler *et al.*, 'Deerhurst 1971–1974', pl. LXXa.

[65] Darby and Terrett, *Domesday Geography*, p. 3, fig. 3; *ECWM*, pp. 79–84 and 238; S 1187; and above, p. 174. Shrawley is the usual identification for S 1187 (cf. *PNE* II, 113–14; *DEPN*, p. 420).

[66] Wills, 'Pleistocene Development', pp. 166, 190 and 206–7. Cf. Dyer, *Lords and Peasants*, p. 94, fig. 8. For Ripple see S 52.

earthwork on the gravel terrace, which raised it up from the flood plain, giving the place its name, 'Cymi's island'.[67]

In the Stour valley the monastery in the province of the *Usmere* (Stour in Ismere) may have stood on the fourth ('Kidderminster' or 'Wilden') terrace; this forms the conspicuous flat upon which upper Kidderminster is built, with patches round about – including some near Ismere House (SO/8679), which preserves the name *Usmere*. As the gravels and sands of this terrace were mainly deposited by water coming down the Stour, long sections of the lower Stour valley are flanked by it.[68] Much of the best land of the monastery's 10 hides must have lain on these deposits and on those of the third (Main) terrace, which flanks it at Wolverley and along the Churchill Brook. The monastery's charter of 736 describes the 10 hides as 'extending in circumference on either side of the river Stour, having to the north the wood called Kinver and to the west another wood which is called Morfe, of which woods the greater part belong to the aforesaid estate'.[69] Some trace of this woodland environment appears from pollen analysis at Cookley, which suggests that while there had been Neolithic arable farming on the light sandy soils there, in the early Anglo-Saxon period there was a resurgence of woodland, to be followed by further clearances.[70] An endorsement to the 736 charter notes that Æthelbald of Mercia also granted an estate at *Brochyl* in Morfe wood to the founder of the monastery; this was apparently of 4 hides.[71]

---

[67] Wills, 'Pleistocene Development', pp. 207–9; H. E. O'Neil, 'Court House Excavations, Kempsey, Worcestershire', *TWAS* 33 (1956), 33–44; Mackney and Burnham, *Soils*, p. 77.

[68] L. J. Wills, 'Pleistocene Development', pp. 165, 179–80, 183–5, 204–5, 225, and pl. XIV, and 'The Geology and Soils of Hartlebury Common', *PBNHPS* 15 (1921–30), 95–101; G. H. Mitchell *et al.*, *Geology of the Country Around Droitwich, Abberley and Kidderminster*, Memoirs of the Geological Society (London, [1962]), pp. 112–14. See above, p. 31 and n. 73.

[69] S 89; Stenton, *Anglo-Saxon England*, p. 286. Cf. Ford, 'Note', and Sawyer, *Roman Britain to Norman England*, p. 145 (who both use the misleading translation in *EHD*, no. 67).

[70] J. Greig, 'Cookley, Hereford and Worcester: Pollen Diagram from Deposit at SO 838 799', *WMA* 23 (1980), 82.

[71] Because Stour in Ismere is assessed at 14 hides in S 1411 and 1257, and S 180 says these were 'duobus in curtis'. The identification of *Brochyl* by Ford, 'Note', is impossible, not lying in the Forest of Morfe as indicated in S 89 or as known from later sources, for which see E. M. Yates, 'Dark Age and Medieval Settlement on the Edge of Wastes and Forests', *Field Studies* 2 (1964–8), 133–53, at 148–51.

The Cotswolds

The other natural focus of settlement in the kingdom of the Hwicce could hardly contrast more with the river terraces. The Cotswold hills run parallel to the lower Severn, and the rivers of their scarp slope, which was formerly very wooded, drain into the Severn; those of the dip slope, with the exception of the (Bristol) Avon, join the Thames. In the Cotswolds there is plenty of evidence for Iron Age and Romano-British occupation (but rarely for *continuity* of occupation), and so-called 'Celtic' Fields, indicating prehistoric agriculture, are increasingly being discovered.[72] The Cotswold soils are closely related to the underlying geological formations, usually Oolitic limestones which give rise to brown and red calcareous soils, most commonly of the Sherborne series.[73] As later medieval records show, these 'stonebrash' soils had less arable potential than the richer soils of river-valley estates, and the area was short of lush river-meadows for raising cattle, which need more water than sheep. Nevertheless, like the prehistoric and Romano-British farmers before them, the Anglo-Saxons must have prized these uplands. If the limestone soils were naturally deficient in certain chemicals, they had the great advantage of being naturally well-drained and not needing heavy or frequent ploughing; indeed, because of their shallowness, they would suffer from it. Their disadvantage, that they are easily eroded by wind, would have been less of a problem in the early Anglo-Saxon period when much of their beech-wood protection survived, or had regenerated; and the danger of erosion might also be offset by folding sheep on the arable to restore both its firmness and its fertility – a policy that would also provide meat and clothing.[74] The Cotswolds were thus suited to a mixed economy of corn growing and sheep grazing. This is probably what they have had, with fluctuations from corn to sheep, since Roman times, even in the heyday of the later medieval Cotswold wool trade.[75]

[72] Kellaway and Welch, *Bristol and Gloucester District*, p. 3; *RCHM Gl* I, xxix and xliv; Fowler, 'Pre-Medieval Fields'.

[73] Osmond, 'Soils', pp. 69–70; Findlay, 'Soils', p. 15; Mackney and Burnham, *Soils*, pp. 30–1, 85 and 101.

[74] Hilton, *A Medieval Society*, pp. 13 and 117; Dyer, *Lords and Peasants*, pp. 68, 70, 134, etc. (and cf. p. 128); Fowler, 'Pre-Medieval Fields'; *RCHM Gl* I, xxiv and xlviii-xlix; *Agrarian History*, ed. Finberg, p. 59; Vince, *Gloucestershire*, pp. 333, 337, 342, 371–3, 397 and 400; Hooke, *Hwicce*, pp. 229–35 and 250.

[75] Hilton, *A Medieval Society*, p. 13; Finberg, *Gloucestershire Landscape*, pp. 57–8; Dyer, *Lords and Peasants*; Darby and Terrett, *Domesday Geography*, p. 50; *PNGl* IV, 6–7.

According to Finberg, who cites his own studies of Withington and Blockley, the Anglo-Saxons colonized the hill-pastures first and tackled the valleys later.[76] This is a generalization. They would certainly have tended to avoid valley bottoms which were lined with clay or liable to flood, but their settlements were generally on the sides of the valleys, just above the spring-line; in this they contrast with the Roman villas, which were usually sited below the spring-line with indifference to the subsoil, paramount importance being given to the need for running water for baths. (The putative villa high and dry above Tetbury is an exception.)[77] Springs of any importance usually occur at the head of the combes which they have formed and enlarged by headward erosion. The water runs out of a porous stratum where it rests on an impervious stratum; spring-lines occur, for instance, where water seeps through the Great Oolite to its junction with the Fuller's Earth clay (in the mid- and southern Cotswolds) or else through the Inferior Oolite (and Upper Lias Sands, where present) to emerge at the junction with the Upper Lias clay or the Snowshill clay.[78] The Oolites and Upper Lias Sands provided good dry sites for settlement, with easily worked land, while the springs provided ample water supplies. In some cases, however, even the valley bottoms could be cultivated and settled where their clays were overlain by the permeable loams resulting from the decalcification of the upper layers of fans of coarse 'taele' gravels (the remains of old Jurassic rocks, mainly Oolitic limestones, whose surface had broken up in Arctic conditions and then been spread over the valleys during seasonal thaws).[79] In any case, the valleys and streams would have provided some valuable meadow (the *pratae* granted in Anglo-Saxon charters), and sometimes these might be suitable for ploughing up for extra crops, as happened in Blockley in the later Middle Ages.[80]

The distribution of Hwiccian monasteries reflects the importance of the

---

[76] *Gloucestershire Studies*, p. 11; cf. Fowler, 'Agriculture and Rural Settlement', pp. 37–9 and 43.

[77] *RCHM Gl* I, 119 (ST/87829572).

[78] *Ibid.* pp. xxiii and xxxviii. For an elementary account see Dreghorn, *Geology*, pp. 87, 106–7, 125–6, 131–2, 134, etc. See also Arkell and Donovan, 'Fuller's Earth'; Arkell, *Geology of Oxford*, pp. 243–4 and 253; Kellaway and Welch, *Bristol and Gloucester District*, pp. 87–8; Vince, *Gloucestershire*, pp. 323 and 362; *PNOx*, pp. xiii–xiv.

[79] Tomlinson, 'Cotswold Sub-Edge Plain'. Cf. Arkell, *Geology of Oxford*, pp. 228–30; Kellaway and Welch, *Bristol and Gloucester District*, pp. 80–1 and 83; Dreghorn, *Geology*, pp. 121 and 187.

[80] Dyer, *Lords and Peasants*, p. 96.

Cotswolds, and interestingly many of them are located near Iron Age or Roman sites. By and large they occupy fairly high, dry sites. A monastery at Bibury (*Beagan byrig*) seems to have begun with a lease of 5 of the see of Worcester's 15 hides there to an Earl Leppa and his daughter Beage. These 5 hides seem to have been at Ablington, a high area with traces of 'Celtic' Fields and Romano-British settlements, for Leppa's name was preserved in the name of some quarries, *Leppan crundlas*, by the saltway on its northern boundary; but presumably it was his daughter who acquired the remaining 10 hides, including Bibury itself, since she gave her name to the latter.[81] A spring named after Beage may be commemorated in the name *Bywell*, an area on the west bank of the Coln in central Bibury.[82] The parish as a whole lies on the Great Oolite and, higher up, on the Forest Marble, but the floor of the Coln valley, on which the present village is sited, is formed of spring-bearing Fuller's Earth. The partly Anglo-Saxon church faces a Roman villa site on the opposite side of the river, and there is an Iron Age hill-fort further upstream at Ablington.[83]

Higher up the Coln, the monastery at Withington had an estate of 20 hides on the west bank at its foundation *c.* 700; a further hide was soon added, probably of sheep-pasture on the east bank.[84] The monastic settlement was presumably around the present church, on a level platform well above the valley bottom, and its arable probably lay to the north around Northfield and towards Foxcote, where there is evidence of Iron Age settlement and Late Roman (or possibly early Anglo-Saxon) burials.[85] As Finberg showed, Withington is one of the most plausible sites for continuity of settlement and agriculture from Romano-British to Anglo-Saxon times. Neighbouring parishes, notably Chedworth and Compton Abdale, had important villas, and Withington's own villa, half-a-mile

---

[81] *RCHM Gl* I, 13; cf. Grundy, *Gloucestershire*, pp. 40–3; *PNGl* I, 26–9; L. Bishop, 'The Bibury Saxon Charter', *Glevensis: The Gloucester and District Archaeological Research Group Review* 18 (1984), 16–18; Hooke, *Hwicce*, p. 127; and above, p. 152.

[82] *PNGl* I, 26 and 28; also Anon., *A Gloucestershire and Bristol Atlas* (Bristol and Gloucestershire Archaeological Society, 1961), p. 5, for a map of 1675 from John Ogilby's *Britannia*.

[83] *VCH Gl* VII, 23; *RCMH Gl* I, 13–15.

[84] S 1429 and 1255; Finberg, *Lucerna*, pp. 34–6 and 40–1.

[85] *Ibid.*, pp. 27–8, 38–9, 46 and 50; *RCHM Gl* I, 131; Fowler, 'Pre-Medieval Fields', p. 45. Cf. above, p. 83, n. 117.

south of the church, stands above a spring called Walwell ('Briton's spring?').[86]

Across the watershed from Withington, but still high up, was a multiple monastic estate centred on Dowdeswell which probably included the Roman villa at Whittington, as well as the Iron Age hill-fort on Dowdeswell Hill.[87] At the other end of the Cotswold scarp an analogous position is occupied by Old Sodbury, whose parish church is overlooked by an unexcavated hill-fort. This early monastic(?) estate, which offers further analogies to Dowdeswell,[88] is centred on the water-bearing Midford (Upper Lias) Sands, between the limestone uplands and the Lower Lias clay lowlands.[89] By contrast, Winchcombe is low-lying, at the foot of a twisting combe (*wincel-cumb*) running into the scarp. The combe's Roman villas at Wadfield and Spoonley Wood were sited just below the spring-line on opposite sides of the combe, and the siting of the Anglo-Saxon ecclesiastical settlement, not further up but on the Lower Lias clay of the Ishbourne valley, may be explained by the spread of 'taele' limestone gravel over the clay of the valley bottom; this had already encouraged settlement in the late Romano-British period. As befitted a royal foundation, Winchcombe monastery had extensive estates, which included the 3 hides of Twyning discussed above and 5 hides at Upton (in Blockley), a Romano-British settlement site on the other side of the Cotswolds, which is now a deserted medieval village.[90]

The Vale of Gloucester

It will be noticed from fig. 1 that there are fewer monasteries in the Vale of Gloucester than in the Cotswolds. This may partly be explained by the

---

[86] *Lucerna*, esp. p. 44; Reece, 'Cotswolds', pp. 186–7; *RCHM Gl* I, 24–9, 37–8 and 131–2; *PNGl* I, 189.

[87] SO/999191. See *RCHM Gl* I, 43–4 and 126–8; and above, p. 155.

[88] See above, p. 156.

[89] *RCHM Gl* I, 66 and 103–4; Kellaway and Welch, *Bristol and Gloucester District*, pp. 56–8 and 87; Arkell and Donovan, 'Fuller's Earth', p. 232.

[90] Tomlinson, 'Cotswold Sub-Edge Plain', p. 395; Wills, *Palaeogeography*, p. 128; Richardson, *Moreton*, p. 123; Dreghorn, *Geology*, pp. 122–3; *RCHM Gl* I, 112–14 and 130; Saville, 'North Street, Winchcombe'; P. Ellis, 'Excavations at Winchcombe, Gloucestershire, 1962–72', *TBGAS* 104 (1986), 95–138. For Upton see *RCHM Gl* I, 17; Dyer, *Lords and Peasants*, pp. 245–6 and reference; and for Twyning, see above, p. 375. For the ecclesiastical topography of Winchcombe see Bassett, 'Winchcombe'; and for Winchcombe estates see above, pp. 133, n. 83, 166 and 172.

supposition that the monastic estates of Gloucester (allegedly 300 *tributarii* originally) and of Berkeley took up large tracts of land in the north; while in the south the monastery of Westbury-on-Trym had 43 hides (plus 12 at Stoke Bishop disputed with Berkeley), and Henbury (20 hides) and Yate (10 hides) were also church properties.[91] On the other hand, the clay, often water-logged, soils of the Vale must have been less attractive than the Cotswold soils, though by modern standards the latter are less rich. By the time of the Domesday survey, when considerable wood-clearance and drainage had been accomplished, the Vale was supporting a population equal to that of the Cotswolds, and its number of plough-teams was comparable; yet it is striking that William of Malmesbury, praising the fertility of the Vale of Gloucester *c.* 1125, lays stress on its fruit-trees and vines rather than on its cereals.[92] A plough-team could operate less efficiently on the heavy soils based on the Keuper Marl and, especially, the Lower Lias clays than it could in the Cotswolds. As late as 1813 it was remarked that 'the plough will not at all times work, and it is an important concern to catch that moment which is most favourable. This kind of land soon becomes either too wet or too dry for work.'[93] The rich alluvial flats of the Lower Severn, now drained and protected by sea-walls, would also have been difficult to exploit in the early Anglo-Saxon period.[94]

The contrast with the Cotswolds must not be exaggerated, however. In the south, towards the Bristol Avon, the simplicity of the Vale's lowlands is interrupted by Carboniferous and Old Red Sandstone inliers denuded of their Keuper and Lias cover, and some of these give rise to fairly good soils: Oldminster in Hinton, thought to be the site of Berkeley monastery, stands on the most northerly stretch of Old Red Sandstone, which gives an acid but freely drained soil.[95] Elsewhere the uniformity of the clays and marls is broken by superficial deposits of water-laid Jurassic gravels and sands, often topped by brown loam or brickearth. (These are due to the

[91] See above, pp. 89, 153 and 175.

[92] Darby and Terrett, *Domesday Geography*, pp. 21 and 50–2; Finberg, *Gloucestershire Landscape*, p. 61; Hilton, *A Medieval Society*, p. 16; *PNGl* IV, 11 and 12, n. 4; *GP*, pp. 291–2.

[93] Vince, *Gloucestershire*, pp. 398–9. Cf. *ibid.*, pp. 323, 333–4, 337, 339, 342, 377, 397–9 and 401; Findlay, 'Soils', pp. 15–16; Osmond, 'Soils', p. 71.

[94] Cf. *ibid.*, p. 71; Findlay, 'Soils', p. 17; Vince, *Gloucestershire*, pp. 381–3; Kellaway and Welch, *Bristol and Gloucester District*, p. 83.

[95] Vince, *Gloucestershire*, pp. 319–21, 339, 368 and 387–9; Findlay, 'Soils', p. 17 and map. Cf. Taylor, 'Berkeley Minster', pp. 81–2; *PNGl* II, 234–5 and IV, 51.

decalcification noted above in connection with the coarser 'taele' gravels.) These sands and gravels occur both as terraces along major streams and as gently sloping fans with no relation to the existing drainage, sometimes filling up depressions in the Lias. They probably influenced the siting of many settlements.[96] Much of the land on which Gloucester itself stands is composed of sand and gravel.[97] Cheltenham, which also had a monastery in the eighth century, originated on a patch of Jurassic gravels and wind-blown quartz sand, though the present town has spread onto the Lower Lias clay. These 'Cheltenham Sands' provided dry settlement sites, plenty of drinking water reachable through shallow wells, and a light, easily worked soil, whose excellence is still reflected in the distribution of market gardens.[98] The parish of St Michael, Bishop's Cleeve has developed on a fan of Cheltenham Sands which fill a basin in the Lias. The estate of its eighth-century monastic church, assessed at 15 hides, seems to have embraced all the neighbouring parishes, giving it a variety of Cotswold woodland and low-lying river-meadow.[99] An inhumation cemetery found during sand-quarrying indicates early Anglo-Saxon settlement at Cleeve.[100] Beckford is sited on the river gravels along the Carrant Brook, which merge with 'taele' gravels on the lower slopes of Bredon Hill. Two sixth-century Anglo-Saxon cemeteries have been discovered in gravel digging, and Romano-British and earlier settlements have been identi-fied.[101] Both Beckford and Cheltenham monasteries formed valued parts of

[96] Tomlinson, 'Cotswold Sub-Edge Plain'; Wills, *Palaeogeography*, pp. 127–9; Arkell, *Geology of Oxford*, pp. 230–1; Kellaway and Welch, *Bristol and Gloucester District*, p. 83. Cf. Findlay, 'Soils', pp. 13 and 16–17; Vince, *Gloucestershire*, p. 333; and *PNGl* IV, 12.

[97] Tomlinson, 'Cotswold-Sub-Edge Plain', p. 397.

[98] *Ibid.*, pp. 389 and 395; Dreghorn, *Geology*, pp. 60–7; Vince, *Gloucestershire*, pp. 324, 348 and 386. Cf. Wills, 'Pleistocene Development', pp. 189, 212 and 228; Arkell, *Geology of Oxford*, p. 231; Tomlinson, 'Stour-Evenlode Watershed', p. 179; Richardson, *Moreton*, p. 123.

[99] Tomlinson, 'Cotswold Sub-Edge Plain', pp. 391 and 395; Dreghorn, *Geology*, p. 61; Richardson, *Moreton*, pp. 123–4; *VCH Gl* VIII, 2–3; Hooke, *Hwicce*, p. 231; and above, p. 157 and n. 69.

[100] SO/94852708. Unpublished, but listed in *MA* 14 (1970), 156.

[101] Tomlinson, 'Cotswold Sub-Edge Plain', pp. 391–3; Richardson, *Moreton*, pp. 125–8; Webster and Hobley, 'Aerial Reconnaissance', p. 13; Webster, 'Prehistoric Settle-ment', pp. 32–4 and 52, n. 10; J. Wills and S. Colledge, 'Beckford, SO 984 364', *WMA* 23 (1980), 78; B. Watson, 'Beckford, Nettlebed Field Romano-British Site', *WMA* 30 (1987), 1; Pretty, 'Welsh Border', pp. 126–7 (for unpublished cemeteries A and B at SO/964355 and 969355).

the Bishop of Hereford's estate, and owed food-renders to the Bishop of Worcester.[102]

Despite irregularities such as those just mentioned, it seems fair to uphold the traditional generalization that the Vale of Gloucester was slow to develop agriculturally. It is significant that although the Vale did support a number of villas in Roman times, particularly around the important centre of Gloucester, they are fewer than in the Cotswolds; that few 'Celtic' Fields have been detected; and that rescue archaeology along the M5 motorway between Tewkesbury and Bristol has produced few extensive Romano-British settlements (by comparison with numerous *minor* sites of that period) and no Iron Age sites at all – the important sites tended to lie where the M5 crossed the 'toes' of the Cotswolds, for instance in Alkington parish, above Berkeley, rather than on the lower Severn plains.[103] All this suggests that large settlements were rare, except on the islands of permeable soil mentioned above, and it may explain why the eighth-century abbesses of Gloucester were so zealous in obtaining estates outside the Vale itself.[104]

PERIPHERAL AREAS

The South

If one were to leave these central areas, the river terraces and Cotswolds, and perambulate the bounds of the kingdom and diocese of the Hwicce, one would pass through some naturally marginal country, and encounter fewer monasteries. There would be notable exceptions, for instance along the southern border with the West Saxons. In the historical period (from *c.* 675), this border seems to have run along the (Bristol) Avon, taking in Bath, and then gone along the Cotswolds, partly following the Fosse Way, before branching eastwards south of Cirencester to meet the Thames near Kempsford.[105] Political power rather than the lie of the land must have

---

[102] See above, pp. 138–9.

[103] *Roman West Country*, ed. Branigan and Fowler, pp. 167 and 177, and maps on pp. 121 and 178; P. J. Fowler, 'Pre-Medieval Fields', fig. 5.1, and 'Archaeology and the M5 Motorway, Gloucestershire 1969–75: A Summary and Assessment', *TBGAS* 95 (1977), 40–6 (with citations of earlier literature).

[104] See above, p. 145.

[105] Smith, 'Hwicce', and *PNGl* IV, 32–3; Hooke, *Hwicce*, pp. 13–16; Sims-Williams, 'Wilfrid', p. 178 and n. 67.

maintained this boundary. The Avon is flanked by terraces of mainly Jurassic gravel, which have offered fine dry sites for settlement since the Stone Age,[106] while the boundary at the Thames ran through high-quality land, and arbitrarily cut off the Saxons of the upper Thames valley from the area towards Cirencester that seems to have been their natural sphere of cultural influence in the sixth century, judging from the grave-goods of cemeteries such as Fairford and Kemble.[107] Whether or not the later diocesan boundary marks the south-eastern border of the Hwicce precisely is uncertain, but the Hwiccian border clearly passed through Kempsford, the site of a battle with the Wilsætan in 802; here there is an extensive river terrace, densely settled from the earliest times, and still the centre of an important wheat producing area.[108] The density of population here may have resulted in smaller socio-economic units than in the Cotswolds, hindering the creation of the large estates that might have supported Roman villas and, in due course, Anglo-Saxon monasteries.[109]

The history of the monasteries of Bath, Malmesbury and Tetbury reflects the critical nature of the West Saxon border. In 675 Osric of the Hwicce granted Abbess Berta 100 hides beside the *ciuitas* of *Hat Bathu* to found a monastery, and it seems that her successor received another 20 hides on the Cherwell in Middle Anglia, perhaps at Islip or Water Eaton.[110] In the following century, against a background of Mercian supremacy, Bath

---

[106] A. B. Hawkins and E. K. Tratman, 'The Quaternary Deposits of the Mendip, Bath and Bristol Areas', *Proceedings of the University of Bristol Spelaeological Society* 14 (1975–7), 197–232; B. Oriel, 'The Avon and its Gravels', *Proceedings of the Bristol Naturalists' Society* 10 (1901–3), 228–40; Kellaway and Welch, *Bristol and Gloucester District*, pp. 80 and 83; A. D. Lacaille, 'Palaeoliths from the Lower Reaches of the Bristol Avon', *AntJ* 34 (1954), 1–27; *Bristol and its Adjoining Counties*, ed. MacInnes and Whittard, pp. 28–9, 147–9, 152, 156, 159, 167, etc.; Fowler, 'Pre-Medieval Fields'.

[107] See above, p. 20. Smith, *PNGl* IV, 34 and 37, attempts some correlation with early types of place-name. His use of S 231 and 234 to show that Kemble was still in West Saxon hands in 682–8 is debatable (*PNGl* IV, 33, n. 3).

[108] See above, p. 9; Vince, *Gloucestershire*, pp. 342 and 370; R. Leech, *The Upper Thames Valley in Gloucestershire and Wiltshire: An Archaeological Survey of the River Gravels* (Bristol, 1977), pp. 14–17; Smith, 'Ring-Ditches', pp. 158–60, 163–4 and pl. XII; *RCHM Gl* I, liv–lv and 68–9; Miles, 'Romano-British Settlement', pp. 193–5.

[109] *Ibid.*, p. 207.

[110] See above, pp. 111–12, and Sims-Williams, 'Bath', p. 3, n. 2.

monastery obtained from the West Saxons first 5 hides at North Stoke, which included a strategic fort on the Great Oolite plateau, and then 30 hides on the south side of the Avon. After the decline of Mercian power in the ninth century, Bath and its monastery were transferred to Wessex, and the Avon boundary collapsed.[111] On the other hand, Malmesbury monastery, further up the Avon, seems always to have stayed on the West Saxon side of the border and to have benefited from the support of the rulers on both sides.[112] It did, however, lose Tetbury (*Tettanminster*) to the bishop of Worcester after Offa defeated the West Saxons at Bensington in 779.[113] The border between Malmesbury and Tetbury ran through inevitably controversial land, for the various geological formations to which it ran roughly parallel provide good arable soils for the most part. The limestone and marl formation which runs through Malmesbury and Fairford gives rise to soils especially suited to cereals, as its name 'Cornbrash' implies, and it is often water-bearing because it frequently overlies clays; hence it has had an importance for settlement disproportionate to its narrow width, and its outcrop is still marked by a line of villages.[114] To the south-east of the Cornbrash is the Oxford Clay, largely masked by dry, fertile gravels of the broad terraces of the Thames and its tributaries; to its north-west the Kemble Beds (the uppermost beds of the Great Oolite limestone) run through Kemble to Cirencester, providing a good arable soil, less porous than the Great Oolite beneath but probably not too heavy to work in the early Middle Ages. The 20 hides of Tetbury would have been centred on a region of Kemble Beds considerably below the level of the surrounding countryside and well suited for cattle raising.[115]

---

[111] See above, pp. 4, n. 9, 159–60 and 174. For North Stoke see also Sims-Williams, 'Bath', p. 9 and n. 7, and Arkell and Donovan, 'Fuller's Earth', p. 230.

[112] See above, pp. 108 and n. 87 and 227.

[113] So William of Malmesbury, *GP*, p. 388: see above, pp. 146, n. 13, and 160.

[114] Kellaway and Welch, *Gloucester and Bristol District*, p. 78; Arkell, *Geology of Oxford*, pp. 35, 38 and 47; J. A. Douglas and W. J. Arkell, 'The Stratigraphical Distribution of the Cornbrash: I. The South-Western Area', *QJGS* 84 (1928), 117–78, at 126 (map); *PNOx*, p. xii.

[115] Kellaway and Welch, *Bristol and Gloucester District*, pp. 71, 76–7 and 79; Osmond, 'Soils', pp. 69 and 71; Arkell, *Geology of Oxford*, pp. 35, 44–7, 213–25 and 250; Vince, *Gloucestershire*, pp. 324, 337–9, 342 and 370; Darby and Terrett, *Domesday Geography*, p. 50; *PNOx*, pp. xii–xiii and xiv–xv.

The East

By contrast the eastern boundary of the Hwicce between Lechlade and Moreton in Marsh, which probably corresponds to the shire boundary of Gloucestershire and Oxfordshire,[116] passed through much marginal land. Wychwood, the 'wood of the Hwicce' (*Huiccewudu*), centred on the high, bleak limestone plateau north-east of Burford, divided the Hwicce from the Saxons of Oxfordshire – its name probably shows that it was regarded as a wood on the Hwiccian border.[117] The northern stretch of the Cotswolds is described in a twelfth-century Worcester forged charter as the 'Hwiccian hill' (*mons Wiccisca*), perhaps a genuine archaism.[118] Its inhabitants were divided from the Oxfordshire Saxons by a large expanse of marshy land around Moreton in Marsh, now reclaimed but formerly named 'Henmarsh' from the moor-hens that frequented it.[119] The kingdom of the Hwicce seems to have extended across this no-man's-land to the foot of the continuation of the Cotswold escarpment on the far side of the Moreton Gap: Whichford, 7 miles east-north-east of Moreton, near the later diocesan boundary, probably denotes a ford leading into Hwiccian territory.[120] The Moreton Gap is floored with heavy Lower Lias clay, and the superficial deposits of gravel and sand on the latter are mostly obliterated by a great spread of boulder clay and clayey outwash (Moreton Drift), left by a tongue of ice which once spread down the Evenlode valley as far south as Wychwood.[121] This naturally water-logged region of clay upon clay

[116] C. S. Taylor in *Gloucestershire Studies*, ed. Finberg, p. 40.

[117] *PNOx*, pp. xii, xiii and 386; Arkell, *Geology of Oxford*, p. 252 (and throughout); *PNGl* IV, 42, n. 1; Gelling, *Place-Names in the Landscape*, p. 229; D. Hooke, 'Early Cotswold Woodland', *Journal of Historical Geography* 4 (1978), 333–41, at 335 and 337, and *Hwicce*, pp. 14–15. For the views that it marks the itinerary of the Hwicce to their homeland or was their common woodland and pasture see Collingwood and Myres, *Roman Britain and the English Settlements*, p. 409, and Ford, 'Settlement Patterns', p. 279. It lay outside the medieval diocese of Worcester and there is no reason to think it was ever part of the kingdom of the Hwicce. Cf. above, p. 365.

[118] S 731; Smith, 'Hwicce', p. 64, n. 18.

[119] *PNWa*, pp. 298–300; *PNGl* I, 230, and IV, 4 and 12; *PNOx*, pp. 338 and 341.

[120] See above, p. 74, n. 76. Note the position of the bishop of Worcester's estates, in Oswaldslow hundred (*PNWo*, map in end-pocket).

[121] Arkell, *Geology of Oxford*, pp. 191–205; Kellaway and Welch, *Bristol and Gloucester District*, p. 82; Richardson, *Moreton*; Tomlinson, 'Stour–Evenlode Watershed'; Wills, *Palaeogeography*, pp. 112 and 114–16; Bishop, 'Three Gaps', pp. 291–8 and 300–3; Millward and Robinson, *West Midlands*, pp. 17 and 165–6; Vince, *Gloucestershire*, pp. 324–5, 350 and 376–7.

provides only a few settlement sites, where patches of wind-blown sands, fans of Oolitic gravels, and the slight terraces of the upper Evenlode mask the Moreton Drift or Lower Lias;[122] the obvious sites for settlement and agriculture were either where older deposits survived, above the level of the Moreton Drift, or on the highlands on either side of the Henmarsh. The latter is the case with the ninth-century monastic settlement at Blockley. This was sited above the marshy ground at the top of Blockley Brook, which is mentioned in an eighth-century charter.[123] Its name, 'Blocca's clearing', suggests that it was a secondary settlement. Finberg argued that it was an offshoot of the neighbouring high settlement at Batsford ('Bæcci's slope'),[124] but it is equally possible that it was related to the Romano-British site at Upton or to the community which used the Anglo-Saxon cemetery north of Blockley Brook on one of the gravel patches towards Paxford.[125] The village of Daylesford, on the other hand, is sited on the Moreton Drift beside the Evenlode; but here the outwash forming the Drift consists chiefly of sands and flinty gravels, and besides, the six-hide monastic estate sloped up from the present church over the more easily cultivated limestone. At the top of the slope stood the Iron Age hill-fort on Chastleton Hill, called 'urbs antiqua' in the bounds.[126] This marks the diocesan and shire boundary.

The Moreton Drift survived because erosion was minimal on the watershed between the Evenlode and the Stour. But north of the Henmarsh the glacial deposits were scoured out and dispersed into the Bristol Channel by the Stour and Avon, with the result that there is no natural frontier in the 'Feldon', the open country south of the Avon.[127] The following

---

[122] Cf. Arkell, *Geology of Oxford*, pp. 217, 230, 239, etc.; Tomlinson, 'Stour–Evenlode Watershed', pp. 171, 173–4 and 186–93; Richardson, *Moreton*; *PNOx*, p. xv. For evidence for agriculture in the Evenlode valley in the later Anglo-Saxon period see Hooke, *Hwicce*, pp. 208–11.

[123] S 101; Finberg, *Gloucestershire Studies*, pp. 7–8.

[124] *Ibid.* He further speculates (pp. 9–10) on a connection between Batsford and the low-lying Roman walled site at Dorn on the Fosse (for which see Todd, 'Vici', pp. 112–14 and *RCHM Gl* I, 12–13). On Blockley monastery see above, p. 172.

[125] Above, p. 380 (for Upton); Meaney, *Gazetteer*, p. 280 (SP/184369); Copley, *Archaeology and Place-Names*, p. 114. For the gravels along the Brook see Richardson, *Moreton*, p. 132; Tomlinson, 'Stour–Evenlode Watershed', p. 167.

[126] *Ibid.*, pp. 164, 181, 184–5 and pl. VI; Bishop, 'Three Gaps', pp. 295–6; Hooke, *Hwicce*, p. 211; Grundy, *Worcestershire*, pp. 70–1, and *Gloucestershire*, pp. 102–4; *PNOx*, p. 341.

[127] Arkell, *Geology of Oxford*, pp. 202, 204–5 and 211.

distinction between Arden (north of the Avon) and Feldon, drawn by John Leland, had some validity even in the early Middle Ages, to judge by the distribution of Romano-British sites and of Anglo-Saxon burials and place-names:

The grownd in Arden is much enclosyd, plentifull of gras, but no great plenty of corne. The other part of Warwyckshire that lyeth on the left hand or ripe of Avon river, muche to the southe, is for the moste parte champion somewhat barren of wood, but very plentiful of corne.[128]

Still less than in the Feldon was there any natural frontier across the Avon valley itself, for, as we have seen, since prehistoric times settlement had extended along this well-terraced valley to Coventry and beyond; perhaps this mattered less because the frontier was with the Hwicce's overlords, the Mercians. Here, at least, it is wrong to envisage a 'belt of undeveloped land', forming 'a natural no-mans-land between the kingdoms of Mercia and the *Hwicce*'.[129] The Mercian boundary seems to have passed through Martimow (*Mercna mere* 'the boundary of the Mercians') in Radway, on the diocesan boundary, and along the *Tach*brook (from **tǣcels*, 'boundary mark') south of Warwick, again on the later diocesan boundary.[130] The irregularity of the course of this boundary through Warwickshire 'shows that it was determined by local conditions of settlement and not by any important continuous natural features',[131] and the same was probably true of the Hwiccian boundary that preceded it. The only natural factor is the increase in altitude above Warwick, which is reflected in lower population and plough-team densities in Domesday statistics.[132] A surmise that the Roman settlement at Chesterton on the Fosse influenced the position of the

---

[128] Quoted by Nicklin, 'Arden', p. 71, Dyer, *Lords and Peasants*, p. 26, and Hooke, *Hwicce*, p. 202. See also Hilton, *A Medieval Society*, p. 15; *PNWa*, pp. xiii–xiv; Ford, 'Settlement Patterns', pp. 274–5 and 283–4; Millward and Robinson, *West Midlands*, pp. 12–13, 41–2 and 152; Thorpe, 'Growth of Settlement', pp. 102 and 105–6; Gelling, 'Evidence', p. 208 (on the British etymology of *Arden* see her 'Notes', p. 74); Darby and Terrett, *Domesday Geography*, pp. 295–6 and 308–9. The extent of later royal forest (*ibid.*, p. 443) is not really relevant being artificially maintained and partly a legal fiction (cf. Hilton, *A Medieval Society*, pp. 13–15).

[129] Ford, 'Settlement Patterns', p. 277.

[130] *PNWa*, pp. xvi–xvii, 258–9 and 272; *DEPN*, p. 458; *PNE* II, 174; *EHD*, no. 113; Smith, 'Hwicce', p. 64, n. 17; Hooke, *Hwicce*, p. 13. Cf. above, p. 70. The diocese of Lichfield extended nearly to Banbury.

[131] *PNWa*, p. xvi, n. 2.   [132] Darby and Terrett, *Domesday Geography*, pp. 309–10.

Hwiccian boundary, and was perhaps even inspired by a still earlier boundary there, is speculation.[133]

The North

The Arden forest, on the heavy soils north of the Avon (mainly Keuper Marls), and the high ground of the Clent and Lickey hills separated the Hwicce of the Avon and Severn valleys both from the Tomsætan of the Tame valley on the other side of the northern watershed and from the latter's Mercian overlords.[134] The marginal nature of much of this northern part of the Hwiccian kingdom is clearly indicated by the distribution of settlements in Worcester diocese documented before 850, or even before 1086, by the distribution of names indicating woodland settlements (especially ones in -*lēah*) relative to other types of settlement (especially ones in -*tūn*), and even by the distribution of post-Conquest assarts and clearances on the episcopal estates.[135] One hesitates to describe an area crossed by two Roman roads and useful for hunting, charcoal-burning and pannage as 'no-man's-land', but the barren Birmingham plateau must have been uninviting to settlers.[136] A partial exception must be made for the

[133] Phythian-Adams, 'Rutland', pp. 77–8 and 82, n. 31 (cf. Sawyer, *Roman Britain to Norman England*, pp. 62–3 and 197). The suggested correlation of the Hwicce and the Dobunnic coinage (of the first centuries BC and AD!), anticipated by D. Allen ('A Study of the Dobunnic Coinage', in *Bagendon: A Belgic Oppidum*, ed. E. M. Clifford (Cambridge, 1961), pp. 68–149, at 75), is not borne out by the southern distribution (*ibid.*, p. 68 and Hooke, *Hwicce*, pp. 5–6), although it has been argued that some of the Wiltshire coinage is secondary (cf. P. H. Robinson, 'A Local Iron Age Coinage in Silver and Perhaps Gold in Wiltshire', *BNJ* 47 (1977), 5–20). Altitude, plus the Anglo-Saxon liking for conspicuous boundary points, probably explains the correlation between the Hwiccian boundary and the early hill-forts noted by Ford, 'Settlement Patterns', pp. 227–8.

[134] For Arden see above, n. 128. For the Tomsætan (S 197 and 1272) see Stenton, *Anglo-Saxon England*, p. 41; *PNWa*, pp. xvii–xviii; Hooke, *Staffordshire*, pp. 12–13 and 19–21. They do not appear in the *Tribal Hidage*, presumably being subsumed under Mercia.

[135] Thorpe, 'Growth of Settlement', p. 101 (the lack of names *outside* Worcester diocese on this map is hardly significant); Ford, 'Settlement Patterns', p. 284; Gelling, 'Evidence', p. 206; *PNWa*, p. xiii, n. 3; Hooke, *Hwicce*, pp. 45–9 and 166–7; Dyer, *Lords and Peasants*, pp. 92–3. On the use of *tūn* and *lēah* names see Gelling, 'Notes', pp. 65–9, and Cox, 'Aspects', pp. 42–3.

[136] Millward and Robinson, *West Midlands*, pp. 25–6; Darby and Terrett, *Domesday Geography*, pp. 228 and 310–11; Webster, 'West Midlands in the Roman Period', p. 55; Thorpe, 'Growth of Settlement', pp. 96 and 99; Hooke, *Hwicce*, pp. 86 and

poor, but high and dry, Clent and Lickey hills which have produced important pre-Roman finds. Mostly on their southern slopes, there are a fair number of English settlements attested by 850 and of *-tūn* names contrasting with the predominance of *-lēah* or absence of both elements in the surrounding districts. According to a ninth-century charter relating to one of these places – Cofton Hackett, a *tūn* in a recess (*cofa*) in the Lickey Hills – the inhabitants of the remote region immediately to the north were called *Pencersætan*.[137] Wychbury, an important Iron Age hill-fort overlooking the Stour valley on a spur at the north-west end of the Clent ridge (SO/919818), may take its name from the Hwicce.[138]

The marginal nature of these northern regions is reflected in the lack of early monastic sites. Hanbury, an exception, is a rather special case, being an Irish foundation within a Romano-British hill-fort.[139] It should not be regarded as a backwater of Celtic asceticism, however; it stood at the centre of an estate of 50 hides (perhaps embracing the 12 sq. miles of the large modern parish) on the Roman road between the Roman industrial centre at Alcester and the salt-making centre at Droitwich, and Hanbury's charters refer to lead-furnaces and salt-pits among its appurtenances: these were perhaps at Alcester and Droitwich.[140] As lead-making and salt-making required large quantities of timber, the wooded nature of the estate would have been turned to positive advantage. Further south, on the Alcester–Worcester *stræt*, the monastery of *Penintanham* ('Inta's *hām* by the hill'?), if correctly identified with Inkberrow ('Inta's hills'), was sited in one of those

173–80. On two ways in Yardley noted in S 786 see *PNWo*, p. 4 and Grundy, *Worcestershire*, pp. 287–8 (cf. *PNWa*, p. 294).

[137] Thorpe, 'Growth of Settlement', pp. 87–93 and 101; Gelling, 'Evidence', p. 206: the *tūn* symbols on her map mark Drayton, Belbroughton (817), Walton, Hunnington, Quinton, and Cofton Hackett (780). For the *Pencersætan* see above, p. 31, n. 70. On the geology of Clent and Lickey see Millward and Robinson, *West Midlands*, pp. 13–14 and 28; Wills, *Palaeogeography*, p. 129.

[138] Thorpe, 'Growth of Settlement', pp. 93 and 108, n. 4; *PNWo*, p. 293.

[139] See above, p. 107.

[140] Cf. Millward and Robinson, *West Midlands*, pp. 37–8; Hooke, 'Droitwich Salt Industry', p. 129. For Alcester and Droitwich see Webster, 'West Midlands in the Roman Period', p. 53, and 'Prehistoric Settlement', pp. 46 and 50. There is a reference to the discovery of ancient iron works at Alcester in the *vitae* of St Ecgwine ptd by Horstman, *Nova Legenda Anglie* I, 376–7 (cf. Hardy, *Descriptive Catalogue* I, 420, n.), and Macray, *Chronicon de Evesham*, pp. 23–7 (cf. Lapidge, 'Hagiography of St Ecgwine', pp. 89–90). The Domesday manor of Hanbury possessed salt-pits at Droitwich (*VCH Wo* I, 298, and III, 374); see also above, p. 11.

places in Arden where outcrops of Arden Sandstone break the uniformity of the Keuper Marl and Lias clays and provide ready water-supplies and patches of lighter soil.[141] The name 'Inta's hills' (*Intanbeorgas*) probably refers to the striking Keuper Marl hills that thrust up through the Arden Sandstone in Inkberrow. The late seventh-century estate of *Penintanham* is assessed at 15 hides plus an unspecified number at *Dyllawidu*, presumably of detached woodland (*widu*).[142] The first abbess of *Penintanham* enhanced her estate by purchasing 5 hides at Ingon, a place centred on a stray patch of the sandy gravels of the Avon's fourth terrace north of Stratford, and another abbess seems to have obtained 6 hides at Bradley, a presumably wooded area (*lēah*), between Inkberrow and Hanbury.[143] The late Anglo-Saxon church at Wootton Wawen, which may well be on or close to the eighth-century monastic site,[144] also lies on a patch of Arden Sandstone, one partially covered by the river-gravels of the Alne, making it a doubly favourable site. Its name *widutūn* indicates the proximity of Arden woodland, but, according to Dr Gelling, 'the general avoidance of known forest areas by *tūn* names is so marked that a Wootton seems more likely to have been a farm or estate on the boundary between forest and open land than a farm in a woodland setting'.[145] Its original hidage – 20 hides –

---

[141] K. M. Buchanan, *Worcestershire*, The Land of Britain, ed. L. D. Stamp, 68 (London, 1944), 422; Millward and Robinson, *West Midlands*, pp. 11–12; Nicklin, 'Arden', pp. 71–2; Thorpe, 'Growth of Settlement', p. 88; Darby and Terrett, *Domesday Geography*, p. 310; Ford, 'Settlement Patterns', p. 289; Wills, *Palaeogeography*, p. 89; Matley, 'Upper Keuper', p. 279; Williams and Whittaker, *Stratford and Evesham*, pp. 18, 23 and 79; Mackney and Burnham, *Soils*, p. 76. For the Inkberrow identification see above, p. 191, n. 63. For the *stræt*, see Grundy, *Worcestershire*, p. 158.

[142] Sims-Williams, 'Cuthswith', pp. 8, n. 8 and 11; Cox, 'Place-Names of the Earliest Records', p. 20. Cf. the fifteen-and-a-half hides of (Great) Inkberrow in Domesday Book.

[143] For Ingon see above, p. 191, n. 64; Williams and Whittaker, *Stratford and Evesham*, p. 62; Matley, 'Upper Keuper', p. 265; Tomlinson, 'Country North of Stratford', p. 439; Slater and Wilson, *Stratford*, pp. 1 bis and 19 bis (crop-marks). For Bradley see above, p. 238, and Millward and Robinson, *West Midlands*, p. 38.

[144] S. R. Bassett, *The Wootton Wawen Project: Interim Report No. 2* (Birmingham, 1984), p. 9. But cf. Bassett, 'Search', p. 242, n. 46.

[145] Matley, 'Upper Keuper', pp. 261 and 270, and pl. XVIII (cf. Tomlinson, 'Country North of Stratford', pl. XXVII); H. James, 'Excavations in Wootton Wawen Churchyard, 1974 and 1975', *TBWAS* 90 (1980), 37–48, at 39–40; Gelling, 'Notes', p. 67.

shows that Wootton Wawen was a large estate, and this was to be reflected in the size of the medieval ecclesiastical parish.[146]

The West

The Hwicce of the Stour and Severn valleys near Kidderminster and Bewdley were divided from the Magonsætan by the woods of Kinver, Morfe and Wyre and by the high ground that culminates in Clows Top; apart from the woodland, the area was made unattractive for settlement by the scarcity of river terraces between Bewdley and Quatford and the lack of drift on both sides of the Severn.[147] The Clows Top watershed marked the boundary between Hwicce and Magonsætan, to judge by the early eleventh-century diocesan bounds; and it may have marked the boundary between the English and Welsh if the settlement-name Pensax ('hill of the Saxon(s)'?) originally denoted Clows Top itself, as has been suggested.[148] South of this there was less barrier to expansion, and the distribution of settlements attested before 850 and of *tūn* names shows that the Hwicce and Magonsætan settled right up to the Teme valley, which constituted the diocesan boundary from Stanford Bridge to Alfrick.[149] Wichenford (SO/7860), which seems to have lain on a *portstrǣt* or *grēnan weg* running through Greenstreet Farm to Worcester, may have been a ford near the

---

[146] Bassett, 'Wootton Wawen Project' (1983), p. 70; Hooke, *Hwicce*, pp. 110 and 134–7.

[147] Wills, 'Pleistocene Development', p. 209 and pl. XIV. For Kinver and Morfe see above, p. 376.

[148] Gelling, 'New Look', p. 66, and *Signposts*, pp. 99–100; Hooke, *Hwicce*, p. 164. Cf. Jackson, *Language and History*, pp. 226 and 539; *DEPN*, p. 362; J. T. Koch, 'The Loss of Final Syllables and the Loss of Declension in Brittonic', *BBCS* 30 (1982–3), 201–33, at 207–8 and 230. For the diocesan boundary see above, p. 43, n. 137. Finberg takes 'of Carc-dune in Eardig-tun, of Eardigtune eft in Sæfern in Quatt-ford' to mean that the bounds went from Carton (SO/7173) along the Dowles Brook to its confluence with the Severn, then upstream to Eardington and Quatford (*ECWM*, p. 226); but it may mean that they went *overland* from Carton to Eardington, taking in Wyre Forest. Hooke, *Hwicce*, pp. 12–13, questions the Carton identification.

[149] Thorpe, 'Growth of Settlement', p. 101; Gelling, 'Evidence', p. 206. Gelling notes (p.208) that *tūn* is 'hardly used at all in forest areas, with the single exception of an area of Worcestershire, northwest of Worcester' – but the afforestation of this area may have been exaggerated (see below). For *tūn* and *lēah* in Herefordshire and Shropshire, see Lloyd Jones, *Wales and the Marches* I, 160–1, and II, 466, and Hooke, *Territorial Organization*, p. 18.

border of the Hwicce. [150] It has often been wrongly supposed that Wyre Forest stretched along the west bank of the Severn as far south as Worcester, but this is based on a mistaken equation of the *Weogorena leag* ('clearing(?) of the Weogoran') mentioned in a charter of 816 with the name Wyre (**Wigora*) – in fact any connection between the two must be at more than one remove, and the tribal name Weogoran may be derived from a different **Wigora*. [151] Nevertheless, the area west of the Severn probably did have more woodland than other parts of the kingdom of the Hwicce. That is indicated by the occurrence of the element *lēah* (as in *Weogorena leag*) and the fact that nearly all the Hwiccian charters including the term *haga* refer to the belt west of the Severn. [152] The heavier soils here, based on Keuper Marls, were relatively unattractive. This is not to say that the Hwicce and Magonsætan were divided by dense forest. In fact we know that Worcester was an important thoroughfare for traffic across the Severn in Roman times, and in the Anglo-Saxon period we know of several roads from Worcester into Herefordshire. [153] The small monastery of Acton Beauchamp (3 hides) lay on a saltway running through Worcester to Droitwich. [154] Although Acton lay within the diocese of the Magonsætan in the early Anglo-Saxon period, its inhabitants were not cut off from the Hwiccian kingdom; this is reflected in the similarity between the sculpture at Acton and the cross-shaft at Cropthorne in Worcestershire. [155]

The diocesan boundary south of Alfrick followed the Malvern hills. This bare range (cf. Welsh *moelfryn* 'bare hill'), perhaps not yet crossed by its solitary saltway, was an effective barrier to expansion from the Severn

[150] *PNWo*, p. 179; *PNGl* IV, 32; Smith, 'Hwicce', p. 59 (cf. *DEPN*, p. 516). Cf. *PNWo*, p. 3 (but S 179 refers to Hawling, not Hallow); Grundy, *Worcestershire*, pp. 125–7; Hooke, 'Hinterland', p. 46, and *Hwicce*, p. 15.

[151] The charter is S 180 (cf. *ECWM*, pp. 184–5), used by Stenton, *Anglo-Saxon England*, p. 284; *DEPN*, pp. 292 and 541; Johansson, *Lēah*, pp. 29 and 137 (cf. Hill, *Atlas*, pp. 16–17). But see Gelling, 'Note on the Name Worcester', and, on the meaning of *lēah*, 'Notes', pp. 67–8, and *Place-Names in the Landscape*, pp. 198–9. For **Wigora* and the Weogoran see above, p. 31, n. 71.

[152] Dyer, *Lords and Peasants*, pp. 24 and 26; Hooke, *Hwicce*, pp. 118 and 159–62; Grundy, *Worcestershire*, p. xi. Hooke equates *haga* with the Domesday *haia* (see Darby and Terrett, *Domesday Geography*, pp. 88–9, 248–9, etc.), but the latter is taken as OE *(ge)hæg* in *PNE* I, 214–15.

[153] See references above, p. 10.

[154] S 786; *PNWo*, p. 8; Grundy, *Worcestershire*, p. 8; Houghton, 'Salt-Ways', p. 15, Route K; Hooke, 'Droitwich Salt Industry', p. 134.

[155] See above, p. 151.

valley; in the twelfth century it could still be described as a 'vast woodland (*saltus*)' by William of Malmesbury.[156] Interestingly, the distribution of both -*tūn* and -*lēah* names shows a remarkable sparsity not only on top of Malvern, as one would expect, but also in a large part of the surrounding area; and this emptiness is also a feature of the Domesday evidence for this western extremity of Worcestershire.[157] The Hwicce and Magonsætan could hardly have agreed a more natural boundary than the Pre-Cambrian Malvern range, which divides the horizontal Triassic rocks of the lowland east from the older, folded Silurian rocks of the highland west. (Not that they would have expressed it like this!)

Further south, contact between the Hwicce and Magonsætan must have been easy, for the diocesan boundary ran down the Leadon and skirted Gloucester to join the Severn at Minsterworth:[158] the Sandstone outcrops of the Newent region and the drift flanking the Leadon provided light arable soils,[159] and two Roman roads bridged the Severn at Gloucester. Below Minsterworth the Severn served as a boundary, and west of it there was the natural barrier of the Forest of Dean. Yet this area, which was remote from the centre of the kingdom of the Magonsætan, had long been accessible by ferries across the Severn and had been exploited for coal and iron working. It must have been at least equally open to influence from the Hwiccian side of the Severn; in fact, later in the Anglo-Saxon period it was to be annexed, for the purposes of secular administration to Gloucestershire.[160]

CONCLUSION

Clearly the borders of the kingdom-diocese of the Hwicce tended, with exceptions, to run through marginal territory, whereas most monasteries

[156] *PNWo*, p. 8; Houghton, 'Salt-Ways', p. 15, Route L (there is better evidence for Route N, south of Malvern, through Redmarley d'Abitot); *GP*, pp. 285–6; Hooke, *Hwicce*, p. 180.

[157] Gelling, 'Evidence', p. 206; Darby and Terrett, *Domesday Geography*, pp. 227–8 and 267.

[158] Cf. (slightly differently) *ECWM*, pp. 225–6. The text runs: 'of Mynster-worpige in Doddes-æsc [near SO/750323?], of Doddes-æsc in Ceolan-heafdan [SO/761335], of Ceolan-heafdan in Mælfern' (Förster, *Themse*, p. 769).

[159] Cf. Wills, 'Pleistocene Development', pp. 167, 169, 171–2, 219 and pl. xv; Vince, *Gloucestershire*, pp. 321, 339, 343, 368 and 390–1.

[160] *PNGl* IV, 17–20, 32, n. 1, and 42–3; *ECWM*, pp. 226–7 and 233.

and the see, like secular settlements, tended to be sited more centrally; this probably contributed to the unification of the region.[161] It is not as clear why they were so sited. It might be argued that it was to avoid pagan sites on the peripheries; on the other hand, the causation here could be vice versa, with paganism surviving longest away from ecclesiastical centres.[162] Again, it might be argued that monasteries were essentially 'central places', founded as foci for the church's pastoral mission;[163] against this it could be argued that they were only incorporated into this pastoral system at a later stage, after many of them had fallen into the spider's web set by the bishops of Worcester. The simplest explanation is that monasteries were sited centrally because the bounds of the kingdom were politically vulnerable (although Bath and Malmesbury survived) and provided the least attractive agricultural land (although the West Saxon border was again exceptional in this respect).

Once the monasteries came to be sited centrally, this would tend to reinforce the labour-intensive, agrarian status of the central estates, and the subsidiary, appurtenance status of the peripheral areas of exploitation, even in the face of geological reality.[164] The monasteries were thus centrally placed to administer the surplus that enabled them to sustain the high culture described in earlier chapters of this book: they could produce skins for manuscripts; they could barter for precious materials to make vessels and vestments; and they could afford the leisure from manual toil that made education, reading, writing, art and liturgy possible. One imagines that, just as the pagan kingdom of the South Saxons, encircled by woods and rocks, was perceived to have a discrete identity,[165] so the kingdom of the Hwicce, also encircled by marginal land, but with a see and monasteries providing central foci for the Christian culture of its aristocracy, would have been regarded as a distinctive, coherent province. But, as yet, we know as little about the 'perceptual geography'[166] of the early Anglo-Saxons as we know about their historical geography.

[161] Cf. above, pp. 7–8.   [162] Cf. above, pp. 74–5.
[163] Blair, 'Minster Churches in the Landscape', p. 35. Cf. above, p. 172.
[164] See above, p. 367.   [165] Above, p. 367.
[166] Cf. Wickham, *The Mountains and the City*, p. 6.

13

Conclusion

In this study, rather than taking a single topic, such as settlement, or monasticism, or literature, and pursuing it across the country up to the Norman Conquest, I have examined a small area over two centuries from as many points of view as the available data suggested. From a purely practical point of view, some geographical and chronological limitation was necessary if I was to handle, and understand the transmission of, very disparate primary material. More positively, a regional approach has made it possible to perceive significant connections between varied types of evidence. Moreover, even where I have not linked up the pieces of the jigsaw, I believe that their juxtaposition in these pages will stimulate the imagination of readers with knowledge, interests and assumptions which differ from my own (which is, surely, one purpose of historical writing).

At present it is probably not practical or useful to generalize about the seven centuries of pre-Conquest England as a whole. Further rounded portraits of restricted areas and periods are likely to shed more light on the Anglo-Saxons than the selectivity and generalization necessitated by broader canvases. Admittedly, by concentrating on a particular area, the historian forgoes the opportunity of demonstrating whether it was a microcosm of the rest of England or was significantly atypical. Only comparative studies can settle such questions and lead towards a future synthesis. Such comparisons, however, would be provisional or even premature before detailed interdisciplinary studies of other regions and periods have been completed. This is not to encourage a myopic parochialism, but to agree with a recent defender of local studies, C. J. Wickham, that 'what local analysis entails, rather, is more sophisticated generalization'.[1]

---

[1] *The Mountains and the City*, p. 2 (he italicizes *sophisticated*).

Dr Wickham also remarks that,

Local histories are often regarded by historians as not fully respectable; they can too often consist of the evaluation or celebration of the history of a single locality – whether a village, or a city, or a river valley – without regard for general historical issues; as pure empiricism, even antiquarianism, for its own sake. But at least such works have a sense of place, a quality too often lacking in professional history-writing. And they force us to recognize that all historical frameworks are inevitably rooted in local realities.[2]

I should not be dismayed if this study were read as an evaluation and celebration of two kingdoms which are almost forgotten (as casual conversation shows). When Milred of Worcester died *c.* 775, the episcopal sees of the Hwicce and Magonsætan had been in existence for less than a century, and the Anglo-Saxons had been settled in much of the area for less than two centuries: if one may believe the *Anglo-Saxon Chronicle*, Gloucester, Cirencester and Bath were still in the hands of British kings in 577.[3] These two centuries had seen the rise of the local royal dynasties and their eclipse by Mercia, the conversion to Christianity, and the establishment of many monasteries under diverse influences. Bishops, abbots and abbesses had built up libraries of imported books, chiefly no doubt as aids for biblical study; they had learnt to produce their own manuscripts, and had played their part in the transmission of patristic culture and the creation of the most distant precursors of the medieval Books of Hours. They had developed the teaching of Latin to the stage where they could write letters in stylistically ambitious Latin and compose passable inscriptions in an alien metrical system. They had established institutions that were to become key elements in the pastoral system of the medieval and modern church.

These achievements were soon forgotten. Already in the eleventh and twelfth centuries writers showed little interest in, and sometimes little awareness of the existence of, the Hwicce and the Magonsætan. 'Florence' of Worcester, who looks back on the glories of Mercia as a whole, even confuses the two ('Huuicciæ uel Magesitaniæ').[4] Hagiographers tended to review England's saintly past as a national heritage in the manner of Bede. Already in the Old English tract on the 'Resting-Places of the English Saints', there are only slight and insignificant traces of a geographical

---

[2] *Ibid.*, p. 1.   [3] Cf. above, p. 23.
[4] *MHB*, p. 662; cf. Dugdale, *Monasticon* I, 607, and above, p. 90, n. 12.

grouping of saints in the old sub-kingdoms (items 42–4 are St Oswald at Worcester, St Ecgwine at Evesham and St Kenelm at Winchcombe) and, insofar as any regional approach is detectable it is to treat the whole of greater Mercia as a unit.[5] There survives no dynastic or hagiographical text about the Hwicce or Magonsætan comparable with the so-called 'Kentish Royal Legend'. The nearest approach to it is the unpublished *vita* of St Mildburg of Wenlock, which also deals with the foundation of Leominster, as well as various Kentish monasteries, on account of their dynastic links with the royal family of the Magonsætan.[6] Yet, by and large, the hagiographers of saints such as Ecgwine of Evesham and Kenelm of Winchcombe were as narrowly concerned with the interests of the monasteries for whom they wrote as were the monastic cartularies themselves. The *vitae* of Ecgwine show interest in the Hwiccian royal family only because they rely on forged charters relating to Ecgwine's acquisition of lands for Evesham.[7] The *Vita S. Kenelmi* anachronistically supposes that after the saint's death, there was a struggle over his body between the men of Worcestershire and Gloucestershire – shires not yet in existence in 821.[8] The *Passio* of Ethelbert of Hereford tells the story of the martyrdom in 794 with a wealth of local topographical detail, yet incomprehendingly introduces Milfrith, a much earlier sub-king, into the tale.[9]

Monastic chroniclers, too, displayed little interest in other early foundations in their dioceses. The twelfth-century *Cronica de Anglia* from the diocese of Worcester records only Gloucester, Pershore, Evesham and Winchcombe among the early foundations in the diocese, and the *Annales de Wigornia* are still weaker.[10] An exception which proves the rule is a letter

---

[5] See Rollason, 'Resting-Places'.

[6] See especially the prefatory *Genealogia beate uirginis Myldburge*: BL, Add. 34633, 206r–210r. See above, pp. 42, 55 and 101.

[7] See above, pp. 33 and 141.

[8] Antropoff, *Entwicklung*, p. xiii; cf. Thacker, 'Pre-Viking Mercia', p. 9. The writer of the *vita* himself compares the case of St Martin (*HF* 1.48); the same motif appears in the twelfth-century *Vita S. Ercenwaldi*, ed. W. Dugdale and H. Ellis, *The History of St Paul's Cathedral* (London, 1818), p. 291.

[9] See above, pp. 50–1 and 342.

[10] *Geschichtsquellen*, ed. Liebermann, pp. 18–19; *Annales Monastici*, ed. Luard IV, 365–7. This is not to say that the monasteries were uninterested in other local monasteries in other respects; note an Old English agreement of 1077 for mutual prayer between Worcester, Evesham, Chertsey (linked to Bath), Bath, Pershore, Winchcombe and Gloucester: *Two Chartularies of the Priory of St Peter at Bath*, ed. W. Hunt, Somerset Record Society (n.p., 1893), pp. 3–4 and 74–5; Ker, *Catalogue*, p. 48.

of Thomas, abbot of Pershore, supporting Gloucester in a mid-twelfth-century property dispute with York: Thomas digresses on the alleged Northumbrian connections of Osric, the founder of Gloucester; but the foundation of Pershore was believed to be intimately connected with that of Gloucester.[11] Even William of Malmesbury, in his diocese by diocese account of the early English church, notes only the foundation of Winchcombe, Evesham and Wenlock, and treats the later re-foundations of Gloucester and Pershore as if they were the first foundations.[12]

It was not until Stubbs published his paper on 'The Cathedral, Diocese, and Monasteries of Worcester in the Eighth Century' in 1862 that a truer picture of the area began to emerge from the charters of the Worcester archive. The contrast between Stubbs's work and the medieval writings mentioned above reveals how selective a memory of the past there was by the eleventh and twelfth centuries, and how much the historiography and hagiography of that period was determined and limited by the continuity and interests of institutions.

Reliable surviving narrative sources provide no more than a skeletal knowledge of Anglo-Saxon England between 600 and 800. One of the least rewarding duties of the modern Anglo-Saxon historian is to strip off the conjectural flesh with which medieval and modern historians, hagiographers and antiquaries have enhanced the bare skeleton, and to restore it to its pristine and enigmatic state. The aim of the present study has been to put some authentic flesh back onto a small part of the skeleton. Principally, I have returned to the documents used by Stubbs. But a document, according to Marc Bloch, 'is a witness; and like most witnesses, it does not say much except under cross-examination. The real difficulty lies in putting the right questions'.[13] My witnesses have volunteered more than enough information for a single book. They certainly have more secrets for sterner interrogators with shrewder questions.

[11] *Historia et Cartularium*, ed. Hart II, 110–11 (cf. above, pp. 33 and 94–5). In connection with the same dispute, David, ex-prior of Worcester, refers to his consultation of *cartae* and *cronica* concerning Gloucester (*ibid.* II, 115).

[12] *GP*, pp. 278–306.

[13] Quoted, with similar dicta, by A. Macfarlane, *The Origins of English Individualism* (Oxford, 1978), p. 190, n. 2.

Bibliography

Åberg, N., *The Anglo-Saxons in England during the Early Centuries after the Invasion* (Uppsala, 1926)

Acta Sanctorum [Bollandists], ed. novissima (Paris and Brussels, 1863–)

Adriaen, M., ed., *S. Hieronymi presbyteri commentarius in Ecclesiasten*, CCSL 72 (Turnhout, 1959), 247–361

Alexander, J. J. G., *Insular Manuscripts 6th to the 9th Century* (London, 1978)

Amat, J., *Songes et visions: L'Au-delà dans la littérature latine tardive* (Paris, 1985)

Andrieu, M., ed., *Les ordines romani du haut moyen âge*, 5 vols. (Louvain, 1931–61)

Antropoff, R. von, *Die Entwicklung der Kenelm-Legende*, Inaugural-Dissertation (Bonn, 1965)

Arndt, W., ed., *Gregorii Episcopi Turonensis Historia Francorum*, MGH, SS. rer. Merov. 1 (Hannover, 1885), 1–450

Arkell, W. J., *The Geology of Oxford* (Oxford, 1947)

Arkell, W. J. and D. T. Donovan, 'The Fuller's Earth of the Cotswolds and its Relation to the Great Oolite', *QJGS* 107 (1951), 227–53

Arnold, C. J., *An Archaeology of the Early Anglo-Saxon Kingdoms* (London, 1988)

Arnold, T., ed., *Symeonis Monachi Opera Omnia*, 2 vols., RS (London, 1882–5)

Atkins, I., 'The Church of Worcester from the Eighth to the Twelfth Century: Part I. The Constitution of the "Familia" from the Foundation of the See to St. Oswald', *AntJ* 17 (1937), 371–91; 'Part II. The Familia from the Middle of the Tenth to the Beginning of the Twelfth Century', *AntJ* 20 (1940), 1–38 and 203–29

Atkins, I. and N. R. Ker, ed., *Catalogus Librorum Manuscriptorum Bibliothecae Wigorniensis, made in 1622–1623 by Patrick Young, Librarian to King James I* (Cambridge, 1944)

Badcock, F. J., 'A Portion of an Early Anatolian Prayer-Book', *JTS* 33 (1932), 167–80

Baesecke, G., *Der Vocabularius Sti. Galli in der angelsächsischen Mission* (Halle, 1933)

Baldwin Brown, G., *The Arts in Early England*, 7 vols. (London, 1903–37)

Bannister, A. T., *The Cathedral Church of Hereford: Its History and Constitution* (London, 1924)

Barb, A. A., 'The Survival of Magic Arts', in *The Conflict Between Paganism and Christianity in the Fourth Century*, ed. A. Momigliano (Oxford, 1963), pp. 100–25

'Die Blutsegen von Fulda und London', in *Fachliteratur des Mittelalters: Festschrift für Gerhard Eis*, ed. G. Keil *et al.* (Stuttgart, 1968), pp. 485–93

Barker, P. *et al.*, 'The Origins of Worcester', *TWAS* 3rd ser. 2 (1968–9), 1–116

Barlow, F., *Edward the Confessor* (London, 1970)

The English Church 1000–1066, 2nd ed. (London, 1979)

Barré, H., *Prières anciennes de l'occident à la mère du Sauveur des origines à saint Anselme* (Paris, 1963)

Bassett, S. R., 'The Wootton Wawen Project', *WMA* 26 (1983), 66–71; 27 (1984), 72; 29 (1986), 62

'A Probable Mercian Royal Mausoleum at Winchcombe, Gloucestershire', *AntJ* 65 (1985), 82–100

'In Search of the Origins of Anglo-Saxon Kingdoms', in *Origins*, ed. Bassett, pp. 3–27 and 237–45

Bassett, S. R., ed., *The Origins of Anglo-Saxon Kingdoms* (Leicester, 1989)

Bede, *Opera*, ed. J. Heerwagen, 8 vols. (Basel, 1563)

Berthod, A., 'Notice du Cartulaire de Simon, manuscrit de la Bibliothèque de St. Bertin', *Nouveaux mémoires de l'Académie impériale et royale des sciences et belles-lettres de Bruxelles* 5, *Histoire* 1 (1788), 227–31

Beyenka, M. M., *Consolation in Saint Augustine*, Catholic University of America Patristic Studies 83 (Washington, 1950)

Biddle, M., 'Towns', in *Archaeology*, ed. Wilson, pp. 99–150

'A Widening Horizon', in *The Archaeological Study of Churches*, ed. P. Addyman and R. Morris, CBA Research Report 13 (London, 1976), 65–71

'Archaeology, Architecture, and the Cult of Saints in Anglo-Saxon England', in *The Anglo-Saxon Church*, ed. Butler and Morris, pp. 1–31

Bieler, L., ed., *The Irish Penitentials*, Scriptores Latini Hiberniae 5 (Dublin, 1963)

Birch, W. de G., 'On the Succession of the Abbots of Malmesbury', *JBAA* 27 (1871), 314–42 and 446–8

Birch, W. de G., ed., *Cartularium Saxonicum*, 3 vols. and Index (London, 1885–99)

    An Ancient Manuscript of the Eighth or Ninth Century Formerly Belonging to St Mary's Abbey, or Nunnaminster, Winchester, Hampshire Record Society (n.p., 1889)

Bischoff, B., *Mittelalterliche Studien*, 3 vols. (Stuttgart, 1966–81)

Bischoff, B. and J. Hofmann, *Libri Sancti Kyliani: Die Würzburger Schreibschule und die Dombibliothek im VIII. und IX. Jahrhundert* (Würzburg, 1952)

Bishop, E., *Liturgica Historica* (Oxford, 1918)

Bishop, T. A. M., 'Notes on Cambridge Manuscripts Part V: MSS. Connected with St Augustine's Canterbury', *TCBS* 2 (1954–8), 323–36, and 3 (1959–63), 93–5

Bishop, W. W., 'The Pleistocene Geology and Geomorphology of Three Gaps in the Midland Jurassic Escarpment', *Philosophical Transactions of the Royal Society of London*, Series B, 241 (1957–8), 255–306

Blackburn, M., 'A Chronology for the Sceattas', in *Sceattas*, ed. Hill and Metcalf, pp. 165–74

Blair, J., 'Secular Minster Churches in Domesday Book', in *Domesday Book: A Reassessment*, ed. P. Sawyer (London, 1985), 104–42

    'Local Churches in Domesday Book and Before', in *Domesday Studies*, ed. J. C. Holt (Woodbridge, 1987), pp. 265–78

    'Minster Churches in the Landscape', in *Anglo-Saxon Settlements*, ed. D. Hooke (Oxford, 1988), pp. 35–58

Blair, J., ed., *Minsters and Parish Churches: The Local Church in Transition 950–1200* (Oxford, 1988)

Blake, E. O., ed., *Liber Eliensis*, Camden Third Series 92 (London, 1962)

Blanchinus, J. [G. Bianchini], ed., *Venerabilis Josephi Mariae Thomasii Opera Omnia* I [all published] (Rome, 1741)

Blume, C., ed., *Die Hymnen des 5.–11. Jahrhunderts und die irisch-keltische Hymnodie*, Analecta Hymnica Medii Aevi 51 (Leipzig, 1908)

Bond, C. J., 'Two Recent Saxon Discoveries in Fladbury', *VEHSRP* 5 (1975), 17–24

'Church and Parish in Norman Worcestershire', in *Minsters and Parish Churches*, ed. Blair, pp. 119–58

Bond, C. J. and A. M. Hunt, 'Recent Archaeological Work in Pershore', *VEHSRP* 6 (1977), 1–76

Bonner, G., ed., *Famulus Christi: Essays in Commemoration of the Thirteenth Centenary of the Birth of the Venerable Bede* (London, 1976)

B[randl], A., 'Chrousts Fund einer des ältesten ags. Aufzeichnungen', *Archiv für das Studien der neueren Sprachen und Literaturen* 107 (1901), 103–5

Branigan, K. and P. J. Fowler, ed., *The Roman West Country: Classical Culture and Celtic Society* (Newton Abbot, 1976)

Brett, M., 'John of Worcester and his Contemporaries', in *The Writing of History in the Middle Ages: Essays presented to Richard William Southern*, ed. R. H. C. Davis and J. M. Wallace-Hadrill (Oxford, 1981), pp. 101–26

Brooke, C. N. L., *The Church and the Welsh Border in the Central Middle Ages* (Woodbridge, 1986)

Brooks, N., 'The Development of Military Obligations in Eighth- and Ninth-Century England', in *England Before the Conquest*, ed. Clemoes and Hughes, pp. 69–84

'Anglo-Saxon Charters: The Work of the Last Twenty Years', *ASE* 3 (1974), 211–31

The Early History of the Church of Canterbury: Christ Church from 597 to 1066 (Leicester, 1984)

Brooks, N., M. Gelling and D. Johnson, 'A New Charter of King Edgar', *ASE* 13 (1984), 137–55

Brou, L., ed., *The Psalter Collects from V–VIth Century Sources (Three Series)*, HBS 83 (London, 1949)

Brown, M. P., 'Paris, Bibliothèque Nationale, lat. 10861 and the Scriptorium of Christ Church, Canterbury', *ASE* 15 (1986), 119–37

Brown, P., *Augustine of Hippo: A Biography* (London, 1967)

Religion and Society in the Age of Saint Augustine (London, 1972)

Brown, T. J., 'The Irish Element in the Insular System of Scripts to Circa A.D. 850', in *Iren und Europa*, ed. Löwe I, 101–19

Brown, T. J., ed., *The Stonyhurst Gospel of Saint John*, Roxburghe Club (Oxford, 1969)

Bruce-Mitford, R. L. S., 'The Art of the Codex Amiatinus', *JBAA* 3rd ser. 32 (1969), 1–25

Bruce-Mitford, R. L. S. *et al.*, *The Sutton Hoo Ship-Burial* (London, 1975–)

Bruckner, A., and R. Marichal, *Chartae Latinae Antiquiores* (Olten and Lausanne, 1954–)

Bullough, D., 'Roman Books and Carolingian *Renovatio*', in *Renaissance and Renewal in Christian History*, ed. D. Baker, Studies in Church History 14 (Oxford, 1977), 23–50

'Burial, Community and Belief in the Early Medieval West', in *Ideal and Reality*, ed. Wormald *et al.*, pp. 177–201

'Alcuin and the Kingdom of Heaven: Liturgy, Theology, and the Carolingian Age', in *Carolingian Essays: Andrew W. Mellon Lectures in Early Christian Studies*, ed. U.-R. Blumenthal (Washington, 1983), pp. 1–69

'Albuinus Deliciosus Karoli Regis: Alcuin of York and the Shaping of the Early Carolingian Court', in *Institutionen, Kultur und Gesellschaft im Mittelalter: Festschrift für Josef Fleckenstein zu seinem 65. Geburtstag*, ed. L. Fenske *et al.* (Sigmaringen, 1984), pp. 73–92

Burnaby, J., *Amor Dei: A Study of the Religion of St. Augustine* (London, 1938)

Butler, C., *Western Mysticism: The Teaching of SS Augustine, Gregory and Bernard on Contemplation and the Contemplative Life*, 2nd ed. (London, 1927)

Butler, L. A. S. *et al.*, 'Deerhurst 1971–1974', *AntJ* 55 (1975), 346–65

Butler, L. A. S. and R. K. Morris, ed., *The Anglo-Saxon Church: Papers in History, Architecture, and Archaeology In Honour of H. M. Taylor*, CBA Research Report 60 (London, 1986)

Cameron, K., ed., *Place-Name Evidence for the Anglo-Saxon Invasion and Scandinavian Settlements: Eight Studies* (Nottingham, 1975)

Campbell, J., *Essays in Anglo-Saxon History* (London, 1986)

'The Debt of the Early English Church to Ireland', in *Irland und die Christenheit*, ed. Ní Chatháin and Richter, pp. 332–46

Campbell, J., ed., *The Anglo-Saxons* (Oxford, 1982)

Carley, J. P., ed., and D. Townsend, trans., *The Chronicle of Glastonbury Abbey: An Edition, Translation and Study of John of Glastonbury's Cronica sive Antiquitates Glastoniensis Ecclesie* (Woodbridge, 1985)

Carozzi, C., 'La géographie de l'Au-delà et sa signification pendant le haut moyen âge', *Settimane* 29 (1983), 423–85

Carver, M. O. H., ed., *Medieval Worcester: An Archaeological Framework* = *TWAS* 3rd ser. 7 (1980).

Casey, P. J., ed., *The End of Roman Britain*, BAR British Series 71 (Oxford, 1979)

Chadwick, H. M., *The Origin of the English Nation*, repr. [with new pagination] (Cambridge, 1924)

Bibliography

Chadwick, O., *John Cassian: A Study in Primitive Monasticism* (Cambridge, 1950)

Chadwick, O., trans., *Western Asceticism*, Library of Christian Classics 12 (London, 1958)

Chaplais, P., 'The Letter from Bishop Wealdhere of London to Archbishop Brihtwold of Canterbury: The Earliest Original "Letter Close" extant in the West', in *Medieval Scribes, Manuscripts and Libraries: Essays presented to N. R. Ker*, ed. M. B. Parkes and A. G. Watson (London, 1978), pp. 3–23

Charles, B. G., 'The Welsh, their Language and Place-Names in Archenfield and Oswestry', in *Angles and Britons (O'Donnell Lectures)*, [ed. H. Lewis] (Cardiff, 1963), pp. 85–110

Charles, R. H., ed., *The Apocrypha and Pseudepigrapha of the Old Testament in English*: II. *Pseudepigrapha* (Oxford, 1913)

Charlesworth, J. H., ed., *The Old Testament Pseudepigrapha*, 2 vols. (London, 1983–5)

Chavasse, A., *Le sacramentaire gélasien (Vaticanus Reginensis 316)* (Tournai, 1958)

Chroust, A., ed., *Monumenta Palaeographica: Denkmäler der Schreibkunst des Mittelalters* (Munich, 1901–)

Ciccarese, M. P., 'Alle origini della letteratura delle visioni: il contributo di Gregorio di Tours', *Studi storico-religiosi* 5 (1981), 251–66

'La *Visio Baronti* nella tradizione letteraria delle *Visiones* dell'aldilà', *Romanobarbarica* 6 (1981–2), 25–52

'Le più antiche rappresentazioni del purgatorio, dalla *Passio Perpetuae* alla fine del IX sec.', *Romanobarbarica* 7 (1982–3), 33–76

'Le visioni di S. Fursa', *Romanobarbarica* 8 (1984–5), 231–303

Ciccarese, M. P., ed., *Visioni dell'aldilà in occidente: fonti, modelli, testi*, Biblioteca Patristica 8 (Florence, 1987)

Clarke, G., *The Roman Cemetery at Lankhills*, Winchester Studies 3.2 (Oxford, 1979)

Clemoes, P. and K. Hughes, ed., *England Before the Conquest: Studies in Primary Sources presented to Dorothy Whitelock* (Cambridge, 1971)

Coens, M., 'Anciennes litanies des saints', *AB* 54 (1936), 5–37

Colgrave, B., ed. and trans., *The Life of Bishop Wilfrid by Eddius Stephanus* (Cambridge, 1927)

Two Lives of Saint Cuthbert: A Life by an Anonymous Monk of Lindisfarne and Bede's Prose Life (Cambridge, 1940)

Felix's Life of Guthlac (Cambridge, 1956)

The Earliest Life of Gregory the Great by an Anonymous Monk of Whitby (Lawrence, KA 1968)

Colgrave, B. and R. A. B. Mynors, ed. and trans., *Bede's Ecclesiastical History of the English People* (Oxford, 1969)

Collingwood, R. G. and J. N. L. Myres, *Roman Britain and the English Settlements*, 2nd ed. (Oxford, 1937)

Constable, G., *Monastic Tithes from their Origins to the Twelfth Century* (Cambridge, 1964)

'Opposition to Pilgrimage in the Middle Ages', *Studia Gratiana* 19 (1976), 123–46

'Monasteries, Rural Churches and the *Cura Animarum* in the Early Middle Ages', *Settimane* 28 (1982), 349–95

Constantinescu, R., 'Alcuin et les "libelli precum" de l'époque carolingienne', *Revue de l'histoire de la spiritualité* 50 (1974), 17–56

Copley, G., *Archaeology and Place-Names in the Fifth and Sixth Centuries*, BAR British Series 147 (Oxford, 1986)

Early Place-Names of the Anglian Regions of England, BAR British Series 185 (Oxford, 1988)

Courcelle, P., *Les Confessions de saint Augustin dans la tradition littéraire: antécédents et postérité* (Paris, 1963)

Recherches sur les Confessions de saint Augustin, 2nd ed. (Paris, 1968)

Cox, B., 'The Place-Names of the Earliest English Records', *JEPNS* 8 (1975–6), 12–66

'Aspects of Place-Name Evidence for Early Medieval Settlement in England', *Viator* 11 (1980), 35–50

Cox, D. C., 'The Vale Estates of the Church of Evesham, *c.* 700–1086', *VEHSRP* 5 (1975), 25–50

Cramp, R., 'Monkwearmouth and Jarrow: The Archaeological Evidence', in *Famulus Christi*, ed. Bonner, pp. 5–18

'Monastic Sites', in *Archaeology*, ed. Wilson, pp. 201–52 and 453–62

Croom, J., 'The Fragmentation of the Minster *Parochiae* of South-East Shropshire', in *Minsters and Parish Churches*, ed. Blair, pp. 67–81

Cross, F. L. and E. A. Livingstone, ed., *The Oxford Dictionary of the Christian Church*, 2nd ed. (Oxford, 1974)

Curran, M., *The Antiphonary of Bangor* (Dublin, 1984)

Curtius, E. R., *European Literature and the Latin Middle Ages*, trans. W. R. Trask (London, 1953)

Daly, L. W., 'A Greek Palindrome in Eighth-Century England', *American Journal of Philology* 103 (1982), 95–7

Daniélou, J., 'Les démons de l'air dans la "Vie d'Antoine" ', *Studia Anselmiana* 38 (1956), 136–47

Darby, H. C. and I. B. Terrett, ed., *The Domesday Geography of Midland England*, 2nd ed. (Cambridge, 1971)

Darlington, R. R., 'Æthelwig, Abbot of Evesham', *EHR* 48 (1933), 1–22 and 177–98

Darlington, R. R., ed., *The Cartulary of Worcester Cathedral Priory (Register I)*, PPRS ns 38 (London, 1968)

Darlington, R. R. and P. McGurk, 'The "Chronicon ex Chronicis" of "Florence" of Worcester and its Use of Sources for English History Before 1066', in *Anglo-Norman Studies V: Proceedings of the Battle Conference 1982*, ed. R. A. Brown (Woodbridge, 1983), pp. 185–96

Davies, W., 'Annals and the Origin of Mercia', in *Mercian Studies*, ed. Dornier, pp. 17–29

An Early Welsh Microcosm: Studies in the Llandaff Charters (London, 1978)

The Llandaff Charters (Aberystwyth, 1979)

'Roman Settlements and Post-Roman Estates in South-East Wales', in *The End of Roman Britain*, ed. Casey, pp. 153–73

Davies, W. and H. Vierck, 'The Contexts of Tribal Hidage: Social Aggregates and Settlement Patterns', *FS* 8 (1974), 223–93

Dekkers, E. and A. Gaar, *Clavis Patrum Latinorum*, 2nd ed. (Bruges, 1961)

de Lubac, H., *Histoire et esprit: l'intelligence de l'écriture d'après Origène* (Paris, 1950)

de Rossi, I. B., ed., *Inscriptiones Christianae Urbis Romae*, 2 vols. (Rome, 1857–88)

de Vogüé, A., ed., and P. Antin, trans., *Grégoire le Grand: Dialogues*, 3 vols., SC 251, 260 and 265 (Paris, 1978–80)

de Vregille, B. and L. Neyrand, ed., *Apponii in Canticum canticorum expositio*, CCSL 19 (Turnhout, 1986)

Dickinson, T. M., 'British Antiquity 1977–78: Post Roman and Pagan Anglo-Saxon', *ArchJ* 135 (1978), 332–44

'The Present State of Anglo-Saxon Cemetery Studies', in *Anglo-Saxon Cemeteries*, ed. Rahtz *et al.*, pp. 11–33

Dinzelbacher, P., *Vision und Visionsliteratur im Mittelalter* (Stuttgart, 1981)

Dodgson, J. McN., 'The English Arrival in Cheshire', *Transactions of the Historic Society of Lancashire and Cheshire* 119 (1968), 1–37 and 241–3

Dold, A. and L. Eizenhöfer, with D. H. Wright, ed., *Das irische Palimpsest-*

sakramentar im Clm 14429 der Staatsbibliothek München, Texte und Arbeiten 53/54 (Beuron, 1964)

Dornier, A., ed., *Mercian Studies* (Leicester, 1977)

Dreghorn, W., *Geology Explained in the Severn Vale and Cotswolds* (Newton Abbot, 1967)

Dronke, P., *Women Writers of the Middle Ages: A Critical Study of Texts from Perpetua (†203) to Marguerite Porete (†1310)* (Cambridge, 1984)

'Towards the Interpretation of the Leiden Love-Spell', *CMCS* 16 (Winter 1988), 61–75

Duckett, E. S., *Anglo-Saxon Saints and Scholars* (New York, 1947)

Duemmler, E., ed., *Epistolae Karolini Aevi* II, MGH, Epistolae 4 (Berlin, 1895)

Dugdale, W., *Monasticon Anglicanum*, ed. J. Caley *et al.*, repr., 6 vols. in 8 (London, 1846)

Dulaey, M., *Le rêve dans la vie et la pensée de saint Augustin* (Paris, 1973)

Dumas, A. and J. Deshusses, ed., *Liber Sacramentorum Gellonensis*, 2 vols., CCSL 149–149A (Turnhout, 1981)

Dumville, D. N., 'The Anglian Collection of Royal Genealogies and Regnal Lists', *ASE* 5 (1976), 23–50

'Kingship, Genealogies and Regnal Lists', in *Early Medieval Kingship*, ed. P. H. Sawyer and I. N. Wood (Leeds, 1977), pp. 72–104

'English Square Minuscule Script: The Background and Earliest Phases', *ASE* 16 (1987), 147–79

Dyer, C., *Lords and Peasants in a Changing Society: The Estates of the Bishopric of Worcester, 650–1540* (Cambridge, 1980)

Edwards, H., 'Two Documents from Aldhelm's Malmesbury', *BIHR* 59 (1986), 1–19

Ehwald, R., ed., *Aldhelmi Opera*, MGH, Auct. antiq. 15 (Berlin, 1919)

Ekwall, E., *The Concise Oxford Dictionary of English Place-Names*, 4th ed. (Oxford, 1960)

Eliade, M., *Shamanism: Archaic Techniques of Ecstasy*, trans. W. R. Trask (London, 1964)

Emerton, E., trans., *The Letters of Saint Boniface*, Columbia University Records of Civilisation 31 (New York, 1940)

Engelbert, P., 'Paläographische Bemerkungen zur Faksimileausgabe der ältesten Handschrift der Regula Benedicti (Oxford Bodl. Libr. Hatton 48)', *RB* 79 (1969), 399–413

Bibliography

Evans, J. G. and J. Rhys, ed., *The Text of the Book of Llan Dâv* (Oxford, 1893)

Everitt, A., *Continuity and Colonization: The Evolution of Kentish Settlement* (Leicester, 1986)

Evison, V. I., 'Sugar-Loaf Shield Bosses', *AntJ* 43 (1963), 38–96

Faller, O., ed., *Sancti Ambrosii Opera, pars VII*, CSEL 73 (Vienna, 1955)

Farmer, D. H., ed., *The Rule of St Benedict: Oxford, Bodleian Library, Hatton 48*, EEMF 15 (Copenhagen, 1968)

Faull, M. L., 'British Survival in Anglo-Saxon Northumbria', in *Studies in Celtic Survival*, ed. L. Laing, BAR British Series 37 (Oxford, 1977), 1–55

Favez, C., *La consolation latine chrétienne* (Paris, 1937)

Fell, C. E., 'Hild, Abbess of Streonæshalch', in *Hagiography and Medieval Literature: A Symposium*, ed. H. Bekker-Nielsen *et al.* (Odense, 1981), pp. 76–99

Ferrari, G., *Early Roman Monasteries: Notes for the History of the Monasteries and Convents of Rome From the V Through the X Century* (Rome, 1957)

Finberg, H. P. R., *Lucerna: Studies of Some Problems in the Early History of England* (London, 1964)

The Early Charters of Wessex (Leicester, 1964)

The Early Charters of the West Midlands, 2nd ed. (Leicester, 1972)

The Gloucestershire Landscape, 2nd ed. (London, 1975)

Finberg, H. P. R., ed., *Gloucestershire Studies* (Leicester, 1957)

The Agrarian History of England and Wales I.2, A.D. 43–1042 (Cambridge, 1972)

Findlay, D. C., 'Soils', in *A Survey and Policy Concerning the Archaeology of the Bristol Region* I, *To the Norman Conquest*, ed. L. V. Grinsell, 2nd ed., Bristol Archaeological Research Group (n.p., 1966), pp. 11–18

Fontaine, J., ed. and trans., *Sulpice Sévère: vie de saint Martin*, SC 133–5 (Paris, 1967–9)

Ford, D., 'A Note on a "Grant by Aethelbald, King of Mercia, to Ealdorman Cyneberht, of Land at Stour in Ismere, Worcs."', *JEPNS* 12 (1979–80), 66–9

Ford, W. J., 'Stretton-on-Fosse, Warws (SP 2182 3831)', *WMANS* 14 (1971), 22

'Some Settlement Patterns in the Central Region of the Warwickshire Avon', in *Medieval Settlement*, ed. Sawyer, pp. 274–94

Förster, M., *Der Flussname Themse und seine Sippe: Studien zur Anglisierung keltischer Eigennamen und zur Lautchronologie des Albritischen*, Sitzungsberichte der Bayerischen Akademie der Wissenschaften, Philos.-hist. Abteilung, 1941, 1 (Munich, 1941)

Foster, I. Ll. and L. Alcock, ed., *Culture and Environment: Essays in Honour of Sir Cyril Fox* (London, 1963)

Fowler, P. J., 'Agriculture and Rural Settlement', in *Archaeology*, ed. Wilson, pp. 23–48

'Lowland Landscapes: Culture, Time, and Personality', in *The Effect of Man on the Landscape: The Lowland Zone*, ed. S. Limbury and J. G. Evans, CBA Research Report 21 (London, 1978), 1–12

'Pre-Medieval Fields in the Bristol Region', in *Early Land Allotment in the British Isles*, ed. H. C. Bowen and P. J. Fowler, BAR British Series 48 (Oxford, 1978), pp. 29–47

'Farming in the Anglo-Saxon Landscape: an Archaeologist's Review', *ASE* 9 (1981), 263–80

Fowler, P. J., ed., *Archaeology and Landscape: Essays for L. V. Grinsell* (London, 1972)

Fraipont, J., ed., *Bedae Venerabilis Opera*, pars IV, *Opera Rhythmica*, CCSL 122 (Turnhout, 1955), 405–70

Frantzen, A. J., 'The Tradition of Penitentials in Anglo-Saxon England', *ASE* 11 (1983), 23–56

The Literature of Penance in Anglo-Saxon England (New Brunswick, NJ, 1983)

Franz, A., *Die kirchlichen Benediktionen im Mittelalter*, 2 vols. (Freiburg im Breisgau, 1909)

Freeman, J., 'Some Place-Names of Archenfield and the Golden Valley Recorded in the Balliol Herefordshire Domesday', *Nomina* 10 (1986), 61–77

Fremantle, W. H. *et al.*, trans., *St Jerome: Letters and Select Works*, Library of Nicene and Post-Nicene Fathers 6 (Oxford and New York, 1893)

Frost, M., ed., 'A Prayer Book from St. Emmeran, Ratisbon', *JTS* 30 (1928–9), 32–45

Fryde, E. B. *et al.*, ed., *Handbook of British Chronology*, 3rd ed. (London, 1986)

Gardner, P. J. *et al.*, 'Prehistoric, Roman, and Medieval Settlement at Stretton-on-Fosse: Excavations and Salvage 1971–76', *TBWAS* 90 (1980), 1–35

Gelling, M., *The Place-Names of Oxfordshire*, 2 vols., EPNS 23–4 (Cambridge, 1953–4)

'A Note on the Name Worcester', in Barker, 'Origins of Worcester', p. 26.

'Some Notes on Warwickshire Place-Names', *TBWAS* 86 (1974), 59–79

'Further Thoughts on Pagan Place-Names', in *Place-Name Evidence*, ed. Cameron, pp. 99–114

'The Evidence of Place-Names', in *Medieval Settlement*, ed. Sawyer, pp. 200–11

Signposts to the Past: Place-Names and the History of England (London, 1978)

'The Place-Name Volumes for Worcestershire and Warwickshire: A New Look', in *Field and Forest*, ed. Slater and Jarvis, pp. 59–78

Place-Names in the Landscape (London, 1984)

Gerchow, J., *Die Gedenküberlieferung der Angelsachsen, mit einem Katalog der "libri vitae" und Necrologien* (Berlin, 1988)

Gibbs, M., 'The Decrees of Agatho and the Gregorian Plan for York', *Speculum* 48 (1973), 213–46

Gibson, E. C. S., trans., *John Cassian: Works*, Library of Nicene and Post-Nicene Fathers 11 (Oxford, 1894), 161–641

Giles, J. A., ed., *Vita Quorundum* [sic] *Anglo-Saxonum: Original Lives of Anglo-Saxons and Others, Who Lived Before the Conquest*, Caxton Society (London, 1854)

Gneuss, H., 'A Preliminary List of Manuscripts Written or Owned in England up to 1100', *ASE* 9 (1981), 1–60

Godden, M., ed., *Ælfric's Catholic Homilies: The Second Series, Text*, EETS Supplementary Ser. 5 (London, 1979)

Godel, W., 'Irisches Beten im frühen Mittelalter: eine liturgie- und frömmig-keitsgeschichtliche Untersuchung', *ZKT* 85 (1963), 261–321 and 389–439

Gougaud, L., 'Étude sur les *loricae* celtiques et sur les prières qui s'en rappro-chent', *Bulletin d'ancienne littérature et d'archéologie chrétiennes* 1 (1911), 265–81; 2 (1912), 33–41 and 101–27

Gover, J. E. B. *et al.*, *The Place-Names of Warwickshire*, EPNS 13 (Cambridge, 1936)

The Place-Names of Wiltshire, EPNS 16 (Cambridge, 1939)

Graham-Campbell, J., 'The Scandinavian Viking-Age Burials in England – Some Problems of Interpretation', in *Anglo-Saxon Cemeteries*, ed. Rahtz *et al.*, pp. 379–82

Grattan, J. H. G. and C. Singer, *Anglo-Saxon Magic and Medicine, Illustrated Especially from the Semi-Pagan Text 'Lacnunga'* (London, 1952)

Green, C. J. S., 'The Significance of Plaster Burials for the Recognition of Christian Cemeteries', in *Burial*, ed. Reece, pp. 46–53

Grierson, P., 'Les livres de l'abbé Seiwold de Bath', *RB* 52 (1940), 96–116

'Relations Between England and Flanders Before the Norman Conquest', *TRHS* 4th ser. 23 (1941), 71–112

Grosjean, P., 'A propos du manuscrit 49 de la Reine Christine', *AB* 54 (1936), 113–36

'La date du Colloque de Whitby', *AB* 78 (1960), 233–74

'Saints anglo-saxons des marches galloises: à propos d'un ouvrage récent [i.e. *ECWM*]', *AB* 79 (1961), 161–9

Gruffydd, R. G., ed., '"Marwnad Cynddylan"', in *Bardos: Penodau ar y Traddodiad Barddol Cymreig a Cheltaidd cyflwynedig i J. E. Caerwyn Williams*, ed. R. G. Gruffydd (Cardiff, 1982), pp. 10–28

Grundy, G. B., *Saxon Charters of Worcestershire*, Birmingham Archaeological Society (n.p., 1931)

Saxon Charters and Field-Names of Gloucestershire, 2 parts [continuously paginated], Bristol and Gloucestershire Archaeological Society (n.p., 1935–6)

Guerout, J., 'Les origines et le premier siècle de l'abbaye', in *L'abbaye royale de Notre-Dame de Jouarre*, ed. Y. Chaussy *et al.*, 2 vols. (Paris, 1961) I, 1–67

Haddan, A. W. and W. Stubbs, ed., *Councils and Ecclesiastical Documents Relating to Great Britain and Ireland*, 3 vols. (Oxford, 1869–71)

Hahn, H., 'Ueber einige Briefe der Bonifazischen Sammlung mit unbestimmter Adresse', *Forschungen zur deutschen Geschichte* 21 (1881), 383–400

Bonifaz und Lul: ihre angelsächsischen Korrespondenten. Erzbischof Luls Leben (Leipzig, 1883)

Haigh, D. H., 'The Monasteries of S. Heiu and S. Hild', *Yorkshire Archaeological and Topographical Journal* 3 (1875), 349–91

Hall, A., ed., *Commentarii de Scriptoribus Britannicis Auctore Joanne Lelando*, 2 vols. [continuously paginated] (Oxford, 1709)

Hamilton, N. E. S. A., ed., *Willelmi Malmesbiriensis De gestis pontificum Anglorum libri quinque*, RS (London, 1870)

Hamman, A., ed., *Early Christian Prayers*, trans. W. Mitchell (Chicago and London, 1961)

Hampe, J. C., *To Die is to Gain*, trans. M. Kohl (London, 1979)

Harden, D. B., 'Glass Vessels in Britain and Ireland, A.D. 400–1000', in *Dark-Age Britain*, ed. Harden, pp. 132–67

Harden, D. B., ed., *Dark-Age Britain: Studies presented to E. T. Leeds* (London, 1956)

Hardwick, C., ed., *Historia Monasterii S. Augustini Cantuariensis by Thomas of Elmham*, RS (London, 1858)

Hardy, T. D., *Descriptive Catalogue of Materials Relating to the History of Great Britain and Ireland* I, *From the Roman Period to the Norman Invasion*, RS (London, 1862)

Harmer, F. E., ed., *Select English Historical Documents of the Ninth and Tenth Centuries* (Cambridge, 1914)

Harrison, K., 'The *Annus Domini* in Some Early Charters', *Journal of the Society of Archivists* 4 (1970–3), 551–7

The Framework of Anglo-Saxon History to A.D. 900 (Cambridge, 1976)

Hart, C. R., 'The Tribal Hidage', *TRHS* 5th ser. 21 (1971), 133–57

'The Kingdom of Mercia', in *Mercian Studies*, ed. Dornier, pp. 43–61

The Early Charters of Northern England and the North Midlands (Leicester, 1975)

'The Early Section of the *Worcester Chronicle*', *Journal of Medieval History* 9 (1983), 251–315

Hart, W. H., ed., *Historia et Cartularium Monasterii Sancti Petri Gloucestriae*, 3 vols. RS (London, 1863–7)

Haslam, J., 'The Towns of Wiltshire', in *Anglo-Saxon Towns*, ed. Haslam, pp. 87–147

Haslam, J., ed., *Anglo-Saxon Towns in Southern England* (Chichester, 1984)

Hausherr, I., 'Comment priaient les pères', *Revue d'ascétique et mystique* 32 (1956), 33–58 and 284–97

Hawkes, S. C., 'Orientation at Finglesham: Sunrise Dating of Death and Burial in an Anglo-Saxon Cemetery in East Kent', *Archaeologia Cantiana* 92 (1976), 33–51

'The Early Saxon Period', in *The Archaeology of the Oxford Region*, ed. G. Briggs *et al.* (Oxford, 1986), pp. 64–108

Healey, A. diP., ed., *The Old English Vision of St. Paul*, Speculum Anniversary Monographs 2 (Cambridge, Mass., 1978)

Hearne, T., ed., *Joannis Lelandi Antiquarii De Rebus Britannicis Collectanea*, 6 vols., 2nd ed. (London, 1774)

Hemingi Chartularium Ecclesiae Wigorniensis, 2 vols. [continuous pagination] (Oxford, 1723)

Heighway, C. M., 'Anglo-Saxon Gloucestershire', in *Archaeology in Gloucestershire*, ed. Saville, pp. 225–47

'Saxon Gloucester', in *Anglo-Saxon Towns*, ed. Haslam, pp. 359–83

'Anglo-Saxon Gloucester to A.D. 1000', in *Studies in Late Anglo-Saxon Settlement*, ed. M. L. Faull (Oxford, 1984), pp. 35–53

Heiming, O., ed., 'Ein benediktinisch-ambrosianisches Gebetbuch des frühen 11. Jahrhunderts (Brit. Mus. Egerton 3763)', *Archiv für Liturgiewissenschaft* 8 (1964), 325–435

Herren, M. W., ed., *The Hisperica Famina*, 2 vols. (Toronto, 1974–87)

Hesbert, R.-J., ed., *Corpus Antiphonalium Officii*, 4 vols. (Rome, 1963–70)

Hilberg, I., ed., *Santi Eusebii Hieronymi Epistulae*, 3 vols., CSEL 54–6 (Vienna, 1910–18)

Hill, D., *An Atlas of Anglo-Saxon England* (Oxford, 1981)

Hill, D. and D. M. Metcalf, ed., *Sceattas in England and on the Continent*, BAR British Series 128 (Oxford, 1984)

Hill, T. D., 'The *æcerbot* Charm and its Christian User', *ASE* 6 (1977), 213–21

Hillaby, J. G., 'The Origins of the Diocese of Hereford', *TWNFC* 42 (1976–8), 16–52

Hillgarth, J. N., ed., *Sancti Iuliani Toletanae Sedis Episcopi Opera, pars I*, CCSL 115 (Turnhout, 1976)

Hills, C., 'The Archaeology of Anglo-Saxon England in the Pagan Period: A Review', *ASE* 8 (1979), 297–329

Hilton, R. H., *A Medieval Society: The West Midlands at the End of the Thirteenth Century*, 2nd ed. (Cambridge, 1983)

Hines, J., *The Scandinavian Character of Anglian England in the Pre-Viking Period*, BAR British Series 124 (Oxford, 1984)

Hirst, S. M., 'Bidford-on-Avon 1979', *WMANS* 22 (1979), 54–5

Holdsworth, C. J., 'Visions and Visionaries in the Middle Ages', *History* 48 (1963), 141–53

'Saint Boniface the Monk', in *The Greatest Englishman*, ed. Reuter, pp. 47–67

Hooke, D., 'Burial Features of West Midland Charters', *JEPNS* 13 (1980–1), 1–40

'The Hinterland and Routeways of Late Saxon Worcester: The Charter Evidence', in *Medieval Worcester*, ed. Carver, pp. 39–49

'The Droitwich Salt Industry: An Examination of the West Midland Charter Evidence', *ASSAH* 2 (1981), 123–69

Anglo-Saxon Landscapes of the West Midlands: The Charter Evidence, BAR British Series 95 (Oxford, 1981)

The Landscape of Anglo-Saxon Staffordshire: The Charter Evidence (Keele, 1983)

The Anglo-Saxon Landscape: The Kingdom of the Hwicce (Manchester, 1985)

Anglo-Saxon Territorial Organization: The Western Margins of Mercia, University of Birmingham Department of Geography Occasional Publication 22 (Birmingham, 1986)

Horstman, C., ed., *Nova Legenda Anglie, as Collected by John of Tynemouth, John Capgrave and Others*, 2 vols. (Oxford, 1901)

Hoskins, W. G., *The Making of the English Landscape*, 3rd ed. by C. Taylor (London, 1988)

Houghton, F. T. S., 'Salt-Ways', *TBAS* 54 (1929–30), 1–17

Worcestershire, 3rd ed., rev. M. Moore, The Little Guides (London, 1952)

Huemer, J., ed., *Sedulii Opera Omnia*, CSEL 10 (Vienna, 1885)

Iuuenci Euangeliorum Libri Quattuor, CSEL 24 (Vienna, 1891)

Hughes, K., 'Some Aspects of Irish Influence on Early English Private Prayer', *Studia Celtica* 5 (1970), 48–61

'Evidence for Contacts Between the Churches of the Irish and English from the Synod of Whitby to the Viking Age', in *England Before the Conquest*, ed. Clemoes and Hughes, pp. 49–67

Celtic Britain in the Early Middle Ages, ed. D. Dumville (Woodbridge, 1980)

'The Celtic Church: Is This a Valid Concept?', *CMCS* 1 (Summer 1981), 1–20

Humphreys, J. *et al.*, 'An Anglo-Saxon Cemetery at Bidford-on-Avon, Warwickshire', *Archaeologia* 73 (1923), 89–116; 74 (1925), 271–88

Hunt, A. M., 'Archaeology in the Avon and Severn Valleys: A Review', *WMA* 25 (1982), 1–24

Hunter Blair, P., *The World of Bede* (London, 1970)

'From Bede to Alcuin', in *Famulus Christi*, ed. Bonner, pp. 239–60

'Whitby as a Centre of Learning in the Seventh Century', in *Learning and Literature*, ed. Lapidge and Gneuss, pp. 3–32

Hurst, D., ed., *Bedae Venerabilis Opera, pars III, Opera Homiletica*, CCSL 122 (Turnhout, 1955)

Hurst, H. R. *Kingsholm: Excavations at Kingsholm Close and Other Sites with a Discussion of the Archaeology of the Area*, Gloucester Archaeological Reports 1 (Gloucester, 1985)

Hyslop, M., 'Two Anglo-Saxon Cemeteries at Chamberlains Barn, Leighton Buzzard, Bedfordshire', *ArchJ* 120 (1963), 161–200

Jaager, W., ed., *Bedas metrische Vita sancti Cuthberti*, Palaestra 198 (Leipzig, 1935)

Jackson, K., *Language and History in Early Britain* (Edinburgh, 1953)

James, E., 'Cemeteries and the Problem of Frankish Settlement in Gaul', in *Names, Words, and Graves: Early Medieval Settlement*, ed. P. H. Sawyer (Leeds, 1979), pp. 55–89

'Merovingian Cemetery Studies and Some Implications for Anglo-Saxon England', in *Anglo-Saxon Cemeteries*, ed. Rahtz *et al.*, pp. 35–55

James, M. R., *A Descriptive Catalogue of the Manuscripts in the Library of Corpus Christi College, Cambridge*, 2 vols. (Cambridge, 1909–13)

The Lost Apocrypha of the Old Testament: Their Titles and Fragments (London, 1920)

A Descriptive Catalogue of the Manuscripts in the Library of Lambeth Palace: The Medieval Manuscripts (Cambridge, 1932)

James, M. R., ed., *The Testament of Abraham*, Texts and Studies 2.2 (Cambridge, 1892)

Apocrypha Anecdota [First Series]: A Collection of Thirteen Apocryphal Books and Fragments, Texts and Studies 2.3 (Cambridge, 1893)

Apocrypha Anecdota, Second Series, Texts and Studies 5.1 (Cambridge, 1897)

'Two Lives of St. Ethelbert, King and Martyr', *EHR* 32 (1917), 214–44

James, M. R., trans., *The Apocryphal New Testament* (Oxford, 1924)

Jenkins, D. and M. E. Owen, 'The Welsh Marginalia in the Lichfield Gospels: Part I', *CMCS* 5 (Summer 1985), 37–66

Johansson, C., *Old English Place-Names and Field-Names Containing 'lēah'*, Stockholm Studies in English 32 (Stockholm, 1975)

John, E., 'St Oswald and the Tenth Century Reformation', *JEH* 9 (1958), 159–72

Land Tenure in Early England (Leicester, 1964)

Orbis Britanniae and Other Studies (Leicester, 1966)

'The Social and Political Problems of the Early English Church', in *Land, Church, and People: Essays presented to H. P. R. Finberg*, ed. J. Thirsk, *Agricultural History Review* 18 (1970), Supplement, pp. 39–63

Jones, G. R. J., 'Early Historic Settlement in Border Territory: A Case-Study of Archenfield and its Environs in Herefordshire', in *Recherches de géographie rurale: hommage au Professeur Frans Dussart*, ed. C. Christians and J. Claude, 2 vols. (Liège, 1979) I, 117–32

Jones, T., trans., *Brut y Tywysogyon, or, The Chronicle of the Princes: Peniarth MS. 20 Version* (Cardiff, 1952)

Junod, E. and J.-D. Kaestli, ed., *Acta Iohannis*, 2 vols., Corpus Christianorum, Series Apocryphorum 1–2 (Turnhout, 1983)

Kamphausen, H. J., *Traum und Vision in der lateinischen Poesie der Karolingerzeit* (Bern and Frankfurt, 1975)

Kantorowicz, E. H., *Laudes Regiae: A Study in Liturgical Acclamations and Mediaeval Ruler Worship* (Berkeley and Los Angeles, 1958)

Kellaway, G. A. and F. B. A. Welch, *Bristol and Gloucester District*, 2nd ed., British Regional Geology (London, 1948)

Kelly, J. N. D., *Jerome: His Life, Writings, and Controversies* (London, 1975)

Kemble, J. M., ed., *Codex Diplomaticus Aevi Saxonici*, 6 vols. (London, 1839–48)

Ker, N. R., *Catalogue of Manuscripts Containing Anglo-Saxon* (Oxford, 1957)

Books, Collectors and Libraries: Studies in the Medieval Heritage, ed. A. G. Watson (London, 1985)

Ker, N. R., ed., *Medieval Libraries of Great Britain: A List of Surviving Books*, 2nd ed. (London, 1964)

Keynes, S., *The Diplomas of King Æthelred 'the Unready'* (Cambridge, 1980)

'King Athelstan's Books', in *Learning and Literature*, ed. Lapidge and Gneuss, pp. 143–201

Kirby, D. P., 'Bede's Native Sources for the *Historia Ecclesiastica*', *Bulletin of the John Rylands Library* 48 (1965–6), 341–71

'Bede, Eddius Stephanus and the "Life of Wilfrid"', *EHR* 98 (1983), 101–14

Kirby, D. P., ed., *Saint Wilfrid at Hexham* (Newcastle upon Tyne, 1974)

Krusch, B., ed., 'Vita Virtutesque Fursei Abbatis Latiniacensis et de Fuilano Additamentum Nivialense', MGH, SS. rer. Merov. 4 (Hannover and Leipzig, 1902), 423–51 and 779–80; 7 (Hannover and Leipzig, 1920), 837–42

Kuypers, A. B., ed., *The Prayer Book of Aedeluald the Bishop, Commonly Called The Book of Cerne* (Cambridge, 1902)

Kylie, E., trans., *The English Correspondence of Saint Boniface* (London, 1911)

Laistner, M. L. W., 'The Study of St. Jerome in the Early Middle Ages', in *A Monument to Saint Jerome: Essays on Some Aspects of his Life, Work and Influence*, ed. F. X. Murphy (New York, 1952), pp. 233–56

'Some Early Medieval Commentaries on the Old Testament', *HThR* 46 (1953), 27–46

Thought and Letters in Western Europe A.D. *500 to 900*, 2nd ed. (London and New York, 1957)

Lambot, C., ed., *North Italian Services of the Eleventh Century: Recueil d'Ordines du XIᵉ siècle provenant de la haute-Italie (Milan, Bibl. Ambros. T. 27. sup.)*, HBS 67 (London, 1931)

Lapidge, M., 'Some Remnants of Bede's Lost Liber Epigrammatum', *EHR* 90 (1975), 798–820

'The Medieval Hagiography of St. Ecgwine', *VEHSRP* 6 (1977), 77–93

'Aldhelm's Latin Poetry and Old English Verse', *Comparative Literature* 31 (1979), 209–31

'The Cult of St Indract at Glastonbury', in *Ireland in Early Mediaeval Europe*, ed. Whitelock *et al.*, pp. 179–212

'A Seventh-Century Insular Latin Debate Poem on Divorce', *CMCS* 10 (Winter 1985), 1–23

'Surviving Booklists from Anglo-Saxon England', in *Literature and Learning*, ed. Lapidge and Gneuss, pp. 33-89

'The School of Theodore and Hadrian', *ASE* 15 (1986), 45–72

Lapidge, M. and D. Dumville, ed., *Gildas: New Approaches* (Woodbridge, 1984)

Lapidge, M. and H. Gneuss, ed., *Learning and Literature in Anglo-Saxon England: Studies presented to Peter Clemoes* (Cambridge, 1985)

Lapidge, M. and M. Herren, trans., *Aldhelm: The Prose Works* (Ipswich and Cambridge, 1979)

Lapidge, M. and J. Rosier, trans., *Aldhelm: The Poetic Works* (Cambridge, 1985)

Lapidge, M. and R. Sharpe, *A Bibliography of Celtic-Latin Literature 400–1200* (Dublin, 1985)

Lattimore, R., *Themes in Greek and Latin Epitaphs*, Illinois Studies in Language and Literature, 28.1–2 (Urbana, 1942)

Leclercq, J., *The Love of Learning and the Desire for God: A Study of Monastic Culture*, trans. C. Misrahi (New York, 1962)

Leeds, E. T., *Early Anglo-Saxon Art and Archaeology* (Oxford, 1936)

A Corpus of Early Anglo-Saxon Great Square-Headed Brooches (Oxford, 1949)

The Archaeology of the Anglo-Saxon Settlements, 2nd ed. (Oxford, 1970)

Leeds, E. T. and M. Pocock, 'A Survey of the Anglo-Saxon Cruciform Brooches of Florid Type', *MA* 15 (1971), 13–36

Le Goff, J., *The Birth of Purgatory*, trans. A. Goldhammer (London, 1984)

Lehmann, P., *Mittelalterliche Büchertitel* II, Sitzungsberichte der Bayerischen Akademie der Wissenschaften, philos.-hist. Klasse, 1953, 3 (Munich, 1953)

Lehner, A., ed., *Florilegia: Florilegium Frisingense (Clm 6433); Testimonia Divinae Scripturae*, CCSL 108D (Turnhout, 1987)

Lennard, R., *Rural England 1086–1135* (Oxford, 1959)

Leo, F., ed., *Venanti Fortunati Opera Poetica*, MGH, Auct. antiq. 4.1 (Berlin, 1881)

Lesne, É., *Histoire de la propriété ecclésiastique en France* IV, *Les livres, 'scriptoria' et bibliothèques du commencement du VIIIe à la fin du XIe siècle* (Lille, 1938)

Levison, W., 'Eine Bearbeitung des 10. Bonifaz-Briefes', *NA* 32 (1907), 380–5

England and the Continent in the Eighth Century (Oxford, 1946)

Levison, W., ed., *Vitae Sancti Bonifatii Archiepiscopi Moguntini*, Scriptores Rerum Germanicarum in Usum Scholarum ex MGH Separatim Editi (Hannover and Leipzig, 1905)

'Visio Baronti Monachi Longoretensis', MGH, SS. rer. Merov. 5 (Hannover and Leipzig, 1910), 368–94, and 7 (Hannover and Leipzig, 1920), 846

'Vita Filiberti Abbatis Gemeticensis et Heriensis', MGH, SS. rer. Merov. 5 (Hannover and Leipzig, 1910), 568–606

'Vita Bertilae Abbatissae Calensis', MGH, SS. rer. Merov. 6 (Hannover and Leipzig, 1913), 95–109

Liebermann, F., *Die Heiligen Englands* (Hannover, 1889)

Liebermann, F., ed., *Ungedruckte Anglo-Normannische Geschichtsquellen* (Strassburg, 1879)

Lloyd, J. E., *A History of Wales from the Earliest Times to the Edwardian Conquest*, 2 vols., 3rd ed. (London, 1939)

Lloyd Jones, M., *Society and Settlement in Wales and the Marches 500 B.C. to A.D. 1100*, 2 vols., BAR British Series 121, (Oxford, 1984)

Lorenz, R., 'Die Anfänge des abendländischen Mönchtums im 4. Jahrhundert', *Zeitschrift für Kirchengeschichte* 77 (1966), 1–61

Lowe, E. A., *Codices Latini Antiquiores*, 12 vols., with 2nd ed. of vol. II only (Oxford, 1934–72)

English Uncial (Oxford, 1960)

Löwe, H., ed., *Die Iren und Europa im früheren Mittelalter*, 2 vols. (Stuttgart, 1982)

Loyn, H. R., 'The Term *Ealdorman* in the Translations Prepared at the Time of King Alfred', *EHR* 68 (1953), 513–25

'Gesiths and Thegns in Anglo-Saxon England from the Seventh to the Tenth Century', *EHR* 70 (1955), 529–49

The Governance of Anglo-Saxon England 500–1087 (London, 1984)

'The Conversion of the English to Christianity: Some Comments on the Celtic Contribution', in *Welsh Society and Nationhood: Historical Essays presented to Glanmor Williams*, ed. R. R. Davies *et al.* (Cardiff, 1984), pp. 5–18

Luard, H. R., ed., *Annales Monastici*, 5 vols., RS (London, 1864–9)

McGurk, P., 'The Gospel Book in Celtic Lands Before AD 850: Contents and Arrangement', in *Irland und die Christenheit*, ed. Ní Chatháin and Richter, pp. 165–89

McGurk, P. *et al.*, ed., *An Eleventh-Century Anglo-Saxon Illustrated Miscellany: British Library Cotton Tiberius B.V Part I Together with Leaves from British Library Cotton Nero D.II*, EEMF 21 (Copenhagen, 1983)

MacInnes, C. M. and W. F. Whittard, ed., *Bristol and its Adjoining Counties* (Bristol, 1955)

Mackney, D. and C. P. Burnham, *The Soils of the West Midlands* (Harpenden, 1964)

McNally, R. E., *Der irische Liber de numeris: Eine Quellenanalyse des pseudo-isidorischen Liber de numeris*, Inaugural-Dissertation (Munich, 1957)

The Bible in the Early Middle Ages, Woodstock Occasional Essays for Theology 4 (Westminster, MD, 1959)

McNamara, M., *The Apocrypha in the Irish Church* (Dublin, 1975)

'Early Irish Exegesis: Some Facts and Tendencies', *PIBA* 8 (1984), 57–96

Macray, W. D., ed., *Chronicon Abbatiae de Evesham ad Annum 1418*, RS (London, 1863)

McWhirr, A. *et al.*, *Romano-British Cemeteries at Cirencester*, Cirencester Excavations 2 (Cirencester, 1982)

Margary, I. D., *Roman Roads in Britain*, 2 vols. (London, 1955–7)

Matley, C. A., 'The Upper Keuper (or Arden) Sandstone Group and Associated Rocks of Warwickshire', *QJGS* 68 (1912), 252–80

Mawer, A. *et al.*, *The Place-Names of Worcestershire*, EPNS 4 (Cambridge, 1927)

Mayr-Harting, H., *The Coming of Christianity to Anglo-Saxon England* (London, 1972)

'St. Wilfrid in Sussex', in *Studies in Sussex Church History*, ed. M. J. Kitch (London, 1981), pp. 1–17

Meaney, A. L., *A Gazetteer of Early Anglo-Saxon Burial Sites* (London, 1964)

Meaney, A. L. and S. C. Hawkes, *Two Anglo-Saxon Cemeteries at Winnall, Winchester, Hampshire*, Society for Medieval Archaeology Monograph Series 4 (London, 1970)

Mellows, W. T., ed., *The Chronicle of Hugh Candidus, A Monk of Peterborough* (London, 1949)

Metcalf, D. M., 'Sceattas from the Territory of the Hwicce', *Numismatic Chronicle* 136 (1976), 64–74

'Monetary Affairs in Mercia in the Time of Æthelbald', in *Mercian Studies*, ed. Dornier, pp. 87–106

'Monetary Circulation in Southern England in the First Half of the Eighth Century', in *Sceattas*, ed. Hill and Metcalf, pp. 27–69

Metz, R., *La consécration des vierges dans l'église romaine* (Paris, 1954)

Meyer, R. T., trans., *St. Athanasius: The Life of Saint Antony*, Ancient Christian Writers 10 (Westminster, Maryland, 1950)

Meyer, W., 'Poetische Nachlese aus dem sogenannten Book of Cerne in Cambridge und aus dem Londoner Codex Regius A.XX', *Nachrichten von der kgl. Gesell-schaft der Wissenschaften zu Göttingen*, Philol.-hist. Klasse, 1917, pp. 597–625

Migne, J.-P., ed., *Patrologia Latina*, 221 vols. (Paris, 1844–64)

Patrologia Graeco-Latina, 162 vols. (Paris, 1857–66)

Miles, D., 'Romano-British Settlement in the Gloucestershire Thames Valley', in *Archaeology in Gloucestershire*, ed. Saville, pp. 191–211

Miles, D. and S. Palmer, *Invested in Mother Earth: The Anglo-Saxon Cemetery at Lechlade* (Oxford, [1986])

Milik, J. T., '4Q visions de 'Amram et une citation d'Origène', *Revue biblique* 79 (1972), 77–97

Millward, R. and A. Robinson, *Landscapes of Britain: The West Midlands* (London, 1971)

Mohlberg, L. C., ed., *Liber sacramentorum Romanae aecclesiae ordinis anni circuli (Cod. Vat. Reg. lat. 316/Paris Bibl. Nat. 7193, 41/56) (Sacramentarium Gelasianum)* (Rome, 1960)

Missale Gothicum (Vat. Reg. lat. 317) (Rome, 1961)

Mohlberg, L. C. *et al.*, ed., *Missale Gallicanum Vetus (Cod. Vat. Palat. lat. 493)* (Rome, 1958)

Mohrmann, C., *Liturgical Latin: Its Origins and Character* (London, 1959)

Études sur le latin des chrétiens, 3 vols. (Rome, 1961–5)

Mommsen, T., ed., *Chronica Minora* III, MGH, Auct. antiq. 13 (Berlin, 1898)

Moore, W. J., *The Saxon Pilgrims to Rome and the Schola Saxonum*, D. ès L. diss., Faculty of Letters (Fribourg, Switz., 1937)

Morris, J., *The Age of Arthur* (London, 1973)

Bibliography

Morris, R., *The Church in British Archaeology*, CBA Research Report 47 (London, 1983)

Morrish, J., 'Dated and Datable Manuscripts Copied in England During the Ninth Century: A Preliminary List', *MS* 50 (1988), 512–38

Muir, B. J., ed., *A Pre-Conquest English Prayer-Book (BL MSS Cotton Galba A.xiv and Nero A.ii (ff.3–13))*, HBS 103 (Woodbridge, 1988)

Myres, J. N. L., *Anglo-Saxon Pottery and the Settlement of England* (Oxford, 1969)

Nees, L., 'The Colophon Drawing in the Book of Mulling: A Supposed Irish Monastery Plan and the Tradition of Terminal Illustration in Early Medieval Manuscripts', *CMCS* 5 (Summer 1983), 67–91

Ní Chatháin, P. and M. Richter, ed., *Irland und die Christenheit: Bibelstudien und Mission* (Stuttgart, 1987)

Nicklin, P. A., 'The Early Historical Geography of the Forest of Arden', *TBAS* 56 (1932), 71–6

Noble, F., *Offa's Dyke Reviewed*, ed. M. Gelling, BAR British Series 114 (Oxford, 1983)

Nordenfalk, C., 'A Note on the Stockholm Codex Aureus', *NTBB* 38 (1951), 145–55

Die spätantiken Zierbuchstaben, 2 vols. (Stockholm, 1970)

Celtic and Anglo-Saxon Painting: Book Illumination in the British Isles 600–800 (London, 1977)

Norman, E. R. and J. K. S. St Joseph, *The Early Development of Irish Society: The Evidence of Aerial Photography* (Cambridge, 1969)

Ntedika, J., *L'évocation de l'Au-delà dans la prière pour les morts: étude de patristique et de liturgie latines (IVᵉ–VIIIᵉ s.)* (Louvain, 1971)

Ó Cróinín, D., 'The Irish Provenance of Bede's Computus', *Peritia* 2 (1983), 229–47

O'Donovan, M. A., 'An Interim Revision of Episcopal Dates for the Province of Canterbury, 850–950: Parts I and II', *ASE* 1 (1972), 23–44; 2 (1973), 91–113

Ó Laoghaire, D., 'Irish Elements in the *Catechesis Celtica*', in *Irland und die Christenheit*, ed. Ní Chatháin and Richter, pp. 146–64

O'Neil, H. E., 'Bevan's Quarry Round Barrow, Temple Guiting, Gloucestershire, 1964', *TBGAS* 86 (1967), 16–41

Ordnance Survey, *Map of Britain in the Dark Ages*, 2nd ed. (Southampton, 1966)

Osmond, D. A., 'The Soils of Gloucestershire, Somerset and Wiltshire', in *Bristol and Its Adjoining Counties*, ed. MacInnes and Whittard, pp. 67–72

Owen, H., ed., *The Description of Penbrokshire* [sic] *by George Owen of Henllys*, 4 pts, Cymmrodorion Record Series 1 (London, 1892–1906)

Ozanne, A., 'The Peak Dwellers', *MA* 6/7 (1962–3), 15–52

Page, R. I., 'Anglo-Saxon Episcopal Lists, Parts I and II', *Nottingham Mediaeval Studies* 9 (1965), 71–95

  'Anglo-Saxon Episcopal Lists, Part III', *Nottingham Mediaeval Studies* 10 (1966), 2–24

Parkes, M. B., 'The Handwriting of St Boniface: A Reassessment of the Problems', *BGDSL* 98 (1976), 161–79

  The Scriptorium of Wearmouth-Jarrow, Jarrow Lecture 1982 (Jarrow, [1982])

  'The Contribution of Insular Scribes of the Seventh and Eighth Centuries to the "Grammar of Legibility"', in *Grafia e interpunzione del Latino nel medioevo*, ed. A. Maierù (Rome, 1987), pp. 15–30

Pattie, T. S., 'Ephraem the Syrian and the Latin Manuscripts of "De Paenitentia"', *British Library Journal* 13 (1987), 1–24

Peacock, D., 'Fladbury', *CA* 1 (1967–8), 123–4

Petersen, J. M., *The Dialogues of Gregory the Great in their Late Antique Cultural Background* (Toronto, 1984)

Petrie, H. and J. Sharpe, ed., *Monumenta Historica Britannica* 1 [all published] (London, 1848)

Petschenig, M., ed., *Iohannis Cassiani Conlationes*, CSEL 13.2 (Vienna, 1886)

Phillimore, E., ed., 'The *Annales Cambriae* and Old-Welsh Genealogies from Harleian MS. 3859', *Y Cymmrodor* 9 (1888), 141–83

Phythian-Adams, C., 'Rutland Reconsidered', in *Mercian Studies*, ed. Dornier, pp. 63–84

Plummer, C., ed., *Venerabilis Baedae Opera Historica*, 2 vols. (Oxford, 1896)

  Irish Litanies, HBS 62 (London, 1925)

  Two of the Saxon Chronicles Parallel, 2 vols. (Oxford, 1892–9)

Poole, R. L., *Studies in Chronology and History*, ed. A. L. Poole (Oxford, 1934)

Porter, W. S., *The Gallican Rite*, Alcuin Club (London, 1958)

Powicke, F. M. and E. B. Fryde, ed., *Handbook of British Chronology*, 2nd ed. (London, 1961)

Pralle, L., 'Ein keltisches Missale in der Fuldaer Klosterbibliothek', *Fuldaer Geschichtsblätter: Zeitschrift des Fuldaer Geschichtsvereins* 31 (1955), 8–21

Pretty, K. B., 'The Welsh Border and the Severn and Avon Valleys in the Fifth and Sixth Centuries A.D.: An Archaeological Survey' (unpubl. PhD dissertation, Cambridge Univ., 1975)

Price, E. A. and B. Watson, 'A Romano-British and Anglo-Saxon Site at Sedgeberrow', *WMA* 27 (1984), 88–95

Rahtz, P., 'Atcham Timber Halls, Salop (SJ/552115)', *WMANS* 18 (1975), 58–60; 19 (1976), 53–4

   Excavations at St Mary's Church, Deerhurst, 1971–73, CBA Research Report 15 (London, 1976)

   'Buildings and Rural Settlement', in *Archaeology*, ed. Wilson, pp. 49–98 and 405–52

   'The Archaeology of West Mercian Towns', in *Mercian Studies*, ed. Dornier, pp. 107–29

   'Late Roman Cemeteries and Beyond', in *Burial*, ed. Reece, pp. 53–64

   'Grave Orientation', *ArchJ* 135 (1978), 1–14

Rahtz, P. *et al.*, *Anglo-Saxon Cemeteries 1979*, BAR British Series 82 (Oxford, 1980)

Rahtz, P. and P. Fowler, 'Somerset A.D. 400–700', in *Archaeology and the Landscape*, ed. Fowler, pp. 187–221

Rau, R., ed. and trans., *Bonifatii Epistulae, Willibaldi Vita Bonifatii* (Darmstadt, 1968)

Redin, M., *Studies on Uncompounded Personal Names in Old English*, Uppsala Universitets Årsskrift 1919, no. 2 (Uppsala, 1919)

Reece, R., 'The Cotswolds: An Essay on Some Aspects and Problems of Roman Rural Settlement', in *Archaeology in Gloucestershire*, ed. Saville, pp. 181–90

Reece, R., ed., *Burial in the Roman World*, CBA Research Report 22 (London, 1977)

Rees, W., *South Wales and the Border in the Fourteenth Century*, map in 4 sheets (Cardiff, 1933)

Rennell of Rodd, Lord, 'The Land of Lene', in *Culture and Environment*, ed. Foster and Alcock, pp. 303–26

Reuter, T., 'Saint Boniface and Europe', in *The Greatest Englishman*, ed. Reuter, pp. 71–94

Reuter, T., ed., *The Greatest Englishman: Essays on St Boniface and the Church at Crediton* (Exeter, 1980)

Reuter, T., ed. and trans., *The Medieval Nobility: Studies on the Ruling Classes of France and Germany from the Sixth to the Twelfth Century* (Amsterdam, 1978)

Richards, M., *Welsh Administrative and Territorial Units* (Cardiff, 1969)

Richardson, L., *The Country Around Moreton in Marsh*, Memoirs of the Geological Survey: Explanation of Sheet 217 (London, 1929)

Riché, P., *Education and Culture in the Barbarian West, Sixth Through Eighth Centuries*, trans. J. J. Contreni (Columbia, SC, 1976)

Rigg, A. G. and G. R. Wieland, 'A Canterbury Classbook of the Mid-Eleventh-Century (The "Cambridge Songs" Manuscript)', *ASE* 4 (1975), 113–30

Rigold, S. E. and D. M. Metcalf, 'A Revised Check-List of English Finds of Sceattas', in *Sceattas*, ed. Hill and Metcalf, pp. 245–68

Rivière, J., 'Rôle du démon au jugement particulier chez les pères', *Revue des sciences religieuses* 4 (1924), 43–64

Robertson, A. J., ed., *Anglo-Saxon Charters*, 2nd ed. (Cambridge, 1956)

Robinson, J. A., *St Oswald and the Church of Worcester*, British Academy Supplemental Papers 5 (London, [1919])

Somerset Historical Essays (London, 1921)

The Times of Saint Dunstan (Oxford, 1923)

Rollason, D. W., 'Lists of Saints' Resting-Places in Anglo-Saxon England', *ASE* 7 (1978), 61–93

The Mildrith Legend: A Study in Early Medieval Hagiography in England (Leicester, 1982)

'The Cult of Murdered Royal Saints in Anglo-Saxon England', *ASE* 11 (1983), 1–22

Roper, M., 'Wilfrid's Landholdings in Northumbria', in *Wilfrid at Hexham*, ed. Kirby, pp. 61–79

Rousseau, P., *Ascetics, Authority, and the Church in the Age of Jerome and Cassian* (Oxford, 1978)

Rowley, T., *The Shropshire Landscape* (London, 1972)

Royal Commission on Historical Monuments, *County of Gloucester* 1, *Iron Age and Romano-British Monuments in the Gloucestershire Cotswolds* (London, 1976)

Royce, D., ed., *Landboc sive Registrum Monasterii Beatae Mariae Virginis et Sancti Cenhelmi de Winchelcumba*, 2 vols. (Exeter, 1892–1903)

Salmon, P., *Analecta liturgica: extraits des manuscrits liturgiques de la bibliothèque Vaticane*, Studi e testi 273 (Vatican, 1974)

'Livrets de prières de l'époque carolingienne', *RB* 86 (1976), 218–34

'Livrets de prières de l'époque carolingienne: nouvelle liste de manuscrits', *RB* 90 (1980), 147–9

Salmon, P. *et al.*, ed., *Testimonia Orationis Christianae Antiquioris*, Corpus Christianorum, Continuatio Mediaevalis 47 (Turnhout, 1977)

Saville, A., 'Salvage Recording of Romano-British, Saxon, Medieval, and Post-Medieval Remains at North Street, Winchcombe, Gloucestershire', *TBGAS* 103 (1985), 101–39

Bibliography

Saville, A., ed., *Archaeology in Gloucestershire from the Earliest Hunters to the Industrial Age: Essays Dedicated to Helen O'Neil and Elsie Clifford* (Cheltenham, 1984)

Sawyer, P. H., *Anglo-Saxon Charters: An Annotated List and Bibliography* (London, 1968)

From Roman Britain to Norman England (London, 1978)

'The Royal *tun* in Pre-Conquest England', in *Ideal and Reality*, ed. Wormald *et al.*, pp. 273–99

Sawyer, P. H., ed., *Medieval Settlement: Continuity and Change* (London, 1976)

Schaller, D., 'Bemerkungen zur Inschriften-Sylloge von Urbana', *Mittellateinisches Jahrbuch* 12 (1977), 9–21

Schaller, D. and E. Könsgen, *Initia Carminum Latinorum Saeculo Undecimo Antiquiorum* (Göttingen, 1977)

Scharer, A., *Die angelsächsische Königsurkunde im 7. und 8. Jahrhundert*, Veröffentlichungen des Instituts für österreichische Geschichtsforschung 26 (Vienna, 1982)

'Die Intitulationes der angelsächsischen Könige im 7. und 8. Jahrhundert', in *Intitulatio* III, *Lateinische Herrschertitel und Herrschertitulaturen von 7. bis zum 13. Jahrhundert*, ed. H. Wolfram and A. Scharer (Vienna, 1988), pp. 9–74

Schneider, D. B., 'Anglo-Saxon Women in the Religious Life: A Study of the Status and Position of Women in an Early Mediaeval Society' (unpubl. PhD dissertation, Cambridge Univ., 1985)

Scholz, B. W., ed., 'Eadmer's Life of Bregwine, Archbishop of Canterbury, 761–764', *Traditio* 22 (1966), 127–48

Schumann, O., *Lateinisches Hexameter-Lexicon: Dichterisches Formelgut von Ennius bis zum Archipoeta*, 6 vols., MGH, Hilfsmittel 4 (Munich, 1979–83)

Scott, J., *The Early History of Glastonbury: An Edition, Translation and Study of William of Malmesbury's De Antiquitate Glastonie Ecclesie* (Woodbridge, 1981)

Searle, W. G., *Onomasticon Anglo-Saxonicum* (Cambridge, 1897)

Anglo-Saxon Bishops, Kings and Nobles (Cambridge, 1899)

Sheerin, D. J., 'John Leland and Milred of Worcester', *Manuscripta* 21 (1977), 172–80

Shepherd, G., 'The Prophetic Cædmon', *RES* ns 5 (1954), 113–22

'Scriptural Poetry', in *Continuations and Beginnings*, ed. Stanley, pp. 1–36

Shoesmith, R., *Hereford City Excavations*, 3 vols., CBA Research Reports 36, 46 and 56 (London, 1980–5)

Sicard, D., *La liturgie de la mort dans l'église latine des origines à la réforme carolingienne*, Liturgiewissenschaftliche Quellen und Forschungen 63 (Münster, Westfalen, 1978)

Silverstein, T., *Visio Sancti Pauli: The History of the Apocalypse in Latin Together with Nine Texts*, Studies and Documents 4 (London, 1935)

'Dante and the Legend of the *Miʿrāj*: The Problem of Islamic Influence on the Christian Literature of the Otherworld', *Journal of Near Eastern Studies* 11 (1952), 89–110 and 187–97

Sims-Williams, P., 'Continental Influence at Bath Monastery in the Seventh Century', *ASE* 4 (1975), 1–10

'Cuthswith, Seventh-Century Abbess of Inkberrow, near Worcester, and the Würzburg Manuscript of Jerome on Ecclesiastes', *ASE* 5 (1976), 1–21

'Thought, Word and Deed: An Irish Triad', *Ériu* 29 (1978), 78–111

'An Unpublished Seventh- or Eighth-Century Anglo-Latin Letter in Boulogne-sur-Mer MS 74 (82)', *MÆ* 48 (1979), 1–22

Review of *Text of the Book of Llan Dâv*, ed. Evans and Rhys (repr. Aberystwyth, 1979), and Davies, *Llandaff Charters* and *Microcosm*, in *JEH* 33 (1982), 124–9

'Milred of Worcester's Collection of Latin Epigrams and its Continental Counterparts', *ASE* 10 (1982), 21–38

'William of Malmesbury and *La silloge epigrafica di Cambridge*', *Archivum Historiae Pontificiae* 21 (1983), 9–33

'Gildas and the Anglo-Saxons', *CMCS* 6 (Winter 1983), 1–30

'The Settlement of England in Bede and the *Chronicle*', *ASE* 12 (1983), 1–41

'Gildas and Vernacular Poetry', in *Gildas: New Approaches*, ed. Lapidge and Dumville, pp. 169–92

Review of Hughes, *Celtic Britain*, in *JEH* 36 (1985), 306–9

'The Visionary Celt: The Construction of an Ethnic Preconception', *CMCS* 11 (Summer 1986), 71–96

Review of *Ideal and Reality*, ed. Wormald *et al.*, in *JEH* 37 (1986), 114–17

'Thoughts on Ephrem the Syrian in Anglo-Saxon England', in *Learning and Literature*, ed. Lapidge and Gneuss, pp. 205–26

'St Wilfrid and Two Charters dated AD 676 and 680', *JEH* 39 (1988), 163–83

'A Recension of Boniface's Letter to Eadburg about the Monk of Wenlock's Vision' (in preparation)

'People and Places in the Anglo-Saxon West Midlands' (in preparation)

Sisam, K., *Studies in the History of Old English Literature* (Oxford, 1953)

Slater, T. R. and P. J. Jarvis, ed., *Field and Forest: An Historical Geography of Warwickshire and Worcestershire* (Norwich, 1982)

Slater, T. R. and C. Wilson, *Archaeology and Development in Stratford-upon-Avon* (Birmingham, 1977)

Smith, A. H., *English Place-Name Elements*, 2 vols., EPNS 25–6 (Cambridge, 1956)

The Place-Names of Gloucestershire, 4 vols., EPNS 38–41 (Cambridge, 1964–5)

'The *Hwicce*', in *Medieval and Linguistic Studies in Honor of Francis Peabody Magoun Jr*, ed. J. B. Bessinger and R. P. Creed (London, 1965), pp. 56–65

Smith, I., 'Ring-Ditches in Eastern and Central Gloucestershire', in *Archaeology and the Landscape*, ed. Fowler, pp. 157–67

Smyth, M., 'Isidore of Seville and Early Irish Cosmography', *CMCS* 14 (Winter 1987), 69–102

Speake, G., *Anglo-Saxon Animal Art and its Germanic Background* (Oxford, 1980)

Stafford, P., *The East Midlands in the Early Middle Ages* (Leicester, 1985)

Stancliffe, C., *St. Martin and his Hagiographer: History and Miracle in Sulpicius Severus* (Oxford, 1983)

Stanford, S. C., *The Archaeology of the Welsh Marches* (London, 1980)

Stanley, E. G., ed., *Continuations and Beginnings: Studies in Old English Literature* (London, 1966)

Stenton, F. M., *The Early History of the Abbey of Abingdon* (Reading, 1913)

The Latin Charters of the Anglo-Saxon Period (Oxford, 1955)

Preparatory to Anglo-Saxon England, being the Collected Papers of Frank Merry Stenton, ed. D. M. Stenton (Oxford, 1970)

Anglo-Saxon England, 3rd ed. (Oxford, 1971)

Stevenson, W. H., ed., *Asser's Life of King Alfred*, 2nd ed. by D. Whitelock (Oxford, 1959)

Stewart, I., 'The London Mint and the Coinage of Offa', in *Anglo-Saxon Monetary History: Essays in Memory of Michael Dolley*, ed. M. A. S. Blackburn (Leicester, 1986), pp. 27–43

Stone, M. E., 'The Metamorphosis of Ezra: Jewish Apocalypse and Medieval Vision', *JTS* ns 33 (1982), 1–18

Storms, G., *Anglo-Saxon Magic* (The Hague, 1948)

Stubbs, W., 'The Cathedral, Diocese, and Monasteries of Worcester in the Eighth Century', *ArchJ* 19 (1862), 236–52

Stubbs, W., ed., *Chronicles of the Reigns of Edward I and Edward II*, 2 vols., RS (London, 1882–3)

Bibliography

Willelmi Malmesbiriensis monachi De gestis regum Anglorum libri quinque, 2 vols., RS (London, 1887–9)

Swanton, M. J., *The Spearheads of the Anglo-Saxon Settlements* (London, 1973)

A Corpus of Pagan Anglo-Saxon Spear-Types, BAR British Series 7 (Oxford, 1974)

Swanton, M. J., ed. and trans., 'A Fragmentary Life of St. Mildred and Other Kentish Royal Saints', *Archaeologia Cantiana* 91 (1975), 15–27

Sweet, H., ed., *The Oldest English Texts*, EETS os 83 (London, 1885)

Tangl, M., ed., *Die Briefe des heiligen Bonifatius und Lullus*, MGH, Epistolae Selectae 1 (Berlin, 1916)

Taylor, C., *Village and Farmstead: A History of Rural Settlement in England* (London, 1983)

Taylor, C. S., 'The Pre-Domesday Hide of Gloucestershire', *TBGAS* 18 (1893–4), 288–319

'Berkeley Minster', *TBGAS* 19 (1894–5), 70–84

'Bath, Mercian and West-Saxon', *TBGAS* 23 (1900), 129–61

'Deerhurst, Pershore, and Westminster', *TBGAS* 25 (1902), 230–50

'Osric of Gloucester', *TBGAS* 26 (1903), 308–25

Taylor, H. M. and J. Taylor, *Anglo-Saxon Architecture*, 3 vols. (Cambridge, 1965–78)

Thacker, A. T., 'Some Terms for Noblemen in Anglo-Saxon England, *c.* 650–900', *ASSAH* 2 (1981), 201–36

'Chester and Gloucester: Early Ecclesiastical Organization in Two Mercian Burhs', *Northern History* 18 (1982), 199–211

'Kings, Saints, and Monasteries in Pre-Viking Mercia', *Midland History* 10 (1985), 1–25

Thomas, C., *The Early Christian Archaeology of North Britain* (London, 1971)

Christianity in Roman Britain to AD 500 (London, 1981)

Thomas, K., *Religion and the Decline of Magic: Studies in Popular Beliefs in Sixteenth- and Seventeenth-Century England* (repr. Harmondsworth, 1985)

Thomas, N., 'An Archaeological Gazetteer for Warwickshire: Neolithic to Iron Age', *TBWAS* 86 (1974), 16–48

Thomson, R., *William of Malmesbury* (Woodbridge, 1987)

Thorpe, H., 'The Growth of Settlement Before the Norman Conquest', in *Birmingham and Its Regional Setting: A Scientific Survey (British Association)* (Birmingham, 1950), pp. 87–112

Thorpe, L., trans., *Gregory of Tours: The History of the Franks* (Harmondsworth, 1974)

Thurn, H., *Die Pergamenthandschriften der ehemaligen Dombibliothek*, Die Handschriften der Universitätsbibliothek Würzburg 3.1 (Wiesbaden, 1984)

Todd, M., 'The *Vici* of Western England', in *The Roman West Country*, ed. Branigan and Fowler, pp. 99–119

Tomlinson, M. E., 'The Drifts of the Stour–Evenlode Watershed and their Extension in the Valleys of the Warwickshire Stour and Upper Evenlode', *PBNHPS* 15 (1921–30), 157–95

'River-Terraces of the Lower Valley of the Warwickshire Avon', *QJGS* 81 (1925), 137–63

'Superficial Deposits of the Country North of Stratford on Avon', *QJGS* 91 (1935), 423–62

'Pleistocene Gravels of the Cotswold Sub-Edge Plain from Mickleton to the Frome Valley', *QJGS* 96 (1940), 385–421

Turner, C. H., ed., *Early Worcester MSS: Fragments of Four Books and a Charter of the Eighth Century Belonging to Worcester Cathedral* (Oxford, 1916)

Twysden, R., ed., *Historiae Anglicanae Scriptores X* (London, 1652)

Unterkircher, F., ed., *Sancti Bonifacii Epistolae: Codex Vindobonensis 751 der Österreichischen Nationalbibliothek*, Codices Selecti 24 (Graz, 1971)

Van der Straeten, J., *Les manuscrits hagiographiques d'Arras et de Boulogne-sur-Mer*, Subsidia Hagiographica 50 (Brussels, 1971)

Victoria County History of Gloucestershire (London, 1907–)

Victoria County History of Warwickshire (London, 1904–)

Victoria County History of Worcestershire (London, 1901–)

Vince, S. W. E., *Gloucestershire*, The Land of Britain: Report of the Land Utilisation Survey of Britain, ed. L. D. Stamp, 67 (London, 1942)

Vogel, C., *Introduction aux sources de l'histoire du culte chrétien au moyen âge* (Spoleto, 1966)

Vollrath, H., *Die Synoden Englands bis 1066* (Paderborn, 1985)

Von Feilitzen, O. and C. Blunt, 'Personal Names on the Coinage of Edgar', in *England Before the Conquest*, ed. Clemoes and Hughes, pp. 183–214

Von Moos, P., *Consolatio: Studien zur mittellateinischen Trostliteratur über den Tod und zum Problem der christlichen Trauer*, 4 vols. (Munich, 1971–2)

Wainwright, F. T., *Archaeology and Place-Names and History: An Essay on Problems of Co-ordination* (London, 1962)

Walker, G. S. M., ed., *Sancti Columbani Opera*, Scriptores Latini Hiberniae 2 (Dublin, 1957)

Wallace-Hadrill, J. M., *Early Germanic Kingship in England and on the Continent* (Oxford, 1971)

Bede's 'Ecclesiastical History of the English People': A Historical Commentary (Oxford, 1988)

Walther, H., *Initia Carminum ac Versuum Medii Aevi Posterioris Latinorum* (Göttingen, 1959)

Warner, G. F., ed., *The Stowe Missal, MS. D.ii.3 in the Library of the Royal Irish Academy, Dublin*, 2 vols., HBS 31–2 (London, 1906–15)

Warner, G. F. and J. P. Gilson, *Catalogue of Western Manuscripts in the Old Royal and King's Collections*, 4 vols. (London, 1921)

Warren, F. E., *The Liturgy and Ritual of the Celtic Church*, 2nd ed. by J. Stevenson (Woodbridge, 1987)

Warren, F. E., ed., *The Antiphonary of Bangor*, 2 vols., HBS 4 and 10 (London, 1893–5)

Waszink, J. H., ed., *Carmen ad Flauium Felicem de resurrectione mortuorum et de iudicio Domini* (Bonn, 1937)

Watson, A. G., *Medieval Libraries of Great Britain edited by N. R. Ker: Supplement to the Second Edition* (London, 1987)

Webster, G., 'The West Midlands in the Roman Period: A Brief Survey', *TBWAS* 86 (1974), 49–58

'Prehistoric Settlement and Land Use in the West Midlands and the Impact of Rome', in *Field and Forest*, ed. Slater and Jarvis, pp. 31–58

Webster, G. and B. Hobley, 'Aerial Reconnaissance over the Warwickshire Avon', *ArchJ* 121 (1965 for 1964), 1–22

Welch, M. G., *Early Anglo-Saxon Sussex*, 2 vols., BAR British Series 112 (Oxford, 1983)

Wharton, H., ed., *Anglia Sacra*, 2 vols. (London, 1691)

Whitelock, D., 'The Conversion of the Eastern Danelaw', *Saga-Book of the Viking Society* 12 (1937–45), 159–76

The Beginnings of English Society (Harmondsworth, 1956)

'The Prose of Alfred's Reign', in *Continuations and Beginnings*, ed. Stanley, pp. 67–103

'William of Malmesbury on the Works of King Alfred', in *Medieval Literature and Civilization: Studies in Memory of G. N. Garmonsway*, ed. D. A. Pearsall and R. A. Waldron (London, 1969), pp. 78–93

Bibliography

'The Pre-Viking Age Church in East Anglia', *ASE* 1 (1972), 1–22

Some Anglo-Saxon Bishops of London, Chambers Memorial Lecture 1974 (London, 1975)

'Some Charters in the Name of King Alfred', in *Saints, Scholars and Heroes: Studies in Medieval Culture in Honour of Charles W. Jones*, ed. M. H. King and W. M. Stevens, 2 vols. (Collegeville, MN, 1979) I, 77–98

Whitelock, D., ed., *Anglo-Saxon Wills* (Cambridge, 1930)

English Historical Documents c. 500–1042, English Historical Documents I, 2nd ed. (London, 1979)

Whitelock, D. *et al.*, ed., *Ireland in Early Mediaeval Europe: Studies in Memory of Kathleen Hughes* (Cambridge, 1982)

Wickham, C. J., *The Mountains and the City: The Tuscan Appennines in the Early Middle Ages* (Oxford, 1988)

Willard, R., *Two Apocrypha in Old English Homilies*, Beiträge zur englischen Philologie 30 (Leipzig, 1935)

Williams, B. J. and A. Whittaker, *Geology of the Country around Stratford-upon-Avon and Evesham*, Memoirs of the Geological Survey: Explanation of Sheet 200 (London, 1974)

Williams, I., ed., *Canu Llywarch Hen*, 2nd ed. (Cardiff, 1953)

Willis, G. G., *Further Essays in Early Roman Liturgy*, Alcuin Club Collections 50 (London, 1968)

Willis, R., *The Architectural History of Canterbury Cathedral* (London, 1845)

Wills, L. J., 'The Pleistocene Development of the Severn from Bridgnorth to the Sea', *QJGS* 94 (1938), 161–242

The Palaeogeography of the Midlands (London, 1948)

Wilmart, A., 'Expositio missae', *Dictionnaire d'archéologie chrétienne et de liturgie*, ed. F. Cabrol and H. Leclercq, 15 vols. (Paris, 1907–53) VI.i (1922), cols. 1014–28

'Les livres de l'abbé Odbert', *Bulletin historique de la Société des antiquaires de la Morinie* 14 (1922–9), 169–88

'Restes d'un très ancien manuscrit de la bibliothèque de Saint-Bertin', *Bulletin historique de la Société des antiquaires de la Morinie* 14 (1922–9), 287–96

'Prières médiévales pour l'adoration de la Croix', *EL* 46 (1932), 22–65

Auteurs spirituels et textes dévots du moyen âge latin (Paris, 1932)

'Le manuel de prières de saint Jean Gualbert', *RB* 48 (1936), 259–99

'Un traité sur la messe copié en Angleterre vers l'an 800', *EL* 50 (1936), 133–9

Wilmart, A., ed., 'The Prayers of the Bury Psalter', *DR* 48 (1930), 198–216

Precum Libelli Quattuor Aevi Karolini (Rome, 1940)

Wilmott, A. R., 'Kenchester (*Magnis*): A Reconsideration', *TWNFC* 43 (1979–81), 116–33

Wilson, D., 'A Note on OE *hearg* and *wēoh* as Place-Name Elements Representing Different Types of Pagan Saxon Worship Sites', *ASSAH* 4 (1985), 179–83

Wilson, D. M., ed., *The Archaeology of Anglo-Saxon England* (London, 1976)

Winterbottom M., ed., *Gildas: The Ruin of Britain and Other Works* (Chichester, 1978)

Wood, S., 'Bede's Northumbrian Dates Again', *EHR* 98 (1983), 280–96

Woods, H., 'Excavations at Wenlock Priory, 1981–6', *JBAA* 140 (1987), 36–75

Wormald, P., 'Bede and Benedict Biscop', in *Famulus Christi*, ed. Bonner, pp. 141–69

Bede and the Conversion of England: The Charter Evidence, Jarrow Lecture 1984 (Jarrow [1984])

'Charters, Law and the Settlement of Disputes in Anglo-Saxon England', in *The Settlement of Disputes in Early Medieval Europe*, ed. W. Davies and P. Fouracre (Cambridge, 1986), pp. 149–68

Wormald, P. *et al.*, ed., *Ideal and Reality in Frankish and Anglo-Saxon Society: Studies presented to J. M. Wallace-Hadrill* (Oxford, 1983)

Wright, D. H., 'Some Notes on English Uncial', *Traditio* 17 (1961), 441–56

Wright, D. H., ed., *The Vespasian Psalter: British Musuem Cotton Vespasian A.1*, EEMF 14 (Copenhagen, 1967)

Wright, F. A., ed. and trans., *Select Letters of St. Jerome*, Loeb Classical Library (London, 1933)

Wright, N., 'Bede and Vergil', *Romanobarbarica* 6 (1981–2), 361–79

Young, B., 'Paganisme, christianisation et rites funéraires mérovingiens', *Archéologie médiévale* 7 (1977), 5–81

Index

Material in footnotes is included in the general page reference.

434

437

Index

Index

Bodleian Library, Lat. Bibl. d. 1 (P):
181
Bodleian Library, Laud. lat. 96: 289,
295–6
Corpus Christi College 157: 41; see also
'Florence' of Worcester
Paris,
BN, lat. 256: 286, 288
BN, lat. 1153: 276, 290, 305, 318,
325
BN, lat. 2421: 331
BN, lat. 2731A: 317–18
BN, lat. 8071: 347–8
BN, lat. 8318: 217–18
BN, lat. 13349: 190
BN, lat. 17177: 202–3
Rochester, Cathedral Library, A.3.5:
41
Saint-Omer, Bibl. Munic., 150: 208
Salisbury, Cathedral Library, 117: 182,
274–5
Shrewsbury, County Record Office, Fragm.
1–2: 183
Spangenberg, Pfarrbibliothek, s.n.: 235
St Gallen, Stiftsbibliothek, 17: 283
Stiftsbibliothek, 1395: 283, 301
St Paul in Carinthia, Stiftsbibliothek, 3 i
(25. 2. 36): 190
Stockholm, Kungliga Biblioteket, A. 135 –
see Codex Aureus
Urbana-Champaign, Univ. of Illinois
Library, 128: 339–59
Vatican, Biblioteca Apostolica, Palat. lat.
67: 276
Biblioteca Apostolica, Reg. lat. 124:
331
Biblioteca Apostolica, Reg. lat. 204:
337
Biblioteca Apostolica, Reg. lat. 316 –
see Gelasian sacramentaries
Biblioteca Apostolica, Reg. lat. 1671:
235
Vienna, Österreichische Nationalbibliothek,
lat. 652: 331
Österreichische Nationalbibliothek, lat.
1888: 297
Österreichische Nationalbibliothek,
Vindobonensis 751: 229–30
Worcester, Cathedral Library, Add. 1: 181,
210, 280
Cathedral Library, Add. 2: 183
Cathedral Library, Add. 3: 136
Cathedral Library, Add. 4: 183
Würzburg, Universitätsbibliothek, M. p.
th. f. 27: 191

Universitätsbibliothek, M. p. th. f. 68
– see Burghard Gospels
Universitätsbibliothek, M. p. th. f. 79:
202
Universitätsbibliothek, M. p. th. q. 2:
15, 190–6, 203, 210, 221,
237–41, 290, 345
Zürich, Zentralbibliothek, Rheinau 140:
335–6
Map, Walter, 14
Marcella 129
Marchamley 50–1
Marcliff 12
Maredudd, king 53
Marmodius 53
Martimow 70, 388
Martin, St 57, 142, 232, 234–5, 398
Matthew Paris 53
Maund 40
Maxims I 221
Medeshamstede, monastery 97, 99, 154, 250
memorial stones, 'Early Christian' 59, 77
Merchelm, king 50–1, 94
Mercians, early history of 5, 16–18, 25–9, 44,
51, 56, 58, 368, 388–9
Merefin 42, 50
Merewald – see Merewalh
Merewalh, sub-king 26, 42, 47–51, 55–6,
60–1, 76, 85, 94, 99, 101, 122
Meurig, son of Tewdrig, king 47, 51
Michael, St 115, 288–9, 352, 382
Middle Angles 5, 20, 26, 30, 33, 47, 56, 58,
87, 103, 384
Mildburg, St and abbess 42, 98, 110–11,
118–19, 122, 244
Mildgyth 42, 50
Mildthryth, St and abbess 42, 48–50, 98, 111
Milfrith, sub-king 40, 50–1, 61, 94, 339,
342, 398
Milred, bishop 2, 14–15, 132, 146–7, 154,
156, 158, 182–3, 193, 198, 212,
227, 230–7, 239, 242, 280,
328–58, 397
'minster' churches 4, 100, 115–17, 122, 130,
132–3, 152, 156, 170–2
Minster-in-Thanet 42, 48–50, 98, 212
Minucius Felix 315
Missale Gothicum 315, 320
Monmouth 47
monuments, 'Early Christian' – see memorial
stones
Moreton in Marsh 22, 386–7
Morfe Forest 148, 376, 392
Moucan – see *Oratio Moucani*
Mozarabic liturgy 313

443